Focus on Strategies

Using Portfolio Assessment

Although this was Mr. Fernandez's first year to use portfolios, he was quickly becoming aware of their usefulness. They were very helpful during parent conferences, because he could show the parents exactly what their children had done during that six-week period—the progress they had made or, in a few cases, the lack of progress. The parents seemed to understand better what their children were doing by looking at their work than by having him try to explain it.

Mr. Fernandez had also found the samples of students' work useful when it was time to give report card grades. He had always believed that grades should be more th...

ts by
as one
nished
ought

Perhaps best of all, most children liked working on their portfolios. They really enjoyed looking back through their papers, recalling different pieces they had worked on and realizing they were getting better. They also liked being able to choose which pieces to include, although sometimes Mr. Fernandez suggested additional pieces.

He had told some of the students that he would meet with them today about their portfolios and asked them to pull their portfolios from the file in the back of the room and have them ready. Now, while they were reading independently, he would begin visiting these children at their seats. Taking along a stool, he seated himself beside Marcus and said quietly, "Marcus, let's see what you've included in your portfolio."

Marcus proudly showed his table of contents, which some of the children had decided to make. Then he turned to the section on his literature log. Marcus confided to Mr. Fernandez, "I really enjoyed reading *Hatchet*. I wanted to include what I wrote about it so I can remember why I liked the book so much." As Mr. Fernandez glanced through Marcus's responses, he could see that Marcus had some remarkable insights about Brian's problem-solving processes as Brian attempted to survive in the wilderness. Marcus had not simply summarized what happened, but had reflected on Brian's survival skills and identified them with his own. "I like the way you refer to Brian's problem-solving skills, Marcus," Mr. Fernandez said. "Can you think how you might learn more about survival skills?".

...arcus to ponder this question, Mr. Fernandez moved on to Tabitha and ...er portfolio. Reluctantly, Tabitha pulled it from her desk and opened it. ...re disorganized: math tests were mixed in with writing samples, and ...s undated. Mr. Fernandez asked her what she might do to get her papers ...w him, and she said she would try to put all the reading and writing ...ter. He agreed to return later. It was strange that some children seemed ...ch about their portfolios, whereas others took little interest in them.

...as next. She had been waiting for Mr. Fernandez and had her portfolio ...y, she produced a letter she had just completed about cleaning up the ..."You know how we've been studying about the environment," Robin ...y got excited about doing something when you read us *A River Ran Wild*, ...to write a letter and send it to the editor of the *Tribune*. Do you think ...it?" As Mr. Fernandez read through the letter, he realized that Robin had ...ideas from the book that she was applying to Simpson's Pond, the one ...come so polluted that fish couldn't live in it anymore. "This letter has ...recommendations in it," Mr. Fernandez told Robin. "I think you should ...n you find the address?"

...g on to Jeremy, Mr. Fernandez asked, "Jeremy, did you include your report ...in your portfolio? You seemed really interested in writing about your find... ...I'd like to see what you've done." After shuffling through some papers, ...und the report and showed it to Mr. Fernandez. "You have some good ...e and a rough draft," said Mr. Fernandez. "Where is your finished paper?" ...dmitted he hadn't done one, adding that he didn't like to have to write ...ver. Reflecting on Jeremy's comment, Mr. Fernandez asked him how he ...el about using the computer to word process his paper. Glancing up, ...aid that idea might work. "Writing it on the computer is better because I can

make the changes easier. Maybe I'll try that." "Be sure to show it to me when you finish," said Mr. Fernandez. "I'm interested in what you write."

Next, Mr. Fernandez came up to Kurt and asked to see his portfolio. "Show me whatever you like," he told Kurt. Kurt pulled out a review he had written of *Maniac Magee*. As Mr. Fernandez looked at the paper, he noticed that this review was little more than a summary and was carelessly written. He knew Kurt had done much better writing than this sample. "Why did you choose this, Kurt?" he asked. "I don't know," Kurt responded. "I guess I just put any old thing in. I don't see what difference it makes." "It's important that you have a reason to place pieces in your portfolio," said Mr. Fernandez. "Think how you can select your most significant work."

When Mr. Fernandez completed his visits for the morning, he realized how much he had learned about the students' work as they explained their portfolios to him. From Kurt he learned that he would need to help students make judgments about their work so that they could decide which selections merited inclusion in their portfolios. He would need to spend more time with Tabitha. She really needed some help with organizing her portfolio and completing her work. Perhaps Robin would help her; they seemed to get along well, and Robin's portfolio was well organized. He needed to find a way to encourage Jeremy to finish his work. The computer seemed to motivate him this time, but he would need to help Jeremy set goals for completing his work. Robin had surprised him with her enthusiasm about the environment. He needed to encourage her to find ways to extend her interest. Marcus was such an avid reader that his responses to *Hatchet* were no surprise. What Marcus needed was a good supply of books, time to read, and opportunities to respond. Mr. Fernandez realized that periodic portfolio reviews were a fine way to get to know his students better and understand their work.

Next year, Mr. Fernandez thought, he would do a few things differently. He had heard of placing an audiotape in each portfolio and recording the children's oral reading periodically. That would be another way to measure their progress. He also needed a better system of weeding out some of their work; their portfolios would be quite bulky by the end of the year. He would try to get some ideas from teachers who were already using portfolios so that he could make the procedure run smoother next time. "We're off to a good start this year, though," Mr. Fernandez thought, "and next year will be even better."

How can portfolios be used for evaluation? No grades should be given on the portfolios themselves (Farr and Tone, 1994), but portfolio assessment can (1) show what students have learned over a period of time, (2) enable students to develop criteria for judging their own work, (3) relate to real-life learning opportunities that reflect day-to-day thinking, (4) offer guidance for setting individual goals, and (5) enable teachers to evaluate teaching practices and curricula (DeFina, 1992).

SELF-CHECK: OBJECTIVE 4 List as many items as you can that are appropriate for inclusion in a portfolio. What is the value of collecting and organizing these items? (See Self-Improvement Opportunities 4, 5, and 10.)

This text includes an abundance of useful classroom strategies and resources. For a special note on the literacy activity that created the art on this text's cover, see page xvi.

Teaching Reading in Today's Elementary Schools

Sixth Edition

Teaching Reading in Today's Elementary Schools

Paul C. Burns

late of University of Tennessee at Knoxville

Betty D. Roe

Tennessee Technological University

Elinor P. Ross

Tennessee Technological University

Houghton Mifflin Company

Boston   Toronto
Geneva, Illinois   Palo Alto   Princeton, New Jersey

*Dedicated to Michael H. Roe
and James R. Ross*

Senior Sponsoring Editor: Loretta Wolozin
Assistant Editor: Lisa Mafrici
Senior Project Editor: Susan Westendorf
Editorial Assistant: Gabrielle Stone
Senior Production/Design Coordinator: Carol Merrigan
Senior Manufacturing Coordinator: Priscilla Bailey
Marketing Associate: Cynthia Voytas

Cover designer: Darci Mehall, Aureo Design
Cover mixed media monotype: *The Most Beautiful Bird*, copyright © 1994 by Fae Kontje,
Max Gibbs, Ben Gramkowski, Katharine Sobotka, and Emily Rodegast.

Chapter opening photo credits:
Chapter 1: Laimute E. Druskis/Stock Boston. Chapter 2: Jean Claude Lejeune. Chapter 3:
David Young Wolf/Photo Edit. Chapter 4: Mary Kate Denny/Photo Edit. Chapter 5:
Erika Stone/Photo Researchers. Chapter 6: Jean Claude Lejeune/Stock Boston. Chapter 7:
Elizabeth Crews. Chapter 8: Elizabeth Crews. Chapter 9: Kalman/The Image Works.
Chapter 10: Jean Claude Lejeune. Chapter 11: Elizabeth Crews. Chapter 12: Paul Conklin/
Monkmeyer Press Photo Service. Chapter 13: Elizabeth Crews/Stock Boston.

Printed in the U.S.A.

Library of Congress Catalog Card Number: 95-76930

ISBN: 0-395-75293-0

A B C D E F G-DH-0 9 8 7 6 5 4 3 2

Contents

Preface   xi

This Book's Cover Art   xvi

Chapter 1
The Reading Act   3

The Importance of Reading   5

Components of the Reading Act   6
The Reading Product 7   The Reading Process 8   The Reading Process: Selected Theories 18

Twelve Principles of Teaching Reading   25

Chapter 2
Emergent Literacy   37

The Concept of Emergent Literacy   39

Development of Cognition and Language   41
Cognitive Development 41   Language Learning 42

The Emergent Literacy Classroom   44
Establishing a Print-Rich Classroom Environment 45   Working with Parents 48

Listening and Speaking   50
*Listening Comprehension 50   Listening Centers 51   Oral Expression 51
Dramatic Play 52   Dramatic Play Centers 53   Creative Dramatics 55*

Reading and Writing   56
Learning to Read 58   Learning to Write 69

Assessment of Emergent Literacy   79
Informal Assessment 79   Formal Tests for Beginning Readers 79

Chapter 3
Word Recognition 91

Word Recognition Strategies   93
*Sight Words 94   Context Clues 103   Phonics 110   Structural Analysis 137
Dictionary Study 146*

Word Recognition Procedure   150

Chapter 4
Meaning Vocabulary 159

Vocabulary Development   161

Vocabulary Instruction   162
Building Readers' Schemata 163   Instructional Procedures 167   Special Words 197

Chapter 5
Comprehension: Part 1 205

The Reader   209
Readers' Schemata 209   Other Aspects Related to the Reader 213

The Reading Situation   214
Purposes for Reading 214   Audience 216   Importance of Task to Student 216

The Text   217
Sentence Comprehension 217   Organizational Patterns 221   Types of Text 222

Interaction of the Reader, the Reading Situation, and the Text   225
*Prereading Strategies and Activities 225   During-Reading Strategies and Activities 229
Postreading Strategies and Activities 237   General Strategies and Activities 238*

Chapter 6
Comprehension: Part 2 253

Types of Comprehension   255
Literal Comprehension 255   Higher-Order Comprehension 261

Effective Questioning   297
*Preparing Questions 298   Helping Students Answer Questions 304   Helping
Students Question 305*

Chapter 7

Major Approaches and Materials for Reading Instruction 311

Published Reading Series   313
  *Traditional Basal Series 313   Literature-Based and Language-Integrated Series 320
  Instructional Procedures Used with Published Reading Series 329*

Literature-Based Approaches   333
  *Whole-Class Reading of a Core Book 335   Literature Response Groups 340
  Thematic Literature Units 340   Individualized Reading Approach 343   Evaluation
  Concerns in Literature-Based Approaches 352*

Language Experience Approach (LEA)   353
  *Implementation in Kindergarten 354   Implementation in the Primary Grades 355
  Implementation in Higher Grades 359   LEA: Pros and Cons 360*

Programmed Instruction   361

Computer Applications   361

Eclectic Approaches   369

What about Whole Language?   371

Chapter 8

Language and Literature: Holistic Learning 377

Whole Language Principles   379

Integrating the Language Arts   380

The Reading-Writing Connection   383
  *A Process Writing Approach 385   Reading and Writing with Journals 387   Writing
  and Reading Workshop 388   Using Computers for Writing 390*

Literature as a Means For Integrating Language   391
  *Creating an Environment for Reading 392   Story Reading and Storytelling 394
  Selecting Literature 396   Responding to Literature 398   Integrating Literature Across
  the Curriculum 406   Thematic Units 408   Working with Support Personnel 417*

Chapter 9

Reading/Study Techniques 425

Study Methods   428
  *SQ3R 428   SQRQCQ 430   Other Techniques to Improve Retention 430
  Test-Taking Strategies 432*

Flexibility of Reading Habits   432
   Adjustment of Approach 433   Adjustment of Rate 433

Locating Information   435
   Books 435   Reference Books 439   Libraries and Media Centers 448
   Computer Databases 453

Organizational Techniques   454
   Note Taking 454   Outlining 456   Summarizing 459

Metacognition   460

Graphic Aids   462
   Maps 463   Graphs 466   Tables 467   Illustrations 470

Chapter 10

Reading in the Content Areas 475

Content Texts Compared to Basal Readers   477

Readability   478
   Cloze Tests 479   Readability Formats 482

Alternatives to Exclusive Use of Content Texts   483

General Techniques for Content Area Reading   485
   Motivating Students to Read 485   Concept-Text-Application (CTA) Approach 486
   Directed Reading-Thinking Activity (DRTA) 486   K-W-L Teaching Model 488
   Study Guides 488   Guided Reading Procedure 495   Question-Only Strategy 495
   Press Conference 495   Creative Mapping 496   Structured Overviews 496   Every-
   Pupil-Response Activities 496   Readers' Theater 496   Sustained Silent Reading
   (SSR) for Expository Materials 497   Learning Text Structure 497   Computer
   Approaches 500   Writing Techniques 501   Using Content Material with
   Reading of Fiction and Writing 503   Manipulative Materials 504   Integrating
   Approaches 504   Creating Instructional Units 505

Specific Content Areas   509
   Language Arts 509   Social Studies 514   Mathematics 520   Science and
   Health 528

Chapter 11

Assessment of Student Progress 539

Movement toward Authentic Assessment   541

Informal (Nonstandardized) Assessment   544
   Observation Strategies 544   Appraising Literary Interests 552

*Portfolio Assessment 553   Self-Appraisal 557   Informal Tests 561
Further Considerations about Informal Assessment 566*

Criterion-Referenced Tests   567

Formal Assessment (Norm-Referenced Tests)   567
*Traditional Achievement Tests 569   Emergence of Performance-Based Achievement
Tests 572*

Chapter 12
Classroom Organization and Management 579

Organizational Patterns   581
*Integrated Language Arts Curriculum 582   Learning in Groups 589
Schoolwide Organizational Plans 596   Making Transitions 598*

Physical Environment   601
Learning Centers 601   Computers 602   Videotapes 603

Role of the Teacher   603
*The Teacher as Facilitator and Manager of Instruction 604   The Teacher as Decision
Maker 605   The Teacher as Researcher 607   The Teacher as Learner 608*

Parents   609
Communicating with Parents 610   General Suggestions 613

Paraprofessionals and Tutors   614

Chapter 13
Readers with Special Needs 621

A View of the Special Learner   623

Laws Affecting Students with Disabilities   624
*Individualized Education Programs 624   Coordination of Special Programs 625
Inclusion 626   General Guidelines 630*

Types of Disabilities   631
*Students with Specific Learning Disabilities 631   Students with Attention-Deficit
Disorders 632   Students with Mental Retardation 633   Students with Visual
Impairments 633   Students with Hearing Impairments 634   Students with Speech
Impairments 634   Students with Emotional/Behavioral Disorders 634   Instructional
Implications and Strategies 635*

Students with Reading Difficulties   635
*Characteristics 635   Instructional Implications 636   Instructional Teaching
Strategies for Students with Reading Difficulties 637   Early Intervention Programs 641*

Gifted Children   642
Characteristics 642   Instructional Implications and Strategies 642

Culturally and Linguistically Diverse Students   645
*Culturally Diverse Students 645   Students with Dialectal Differences 648
Bilingual Students 649*

Chapter Appendix: Multicultural Literature   661

Glossary   699

Appendix: Answers to "Test Yourself"   707

Index   709

Preface

Currently we are in the best of times for reading education. There are moves toward using more authentic literature as a basis for reading instruction, toward integrating more instruction in the language arts and across the curriculum, toward using more holistic instruction, toward actively involving students more in learning activities, and toward applying newer methods of assessment that relate more closely to newer views of the reading process. This sixth edition of *Teaching Reading in Today's Elementary Schools* addresses all of these movements, including new information on theory, research, and techniques while retaining solid, time-tested ideas and procedures—all within the familiar and practical framework of previous editions. We have included new concepts, materials, techniques, and positions and integrated them with valid traditional ideas in the balanced, even-handed way that has characterized our book from the start.

We hope to empower teachers to become decision-makers, rather than merely followers of plans provided by others. Thus, we have offered information about many methods and materials for reading instruction, along with principles to help teachers choose among these options for their specific students and situations.

Audience and Purpose

Teaching Reading in Today's Elementary Schools is intended for use in introductory reading education courses for both preservice and inservice elementary school classroom teachers. It will also be beneficial in introductory courses training teachers as reading specialists, and it contains much information to help administrators direct their schools' reading programs.

This book is designed to familiarize teachers with all important aspects of elementary reading instruction. It presents much practical information about the process of teaching reading. Theoretical background and the research base behind suggestions have also been included to give the teacher or prospective teacher a balanced perspective.

The primary aim of the book is to prepare teachers to develop their students' abilities to read fluently and to foster their students' full use and enjoyment of reading in their lives. The large amount of the school day spent on reading instruction in the primary grades makes this content especially important to the primary grade teacher. In the intermediate grades students must handle reading assignments in the content areas as well as in reading periods. Our book—particularly the chapters on content area reading and reading/study techniques—contains information that will help teachers implement reading instruction across the curriculum.

Revisions in this Edition

This edition represents a substantial revision. Important new understandings about the reading process have been included throughout the book, and the research base for these understandings has been fully updated. A number of topics of recent and far-reaching concern, such as varying theoretical views of the reading process; the whole language philosophy; literature-based reading instruction; the integration of the language arts, including the reading-writing connection; thematic teaching; teacher modeling techniques; new computer technology uses; authentic assessment; cultural diversity; and inclusion of special learners in regular classrooms are each thoroughly addressed.

Each chapter has been completely revised. A new graphic organizer developed for the beginning of each chapter shows chapter organization concretely. Chapter 1 has new information about Rosenblatt's transactive theory of the reading process. It addresses the whole language philosophy, which is also discussed in Chapter 7 and given extensive treatment in Chapter 8. Chapter 2 has expanded discussions of print conventions, of using centers for developing oral and written language, and of language development through oral expression and dramatic play. It includes more strategies for teaching beginning reading and writing and gives additional examples of invented spelling. Chapter 3 now includes a section on onsets and rimes and examples of teaching phonics through use of literature. Chapter 4 has updated research, along with minor organizational changes. Chapters 5 and 6 have been reorganized to eliminate overlap. Chapter 5 has additional diagrams to clarify material, the incorporation of a new child-produced example, and new material on metacognition. New charts and graphic organizers to clarify material are included in Chapter 6. The section on linguistic approaches has been deleted from Chapter 7, but some information exists in a condensed form under Types of Basal Reading Programs. A new thematic literature unit contains more detail to help teachers plan such a unit. Computer applications for reading instruction have been updated. Opening with a discussion of whole language concepts, Chapter 8 continues with current coverage of reading/writing workshops, use of literature-based themes, the addition of responses to literature through music, and examples of theme development through webbing and K-W-L. Chapter 9 now has an example of a computerized card catalog entry. Chapter 10 includes material from newer textbooks in several examples, a new example of the K-W-L, and a recently developed pattern guide. Chapter 11 reflects current thinking on assessment by presenting material on authentic assessment, rubrics (an added feature), new samples of informal written teacher observations, and additional information about portfolio assessment. Chapter 12 opens with a new, in-depth discussion of integrated curriculum, including scheduling and program evaluation. It features new material related to grouping for reading communities of learners, multiage classrooms, and cross-grade arrangements. Beginning with discussions of recent laws affecting special learners, Chapter 13 moves into a description and classroom vignette of inclusion. In addition to updated material and use of current terminology, new topics such as multiple intelligences and early intervention programs are included, and the sections on culturally diverse students have been revised.

Facsimiles of elementary school reading materials, exemplary activities, model activities, and classroom scenarios are plentiful; many have been revised. New to this edition are Focus on Strategies vignettes that describe using strategies for literacy instruction in authentic classroom situations.

Three information strands—literature-centered instruction, reading-writing connections, and thematic learning approaches—are emphasized throughout the text. They are indicated by special labels in the margins of pages where they begin. Although the labels do not appear beside Examples, Classroom Scenarios, Model Activities, and Focus on Strategies sections, many of these features relate to the central strands. Note that these strands often overlap, so that the beginning of a new strand does not necessarily end the previously marked strand.

Coverage/Organization

The first chapter discusses components of the reading act, theories related to reading, and principles of teaching reading. Chapter 2 presents information on emergent literacy. The next two chapters are devoted to techniques of teaching word recognition and meaning vocabulary. Comprehension strategies and skills are covered in the two comprehension chapters, 5 and 6. Major approaches and materials for reading instruction are described in Chapter 7. Chapter 8 deals with language and literature; Chapter 9 discusses methods of teaching reading/study techniques; and Chapter 10 tells how to present the skills necessary for reading in individual content areas. Assessment of student progress is discussed in Chapter 11, and classroom management and organization are treated in Chapter 12. Chapter 13 covers teaching reading to special needs students. The Appendix contains answers to Test Yourself quizzes.

Features of the Text

This text provides abundant practical activities and strategies for improving students' reading performance. The ***Examples***, ***Model Activities***, ***Classroom Scenarios***, and ***Focus on Strategies*** sections clarify the text material and put it into perspective. The new ***Focus on Strategies*** sections show how a teacher might actually use a strategy advocated in the chapter. Thus, this book will remain a valuable resource for inservice teachers.

In order to make this text easy for studying and learning, we have included the following features:

Setting Objectives, part of each chapter's opening material, provides objectives to be met as the chapter is read.

Key Vocabulary, a list of important terms which readers should know, is included to help students focus on key chapter concepts.

Self-Checks are keyed to the objectives and located at strategic points throughout each chapter to help readers check their grasp of the ideas presented.

Test Yourself, a section at the end of each chapter, includes questions that check retention of the chapter's material as a whole; these questions may also serve as a basis for discussion.

Self-Improvement Opportunities are activities in which readers can participate to further their understanding of the chapter's ideas and methods.

A **Glossary** contains meanings of special terms used in this book.

Special icons that label information strands in the text appear in the margins of pages to mark the beginnings of material about literature-centered instruction, reading-writing connections, and thematic learning material.

Instructional Components That Accompany the Text

Instructor's Resource Manual with Test Items   This teaching aid provides supplementary material including model syllabi, chapter outlines, key vocabulary terms and definitions, instructional media selections, suggested teaching strategies, and suggested readings. It also lists resources for independent reading activities, multimedia materials, and computer software. In addition, essay and objective questions as well as ideas for implementing authentic assessment are provided for each chapter.

Computerized Test Generator   Questions from the *Instructor's Resource Manual* are also available in computerized format.

Transparencies   A set of 80 overhead transparencies reproduce important text figures, lists, strategies, and activities as well as present new graphics designed for the transparency package. This package is available upon adoption of the text.

Acknowledgments

We are indebted to many people for assisting in preparing this text. In particular, we would like to recognize the contribution Paul C. Burns made to the first and second editions of this book. His death in the summer of 1983 was a loss to us as his colleagues and friends as well as a loss to the field of reading. As a prolific writer and an outstanding teacher, his contributions to reading education were exceptional.

Although we would like to acknowledge the many teachers and students whose inspiration was instrumental in developing this book, we cannot name all of them. We offer grateful recognition to the following reviewers, whose constructive advice and criticism helped immensely in the writing and revision of the manuscript:

Betty Fortner   *Penn State, Harrisburg*

Anna Ruth Hille   *Cedarville College*

Linda Payne   *Clarion University of Pennsylvania*

Norma Jean Prater   *Auburn University at Montgomery*

Peter Quinn   *St. John's University*

Candace Schulhauser   *University of Washington, Tacoma*

Katherine Matthews Stroup   *Southeastern Oklahoma State University*

Dana Thames   *The University of Southern Mississippi*

Linda Wason-Ellam   *University of Saskatchewan*

In addition, we express appreciation to those who have granted permission to use sample materials or citations from their respective works. These contributions have been credited in the footnotes.

The invaluable assistance provided by Michael Roe in proofreading, obtaining permissions, and resolving computer problems is greatly appreciated. Grateful acknowledgment is also given to our editors—Lisa Mafrici, Susan Westendorf, and Loretta Wolozin—for their assistance throughout the book's development and production.

Betty D. Roe
Elinor P. Ross

This Book's Cover Art, or the Story of the Story

Time: Summer 1994
Place: A Studio/Classroom on Martha's Vineyard, Massachusetts
Action: A collaborative group lesson, developing oral and visual literacy skills with teacher and artist Fae Kontje and students (ages 5–7) Max Gibbs, Ben Gramkowski, Emily Rodegast, and Katharine Sobotka.

Ms. Kontje begins by starting to tell a story, coming up with only its first sentence. Each child then takes a turn orally contributing the next sentence, and then the next, until the story reaches its conclusion. As the children create their story, they support one another, chiming in with suggestions and help as needed. As each line is composed, Ms. Kontje writes it down on paper.

One day, the most beautiful bird in the world was flying toward the sun when it saw a bright house caught up in a tornado. The house was about to hit the sun, so the bird clinged onto it and put it back on the ground (Strong bird). Along came a person. It was the President (Clinton) eating a chocolate ice cream cone. He went into the house to see if there was anyone inside. There was. It was an old lady, a tiny, skinny old lady swimming underwater in a fish tank, but she couldn't swim; she was drowning.

The President decided to move into the house. First, he moved in his suitcase, which was full of clothes. Then, he put his hand down into the fish tank and the old lady grabbed onto his finger and he pulled her up. He dried her off with a paper towel, then he went to get his pet lion. Next, he moved his house into the house. While he was doing that, the lion ate the old lady. The president was horrified! . . . for ten minutes. So he and his lion went out for a walk, where they saw the most beautiful bird in the world. Suddenly, his pet bald eagle, his pet griffin, and his pet dragon swooped up the lion to the sun and clawed the most beautiful bird. The lion got hot next to the sun, and started shedding. They dropped the lion, who fell on the beautiful bird. People came along and put the lion in a zoo and set the beautiful bird free.

After the initial story development-story telling, each child then creates a stencil of an image or element from it (the griffin, the lion, the ice cream cone . . .). They then work together on a large piece of blank paper, coloring its border using wax oil crayons and painting its center with watercolors. Next, with a Plexiglas plate rolled with black lithographic ink, the children print their stencils on top of the watercolor. *What emerges is the total piece of art which is on the cover of this book.* After the larger collective print is completed, the children again use their stencils to print out their own individual pieces of art. So, at the end of this lesson, each child has his or her own artwork to take home.

These children use multiple modes, media, and methods in their learning to create—their story and the story of their story in their art. Ms. Kontje observes that in collaborative projects children often experience a much greater sense of success in seeing the whole work than in merely seeing their individual pieces. Within the community context, a sense of individual achievement occurs. Integrating oral and visual arts, the teacher involves children in dynamic projects which at once advance learning and motivate continuing literacy learning.

Teaching Reading in Today's Elementary Schools

Chapter 1

Key Vocabulary

Pay close attention to these terms when they appear in the chapter.

affective

auditory acuity

auditory discrimination

automaticity

bottom-up models

fixations

grapheme

interactive theories

kinesthetic

metacognitive
  strategies

modality

motivation

perception

phoneme

regressions

reinforcement

schemata

self-concept

semantic clues

subskill theories

syntactic clues

tactile

top-down models

transactive theories

vicarious experience

visual acuity

visual discrimination

whole language
  philosophy

The Reading Act

Setting Objectives

When you finish reading this chapter, you should be able to

1. Discuss the reading product.
2. Describe the reading process.
3. Explain three types of theories of the reading process: subskill, interactive and transactive.
4. Identify some attributes of the whole language philosophy.
5. Name some principles on which effective reading instruction is based.

Figure 1.1 *Chapter 1 Organization*

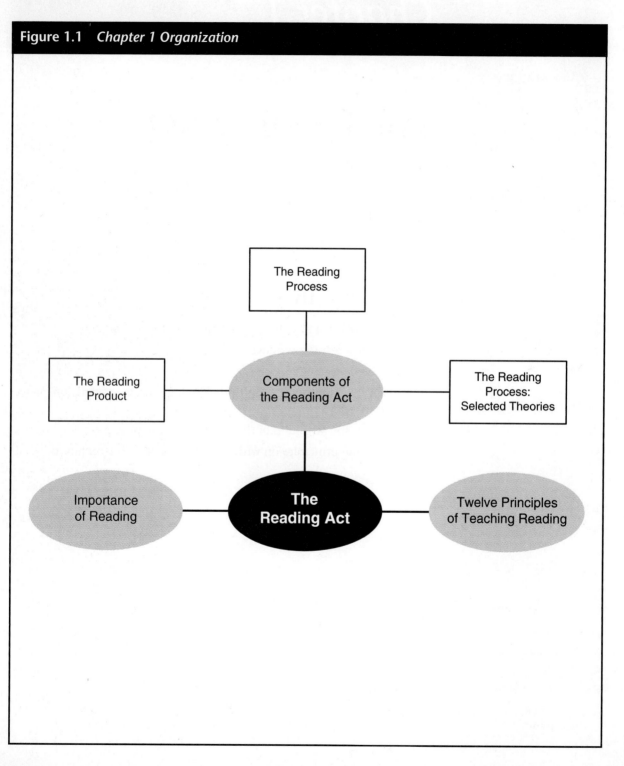

Few adults would question the importance of reading to effective functioning in our complex technological world. Educators have long made reading instruction a priority in the school curriculum, and many children come to school with a sense of the importance of reading in their lives. Unfortunately, however, not all students have this vision. One of the tasks teachers face is to help students see the importance of acquiring reading ability for performing everyday tasks effectively and the value of reading as a source of information, enjoyment, and recreation. To accomplish this task effectively, teachers need to know something about the reading act, know some useful principles of reading instruction, and understand some of the theories on which instructional practices in reading are based. They will also benefit from exposure to current philosophical positions related to reading instruction, such as the whole language philosophy.

Reading is a highly complex act. It includes two major components—a process and a product—each of which is also complicated. Teachers need to be aware of these components and their different aspects in order to respond effectively to their students' reading needs.

This chapter analyzes the reading product and process. It describes three theories of the reading process and presents some sound principles for reading instruction, with explanatory comments.

thematic learning
reading-writing connection
literature-centered reading

Beginning in this chapter and continuing throughout this text, we have woven three strands of information about teaching that we believe are central to reading instruction. These three strands are literature-centered instruction, reading-writing connections, and thematic learning approaches. The beginnings of various discussions pertaining to these strands are indicated in the margins of the pages with special labels. In addition to the text that is marked with marginal labels, many of the Examples, Classroom Scenarios, Focus on Strategies sections, and Model Activities sections relate to these vital strands. Note that often these strands overlap, so that the beginning of a new strand does not necessarily end the previously marked strands. We hope that the marking of these strands will help readers locate information of interest.

The Importance of Reading

The ability to read is vital to functioning effectively in a literate society such as ours. However, children who do not understand the importance of learning to read will not be motivated to learn. Learning to read takes effort, and children who see the value of reading in their personal activities will be more likely to work hard than those who fail to see the benefits.

Teachers should have little trouble demonstrating to children that reading is important. Every aspect of life involves reading. Road signs direct travelers to particular destinations, inform drivers of hazards, and remind people about traffic regulations. There are menus in restaurants, labels on cans, printed advertisements, newspapers, magazines, insurance forms, income tax forms, and campaign and travel brochures. These reading situations are inescapable. Even very young children can be helped to see the need to read the signs on restrooms, the labels on individual desks in their classrooms, and the labeled areas for supplies. In fact, these young children are often eager to learn to read and are ready to attack the task enthusiastically.

Anderson (1988) points out that middle-grade students who have achieved basic literacy may become complacent and cease to see reading improvement as a priority. However, reading tasks become increasingly complex as students advance through the grades and require continuing improvement. Anderson suggests sparking the interest of these older children through career education activities, helping them in this way to see that reading is a life skill that is relevant to their future success. The children can choose occupations that interest them and list the reading skills each occupation requires. They can take one or more field trips to businesses to see workers using reading to carry out their jobs, and they can hear resource people speak to their classes about how they personally need reading in their jobs. These resource people may bring to class examples of the reading materials they must use to perform their daily tasks. The students may also interview parents and others to learn about reading demands in a wide variety of careers.

As important as functional reading is to everyday living, another important goal of reading is enjoyment. Teachers must attempt to show students that reading can be interesting to them for reasons other than strictly utilitarian ones. Students may read for relaxation, vicarious adventure, or aesthetic pleasure as they immerse themselves in tales of other times and places or those of the here

thematic learning

literature-centered reading

and now. They may also read to obtain information about areas of interest or hobbies to fill their leisure time. To help children see reading as a pleasurable activity, teachers should read to them each day on a variety of themes and topics, from a variety of genres, and from the works of many authors. They should also make many books available for children to look at and read for themselves, and

reading-writing connection

they should set aside time for children to read from self-selected materials. Students should be given opportunities to share information from and reactions to their reading in both oral and written forms. They should be encouraged to think about the things they are reading and to relate them to their own experiences.

Components of the Reading Act

The reading act is composed of two parts: the *reading process* and the *reading product*. As Example 1.1 shows, nine aspects of the reading process combine to produce the reading product. When these aspects blend and interact harmoniously, good communication between the writer and reader results. But the sequences involved in the reading process are not always exactly the same, and they are not always performed in the same way by different readers.

The product of reading is the communication of thoughts and emotions by the writer to the reader. Communication results from the reader's construction of meaning through integrating his or her prior knowledge with the information presented in the text. Because the goal of communication is central to reading instruction, we will discuss the reading product first.

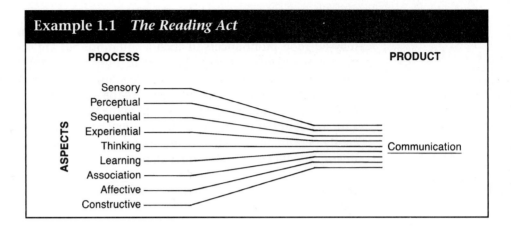

Example 1.1   *The Reading Act*

The Reading Product

As we have pointed out, the product of the reading act is communication, the reader's understanding of ideas that the writer has put into print. Today's readers have a wealth of knowledge available to them because they are able to read material that others wrote in the past. Americans can read of events and accomplishments that occur in other parts of the globe. Knowledge of great discoveries need not be laboriously passed from person to person by word of mouth; such knowledge is available to all who can read.

In addition to being a means of communicating generally, reading is a means of communicating specifically with friends and acquaintances. A note may tell a child that Mother has gone to the store or inform a baby-sitter about where to call in case of an emergency. A memo from a person's employer can identify the work to be done.

Reading can be a way to share another person's insights, joys, sorrows, or creative endeavors. Reading can also enable a person to find places he or she has never visited before (through maps and directional signs), to take advantage of bargains (through advertisements), or to avert disaster (through warning signs). It is difficult to imagine what life would be like without this vital means of communication.

Communication depends on comprehension, which is affected by all aspects of the reading process. Word recognition strategies, a part of the associational aspect of the reading process, are essential, but comprehension involves much more than decoding symbols into sounds; the reader must construct meaning while interacting with the printed page. Some people mistakenly view reading as a single skill, that of pronouncing words, rather than a combination of many skills that lead to the derivation of meaning. Thinking of reading in this way may have fostered the misguided practice of using a reading period for extended drill on word calling, in which the teacher asks each child to "read" aloud while classmates follow in their books. When a child cannot pronounce a word, the teacher may supply the pronunciation or ask another child to do so. When a child miscalls, or mispronounces, a word, the teacher usually corrects the mistake. Some students may be good pronouncers in such a situation, but are they readers? They may pronounce words perfectly, but fail to understand anything they have read. Although pronunciation is important, reading involves much more.

Teachers who realize that all aspects of the reading process affect comprehension of written material will be better able to diagnose children's reading difficulties and, as a result, offer effective instructional programs based on children's needs. Faulty performance related to any aspect of the reading process may result in an inferior product or in no product at all.

SELF-CHECK: OBJECTIVE 1   Discuss the product of the reading process. (See Self-Improvement Opportunities 1 and 2.)

The Reading Process

Reading is an extremely complex process. When they read, children must be able to

1. Perceive the symbols set before them (*sensory* aspect)

2. Interpret what they see (*perceptual* aspect)

3. Follow the linear, logical, and grammatical patterns of the written words (*sequential* aspect)

4. Relate words back to direct experiences to give the words meaning (*experiential* aspect)

5. Make inferences from and evaluate the material (*thinking* aspect)

6. Remember what they learned in the past and incorporate new ideas and facts (*learning* aspect)

7. Recognize the connections between symbols and sounds, between words and what they represent (*associational* aspect)

8. Deal with personal interests and attitudes that affect the task of reading (*affective* aspect)

9. Put everything together to make sense of the material (*constructive* aspect)

Reading seems to fit into the category of behavior called a *skill*, which Frederick McDonald has defined as an act that "demands complex sets of responses—some of them cognitive, some attitudinal, and some manipulative" (Downing, 1982, p. 535). Understanding, rather than simple motor behavior, is essential. The key element in skill development is *integration* of the processes involved, which "is learned through practice. Practice in integration is only supplied by performing the whole skill or as much as is a part of the learner's 'preliminary fix.' . . . one learns to read by reading" (Downing, 1982, p. 537). Whereas reading can be broken down into subskills, reading takes place only when these subskills are put together into an *integrated* whole. Performing subskills individually is not reading (Anderson et al., 1985).

Reading is not a single skill but a combination of many skills and processes in which a reader interacts with print to derive both meaning and pleasure from the written word. (© Laimute E. Druskis/Stock Boston)

Not only is the reading process complex, but each aspect of the process is complex as well. As Example 1.2 shows, the whole process can be likened to a series of books, with each aspect represented by a hefty volume. A student would have to understand the information in every volume to have a complete grasp of the subject. Therefore, the student would have to integrate information from *all* of the volumes in order to perform effectively in the area of study. The *series* would be more important than any individual volume.

Sensory Aspects of Reading

The reading process begins with a sensory impression, either visual or tactile. A normal reader perceives the printed symbol visually; a blind reader uses the tactile sense. (Discussion of the blind reader is beyond the scope of this text.) The auditory sense is also very important, since a beginning stage in reading is the association of printed symbols with spoken language. A person with poor auditory discrimination may find some reading skills, especially those involved with phonics, difficult to master.

Example 1.2 *Aspects of the Reading Process*

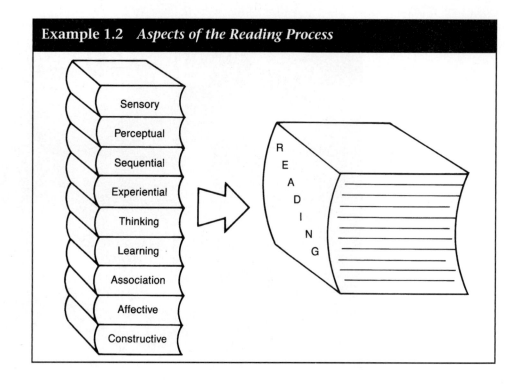

Vision. The reading act imposes many visual demands on children. They must be able to focus their eyes on a page of print that is generally fourteen to twenty inches away, as well as on various signs and visual displays that may be twenty or more feet away. Besides possessing *visual acuity* (or sharpness of vision), children must learn to discriminate visually among the graphic symbols (letters or words) that are used to represent spoken language. Reading is impossible for a person who cannot differentiate between two unlike graphic symbols. Because of these demands, teachers should be aware of the way in which a child's sight develops and of the physical problems that can handicap reading.

Many first graders have not yet attained 20/20 vision. Farsighted first graders may learn reading skills more easily by working on charts and chalkboards than by using workbooks and textbooks. Teachers should avoid requiring farsighted children to do a great deal of uninterrupted reading, and they should also use large print for class handouts (Biehler and Snowman, 1986). Although nearsighted children may do well when working with books, they are often unable to see well enough to respond to directions or exercises written on charts or chalkboards.

Some children may have an eye disorder called *astigmatism*, which results in blurred vision. This problem, as well as nearsightedness and farsightedness, can generally be corrected by glasses.

If a child's eyes do not work well together, he or she may see two images instead of one. Sometimes when this occurs, the child manages to suppress the image from one eye. If suppression continues over a period of time, he or she may lose sight in that eye entirely. If suppression occurs for only short periods, the child may lose the appropriate place on the page when reading and become confused and frustrated.

To the casual observer, eye movement during reading appears as a smooth sweep across a line of print. Actually, a reader makes numerous stops, or *fixations*, to take in the words and phrases and react to them. A high proportion of total reading time is spent on fixations; therefore, fixation time is closely related to reading speed. Both the time and the frequency of fixations will vary according to the difficulty of the material. Easy material involves fewer and briefer fixations.

Eye movements back to a previously read word or phrase in order to reread are called *regressions*. Although regressions can become an undesirable habit, they are useful if the reader performs them to correct false first impressions.

It takes time for children to learn to move their eyes across a page in a left-to-right progression and to execute a return sweep from the end of one line to the beginning of the next line. This is a difficult maneuver. Children who have not yet mastered the process will find themselves rereading and skipping lines, both of which hamper comprehension. Although teachers often attempt to correct faulty eye movements, such movements may be *symptoms* of other problems (for example, poor muscle coordination or poor vocabulary) rather than *causes* of problems. When the other problems are removed, these symptoms usually disappear.

Hearing.   A child who cannot discriminate among the different sounds (*phonemes*) represented by graphic symbols will be unable to make the sound-symbol associations necessary for decoding unfamiliar words. Of course, before a child can discriminate among sounds, he or she must be able to hear them; that is, *auditory acuity* must be adequate. Thus, deaf and hearing-impaired children are deprived of some methods of word identification.

Perceptual Aspects of Reading

Perception involves interpretation of the sensory impressions that reach the brain. Each person processes and reorganizes sensory data according to his or her background of experiences. When a person is reading, the brain receives a visual sensation of words and phrases from the printed page. It recognizes and gives meaning to these words and phrases as it associates them with the reader's previous experience with the objects, ideas, or emotions represented.

Because readers' experiences vary, different readers may interpret a single text differently (Anderson et al., 1985). For example, the printed words *apple pie* have no meaning for a person until that person associates them with the object they represent. Perception of the term *apple pie* can result not only in a visual image of a pie but also in a recollection of its smell and taste. Of course, the person must have prior experience with the thing named by the word(s) in order to make these associations.

Since different people have had different experiences with apple pies, and apple pies can vary in smell, taste, and appearance, people will attach different meanings to *apple pie*. Therefore, individuals will have slightly different perceptions when they encounter these or any other words. The clusters of information that people develop about things (such as apple pies), places (such as restaurants or airports), or ideas (such as justice or democracy) are sometimes referred to as *schemata*. Every person has many schemata. Recent theories describe reading comprehension as the act of relating textual information to existing schemata (Pearson et al., 1979). Chapter 5 presents more information about this relationship.

Visual Perception. Visual perception involves identification and interpretation of size, shape, and relative position of letters and words. *Visual discrimination,* the ability to see likenesses and differences in visual forms (for example, between the printed words *big* and *dig*), is an important part of visual perception because many letters and words are very similar in form but very different in pronunciation and meaning. Accurate identification and interpretation of words results from detecting the small variations in form. A child may have good visual acuity (see images clearly) but be unable to discriminate well visually. Teachers can help children develop this skill through carefully planned activities (discussed in Chapter 3). The final step in visual perception, of course, is attaching meaning to the words by using past experiences, as described earlier.

Auditory Perception. Auditory perception involves *auditory discrimination*, detecting likenesses and differences in speech sounds (for example, recognizing the difference in the spoken words *big* and *dig*) and interpreting the result. Children must be able consciously to separate a phoneme (sound) from one spoken word and compare it with another phoneme separated from another word. Since many children have not developed the ability to perform this task well by the age of five or six years, a phonics-oriented beginning reading program can be very demanding (Pearson et al., 1979). As is true of visual discrimination, a child can have good auditory acuity (hear sounds clearly), but be unable to discriminate well auditorily. The skill can be taught, however. (Instructional activities for enhancing auditory discrimination are discussed in Chapter 3.) The final step in auditory perception is to attach meaning to the words heard by using past experiences.

Sequential Aspects of Reading

English-language printed material generally appears on a page in a left-to-right, top-to-bottom sequence. A person's eyes must follow this sequence in order to read. We pointed out earlier that readers occasionally regress, or look back to earlier words and phrases, as they read. Although these regressions momentarily interrupt the reading process as the reader checks the accuracy of initial impressions, the reader eventually returns to the left-to-right, top-to-bottom sequence.

Another reason reading is a sequential process is that oral language is strung together in a sequential pattern of grammar and logic. Since written language is a way of representing speech, it is expressed in the same manner. The reader must be able to follow the grammatical and logical patterns of spoken language in order to understand written language.

Experiential Background and Reading

As indicated in the section on perceptual aspects, meaning derived from reading is based on the reader's experiential background. Children with rich background experiences have had more chances to develop understanding of the vocabulary and concepts they encounter in reading than have children with limited experiences. For example, a child who has actually been in an airport is more likely to be able to attach appropriate meaning to the word *airport* when he or she encounters it in a reading selection than a child who has not been to an airport. Direct experiences with places, things, and processes described in reading materials make understanding of the materials much more likely.

Vicarious (indirect) *experiences* also enhance conceptual development, although they are probably less effective than concrete experiences. Hearing other people tell of or read about a subject; seeing photos or a movie of a place, event, or activity; and reading about a topic are examples of vicarious experiences that can build concept development. Since vicarious experiences involve fewer senses than do direct, concrete experiences, the concepts gained from them may be developed less fully.

literature-centered reading

Some parents converse freely with their children, read to them, tell them stories, show them pictures, and take them to movies and on trips. These parents are providing rich experiences. Other parents, for a variety of reasons, do not offer these experiences to their children. A child's experiential background may be affected by parental rejection, indifference, or overprotection; by frequent illness; by the use of a nonstandard dialect in the home; or by any number of other reasons. Consider an example of how overprotection can limit a child's experiences: a first-grade boy enters school unable to use scissors, color, or play games effectively. At home he has been denied the use of scissors so that he will not hurt himself, the use of crayons so that he will not mar the walls, and permission to play outside or on the floor so that he will not get dirty. This child's teacher will need to give him a great deal of help to build his experiential background.

literature-centered reading

Teachers can help broaden children's concrete experiences through field trips, displays of objects, and class demonstrations. They can also help by providing rich vicarious experiences, such as photographs, filmstrips, movies, records and tape recordings, classroom discussions, and storytelling and story-reading sessions.

If reading materials contain vocabulary, concepts, and sentence structures that are unfamiliar to children, teachers must help them develop the background they need to understand the materials. Because children's experiential backgrounds differ, some need more preparation for a particular selection than others do.

Teachers can help children learn the standard English found in most books by telling and reading stories, encouraging show-and-tell activities, leading or encouraging class discussions, using language experience stories (accounts developed cooperatively by teacher and class members about actual events), and encouraging dramatic play (enactment of roles or imitation of people or things). The new words encountered during field trips and demonstrations will also be valuable.

Good readers can skillfully integrate information in the text with prior knowledge about the topic, but poor readers may either overemphasize the symbols in the text or rely too heavily on their prior knowledge of the topic. Poor readers who focus primarily on the text may produce nonsense words that are graphically similar to the ones in the text. This occurs because such readers are not attempting to connect what they read to their experiences or to demand sense from reading. Poor readers who depend too much on prior knowledge may fail to make sufficient use of clues in the text to come close to the intended message (Anderson et al., 1985).

The Relationship Between Reading and Thinking

Reading is a thinking process. The act of recognizing words requires interpretation of graphic symbols. To comprehend a reading selection thoroughly, a person must be able to use the information to make inferences and read critically and creatively—to understand the figurative language, determine the author's purpose, evaluate the ideas presented, and apply the ideas to actual situations. All of these skills involve thinking processes.

Teachers can guide students' thinking by asking appropriate questions. Students will be more likely to evaluate the material they are reading if they have been directed to do so. *How* and *why* questions are particularly good. Appropriate questions can help involve a reader in the material and help the reader make personal connections with it. Questions can also limit thinking, however; if children are asked only to locate isolated facts, they will probably not be very concerned about main ideas in a passage or about the author's purpose. Test questions also affect the way students read assignments: if the usual test questions ask for evaluation or application of ideas, children will be apt to read the material more thoughtfully than they will if they are asked to recall isolated facts.

The Relationship of Reading to Learning

Reading is a complex act that must be learned. It is also a means by which further learning takes place. In other words, a person learns to read and reads to learn.

Learning to read depends on motivation, practice, and reinforcement. Teachers must show children that being able to read is rewarding in many ways: it increases success in school, helps in coping with everyday situations outside of school, bestows status, and provides recreation. Children are motivated by the expectation that they will receive these rewards, which then provide reinforcement to continue reading. Reinforcement encourages them to continue to make associations between printed words and the things to which they refer and to practice the skills they need for reading.

After children have developed some facility in reading, it becomes a means through which they learn other things. They read to learn about science, mathematics, social studies, literature, and all other subjects, a topic treated in depth in Chapter 10.

Reading as an Associational Process

Learning to read depends on a number of types of associations. First, children learn to associate objects and ideas with spoken words. Next, they are asked to build up associations between spoken words and written words. In some cases—for instance, when a child encounters an unfamiliar written word paired with a picture of a familiar object—the child makes a direct association between the object or event and the written word without an intermediate connection with the spoken word. In teaching phonics, teachers set up associations between graphic symbols (*graphemes*) and sounds (*phonemes*).

When children practice the associations through classroom activities, immediate reinforcement of correct answers and correction of wrong ones can help to establish the associations. The sooner the teacher provides the reinforcement after the child makes the response, the more effective the reinforcement is likely to be. For example, the teacher might show a child the word *time* and say that this printed word is *time*. Then the teacher would show the word again and ask the child to respond with the word *time*. The teacher may offer the child opportunities for repetition of this response in a variety of situations, and the child can respond appropriately, using the association each time he or she sees that word.

Practice in and of itself, however, is not always enough to set up lasting associations. The more meaningful an association is to a child, the more rapidly he or she will learn it. Children can learn words after only a single exposure if the words have vital meaning for them (Ashton-Warner, 1963).

Affective Aspects of the Reading Process

Interests, attitudes, and self-concepts are three affective aspects of the reading process. These aspects influence how hard children will work at the reading task. For example, children who are interested in the materials presented to them will put forth much more effort in the reading process than will children who have no interest in the available reading materials.

In the same manner, children with positive attitudes toward reading will expend more effort on the reading process than will children with negative attitudes. Positive attitudes are nurtured in homes where the parents read for themselves and to their children and where reading materials are provided for children's use. In the classroom, teachers who enjoy reading, who seize every opportunity to provide pleasurable reading experiences for their students, and who allow time for recreational reading during school hours are encouraging positive attitudes. Reading aloud to the children regularly can also help accomplish this objective, and this activity should continue beyond the primary grades (Daisey, 1993; Duchein and Mealey, 1993; Schumm and Saumell, 1994). Also, if a child's peers view reading as a positive activity, that child is likely to view reading in the same way.

According to Mathewson (1994), a person's attitude toward reading, which includes feelings about reading, readiness for reading, and beliefs about reading, can result in an intention to read or to continue reading, which leads to the act of reading. The intention to read, however, may also be affected by external motivators, such as incentives to read, purposes for reading, expectations of other people, and the setting, as well as by the person's internal emotional state. Ruddell (1992) believes internal motivation and identification with a piece of literature can take several forms: seeing oneself as a successful problem solver, viewing oneself

as a person of significance, evoking an aesthetic sense, finding escape from daily life, piquing intellectual curiosity, and understanding oneself. These types all invite the reader to "step into the story" and be a part of it. External motivations for reading may include peer pressure, teacher expectations, or means to meet responsibilities.

Negative attitudes toward reading may develop in a home environment where parents, for a variety of reasons, do not read. Children from some homes may be told that "reading is for sissies." As the accompanying Focus on Strategies shows, they may bring this idea to the classroom and spread it among children who have not previously been exposed to it. The "reading is for sissies" attitude affects everyone in the classroom negatively, regardless of gender.

Focus on Strategies

Attitude Toward Reading

James, a sixth grader, grumbled about being asked to participate in any reading activities. One day he told Mr. Hyde, his teacher, "I don't need to be able to read. My dad is a construction worker who drives heavy equipment, and that's what I'm going to be. I won't need to read to do that."

Mr. Hyde responded, "What will you do if you are given written instructions to get to the construction site? Won't you need to read then?"

"I'll ask somebody," James replied.

"What if nobody else is there?" Mr. Hyde persisted.

"I don't think that will happen," James countered.

"Well, what if you can't read the road signs to find the place that you are going? You might even need to read a map to find the place. Or what will you do if you get letters from people? You may not want to ask someone else to read them to you. They could be private. Can't you see some advantages to being able to read, even if you don't have to read a lot at work?"

"I guess so," James mumbled reluctantly.

Mr. Hyde had some arguments that were difficult to refute, but probably did not change James's attitude with this one conversation. He needed to be shown repeatedly the benefits that could accrue from reading ability. He also needed to be helped to see that reading can be fun. Mr. Hyde found an informational book containing lots of pictures of heavy equipment and gave James the book to look through whenever he had some time. He did not choose to look at it immediately, but a couple of days later, when the children were having a supervised study time, he took out the book in preference to doing mathematics homework. At first he just thumbed through the pages, but eventually he began to pay closer attention to specific parts of the book. After a day or two, he returned the book and remarked that it was "okay." Mr. Hyde saw a possible avenue to helping James become a reader and pursued it for the rest of the year.

Maudeville (1994) believes that, if readers make decisions about what interested them or what information was important to them in a selection they have just read, they will understand and retain that information better. Reflecting on changes in attitude about the topic may also help. Discussion of these personal responses is also important.

Children with poor opinions of themselves may be afraid to attempt a reading task because they are sure they will fail. They find it easier to avoid the task altogether and to develop "don't care" attitudes than to risk looking "dumb." Children with positive self-concepts, on the other hand, are generally not afraid to attack a reading task, since they believe they are going to succeed.

There are several ways to help children build positive self-concepts. First, in every possible way, the teacher should help the children feel accepted. A definite relationship exists between a teacher's attitude toward a child, as the child perceives it, and the child's self-concept. One of the best ways to make children feel accepted is for the teacher to share their interests, utilizing those interests in planning for reading instruction. The teacher should also accept children's contributions to reading activities even if they are not clearly stated.

Second, the teacher can help children feel successful by providing activities that are simple enough to guarantee satisfactory completion. For poorer readers, we recommend the language experience approach (see Chapter 7), as well as appropriate materials such as high-interest books with lower difficulty levels.

Third, the teacher should avoid comparing a child with other children. Instead, reading progress should be compared with the child's own previous work. Private records of books read, skills mastered, or words learned are much better than public records in which one child consistently compares unfavorably with others.

Fourth, if the teacher uses reading groups, he or she should minimize the focus on the differences among these groups to avoid giving children the idea that unless they are members of the top group they are not worthy people. Comparisons and competition among groups should be avoided, and the bases on which groups are formed should be varied.

Constructive Aspect of the Reading Process

The reader puts together input from sensory and perceptual channels with experiential background and affective responses and constructs a personal meaning for the text. This meaning is based on the printed word, but does not reside completely in it; it is transformed by the information the reader brings to the text, the reader's feelings about the material, the purposes for the reading, and the context in which the reading takes place. Readers with different backgrounds of experience and different affective reactions will derive different meanings from the same text, as may those with divergent purposes and those reading under varying conditions. A person from the Middle East will understand an article about dissension among Middle Eastern countries differently than will one from the United

States. A person reading to find a single fact or a few isolated facts will derive a different meaning from an article from someone reading to get an overall picture of the topic. A person reading a horror story alone in the house at night may well construct a different understanding of the text from one reading the same story in broad daylight in a room full of family members.

Construction of meaning from text is an active process. Readers do not just absorb meaning by taking in the words with their eyes; they must interact with the text by bringing background information and personal reactions to bear on it.

SELF-CHECK: OBJECTIVE 2   List the nine aspects of the reading process presented in this section, and explain each one briefly. Reread the section to check your explanations. (See Self-Improvement Opportunity 1.)

The Reading Process: Selected Theories

A theory is a set of assumptions or principles designed to explain phenomena. Theories that are based on good research and practical observations can be helpful when planning reading instruction, but teachers should not lose sight of the fact that current theories do not account for all aspects of this complex process. In addition, theories grow out of hypotheses—educated guesses. New information may be discovered that proves part or all of a theory invalid.

It would not be practical to present all the theories related to reading in the introductory chapter of a survey textbook. Therefore, we have chosen to discuss three theoretical approaches—subskill, interactive, and transactive theories—to give you a feeling for the complexities inherent in choosing a theoretical stance. The choices that teachers make about types of instruction and emphases in instructional programs are affected by their theoretical positions concerning the reading process.

Subskill Theories

Some educators see reading as a set of *subskills* that children must master and integrate. They believe that, although good readers have learned and integrated these subskills so well that they use them automatically, beginning readers have not learned them all and may not integrate well those that they have learned. Beginning readers, therefore, may exhibit slow, choppy reading and perhaps have reduced comprehension, because the separate skills of word recognition take so much concentration. Teaching these skills until they become automatic and smoothly integrated is thus the approach these educators take to reading instruction (Weaver and Shonhoff, 1984). *Automaticity* is "the ability to perform a task with little attention" (Samuels, 1994, p. 819). It is evident when a high level of accuracy is combined with speed, and readers who read orally with good expression are exhibiting automaticity in word recognition.

R. J. Smith and colleagues (1978) assert that teachers need to teach specific skills in order to focus instruction. Otherwise, instruction in reading would be reduced to assisted practice—a long, laborious trial-and-error approach. Weaver and Shonhoff (1984) state that "although some research suggests that *skilled* reading is a single, holistic process, there is no research to suggest that children can learn to read and develop reading skill if they are taught using a method that treats reading as if it were a single process. Therefore, for instructional purposes, it is probably best to think of reading as a set of interrelated subskills" (p. 36).

Similarly, LaBerge and Samuels (1985) believe that a teacher watching a bright student learning to read may observe that the student is attaining one skill (reading) slowly. On the other hand, the same teacher watching a slow learner attempting to learn to read may observe that the student is slowly learning many skills (phonics, etc.). "This comes about because the child often must be given extensive training on each of a variety of tasks, such as letter discrimination, letter-sound training, blending, etc. In this manner a teacher becomes aware of the fact that letter recognition can be considered a skill itself" (p. 713). LaBerge and Samuels's hierarchical model of perceptual learning suggests that students master smaller units before larger ones and integrate them into larger units after mastery (Samuels and Schachter, 1984).

Since fluent readers have mastered each of the subskills to the point where they use and integrate the subskills automatically, they do not clearly see the dividing lines among these skills during their daily reading. "One of the hallmarks of the reader who learned the subskills rapidly is that he was least aware of them at the time, and therefore now has little memory of them as separate subskills" (LaBerge and Samuels, 1985, p. 714). Guthrie (1973) found that reading subskills correlated highly with one another for students who were good readers. The correlations among reading subskills for poor readers were low. These students seemed to be operating at a level of separate rather than integrated skills. Guthrie's findings led to the conclusion that "lack of subskill mastery and lack of integration of these skills into higher order units" were sources of disability among poor readers (Samuels and Schachter, 1984, p. 39).

Samuels and Schachter (1984) report a study in which Donald Shankweiler and Isabelle Liberman tried to determine how well a child's fluency in oral reading of paragraph material could be predicted from his or her ability to read selected words in tests. They found that "roughly 50 percent of the variability in oral reading of connected words is associated with how well one can read these words in isolation" (p. 40). In other words, a child's oral reading of connected discourse tended to be only as good as his or her oral reading of individual words. Recognition of words in isolation (sight words) is one decoding subskill, so this study tends to support subskill theory.

Those who teach a set of subskills as a means of instructing children in reading generally recognize the importance of practicing the subskills in the context of actual reading in order to ensure integration. But some teachers overlook this vital phase and erroneously focus only on the subskills, overlooking the fact that they are the means to an end and not an end in themselves. Samuels (1994) points out that students can build automaticity only by spending much time reading. Although he acknowledges the need for practice with important subskills, he cautions that practice time must also be "spent on reading easy, interesting, meaningful material" (p. 834).

Adams (1994) feels much the same way. She says, "Deep and ready working knowledge of letters, spelling patterns, and words, and of the phonological translations of all three, are of inescapable importance to both skillful reading and its acquisition—not because they are the be all or the end all of the reading process, but because they enable it" (p. 859). She points out that frequent broad reading is important in developing reading proficiency.

Whereas beginning readers first focus on decoding and then switch their attention to comprehension, fluent readers decode automatically, and thus can focus attention on comprehension. Samuels (1994) points out that although the meanings of familiar words may be automatic for skilled readers, "the ability to get the meaning of each word in a sentence, however, is not the same as the ability to comprehend a sentence. In comprehending a sentence one must be able to interrelate and combine the separate meanings of each of its words. From this point of view, comprehension is a constructive process of synthesis and putting word meanings together in special ways, much as individual bricks are combined in the construction of a house" (p. 820).

Interactive Theories

An *interactive* theoretical model of the reading process depicts reading as a combination of two types of processing—top-down (reader based) and bottom-up (text based)—in continuous interaction. In *top-down* processing, the act of reading begins with the reader generating hypotheses or predictions about the material, using visual cues in the material to test these hypotheses as necessary (Walberg, Hare, and Pulliam, 1981). For instance, the reader of a folktale that begins with the words "Once upon a time there was a man who had three sons . . . " forms hypotheses about what will happen next, predicting that there will be a task to perform or a beautiful princess to win over and that the oldest two sons will fail but the youngest will attain his goal. Because of these expectations, the reader may read the material fairly quickly, giving attention primarily to words that confirm the expectations. Close reading occurs only if the hypothesis formed is not confirmed and an atypical plot unfolds. Otherwise, the reader can skip many words while skimming for key words that move the story along. Processing of print obviously cannot be a totally top-down experience, because a reader must begin by focusing on the print (Gove, 1983).

In *bottom-up* processing, reading is initiated by examining the printed symbols and requires little input from the reader (Walberg, Hare, and Pulliam, 1981). Gove (1983) says, "Bottom-up models assume that the translation process begins with print, i.e., letter or word identification, and proceeds to progressively larger linguistic units, phrases, sentences, etc., ending in meaning" (p. 262). A reader using bottom-up processing might first sound out a word letter by letter and then pronounce it, consider its meaning in relation to the phrase in which it is found, and so on. A reading teacher embracing this approach would expect a child to reproduce orally the exact words printed on the page.

An interactive model assumes parallel processing of information from print and information from background knowledge. Recognition and comprehension of printed words and ideas are the result of using both types of information (Gove, 1983). Not all interactive models, however, agree about the degree of influence of each type of processing, about the kind of processing that initiates the reading process, or about whether or not the two types of processing occur simultaneously (Harris and Sipay, 1985).

Rumelhart's early model indicated that, "at least for skilled readers, top-down and bottom-up processing occur simultaneously. . . . Because comprehension depends on both graphic information and the information in the reader's mind, it may be obstructed when a critical skill or a piece of information is missing" (Harris and Sipay, 1985, p. 10). For example, a reader who is unable to use context clues may fail to grasp the meaning of an unfamiliar word that is central to understanding the passage. Similarly, a reader who has no background knowledge about the topic may be unable to reconstruct the ideas the author is trying to convey.

Ruddell and Unrau (1994) bring social context into the picture, along with the reader and the text. They assert that "meaning results from the reader's meaning-construction process. That meaning is not entirely in either the text or the reader but is created as a result of the interactions among reader, text, teacher, and classroom community" (p. 1032).

Transactive Theories

Rosenblatt (1994) believes that "every reading act is an event, or a transaction involving a particular reader and . . . a text, and occurring at a particular time in a particular context. . . . The meaning does not reside ready-made 'in' the text or 'in' the reader but happens or comes into being during the transaction between reader and text" (p. 1061). Meaning results during the transaction. McGee (1992) points out that readers employ knowledge gained through past experiences to help them select interpretations, visualize the message, make connections between the new information and what they know, and relate affectively to the material. The transaction between reader and text is dynamic. The reader is highly important to this view of reading, and the stance the reader chooses must be considered. The reader may focus on obtaining information from the text (an efferent stance) but may also focus on the experience lived through during the reading, the feelings and images evoked and the memories aroused by the text (an aesthetic stance). Both stances are appropriate at times, and it is up to the reader to choose the approach to the reading. Even when reading a single work, readers may shift their stances from more efferent to more aesthetic, or vice versa, but fiction and poetry should involve a more aesthetic stance (Probst, 1988; Rosenblatt, 1978, 1991; McGee, 1992). Beach and Hynds (1991) believe that reading must be viewed as constructing an evolving experience, instead of a static meaning. The readers' stances, beliefs, and attitudes affect their responses, as does the context.

Rosenblatt's idea of an efferent–aesthetic continuum helps teachers see that there are both cognitive and affective aspects of all reading activities for both fiction and nonfiction and that the relative importance of each aspect will vary with the text and the reading situation. Frager (1993) suggests encouraging a wider range of aesthetic responses to content area reading by asking readers what feelings the text aroused in them. Students should both think about the concepts and experience the feelings evoked by the words.

Reading, according to Goodman (1973, p. 31), is a psycholinguistic guessing game in which readers "select the fewest, most productive cues necessary to produce guesses which are right the first time." Goodman believes that, although the ability to combine letters to form words is related to learning to read, it has little to do with the process of fluent reading. A person who is reading for meaning does not always need to identify individual words; a reader can comprehend a passage without having identified all the words in it. The more experience a reader has had with language and the concepts presented, the fewer clues from visual configurations (graphophonic clues) he or she will need to determine the meaning of the material. Fluent readers make frequent use of *semantic* (meaning) and *syntactic* (word-order) clues within the material as well (Cooper and Petrosky, 1976). Goodman points out the importance of the reader's ability to anticipate material that he or she has not yet seen. He also stresses that readers bring to their reading all their accumulated experience, language development, and thought in order to anticipate meanings in the printed material (p. 34).

Goodman acknowledges that Rosenblatt (1938/1983) influenced his thinking (Aaron et al., 1990), and he moved from a psycholinguistic focus to embrace a *transactive* focus. "The reader . . . constructs a text during reading through transactions with the published text and the reader's schemata are also transformed in the process. . . . In the receptive processes (listening and reading), meaning is constructed through transactions with the text and indirectly through the text with the writer" (Goodman, 1985, p. 814). He now asserts that the text a writer constructs has a meaning potential, although the text itself does not have meaning. Readers will use this meaning potential to construct their own meaning (Goodman, 1994).

reading-writing connection

The transactive theory appeals to advocates of a *whole language philosophy* toward reading. These educators want students to be involved with authentic reading, writing, listening, and speaking activities, that is, activities that are not just contrived to teach particular skills but are designed to communicate. They

literature-centered reading

advocate reading and writing whole pieces of literature, discussing these reading and writing experiences in class, and having students choose personally meaningful reading and writing experiences. The whole language philosophy is basically child centered. It emphasizes indirect instruction and the processes of speaking, listening, reading, and writing in the context of real-life activities (Slaughter, 1988). Further description of the whole language philosophy appears later in this chapter.

SELF-CHECK: OBJECTIVE 3   Compare and contrast subskill, transactive, and interactive theories of the reading process. (See Self-Improvement Opportunity 1.)

Teacher's Dilemma

The current educational situation in many areas poses a dilemma for teachers. Accountability is a big issue, and in most cases it is monitored by standardized tests. In general, the standardized tests of reading consist of performance of isolated skill activities rather than reading of whole pieces of text and responding to the text in a variety of ways. To prepare their students to score well on standardized tests, teachers may choose to follow a subskill approach to reading, even if they would more likely embrace an interactive or a transactive theory and set up classrooms filled with activities related to reading and writing whole pieces of literature, if left to their own decisions about what would be best for the students. Mosenthal (1989) says that these teachers are "between a rock and a hard place" and suggests that researchers need to focus on the complementarity between the approaches (subskills and holistic) rather than on their incompatibility, possibly by "creating a third approach that incorporates the best of both approaches while minimizing their weaknesses" (p. 629). This is essentially an eclectic attitude that many teachers have adopted as they have analyzed their instructional options.

Whole Language Philosophy

Whole language is a curricular philosophy, or belief system, in which the teacher is an initiator and mediator of learning experiences, a kidwatcher (observer of children), a liberator from constraints on learning, and a curriculum developer who links the curriculum to the learner. The social context for whole language instruction is a collaborative, mutually supportive, learner-centered classroom in which all learners are viewed positively and accepted as a part of the community of learners regardless of individual differences. Language is seen as central to learning; whole literature selections are used in reading programs; writing and reading are connected; functional language, reading comprehension, and written expression are emphasized; and teachers and students, rather than textbooks and tests, are in control of the curriculum. There is no packaged set of materials to rely on. The teacher, with student input, must be the decision maker. Students are involved in making choices, self-evaluating, and taking responsibility for their learning. In addition, learning is viewed as fulfilling and joyous (Goodman, 1992; Cullinan, 1992; Pahl and Monson, 1992; Oldfather, 1993; Walmsley, 1993; Moss and Noden, 1993/1994; Church, 1994; Watson, 1994). Students are motivated to learn when they are given opportunities to express themselves and have choices about their learning. They need to know that they will have a chance to share their ideas and products with others and that the teacher and other students will listen and respond to their spoken and written ideas (Oldfather, 1993).

Whole language classrooms are not devoid of skills instruction. Phonics *is* taught, but not separately from reading and writing. Spelling and grammar are viewed as means to an end (Newman and Church, 1990).

literature-centered reading

reading-writing connection

Church (1994) points out that "the shift to a whole language perspective involves fundamental changes in how teachers work. To implement a whole language philosophy, teachers need to know about language and literacy development, about language itself, about collaborative learning, about children's literature, about the reading and writing processes, and about language for learning across subject disciplines" (p. 368). There is no "one way" to be a whole language teacher (Newman and Church, 1990).

literature-centered reading

Whole language classrooms make much use of literature. Literature-based reading approaches are discussed in Chapters 7 and 8. Sustained silent reading, a technique in which everyone reads a self-selected book without interruption for a predetermined period of time, is a particularly appropriate technique for use in a school that embraces a whole language philosophy. (See more about this in Chapter 8.) The following Classroom Scenario describes a successful sustained silent reading period.

**Classroom
Scenario**

Sustained Silent Reading

A group of educators visited a middle school in West Tennessee shortly after 8 o'clock one morning. When they entered the school, it was so quiet that you could hear a pin drop. They went directly to the office, where they found the secretary reading a paperback book. One member of the group explained that they had entered the building during the sustained silent reading period and would not be able to talk to anyone until it was over, because interruptions to the reading of students, teachers, and staff members were not allowed. The visitors walked quietly through the school, observing the reading that was going on in every classroom. In some classrooms, students were sitting in chairs in a variety of postures or were sprawled on the carpet on their backs or stomachs. All seemed to be completely absorbed in reading books, magazines, or newspapers. At the end of the period a bell rang and the students, many reluctantly, put aside their reading materials and readied themselves for classwork. Some whispered excitedly to their neighbors, perhaps about the materials they had been reading. The overall impression the visitors received was that children and adults alike were pleased with the opportunity to read self-chosen material without interruption.

Analysis of Scenario
The use of sustained silent reading in this classroom obviously gave students the opportunity to read entire stories independently. The students were also allowed to select their own reading material, making it more likely that the material would be meaningful to them. Motivation to read was high under these conditions.

More on the whole language philosophy, whole language learning, whole language classrooms, and whole language evaluative techniques is found throughout this text, but especially in Chapter 8.

Twelve Principles of Teaching Reading

Principles of teaching reading are generalizations about reading instruction based on research in the field of reading and observation of reading practices. The principles listed here are not all-inclusive; many other useful generalizations about teaching reading have been made in the past and will continue to be made in the future. They are, however, the ones we believe are most useful in guiding teachers in planning reading instruction.

> *Principle 1   Reading is a complex act with many factors that must be considered.*

The discussion earlier in this chapter of the nine aspects of the reading process makes this principle clear. The teacher must understand all parts of the reading process in order to plan reading instruction wisely.

> *Principle 2   Reading involves the construction of the* **meaning** *represented by the printed symbols.*

A person who fails to derive meaning from a passage has not been reading, even if he or she has pronounced every word correctly. Chapters 4, 5, and 6 focus on constructing meaning from reading materials. "In addition to obtaining information from the letters and words in a text, reading involves selecting and using knowledge about people, places, and things, and knowledge about texts and their organization. A text is not so much a vessel containing meaning as it is a source of partial information that enables the reader to use already-possessed knowledge to determine the intended meaning" (Anderson et al., 1985, p. 8).

Readers construct the meanings of passages by using both the information conveyed by the text and their prior knowledge, which is based on their past experiences. Obviously, different readers construct meaning in somewhat different ways because of their varied experiential backgrounds. Some readers do not have enough background knowledge to understand a text; others fail to make good use of the knowledge they have (Anderson et al., 1985). For example, suppose a text mentions how mountains can isolate a group of people living in them. Students familiar with mountainous areas will picture steep grades and rough terrain, which make road building difficult, and will understand the source of the isolation, although the text never mentions it. Affective factors, such as the reader's attitudes toward the subject matter, also influence the construction of meaning, as does the context in which the reading takes place.

> *Principle 3   There is no one correct way to teach reading.*

Some methods of teaching reading work better for some children than for others. Each child is an individual who learns in his or her own way. Some children are visual learners; some are auditory learners; some are kinesthetic learners. Some need to be instructed through a combination of modalities, or avenues of perception, in order to learn. The teacher should differentiate instruction to fit the diverse needs of the students. Of course, some methods also work better for some teachers than they do for others. Teachers need to be acquainted with a

Teachers need to be acquainted with a variety of methods for teaching reading, since there is not just one correct way. (© Elizabeth Crews/Stock Boston)

variety of methods so that they can help all of their students. Chapter 7 covers a number of approaches to reading instruction.

> *Principle 4   Learning to read is a continuing process.*

Children learn to read over a long period of time, acquiring more advanced reading skills after they master prerequisite skills. Even after they have been introduced to all reading skills, the process of refinement continues. No matter how old they are or how long they have been out of school, readers continue to refine their reading skills. Reading skills require practice. If readers do not practice, the skills deteriorate; if they do practice, their skills continue to develop.

> *Principle 5   Students should be taught word recognition strategies that will allow them to unlock the pronunciations and meanings of unfamiliar words independently.*

Children cannot memorize all the words they will meet in print. Therefore, they need to learn techniques for figuring out unfamiliar words so that they can read when the assistance of a teacher, parent, or friend is not available. Chapter 3 focuses on word recognition strategies that children need.

Principle 6   The teacher should assess each student's reading ability and use the assessment as a basis for planning instruction.

Teaching all children the same reading lessons and hoping to deal at one time or another with all the difficulties students encounter is a shotgun approach and should be avoided. Such an approach wastes the time of those children who have attained the skills currently being emphasized and may never meet some of the desperate needs of other children. Teachers can avoid this approach by using assessment instruments and techniques to pinpoint the strengths and weaknesses of each child in the classroom. Then they can either divide the children into needs groups for pertinent instruction or give each child individual instruction. Chapter 11 describes many useful tests and other assessment procedures.

Principle 7   Reading and the other language arts are closely interrelated.

Reading—the interaction between a reader and written language through which the reader tries to reconstruct the writer's message—is closely related to all of the other major language arts (listening, speaking, and writing). Learning to read should be treated as an extension of the process of learning spoken language, a process that generally takes place in the home with little difficulty if children are given normal language input and feedback on their efforts to use language. Extensive input of natural language, opportunities to respond to this language, and feedback on appropriateness of responses provide children with a good learning environment (Hart, 1983).

A special relationship exists between listening and reading, which are *receptive* phases of language, as opposed to the *expressive* phases of speaking and writing. Mastering listening skills is important in learning to read, for direct association of sound, meaning, and word form must be established from the start. The ability to identify sounds heard at the beginning, middle, or end of a word and the ability to discriminate among sounds are essential to successful phonetic analysis of words. Listening skills also contribute to the interpretation of reading material.

Students' listening comprehension is generally superior to their reading comprehension in the elementary school years. Listening and reading become more equal in both word recognition rate and in word-per-minute rate later on. Not until the latter part of the sixth or seventh grade does reading proficiency reach the stage where most students prefer reading to listening in many learning situations. This implies that it is profitable to present instruction orally in the elementary school. Generally, more advanced children prefer to learn by reading; slower ones prefer to learn by listening, particularly when the concepts and vocabulary are especially difficult. Although reading and listening are not identical and each has its own advantages, they are alike in many ways. For example, both are constructive processes. In reading, the reader constructs the message from a printed source with the help of background knowledge; in listening, the listener constructs the message from a spoken source with the help of that same background knowledge. Teachers must be aware of the similarities so that they can provide effective instruction.

People learn to speak before they learn to read and write. Through experience with their environments, they begin to associate oral symbols or words with certain people, places, things, and ideas. Children's reading vocabularies generally consist largely of words in their oral language (listening and speaking) vocabularies. These are words for which they have previously developed concepts and thus, can comprehend.

reading-writing connection

Speaking, like the other language arts, is a constructive process. The speaker puts together words in an attempt to convey ideas to one or more listeners. The reader works at constructing meaning from the words the writer has put on paper.

The connection between reading and writing is particularly strong. First, both reading and writing are basically constructive processes. Readers must construct or attempt to reconstruct the message behind a written text. Their purposes for reading will affect the result of the reading activity, as will their knowledge about the world and about written language. Because of their differing purposes and backgrounds of experience, not all readers will interpret the same passage in the same way. Readers evaluate the accuracy of their message construction as they monitor their reading processes; they may revise the constructed meaning if the need is apparent.

Starting with purposes for writing that affect the choice of ideas and the way these ideas are expressed, writers work to create written messages for others to read. In completing the writing task, they draw on their past experiences and their knowledge of writing conventions. As they work, they tend to read and review their material in order to evaluate its effectiveness and to revise it, if necessary.

One means of relating early writing experiences to reading experiences—the language experience approach—is described in Chapter 7. Chapters 7 and 8 describe having children construct written responses to their reading of literature. Writing is also sometimes used as a follow-up or enrichment activity in basal reading lessons.

The strategies and skills needed for all four language arts are interrelated. For example, the need to develop and expand concepts and vocabulary, which is essential to reading, is evident in the entire language arts curriculum. Concepts and vocabulary terms to express these concepts are basic to listening, speaking, and writing as well as to reading activities. Spoken and written messages are organized around main ideas and supporting details, and people listen and read to identify the main ideas and supporting details conveyed in the material. Chapter 6 contains many examples of reading skills that have parallel listening skills and related writing and speaking skills.

literature-centered reading

Principle 8   *Using complete literature selections in the reading program is important.*

Students need to experience the reading of whole stories and books to develop their reading skills. Reading isolated words, sentences, and paragraphs does not give them the opportunity to use their knowledge of language and story structure to the fullest, and reading overly simplified language both reduces the opportunities to use their language expertise *and* dampens interest in reading the material. Whole pieces of literature can include students' own writing and the writing of other children as well as the works of commercial authors.

Principle 9   Reading is an integral part of all content area instruction within the educational program.

Teachers must consider the relationship of reading to other subjects within the curriculum of the elementary school. Frequently other curricular areas provide applications for the skills taught in the reading period. Textbooks in the various content areas are often the main means of conveying content concepts to students. Supplementary reading of library materials, magazines, and newspapers is also frequently used. Inability to read these materials with comprehension can mean failure to master important ideas in science, mathematics, social studies, and other areas of the curriculum. Students who have poor reading skills may therefore face failure in other areas of study because of the large amount of reading these areas often require. In addition, the need to write reports in social studies, science, health, or other areas can involve many reading and study skills: locating information (using the alphabet and the dictionary); organizing information (outlining, note taking, and preparing bibliographies); and using the library (using the card catalog, call numbers, classification systems, and references such as encyclopedias and atlases).

Teachers who give reading and writing instruction only within isolated periods and treat reading and writing as separate from the rest of the curriculum will probably experience frustration rather than achieve student change and growth. Although a definite period scheduled specifically for language instruction (listening, speaking, reading, and writing) may be recommended, this does not mean that teachers should ignore these areas when teaching content subjects. The ideal situation at any level is not "reading" and "writing" for separate time periods, followed by "study" of social science or science for the next period. Instead, although the emphasis shifts, language learning and studying should be integrated during all periods at all levels.

Chapters 9, 10, and 12 elaborate on these points, but we should clarify one additional idea at this time. Teachers sometimes assume the existence of a dichotomy: that children "learn to read" in the primary grades and "read to learn" in the intermediate and upper grades. Although it may be true that teachers devote less attention to the actual process of learning to read at the intermediate level, there is still a need there for attention to primary, as well as higher-level, strategies. On the other hand, primary students can and do read for information.

Principle 10   The student needs to see that reading can be an enjoyable pursuit.

It is possible for our schools to produce capable readers who do not read; in fact, today this is a common occurrence. Reading can be entertaining as well as informative. Teachers can help students realize this fact by reading stories and poems to them daily and setting aside a regular time for pleasure reading, during which many good books of appropriate levels and from many interest areas are

literature-centered reading

readily available. Teachers can show children that reading is a good recreational pursuit by describing the pleasure they personally derive from reading in their spare time and by reading for pleasure in the children's presence. When the children read recreationally, the teacher should do this also, thereby modeling desired behavior. Pressures of tests and reports should not be a part of recreational reading times. Chapter 8 provides some guidance for teachers in this area. Students in literature-based reading instructional programs that include self-selection of reading materials and group discussion of chosen reading materials are likely to discover the enjoyable aspects of reading for themselves. Chapter 7 discusses such programs.

>*Principle 11 Reading should be taught in a way that allows each child to experience success.*

The stage of the child's literacy development should be considered for all instructional activities throughout the grades. Not only when reading and writing instruction begins, but whenever instruction in any language strategy takes place, at all grade levels, teachers should consider each child's readiness for the instructional activity. If the child's literacy development is not adequate for the task, the teacher should adjust the instruction so that it is congruent with the student's literacy level. This may involve instruction to provide a child with readiness to incorporate the new learning into his or her store of concepts.

Asking children to try to learn to read from materials that are too difficult for them ensures that a large number will fail. Teachers should give children instruction at their own levels of achievement, regardless of grade placement. Success generates success. If children are given a reading task at which they can succeed, they gain the confidence to attack the other reading tasks they must perform in a positive way. This greatly increases the likelihood of their success at these later tasks. In addition, some studies have shown that if a teacher *expects* students to be successful readers, they will in fact *be* successful.

Teachers tend to place poor readers in materials that are too hard for them more frequently than they place good readers in such materials. Children who are given difficult material to read use active, comprehension-seeking behaviors less often than do children who are reading instructional-level material (material they can understand with a teacher's assistance). Placing poor readers on levels that are too high tends to reinforce the inefficient reading strategies that emerge when material is too difficult, making it less likely that these readers will develop more efficient strategies. Poor readers give up on reading tasks more quickly than do good readers. Although they do not have high expectations of success under any circumstances, their expectations of success decrease more after failure than do those of good readers (Bristow, 1985).

Teachers should place poor readers in material they can read without undue focus on word recognition. This approach allows poor readers to focus on comprehending the text. Also, because poor readers may not have had the idea that reading should make sense, urging them to make sense of written messages can be helpful. Poor readers' comprehension skills can be improved if teachers help them acquire the appropriate background for reading selections and help them develop such metacognitive (self-monitoring) strategies as rereading, self-questioning, purpose-setting, and predicting. Finally, poor readers must be convinced that they will gain greater understanding during reading if they apply specific strategies they have learned. They must believe that success lies within their reach (Bristow, 1985).

Hart (1983) states that threat of failure (especially public failure) may cause students to "downshift" to a less sophisticated part of the brain that lacks the pattern detection capabilities and program-storing capabilities of the cerebrum, which is the locus of language functions. Therefore, threat of failure can induce failure.

Asking children to read from materials that do not relate to their backgrounds of experiences can also result in less successful experiences. In view of the wide cultural diversity found in schools today, teachers must be particularly sensitive to this problem and must provide relevant materials for children that offer them a chance for success.

> *Principle 12   Encouragement of self-direction and self-monitoring of reading is important.*

Good readers direct their own reading, making decisions about how to approach particular passages, what reading speed is appropriate, and *why* they are reading the passages. They are able to decide when they are having difficulties with understanding and can take steps to remedy their misunderstandings (Anderson et al., 1985). When they do this, they are using metacognitive strategies. Chapters 5 and 9 present more information about the way good readers read flexibly and monitor their reading.

No matter what teaching approaches are used in a school or what patterns of organization predominate, these principles of teaching reading should apply. Each teacher should consider carefully his or her adherence or lack of adherence to such principles.

SELF-CHECK: OBJECTIVE 4   We have discussed twelve principles related to teaching reading. Explain how knowledge of each principle should affect your teaching of reading. (See Self-Improvement Opportunity 3.)

Summary

The reading act is composed of two major parts: the reading process and the reading product. The reading process has nine aspects—sensory, perceptual, sequential, experiential, thinking, learning, association, affective, and constructive—that combine to produce the reading product, communication.

Three of the many types of theories about the reading process are subskill theories, interactive theories, and transactive theories. Subskill theories depict reading as a series of subskills that children must master so that they become automatic and smoothly integrated. Interactive theories depict reading as the interaction of two types of processing: top-down and bottom-up. Both types of processing are used to recognize and comprehend words. According to the bottom-up view, reading is initiated by the printed symbols (letters and words) and proceeds to larger linguistic units until the reader discovers meaning. According to the top-down view, reading begins with the reader's generation of hypotheses or predictions about the material, with the reader using the visual cues in the material to test these hypotheses as necessary. Therefore, according to interactive theories, both the print and the reader's background are important in the reading process. Transactive theories depict every reading act as a transaction involving a reader and a text at a particular time in a specific context. Readers generate and test hypotheses about the reading material and get feedback from the material. Whole language activities fit well with the transactive theoretical stance, since the whole language philosophy embraces the idea of encouraging authentic transactions with text. Whole language philosophy also encourages collaborative, learner-centered classroom environments, much reading and writing of whole selections, and student choice.

Some principles related to reading instruction that may be helpful to teachers include the following:

1. Reading is a complex act with many factors that must be considered.
2. Reading involves the construction of the *meaning* represented by the printed symbols.
3. There is no one correct way to teach reading.
4. Learning to read is a continuing process.
5. Students should be taught word recognition skills that will allow them to unlock the pronunciations and meanings of unfamiliar words independently.
6. The teacher should assess each student's reading ability and use the assessment as a basis for planning instruction.
7. Reading and the other language arts are closely interrelated.
8. Using complete literature selections in the reading program is important.
9. Reading is an integral part of all content area instruction within the educational program.
10. The student needs to see that reading can be an enjoyable pursuit.
11. Reading should be taught in a way that allows each child to experience success.
12. Encouragement of self-direction and self-monitoring of reading is important.

Test Yourself *True or False*

_____ 1. Over a period of time a single, clear-cut definition of reading has emerged.

_____ 2. Reading is a complex of many skills.

_____ 3. When children read, their eyes move smoothly over the page from left to right.

_____ 4. Faulty eye movements usually cause serious reading problems.

_____ 5. Regressions are always undesirable.

_____ 6. Perception involves interpretation of sensation.

_____ 7. Prereading questions can affect the way students think while reading.

_____ 8. The more meaningful learning is to a child, the more rapidly associative learning takes place.

_____ 9. Word calling and reading are synonymous.

_____ 10. Teachers go to school so that they can learn the one way to teach reading.

_____ 11. People can continue to refine their reading skills as long as they live.

_____ 12. Assessing the reading problems of every child in a class is a waste of a teacher's valuable time.

_____ 13. Assessment can help a teacher plan appropriate instruction for all children in a class.

_____ 14. Reading and the other language arts are closely interrelated.

_____ 15. Content area instruction should not have to be interrupted for teaching of reading strategies; reading instruction should remain strictly within a special reading period.

_____ 16. Understanding the importance of reading is unimportant to a child's reading progress.

_____ 17. Teachers should stress reading for enjoyment as well as for information.

_____ 18. Reading seems to fit in the "skill" category of behavior.

_____ 19. Current theories about reading account for all aspects of the reading process.

_____ 20. No research supports the view that reading is a set of subskills that must be mastered and integrated.

_____ 21. A bottom-up model of the reading process assumes that reading is initiated by the printed symbols, with little input required from the reader.

_____ 22. According to an interactive model of reading, parallel processing of information from print and from background knowledge takes place.

_____ 23. Reading involves constructing the meaning of a written passage.

_____ 24. Reading and writing are both constructive processes.

_____ 25. Teachers give good readers materials that are too hard for them more often than they give poor readers such materials.

_____ 26. Metacognitive processes are self-monitoring processes.

_____ 27. A whole language philosophy is not compatible with a skill-and-drill approach to teaching.

_____ 28. Whole language teachers personally make all of the decisions about classroom materials and activities.

_____ 29. Transactive theories of the reading process take into account the reader, the text, and the context in which the reading takes place.

_____ 30. A transactive theory would support the position that the meaning resides in the text.

Self-Improvement Opportunities

1. Study the following definitions of reading, which have been suggested by well-known authorities. Decide which aspect or combination of aspects of the reading process each definition emphasizes most.

   a. "Reading is a process in which information from the text and the knowledge possessed by the reader act together to produce meaning." (Richard C. Anderson et al., *Becoming a Nation of Readers*. Washington, D.C.: National Institute of Education, 1985, p. 8.)

   b. "Reading is a sampling, selecting, predicting, comparing and confirming activity in which the reader selects a sample of useful graphic cues based on what he sees and what he expects to see." (Kenneth Goodman, quoted in *A Dictionary of Reading and Related Terms*, edited by Theodore L. Harris and Richard E. Hodges. Newark, Del.: International Reading Association, 1981, p. 265.)

   c. "Reading means getting meaning from certain combinations of letters. Teach the child what each letter stands for and he can read." (Rudolph Flesch, *Why Johnny Can't Read and What You Can Do about It*. New York: Harper & Row, 1955, pp. 2–3.)

   d. "Reading is a process of looking at written language symbols, converting them into overt or covert speech symbols, and then manipulating them so that both the direct (overt) and implied (covert) ideas intended by the author may be understood." (Lawrence E. Hafner and Hayden B. Jolly, *Teaching Reading to Children*, 2d ed. New York: Macmillan, 1982, p. 4.)

   e. "Reading is thinking . . . reconstructing the ideas of others." (Robert Karlin, *Teaching Elementary Reading: Principles and Strategies*, 3d ed. New York: Harcourt Brace Jovanovich, 1980, p. 7.)

   f. "Reading involves the identification and recognition of printed or written symbols which serve as stimuli for the recall of meaning built up through past experience, and further the construction of new meanings through the reader's manipulation of relevant concepts already in his possession. The resulting meanings are organized into thought processes according to the purposes that are operating in the reader." (Miles A. Tinker and Constance M. McCullough, *Teaching Elementary Reading,* 4th ed. Englewood Cliffs, N.J.: Prentice-Hall, 1975, p. 9.)

g. "Reading involves nothing more than the correlation of a sound image with its corresponding visual image, that is, the spelling." (Leonard Bloomfield and Clarence L. Barnhart, *Let's Read: A Linguistic Approach.* Detroit: Wayne State University Press, 1961, dustjacket.)

h. "Reading typically is the bringing of meaning *to* rather than the gaining of meaning *from* the printed page." (Henry P. Smith and Emerald V. Dechant, *Psychology in Teaching Reading.* Englewood Cliffs, N.J.: Prentice-Hall, 1961, p. 22.)

2. Note the points of agreement in the various definitions given in item 1.

3. Find more recent definitions of reading in this text or in journal articles, and compare them to the definitions in item 1.

4. After studying the principles of reading instruction presented in this chapter, see if you can formulate other principles based on your reading in other sources.

5. To help you in your further study of elementary school reading, participate in the activities of organizations such as the International Reading Association and the National Council of Teachers of English. The meetings, publications (particularly *The Reading Teacher* and *Language Arts*), and projects these organizations sponsor provide some of the best ways to keep informed about new ideas on teaching reading, as well as the other language arts.

Emergent Literacy

Key Vocabulary

Pay close attention to these terms when they appear in the chapter.

alphabetic principle

big book

cognitive development

creative dramatics

dramatic play

emergent literacy

environmental print

experience chart

invented spelling

phonemic awareness

predictable story

preoperational period

print convention

reading readiness

shared-book
  experience

sight word

Setting Objectives

When you finish reading this chapter, you should be able to

1. Understand the concept of *emergent literacy.*

2. Discuss the relationship between cognitive development and language learning.

3. List some features of a print-rich classroom environment.

4. Explain the influence of the home on a child's early language growth.

5. Discuss the roles of listening comprehension and oral expression in the development of literacy.

6. Identify some ways children learn to read in an emergent literacy classroom.

7. Explain how children's growth in writing occurs.

8. Describe some appropriate assessment techniques.

Figure 2.1 *Chapter 2 Organization*

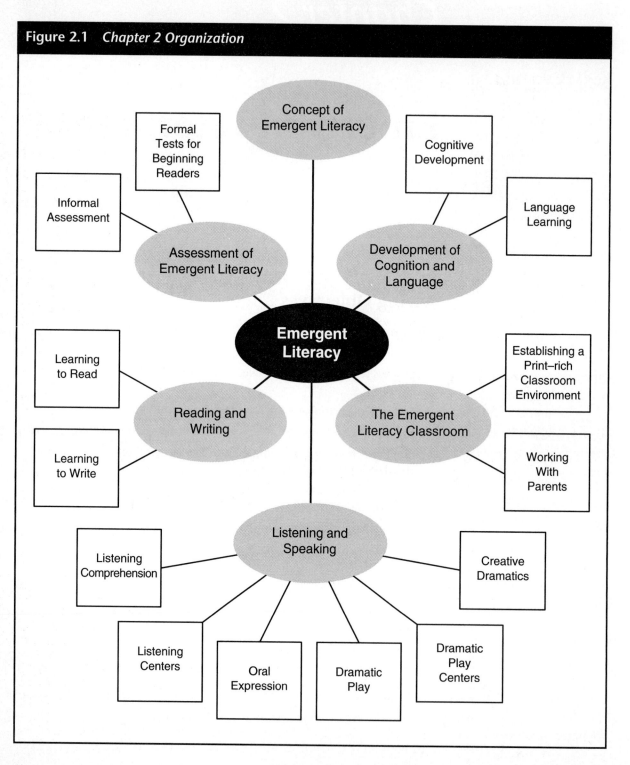

This chapter begins with a discussion of the differences between the concepts of reading readiness and emergent literacy. Then it demonstrates the close relationship between cognitive development and language learning. The emergent literacy classroom places the child at the center of the learning experiences and provides many opportunities for language development. A central emergent literacy concept is that most children know a great deal about literacy from early experiences in the home, and the teacher should build on this knowledge when planning classroom learning activities. The teacher should provide a print-rich environment to nurture growth in reading and writing and should offer children authentic purposes for learning language. As in the home, reading and writing should develop concurrently through the use of a wide variety of literacy experiences and materials.

The chapter presents a variety of ways teachers can facilitate language development in young children. It discusses ideas for enhancing listening comprehension and oral expression and gives special attention to informal drama as a means of stimulating such development. Then it examines the ways children learn to read and write by applying knowledge they have gained from their background experiences and their familiarity with print. Strategies for encouraging children to use invented spellings are considered for promoting both writing and reading. A discussion of assessment techniques concludes the chapter.

The Concept of Emergent Literacy

A current view of beginning reading supports the position that, during early childhood and beyond, youngsters go through a period of *emergent literacy*, or a developing awareness of the interrelatedness of oral and written language (Teale and Sulzby, 1986). The word *emergent* implies that development occurs from within the child, that it happens gradually over time, that some fundamental abilities for making sense of the world must already exist within the child, and that *literacy* (the ability to read and write) will emerge when conditions are right (Hall, 1987).

This viewpoint has largely supplanted the concepts of *reading readiness* and *reading readiness period*. Educators used these terms for many decades, and teachers will undoubtedly still encounter them. Reading readiness was regarded as mastery of a set of discrete skills, such as visual and auditory discrimination, necessary for learning to read and write. The readiness period was thought to occur before formal reading instruction, usually from kindergarten through the early part of first grade. When children mastered a sufficient number of readiness skills, teachers introduced them to preprimers and, sometime later, to writing. It was assumed that children knew little about literacy when they entered school and needed to learn specific skills before they were ready to read and write.

Emergent literacy, in contrast, is based on the assumption that language learning occurs naturally in the home and community as children see print and understand its function in their environment. They learn about literacy from adult models, particularly family members, and their knowledge of reading and

reading-writing connection

writing develops concurrently. Before they understand letter-sound associations, they scribble messages or draw letterlike forms that have meaning for them and then "read" their messages to others.

Researchers have found that many kindergarten children already understand numerous concepts about language, including the following (Mavrogenes, 1986; McLane and McNamee, 1990):

1. They make sense out of the writing in their environment by relating words (such as *McDonald's*) to corresponding places (a restaurant).

2. They expect print to be meaningful and to communicate ideas.

3. They understand some characteristics of written language, such as directionality, spacing, sequencing, and form.

4. They have some knowledge of letter names, auditory and visual discrimination, and correspondence between written and spoken words.

5. They know what books are and how to use them.

What the child learns quite naturally about language at home should be the foundation for literacy learning in the classroom, and it makes sense for continued language growth to occur in much the same way that it did during the preschool years. In other words, language learning in the classroom should grow out of the child's natural curiosity about language, functional use of language in authentic situations, and experimentation with ways to use language for effective communication. The following activities are recommended for promoting literacy:

1. Listening to stories

2. Writing messages

3. Retelling stories

4. Engaging in dramatic play that involves authentic reading and writing activities

5. Sharing in big book story reading

6. Learning to spell one's name

7. Recognizing environmental print, such as *STOP*

reading-writing connection

Early experiences with written language that may occur during the first year of life, such as playing with alphabet blocks and listening to stories read from books, lay the foundation for a lifelong process of learning to read and write (Teale and Sulzby, 1989). Children progress through developmental stages in oral language (from babbling to mature speech) and written language (from scribbling to legible writing), moving toward ever-higher levels of language proficiency. Thus, literacy evolves in a natural, connected way over an extended period of time as the learner discovers new insights about language and how it works.

SELF-CHECK: OBJECTIVE 1   What are some differences between the concepts of reading readiness and emergent literacy? (See Self-Improvement Opportunities 5, 6, and 13.)

Development of Cognition and Language

In recent years, the study of language development in isolation has shifted to the study of language learning in relation to *cognitive development* (Finn, 1985). This means there is a connection between the way children learn to use language and the way they grow in the ability to know and understand concepts or ideas. Thinking skills are closely related; language is a vehicle for understanding and communicating thoughts.

Cognitive Development

Jean Piaget, a Swiss psychologist highly respected for his theory of cognitive development, asserted that thought comes before language and that language is a way of representing thought. Piaget divided cognitive development into four periods: sensorimotor, preoperational, concrete-operational, and formal-operational. Because this chapter deals with the child's early school years, this discussion of Piaget's theory will focus on the *preoperational period.*

The preoperational period is divided into two stages, the *preconceptual stage* from age two to four and the *intuitive stage* from age four to six or seven (Burmeister, 1983). During the preconceptual stage, children begin to engage in symbolic thought by representing ideas and events with words and sentences, drawings, and dramatic play. As they begin to use symbols to stand for spoken words, they realize that writing represents meaning, a concept that is basic to reading comprehension (Waller, 1977).

At the intuitive stage, children are rapidly developing concepts but are limited in their ability to use adult logic. They are egocentric; that is, they consider things only from their own points of view. This characteristic prevents children from thinking clearly about the events in a story, except from their own limited perspectives. Although most children at this stage are unable to state the rules governing syntax, they do demonstrate syntactic or grammatical awareness in their speech; that is, they are able to use words in a logical order as they form sentences.

reading-writing connection　Children at the preoperational level lack many of the concepts needed to understand reading and writing processes, and they are often frustrated when teachers expect them to perform such beginning reading tasks as memorizing rules and deciding which words follow the rule, understanding that a single letter can represent multiple sounds, and changing letters to sounds and back to letters (Harp, 1987). Children at this level would probably be more successful in whole language or child-centered classrooms with a wide variety of language materials and experiences that would allow them to form their own concepts about print.

Basing her experiments with children on principles of Piaget's theory, Ferreiro (1990) found that children attempt to assimilate information about the writing system by drawing on their observations of the environment. As they encounter new information about language, they struggle to make sense of it and actively construct their own interpretation systems in their search for coherence. These systems are illogical and incomplete by adult standards, but for children they represent their best concepts of the nature and function of written language at a given stage of cognitive development. As children receive new information that contradicts the knowledge they already have, they must modify their language systems (Ferreiro and Teberosky, 1982).

Language Learning

Developmental learning occurs naturally, with minimal instruction, as a child grows up. It "is highly individual and noncompetitive; it is short on teaching and long on learning; it is self-regulated rather than adult-regulated; it goes hand in hand with the fulfillment of real life purposes; it emulates the behavior of people who model the skill in natural use" (Holdaway, 1979, p. 14). Speech develops in this way, and many educators argue that literacy should develop in a similar manner.

Language learning is a continuous, interactive, and purposeful process (Loughlin and Martin, 1987). Children learn to speak without instruction by imitating speech sounds and observing the interactions of language users. Language learning is more than imitation, however, because each individual constructs language according to personal needs and motivations. The child acquires speech through immersion in a language environment that provides speech models, motivation for speaking, and interactions with other speakers. The beginning speaker engages in trial and error and takes risks to establish communications with others.

The following assumptions about language learning have some implications for instruction that will be discussed later in this chapter (Cambourne, 1984; *Cases in Literacy*, 1989; Hall, 1987; Strickland, 1990; Teale and Sulzby, 1989):

1. Children begin to read and write early in life without formal instruction.

2. Social interactions with family members and feedback from them are important for developing literacy.

3. Exposure to print in many forms and for many purposes enhances literacy. Shared-book experiences are especially valuable.

4. The cultural group in which children grow up greatly affects their emerging literacy.

5. The language children hear is meaningful and whole, not nonsensical or fragmented.

6. Children are responsible for their own learning. They construct language individually according to their understandings and purposes.

7. Expectations affect how children learn; high expectations often lead learners to live up to them.

8. Reading and writing develop interrelatedly and concurrently.

9. Children learn language by using it in meaningful ways.

10. Language learning is continuous: it begins at birth and continues throughout life.

A child's early attempts at language are intuitive; that is, the child uses language reasonably well but lacks metalinguistic awareness, the ability to think about language and manipulate it objectively. For example, a youngster may say, "I want some candy," but may be unable to tell how many words were spoken or recognize that this group of words is called a *sentence*. A discrepancy exists between the use of language and an awareness of the meanings of terms, such as *word, sentence, sound,* and *letter,* that refer to language (Hare, 1984). A teacher who wishes to develop children's skill in recognizing words as basic elements of speech might use the following Model Activity.

Model Activities

Recognition of the Concept of *Word*

Make two copies of a chart story based on an experience that children have shared. Run your fingers under the first sentence on one of the charts as you say to the children: "Read this sentence with me." Then use your hands to block off individual words as you say to them: "Look at the groups of letters between the spaces. We call each group of letters a *word*." Ask them: "How many words are in this sentence?" Do the same thing with the other sentences on the chart. Then cut the sentences into strips and ask several children to cut the strips into words. Give each child a word. Say to the children: "Can you find your word on our other chart? If you can, put your word with the word on the chart."

It is important to realize that children develop an understanding of the concept of *word* gradually through many experiences. Also, because individual children are at various developmental levels for acquiring this concept, for some the lesson will verify what they were already beginning to realize and for others, who are less ready, the lesson will have little or no meaning. Another Model Activity, on page 44, reinforces the concept of *word* and helps children begin to develop a concept of *sentence*.

Because many children fail to understand linguistic terminology, they cannot make sense of instruction based on these terms. If a child does not understand the meanings of language-related terms, he or she must experience considerable confusion when a teacher says, "Look at the *middle letter* of this *word*. The *vowel* has its *short sound* because it is followed by a *consonant*."

Having children perform isolated drills and memorize rules without understanding their meanings is unlikely to help them learn to read. Beginning reading instruction should be based on language experiences and predictable or repetitive stories rather than on isolated phonics and structural analysis. It is the teacher's responsibility to provide a print-rich environment, ask questions about language and help children discover answers, read to and with the children, provide authentic reading and writing tasks, and encourage and guide children in their developing sense of language.

Model Activities

Recognition of the Concept of *Sentence*

Say to the children: "Today we're going to put some sentences on the board. A sentence is a group of words. Who can tell me a sentence about what day it is?"

Mike: "Tuesday."

Then say: "You're right, Mike; it's Tuesday. Can you put the word *Tuesday* in a sentence with some other words?"

Mike: "Today is Tuesday."

Say: "That's right," and write the sentence on the board. Then say: "Now look at the sentence I've written and tell me how many words are in it. Remember to look for the spaces between the groups of letters."

Mike: "Three."

Then say: "Good. Can someone tell me a sentence about the weather today?"

Tina: "It's cloudy outside."

Say: "That's a good sentence, Tina," and write the sentence on the board. Say: "Look at Tina's sentence and tell me how many words there are." (You may continue by asking other questions for the children to answer in sentences and then follow the same procedure.)

SELF-CHECK: OBJECTIVE 2   What are some ways that levels of cognitive development and language learning affect a child's ability to learn to read and write? (See Self-Improvement Opportunity 8.)

The Emergent Literacy Classroom

reading-writing connection

In the emergent literacy classroom, children are the center of learning, many forms of print are available, and activities are purposeful, always moving children toward the acquisition of literacy. Reading and writing develop concurrently, with teacher guidance and encouragement. This does not mean skills are unimportant; indeed, children must learn them to become successful readers, writers, and speakers. The perspective has changed, however. The teacher's role is now one of setting conditions that enable children to explore language and make discoveries that will lead them to internalize reading and writing skills. The teacher is there sometimes to provide direct instruction, but more often to assist learners and intervene when they need help.

The teacher must build on children's existing knowledge about language by understanding each child and providing appropriate literacy experiences. It is important to remember that every child who enters school is an individual with a unique personality, a specific set of experiences, and special interests. Most children come to the classroom with reasonable control over oral language, but they are likely to have many misconceptions and incompletely formed concepts about written language. According to Kenneth Goodman (1986), teachers should accept children as natural and curious learners, recognize their special competencies and needs, find ways to serve them, and support them with patience and encouragement.

Children whose teachers adhere to these ideas are likely to flourish. No matter how unconventional their literacy appears to adults, they view themselves as readers and writers. They are risk takers, experimenting and learning with language, unafraid of making mistakes. Through their writing and interactions with their teacher and peers, they become thinkers who search for meaning and try to clarify their concepts (Avery, 1987). These children also value their ability to make choices—what to do, with whom to work, where to work, and how best to do the chosen tasks (Rasinski, 1988). The following Classroom Scenario illustrates this point.

Classroom Scenario

Freedom to Choose

Following a unit on giants that included a section on whales, a prefirst grader chose to draw pictures of whales during language workshop. Sprawled on the floor in a corner or the room, Danny carefully sketched a different kind of whale in each of six frames of large segmented paper to be used for a roll movie. He marked the distinguishing features of each whale, then labeled each picture by copying the name of the type of whale. For Danny, such sustained attention was unusual, but whales fascinated him.

Analysis of Scenario
When children are free to choose their activities, their concentration and determination enable them to accomplish remarkable tasks.

Establishing a Print-Rich Classroom Environment

reading-writing connection   By establishing print-rich environments, teachers can encourage children to become aware of purposes for reading and writing. Charts on which teachers record dictations about students' experiences, as well as labels for identifying objects, remind students that print communicates meaning. Attractively displayed books invite children to read, and writing materials at play centers encourage them to write lists and memos (Booth, 1994).

Many children learn to read *environmental print*—words they frequently see around them—long before they enter school. By using advertisements and promotional materials for familiar products such as Crest or popular cereals, teachers link the home/community environment with that of the classroom (Neuman and Roskos, 1993; Sabey and Squier, 1993). Another advantage of using environmental print is that it is free and readily available. Often children bring examples to share, read them, and display them for others to read. Using the children's knowledge of environmental words, the teacher can begin teaching letter-sound relationships. See the following Model Activity.

**Model
Activities**

Environmental Print

Since you have been encouraging the children to share examples of environmental print, they have responded enthusiastically. Today, as the children present their treasures, you notice a teaching opportunity. Say: "Tina and Jeff, will you please tell us what you brought?" (Tina has a label from a pizza box, and Jeff has an empty bag of potato chips.) Then say: "Who can tell me the name of the letter we see at the beginning of *pizza*? What letter do we see at the beginning of *potato chip*? Now let's say these words and listen to see if they sound alike at the beginning."

When the children have identified the letter and realized that the words begin with the same sound, say: "Can you find another word in the room that starts with the same letter?" When Carole finds the word *party* in a chart story about last week's Halloween party, ask: "Does *party* begin with the same sound we hear at the beginning of *pizza* and *potato chip*?" When the children reply affirmatively, put the letter *p* at the top of a chart and write *pizza*, *potato chip*, and *party* under the letter. Say: "Let's read these words again and listen for the sound that *p* makes. When we find other words that begin with the letter *p*, we can add them to our chart."

A teacher's daily reading aloud to children helps them develop an awareness of story structure, acquaints them with new words, and fosters their interest in reading. (*Barbara Alper/Stock Boston*)

In a developmental classroom, the environment should provide opportunities for language growth that are similar to those provided in a natural home environment (Holdaway, 1979). Here are some guidelines based on this concept (Fisher, 1989; Wood and Nurss, 1988):

reading-writing connection

1. Provide a wide variety of materials for purposeful writing and reading.

2. Place labels and key words around the room at the children's eye level.

3. Organize the room so that children can follow the classroom routine and take care of their belongings independently.

4. Display children's work so that they can see it and discuss it with others. (In one room, the bulletin board is on the floor.)

5. Use reading materials that relate to ongoing class activities, as shown in the following Model Activity.

Model Activities

Duty Chart

Say to the children: "In our classroom, we need many helpers. What kinds of helpers do we need?" The children suggest answers. Then say: "We will need different boys and girls to help us each week. I have made a duty chart to help us remember whose turn it is to help. Each week we will change the names beside the jobs. Let's read the chart together. We'll see who has a job this week."

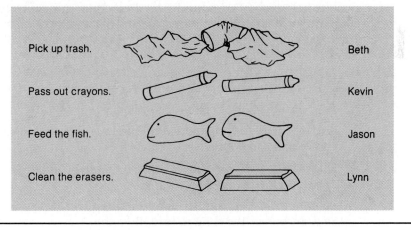

Pick up trash.		Beth
Pass out crayons.		Kevin
Feed the fish.		Jason
Clean the erasers.		Lynn

Following are some items that might be found in a print-rich, literate classroom environment:

books of all types	stamp pads
typewriter and computer	variety of writing materials

captioned photographs	nature center with labels
individual chalkboards	displays of children's work
chart stories	calendars, weather reports
newspapers, magazines	unit displays and models
message boards	labels from familiar foods
children's books	files of children's work
labels around classroom	pocket charts

Many of these items appear on bulletin boards, on walls, and even suspended from the ceiling; others are located at centers in the room. Examples of tasks and materials appropriate for listening, reading, writing, and dramatic play centers are presented later in this chapter.

SELF-CHECK: OBJECTIVE 3   Brainstorm as many types of materials as you can for a print-rich classroom. (See Self-Improvement Opportunities 1, 2, 6, 10, and 11.)

Working with Parents

It is important that parents provide a positive environment for their youngsters' emerging literacy. Parents need to become aware that they are their children's first teachers and that the language experiences they provide will have a powerful effect on the children's growth in literacy. Teachers can help parents better understand and execute their critical role in promoting early literacy by encouraging them to respond enthusiastically to their children's curiosity about print. The continuity—or lack of continuity—between literacy experiences at home and in school strongly affects learning (McLane and McNamee, 1990).

Although teachers should not expect parents to provide direct instruction for their children, which may create anxieties and tensions (Clay, 1979), they can offer parents the following suggestions for guiding literacy development at home:

1. Read picture books, beginning at infancy.

2. Listen patiently and supportively when the child struggles to express an idea, and respond appropriately.

3. Share letters that come in the mail so that the child understands that writing can communicate messages.

4. Point out and read familiar signs, such as ones that say *Sears, Wendy's,* and *Stop.* Encourage the child to read them too.

5. Provide writing materials (including typewriters and computers, if possible) and encourage their use for writing messages, shopping lists, and letters.

6. Model good reading practices by reading books for your own pleasure. Explain why you are enjoying your book.

7. Carry on conversations with the child. Answer questions and explain "why" and "how."

8. Share newspapers and magazines. Encourage the child to find familiar words that appear in advertisements.

9. Sing songs, do finger plays, recite nursery rhymes, and play guessing games.

10. Take the child with you on visits and trips. Use specific terms when discussing the experience, such as *flight attendant, pilot, gate,* and *baggage area.*

11. Involve the child in activities around the home, such as cooking, gardening, and paying bills. Point out the usefulness of recipes, instructions on seed packets, and checkbooks.

12. Visit the children's section of the library; let the child get a library card and check out lots of books.

13. Read together cereal boxes, menus, place mats, street signs, coupons, and other forms of print.

14. Encourage the child to "talk like a book" when sharing a storybook with you.

literature-centered reading

Because of the importance of story reading with children, teachers might offer parents some specific pointers. Story reading can be a pleasurable experience for both the reader and the child, especially when accompanied by a lively verbal exchange about the story and the illustrations. Research on home storybook reading has supported the following interactive behaviors for their positive effects on literacy: questioning, praising, offering information, directing discussion, relating concepts to life experiences, modeling dialogue and responses, and sharing personal reactions (Strickland and Morrow, 1990). Here are examples of appropriate questions and comments based on *The Three Little Pigs.*

How is this little pig's house different from our house?

Uh-oh, that wolf is going to cause trouble! Can you read this part with me? (*I'll huff, and I'll puff, and I'll blow your house down.*)

What do you think will happen next?

That's a good idea! Let's read so that we can find out for sure.

I think this third little pig is pretty smart. What do you think?

By sharing alphabet books with their children, parents can make them aware of many print conventions. Behaviors such as pointing to words and letters, talking about words with similar sounds, and observing upper- and lower-case letters occur naturally during parent-child reading. Smolkin and Yaden (1992) found that children whose parents read with them were using correct linguistic terms (for example, *letter* and *word*) and becoming aware of directionality, letter forms, and sound-letter relationships. In addition, they were learning new word meanings and using prior knowledge to make sense of text.

SELF-CHECK: OBJECTIVE 4   List several suggestions teachers can offer parents about supporting a child's emerging literacy. (See Self-Improvement Opportunity 13.)

Listening and Speaking

The language skills children have learned at home are the foundation for their further language development. Throughout the school day, children should have many opportunities to develop oral communication skills. In the accompanying Classroom Scenario, the children follow a procedure for sharing time that stresses courtesy in both speaking and listening behaviors.

Classroom Scenario

Sharing Time

At the beginning of school, Paula Franck modeled sharing time with her kindergartners, but now they are conducting it themselves. Paula and the children are sitting on the rug with Kelly, today's leader, on a chair in front of them. Kelly begins by saying: "Who has something to share today?" Jenny's hand goes up, and Kelly invites her to share. Jenny begins: "This is what my dad brought me from Washington." She shows a model of the Washington Monument and continues to talk about it. When Jenny finishes, she calls on the listeners to make comments and ask questions. Ted says: "I really like what you told us. What is it made of?" Jenny answers, then calls on Chris, who says: "That is very interesting. How big is the real one?"

Analysis of Scenario
Children who speak must be prepared to share and then be able to direct the discussion that follows. Based on careful listening, members of the audience must say something positive and then ask questions or make comments. Paula intervenes only when no one has a question or comment, which rarely occurs.

Listening Comprehension

In teaching children to listen, the teacher should choose topics that interest them and make use of words and concepts they understand. To be members of an audience, children need to learn to concentrate and become good listeners.

literature-centered reading   Teachers can help children improve their listening comprehension by reading both story and informational books to them. When reading these books to the class, teachers should relate the children's experiences to the content of the books. They should read relevant books and make them available to children before and after visiting various places on field trips. In other words, books should be an integral part of many classroom activities and experiences.

The following Model Activity shows how books could be used in a lesson on plants in a kindergarten room.

Model Activities

Listening for Information

Set up a science center with books and displays about plants. Say to the children: "Today we are going to talk about plants. First, I am going to read you a book about plants. Listen to see if you can find out how plants grow. Then we will plant something for our room." Read the book and ask questions like the following:

Questions

Where do seeds come from?

What do plants need to make them grow?

How are seeds planted?

If we want to plant something, what will we need?

Sources for Center

Eat the Fruit, Plant the Seed by Millicent Selsam and Jerome Wexler. New York: Morrow, 1980.

Desert Giant: The World of Sagura Cactus by Barbara Bash. New York: Sierra Club/Little, Brown, 1989.

Seeds Pop! Stick! Glide! by Patricia Lauber. New York: Bradbury, 1981.

The Tiny Seed by Eric Carle. Saxonville, Mass.: Picture Book Studios, 1987.

Growing Vegetable Soup by Lois Ehlert. San Diego: Harcourt Brace Jovanovich, 1987.

Planting a Rainbow by Lois Ehlert. Orlando: Harcourt Brace Jovanovich, 1988.

Listening Centers

The listening area has tape recorders, headsets, story tapes, and multiple copies of read-along books. By recording themselves as they read stories to the children, teachers can provide a wide variety of tapes easily and inexpensively (Ollila and Mayfield, 1992). Tapes of nonfiction books expose children to expository text, and recorded commentaries on field trips recall special events with appropriate specialized vocabulary. Other ideas for listening center tapes include jump-rope rhymes, riddles and jokes, interviews, tongue twisters, and poems or jingles.

Children may wish to make their own tape recordings, with younger children reciting Mother Goose rhymes and older ones reading stories for young listeners. By giving individual responses on tape to such questions as "What is your favorite pet?", each child can participate in a class survey. Children can also record their reactions to stories or share personal experiences on tape.

Oral Expression

Children learn about using language through informal conversations with other children and with the teacher. These conversations may be carried on while the children work together at centers or on projects. The schoolroom environment provides many subjects and opportunities for descriptive talk. Children can compare different building blocks and note their relationships (size, weight, color); they can observe several kinds of animals and consider differences in the animals' feet, skin covering, and size; and they can compare a variety of fabrics for texture, weight, and purpose.

Such uses of language develop the ability to communicate orally with reasonable fluency, to articulate common sounds clearly, to choose words, and to use a variety of sentence structures. In all their communications with children, teachers should model good speech. They should encourage the children's efforts to use new words and speak in correctly formed sentences.

Opportunities for oral expression occur frequently during the day. Teachers should encourage children to use these opportunities to develop their skills in oral communication. Here are some good ideas for class activities that develop oral expression:

> making the daily schedule
>
> choosing a current event to record on the chalkboard
>
> planning projects, activities, or experiences
>
> discussing a new bulletin board display
>
> interpreting pictures
>
> discussing what to include in an experience story
>
> brainstorming ideas from "What if . . . " situations (Example: "What if we had four arms instead of two arms?")
>
> acting out stories
>
> carrying on pretend telephone conversations with toy telephones
>
> reviewing the day's events
>
> engaging in dramatic play

Some teachers may wish to set up language centers to combine verbal communication with cognitive development (Hunter-Grundin, 1990). An adult (teacher, parent, or teaching assistant) leads a small group of children in a discussion that enables them to express opinions, justify points of view, challenge the opinions of others, or suggest possible alternatives. Appropriate topics include ideas for books children are coauthoring, solutions to problems, and subjects related to a theme. The discussion is not a question-answer session, but an open expression of thoughts and ideas. It should help students gain confidence in their ability to communicate, and it should stimulate them to think deeply about matters that concern them.

Dramatic Play

Dramatic play occurs when children simulate real experiences, such as cooking dinner or being a cashier. It requires both speaking and listening but often incorporates reading and writing as well. It is spontaneous and unrehearsed, and children assume the roles of people they have observed from real-life experiences. They think, feel, move, react, and speak according to their interpretations of how these people perform their roles.

In the following Model Activity, children are able to practice language skills as they play the roles of customer, cashier, food preparer, and order taker. They learn to follow directions, fill out forms, and recognize the words for menu items. They also develop mathematical skills as they use play money to pay for their orders and make change.

Model Activities

Dramatic Play

After the children have discussed their experiences at various fast-food restaurants, say to them: "How could we make a pretend fast-food restaurant in our own classroom? Where could we put it? What are some things we would need? How could we get these things?" Have the children come up with answers and develop a plan. Ask some children to bring in cups, napkins, bags, and plastic containers from a fast-food restaurant, and have others paint a sign. One child can bring in a toy cash register.

Make an illustrated price list to place above an improvised counter, and provide copies of order forms for the children to use. Help the children learn to read the food words and the prices by asking: "What is the first item on the list? How much does it cost? Can you find it on the order form?" Keep the list simple at first, and add new items later. When the fast-food center is ready, different children can assume the roles of customers and workers.[1]

Dramatic Play Centers

thematic learning

Ideally, themes for dramatic play centers originate from the children's interests and ideas, with the teacher facilitating the development of the centers. A field trip to a grocery store or fire station may be the stimulus for a dramatic play center. Other typical centers are a kitchen, bakery, post office, bank, business office, hospital, beauty parlor, travel agency, aquarium, and restaurant (Dailey and Owen, 1994; Fields and Hillstead, 1990; Fisher, 1991). See Example 2.1 for an example of a library center.

The children can plan and prepare each center by bringing supplies, arranging the area, and painting cardboard walls or counters. The teacher should see

---

[1] For a detailed account of setting up a McDonald's center, see Gaye McNutt and Nancy Bukofzer, "Teaching Early Reading at McDonald's," *The Reading Teacher* 35 (April 1982), 841–842.

Example 2.1   *Library Center*

Discussion:

To create interest in this center, have the children take a trip to the public library, or have the school librarian introduce the children to their library and its facilities. The children should understand that the library exists so that people may borrow books to read and that borrowers must take good care of the books.

Preparation:

The teacher writes an experience story about the library visit from the children's dictation. Together, the children and teacher plan their own library, including the arrangement of the area and the supplies needed. With the teacher's help, the children plan ways to organize their space, put up signs, create shelves for books, decorate the walls, and get the books they'll use.

Center Props:

check-out table or desk	bookshelves
mats for sitting	book and author posters
books and magazines	telephone

Literacy Materials:

library cards (personal)	library book return cards
pencils, pens, markers	telephone directory
stamp pad	check-out/check-in paper
index cards	telephone pad
bookmarks	calendar

signs and labels (for library hours, book classifications, etc.)

that materials are available to stimulate the use of written language for communication, such as the following:

recipes	note paper
writing tools	envelopes
clipboards	briefcases
file folders	newspapers
coupons	menus
grocery lists	junk mail
bank checks	strips of tickets

Only a few materials should be available at first, and others may be added as needed. These items should be safe for children to handle, authentic in terms of their real-world environment, and useful for carrying out their roles (Neuman and Roskos, 1993; Roskos and Vukelich, 1991).

During dramatic play, the teacher acts primarily as an observer, but may also participate briefly to model appropriate behaviors and promote interaction. For instance, at a grocery store, the teacher might ask, "Do you have any specials today?" or "May I use my coupon to buy this soap?"

Dramatic play has many benefits. Because children need to carry on conversations, they must use good language skills. Frequently children use printed words in their play, which later become sight words. These words may be found on package labels, order forms, street signs, or ticket booths. Children discover the need to read when they have to recognize words to play the situation. Perceiving this need stimulates their interest in learning to read.

Creative Dramatics

literature-centered reading   Acting out stories spontaneously, or *creative dramatics*, builds interest in reading because children love to hear stories and then perform them. As the teacher reads a story, the children need to pay close attention to the sequence of events, the personalities of the characters, the dialogue, and the mood. Before acting out the story, the class reviews what happened and identifies the characters. As they act, the children must use appropriate vocabulary, enunciate distinctly, speak audibly, and express themselves clearly. Children will want to dramatize some stories several times, switching roles each time. The rest of the class forms the audience and must listen carefully. There is little or no need for props, sets, or costumes. Here are some good stories:

Polar Bear, Polar Bear, What Do You Hear? by Bill Martin, Jr. New York: Henry Holt, 1991.

One Fine Day by Nonny Hogrogian. New York: Macmillan, 1971.

Caps for Sale by Esphyr Slobodkina. New York: William R. Scott, 1947.

The Three Billy Goats Gruff by Peter Asbjornsen and Jorgan Moe. New York: Harcourt Brace Jovanovich, 1957.

The Ox-Cart Man by Barbara Cooney. New York: Viking, 1979.

Where the Wild Things Are by Maurice Sendak. New York: Harper & Row, 1963.

Seven Blind Mice by Ed Young. New York: Philomel, 1992.

Puppets are also useful in creative dramatics. Some shy children who are unwilling to speak as themselves are willing to talk through puppets. Children develop good language skills as they plan puppet shows and spontaneously speak their lines. See the following Model Activity.

**Model
Activities**

Puppets

Provide a simple puppet theater and a box of puppets that can be used to represent different characters. The puppet theater can be an old appliance carton with the back cut out and a hole cut near the top of the front.

Here are some of the kinds of puppets the children may use, along with directions for making them:

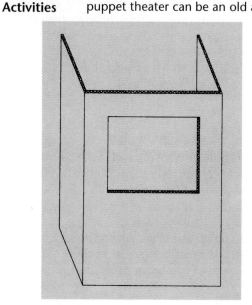

1. *Finger puppets.* Use fabric or construction paper to make a snug tube that fits over a finger. Decorate it to make it resemble a character.

2. *Paper-bag puppets.* Use paper lunch bags and apply facial features with scraps of fabric or construction paper. The mouth opening should fall on the fold of the bag.

3. *Sock puppets.* Using a child's sock that can fit over the hand, apply buttons, yarn, and bits of felt to make a character's head.

4. *Stick puppets.* Cut out characters that children have colored from coloring books. Mount them on the ends of rules or sticks.

literature-centered reading   Dramatic story reenactments may be stimulated by frequent exposure to stories through a literature-rich environment, an enticing classroom library, and an active read-aloud program with response activities. Story reenactments heighten children's awareness of story structure and characterization, which in turn helps them comprehend and recall stories (Martinez, 1993).

SELF-CHECK: OBJECTIVE 5   In what ways are listening and speaking the foundation of literacy? How can a teacher create a strong listening-speaking program? (See Self-Improvement Opportunities 2, 3, and 4.)

Reading and Writing

reading-writing connection   Several concepts, some of which have already been presented, are basic to understanding how growth in reading and writing occurs in an emergent literacy classroom (Strickland and Morrow, 1988):

1. Literacy is a complex ability with linguistic, social, and psychological aspects.

2. Literacy development starts earlier than once thought, usually by age two or three. Most children enter school knowing a great deal about the use of written language.

3. Children construct their own knowledge of reading and writing through experimentation and discovery. By bringing the knowledge they already have to new situations, they make connections and look for patterns in printed words.

4. Growth in reading and writing occurs jointly and along with growth in oral language. Each language art supports the others in an interrelated way.

5. Children learn reading and writing by actively using them for real purposes. A major task for the teacher is to structure the environment so that children can explore language in meaningful ways.

6. Children have different kinds of experiences with literacy in the home. These experiences help children understand that reading and writing are important for daily living. Teachers need to consider individual differences in children's abilities, interests, and experiences when planning instruction.

7. Instead of providing practice in the subskills of reading, teachers set conditions for letting children participate in meaningful literacy activities in the classroom.

8. When necessary, teachers intervene in language learning to help children make connections and move ahead.

9. Hands-on experiences provide the basis for understanding concepts, which are then extended through books.

10. Reading and writing activities take place throughout the school day, not in separate instructional periods.

In the Classroom Scenario "Kindergarten Literacy Activities," the teacher is using many of these concepts.

**Classroom
Scenario**

Kindergarten Literacy Activities

Before the school day officially begins in Linda Edwards's whole language kindergarten, the children are sitting at tables writing journal entries, gathering around the incubator watching newly hatched ducklings, or sharing books at the reading center. When Linda calls the children together, they discuss the date and the weather. They mark the calendar, and one child calculates the number of 1s and 10s in May 17. Linda then reads them a story from a big book, moving a pointer under the words as she reads. The children sing a song from the big book, with a parent using the pointer while the teacher plays the autoharp. When Linda questions the children about their favorite part, they respond enthusiastically. Then they read the story with her as she moves the pointer below the words again.

Analysis of Scenario

This scenario contains many opportunities for observing and discussing, writing purposely, and reading independently, as well as learning math concepts, singing songs, and making decisions as a class. Reading and writing are not lessons to be taught during specific time periods but occur in various forms throughout the day.

It is important to keep in mind that reading and writing are complementary processes; children learn them interrelatedly. To give each process due consideration, however, we will examine them separately.

Learning to Read

Learning to read does not happen all at once when children enter school; it is a process that builds gradually from an early age as children acquire new understandings about reading and writing as communication. Let us consider some of the various factors that enter into a child's ability to read.

Experiential Background

A broad experiential background is essential for success in reading, because children must be familiar with the concepts and vocabulary they will see in written form to gain meaning from them. Through their individual experiences, children gain an understanding of concepts and learn words, or labels, for them. As children encounter a variety of experiences, they modify and refine their perceptions until they get a clear picture of each concept they have acquired. A child may need many experiences to attain a well-rounded impression of a single idea. *School,* for example, is a concept that children do not completely understand until they have experienced it in different ways.

Teachers may help children build broad backgrounds of experience in a variety of ways. The important things to keep in mind are the needs of the children and the available resources.

Teachers should read aloud to children several times a day, because story sharing creates far-reaching benefits for the listener. Stories introduce children to new vocabulary, language patterns, concepts, cultures, and lifestyles. Children develop an awareness of story structure by listening to stories and discussing them. Hearing stories read aloud may bring about an interest in reading and a desire to learn to read. Well-chosen stories can be the basis for creative expression such as drama, music, and art.

Having a news period can be useful. The teacher can make a chart of classroom news, including items like "We had a fire drill today" or "We talked about the farm." Students can help compile the week's news, decide on headlines, and make illustrations for some items.

It is important to use both planned and unplanned experiences to develop concepts and language. Teachers should use correct vocabulary and specific terms such as *printing press* and *card catalog* in class discussions. They should elicit descriptive words from the children or introduce these words as they ask the children to recall their sensory impressions of experiences. Both before and after experiences, teachers should involve children in related language activities. In this way, the children increase their verbal ability; that is, their vocabularies and concepts expand as they use new words to talk about their ideas.

Experiences may be either direct or vicarious. Children generally remember direct experiences with actual physical involvement best, but it may not always be feasible to provide direct experiences. Good vicarious experiences, such as listening to stories and watching films, provide opportunities to expand concepts and vocabulary indirectly. Some appropriate experiences of both types are

field trips	films, filmstrips, slides, and tapes
resource people	selected television programs
story reading	photographs, pictures, posters
demonstrations	neighborhood walks
exhibits	class holiday celebrations

A class project like the following Model Activity can promote growth in vocabulary and concept development.

Model Activities

Direct Experience

Start by saying to the children: "Tomorrow we will make some vegetable soup. Try to remember to bring a vegetable to put in the soup. Now we will write a chart story about the ingredients we will need for our soup."

The next morning, say: "Tell us about your vegetable. What is it called? What color is it? How does it feel? How does it smell?" Give each child a chance to handle and talk about the vegetables. Then ask: "What do we need to do first to make the soup? What must we do to the vegetables before we put them in the pot? What else should we add?"

(Answers include getting and heating the water, washing and cutting up the vegetables, and adding spices and alphabet noodles.)

When the soup is ready to eat, give each child a cupful. As the children eat, ask: "How does your soup taste? Are the colors of the vegetables the same as when we put them into the soup? How have the alphabet noodles changed? Can you name some of the letters that are in your soup?" After they have finished eating, let the children dictate another chart story about the sequence of making the soup and/or their reactions to eating it, or have the children write their own stories.

Some of the concepts you can help children acquire from this experience and related discussions are (1) soup can be made from firm, fresh, brightly colored vegetables; (2) after they are cooked, the vegetables change in texture and appearance; (3) the noodles get larger from absorbing the water; (4) it takes time to heat water and cook soup; (5) the water absorbs flavor and color from the vegetables and spices; (6) cold water becomes hot when it is placed on a heated surface; (7) certain foods are classified as vegetables.

As a result of the experience, children's vocabularies might now include *boil, simmer, dissolve, ingredients, squash, celery, turnips, slice, chop, shred, dice, liquid,* and *flavor.* A bonus comes from letting the children manipulate the alphabet letters—identifying them, matching them, and finding the first letters of their names.

Wordless picture books and pictures can provide vicarious experiences. By looking at the pictures in wordless picture books, children can use their own words to describe events and characters, thus building their experiences along with vocabulary and concepts. Pictures, particularly those that tell a story, are extremely fruitful sources of new ideas and experiences. To help children interpret pictures fully, teachers should ask them questions like those in the following Model Activity.

reading-writing connection   Story writing can be a logical extension of either direct or vicarious experiences. If a class writes a story after a field trip, the students should first discuss the trip. By asking carefully selected questions, the teacher can encourage them to form valid concepts and use appropriate vocabulary words. The students then dictate sentences for the teacher to write on an *experience chart* like that in Example 2.2. Dictated story experiences provide excellent opportunities to introduce the coordinated language experience approach, discussed in Chapter 7.

Stories about an experience may be dictated by a whole class, a group, or a single child. When individual children tell stories, parents, teaching assistants, older children, classroom volunteers, or the teacher can act as scribes. These stories should be about things that are important to the children, such as their families, pets, or favorite activities. The children may illustrate them and combine them into booklets that are then shared around the library table and eventually taken home by the authors. Following are some appropriate experiences for story writing:

taking a field trip	observing an animal
watching an experiment	popping corn
visiting a science or book fair	experimenting with paints
tasting unusual foods	planting seeds or bulbs
entertaining a visitor	building a pretend space ship

Perhaps the most important reason for story writing is that children begin to realize that speech can be recorded and that print makes sense. This awareness occurs as the teacher reads the story back to the children in the words they have just dictated. After repeated readings by the teacher, the children may also be able to "read" the story. The teacher can make copies of the story for all the children to take home and share with their families. As a result of their involvement with

Model Activities

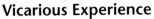

Vicarious Experience

Show the children the picture and then ask the following questions:

1. Where is the little boy? How do you know?

2. What kinds of things usually happen at the veterinarian's office?

3. Why do you think he took his cat there?

4. Why are the other people there?

5. Who is at the door? How do you know?

6. Why is the boy there without his father or mother?

7. What is the boy doing?

8. What do you think will happen soon?

the story, children may learn to recognize some high-interest words and words used more than once (such as *we*, *zoo*, and *bus* in the experience chart story).

Children learn many literacy concepts through story writing. They watch as the teacher forms letters that make up words. They notice that language consists of separate words that are combined into sentences. They see the teacher begin at the left side and move to the right and go from top to bottom. They become aware that dictated stories have titles in which the first letter of each important word is capitalized. They realize that sentences begin with capital letters and end with punctuation marks. Besides becoming familiar with mechanical writing skills, children develop their thinking skills. The teacher's questions help them develop skill in organizing and summarizing. As the children retell events in the order of occurrence, they begin to understand sequence. As they recall the important points, they begin to form a concept of *main idea*.

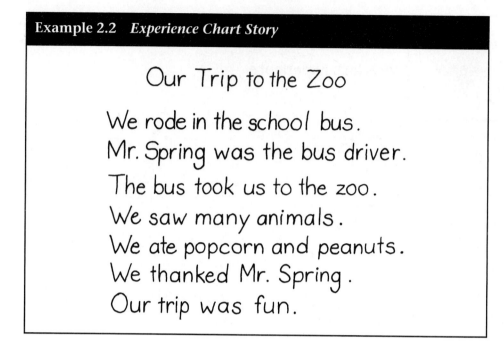

Example 2.2 *Experience Chart Story*

Our Trip to the Zoo

We rode in the school bus.
Mr. Spring was the bus driver.
The bus took us to the zoo.
We saw many animals.
We ate popcorn and peanuts.
We thanked Mr. Spring.
Our trip was fun.

Print Conventions

Many children, especially those who have been read to often, begin to "talk like a book" at a very young age (Clay, 1979; Dickinson, 1987; Hall, 1987). They pretend to read by imitating literary style and content instead of using conversational style. Illustrations and previous readings by adults help children construct the text they pretend to read, but of course these children are not yet able to read the actual words. Youngsters often practice "pretend reading" to a younger sibling or a grandparent. "Talking like a book" is an important step in learning to read because it helps children acquire basic literacy concepts, such as realizing that print can be turned into spoken words and that books use a special type of language. These and similar concepts are sometimes called *print conventions*, that is, generally accepted concepts about reading and writing. The reader expects the writer to use certain conventions, and the writer assumes the reader will follow them (Butler and Turbill, 1984).

reading-writing connection

Fisher (1991) focuses on four major types of print conventions as she helps her kindergartners increase their awareness of written language:

1. Book knowledge (awareness of title and author, knowing how to hold a book and turn pages)

2. Directionality (moving from top to bottom and left to right)

3. Visual connections (distinguishing between letter and word, understanding uses of punctuation, recognizing upper- and lower-case letters)

4. Auditory conventions (awareness of sound-letter relationships)

By demonstrating these conventions while reading, Fisher helps her children become more aware of them. She records the concepts she stresses during each lesson and evaluates the children's progress toward understanding and applying them in their reading and writing.

Sight Words

Children who enter school are rapidly acquiring *sight words*, words they recognize instantly without analyzing them. Teachers can encourage sight word recognition by exposing children to commonly used words, such as names, number and color words (see the following Model Activity), and environmental words.

Model Activities

Sight Word Recognition

Make a color chart like the one pictured here. On one side of the chart, print a list of color words in their corresponding colors. On the other side, make some color splotches that match the words, but arrange them in a different sequence from the words. Attach colored yarn tipped with tape or glue to the appropriate color words. Punch a hole beside each splotch of color on the right side of the chart. While working with a small group of children, say: "Here are some colors that you know. Let's name the colors together." Say the color names with the children. Then say: "Now let's read these color words together." Read the color words with the children. Then say: "Frank, I would like you to read us one of the color words. Then put the piece of yarn from that word through the hole that is beside the same color as the word." Continue in the same way with the other children.

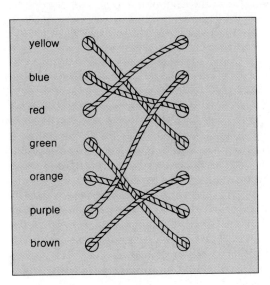

yellow

blue

red

green

orange

purple

brown

Sight vocabulary can be learned in a number of meaningful ways. Ashton-Warner (1963) described the use of *organic words*, words that are meaningful or emotionally charged, such as *ghost, kiss,* and *Mother.* Each child chooses a word that has special personal meaning, and the teacher writes that word on a card and gives it to the child. A word card is kept as long as the word is known; when a word is forgotten or is no longer meaningful to the child, the card is discarded.

reading-writing connection

Another child-centered strategy for teaching sight words is to create a "word wall" of words that children find interesting or important. Martha Dawson demonstrates how her children use their word wall in the following Classroom Scenario.

Classroom Scenario

Word Wall

Toward the end of the year, the word wall in her classroom contained a large number of words that Martha Dawson's kindergartners wanted to know. Martha had started the collection of words when the children asked how to spell words they needed to use. She encouraged them to suggest words for her to write on cards made from colored poster board strips. She attached the cards to the wall in alphabetical order, and the children read them daily—sometimes all of them in alphabetical order and sometimes just similar words classified by colors, such as blue words or yellow words.

Today Andy had a word to add to the wall. His word was *TV.* The children agreed this was an important word and should go with the group of words near the end of the list that began with *t.* There were already two *t* words, *thank* and *train,* so the children needed to decide where *TV* should go. With Martha's help, they checked the alphabet strip at the front of the room and decided that *TV* should go after *thank* and *train* because *V* comes after *h* and *r.* Martha then taped the word card in its proper place, and the class read all of the words on the wall, including the new one.

Analysis of Scenario

In Martha's classroom, children chose words they considered important, so they felt a sense of ownership with their word wall. It provided a quick reference for accurate spelling of frequently used words, and the children were learning to recognize these words by reading them often. They also found that alphabetical order was a convenient way to organize and locate words. By learning at this early stage to look at the first and second letters of a word for its alphabetical placement, they should find later dictionary study an easy task.

Letters and Sounds

To learn to read, children must acquire knowledge of letters and their corresponding sounds.

Letter Recognition.   Teachers need to keep several points in mind while helping beginning readers learn letters and words. Children should learn letter names early so that the teacher and the class have a common referent—for example, understanding when the teacher talks about the letter *f* or the letter *n* (Farr and Roser, 1979). Knowledge of letter *names* is important for talking about similarities and differences among printed words, but knowledge of letter *sounds* is more useful in decoding words (Hafner and Jolly, 1982). Children who learn both the names and sounds of letters can read better than children who learn only letter names (Anderson et al., 1985).

Phonemic Awareness.   *Phonemic awareness*, an understanding that speech consists of a series of small sound units, is a powerful predictor of success in reading (Adams, 1990; Pearson, 1993; Stanovich, 1993/1994; Yopp, 1992). It is both a prerequisite for learning to read and a consequence of an increased awareness of language that comes from learning to read (Yopp, 1992).

reading-writing connection

Teachers can help students develop phonemic awareness by encouraging them to use invented spellings so that they become conscious of the sounds that make up words (Pearson, 1993), exposing them to literature that plays with the sounds of language (Griffith and Olson, 1992), and involving them in songs and games that draw attention to the sounds of language (Yopp, 1992).

Alphabetic Principle.   It is critical that beginning readers understand the *alphabetic principle*, the concept that letters represent speech sounds (Pikulski, 1989). Some children learn this principle intuitively, but most need help. Holdaway (1979) suggests introducing two contrasting letter-sound combinations, such as *m* and *f*, and having children find these letters in familiar stories that the teacher has read with them. After they find many examples, which they can readily identify because of their familiarity with the stories, they work with other letter-sound relationships, including *b, g, s,* and *t*. Because of the insights they have gained, many children are now able to learn the remaining initial consonants and consonant blends on their own.

Reading Centers

literature-centered reading

A reading center is an area in which children gather to read and listen to stories. Books are arranged on shelves by categories, placed in storage crates by favorite authors, or enticingly displayed with their full covers showing. The classroom library should contain about five to eight books per child. These books should represent different levels of difficulty and should be rotated from time to time (Strickland and Morrow, 1988). Big books open to familiar stories rest on easels; smaller versions are nearby for independent reading. A carpeted area with a rocking chair and pillows completes the scene.

At reading centers, children may read independently or with partners from books, magazines, or newspapers. They may make and use such materials as roll movies, flannel boards, and puppets to expand on stories they have heard or read. If a library check-out system is operating, youngsters can write their names and dates on cards and file them. The children may find ways to make the center more attractive and meaningful for them, perhaps by decorating it with their own stories and illustrations.

Reading Materials

In a print-rich classroom environment, words are everywhere—on bulletin boards and walls, on children's work and book jackets, and as labels on objects around the room. There are charts dictated by the children and books on shelves and at centers.

literature-centered reading

Big books with enlarged pictures and print that the entire class can read together offer an excellent way for children to learn to read, even on the first day of school. (See the Classroom Scenario "First Day of School.") Many big books have *predictable* or patterned stories—stories that use repetition, rhythmic language patterns, and familiar concepts. (See Appendix A at the end of this chapter.) Even during a first reading by the teacher, children join in on the repetitive lines or familiar chants. For example, when the teacher reads, "And the little red hen said—," the children respond, "I'll do it myself!" This procedure enables a child to "confirm the predictability of written language" (Wiseman, 1984, p. 343). Stories such as Bill Martin, Jr.'s *Brown Bear, Brown Bear* and Audrey Wood's *The Napping House* contain familiar sequences of this sort. Children will soon read these books by themselves if the teacher has reread them and pointed out the corresponding words.

Classroom Scenario

First Day of School

Early in the day, Oliver Jordan calls the children to the story rug and introduces the big book version of Bill Martin, Jr.'s *Brown Bear, Brown Bear, What Do You See?* Eagerly the children listen as he reads and watch as he turns the brightly colored pages. Soon they are chiming in on some of the words, helped along by the picture clues. When they beg him to read it again, he does so and invites all of them to read it with him. In additional readings throughout the day, children read pages by themselves and with partners. They listen with headphones as they follow along in small book versions, and by the end of the day they believe they are readers.

Across the hall, Mary Hill is also introducing her children to reading, but she does so by asking them to return to their seats and giving them new workbooks. She tells them to turn to the first page and explains the directions for marking the words that begin with the same letter. "Our letter today is the letter *m*," she says, "and I'd like you to take your pencil or crayon and mark each word that begins with this letter." The children finish the exercise, watch as Mary shows them how to print the letter *m*, and then make rows of *m*s.

Analysis of Scenario

Many children come to school eager to learn to read. In Oliver's class, the children were excited because they believed they were really reading. In Mary's class, the children were disappointed because they had not learned to read; they were unable to see any connection between their work and reading stories. According to Booth (1994), the way children encounter print at the beginning of school may determine their attitudes toward reading for the rest of their lives.

literature-centered reading Commercial publishers produce big books, but teachers can make their own. Teachers often run a pointer slowly under the words while reading them so that the children can connect the spoken words with the written words. As the children read and reread the stories—by themselves and to one another—and engage in reading and writing activities related to the stories, they are participating in what Holdaway (1979) calls the *shared-book experience*.

Teachers may use the following procedure for sharing big books with their children, which is an extension of the bedtime story shared between parent and child (Holdaway, 1979; Strickland, 1988):

1. Introduce the story by stimulating a discussion that relates students' experiences to the text, presenting the title and author (using these terms), guiding the children to make predictions about the story, and showing eager anticipation for reading the story.

2. Read the story with lively expression. Point to the words as you read them so that the children can match the spoken words with the print and observe the directionality. While reading, think aloud about aspects of the story ("I wonder what will happen now!" or "Little Bear must feel very happy!"). Encourage children to make predictions and read familiar parts with you.

3. When the story is over, guide a discussion about major points; then find and reread corresponding parts of the text to confirm the points. Help the children reread the text together until they become fluent and confident.

A number of optional variations and follow-up activities are also useful. To focus on meaning, the teacher may use adhesive notes or flaps to cover meaningful, predictable words and then ask the children to identify the words underneath. The teacher may also select certain phonics or structural elements that are well represented in the story, call the children's attention to them, and lead the children to discover word recognition strategies for decoding words with these elements. The children may wish to illustrate parts of the text, write their own versions, find other books related to the same topic, or extend the text in some other way. Since many big books have accompanying audiotapes and sets of small books, the children may read a small version to a listener or listen to a tape of the big book while following along in the smaller one.

Believing that children gain confidence and skill in reading from free selection, Fisher (1991) explains her procedure for daily *choice time* reading. The children may choose whatever they wish to read: big books or small versions of them, trade books, magazines, books published by other children, poems, or songs written on charts around the room. They may follow along in a book as they listen to a tape of a familiar story, or they may read with her, with a friend, with a visitor, or alone. Sometimes they role-play a shared reading session, taking turns being the teacher and inviting a small group to respond.

The McCrackens (1987) use a *pocket chart* for teaching children to read. This consists of a large chart with rows of "pockets" that hold words, pictures that represent words, and sentence strips. The teacher has the children manipulate the words and sentences so that they can learn the story, become aware of print, match words, and build the story or sequence of events. See the following Classroom Scenario.

**Classroom
Scenario**

Reading from a Pocket Chart

As part of the morning activities, Tina DeStephen's prefirst graders read their daily schedule from a pocket chart.

Morning	Afternoon
Attendance/Tally	Lunch
Pledge/Song	Storytime
Calendar/Weather	Quiet self-selected reading
Language workshop	Buddy reading
Author's Chair	Reading conferences
Something Special	Self-selection
Recess	Clean-up
Math	Time to go home

Tina discusses the day's schedule with the children and talks about "something special," which may be a visitor, a trip, or an invitation to see another class perform a play. "Self-selection" refers to such options as playing with blocks, doing handwriting, reading to the bear, making a puppet show, playing instruments, painting at the easel, using math manipulatives, and playing in the housekeeping center. Before releasing the children to work independently, Tina makes sure that each child has decided what to do.

Analysis of Scenario
This daily ritual serves many purposes. Tina and the children anticipate the day's events together as they read and discuss the activities. The children are comfortable and secure in this familiar routine, and they consider their choices and make decisions about what they will do. They realize that reading is purposeful, they reread now familiar words, and they become aware of sequence.

Basal reader series publish activity books, with accompanying teacher's manuals, for beginning readers. Example 2.3 presents a shared reading lesson from the *Teacher's Book, Kindergarten Part 2* (Boston: Houghton Mifflin, 1991). The teacher introduced the poem during a previous lesson and now asks the children to join in the oral reading. The teacher next encourages the children to respond by drawing pictures in their journals or retelling what happened.

SELF-CHECK: OBJECTIVE 6 What classroom activities and materials contribute to a child's progress in learning to read? What does a child need to know in order to read? (See Self-Improvement Opportunities 1, 3, 5, 9, 10, and 11.)

Learning to Write

We have stressed that many youngsters know a great deal about written language before entering school. They realize that the purpose of writing is to communicate messages, that writing contains certain elements, and that it appears in certain forms (Hall, 1987). Children actually perceive themselves as writers long before they can write conventionally. They experiment with making scribbles, sometimes interspersing pictures and letterlike shapes, and believe that their "writing" conveys messages.

When teachers invite children to write in kindergarten, they should follow certain basic guidelines (based on Sulzby, Teale, and Kamberelis, 1989; Sulzby, 1994; Ollila and Mayfield, 1992):

1. Accept the form of writing the child can use; it does not have to be adult writing.

2. Allow children to share their writing and respond to what other children have written.

3. Let children "write" their own names on their work to give them a sense of ownership.

4. Encourage children to use writing to communicate with other people.

5. Provide a variety of writing materials that are readily available.

6. Be a model by letting children see you writing purposefully.

Example 2.3 *Shared Reading Lesson*

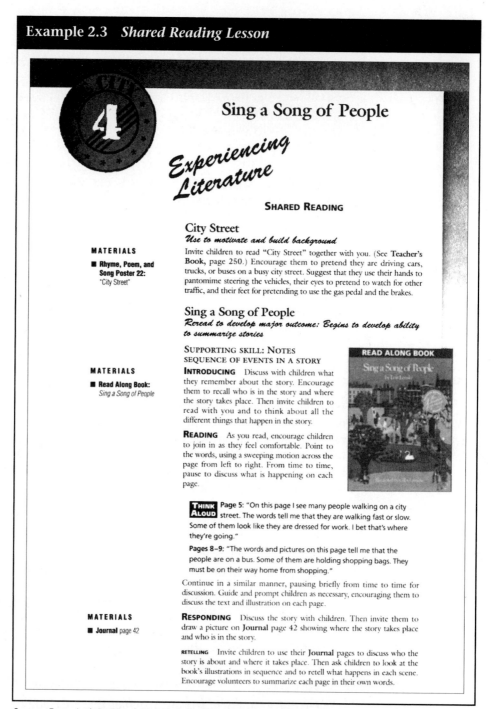

4

Sing a Song of People

Experiencing Literature

SHARED READING

City Street
Use to motivate and build background

MATERIALS

■ Rhyme, Poem, and Song Poster 22: "City Street"

Invite children to read "City Street" together with you. (See **Teacher's Book**, page 250.) Encourage them to pretend they are driving cars, trucks, or buses on a busy city street. Suggest that they use their hands to pantomime steering the vehicles, their eyes to pretend to watch for other traffic, and their feet for pretending to use the gas pedal and the brakes.

Sing a Song of People
Reread to develop major outcome: Begins to develop ability to summarize stories

SUPPORTING SKILL: NOTES SEQUENCE OF EVENTS IN A STORY

MATERIALS

■ Read Along Book: *Sing a Song of People*

INTRODUCING Discuss with children what they remember about the story. Encourage them to recall who is in the story and where the story takes place. Then invite children to read with you and to think about all the different things that happen in the story.

READING As you read, encourage children to join in as they feel comfortable. Point to the words, using a sweeping motion across the page from left to right. From time to time, pause to discuss what is happening on each page.

READ ALONG BOOK
Sing a Song of People
by Lois Lenski

THINK ALOUD **Page 5:** "On this page I see many people walking on a city street. The words tell me that they are walking fast or slow. Some of them look like they are dressed for work. I bet that's where they're going."

Pages 8–9: "The words and pictures on this page tell me that the people are on a bus. Some of them are holding shopping bags. They must be on their way home from shopping."

Continue in a similar manner, pausing briefly from time to time for discussion. Guide and prompt children as necessary, encouraging them to discuss the text and illustration on each page.

MATERIALS

■ Journal page 42

RESPONDING Discuss the story with children. Then invite them to draw a picture on **Journal** page 42 showing where the story takes place and who is in the story.

RETELLING Invite children to use their **Journal** pages to discuss who the story is about and where it takes place. Then ask children to look at the book's illustrations in sequence and to retell what happens in each scene. Encourage volunteers to summarize each page in their own words.

Source: From *Let's Be Friends* Teacher's Book in *Houghton Mifflin Reading* by John G. Pikulski, et al. Copyright © 1991 Houghton Mifflin Company. Reprinted by permission of Houghton Mifflin Company. All rights reserved.

7. Provide ample time for children to write.

8. Help children realize the importance of writing in their lives.

Early Writing Strategies

For young children, writing is often a social event. Children confer with one another, sharing their skills and searching for resources and examples (Loughlin and Martin, 1987). They may tentatively compose stories and tell them to their friends before writing them. When children actually get down to the serious business of writing, Graves claims, they talk to themselves, audibly or subaudibly (Walshe, 1986). They verbalize as they physically form letters and words in the process of formulating their stories.

When children begin kindergarten and are given opportunities to write, some are in the prephonetic stage and place letters on paper without regard for the sounds they make, as in Example 2.4. They tell the teacher what they have written, and the teacher records what they dictate while helping them see relationships between spoken and written words (Coate and Castle, 1989). In kindergarten most children continue to scribble, draw, and use nonphonetic strings of letters (Sulzby, Teale, and Kamberelis, 1989).

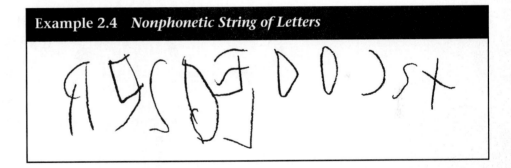

Example 2.4 *Nonphonetic String of Letters*

Once children have a sense of letter-sound relationships, they begin to use *invented spellings*. Richgels (1987, p. 523) defines invented spelling as "beginning writers' ability to write words by attending to their sound units and associating letters with them in a systematic, though unconventional, way." Writing with invented spellings enables children to apply their knowledge of letter-sound relationships for their own purposes. Example 2.5 shows how a kindergartner reacted to a dinosaur theme by drawing a picture and writing a story with invented spellings. Example 2.6 shows a first grader's use of invented spellings in a message to a friend.

reading-writing connection
Close observation of children's invented spellings provides insights into their awareness of letter-sound relationships. Because consonant sounds are more distinctive than vowel sounds, children often use them to represent the key sounds in the words they are trying to spell, either omitting or misrepresenting vowel

Example 2.5 *Kindergartner's Use of Invented Spellings*

This story reads as follows: The meat eater of the dinosaurs. Will Tyrannosaurus Rex survive?

Source: Taylor Bennett, Sycamore Elementary School, Cookeville, Tennessee, 1987. Used with permission.

sounds. Sometimes, in fact, beginning spellers use only the initial consonant of the word they wish to spell. In Example 2.5, Taylor shows considerable knowledge of phonics by systematically sounding through each word and representing each sound with the letter he hears, as in *dinaswrs*. Taylor also mixes some conventional

---

Example 2.6 *First Grader's Use of Invented Spellings*

This story reads as follows: Roses are red. Violets are blue. These golden flowers remind me of you. Dedicated to Janet.

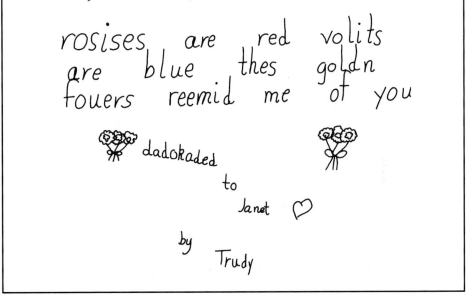

Source: Trudy Walker, Capshaw Elementary School, Cookeville, Tennessee, 1987. Used with permission.

spelling (i.e., *of* and *the*) with his spelling inventions. Trudy (Example 2.6) also reveals excellent awareness of letter-sound relationships in the word *dadokaded*.

With each writing sample, the teacher can learn a great deal about a child's beginning reading and writing competencies. In Example 2.7, the teacher observes that Sheila, a kindergartner, writes from left to right, leaves spaces between words, and writes in complete sentences. She has a good sense of sound-letter relationships, although she sometimes omits some sounds (*WH* for *went*). She spells the *ing* ending correctly. She is not clear about when to use upper- and lower-case letters, however, and she does not use punctuation.

Knowledge of which letters represent certain sounds within words is useful not only for writing, but also for decoding words in reading. Using invented spelling helps children develop phonemic awareness and understanding of the alphabetic principle (Adams, 1990). According to Cunningham and Cunningham (1992, p. 106), research indicates that "invented spelling and decoding are mirror-like processes that make use of the same store of phonological knowledge." Thus, as children learn to associate sounds with letters, they advance their knowledge of both reading and writing. The Model Activity on invented spelling and the Focus on Strategies demonstrate ways teachers can help children begin to write and read.

Example 2.7 *Beginning Writing*

The story reads as follows: I went to get a present for my mom. Everybody was shouting hoorah and singing happy birthday.

I WH to GH A
PREST FOR my
mom eVRX BUDY
WUS ShowINg
hURA AND
SEINg hBe BRDA

Source: Sheila Vogel, Kingston Elementary School, Kingston, Tennessee, 1994. Used with permission.

Model Activities

Demonstrating Invented Spelling

Say to the children: "We've been talking about going camping, and today we set up a tent in our room. Some of you may want to write about tents in your journals. Can you help me spell *tent*?" The children eagerly agree. "Let's say *tent* slowly together and listen for the sounds. What letter makes the sound we hear at the beginning?" Most children suggest *t*, so write *t* on the board. Then ask: "Let's say *tent* again and stretch it out. Think about the sound we hear next. What let-ter makes that sound?" The children aren't quite sure; some say *t*; some say *n*; and a few offer other letters. For now, write *n*. Then say "Is there another sound? Let's say *tent* once more, very slowly." After repeating the word, the children quickly say: "*t*, another *t* at the end." Complete the word for them by adding *t*.

To reinforce the sound-letter relationships, ask: "Can you find a word in our room that begins like *tent*?" The children turn to the charts and labels. Jamie finds *turtle*, and Allyson sees *ten*. She says excitedly:

"*Tent* and *ten* sound almost alike! Can we put an *e* in *tent*?" Ask Allyson to come to the board and put the *e* where it should go; then ask the other children if they agree. After receiving an affirmative answer, ask the children to say the letters in *tent* and remind them to use these letters if they write about tents.

Focus on Strategies

Getting Children Started in Writing

Ms. McLoughlin paused a moment as she moved from one kindergartner to another, offering encouragement as they worked in their journals. She thought back to the beginning of the year when only a few of them could even print their names. For the first few weeks, she had to write in their journals a sentence or two that they had dictated to her to help them grasp the concept that what they said could be written down.

When she had first asked the children to write, they told her they didn't know how. She supplied them with paper and a variety of writing tools, however, and encouraged them to first draw a picture and then write something about it. Some did this with scribbles, some with pictures only, and some with a few letters strewn haphazardly on the page. She accepted their work and asked them to read their stories to her, but she realized she needed to help them discover sound-letter relationships so that they could begin using the letters they needed to make words.

Ms. McLoughlin helped her children discover associations between sounds and letters by pointing them out during shared book reading and having the children pay attention to the letters and sounds in the environmental words at play centers. When the children had developed some knowledge of sound-letter relationships, she demonstrated how to spell words. Even though it took time, she shared individually with each child every day and noted in their journals if she helped them sound the words.

In a few weeks, some children were still scribble writing or drawing pictures, but a few had begun to string letters together, often using invented spelling to make words. Ms. McLoughlin remembered the day Tony asked her to spell *duck* and she had said, "What sounds do you hear? Stretch out the word so that you can hear all of its sounds." Slowly, Tony said the word, then wrote *dk*—a real breakthrough for him. As the children discovered sound-letter relationships, they eagerly attempted to spell any word they wanted to use in their stories.

Now, near the end of the school year, Ms. McLoughlin found that most of her children were writing longer and more readable journal entries. They were working on refining sentence structure, making sure there were spaces between words, and placing punctuation marks correctly. She looked at Hank's story and asked him to read it to her. He read:

> Once upon a time there was a tree that wanted to be yellow and he could not decide. So he waited for fall . . . And he turned yellow. The end. By Hank

Ms. McLoughlin complimented him on the way his story had a beginning, a middle, and an end—something she encouraged her children to consider as they wrote. They often discussed story structure as they read stories together.

THE TREE THeT COd hotbs
Ohce apon a time. Theyr
Wus a tree thet Wott too
be. Yellow and he Cob hot
bsieb. So be Waebb for
foll....
Anb He
turb Yellow. The Ead
By Hank

Source: Hank Replogle, Carthage Elementary School, Carthage, Tennessee, 1994.
Used with permission.

Looking over at Judy's paper, Ms. McLoughlin could see that Judy still had not made the breakthrough to understanding the relationship between sounds and letters. She looked frustrated, so Ms. McLoughlin asked Hank to help Judy with the words she needed. Ms. McLoughlin smiled to herself as she heard Hank using her exact words: "Think of the sounds in *dinner*. What letter makes the sound you hear at the beginning of the word?"

Moving on, Ms. McLoughlin overheard two children conferring. Al said, "You know. When we write *running*, all we have to do is think how to spell *run* and add *ing*.

That's easy." When Chris asked Karen how to spell a word, Karen reminded him he could copy the word he needed from yesterday's chart. Ms. McLoughlin was pleased to hear that exchange, because she always encouraged the children to use the words displayed in the room to get the correct spelling. Tara wanted someone to listen to her story, and Joshua was asking Jeff to help him write his next word. The children learn so much from each other, Ms. McLoughlin thought as she watched them work.

When most of the children had finished, Ms. McLoughlin told them she was ready for them to read their journals to her. Martha came first with a two-page story about her big sister's birthday party. After letting Martha stamp the date on her story, Ms. McLoughlin asked her to select a book to read while the others came to her with their journals. Chuck came next with four pages filled with writing. He eagerly read her a long, involved story about dinosaurs, but she noted that his words were made of letters that had no relationship to the sounds in them. Chuck was a bright child and knew a great deal about dinosaurs, but he still could not use letter-sound relationships.

Even though Ms. McLoughlin sometimes asked the children to write about special topics related to holidays or themes, she often let them choose their own topics. Free choice worked well for Matt; his last entry was only three words, but today he produced a full-page story about his camping trip with his dad.

Glancing around, Ms. McLoughlin could see that nearly all the children had read their journals to her and were comfortably looking at books. Establishing this routine had taken considerable time and effort, but most of the children now understood the schedule and responded well. Even better, many of them were now able to write simple, well-constructed stories with invented spelling.

SELF-CHECK: OBJECTIVE 7   What is invented spelling? What role does it play in learning to read and write? What can you say about Hank's knowledge of sound-letter relationships, use of lower- and upper-case letters, punctuation, letter formation, and sense of story? (See Self-Improvement Opportunities 7 and 12.)

Purposes for Writing

When children write to communicate meaning, their writing is purposeful. The writing center and the entire classroom contain many examples of purposeful print. Martinez and Teale (1987) describe a kindergarten classroom featuring an Author of the Week program that allows children to share their writing with an audience of their peers during a weekly Author's Circle. This class also supports a postal system/penpal program with individual mailboxes for receiving letters and a central mailbox for sending letters. Many reasons for writing also occur at dramatic play centers, where children write telephone messages, take orders for food, make shopping lists, and so on. Other purposeful writing activities include sending messages to school personnel, making greeting cards, sending thank-you notes, writing stories, writing letters, and recording information.

Journal writing offers another purposeful writing activity. The teacher gives each child a booklet, often made of folded unlined sheets of paper stapled together, to write in during a special time each day. Children may copy, scribble, print, or draw anything they wish in their journals, and sometimes the teacher records in conventional print what the children dictate (McGee and Richgels, 1990). A variation suggested by Strickland and Morrow (1990) is group journal writing/reading, a procedure similar to writing and reading language experience charts dictated by the class. Although children are not asked to read parts of the chart independently, they are asked to look for letters they can identify, repeated words, and other interesting print elements. The entries may be narratives, lists, recipes, directions, or chants and poems—whatever contributions the children wish to dictate. These group journals then become part of the classroom's environmental print.

Writing Centers

A writing center should have a table with chairs around it, containers of writing tools, and newsprint or unlined paper in various sizes and colors. Children like to experiment with colored felt-tipped pens, crayons, pencils, and chalk for individual chalkboards. Resource materials to encourage children to write include greeting cards, note pads, books and magazines, envelopes, special words related to a unit or holiday, magnetic letters, and the alphabet in upper- and lower-case letters. Writing centers may also contain notice or message boards for the children and teacher to use for exchanging information. Computers and even old typewriters should be available at writing centers to provide an option for communicating ideas. Ideally, each center should be partially enclosed by arranging portable chalkboards, bookshelves, and other pieces of furniture. This arrangement provides privacy from the rest of the classroom as well as "walls" for displaying written work.

Children may write journal entries and stories on unlined paper. They can also write in blank books made of several sheets of plain paper folded and stapled together and covered with construction paper. Children can place their work-in-progress in folders and display their finished work on bulletin boards or other available space. Children should assume responsibility for maintaining and managing the center.

Using Computers

Computers have many uses in the emergent literacy classroom (DeGroff, 1990). Beginning writers use word processors to write imaginative stories and personal narratives.

Schaeffer (1987) suggests that teachers should introduce kindergartners to the computer by presenting various components, including the keyboard, printer, monitor, and disk drive. The teacher should demonstrate the functions of the components so that the children understand what causes changes on the monitor. Since the children are becoming familiar with the letters of the alphabet, they can begin learning the positions of letters on the keyboard.

Discis Books (Discis Knowledge Research Inc., P.O. Box 66, Buffalo, N.Y. 14223-0066) offer materials at all levels, but their interactive picture book format makes them particularly appealing to younger children. Youngsters can listen to a story, click on a word or a sentence to hear it read aloud, or click on part of a picture to learn more about it. Particularly appropriate for kindergartners are Discis's *Colors*, *Opposites*, *Counting*, *ABC's*, and picture storybooks.

reading-writing connection   To help children grasp the relationship between spoken and written language, *Wiggleworks: Scholastic Beginning Literacy System* enables them to record in their own voices what they want to write. They can play back what they have said at any time and compare it with what they are composing. By clicking a button beside the text, children can hear the computer read aloud in synthetic speech the actual text they have written (Rose and Meyer, 1994).

Intended for first and second graders, Houghton Mifflin's *C.D.'s Story Time* consists of Reading, Writing, and Story Support Centers. With an interactive format and attractive graphics, it motivates, teaches, and evaluates students as they explore literature and develop reading and writing skills. Teachers can also use *C.D.'s Story Time* for students moving from Spanish reading to English reading.

Assessment of Emergent Literacy

Assessment of each child's progress toward literacy is an essential component of the instructional program. Both informal and formal measures may be used. Chapter 11 presents additional information on assessment in the elementary grades.

Informal Assessment

Teachers can evaluate children's awareness of the function or purpose of writing by observing their responses to printed labels and messages. They can learn about children's comprehension strategies by noting their answers to questions about stories read to them. Children reveal a great deal about their emergent literacy when they pretend to read books, especially by the way they use pictures or print as a guide, by *reading-writing connection*   the formality of their language, and by their ability to construct stories. Their use of invented spellings when they write and their perceptions of the connections between reading and writing as they "read" their writings also indicate their literacy development. Other indications include the ability to dictate coherent stories and to recognize environmental print (words on signs, for example).

Teachers can create their own informal checklists of literacy skills and behaviors. By filling out the forms periodically and dating each form, the teacher creates a written record of each child's progress. A sample checklist of emergent literacy behaviors is given in Example 2.8, and a checklist for writing appears in Example 2.9. These checklists may be modified according to individual situations.

Formal Tests for Beginning Readers

Teachers sometimes administer reading readiness tests at the end of kindergarten and/or the beginning of first grade to predict a child's likelihood of success in

Example 2.8 *Checklist of Emergent Literacy Behaviors*

Child _____ Grade _____ Teacher _____ Date_____

Ratings of child's interest/investment in different classroom contexts
(based on observations over a period of several weeks)

Settings and activities	Degree of interest/investment				
	Very interested, intense		Moderately interested		Uninterested attention is elsewhere
Story time: Teacher reads to class (responses to story line: child's comments, questions, elaborations)	____	____	____	____	____
Independent reading: Book time (nature of books child chooses or brings in, process of selecting, quiet or social reading)	____	____	____	____	____
Writing (journal, stories, alphabet, dictation)	____	____	____	____	____
Reading group/individual (oral reading strategies: discussion of text, responses to instruction)	____	____	____	____	____
Reading related activities tasks (responses to assignments or discussions focusing on word letter properties, word games/experience charts)	____	____	____	____	____
Informal settings (use of language in play, jokes, storytelling, conversation)	____	____	____	____	____
Books and print as resource (use of books for projects; attention to signs, labels, names; locating information)	____	____	____	____	____
Other	____	____	____	____	____

Source: Edward Chittenden and Rosalea Courtney, "Assessment of Young Children's Reading: Documentation as an Alternative to Testing." In *Emerging Literacy* by Dorothy Strickland and Lesley Morrow, eds. International Reading Association, 1989, p. 111. Reprinted by permission of Edward Chittendon and the International Reading Association.

reading. These tests frequently measure listening skills, letter recognition, visual-motor coordination, auditory discrimination, and visual discrimination. Some basal reading programs also provide teachers with readiness tests designed to measure the skills covered in their own programs.

Example 2.9 *Writing Checklist*

Name _____

Six-Week Periods						Criteria for Evaluation
1	2	3	4	5	6	
						Shows interest in writing
						Writes name
						Draws recognizable picture and can tell story to go with it
						Writes letters or scribblings to represent words
						Reads back own writing
						Writes letter(s) for beginning sounds
						Writes letter(s) for ending sounds
						Writes some intermediate letters
						Copies words from various sources
						Writes from left to right and top to bottom
						Leaves spaces between words
						Uses punctuation appropriately
						Uses upper- and lower-case letters appropriately
						Writes complete sentences
						Writes complete stories

Key:

__+__ Shows normal progress.

__−__ Needs improvement.

__0__ Not expected at this time.

Traditional readiness tests have several limitations, according to Lipson and Wixson (1991). Despite expectations to the contrary, few such tests can reliably predict student performance. Many are too unreliable to use for making instructional decisions, and the test results of young children tend to be unstable. Also, many reading readiness tests fail to reflect recent knowledge about literacy development.

For a holistic or process-oriented assessment of a young child's literacy development, Marie Clay offers an alternative to traditional readiness tests. Clay's *Con-*

An older sibling or a parent who reads to a young child helps promote literacy. (© Judith D. Sedwick/The Picture Cube)

cepts about Print Test: Sand and *Concepts about Print Test: Stones* (both from Heine-mann Educational Books, Portsmouth, New Hampshire, 1979) can provide insight into a child's knowledge of written language. The 20-page booklets used for administering the tests are similar to children's picture storybooks. They enable the teacher to observe how a child responds to print as the teacher reads, discover what should be taught as the child interacts with the printed page, and find out which aspects of language the child is learning to control.

The teacher gives the test individually in about five or ten minutes using the following procedure (Clay, 1979). The teacher says to the child, "I'm going to read you this story, but I want you to help me." Teacher and child proceed through the test booklet, with the teacher questioning the child about significant concepts of written language. On the sample page given here (Example 2.10), the teacher tests for awareness of directionality and word-by-word pointing.

1. For directional rules.

   a. The teacher says: Show me where to start.
      Score: 1 for top left

Example 2.10 *Test Page from Sand Booklet*

I dug a little hole
and the waves
splashed in.

4

Source: *SAND—Concepts About Print Test*. Marie M. Clay, Heinemann Publishers, Auckland, New Zealand, Heinemann Educational Books, Inc., Portsmouth, N.H., 1989.

b. The teacher says: Which way do I go?
Score: 1 for left to right

c. The teacher says: Where do I go after that?
Score: 1 for return sweep to left.

2. Word-by-word pointing.

a. The teacher says: Point to it while I read it. (The teacher reads slowly, but fluently.)
Score: 1 for exact matching.

SELF-CHECK: OBJECTIVE 8   What are some procedures for assessing children's literacy? Which procedures would you use? (See Self-Improvement Opportunity 14.)

Summary

Among educators the concept of *reading readiness*, a specific period before formal reading instruction, is giving way to the concept of *emergent literacy*, a continuum of literacy growth beginning at birth. This viewpoint assumes that children already know a great deal about reading and writing before entering school and that teachers should build on and expand children's growing awareness of language as purposeful communication. Cognitive development and language learning occur together. Children learn language naturally by observing and imitating language users and then constructing language to meet their needs.

In the emergent literacy classroom, the teacher acts as a facilitator of learning by creating activities to meet the children's needs and interests. A print-rich classroom environment with books, charts, labels, environmental print, and centers provides a further stimulus for language development. Realizing the value of a literate home environment, the teacher may suggest strategies to parents for guiding their youngsters toward literacy.

Many children's listening and speaking skills are well developed when they enter school, and teachers provide opportunities for further growth in listening comprehension and oral expression. Through exposure to reading and writing materials and experiences, children gain knowledge of print conventions and sight words. Children's growth in reading and writing, based on what they already know, occurs concurrently and interrelatedly through experiences with big books, journal writing, listening to stories, and working on computers. Invented spelling helps children to connect letters with sounds. Although teachers may sometimes use formal assessment techniques, they are more likely to evaluate young children's progress through observation and checklists.

Test Yourself   *True or False*

_____ 1. Language learning begins at birth and is continuous.

_____ 2. The term *emergent literacy* refers to a child's language development after entering school.

_____ 3. A child's phonemic awareness is a good predictor of future reading success.

_____ 4. A close relationship exists between cognitive development and the growth of concepts about language.

_____ 5. The preferred frequency for teachers to read aloud to children is once a week.

_____ 6. Picture reading is an example of a direct experience through which a child can learn concepts and vocabulary.

_____ 7. Jean Piaget developed a philosophy of whole language.

_____ 8. According to Piaget, children at the preoperational level are more likely to be successful in child-centered classes than in classes where they are required to memorize rules.

_____ 9. According to Piaget, language comes before thought.

_____ 10. Reading readiness workbooks are used extensively in emergent literacy classrooms.

_____ 11. The only way children can learn language is by imitation.

_____ 12. Many children engage in unconventional forms of reading and writing before they enter school.

_____ 13. Dramatic play centers should include materials for motivating written communication.

_____ 14. Young children need direct instruction in how to speak when they first begin talking.

_____ 15. Traditional readiness tests are the most appropriate form of assessment for young children.

_____ 16. Home environment has little or no effect on language learning.

_____ 17. In shared big book reading, children take turns reading from a large book.

_____ 18. When children "talk like a book," they are most likely reading the exact words.

_____ 19. Interactive story reading is a more worthwhile literacy experience than simply reading a story aloud without comments or questions.

_____ 20. Parents should discourage a child who wants to read before entering school.

_____ 21. Children must learn to read before they can learn to write.

_____ 22. As presented in this chapter, a writing center is a place where children go to practice handwriting skills.

_____ 23. Children use invented spellings to express the ways they perceive letter-sound associations.

_____ 24. Isolated drills and memorization of rules are better than language experiences for helping children understand written communication.

_____ 25. Early reading of environmental words helps children realize that print represents meaning.

_____ 26. A teacher should intervene in language learning by providing help when students are having problems.

_____ 27. Many big books have predictable language patterns.

_____ 28. Children in the primary grades are too young to use computers.

Self-Improvement Opportunities

1. Start a collection of read-aloud books and stories for young children. Make a card for each book or story that gives bibliographic information, a brief summary, and ideas for using it with children.

2. Ask a child to interpret a picture. Report your findings and start your own picture file.

3. Use a trade book to help develop concepts and vocabularies with a small group of children. Report your results.

4. Ask a child to dictate a story to you. Print it in large letters and help the child read it with you. Give the story to the child, but make yourself a copy to bring to class and share.

5. Visit a preschool. How much direct or indirect reading instruction is part of the program?

6. Find some common logos from food package labels, and ask a young child to read them. Then see if the child can read words from the logos when the words are printed in black on white cards. On the basis of your observations, write your conclusions about the effects of the background color and design on a child's ability to recognize environmental words by sight.

7. Read the following story by a kindergartner, and analyze it according to the writing checklist presented in Example 2.9.

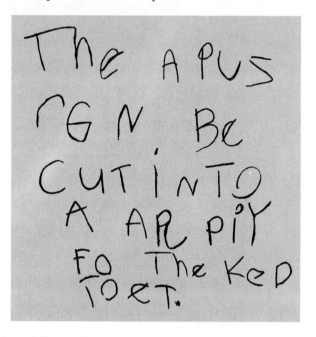

The story reads as follows: The apples are going to be cut into a apple pie for the kid to eat.

Source: Thor McCormick, Kingston Elementary School, Kingston, Tennessee, 1994. Used with permission.

8. Interview a kindergartner to discover his or her knowledge of concepts about print. While reading a simple story with the child, ask such questions as "Where should I start reading?" "Can you point to the words on this page?" "What do you think these marks mean?" Write your questions and the child's answers, followed by a conclusion.

9. Locate a big book and practice using it with a group of children. Try some techniques mentioned in the text, such as using a pointer and using flaps to cover meaningful, predictable words. Summarize your problems and successes with this lesson.

10. Collect environmental words from advertisements, fast-food restaurants, and other sources. Mount them on a large poster board.

11. Using the theme about a library as a model, develop a dramatic play center for one of the following themes: bank, post office, doctor's office, or grocery store. What literacy resources can you use?

12. At the beginning of the course, choose one child who is writing with invented spelling. Each week get a sample of this child's writing, date it, and keep it in a folder. At the end of the course, write a report on the child's progress in learning sound-letter relationships.

13. Visit a home where a preschooler lives. Interview a parent to find out what support is provided for the child's language growth. Share your results in a small group during class.

14. Look at the assessment checklist in Example 2.8. Add other appropriate items, or design your own informal observation form.

Chapter Appendix A

Predictable/Repetitive Books

Aardema, V. *Why Mosquitoes Buzz in People's Ears*. New York: Dial, 1978.
Aliki. *Go Tell Aunt Rhody*. New York: Macmillan, 1974.
Allen, R. V., ed. *The Dinosaur Land*. Allen, Tex.: DLM, 1989.
Allen, R. V. *I Love Ladybugs*. Allen, Tex.: DLM, 1985.
Asch, F. *Just Like Daddy*. Englewood Cliffs, N.J.: Prentice-Hall, 1981.
Baer, G. *THUMP, THUMP, Rat-a-Tat-Tat*. Singapore: Harper & Row, 1989.
Barrett, J. *Animals Should Definitely Not Act Like People*. New York: Aladdin, 1987.
Carle, E. *Today Is Monday*. New York: Scholastic, 1993.
Carle, E. *The Very Busy Spider*. New York: Philomel, 1985.
Carle, E. *The Very Hungry Caterpillar*. Cleveland: Collins World, 1969.
Cooney, B. *Miss Rumphius*. New York: Puffin, 1985.
Cowley, J. *Mrs. Wishy-Washy*. San Diego: The Wright Group, 1987.
Emberley, D. *Drummer Hoff*. Englewood Cliffs, N.J.: Prentice-Hall, 1967.
Fox, M. *Shoes from Grandpa*. Sydney, Australia: Ashton Scholastic, 1989.
Fox, M. *Time for Bed*. San Diego: Gulliver, 1993.
Galdone, P. *The Teeny, Tiny Woman*. New York: Clarion, 1984.
Hutchins, P. *The Doorbell Rang*. New York: Greenwillow, 1986.
Hutchins, P. *Rosie's Walk*. New York: Macmillan, 1968.
Hutchins, P. *Titch*. New York: Penguin, 1985.
Johnson, T. *Yonder*. New York: Dial, 1988.
Kent, J. *The Fat Cat*. New York: Scholastic, 1987.
Langstaff, J. *Oh, A-Hunting We Will Go*. New York: Atheneum, 1974.
Langstaff, J. *Ol' Dan Tucker*. New York: Harcourt Brace & World, 1963.
Livingston, M. C. *Dilly Dilly Piccalilli*. New York: McElderry, 1988.
Lobel, A. *The Rose in My Garden*. New York: Greenwillow, 1984.
Martin, B. *Brown Bear, Brown Bear*. New York: Holt, Rinehart and Winston, 1970.
Martin, B. *Fire! Fire! Said Mrs. McGuire*. New York: Holt, Rinehart and Winston, 1970.
Martin, B., and Archambault, J. *The Braggin' Dragon*. Allen, Tex.: DLM, 1988.

Martin, B., and Archambault, J. *Good Night, Mr. Beetle*. Allen, Tex.: DLM, 1988.

Mayer, M. *What Do You Do with a Kangaroo?* New York: Scholastic, 1973.

Munsch, R. *Mud Puddle*. Scarborough, Ontario: Firefly, 1982.

Munsch, R. *Mortimer*. Scarborough, Ontario: Firefly, 1982.

Nelson, J. *Peanut Butter and Jelly.* Cleveland: Modern Curriculum Press, 1989.

Quackenbush, R. *She'll Be Coming 'Round the Mountain*. New York: Lippincott, 1973.

Sendak, M. *Pierre*. New York: Harper & Row, 1962.

Shaw, C. B. *It Looked Like Spilt Milk*. New York: Harper & Row, 1947.

Stevens, J. *The House that Jack Built*. New York: Holiday House, 1985.

Westcott, N. *I Know an Old Lady Who Swallowed a Fly*. New York: Little, Brown, 1980.

Wood, A. *King Bidgood's in the Bathtub*. New York: Harcourt Brace Jovanovich, 1985.

Wood, A. *The Napping House*. San Diego: Harcourt Brace Jovanovich, 1984.

Wood, D. and Wood, A. *The Little Mouse, the Red Ripe Strawberry, and the Big Hungry Bear.* New York: Scholastic, 1984.

Yolen, J. *Owl Moon*. New York: Philomel, 1987.

Chapter 3

Key Vocabulary

Pay close attention to these terms when they appear in the chapter.

analytic approach to phonics instruction

cloze procedure

context clues

homographs

inflectional endings

onset

phonemic awareness

phonics

rime

semantic clues

sight words

structural analysis

syntactic clues

synthetic approach to phonics instruction

word configuration

In addition, pay close attention to the specific phonics terms discussed in this chapter.

Word Recognition

Setting Objectives

When you finish reading this chapter, you should be able to

1. Describe some ways to help a child develop a sight vocabulary.
2. Describe some activities for teaching use of context clues.
3. Discuss the role of phonics in the reading program.
4. Define each of the following terms: *consonant blend, consonant digraph, vowel digraph, diphthong.*
5. Describe how to teach a child to associate a specific sound with a specific letter or group of letters.
6. Discuss ways to teach the various facets of structural analysis.
7. Identify the skills children need in order to use a dictionary as an aid in word recognition.

Figure 3.1 *Chapter 3 Organization*

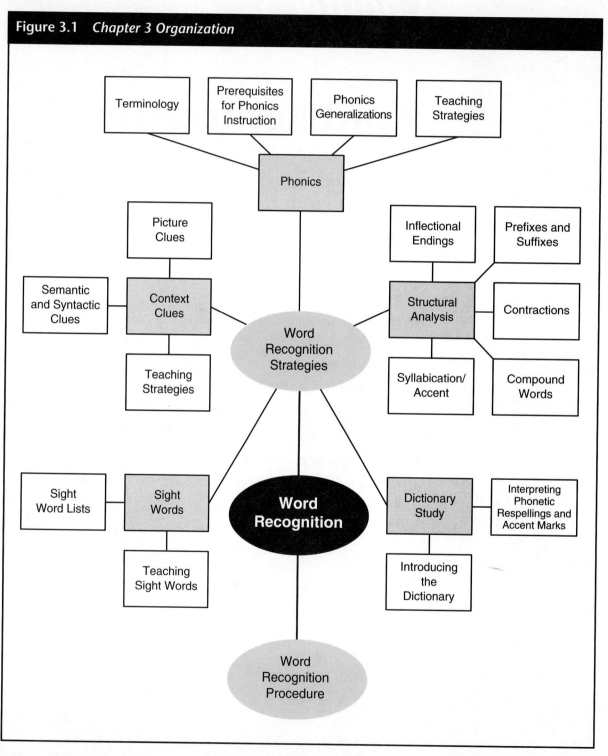

Good readers differ from poor readers in both the size of sight vocabularies and the ability to decode words. Good readers tend to have larger sight vocabularies than poor readers, thereby decreasing their need to stop and analyze words. When they do have to analyze words, good readers often have a more flexible approach than poor readers do because they generally have been taught several strategies and have been encouraged to try a new one if one strategy fails (Jenkins et al., 1980). Poor readers frequently know only a single strategy for decoding words. No one strategy is appropriate for all words, however, and thus these children are at a disadvantage when they encounter words for which their strategy is not useful. Even if they have been taught several strategies, poor readers may have failed to learn a procedure that will allow them to decode unfamiliar words as efficiently as possible. "Research suggests that, no matter which strategies are used to introduce them to reading, the children who earn the best scores on reading comprehension tests in the second grade are the ones who made the most progress in fast and accurate word identification in the first grade" (Anderson et al., 1985, pp. 10–11).

Samuels (1988) sees word recognition skills as "a necessary prerequisite for comprehension and skilled reading" and points out that "we need a balanced reading program, one which combines decoding skills and the skills of reading in context" (pp. 757, 758). He has long supported the idea that accurate and automatic word recognition is necessary for reading fluency. This automaticity (application without conscious thought) in word recognition is achieved through extended practice. Repeated readings of the same passages can help move students from accuracy to automaticity in word recognition.

Adams (1991) also endorses the need for word recognition skills along with strategies for acquiring meaning. She encourages "thorough overlearning of letters, spelling patterns, and spelling-sound correspondences—and also of vocabulary, syntactic patterns, rhetorical devices, text structures, conceptual underpinnings, and modes of thought on which the full meaning of text depends." However, she denounces "'ponderous drills' on 'isolated skills'" (Adams, 1991, p. 394). She also emphasizes the need for automaticity in decoding to free students' attention for comprehension ("A Talk with Marilyn Adams," 1991).

This chapter presents a variety of methods of word recognition and stresses a flexible approach to unfamiliar words, encouraging application of those word recognition strategies that are most helpful at the moment. It also explains ways to show children how to use a number of word recognition strategies jointly to help in decoding words.

Word Recognition Strategies

Word recognition strategies and skills help a reader recognize written words. They include development of a store of words that can be recognized immediately on sight and the ability to use context clues, phonics, structural analysis, and dictionaries for word identification where each strategy is appropriate. The last four types are sometimes referred to as *word attack* strategies or skills.

Children need to be able to perform all of the word recognition strategies because some will be more helpful than others in certain situations. Teaching a single approach to word identification is not wise, because children may be left without the proper tools for specific situations. In addition, depending on their individual abilities, children find some word recognition strategies easier to learn than others. A child who has a hearing loss, for example, may not become very skillful at using phonics but may learn sight words easily and profit greatly from the use of context clues.

Instruction in word recognition should not dominate reading time. Much time should be spent in reading connected text; Stahl (1992) suggests half of the time or more. Attention to comprehension instruction should also receive ample attention.

Gill (1992, p. 450) warns that instruction in word recognition "hinders progress when it places the child in reading material on his frustration level," because this prevents the child from extracting information from patterns that he or she is capable of detecting in the text. When children are taught with materials that emphasize repetitions of spelling patterns, they tend to develop strategies based on alphabetic principles. To accomplish this, they need to be exposed to texts that contain unchanging patterns that they are able to detect. Some children also need assistance in detecting these patterns.

Sight Words

Young readers also need to develop a store of sight words, words that are recognized immediately without having to resort to analysis. The larger the store of sight words a reader has, the more rapidly and fluently he or she can read a selection. Comprehension and reading speed suffer if a reader has to pause too often to analyze unfamiliar words. The more mature and experienced a reader becomes, the larger his or her store of sight words becomes. (Most, if not all, of the words used in this textbook, for example, are a part of the sight vocabularies of college students.) Thus, one goal of reading instruction is to turn all the words students continuously need to recognize in print into sight words.

A *sight word approach* (also referred to as a *look-and-say* or *whole word approach*) to teaching beginning reading may be used for several reasons:

1. The English language contains a multitude of irregularly spelled words, that is, words that are not spelled the way they sound. Many of these are among the most frequently used words in our language. The spellings of the following common words are highly irregular in their sound-symbol associations: *of, through, two, know, give, come,* and *once.* Rather than trying in vain to sound out these words, children need to learn to recognize them on sight as whole configurations.

2. Learning several sight words at the very beginning of reading instruction gives the child a chance to engage in a successful reading experience very early and consequently promotes a positive attitude toward reading.

3. Words have meaning for youngsters by the time they arrive at school, but single letters have no meaning for them. Therefore, presenting children with whole words at the beginning allows them to associate reading with meaning rather than with meaningless memorization.

4. After children have built up a small store of sight words, the teacher can begin phonics instruction with an analytic approach. (More about the analytic approach appears later in this chapter.)

Most children know some sight words when they first come to school. They have learned the names of some of their favorite fast-food restaurants and other businesses from signs, the names of some of their favorite foods and drinks from the packages or labels, or both categories of words, as well as others, from television commercials. Children who have been read stories while sitting on their parents' laps may well have picked up vocabulary from favorite stories that were repeatedly shared. Still, the sight vocabularies of beginning students are meager compared to those mature readers need.

literature-centered reading

A teacher must carefully choose which words to teach as sight words. Extremely common irregularly spelled words (*come, to, two*) and frequently used regularly spelled words (*at, it, and, am, go*) should be taught as sight words so that children can read connected sentences early in the program. The first sight words should be useful and meaningful. A child's name should be one of those words; days of the week, months of the year, and names of school subjects are other prime candidates. Words that stand for concepts unfamiliar to youngsters are poor choices. Before children learn *democracy* as a sight word, for example, they need to understand what a democracy is; therefore, this is not a good word to teach in the primary grades.

Teaching some words with regular spelling patterns as sight words is consistent with the beliefs of linguists who have become involved in developing reading materials (see Chapter 6 for further details). Words with regular spelling patterns are also a good base for teaching "word families" in phonics; the *an* family, for example, includes *ban, can, Dan, fan, man, Nan, pan, ran, tan,* and *van.*

Sight Word Lists

Lists of basic sight words may give teachers an indication of the words that are most frequently used in reading materials and therefore needed most frequently by students. The Dolch list of the 220 most common words in reading materials (excluding nouns), though first published in the 1930s, has repeatedly been found to be relevant and useful in more recent materials (Mangieri and Kahn, 1977; Palmer, 1985).

Another well-known list of basic sight words is Fry's "Instant Words," shown in Table 3.1. This list presents the words most frequently used in reading materials.

Dreyer, Futtersak, and Boehm (1985) have compiled a supplementary list of words found in computer-assisted instructional materials for elementary school children. This list is helpful because many of the special terms used in these materials are not found on traditional word lists. The list contains major procedural

Table 3.1   *Fry's List of "Instant Words"*

First hundred words (approximately first grade)					Second hundred words (approximately second grade)					Third hundred words (approximately third grade)			
Group 1a	Group 1b	Group 1c	Group 1d		Group 2a	Group 2b	Group 2c	Group 2d		Group 3a	Group 3b	Group 3c	Group 3d
the	he	go	who		saw	big	may	fan		ask	hat	off	fire
a	I	see	an		home	where	let	five		small	car	sister	ten
is	they	then	their		soon	am	use	read		yellow	write	happy	order
you	one	us	she		stand	ball	these	over		show	try	once	part
to	good	no	new		box	morning	right	such		goes	myself	didn't	early
and	me	him	said		upon	live	present	way		clean	longer	set	fat
we	about	by	did		first	four	tell	too		buy	those	round	third
that	had	was	boy		came	last	next	shall		thank	hold	dress	same
in	if	come	three		girl	color	please	own		sleep	full	tell	love
not	some	get	down		house	away	leave	most		letter	carry	wash	hear
for	up	or	work		find	red	hand	sure		jump	eight	start	yesterday
at	her	two	put		because	friend	more	thing		help	sing	always	eyes
with	do	man	were		made	pretty	why	only		fly	warm	anything	door
it	when	little	before		could	eat	better	near		don't	sit	around	clothes
on	so	has	just		book	want	under	than		fast	dog	close	through
can	my	them	long		look	year	while	open		cold	ride	walk	o'clock
will	very	how	here		mother	white	should	kind		today	hot	money	second
are	all	like	other		run	got	never	must		does	grow	turn	water
of	would	our	old		school	play	each	high		face	cut	might	town
this	any	what	take		people	found	best	far		green	seven	hard	took
your	been	know	cat		night	left	another	both		every	woman	along	pair
as	out	make	again		into	men	seem	end		brown	funny	bed	now
but	there	which	give		say	bring	tree	also		coat	yes	fine	keep
be	from	much	after		think	wish	name	until		six	ate	sat	head
have	day	his	many		back	black	dear	call		gave	stop	hope	food

Table 3.1   *Fry's List of "Instant Words" (cont.)*

**The second 300 words
(approximately fourth grade)**

Group 4a	Group 4b	Group 4c	Group 4d	Group 4e	Group 4f	Group 4g	Group 4h	Group 4i	Group 4j	Group 4k	Group 4l
told	time	word	wear	hour	grade	egg	spell	become	herself	demand	aunt
Miss	yet	almost	Mr.	glad	brother	ground	beautiful	body	idea	however	system
father	true	thought	side	follow	remain	afternoon	sick	chance	drop	figure	line
children	above	send	poor	company	milk	feed	became	act	river	case	cause
land	still	receive	lost	believe	several	boat	cry	die	smile	increase	marry
interest	meet	pay	outside	begin	war	plan	finish	real	son	enjoy	possible
government	since	nothing	wind	mind	able	question	catch	speak	bat	rather	supply
feet	number	need	Mrs.	pass	charge	fish	floor	already	fact	sound	thousand
garden	state	mean	learn	reach	either	return	stick	doctor	sort	eleven	pen
done	matter	late	held	month	less	sir	great	step	king	music	condition
country	line	half	front	point	train	fell	guess	itself	dark	human	perhaps
different	remember	fight	built	rest	cost	hill	bridge	nine	themselves	court	produce
bad	large	enough	family	sent	evening	wood	church	baby	whose	force	twelve
across	few	feet	began	talk	note	add	lady	minute	study	plant	rode
yard	hit	during	air	went	past	ice	tomorrow	ring	fear	suppose	uncle
winter	cover	gone	young	bank	room	chair	snow	wrote	move	law	labor
table	window	hundred	ago	ship	flew	watch	whom	happen	stood	husband	public
story	even	week	world	business	office	alone	women	appear	himself	moment	consider
sometimes	city	between	airplane	whole	cow	low	among	heart	strong	person	thus
I'm	together	change	without	short	visit	arm	road	swim	knew	result	least
tired	sun	being	kill	certain	wait	dinner	farm	felt	often	continue	power
horse	life	care	ready	fair	teacher	hair	cousin	fourth	toward	price	mark
something	street	answer	stay	reason	spring	service	bread	I'll	wonder	serve	president
brought	party	course	won't	summer	picture	class	wrong	kept	twenty	national	voice
shoes	suit	against	paper	fill	bird	quite	age	well	important	wife	whether

Source: From *Elementary Reading Instruction* (p. 73) by Edward Fry. Copyright © 1977. Used with permission of the author.

and feedback words found in thirty-five representative computer programs in the areas of reading comprehension, grammar, spelling, word processing, logic/problem solving, basic verbal concepts, and mathematics. This list will help the teacher introduce children to the words they need to know in order to use computer-assisted instructional programs successfully.

Teaching Sight Words

Before children begin to learn sight words, they must have developed visual discrimination skills; that is, they must be able to see likenesses and differences among printed words. It is also helpful, although not essential, for them to know the names of the letters of the alphabet, because this facilitates discussion of likenesses and differences among words. For example, a teacher could point out that, whereas *take* has a *k* before the *e*, *tale* has an *l* in the same position.

A potential sight word must initially be identified for learners. A teacher should show the children the printed word as he or she pronounces it, or pair the word with an identifying picture. Reading aloud to children as they follow along in the book is one way to identify vocabulary for children within a meaningful context. Regardless of the method of presentation, one factor is of paramount importance: the children must *look* at the printed word when it is identified in order to associate the letter configuration with the spoken word or picture. If children fail to look at the word when it is pronounced, they have no chance of remembering it when they next encounter it.

Teachers should also encourage children to pay attention to the details of the word by asking them to notice ascending letters (such as *b, d, h*), descending letters (such as *p, g, q*), word length, and particular letter combinations (such as double letters). Careful scrutiny of words can greatly aid retention.

The most natural, holistic approach to sight word instruction is reading to children as they follow along. Teachers may use this approach with groups of students when big books are available, allowing all children in the group to see the words. They may also read from books that are available in multiple copies in the classroom, with each child or pair of children following along on his or her own copy of the story. Books with accompanying tapes or records can promote sight vocabulary in a similar way.

Children learn early to recognize some sight words by their visual *configurations*, or shapes. Teachers should not overly stress this technique, because many words have similar shapes. But since many children seem to use the technique in the early stages of reading, regardless of the teacher's methods, a teacher can use configuration judiciously to develop early sight words. One way to call attention to shape is to have the children frame the words to be learned:

The limitation of configuration as a sight word recognition clue is demonstrated by the following words:

Teachers can call attention to word makeup through comparison and contrast, comparing a new word to a similar known word: *fan* may be compared to *can* if the children already have *can* in their sight vocabularies. Either the teacher can point out that the initial letters of the words are different and the other letters are the same, or the students can discover this on their own. The latter method is preferable, because the students are likely to remember their own discoveries longer than they will remember something the teacher has told them.

Few words are learned after a single presentation, although Ashton-Warner (1963) claims that children will instantly learn words that are extremely important to them. Generally, a number of repetitions are necessary before a word actually becomes a sight word.

The teacher should carefully plan practice with potential sight words. This practice should be varied and interesting, because children will more readily learn those things that interest them. Games are useful if they emphasize the words being learned rather than the rules of the game.

Practice with potential sight words should generally involve using the words *in context*. Children cannot pronounce many words out of context with certainty—for example, *read, desert,* and *record.* The following sentences indicate the importance of context:

I *read* that book yesterday.

I can't *read* without glasses.

We drove for miles through the *desert.*

How can you *desert* him when he needs you most?

Will you *record* these figures for me?

I bought a new *record* today.

Another reason for using context when presenting sight words is that many commonly used words have little meaning when they stand alone. Prime examples are *the, a,* and *an.* Context for words may be a sentence (*The* girl ate *a* pear and *an* apple.) or short phrases (*the* girl, *a* pear, *an* apple). Context is also useful if pronunciation is less clear than it should be. Children may confuse the word *thing* with *think* unless the teacher has presented context for the word: "I haven't done a useful thing all day."

literature-centered reading   McGill-Franzen (1993) points out the value of highly predictable books, such as those used in the Reading Recovery Program, for beginning readers. Peterson (1991) has arranged a continuum of Reading Recovery books from easy to more complex, based partially on the context provided. The books at the easiest levels are highly predictable from the pictures and repetitive sentence patterns.

reading-writing connection

The language experience approach, in which students' own language is written down and used as the basis for their reading material, is good for developing sight vocabulary. This approach (described in detail in Chapter 7) provides a meaningful context for learning sight words, and it can be used productively with individuals or groups. The word-bank activities associated with this approach are particularly helpful.

Teachers may also present words in conjunction with pictures or with the actual objects the words name, such as chairs and tables, calling attention to the fact that the labels name the items. These names can be written on the board so that youngsters can try to locate the items in the room by finding the matching labels.

reading-writing connection

Constructing picture dictionaries, in which children illustrate words and file the labeled pictures alphabetically in a notebook, is a good activity for helping younger children develop sight vocabulary. This procedure has been effective in helping children whose primary language is not English learn to read and understand English words.

Teachers can use labels to help children learn to recognize their own names and the names of some of their classmates. On the first day of school, the teacher can give each child a name tag and label each child's desk with his or her name. The teacher may also label the area where the child is supposed to hang a coat or store supplies. The teacher should explain to the children that the letters written on the name tags, desks, and storage areas spell their own names and that no one else is supposed to use these areas. The children should be encouraged to look at the names carefully and try to remember them when locating their belongings. Although the children may initially use the name tags to match the labels on the desks and storage areas, by the time the name tags are worn out or lost, the children should be able to identify their printed names without assistance.

reading-writing connection

The teacher can generally accelerate this process by teaching children how to write their names. Children may first trace the name labels on their desks with their fingers. Next, they can try to copy the names on sheets of paper. At first, the teacher should label all students' work and drawings with the students' names, but as soon as the children are capable of writing their names, they should label their own papers. From the beginning, the children's names should be written in capital and lower-case letters, rather than all capitals, since this is the way names most commonly appear in print.

The days of the week can also be taught as sight words. Each morning, the teacher can write "Today is" on the chalkboard and fill in the name of the appropriate day. At first the teacher may read the sentence to the children at the beginning of each day, but soon some children will be able to read the sentence successfully without help.

Function words—words, such as *the* and *or,* that have only syntactic meaning rather than concrete content—are often particularly difficult for children to learn because they lack concrete meaning and because many of them are similar in physical features. These words need to be presented in context repeatedly so that the surrounding words can provide meaning (Hargis et al., 1988). Jolly (1981) suggests teaching these troublesome words by presenting only one word at a time of a pair of words that are likely to be confused (for example, *was* and *saw*). He also suggests teaching words with more obvious differences in features first, then those with subtler differences. For example, teach *that* with words like *for* and *is* before presenting it with *this* and *the*. Teachers can also delete the words from passages, leaving blanks for the students to fill in with the target words.

reading-writing connection

Much teaching of sight word recognition takes place as a part of basal reader lessons. The teacher frequently introduces the new words, possibly in one of the ways discussed here, before reading, discussing meanings at the same time. Then students have a guided silent reading period during which they read material containing the new words in order to answer questions asked by the teacher. Purposeful oral rereading activities offer another chance to use the new words. Afterward, teachers generally provide practice activities suggested in the teacher's manual of the basal reading series. Follow-up activities may include skill sheets, games, manipulative devices, and special audiovisual materials. Writing new words is helpful for some learners, especially for kinesthetic learners (those who learn through muscle movement).

reading-writing connection

Games such as word bingo are useful for practice with sight words. The teacher or a leader calls out a word, and the children who recognize that word on their cards cover it. (Cards may look something like the ones shown here.) When a child covers an entire card, he or she says, "Cover," and the teacher or leader checks the card to see if all the covered words were actually called.

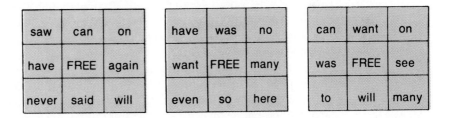

Another technique is to list sight words on a circular piece of cardboard and have children paper-clip pictures to appropriate words. The teacher can make this activity self-scoring by printing the matching words on the backs of the pictures, as shown on the next page.

Dickerson (1982) compared the use of physically active games, passive games, and worksheets in an attempt to discover which would be most effective in increasing the sight vocabularies of remedial first graders. The physically active games proved to be most effective, followed by the passive games. Worksheets were the least effective, although the children who used the worksheets did gain some sight vocabulary. Teachers may consider increasing use of more active games, such as those in which children stand and act out action verbs. The Classroom Scenario on page 102 describes such an activity.

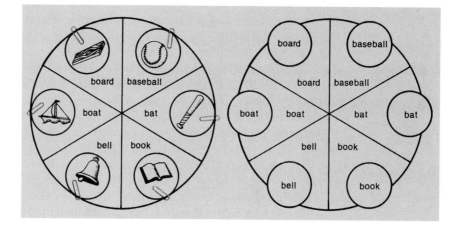

Developing Sight Vocabulary

Mr. Barkley, a first-grade teacher, found that three children were having trouble remembering the action words in the stories they were reading. He called these children over to a corner of the room near the chalkboard and wrote these words on the board: jump, walk, run. He introduced the words by saying, "We have seen these words in our stories this week, but they have been hard for you to remember, so we are going to practice reading them as we play a game. This word is jump. Can you jump for me?" The children jumped. Then he said, "Good. Whenever you read the word jump for this game, I want you to jump just like that."

Mr. Barkley introduced *walk* and *run* in the same way. The students readily demonstrated each one.

Then Mr. Barkley brought out a board game with a racetrack oval drawn on it. Each space in the path around the oval had a simple sentence containing either *jump, walk,* or *run* written on it. The children took turns spinning a spinner and moving the number of spaces indicated around the racetrack with a personally selected token (one of several different miniature race cars). A child who landed on a space had to read the sentence, tell what it meant, and perform the action in the sentence. For example, the child might read, "Mary can jump," and then say, "That means Mary can do this." Then the child would stand up and jump. If a child could not read the sentence or tell/show what it meant, another player could "steal his or her play" by reading the sentence and performing the action. The player who got to try this would be determined by having the opponents of the player who missed spin the spinner for a high number.

The first child around the track won the game, but all three children were actively involved with the action words and made progress in reading them correctly as the game continued.

Analysis of Scenario
Mr. Barkley used a physically active game to develop the children's sight vocabularies after more passive reading activities had failed to be effective with these children. He targeted the activity for the children who were having difficulty, not forcing the repetitive practice on those who had mastered the words. He presented the words in sentence contexts to encourage children to recognize the words in typical reading situations, rather than as isolated entities.

Ceprano (1981) reviewed research on methods of teaching sight words and found that no one method alone was best for every student. She found evidence that teaching the distinctive features of words helped children learn. She also found evidence that use of picture clues along with specific instruction to focus attention on the words facilitated learning. She reported, however, that some research indicates that teaching words in isolation or with pictures does not ensure the ability to read words in context. In fact, indications are that "most learners need directed experience with written context while learning words in order to perceive that reading is a language process and a meaning-getting process" (p. 321). Therefore, when teachers are working with sight-word instruction, it seems wise to present words in context rather than just in isolation.

SELF-CHECK: OBJECTIVE 1   Should sight words be presented alone or in context? Justify your answer. Describe two activities that can be used for teaching sight words. (See Self-Improvement Opportunities 1 and 2.)

Context Clues

Context clues—the words, phrases, and sentences surrounding the words to be decoded—help readers determine what the unfamiliar words are. Here we will focus on the function of context clues as *word recognition* aids; Chapter 5 considers the function of context clues as *comprehension* aids.

Since research has found that syntactic and semantic context influence readers' identification of words, it is important that word recognition skills be introduced and practiced in context (Jones, 1982). Much of the written material to which primary-level readers are introduced falls well within their comprehension as far as vocabulary and ideas are concerned, but these youngsters cannot always recognize in printed form the words that are familiar in oral form. Context clues can be extremely helpful in this process. Research also shows that context clues help younger and poorer readers recognize words more than they help older and better readers (Gough, 1984; Daneman, 1991).

The teacher should carefully plan practice with potential sight words. (© *Tony Freeman/ Photo Edit*)

Picture Clues

Picture clues are generally the earliest context clues children use. If children are exposed to many pictures of a character, such as one named Julie, in beginning reading materials, they may come to recognize the character instantly. When they are shown a page containing a picture of Julie and a single word, they may naturally assume that the word names the picture and that the word is *Julie.* If they do not relate the picture to the word in this manner, the teacher can ask a question such as "Who is in the picture?" to lead them toward understanding the relationship. If a child responds, "A girl," the teacher might ask, "What kind of letter is at the beginning of the word?" The response "A capital letter" would prompt the question "What kinds of words have we talked about that begin with capital letters?" After eliciting the answer "Names," the teacher can then ask, "What is the name of the girl in the picture?" This question should produce the response "Julie." Finally, the teacher asks, "Now what do you think the word is?" At this point, a correct response is extremely likely. The teacher should use a procedure that encourages the use of picture clues *along with,* rather than apart from, the clues available in the printed word.

Teachers should not overemphasize picture clues. These clues may be useful in the initial stages of instruction, but they become less useful as the child advances to more difficult material, which has a decreasing number of pictures and an increasing proportion of print. Encouraging too much reliance on pictures may result in too little time spent on developing word analysis skills.

Semantic and Syntactic Clues

As soon as possible, teachers should encourage first-grade children to use written context as a clue to unknown words. The idea of using context clues can be introduced by oral activities like the following one. The sentences can often be drawn from stories that have just been read or listened to in class.

Model Activities

Use of Oral Context

Read sentences such as the following to the children, leaving out words as indicated by the blanks. Sentences can be drawn from books the teacher plans to share later in class. After reading each sentence, ask the children what word they could use to finish the sentence in a way that would make sense. The children will find that the sentences that have missing words at the end are easier. In some cases, the children may suggest several possibilities, all of which are appropriate. Accept all of these contributions with positive comments.

Sample sentences:

1. Jane went out to walk her _____.
2. John was at home reading a _____.
3. They were fighting like cats and _____.
4. I want ham and _____ for breakfast.
5. Will you _____ football with me?

In these sample sentences, children can use both semantic (meaning) and syntactic (grammar) clues in choosing words to fill in the blanks. Youngsters generally use these two types of clues in combination, but for the purpose of clarifying their differences, we will consider them separately first.

Semantic clues are clues derived from the meanings of the words, phrases, and sentences surrounding the unknown word. In the example just given, children can ask themselves the following questions to decide what words would make sense:

Sentence 1. What are things that can be walked?

Sentence 2. What are things that can be read?

Sentence 3. What expression do I know about fighting that has *like cats and* in it?

Sentence 4. What food might be eaten with ham for breakfast?

Sentence 5. What things can you do with a football?

Various kinds of semantic clues exist, including the following:

1. *Definition clues.* A word may be directly defined in the context. If the child knows the word in oral form, he or she can recognize it in print through the definition.

   The *register* is a book in which the names of the people who come to a wedding are kept.

   The *dictionary* is a book in which the meanings of words can be found.

2. *Appositive clues.* An appositive may offer a synonym or a description of the word that will cue its recognition. Children need to be taught that an appositive is a word or phrase that restates or identifies the word or expression it follows and that it is usually set off by commas, dashes, or parentheses.

   They are going to *harvest,* or gather in, the season's crops.

   That model is *obsolete* (outdated).

   The *rodents*—rats and mice—in the experiment learned to run a maze.

3. *Comparison clues.* A comparison of the unfamiliar word with a word the child knows may offer a clue. In the examples, the familiar words *sleepy* and *clothes* provide the clues for *drowsy* and *habit.*

   Like her sleepy brother, Mary felt *drowsy.*

   Like all the clothes she wore, her riding *habit* was very fashionable.

4. *Contrast clues.* A contrast of the unknown word with a familiar one may offer a clue. In the examples, the unfamiliar word *temporary* is contrasted with the familiar word *forever,* and the unfamiliar word *occasionally* is contrasted with the familiar word *regularly.*

   It will not last forever; it is only *temporary.*

   She doesn't visit regularly; she just comes by *occasionally.*

5. *Common-expression clues.* Familiarity with the word order in many commonly heard expressions, particularly figurative expressions, can lead children to

the identity of an unknown word. In the context activity discussed earlier, children needed to know the expression "fighting like cats and dogs" to complete the sentence. Children with varied language backgrounds are more likely to be able to use figurative expressions to aid word recognition than are children with less developed backgrounds.

He was as quiet as a *mouse.*

Daryl charged around like a bull in a *china* shop.

6. *Example clues.* Sometimes examples are given for words that may be unfamiliar in print, and these examples can provide the clues needed for identification.

Mark was going to talk about *reptiles*—for example, snakes and lizards.

Andrea wants to play a *percussion* instrument, such as the snare drum or the bells.

Syntactic clues are provided by the grammar or syntax of our language. Certain types of words appear in certain positions in spoken English sentences. Thus, word order can give readers clues to the identity of an unfamiliar word. Because most children in schools in the United States have been speaking English since they were preschoolers, they have a feeling for the grammar or syntax of the language. Syntactic clues help them discover that the missing words in sentences 1 through 4 in the oral-context activity presented earlier in this section are nouns, or naming words, and that the missing word in sentence 5 is a verb, or action word.

Looking at each item, we see that in sentence 1 *her* is usually followed by a noun. *A* is usually followed by a singular noun, as in sentence 2. Sentences 3 and 4 both employ *and,* which usually connects words of the same type. In sentence 3, children are likely to insert a plural animal name because of the absence of an article (*a, an, the*). Similarly, in sentence 4 *and* will signal insertion of another food. Sentence 5 has the verb marker *will,* which is often found in the sequence "Will you (verb) . . . ?"

As we pointed out earlier, semantic and syntactic clues should be used *together* to unlock unknown words.

Teaching Strategies

Early exercises with context clues may resemble the oral-context exercise explained earlier. It is good practice for a teacher to introduce a new word in context and let children try to identify it, rather than simply telling them what the word is. Then children can use any phonics and structural analysis knowledge they have, along with context clues, to help them identify the word. The teacher should use a context in which the only unfamiliar word is the new word; for example, use the sentence "My *umbrella* keeps me from getting wet when it rains" to present the word *umbrella.* The children will thus have graphic examples of the value of context clues in identifying unfamiliar words.

When a child encounters an unfamiliar word when reading orally to the teacher, instead of supplying the word, the teacher can encourage the child to skip it for the time being and read on to the end of the sentence (or even to the next sentence) to see what word would make sense. The teacher can encourage use of the sound of the initial letter or cluster of letters, sounds of other letters in the word, or known structural components, along with context. In a sentence where *hurled* appears as an unknown word in the phrase *hurled the ball,* a child might guess *held* from the context. The teacher could encourage this child to notice the letters *ur* and try a word that contains those sounds and makes sense in the context. Of course, this approach will be effective only if the child knows the meaning of *hurled.* Encouraging the child to read subsequent sentences could also be helpful, since these sentences might disclose situations in which *held* would be inappropriate but *hurled* would fit.

A cloze passage, in which words have been systematically deleted and replaced with blanks of uniform length, can be a good way to work on context clue use. For this purpose, the teacher may delete certain types of words (nouns, verbs, adjectives, etc.) rather than using random deletion. The students should discuss their reasons for choosing the words to be inserted in the blanks, and the teacher should accept synonyms and sometimes nonsynonyms for which the students have a good rationale. The point of the exercise is to have the students think logically about what makes sense in the context. (Other uses for the *cloze procedure* and more details about it are found in Chapters 5, 10, and 11.)

Use of context clues can help children make educated guesses about the identities of unfamiliar words. Context clues are best used with phonics and structural analysis skills because they help identify words more quickly than phonics or structural analysis clues alone would. But without the confirmation of phonics and structural analysis, context clues provide only guesses. As we mentioned earlier, when a blank is substituted for a word in a sentence, students can often use several possibilities to complete the sentence and still have it make sense. When children encounter unknown words, they should make educated guesses based on the context and verify those guesses by using other word analysis skills.

A modified cloze procedure can be used with a story summary to develop children's skill in decoding in a meaningful context. The first letter of the deleted word is provided, helping children use their knowledge of sound-symbol relationships as well as choosing words that make sense in the context (Johnson and Louis, 1987).

reading-writing connection

DeSerres (1990) introduces basal reader stories' mastery vocabulary by presenting each word on the board in sentence context, having students write the word in another sentence or phrase context on 3" × 5" word cards for their word banks, and letting them share their sentences. Later she uses modified cloze stories (in which selected words, rather than regularly spaced words, are deleted) with the mastery words as the words chosen for omission. Students fill in the blanks by choosing from their word cards as the class reads the story together. Then they fill in the blanks on individual copies of the stories and read them to partners. Partners point out parts that do not make sense. Later, students produce their own stories. This procedure gives practice with using context.

A child who encountered the following sentence with a blank instead of a word at the end might fill in the blank with either *bat* or *glove:*

Frank said, "If I am going to play Little League baseball this year, I need a new ball and _____."

If the sentence indicated the initial sound of the missing word by presenting the initial letter *g*, the child would know that *glove*, rather than *bat*, was the appropriate word.

Frank said, "If I am going to play Little League baseball this year, I need a new ball and g_____."

Structural analysis clues can be used in the same way. In the following sentence, a child might insert such words as *stop* or *keep* in the blank.

I wouldn't want to _____ you from going on the trip.

The child who had the help of the familiar prefix *pre-* to guide his or her choice would choose neither. The word *prevent* would obviously be the proper choice.

I wouldn't want to pre_____ you from going on the trip.

Suffixes and ending sounds are also very useful in conjunction with context to help in word identification. Teachers can use exercises similar to the following to encourage children to use phonics and structural analysis clues along with context clues. Sample sentences can be drawn from stories that the children are about to read in class.

literature-centered reading

Word Identification

Model Activities

Write the following sentences on the board.

1. This package is too h _ _ _ y for me. Let someone else carry it.

2. I want to join the Navy and ride in a sub _ _ _ _ _ _ .

3. If you keep up that arguing, you will sp _ _ _ the party for everyone.

4. You can't hurt it. It's in _ _ str _ _ _ ible

5. She lives in a pent _ _ _ _ _ apartment.

6. My grandmother has a home r _ _ _ dy for any disease.

Ask the children to read the sentences silently and to try to identify the incomplete words from the clues in the surrounding words and the letters or groups of letters that have been supplied. Let volunteers go to the board and complete the incomplete words. Ask these volunteers if they can tell how the clues in the sentences helped them decide on the words to write. Encourage the students to use the same strategy to figure out other unfamiliar words in the story they are about to read.

Some words are difficult to pronounce unless they appear in context. *Homographs*—words that look alike but have different meanings and pronunciations, such as *row, wind, bow, read, content, rebel, minute, lead, record,* and *live*—are prime examples. Here are some sentences that demonstrate how context can clarify the pronunciations of such words:

1. The *wind* is blowing through the trees.
   Did you *wind* the clock last night?

2. She put a *bow* on the gift.
   You should *bow* to the audience when you finish your act.

3. Can you *read* the directions to me?
   I *read* that book to my class last year.

4. Would you *rebel* against that law?
   I have always thought you were a *rebel*.

5. Did your father *record* his gas mileage?
   Suzanne broke Jill's *record* for the highest score in one game.

6. I *live* on Main Street.
   We saw a *live* octopus.

Although most of the examples in this section show only a single sentence as the context, children should be encouraged to look for clues in surrounding sentences as well as in the sentence in which the word occurs. Sometimes an entire paragraph will be useful in defining a term.

SELF-CHECK: OBJECTIVE 2   Describe a procedure to help children learn to use context clues. (See Self-Improvement Opportunities 6 and 7.)

Phonics

Before you read this section, go to "Test Yourself" at the end of the chapter and take the multiple-choice phonics test. It will give you an idea of your present knowledge of phonics. After you study the text, go back and take the test again to see what you have learned.

Phonics is the association of speech sounds (*phonemes*) with printed symbols (*graphemes*). In some languages, this sound-symbol association is fairly regular, but not in English. A single letter or combination of letters in our alphabet may stand for many different sounds. For example, the letter *a* in each of the following words has a different sound: *cape, cat, car, father, soda*. On the other hand, a single sound may be represented by more than one letter or combination of letters. The long *e* sound is spelled differently in each of the following words: *me, mien, meal, seed,* and *seize*. To complicate matters further, the English language abounds with words that contain letters that stand for no sound, as in is*l*and, *k*ni*gh*t, *w*rite, lam*b*, *g*nome, *p*salm, and *rh*yme.

The existence of these spelling inconsistencies does not imply that phonics is not useful in helping children decode written English. We discuss inconsistencies to counteract the feeling of some teachers that phonics is an infallible guide to pronouncing words in written materials. Teaching phonics does not constitute a complete reading program; rather, phonics is a valuable aid to word recognition when used in conjunction with other skills, but it is only *one* useful skill among many. Mastering this skill, with the resulting ability to pronounce most unfamiliar words, should not be considered the primary goal of a reading program. Children can pronounce words without understanding them, and deriving *meaning* from the printed page should be the objective of all reading instruction.

Groff (1986) found that, if beginning readers can attain an approximate pronunciation of a written word by applying phonics generalizations, they can go on to infer the true pronunciation of the word. He found, for example, that "100% of the second graders tested could infer and produce the *o* of *from* as /u/ after first hearing it as /o/. The pronunciation /from/ was close enough to /frum/ for these young pupils to infer its correct pronunciation" (p. 921). Groff concluded that children need practice in making such inferences. First, they need to apply phonics generalizations to unfamiliar words, producing approximate pronunciations of the words. Then they can infer the real pronunciations of the words by thinking of words they know that are close in sound to the approximations achieved by the generalizations.

Skilled readers appear to identify unfamiliar words by finding similarities with known words (Anderson et al., 1985). For example, a reader might work out the pronunciation of the unknown word *lore* by comparing it with the known word *sore* and applying the knowledge of the sound of *l* in other known words, such as *lamp*. Cunningham (1978, 1979) suggests using a similar approach to identify polysyllabic words as well as single-syllable words.

Carnine (1977) studied the transfer effects of phonics and whole word approaches to reading instruction and found superior transfer to new words among the students who were taught phonics. The phonics group even had greater transfer to irregular words, although it was not extensive. Research with adults has been interpreted as indicating that teachers should present *several* sound-symbol correspondences for each grapheme rather than one-to-one correspondences, thereby providing their students with a set for diversity. If such a procedure had been used in this study, it might have produced more transfer to irregular words.

Phonics techniques are not intended to be ends in themselves; rather, they are means to the end of successful reading. Maclean (1988) sees phonics as "a catalyst which triggers the process of learning to read" (p. 517). It helps students pair spoken and written words and lays the groundwork for them to develop their own decoding routines, which may bear little resemblance to the rules used in phonics instruction. In order for the phonics catalyst to produce a reaction, children must be allowed to do large amounts of reading in appropriate materials. The following Classroom Scenario shows one way that phonics principles begin to form in classes.

**Classroom
Scenario**

Development of Phonics Knowledge

Marty, a first grader, was turning the pages of a calendar in his classroom, finding numbers that he recognized on each page. Suddenly he called to his teacher excitedly, "Mrs. Overholt, this is almost like my name!"

Mrs. Overholt joined Marty at his table. "Yes, it is," she replied. "Show me the part that is the same."

Marty pointed to the letters *M, a, r,* in sequence.

"That's right," Mrs. Overholt said. "Can you tell me what month this is?"

"No," Marty said.

"The month is March," said Mrs. Overholt. "Does it sound a little like your name, too?"

"Yes," Marty almost squealed. "The beginning of it sounds like the beginning of my name."

"You really listened carefully to hear that," Mrs. Overholt said. "Those letters stand for the same sounds in your name and in the word *March.* Keep your eyes open for other words like this. You may be able to figure out what they are by remembering what you found out about letters and sounds."

Analysis of Scenario
Mrs. Overholt used a teachable moment with Marty. He had made a discovery about words that excited him and his teacher helped him to expand it.

A good phonics program provides sufficient reinforcement for a skill that is being taught and offers a variety of reinforcement opportunities (Spiegel, 1990). The practice activities in this text offer some ideas for reinforcement opportunities. Although reinforcement in phonics instruction may include practice with single letters and sounds, it must include application of the strategy or skill with whole words and longer pieces of discourse, such as sentences and paragraphs. Spiegel (1990) suggests the following sequence: "auditory discrimination of the sound of interest, visual discrimination of the letter pattern, and then work with *literature-centered reading* words, sentences, and short paragraphs" (p. 328). We believe this practice should be expanded to include work with whole selections, such as predictable books that contain the letter-sound association that is being emphasized. In fact, a whole selection, in the form of a big book, may be shared with the children orally, with children chiming in on the highly predictable parts wherever possible. From this beginning, the teacher may have students locate the letter representing the sound under consideration, listen for the sound as he or she reads portions of the story aloud again, and make their own generalizations about the relationship between the sound and the letter that represents it. The children will not state their personal generalizations in the same form as the rules that would be found in a reading text, but they will understand the connection more deeply and retain it better if they have discovered it themselves.

If students are to learn phonics associations effectively, they need to see a reason for doing so. The relevance of learning sound-symbol associations is much clearer when students can see the letters and sounds as a part of a meaning-bearing system, rather than as isolated bits of meaningless information.

If basal reading series consistently designed the stories and phonics instruction to support each other, the connection between the phonics instruction and achieving meaning when reading might be much clearer. Anderson and others (1985, p. 47) found that "a high proportion of the words in the earliest selections children read should conform to the phonics they have already been taught."

Adams sees the instructional goal of phonics as students' understanding of the alphabetic principle in written English. She points out that participating in language experience activities, writing with invented spelling, sharing books, and reading interesting texts can help in reaching this goal ("A Talk with Marilyn Adams," 1991).

SELF-CHECK: OBJECTIVE 3   Can you justify teaching phonics as the only approach to word recognition? Why or why not? (See Self-Improvement Opportunity 3.)

Terminology

To understand written material about phonics, teachers need to be familiar with the following terms.

Vowels.   The letters *a, e, i, o,* and *u* represent vowel sounds, and the letters *w* and *y* take on the characteristics of vowels when they appear in the final position in a word or syllable. The letter *y* also has the characteristics of a vowel in the medial (middle) position in a word or syllable.

Consonants.   Letters other than *a, e, i, o,* and *u* generally represent consonant sounds. *W* and *y* have the characteristics of consonants when they appear in the initial position in a word or syllable.

Consonant Blends (or Clusters).   Two or more adjacent consonant letters whose sounds are blended together, with each individual sound retaining its identity, constitute a consonant blend. For example, although the first three sounds in the word *strike* are blended smoothly, listeners can detect the separate sounds of *s, t,* and *r* being produced in rapid succession. Other examples are the *fr* in *frame,* the *cl* in *click,* and the *br* in *bread,* to mention only a few. Many teaching materials refer to these letter combinations as consonant clusters rather than consonant blends.

Consonant Digraphs.   Two adjacent consonant letters that represent a single speech sound constitute a consonant digraph. For example, *sh* is a consonant digraph in the word *shore* because it represents one sound and not a blend of the sounds of *s* and *h.* Additional examples of consonant digraphs appear on page 120.

Vowel Digraphs.   Two adjacent vowel letters that represent a single speech sound constitute a vowel digraph. In the word *foot, oo* is a vowel digraph. Additional examples of vowel digraphs appear on page 121.

Diphthongs.   Vowel sounds that are so closely blended that they can be treated as single vowel units for the purposes of word identification are called *diphthongs*. These sounds are actually vowel blends, since the vocal mechanism produces two sounds instead of one, as is the case with vowel digraphs. An example of a diphthong is the *ou* in *out*. Additional examples of diphthongs appear on page 121.

SELF-CHECK: OBJECTIVE 4   Define and give an example of a consonant blend, a consonant digraph, a vowel digraph, and a diphthong.

Prerequisites for Phonics Instruction

There seems to be agreement that good auditory and visual discrimination are prerequisites for learning sound-symbol relationships. We know that children must be able to distinguish one letter from another and one sound from another before they can associate a given letter with a given sound. *Visual discrimination* refers to the ability to distinguish likenesses and differences among forms, and *auditory discrimination* refers to the ability to distinguish likenesses and differences among sounds. To achieve these skills, children must first understand the concepts of *like* and *different*. Also, to achieve auditory discrimination, children must have *phonemic awareness*, or the awareness that speech is composed of separate sounds (phonemes). They must be able to hear sounds within words, or they will be unable to form mental connections between sounds and letters (Griffith and Olsen, 1992; Juel, 1988, 1991; Ball and Blachman, 1991; Lundberg et al., 1988; Pearson, 1993; Adams, 1990; Gill, 1992). Training in phonemic awareness has been shown to be effective and to have a positive effect on reading acquisition (Lundberg et al., 1988; Yopp, 1992; Bradley and Bryant, 1983). Phonemic awareness activities may ask children "to match words by sounds, isolate a sound in a word, blend individual sounds to form a word, substitute sounds in a word, or segment a word into its constituent sounds" (Yopp, 1992, p. 699). Yopp (1992) points out that playful, gamelike activities such as riddles and guessing games are best because they engage children in the tasks.

Phonemic awareness can be taught directly and may also "develop as a consequence of learning phonics, learning to read, or even learning to write, especially when teachers encourage students to use invented spellings" (Pearson, 1993, p. 507). In whole language classrooms, phonemic awareness and phonics may be learned through invented-spelling activities.

Activities requiring children to discriminate among letter and word forms are more useful to beginning readers than activities requiring them to identify similarities and differences among geometric forms (Sippola, 1985). Unless children need practice in developing the concepts of *like* and *different*, it is pointless to have them make distinctions among shapes and forms. Instead, they need practice with simultaneous and successive visual discrimination of letters and words. Simultaneous discrimination occurs when children match printed symbols that are alike while they can see both symbols. Successive discrimination occurs when children find a duplicate symbol after a stimulus card is no longer visible. Similarly, attention to general sounds in the environment has value only in teaching concepts of *like* and *different* (Sippola, 1985). Beginning readers need to focus primarily on observing similarities and differences in the initial sounds and rhyming sounds of words.

Introducing children to simple rhymes is a good way to sensitize them to the likenesses and differences in verbal sounds. The teacher can ask children to pick out the words that rhyme and to supply words to rhyme with a given word. This ability is fundamental to the construction of "word families." Children should also be able to hear similarities and differences in word endings and in middle vowels; for example, they should be able to tell whether *rub* and *rob,* or *hill* and *pit,* have the same middle sound. Finally, they should be able to listen to the pronunciation of a word sound by sound and mentally fuse or blend the sounds to recognize the intended word.

The following model activities should help children develop visual and auditory discrimination abilities.

Model Activities

Visual Discrimination

Write on the board some letters that are similar in appearance (*b, d,* and *p,* for example) Say to the children: "Let's look at these letters. Are any of them alike? How are the first two letters different? What is different about the other letter?"

Then say to them: "Now I am going to give you a copy of a page of the story that we read today. Look at the first letter on the board. (Point to the letter.) Then look at the page from the story. Every time you see this letter in the story, circle it with your green crayon. (Give them time to search for the letter *b* and mark their pages.) Now look at the second letter.

(Point to it.) Every time you see this letter in the story, circle it with your red crayon. (Give them time to do this.) Now look at the third letter. (Point to it.) Every time you see this letter in the story, circle it in yellow. (Give them time to do this.) Then display a large copy of the story and let individuals come up and point to the letters that should have been circled in the different colors, while children check their own papers.

Repeat the activity with a set of words containing these letters, such as *big, pet*, and *dog*. Ask the same questions about the words. Then have the children perform a similar activity with the words, using fresh pages from the story so that their previous marks will not confuse them.

Model Activities

Auditory Discrimination (Beginning Sounds)

Name several puppets with double names to stress initial consonant sounds (Molly Mouse, Freddie Frog, Dolly Duck, and Bennie Bear). While

holding a puppet, say: "I'd like you to meet Molly Mouse. Molly Mouse only likes things that begin the same way that her name begins. Molly Mouse likes milk, but she doesn't like water. I am going to name some things that Molly Mouse likes or doesn't like. You must listen closely to the way each word begins. Raise your hand if I say something that Molly Mouse likes. Keep your hand down if I say something that Molly Mouse doesn't like. Let's begin. Molly Mouse likes meat." The children should raise their hands. If they don't seem to understand why she likes meat, talk about the beginning sound and give additional examples. Then say: "Molly Mouse likes cheese." The children should keep their hands down.

Model Activities

Auditory Discrimination (Whole Word)

Give each child in the group or class two cards that are identical except that one has *S* written on it and one has *D* written on it. Say to the children: "Each of you has two cards. Hold up the one that has *S* on it." Demonstrate which card has the *S* by holding it up. Then follow the same procedure with the *D* card. Continue by saying: "I am going to say two words. If the two words sound exactly the same, hold up the card with *S* on it. If the two words do not sound exactly the same, hold up the card with *D* on it. The *S* card means *same*. The *D* card means *different*. The first two words are *boy* and *horse*. All of you should be holding up the *D* card, because these two words sound different. The next two words are *funny* and *funny*. Now everyone should be holding up the *S* card, because these two words sound the same." Continue with other examples.

Activities

Additional Visual and Auditory Discrimination Activities

Visual Discrimination

1. Locate a page in a big book that has pairs of similar-looking letters close to each other, and help students discover how the letters are alike and how they differ. Examples of letter pairs to use: *d b, p q, m n.*

2. Choose a word that is frequently confused with a similarly shaped word from a big book story that is being shared. Write this word on the board once, along with several repetitions of the word with which it may be confused. Have the children find the word on the board that is different. Then have them locate the same word in the big book story. Read aloud the sentence in which the word appears. Example of words that could be used: *on on no on.*

Auditory Discrimination (beginning sounds)

1. Say a group of words and ask the children to indicate, by raising their hands, which one starts with a different sound. Begin with vastly different sounds and move to similar sounds. Example: *hat, head, mask, home.*

2. Play a guessing game. Ask if there is anyone in the room whose name starts with the same sound as the beginning of the word *top*. The first child who replies whose name starts with this sound may give the next clue.

3. Find poems that repeat certain sounds. Examples: "Wee Willie Winkie," "Lucy Locket," "Bye-Baby Bunting," "Deedle, Deedle, Dumpling."

4. Use a commercial game such as *Carnival of Beginning Sounds* (Judy/Instructo, Minneapolis) that Spiegel (1990) recommends for developing auditory discrimination.

Auditory Discrimination (medial and final sounds, whole word)

1. Use pictures and ask questions. Example: "Is this a pat or a pet?"

2. Use riddles to relate sounds to words. For example, ask each child to guess what word, illustrated by the following riddle, begins with the same sound as *pig*.

I am good to eat.
I rhyme with *teach*.
I am a fruit.
What am I?

3. Let the children supply the missing rhyming word in a familiar verse.

Phonics Generalizations

Some teachers believe that good phonics instruction is merely the presentation of a series of principles that children are expected to internalize and use in the process of word identification. Difficulties arise from this conception, however.

First, pupils tend to internalize a phonics generalization more rapidly and effectively when they can arrive at it inductively. That is, by analyzing words to which a generalization applies and by deriving the generalization themselves from this analysis, children will understand it better and remember it longer.

Second, the irregularity of the English spelling system results in numerous exceptions to phonics generalizations. Children must be helped to see that generalizations help them to derive *probable* pronunciations rather than infallible results. When applying a generalization does not produce a word that makes sense in the context of the material, readers should try other reasonable sound possibilities. For example, in cases where a long vowel sound is likely according to a generalization but results in a nonsense word, the child should be taught to try other sounds, such as the short vowel sound, in the search for the correct pronunciation. Some words are so totally irregular in their spellings that even extreme flexibility in phonic analysis will not produce close approximations of the correct pronunciations. In such situations, the child should be taught to turn to the dictionary for help in word recognition. Further discussion of this approach to word recognition can be found later in this chapter.

Third, students can be so deluged with rules that they cannot memorize them all. This procedure may result in their failure to learn any generalization well.

Teachers can enhance a phonics program by presenting judiciously chosen phonics generalizations to youngsters, as long as they are taught, not as unvarying rules, but as guides to best guesses. Authorities vary on which generalizations to present (Bailey, 1967; Burmeister, 1968; Clymer, 1963; Emans, 1967), but they agree on some. Considering the findings of phonics studies and past teaching experience, we believe the following generalizations are among the most useful:

1. When the letters *c* and *g* are followed by *e, i,* or *y,* they generally have soft sounds: the *s* sound for the letter *c* and the *j* sound for the letter *g.* (Examples: *cent, city, cycle, gem, ginger, gypsy.*) When *c* and *g* are followed by *o, a,* or *u,* they generally have hard sounds: *g* has its own special sound, and *c* has the sound of *k.* (Examples: *cat, cake, cut, go, game, gum.*)

2. When two like consonants are next to each other, only one is sounded. (Examples: *hall, glass.*)

3. *Ch* usually has the sound heard in *church,* although it sometimes sounds like *sh* or *k.* (Examples of usual sound: *child, chill, china.* Examples of *sh* sound: *chef, chevron.* Examples of *k* sound: *chemistry, chord.*)

4. When *kn* are the first two letters in a word, the *k* is not sounded. (Examples: *know, knight.*)

5. When *wr* are the first two letters in a word, the *w* is not sounded. (Examples: *write, wrong.*)

6. When *ck* are the last two letters in a word, the sound of *k* is given. (Examples: *check, brick.*)

7. The sound of a vowel preceding *r* is neither long nor short. (Examples: *car, fir, her.*)

8. In the vowel combinations *oa, ee, ai,* and *ay,* the first vowel is generally long and the second one is not sounded. This may also apply to other double vowel combinations. (Examples: *boat, feet, rain, play.*)

9. The double vowels *oi, oy,* and *ou* usually form diphthongs. Whereas the *ow* combination frequently stands for the long *o* sound, it may also form a diphthong. (Examples: *boil, boy, out, now.*)

10. If a word has only one vowel and that vowel is at the end of the word, the vowel usually represents its long sound. (Examples: *me, go.*)

11. If a word has only one vowel and that vowel is *not* at the end of the word, the vowel usually represents its short sound. (Examples: *set, man, cut, hop, list.*)

12. If a word has two vowels and one is a final *e,* the first vowel is usually long and the final *e* is not sounded. (Examples: *cape, cute, cove, kite.*)

Rosso and Emans (1981) tried to determine whether knowledge of phonic generalizations helps children decode unrecognized words and whether children have to be able to state the generalizations to use them. They found statistically significant relationships between knowledge of phonic generalizations and reading achievement, but pointed out that this link does not necessarily indicate a cause-and-effect relationship. They also discovered that "inability to state a phonics rule did not seem to hinder these children's effort to analyze unfamiliar words . . . this study supports Piaget's theory that children in the concrete operations stage of development may encounter difficulty in describing verbally those actions they perform physically" (p. 657). Teachers may need to investigate techniques for teaching phonics generalizations that do not require children to verbalize the generalizations.

It is wise to teach only one generalization at a time, presenting a second only after students have thoroughly learned the first. The existence of exceptions to generalizations should be freely acknowledged, and children should be encouraged to treat the generalizations as *possible* rather than *infallible* clues to pronunciation.

In their summary of *Beginning to Read: Thinking and Learning about Print* by Adams (1990), Stahl, Osborn, and Lehr (1990) emphasize that rote knowledge of abstract generalizations will not produce a skillful decoder. They point out the importance of the connection of generalizations with experience. "Rules are intended to capture the patterns of spelling. But productive use of those patterns depends on relevant experience, not on rote memorization" (p. 83). They conclude that phonics generalizations have only temporary value; in fact, "Once a child has learned to read the spellings to which they pertain, they are superfluous" (p. 126).

Consonants.   Although consonant letters are more consistent in the sounds they represent than vowel letters are, they are not perfectly consistent. The following list shows some examples of variations with which a child must contend.

Variations	Consonant	Variations	Consonant
b	board, lamb	n	never, drink
c	cable, city, scene	p	punt, psalm
d	dog, jumped	q(u)	antique, quit
f	fox, of	s	see, sure, his, pleasure, island
g	go, gem, gnat		
h	hit, hour	t	town, listen
j	just, hallelujah	w	work, wrist
k	kitten, knee	x	fox, anxiety, exit
l	lamp, calf	z	zoo, azure, quartz

Consider the cases in which *y* and *w* take on vowel characteristics. Both of these letters represent consonant sounds when they are in the initial position in a word or syllable, but they represent vowel sounds when they are in a final or medial position. For example, *y* represents a consonant sound in the word *yard,* but a vowel sound in the words *dye, myth,* and *baby.* Notice that actually three different vowel sounds are represented by *y* in these words. *W* represents a consonant sound in the word *watch,* but a vowel sound in the word *cow.*

Consonant Digraphs.   Several consonant digraphs represent sounds not associated with either of the component parts. These are as follows:

Consonant Digraph	*Example*
th	then, thick
ng	sing
sh	shout
ph	telephone
gh	rough
ch	chief, chef, chaos

Other consonant digraphs generally represent the usual sound of one of the component parts, as in *write,* *pn*eumonia, and *gn*at. Some sources consider one of the letters in each of these combinations as a "silent" letter and do not refer to these combinations as digraphs.

Vowels.   The variability of the sounds represented by vowels has been emphasized before. Some examples of this variability are as follows:

Vowel Letter	*Variations*
a	ate, cat, want, ball, father, sofa
e	me, red, pretty, kitten, her, sergeant
i	ice, hit, fir, opportunity
o	go, hot, today, women, button, son, work, born
u	use, cut, put, circus, turn

In the examples here, the first variation listed for each vowel is a word in which the long vowel sound, the same as its letter name, is heard. In the second variation the short sound of the vowel is heard. These are generally the first two sounds taught for each vowel.

Another extremely common sound that children need to learn is the schwa sound, a very soft "uh" or grunt usually found in unaccented syllables. It is heard in the following words: sof*a,* kitt*e*n, opportun*i*ty, butt*o*n, circ*u*s. As you can see, each of the vowel letters can represent the schwa sound in some words.

Three types of markings represent the three types of vowel sounds we have discussed:

Marking	*Name of Mark*	*Designation*
ā, ē, ī, ō, ū	macron	long vowel sound

| ă, ĕ, ĭ, ŏ, ŭ | breve | short vowel sound |
| ə | schwa | soft "uh" sound |

Some dictionaries place no mark at all over a vowel letter that represents the short sound of the vowel.

Vowel Digraphs. Some vowel digraphs represent sounds not associated with either of the letters involved. These are as follows:

Vowel Digraph	*Example*
au	taught
aw	saw
oo	food, look

Other vowel digraphs generally represent the usual sound of one of the component parts, as in br*ea*k, br*ea*d, b*oa*t, s*ee*d, and *ai*m. Some sources treat one of the letters in these combinations as "silent" and do not refer to them as digraphs.

Diphthongs. There are four common diphthongs, or vowel blends.

Diphthong	*Example in Context*
oi	foil
oy	toy
ou	bound
ow	cow

Notice that the first two diphthongs listed (*oi* and *oy*) stand for identical sounds, as do the last two (*ou* and *ow*). Remember that the letter combinations *ow* and *ou* are *not always diphthongs*. In the words *snow* and *blow*, *ow* is a vowel digraph representing the long *o* sound. In the word *routine*, *ou* represents the $\overline{oo}$ sound, and in the word *shoulder*, *ou* represents the long *o* sound.

Teaching Strategies

There are two major approaches to phonics instruction: the synthetic and the analytic.

In the *synthetic approach*, the teacher first instructs children in the speech sounds that are associated with individual letters. Because letters and sounds have no inherent relationships, this task is generally accomplished by repeated drill on sound-symbol associations. The teacher may hold up a card on which the letter *b* appears and expect the children to respond with the sound ordinarily associated with that letter. The next step is to blend the sounds together to form words. The teacher encourages the children to pronounce the sounds associated with the letters in rapid succession so that they produce a word or an approximate pronunciation of a word, which they can then recognize and pronounce accurately. This blending process generally begins with two- and three-letter words and proceeds to much longer ones.

Although blending ability is a key factor in the success of a synthetic phonics approach, many commercial materials for reading instruction give little attention to its development. Research indicates that children must master both segmentation of words into their component sounds and blending before they are able to apply phonics skills to the decoding of unknown words and that the ability to segment is a prerequisite for successful blending. Research also indicates that a teacher cannot assume children will automatically transfer the skills they have been taught to unknown words. Direct instruction for transfer is needed to ensure that it will occur (Johnson and Baumann, 1984).

In the synthetic phonics approach, children are sometimes asked to pronounce nonsense syllables because these syllables will appear later in written materials as word parts. Reading words in context does not generally occur until these steps have been repeatedly carried out and the children have developed a moderate stock of words.

The *analytic approach* involves teaching some sight words, followed by teaching the sounds of the letters within those words. Many educators prefer this approach, and it is used in many basal reader series, partly because it avoids the distortion that occurs when consonants are pronounced in isolation. For example, trying to pronounce a *t* in isolation is likely to result in the sounds *tə*. Pronouncing a schwa sound following the consonant can adversely affect the child's blending because the word *tag* must be sounded as *tə-a-gə*. No matter how fast children make those sounds, they are unlikely to come very close to *tag*. With an analytic approach, the teacher would refer to "the sound you hear at the beginning of the word *top*," when cueing the first sound in *tag*. The same process may be used to introduce other consonants, consonant blends, consonant digraphs, vowels, diphthongs, and vowel digraphs in initial, medial, and final positions. One possible problem when using analytic phonics, however, is that children may not be able to extract an individual sound just from hearing it within a word. Partly for this reason and partly because some analytic phonics instruction is worded in a confusing manner, Adams's (1990) findings seem to indicate that even though trying to isolate phonemes can result in distortion, the advantages of asking students to produce phonemes in isolation can outweigh the disadvantages.

literature-centered reading   Trachtenburg (1990) suggests a procedure that is basically an analytic approach in which phonics instruction occurs within the context of reading quality children's literature. Here the progression is from the whole literature selection to the phonic element within the selection and back to another whole literature selection for application of the new knowledge. This procedure is consistent with Harp's (1989) statement: "While the process may be broken down to examine individual pieces, before the instruction ends the process should be 'put back together' so that the children see the relationship between the part and the whole" (p. 326).

Trachtenburg's method proceeds as follows:

- First, the teacher reads to the class a literature selection that contains many examples of the phonic element in question. Students may discuss or dramatize the story, when the teacher has finished.

- The teacher introduces the phonic element that is the target for the lesson (long *a, e, i, o,* or *u*; short *a, e, i, o,* or *u*; or some other element) by explaining that the children are going to learn one of the sounds for a specific letter or letter combination.

- Then the teacher writes a portion of the story that contains the target element on the chalkboard or a transparency. The teacher reads this portion of the story aloud, pausing to underline the words containing the target element.

- The teacher identifies the sound involved and asks the children to read the story portion with him or her and listen for the sound. The teacher may suggest a key word that will help them remember the sound in the future.

- The teacher guides practice with the new sound, using a mechanical device in which initial consonants can be varied while the medial vowel remains stationary or a similar device in which both initial and final consonants can be varied. (An example of such a device is shown in Activity 4 (page 135) for phonics practice in this chapter.) The teacher may also provide practice with a similar device that allows sentence parts to be substituted, which enables children to practice the sound in larger language chunks. For example, adjectives, verbs, or adverbs could be varied, as could prepositional phrases, verb phrases, or any other sentence part.

- Finally, the teacher presents another book that has numerous examples of the phonic element. Children may then be allowed to read this book independently, read it in unison from a big book, or read it with a partner, depending on their individual achievement levels.

Trachtenburg (1990) offers the following list of trade books that repeat long and short vowel sounds.

Short a

Flack, Marjorie. *Angus and the Cat.* Doubleday, 1931.

Griffith, Hellen. *Alex and the Cat.* Greenwillow, 1982.

Kent, Jack. *The Fat Cat.* Scholastic, 1971.

Most, Bernard. *There's an Ant in Anthony.* William Morrow, 1980.

Nodset, Joan. *Who Took the Farmer's Hat?* Harper & Row, 1963.

Robins, Joan. *Addie Meets Max.* Harper & Row, 1985.

Schmidt, Karen. *The Gingerbread Man.* Scholastic, 1985.

Seuss, Dr. *The Cat in the Hat.* Random House, 1957.

Long a

Aardema, Verna. *Bringing the Rain to Kapiti Plain.* Dial, 1981.

Bang, Molly. *The Paper Crane.* Greenwillow, 1985.

Blume, Judy. *The Pain and the Great One.* Bradbury, 1974.

Byars, Betsy. *The Lace Snail.* Viking, 1975.

Henkes, Kevin. *Sheila Rae, the Brave.* Greenwillow, 1987.

Hines, Anna G. *Taste the Raindrops.* Greenwillow, 1983.

Short and long a

Aliki. *Jack and Jake.* Greenwillow, 1986.

Slobodkina, Esphyr. *Caps for Sale.* Addison-Wesley, 1940.

Short e

Ets, Marie Hall. *Elephant in a Well.* Viking, 1972.

Galdone, Paul. *The Little Red Hen.* Scholastic, 1973.

Ness, Evaline. *Yeck Eck.* E. P. Dutton, 1974.

Shecter, Ben. *Hester the Jester.* Harper & Row, 1977.

Thayer, Jane. *I Don't Believe in Elves.* William Morrow, 1975.

Wing, Henry Ritchet. *Ten Pennies for Candy.* Holt, Rinehart & Winston, 1963.

Long e

Galdone, Paul. *Little Bo-Peep.* Clarion/Ticknor & Fields, 1986.

Keller, Holly. *Ten Sleepy Sheep.* Greenwillow, 1983.

Martin, Bill. *Brown Bear, Brown Bear, What Do You See?* Henry Holt, 1967.

Oppenheim, Joanne. *Have You Seen Trees?* Young Scott Books, 1967.

Soule, Jean C. *Never Tease a Weasel.* Parents' Magazine Press, 1964.

Thomas, Patricia. *"Stand Back," said the Elephant, "I'm Going to Sneeze!"* Lothrop, Lee & Shepard, 1971.

Short i

Browne, Anthony. *Willy the Wimp.* Alfred A. Knopf, 1984.

Ets, Marie Hall. *Gilberto and the Wind.* Viking, 1966.

Hutchins, Pat. *Titch.* Macmillan, 1971.

Keats, Ezra Jack. *Whistle for Willie.* Viking, 1964.

Lewis, Thomas P. *Call for Mr. Sniff.* Harper & Row, 1981.

Lobel, Arnold. *Small Pig.* Harper & Row, 1969.

McPhail, David. *Fix-It.* E. P. Dutton, 1984.

Patrick, Gloria. *This Is . . .* Carolrhoda, 1970.

Robins, Joan. *My Brother, Will.* Greenwillow, 1986.

Long i

Berenstain, Stan and Jan. *The Bike Lesson.* Random House, 1964.

Cameron, John. *If Mice Could Fly.* Atheneum, 1979.

Cole, Sheila. *When the Tide Is Low.* Lothrop, Lee & Shepard, 1985.

Gelman, Rita. *Why Can't I Fly?* Scholastic, 1976.

Hazen, Barbara S. *Tight Times.* Viking, 1979.

Short o

Benchley, Nathaniel. *Oscar Otter.* Harper & Row, 1966.

Dunrea, Olivier. *Mogwogs on the March!* Holiday House, 1985.

Emberley, Barbara. *Drummer Hoff.* Prentice-Hall, 1967.

McKissack, Patricia C. *Flossie & the Fox.* Dial, 1986.

Miller, Patricia, and Iran Seligman. *Big Frogs, Little Frogs.* Holt, Rinehart & Winston, 1963.

Rice, Eve. "The Frog and the Ox" from *Once in a Wood.* Greenwillow, 1979.

Seuss, Dr. *Fox in Socks.* Random House, 1965.

Long o

Cole, Brock. *The Giant's Toe.* Farrar, Straus & Giroux, 1986.

Gerstein, Mordicai. *Roll Over!* Crown, 1984.

Johnston, Tony. *The Adventures of Mole and Troll.* G. P. Putnam's Sons, 1972.

Johnston, Tony. *Night Noises and Other Mole and Troll Stories.* G. P. Putnam's Sons, 1977.

Shulevitz, Uri. *One Monday Morning.* Charles Scribner's Sons, 1967.

Tresselt, Alvin. *White Snow, Bright Snow.* Lothrop, Lee & Shepard, 1947.

Short u

Carroll, Ruth. *Where's the Bunny?* Henry Z. Walck, 1950.

Cooney, Nancy E. *Donald Says Thumbs Down.* G. P. Putnam's Sons, 1987.

Friskey, Margaret. *Seven Little Ducks.* Children's Press, 1940.

Lorenz, Lee. *Big Gus and Little Gus.* Prentice-Hall, 1982.

Marshall, James. *The Cut-Ups.* Viking Kestrel, 1984.

Udry, Janice May. *Thump and Plunk.* Harper & Row, 1981.

Yashima, Taro. *Umbrella.* Viking Penguin, 1958.

Long u

Lobel, Anita. *The Troll Music.* Harper & Row, 1966.

Segal, Lore. *Tell Me a Trudy.* Farrar, Straus & Giroux, 1977.

Slobodkin, Louis. *"Excuse Me—Certainly!"* Vanguard Press, 1959.

Source: Reprinted with permission of Phyllis Trachtenburg and the International Reading Association.

Focus on Strategies

The following Focus on Strategies tells how a teacher introduced the long *e* sound in story context, thus using an analytic approach to phonics.

Teaching Phonics Through Literature

Ms. Mahan started her class by reading the predictable book *Peanut Butter and Jelly* (JoAnne Nelson, Modern Curriculum Press, 1989) to her first graders. By the time she got to page 13, the children were chiming in on the repeated line "But peanut butter and jelly is my favorite thing to eat," as she always encouraged the children to do when they discovered the predictable pattern. When the story had been completed, the teacher responded to requests to "read it again" by doing so. This time the children joined in on the repeated line from the beginning.

The children discussed the story, and Ms. Mahan made a list on the board of the children's personal favorite things to eat.

Then Ms. Mahan wrote the letter combination *ea* on the board. One of the words on the list of the children's favorite foods was *beans*. Another one was *peanuts*. She pronounced each of these words and pointed out that both contained a long *e* sound. Then she displayed transparencies of pages from the story *Peanut Butter and Jelly*. As she read page 5, she underlined the words *meat*, *peanut*, and *eat*. She then reread each underlined word and asked the children to listen to the sounds. She told the class that the letter combination *ea* often has the long *e* sound. Then she read the words again as they listened specifically for the long *e* sound.

She proceeded to display subsequent pages from the story, asking the children to watch for the *ea* combination in the words and raise their hands when they saw it. When hands were raised, she let the children identify the words with the *ea* combination. Then the children listened for the long *e* sound in each word. The following words from this story fit this pattern: *eat, meat, peanut, cream, wheat, treat, heat,* and *beat*. They also found the word *cereal* and recognized that they heard the long *e* sound. Since they had not yet had instruction on syllabication or schwa sounds, Ms. Mahan simply agreed that there was a long *e* sound after the *r* and went on to the next word. On page 18 they saw a word with the ea combination that did not have the long *e* sound: *bread*. The presence of this word allowed Ms. Mahan to point out that sounds are not always consistent and that the sound-letter clues only helped the children make "best guesses" about pronunciations, not absolute certainties.

Ms. Mahan then encouraged the children to play with the words that had been located. She wrote *eat* on the board and asked them how to turn it into *meat*. She let Tammy come to the board and add the needed letter. Then she wrote *eat* again and asked who could turn it into *wheat*, then *treat*, then *heat*, then *beat*. Finally, she branched out from words that were found directly in the story and let the children form *neat* and *seat*. She also let them transform *cream* into *team*, *seam*, and *dream* by removing the initial blend and replacing it with other letters.

Then Ms. Mahan pointed out that sometimes there are several ways to spell a particular sound. She used the transparencies of the story again, encouraging the children to listen for the long *e* sound in words other than the ones already underlined. They located *sweet, street, beet, even,* and *cheese.* Ms. Mahan asked if they could suggest any other letter patterns that could spell the long *e* sound. They quickly identified the *ee* combination, and eventually Tommy said that the *e* by itself could also spell the sound.

Ms. Mahan then shared the books *Ten Sleepy Sheep* (Holly Keller, Greenwillow, 1983) and *Never Tease a Weasel* (Jean C. Soule, Parents' Magazine Press, 1964) with the children and put them in the reading center, along with *Peanut Butter and Jelly,* to be reread by the children independently or with partners.

The children were then given time to write their own stories about favorite foods. Ms. Mahan asked them to notice which words had the long *e* sound as they wrote. She let them share their stories orally with small groups of their peers.

The following three sample lesson plans further illustrate the analytic method. The first two lesson plans are *inductive:* the children look at a number of specific examples related to a generalization and then derive the generalization. The third is *deductive:* the teacher states a generalization and then has the children apply the generalization in decoding unfamiliar words.

Analytic-Inductive Lesson Plan for Initial Consonant

Model Activities

Write on the chalkboard the following words, all of which the children have learned previously as sight words:

dog   did

daddy   donkey

do   Dan

Ask the children to listen carefully as you pronounce the words. Then ask: "Did any parts of these words sound the same?" If you receive an affirmative reply, ask: "What part sounded the same?" This should elicit the answer that the first sound in each word is the same or that the words sound alike at the beginning.

Next, ask the children to look carefully at the words written on the board. Ask: "Do you see anything that is the same in all these words?" This should elicit the answer that all of the words have the same first letter or all of the words start with *d.*

Then ask what the children can conclude about words that begin with the letter *d.* The expected answer is that words that begin with the letter *d* sound the same at the beginning as the word *dog* (or any other word on their list).

Next, invite the children to name other words that have the same beginning sound as *dog.* Write each word on the board. Ask the children to observe the words and draw another conclusion. They may say, "Words that sound the same at the beginning as the word *dog* begin with the letter *d.*"

Ask the children to watch for words in their reading that begin with the letter *d* to check the accuracy of their conclusions.

Model Activities

Analytic-Inductive Lesson Plan for Short Vowel Sound Generalizations

Write the following list of words on the board, all of which are part of the children's sight vocabularies:

sit	in
at	man
hot	Don
met	wet
cut	bun

Ask the children how many vowels they see in each word in the list. When you receive the answer "One," write on the board: "One vowel letter."

Then ask: "Where is the vowel letter found in these words?" The children will probably say, "At the beginning in some and in the middle in others." Write on the board: "At the beginning or in the middle."

Then ask: "Which of its sounds does the vowel have in the word *sit*? In the word *at*?" and so on until

the students have discovered that the short sound is present in each word. Then write on the board: "Short sound."

Next, ask the children to draw a conclusion about the vowel sounds in the words they have analyzed. The generalization may be stated: "In words that contain only one vowel letter, located at the beginning or in the middle of the word, the vowel usually has its short sound." The children will be likely to insert the word *usually* if they have been warned about the tentative nature of phonics generalizations.

Finally, ask the children if they should have included in their generalization words having only one vowel letter located at the end of the word. The children can check sight words such as *he, no,* and *be* in order to conclude that these words do not have a short vowel sound and therefore should not be included in the generalization.

Model Activities

Analytic-Deductive Lesson Plan for Soft Sound of *c*

Tell the children: "When the letter *c* is followed by *e, i,* or *y,* it generally has its soft sound, which is the sound you have learned for the letter *s.*" Write the following examples on the chalkboard: *city, cycle,* and *cent.* Point out that in *cycle* only the *c* that is followed by *y* has the soft sound. Follow this presentation with an activity designed to check the children's understanding of the generalization. The activity might involve a worksheet with items like this:

Directions: Place a check beside the words that contain a soft *c* sound.

_____ cite	_____ cider
_____ cape	_____ cord
_____ cede	_____ cymbal
_____ cut	_____ cod
_____ cell	

The soft *c* sound is the sound we have learned for the letter_____.

An approach that has some aspects of both the synthetic and analytic approaches is the teaching of *onsets* and *rimes*. In this approach, the teacher breaks down a syllable into the part of the syllable before the vowel (onset) and the remainder of the syllable (rime) that begins with the vowel. In the past, these rimes were referred to as *phonograms*. (See Example 3.1.) In one rime-based instructional program, "children are taught to compare an unknown word to already known words and to use context to confirm their predictions" (Stahl, 1992, p. 623; Gaskins et al., 1988; Gaskins et al., 1991). Such an approach may be referred to as an *analogy approach* or a *compare/contrast approach*. The children are taught an initial set of "key words," containing the phonograms or rimes. After comparing the unknown word to a known one and coming up with a tentative decision about the pronunciation of the unknown word, a child would be expected to check to see whether the new word produced made sense in the sentence in which it was found. According to Adams (1990), the letter-sound correspondences in rimes are more stable than the correspondences found when the letters are taken in isolation.

Example 3.1 *Onsets and Rimes*

Word	Onset	Rime
black	bl–	–ack
may	m–	–ay
am	—	am

Gaskins et al. (1991) found that direct instruction was useful in teaching phonics through the analogy approach. In every lesson, teachers inform the children about "*what* they are going to teach, *why* it is important, *when* it can be used, and *how* to use it" (p. 215). This explanation is followed by teacher modeling and group and individual guided practice for the students. Every-pupil response activities and teacher feedback are important program features. Key words are introduced through a structured language experience activity (the writing of a group story with the key words just presented). Phonemic awareness activities are also included to facilitate the learning of onsets such as the initial consonant *f* or the initial consonant blend *fr*. The Model Activity on the next page shows use of an analogy or compare/contrast approach.

reading-writing connection

Spiegel (1990) recommends the commercial games *Road Race* (Carpenter, Curriculum Associates, 1987) and *Word Trek* (Collgrove, DLM, 1977) as educationally valid decoding games that work well with the compare/contrast, onset-rime, and word family approaches to phonics instruction.

Ehri and Robbins (1992) found that students needed some knowledge of phoneme-grapheme correspondences in order to be able to use onset-rime units. Bruck and Treiman (1992) discovered that beginning readers can use analogies, but tend to rely more on individual phoneme-grapheme correspondences to

**Model
Activities**

Analogy or Compare/Contrast Approach

The teacher writes the key words *be* and *rain* on the board and pronounces them. Then he or she writes: "The student hopes to <u>remain</u> in that group." The teacher verbalizes the thought pattern needed to decode the word in this way: "If this (pointing to *be*) is *be*, then this is *re*. If this (pointing to *rain*) is *rain*, then this is *main*." (Note: The sounds of the initial consonants *r* and *m* must have been taught previously.) The teacher continues: "The word is *remain*. Does that make sense in the context?" After receiving an affirmative reply, the teacher says: "Yes, *remain* means to stay."

Then the teacher provides a list of key words the students have already studied and turned into sight words, as well as several paragraphs, preferably from a story they are about to read, with difficult words underlined. The teacher asks the students to decode these underlined words, using the key words and the strategy that has just been modeled. After the children have worked at this task independently, the teacher calls on several students to verbalize their strategies for the difficult words.

decode new words. Their findings suggest that students need instruction on individual phoneme-grapheme correspondences, especially for vowels, rather than just on relationships between groups of phonemes and groups of graphemes. They warn that rime instruction is not sufficient by itself.

Johnson and Baumann (1984) cite research indicating that "programs emphasizing a phonics or code approach to word identification produce superior word-calling ability when compared to programs applying an analytic phonics or meaning emphasis" (p. 590). But, they continue, "there seem to be distinct differences in the quality of error responses made by children instructed in the two general methodologies—readers' errors tend to be real words, meaningful, and syntactically appropriate when instruction emphasizes meaning, whereas code-emphasis word-identification instruction results in more nonword errors that are graphically and aurally like the mispronounced words" (p. 590). Because the goal of reading is comprehension, not word calling, the analytic approach, which uses meaning-emphasis techniques, seems to be the better choice for instruction.

Teachers should keep in mind a caution about the teaching of phonics generalizations that involve the use of such terms as *sound* and *word*. Studies by Reid and Downing indicate that young children (five year olds) have trouble understanding terms used to talk about language, such as *word, letter,* and *sound* (Downing, 1973), and Meltzer and Herse (1969) found that first-grade children do not always know where printed words begin and end. In addition, Tovey (1980) found that the group of second through sixth graders he studied had difficulty in dealing with abstract phonics terms such as *consonant, consonant blend, consonant digraph, vowel digraph, diphthong, possessive, inflectional ending,* and others. His study also showed that the children had learned sound-symbol associations without being able to define the phonics terms involved. Lessons such as those described in this chapter are worthless if the students lack these basic concepts. Before teaching a lesson using linguistic terms, the teacher should check to be sure that students grasp such concepts. Technical terminology should be deemphasized when working with students who have not mastered the terms.

Cordts (1965) suggests using key words to help children learn the sounds associated with vowels, consonants, vowel digraphs, consonant digraphs, diphthongs, and consonant blends. In all cases, these words should already be part of the children's sight vocabularies. Cordts suggests that a key word for a vowel sound be one that contains that vowel sound and can be pictured, whereas a key word for a consonant sound should be one that can be pictured and has that consonant sound at the end. She believes that consonant sounds can be heard more clearly at the ends than at the beginnings of words.

Other authorities also encourage the use of key words, but most suggest using words with the consonant sounds at the beginning. The sounds may be harder to distinguish, but usable key words are much easier to find when initial sounds are used.

Learning phonics skills involves learning about letter-sound associations such as those of consonants, consonant digraphs, and consonant clusters (or blends). (*Jean Claude Lejeune*)

Key words are valuable in helping children remember sound-symbol associations that are not inherently meaningful. People remember new things through associations with things they already know. The more associations a person has for an abstract relationship, such as the letter *d* and the sound of *d*, the more quickly that person will learn to link the sound and the symbol. The person's retention of this connection will also be more accurate. Schell (1978) refers to a third-grade boy who chose as key words for the consonant blends *dr, fr,* and *sp* the character names *Dracula, Frankenstein,* and *Spiderman.* These associations were both concrete and personal for him. The characters were drawn on key-word cards to aid his memory of the associations.

Consonant substitution activities are useful for helping students see how their knowledge of some words helps them to decode other words. Following is a Model Activity for teaching consonant substitution.

**Model
Activities**

Consonant Substitution

Write a known word, such as *pat,* on the board and ask the students to pronounce the word. Then write on the board a letter for which the sound has been taught (for example, *m*). If the letter sound can be pronounced in isolation without distortion, ask the students to do so; if not, ask for a word beginning with this sound. Then ask the students to leave the *p* sound off when they pronounce the word on the board. They will respond with *at.* Next, ask them to put the *m* sound in front of the *at,* and they will produce *mat.* The same process is followed with other sounds, such as *s, r,* and *b.*

This procedure is also useful with sounds at the ends of words or in medial positions. Vowel substitution activities, in which you may start with a known word and have the students omit the vowel sound and substitute a different one (for example: s*a*t, s*e*t, s*i*t; p*a*t, p*e*t, p*i*t, p*o*t), can also be helpful.

---

reading-writing connection   Cunningham and Cunningham (1992) suggest an activity called Making Words, which is a guided group invented-spelling instructional strategy designed to take advantage of the values of writing with invented spelling while offering a more direct instructional procedure. In it the children use the letters of a long word to spell short words of varying lengths, eventually trying to actually spell the long word from which the others were made. They then sort the words they have made according to a variety of patterns. This activity is designed to be used along with writing activities that involve invented spelling. Table 3.3 presents the steps in planning and the steps in teaching a Making Words lesson. Before teaching the lesson, the teacher constructs large letter cards with the capital letter on one side and the lower-case letter on the other side of each card for use with the group and sets of small letter cards that allow each student to have a set at his or her desk. The small cards for each letter may be stored in separate reclosable bags.

Table 3.3 *Making Words*

Steps in planning a Making Words lesson

1. Decide what the final word in the lesson will be. In choosing this word, consider its number of vowels, child interest, curriculum tie-ins you can make, and letter-sound patterns you can draw children's attention to through the word sorting at the end.

2. Make a list of shorter words that can be made from the letters of the final word.

3. From all the words you listed, pick 12–15 words that include: (a) words that you can sort for the pattern(s) you want to emphasize; (b) little words and big words so that the lesson is a multilevel lesson; (c) words that can be made with the same letters in different places (e.g., *barn*, *bran*) so children are reminded that when spelling words, the order of the letters is crucial; (d) a proper name or two to remind them where we use capital letters; and (e) words that most of the students have in their listening vocabularies.

4. Write all the words on index cards and order them from shortest to longest.

5. Once you have the two-letter, three-letter, etc., words together, order them further so that you can emphasize letter patterns and how changing the position of the letters or changing or adding just one letter results in a different word.

6. Store the cards in an envelope. Write on the envelope the words in order and the patterns you will sort for at the end.

Steps in teaching a Making Words lesson

1. Place the large letter cards in a pocket chart or along the chalk ledge.

2. Have designated children give one letter to each child. (Let the passer keep the reclosable bag containing that letter and have the same child collect that letter when the lesson is over.)

3. Hold up and name the letters on the large letter cards, and have the children hold up their matching small letter cards.

4. Write the numeral 2 (or 3, if there are no two-letter words in this lesson) on the board. Tell them to take two letters and make the first word. Use the word in a sentence after you say it.

5. Have a child who has the first word made correctly make the same word with the large letter cards. Encourage anyone who did not make the word correctly at first to fix the word when they see it made correctly.

6. Continue having them make words, erasing and changing the number on the board to indicate the number of letters needed. Use the words in simple sentences to make sure the children understand their meanings. Remember to cue them as to whether they are just changing one letter, changing letters around, or taking all their letters out to make a word from scratch. Cue them when the word you want them to make is a proper name, and send a child who has started that name with a capital letter to make the word with the big letters.

Table 3.3   *Making Words (cont.)*

7. Before telling them the last word, ask "Has anyone figured out what word we can make with all our letters?" If so, congratulate them and have one of them make it with the big letters. If not, say something like, "I love it when I can stump you. Use all your letters and make _____."

8. Once all the words have been made, take the index cards on which you have written the words, and place them one at a time (in the same order children made them) along the chalk ledge or in the pocket chart. Have children say and spell the words with you as you do this. Use these words for sorting and pointing out patterns. Pick a word and point out a particular spelling pattern, and ask children to find the others with that same pattern. Line these words up so that the pattern is visible.

9. To get maximum transfer to reading and writing, have the children use the patterns they have sorted to spell a few new words that you say.

Note: Some teachers have chosen to do steps 1–7 on one day and steps 8 and 9 on the following day.

Source: Patricia M. Cunningham and James W. Cunningham, "Making Words: Enhancing the Invented Spelling-Decoding Connection," *The Reading Teacher*, 46 (October 1992), p. 108. Reprinted by permission of the author and the International Reading Association.

literature-centered reading

Oleneski (1992) used the jump rope rhyme "Teddy Bear" to teach sounds in an analytic manner with authentic material. She duplicated the rhyme, which the children knew well, and let them engage in activities such as reading it and sequencing its parts with sentence strips. Then she covered up certain words and had the children figure out what these words were. She then asked them to predict which letters would represent the beginning and ending sounds of the target words. Students continued to use the poem for reading and writing activities to keep the instruction on sounds in context. This procedure could be used with other jump-rope rhymes or ball-bouncing rhymes.

reading-writing connection

Drill on letter-sound associations need not be dull. Teachers can use many game activities, and activities that are more formal will not become boring if they are not overused. When planning games, teachers should always remember that, although competitive situations are motivational for some youngsters, other children are adversely affected by being placed in win/lose situations, especially if they have little hope of being winners at least part of the time. Constantly being forced into losing situations can negatively affect a child's self-concept and can promote negative attitudes toward the activity involved in the game (in this instance, reading). This effect is less likely if children with similar abilities compete with one another; even then, however, competitive games should be used with caution. Game situations in which children cooperate or in which they compete with *their own previous records* rather than with one another are often more acceptable. Following are some practical examples of both competitive and noncompetitive games.

Activities

1. Construct cards resembling bingo cards, like the ones shown here. Pronounce a word beginning with the sound of one of the listed consonants or consonant digraphs. Instruct the children to check their cards for the letter or letter combination that represents the word's initial sound. Tell those whose cards have the correct letter or letter combination to cover it with a token. Continue to pronounce words until one child has covered his or her entire card. The first child to do this can be declared the winner, or the game may continue until all cards are covered.

b	d	f	g
h	j	k	l
m	n	p	r
s	t	v	w

y	z	th	sh
h	ch	b	p
r	m	t	k
n	s	g	n

d	y	g	th
h	ch	k	p
m	r	s	v
sh	n	l	j

2. Give each child a sheet of paper that is blank except for a letter at the top. Have the children draw pictures of as many items as they can think of that have names beginning with the sound of the letter at the top of the page. Declare the child with the most correct responses the winner.

3. Make five decorated boxes, and label each box with a short vowel. Have the children locate pictures of objects whose names contain the short vowel sounds and file them in the appropriate boxes. Each day take out the pictures, ask the children to pronounce the names, and check to see if the appropriate sounds are present. Do the same thing with long vowel sounds, consonant sounds, consonant blends, digraphs, diphthongs, and rhyming words.

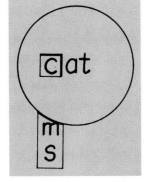

4. Place a familiar word ending on a cardboard disk like the one pictured here. Pull a strip of cardboard with initial consonants on it through an opening cut in the disk. Show the children how to pull the strip through the disk, pronouncing each word that is formed.

5. Divide the children into two groups. Give half of them initial consonant, consonant blend, or consonant di-graph cards. Give the other half word-ending cards. Instruct the children to pair up with other children holding word parts that combine with their parts to form real words. Have each pair hold up their cards and pronounce the word they have made when they have located a combination. Then let them search for other possible combinations for their word parts.

6. Use riddles. For example: "I have in mind a word that rhymes with far. We ride in it. It's called a _____."

7. Give students silly sentences to read orally. Construct these sentences so that they require the application of phonics skills taught previously. Examples: Her mate sat on the mat. He charged a high rate to kill the rat.

Let the children find a hidden picture by shading in all the spaces that contain words with long vowel sounds.

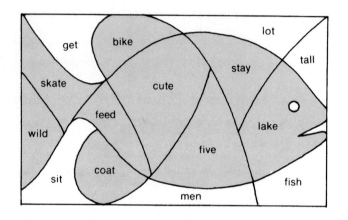

To be effective, practice exercises should always be preceded by instruction and followed by feedback on results. The absence of prior instruction may cause students to practice the wrong response. Feedback, which should come either directly from the teacher or through a self-correcting procedure (posted answers, for example), will inform students of errors immediately so that they do not learn incorrect responses. When students fail to see reasons for errors, the teacher will need to provide explanations and reteach the strategy or skill.

A phonics strategy or skill is a means to an end, not an end in itself. Readers who can recognize words without resorting to letter-by-letter sounding will recognize them more quickly than those who must sound out the words, and the process will interfere less with their train of thought than sounding out the words would have. When the words to be recognized are seen in context, as in most normal reading activities, the sound of the first letter alone may elicit recognition of the whole word. Context clues can provide a child with an idea about the word's identity, and the initial sound can be used to verify an educated guess. This procedure is efficient and is a good way to identify unfamiliar words quickly. Of course, the ultimate goal of instruction in phonics and other word identification skills is to turn initially unfamiliar words into automatically recognized sight words.

SELF-CHECK: OBJECTIVE 5 Describe a procedure for teaching one of the phonics generalizations presented in this section. (See Self-Improvement Opportunities 3, 4, and 9.)

Structural Analysis

Structural analysis is closely related to phonics and has several significant facets:

1. Inflectional endings
2. Prefixes, suffixes
3. Contractions
4. Compound words
5. Syllabication and accents

Structural analysis strategies and skills enable children to decode unfamiliar words by using units larger than single graphemes; this procedure generally expedites the decoding process. Structural analysis can also help in understanding word meanings, a function discussed in Chapter 4.

Inflectional Endings

Inflectional endings are added to nouns to change number, case, or gender; added to verbs to change tense or person; and added to adjectives to change degree. They may also change a word's part of speech. Since inflectional endings are letters or groups of letters added to the endings of root words, some people call them *inflectional suffixes*. Here are some examples of words with inflectional endings.

Root Word	New Word	Change
boy	boys	Singular noun changed to plural noun
host	hostess	Gender of noun changed from masculine to feminine
Karen	Karen's	Proper noun altered to show possession (change of case)
look	looked	Verb changed from present tense to past tense
make	makes	Verb changed from first or second person singular to third person singular
mean	meaner	Simple form of adjective changed to the comparative form
happy	happily	Adjective changed to adverb

Generally, the first inflectional ending to which children are exposed is *-s*. This ending often appears in early reading materials and should be learned early in the first grade. Other inflectional endings children are likely to encounter in these early materials are *-ing* and *-ed*.

A child can be shown the effect of the addition of an *-s* to a singular noun through use of illustrations of single and multiple objects. An activity such as that shown in the following Model Activity: Recognizing Inflectional Ending *-s* can be

literature-centered reading

used to practice this skill. A second Model Activity for various inflectional endings demonstrates further possibilities for practice with different inflectional endings.

Children in the primary grades are frequently exposed to the possessive case formed by -*'s*. Here is an activity designed for work with this inflectional ending.

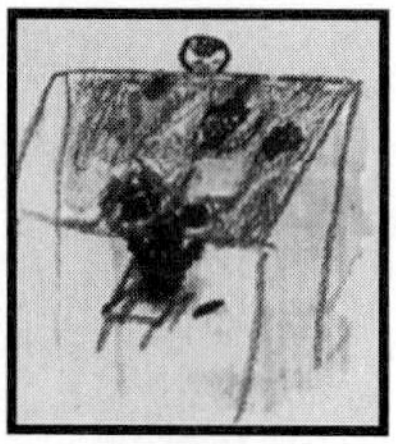

Model Activities

Recognizing Inflectional Ending -*s*

Give the following practice sheet to the children.

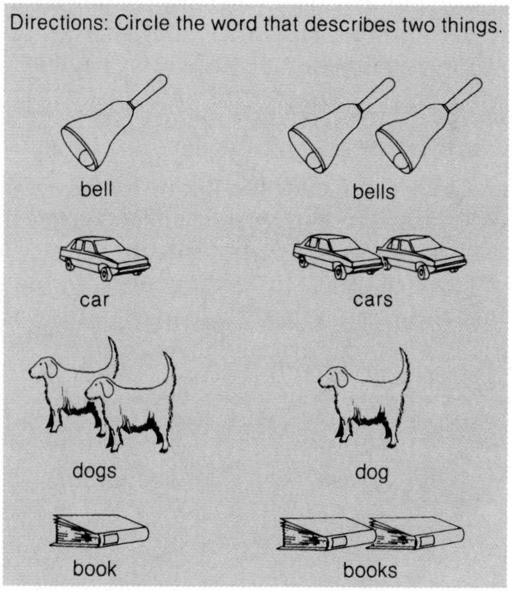
Directions: Circle the word that describes two things.
bell
bells
car
cars
dogs
dog
book
books

Ask the children to read and follow the directions. Then go over the practice sheet with them orally, asking how each word that shows more than one thing looks different from the word that shows only one thing. They should come to the conclusion that -*s* at the ends of the words indicates more than one thing.

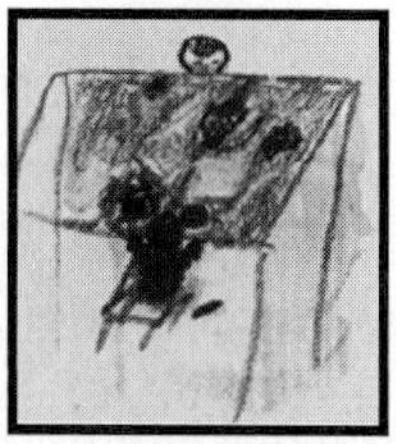

Model Activities

Recognizing Inflectional Endings

Write on the board sentences containing inflectional endings that have already been discussed, taken from a book that has been shared in class. Ask the children to read the sentences silently, looking for the inflectional endings they have studied in class. After the silent reading, let volunteers go to the board, circle the inflectional endings in the sentences, and tell how each ending affects word meaning or word use.

You may not wish to use all possible examples from the book in this activity. Instead, you can encourage students to go back to the book itself, either individually or in pairs, locate the inflectional endings under consideration, and make a list of the words they find. These words can be discussed later in a group discussion, with the students finding the words in the story and reading the sentences in which they appear.

As an example, *Ox-Cart Man* (Hall, Puffin Books, 1979) could be used for sentences containing the words *backed, filled, packed, sheared, spinning, pairs,* *mittens, candles, shingles, brooms, carved, borrowed, potatoes, counted, apples, honeycombs, turnips, cabbages, maples, tapped, boiled, feathers, collected, waved, walked, ox's, days, hills, valleys, streams, farms, villages, kissed, pockets, coins, pounds, candies, tucked, kettle's, waiting, stitching, whittling, cooked, sawed, embroidered, trees, knitted, planted, blossoms, bloomed, bees, starting, squawked, dropping,* and *clouds.* From this short book, you could effectively review the inflectional endings *-ed, -s, -'s,* and *-ing.* You may decide to handle each inflectional ending in a separate lesson.

Model Activities

Using -'s for the Singular Possessive

Tell the children: "When I say, 'This is the book of my brother,' I mean that the book belongs to my brother. Another, shorter, way to say the same thing is 'This is my brother's book.' The apostrophe *s* on the end of the word *brother* shows that the noun following *brother* (*book*) belongs to *brother.*"

Have the children examine stories they have read recently for examples of the use of -'s. Let them read the sentences they found that contained -'s and tell the meanings of the phrases in which it occurs.

SELF-CHECK: OBJECTIVE 6   Describe a procedure for teaching the inflectional ending *-s.* (See Self-Improvement Opportunity 9.)

Prefixes and Suffixes

Prefixes and suffixes are *affixes,* letters or sequences of letters that are added to root words to change their meanings and/or parts of speech. A *prefix* is placed before a root word, and a *suffix* is placed after a root word.

Children can learn the pronunciations and meanings of some common prefixes and suffixes. Good readers learn to recognize common prefixes and suffixes instantly; this helps them recognize words more rapidly than they could if they had to resort to sounding each word letter by letter. Knowledge of prefixes and suffixes can help readers decipher the meanings as well as the pronunciations of unfamiliar words. Following are some common, useful prefixes and suffixes.

Prefix	Meaning	Example
un-	not	unable
in-	in or not	inset, inactive
bi-	two, twice	bicycle, biweekly
dis-	apart from, reversal of	displace, dismount
multi-	many	multicolored
non-	not	nonliving
pre-	before	preview
re-	again, back	reread, repay
pro-	in favor of	prolabor
post-	after	postscript
semi-	partly	semicircle
sub-	under	subway
super-	over	superhuman
trans-	across	transatlantic
tri-	three	tricycle

Suffix	Meaning	Example
-ful	full of	careful
-less	without	painless
-ment*	state of being	contentment
-ship*	state of being	friendship
-ous	full of	joyous
-ward	in the direction of	westward
-tion*	state of being	action
-sion*	state of being	tension
-able*	capable of being	likable
-ness*	state of being	happiness

Note: The starred (*) suffixes are best taught simply as visual units because their meanings are abstract.

Some very common prefixes, such as *ad-, com-,* and *con-,* are not included in this list because they generally occur with word parts that do not stand alone and are not recognizable meaning units to children. Examples are *admit, advice, combine, commerce, commit, conceal,* and *condemn.*

The suffixes *-ment, -ous, -tion,* and *-sion* have especially consistent pronunciations and thus are particularly useful to know. The suffixes *-ment* and *-ous* generally have the pronunciations heard in the words *treatment* and *joyous.* The suffixes *-tion* and *-sion* have the sound of *shun,* as heard in the words *education* and *mission.*

Whereas prefixes simply modify the meanings of the root words, suffixes may change the parts of speech as well as modify the meanings. Some of the resulting modifications are listed here.

Root Word	Affix	New Word	New Meaning or Change
happy	un-	unhappy	not happy
amuse	-ment	amusement	verb is changed to noun
worth	-less	worthless	meaning is opposite of original meaning

literature-centered reading   Use activities like the two following Model Activities.

Recognition of Prefixes and Suffixes

Model Activities

After instruction in prefixes and suffixes, give the students duplicated sheets containing paragraphs from a story that has just been shared in class. Ask them to circle the prefixes and suffixes they see in the paragraphs, working independently. Then divide them into small groups and have them compare and discuss their responses. Each group should come to an agreement about the correct answers. Finally, check the group responses in a whole-class discussion, calling on small-group representatives to give each group's responses to various items.

For example, in *Nadia the Willful* (Alexander, Knopf, 1983), the following words appear: *stubbornness, willful, kindness, graciousness, return, emptiness, punishment, remind, uneasily, hardness, coldness, unhappiness, bitterness, inside, recall, recalled, unbidden, happiness, sharpness,* and *forward.* Some of the words occur several times. The paragraphs in which these words appear can be duplicated for this exercise.

Not all of the words need to be used in a single lesson. You may wish to use one prefix or suffix at a time.

Adding Prefixes and Suffixes

Model Activities

Write the following root words on the chalkboard.

1. agree 2. move 3. construct

Ask the children to write on their papers as many new words as they can by adding

prefixes and suffixes to these root words. Then have the children form small groups and share the words they have formed with the other group members. Group members may question some of the words their classmates have formed and may consult reference books or the teacher to confirm or discredit words formed. Then representatives from the small groups may share the groups' word collections with the rest of the class.

The children may then be encouraged to produce small-group or individual stories using some of the words they constructed. These stories can be shared orally or in written form (perhaps on the bulletin board or in a reading center) with the rest of the class.

In the third and fourth grades, children begin to encounter more words that contain prefixes, suffixes, or both (White, Sowell, and Yanagihara, 1989; Nagy and Anderson, 1984). White, Sowell, and Yanagihara (1989) have identified nine prefixes (*un-*; *re-*; *in-*, *im-*, *ir-* [meaning *not*]; *dis-*; *en-*, *em-*; *non-*; *in-*, *im-* [meaning *in* or *into*]; *over-* [meaning *too much*]; and *mis-*) that cover 76 percent of the prefixed words in the *Word Frequency Book* (Carroll, Davies, and Richman, 1971). They recommend that these prefixes be taught systematically during grades three through five, beginning with *un-*, which alone accounts for 26 percent of the prefixed words. An analysis of their word counts would lead us to add *sub-*, *pre-*, *inter-*, and *fore-* to the recommended list, since they occur as frequently as *over-* and *mis-*, thereby covering 88 percent of the prefixed words.

White, Sowell, and Yanagihara (1989) have identified ten suffixes and inflectional endings that are part of 85 percent of the suffixed words in the *Word Frequency Book*: *-s*, *-es*; *-ed*; *-ing*; *-ly*; *-er*, *-or* (agentive); *-ion*, *-tion*, *-ation*, *-ition*; *-ible*, *-able*; *-al*, *-ial*; *-y*; and *-ness*. The three inflectional endings *-s/-es*, *-ed*, and *-ing* alone account for 65 percent of the incidences of suffixed words in the sample.

Contractions

The apostrophe used in contractions indicates that one or more letters have been left out when two words were combined into one word. Children need to be able to recognize the original words from which the contractions were formed. The following are common contractions, with their meanings, that teachers should present to children:

can't/cannot	I'll/I will
couldn't/could not	I'm/I am
didn't/did not	I've/I have
don't/do not	isn't/is not
hadn't/had not	let's/let us
hasn't/has not	she'd/she would or she had
he'll/he will	she'll/she will
he's/he is or he has	she's/she is or she has
I'd/I had or I would	shouldn't/should not
they'd/they had or they would	we've/we have

they'll/they will

they're/they are

they've/they have

wasn't/was not

we're/we are

weren't/were not

won't/will not

wouldn't/would not

you'll/you will

you're/you are

you've/you have

The teacher may wish to teach contractions in related groups—for example, those in which *not* is the reduced part, those in which *have* is the reduced part, and so on. Students should locate these contractions and their uncontracted referents in context and use them in writing to enhance their learning.

Use an activity such as the following for practice with contractions.

Model Activities

Contractions

On a bulletin board, place the following two columns of words, with protruding tacks beside each item in each column. Attach lengths of yarn to the tacks beside the contractions. Ask the children who manipulate the board to match the contractions in Column 1 with their proper meanings in Column 2 by connecting the other end of the length of yarn beside each contraction to the tack beside the contraction's meaning.

Column 1	Column 2
don't	cannot
can't	do not
he's	we are
we're	I am
you'll	he is
I'm	will not
won't	you will

Compound Words

Compound words consist of two (or occasionally three) words that have been joined together to form a new word. The original pronunciations of the component words are usually maintained, and their meanings are connected to form the meaning of the new word: *dishpan*, for example, is a pan in which dishes are washed. Children can be asked to underline or circle component parts of compound words or to put together familiar compound words as practice activities. Two exercises that illustrate these activities are found on page 144.

Syllabication/Accent

Since many phonics generalizations apply not only to one-syllable words but also to syllables within longer words, many people believe that breaking words into syllables can help determine pronunciation. Some research indicates, however, that

Model Activities

Recognizing Parts of Compound Words

Display a page from a big book (or a transparency made from a regular-size book) that contains several compound words. Let students come to the book (or the projected image) and point out the words that are made up of two or more words (for example, in *Song and Dance Man* [Ackerman, Knopf, 1988], the words *Grandpa,* *Grandma, cardboard, leather-trimmed, inside, half-moon, spotlight, woodpecker, somebody's, bathroom, gold-tipped*, and *stairway*). Write the words on the chalkboard. Let volunteers come to the board and circle the separate words that make up each compound word. Have a class discussion about the way to decide how to pronounce compound words.

Model Activities

Building Compound Words

Write the words in Column 1 on white index cards. Write the words in Column 2 on blue index cards. Distribute the words randomly to ten children, one card to each child. Have each child try to locate another child with a different-colored card with whom he or she can combine cards to form a compound word. Have each pair go to the board and write the word they have formed. An example of one combination is shown below.

Column 1	Column 2	Chalkboard
pocket	burn	pocketbook
letter	hive	
sun	book	
grass	carrier	
bee	hopper	

Finally, have each pair use the newly formed word in a sentence that shows the word's meaning.

syllabication is usually done after the reader has recognized the word and that readers use the sounds to determine syllabication rather than syllabication to determine the sounds (Glass, 1967). If this procedure is the one children normally use in attacking words, syllabication would seem to be of little use in a word analysis program. On the other hand, many authorities firmly believe that syllabication is helpful in decoding words. For this reason, a textbook on reading methods would be incomplete without discussions of syllabication and a related topic, stress or accent.

A *syllable* is a letter or group of letters that forms a pronunciation unit. Every syllable contains a vowel sound. In fact, a vowel sound may form a syllable by itself (*a mong*). Only in a syllable that contains a diphthong is there more than one vowel sound. Diphthongs are treated as single units, although they are actually vowel blends. While each syllable has only one vowel sound or diphthong, a syllable may have more than one vowel letter. Letters and sounds should not be confused. The word *peeve*, for example, has three vowel letters, but the only vowel sound is the long *e* sound. Therefore, *peeve* contains only one syllable.

There are two types of syllables: open and closed. Open syllables end in vowel sounds; closed syllables end in consonant sounds. Syllables may in turn be classified as accented (given greater stress) or unaccented (given little stress). Accent has much to do with the vowel sound we hear in a syllable. Multisyllabic words may have primary (strongest), secondary (second strongest), and even tertiary (third strongest) accents. The vowel sound of an open accented syllable is usually long (*mī' nus, bā' sin*); the second syllable of each of these example words is unaccented, and the vowel sound represented is the schwa, often found in unaccented syllables. A single vowel in a closed accented syllable generally has its short sound, unless it is influenced by another sound in that syllable (*căp' sule, cär' go*).

Following are several useful generalizations concerning syllabication and accent:

1. Words contain as many syllables as they have vowel sounds (counting diphthongs as a unit). Examples: *se/vere* (final *e* has no sound); *break* (*e* is not sounded); *so/lo* (both vowels are sounded); *oil* (diphthong is treated as a unit).

2. In a word with more than one sounded vowel, when the first vowel is followed by two consonants, the division is generally between the two consonants. Examples: *mar/ry, tim/ber.* If the two consonants are identical, the second one is not sounded.

3. Consonant blends and consonant digraphs are treated as units and are not divided. Examples: *ma/chine, a/bridge.*

4. In a word with more than one sounded vowel, when the first vowel is followed by only one consonant or consonant digraph, the division is generally after the vowel. Examples: *ma/jor, ri/val* (long initial vowel sounds). There are, however, many exceptions to this rule, which make it less useful. Examples: *rob/in, hab/it* (short initial vowel sounds).

5. When a word ends in *-le* preceded by a consonant, the preceding consonant plus *-le* constitute the final syllable of the word. This syllable is never accented, and the vowel sound heard in it is the schwa. Examples: *can/dle, ta/ble.*

6. Prefixes and suffixes generally form separate syllables. Examples: *dis/taste/ful, pre/dic/tion.*

7. A compound word is divided between the two words that form the compound, as well as between syllables within the component words. Examples: *snow/man, thun/der/storm.*

8. Prefixes and suffixes are usually not accented. Example: *dis/grace' ful.*

9. Words that can be used as both verbs and nouns are accented on the second syllable when used as verbs and on the first syllable when used as nouns. Examples: *pre/sent'* —verb; *pres' ent*—noun.

10. In two-syllable root words, the first syllable is usually accented, unless the second syllable has two vowel letters. Examples: *rock' et, pa/rade'*.

11. Words containing three or more syllables are likely to have secondary (and perhaps tertiary) accents, in addition to primary accents. Example: *reg' i/men/ta'tion*.

Readiness for learning syllabication includes the ability to hear syllables as pronunciation units. Here is an early exercise on syllabication.

Model Activities

Syllabication

Teachers can have children as young as first graders listen to words and clap for every syllable heard. Following is a list of words you may use for this purpose. Ask the children to say the words aloud and listen for the syllables. Let them clap once for each syllable as it is pronounced.

1. rule	3. table	5. middle	13. fingertip
2. break	4. meaningful	6. excitement	14. hotel
		7. disagreement	15. grandmother
		8. human	16. elephant
		9. cheese	17. name
		10. happen	18. schoolhouse
		11. right	19. scream
		12. person	20. prepare

Generalizations about syllabication can be taught using the same process as that for phonic generalizations, described earlier in this chapter. The teacher can present many examples of a particular generalization and lead the children to state the generalization.

Waugh and Howell (1975) point out that in dictionaries it is the syllable divisions in the phonetic respellings, rather than the ones indicated in the boldface entry words, that are useful to students in pronouncing unfamiliar words. The divisions of the boldface entry words are a guide for hyphenations in writing, not for word pronunciation.

Accentuation generally is not taught until children have a good background in word attack skills and is often presented in conjunction with dictionary study as a tool for word attack. More will be said on this topic in the next section of this chapter.

Dictionary Study

Dictionaries are valuable tools that can help in completing many kinds of reading tasks. They can help students determine pronunciations, meanings, derivations, and parts of speech for words they encounter in reading activities. They can also help with word spellings, if children have some idea of how the words are spelled and need only to confirm the order of letters within the words. Picture dictionaries are used primarily for sight word recognition and spelling assistance. This section deals mainly with the role the dictionary plays in helping children with word recognition; Chapter 4 discusses the dictionary as an aid to comprehension of word meanings. Study skills related to dictionary use, such as use of guide words, are covered in Chapter 9.

Although the dictionary is undeniably useful in determining the pronunciation of unfamiliar words, students should turn to it only as a last resort for this purpose. They should consult it only after they have applied phonics and structural analysis clues along with knowledge of context clues. There are two major reasons for following this procedure. First, applying the appropriate word recognition skills immediately, without having to take the time to look up the word in the dictionary, is less of a disruption of the reader's train of thought and therefore less of a hindrance to comprehension. Second, a dictionary is not always readily available; thoroughly mastered word recognition skills, however, will always be there when they are needed.

When using other word attack skills has produced no useful or clear result, children should turn to the dictionary for help. Obviously, before children can use the dictionary for pronunciation, they must be able to locate words in it. This skill is discussed in Chapter 9.

After children have located particular words, they need two more skills to pronounce the words correctly: the ability to interpret phonetic respellings and to interpret accent marks.

Interpreting Phonetic Respellings and Accent Marks

The pronunciation key, along with knowledge of sounds ordinarily associated with single consonants, helps in interpreting phonetic respellings in dictionaries. A pronunciation key is present somewhere on every page spread of a good dictionary. Students should not be asked to memorize the diacritical (pronunciation) markings used in a given dictionary, because different dictionaries use different markings; learning the markings for one could cause confusion when students use another. The sounds ordinarily associated with relatively unvarying consonants may or may not be included in the pronunciation key. Because they are not always included, it is important that children have a knowledge of phonics.

Here are four activities related to interpretation of phonetic spellings.

Activities

1. Have the students locate a given word in their dictionaries (example: *cheat* [*chēt*]). Call attention to the phonetic respelling beside the entry word. Point out the location of the pronunciation key and explain its function. Have the children locate each successive sound-symbol in the key—*ch, ē, t*. (If necessary, explain why the *t* is not included in the key.) Have the children check the key word for each symbol to confirm its sound value. Then have them blend the three sounds together to form a word. Repeat with other words. (Start with short words and gradually work up to longer ones.)

2. Code an entire paragraph or a joke using phonetic respellings. Provide a pronunciation key. Let groups of children compete to see who can write the selection in the traditional way first. Let each group of students who believe they have done so come to your desk. Check their work. If it is correct, keep it and give it a number indicating the order in which it was finished. If it is incorrect, send the students back to work on it some more. Set a time limit for the activity. The activity may be carried out on a competitive or a noncompetitive basis.

3. Give the children a pronunciation key, and let them encode messages to friends. Check the accuracy of each message before it is passed on to the friends to be decoded.

4. Use an activity such as the following Model Activity.

Model Activities

Pronunciation Key

Write the following hypothetical pronunciation key on the board. Tell the children: "Pretend that this list of words is part of the pronunciation key for a dictionary. Choose the key word or words that would help you pronounce each of the words listed below it. Hold up your hand when you have written the number of the appropriate key word on your paper beside the number of each entry word." (You may form the list of words from a book the children are about to read, thereby giving them some advance preparation for the words that they will meet in the book.)

Pronunciation Key: (1) cat, (2) āge, (3) fär, (4) sōfə, (5) sit

1. cape (kāp)
2. car (kär)
3. ago (ə/gō)
4. aim (ām)
5. fad (fad)
6. race (rās)
7. rack (rak)
8. affix (ə/fiks′)

When all the children have made their choices, call on a volunteer to reply to each one, telling why he or she chose a particular answer.

Some words will have only one accent mark, whereas others will have marks showing different degrees of accent within a single word. Children need to be able to translate the accent marks into proper stress when they speak the words. Here are two ideas for use in teaching accent marks.

Activities

1. Write several familiar multisyllabic words on the board. (*Bottle* and *apartment* are two good choices.) Explain that when words of more than one syllable are spoken, certain syllables are stressed or emphasized by the speaker's breath. Pronounce each of the example words, pointing out which part (or parts) of each

word receives stress. Next, tell the class that the dictionary uses accent marks to indicate which parts of words receive stress. Look up each word in the dictionary, and write the dictionary divisions and accent marks for the word on the board. Pronounce each word again, showing how the accent marks indicate the parts of the words that you stress when you pronounce them. Then have the children complete the following Model Activity.

Model Activities

Accent Marks

Write the following words on the board.

1. truth ful	6. peo ple
2. lo co mo tion	7. gig gle
3. fric tion	8. emp ty
4. at ten tion	9. en e my
5. ad ven ture	10. ge og ra phy

Call on volunteers to pronounce these words and decide where the accent is placed in each one.

Have them come to the board and indicate placements of the accents by putting accent marks (′) after the syllables where they think the accents belong. Then have all the students look up the words in the dictionary and check the placements of the accents. Anyone who finds an incorrectly marked word can come to the board, make the correction, and pronounce the word with the accent correctly placed.

2. Introduce the concept of accent in the same way described in the first activity. Then distribute sheets of paper with a list of words such as the following.

(1) des′ ti na′ tion

(2) con′ sti tu′ tion

(3) mys′ ti fy′

(4) pen′ nant

(5) thun′ der storm

Ask volunteers to read the words, applying the accents properly. When they have done so, give them a list of unfamiliar words with both accent marks and diacritical (pronunciation) marks inserted. (Lists will vary according to the children's ability. Use of words from their classroom reading material is preferable to use of random words.) Once again, ask the children to read the words, applying their dictionary skills.

literature-centered reading

SELF-CHECK: OBJECTIVE 7 Name two skills a child needs to pronounce correctly words found in a dictionary. (See Self-Improvement Opportunity 8.)

Introducing the Dictionary

reading-writing connection
Children can be introduced to picture dictionaries as early as the first grade. They can learn how dictionaries are put together and how they function by making their own picture dictionaries. Intermediate-grade pupils can develop dictionaries of special terms like *My Science Dictionary* or *My Health Dictionary*. From these they can advance to beginning and intermediate dictionaries. Example 3.2 shows a sample page from an intermediate dictionary.

Word Recognition Procedure

It is helpful for children to know a strategy for decoding unfamiliar words independently. A child may discover the word at any point in the following procedure; he or she should then stop the procedure and continue reading. Sometimes it is necessary to try all of the steps.

Step 1. Apply context clues. This may involve reading to the end of the sentence or paragraph in which the word is found to intake enough context to draw a reasonable conclusion about the word.

Step 2. Try the sound of the initial consonant, vowel, or blend along with context clues.

Step 3. Check for structure clues (prefixes, suffixes, inflectional endings, compound words, or familiar syllables).

Step 4. Begin sounding out the word using known phonics generalizations. (Go only as far as necessary to determine the word.)

Step 5. Consult the dictionary.

A teacher may explain this five-step strategy in the following way:

1. First, try to decide what word might reasonably fit in the context in which you found the unfamiliar word. Ask yourself: "Will this word be a naming word? A word that describes? A word that shows action? A word that connects two ideas?" Also ask yourself: "What word will make sense in this place?" Do you have the answer? Are you sure of it? If so, continue to read. If not, go to Step 2.

2. Try the initial sound(s) along with the context clues. Does this help you decide? If you are sure you have the word now, continue reading. If not, go to Step 3.

3. Check to see if there are familiar word parts that will help you. Does the word have a prefix or suffix that you know? If this helps you decide on the word, continue reading. If not, go to Step 4.

4. Begin sounding out the word, using all of your phonics skills. If you discover the word, stop sounding and go back to your reading. If you have sounded out the whole word and it does not sound like a word you know, go to Step 5.

Example 3.2   *Sample Page from an Intermediate Dictionary*

liken • limit

liken *verb* To describe as being like something else; compare: *Politics has often been likened to a game of chess.*
lik·en (lī′kən) ◊ *verb* **likened, likening**
‖*These sound alike:* **liken, lichen**

likeness *noun* **1.** The state of being similar: *There is a close likeness between parent and child.* **2.** A picture of a person.
like·ness (līk′nĭs) ◊ *noun, plural* **likenesses**

> **SYNONYMS**
>
> **likeness, resemblance, similarity**
>
> I see a real *likeness* between the plots of those two stories. There is a clear *resemblance* in appearance between you and your cousin. The *similarity* between those two ideas is not that close.

likewise *adverb* **1.** In a similar manner: *The kittens watched the mother cat climb the tree and did likewise.* **2.** In addition; also: *The football player is likewise a good student.*
like·wise (līk′wīz′) ◊ *adverb*

liking *noun* A feeling of fondness or affection: *I have a special liking for horses.*
lik·ing (lī′kĭng) ◊ *noun, plural* **likings**

lilac *noun* A shrub having clusters of fragrant purplish or white flowers.
li·lac (lī′lək) ◊ *noun, plural* **lilacs**

Lilliputian *or* **lilliputian** *adjective* Very small; tiny.
◊ *noun* A very small person or thing.
Lil·li·pu·tian *or* **lil·li·pu·tian** (lĭl′ə pyōō′shən) ◊ *adjective* ◊ *noun, plural* **Lilliputians** *or* **lilliputians**

lily *noun* Any of several related plants that grow from bulbs and have white or brightly colored flowers that are shaped like trumpets.
lil·y (lĭl′ē) ◊ *noun, plural* **lilies**

lily of the valley *noun* A low-growing plant related to the lilies that has a slender cluster of white, sweet-smelling, bell-shaped flowers.
lily of the valley ◊ *noun, plural* **lilies of the valley**

▲ **lily of the valley**

lima bean *noun* A large, flat, light green bean that is often cooked and eaten as a vegetable.
li·ma bean (lī′mə) ◊ *noun, plural* **lima beans**

limb *noun* **1.** A paired and jointed animal part, such as a leg, arm, wing, or flipper. **2.** One of the larger branches of a tree.
limb (lĭm) ◊ *noun, plural* **limbs**

lime¹ *noun* A small green citrus fruit that is related to the lemon. Limes have sour juice that is used as flavoring.
lime¹ (līm) ◊ *noun, plural* **limes**

lime² *noun* A white powder that is made by heating limestone. Lime is used in making cement and as a fertilizer.
lime² (līm) ◊ *noun*

> **HISTORY • lime¹, lime²**
>
> **Lime¹** comes from the Arabic name for this fruit. **Lime²** comes from an old English word that meant "something sticky."

limerick *noun* An amusing poem of five lines.
lim·er·ick (lĭm′ər ĭk) ◊ *noun, plural* **limericks**

limestone *noun* A rock that is formed especially from shells or coral and is used in building and in making lime and cement.
lime·stone (līm′stōn′) ◊ *noun*

limit *noun* **1.** A point beyond which someone or something cannot go: *The speed limit is 55 miles per hour.* **2.** Often **limits** The boundary

ă	pat	ĭ	pit	oi	oil	th	bath
ā	pay	ī	ride	ŏŏ	book	th	bathe
â	care	î	fierce	ōō	boot	ə	ago, item
ä	father	ŏ	pot	ou	out		pencil
ĕ	pet	ō	go	ŭ	cut		atom
ē	be	ô	paw, for	û	fur		circus

424

Source: Copyright © 1994 by Houghton Mifflin Company. Reprinted by permission from *The American Heritage Children's Dictionary,* p. 424.

5. Look up the word in the dictionary. Use the pronunciation key to help you pronounce the word. If the word is one you have not heard before, check the meaning. Be sure to choose the meaning that fits the context.

For example, a reader who is confronted with the unfamiliar word *chamois* might apply the strategy in the following way:

1. "'He used a chamois to dry off the car.' I've never seen the word *c-h-a-m-o-i-s* before. Let's see. . . . Is it a naming word? . . . Yes, it is, because *a* comes before it. . . . What thing would make sense here? . . . It is something that can be used to dry a car. Could it be *towel?* . . . No, that doesn't have any of the right sounds. Maybe it is *cloth?* . . . No, *cloth* starts with *cl*."

2. "*Ch* usually sounds like the beginning of *choice*. . . . I can't think of anything that starts that way that would fit here. . . . Sometimes it sounds like *k* . . . . I can't think of a word that fits that either . . . . *Ch* even sounds like *sh* sometimes. . . . The only word I can think of that starts with the *sh* sound and fits in the sentence is *sheet,* and I can tell that none of the other sounds are right."

3. "I don't see a prefix, suffix, or root word that I recognize, either."

4. "Maybe I can sound it out. Chămois. No, that's not a word. Kămois. That's not a word either. Shămois. I don't think so. . . . Maybe the *a* is long. Chāmois. No. Kāmois. No. Shāmois. No."

5. "I guess I'll have to use the dictionary. What? Shăm' ē? Oh, I know what that is. I've seen Dad use one! Why is it spelled so funny? Oh, I see! It came from French."

A crucial point for teachers to remember is that children should not consider use of word recognition skills important *only* during reading classes. They should apply these skills whenever they encounter an unfamiliar word, whether it happens during reading class, science class, a free reading period, or in out-of-school situations. Teachers should emphasize to their students that the strategy explained here is applicable to *any* situation in which an unfamiliar word occurs.

Teachers should also encourage students to self-correct their reading errors when the words they read do not combine to make sense. This can be accomplished with some well-planned instruction. Taylor and Nosbush (1983) had children individually read orally from material at their instructional levels. They praised each child for things he or she did well when reading, especially any self-correcting behavior the student exhibited when miscues (unexpected responses) affected the meaning. They encouraged each student to try to make sure the material being read made sense. They also discussed some miscues that the student did not self-correct, particularly ones that did not make sense but for which good context clues were available. Students instructed in this way did better at self-correction than did students who read orally without being asked to pay attention to meaning.

Summary

Word recognition skills help readers identify words while reading. One skill is sight word recognition, the development of a store of words a person can recognize immediately on sight. Use of context clues to help in word identification involves using the surrounding words to decode an unfamiliar word. Both semantic and syntactic clues can be helpful. Phonics, the association of speech sounds (phonemes) with printed symbols (graphemes), is very helpful in identifying unfamiliar words, even though the sound-symbol associations in English are not completely consistent. Structural analysis skills enable readers to decode unfamiliar words using units larger than single graphemes. The process of structural analysis involves recognition of prefixes, suffixes, inflectional endings, contractions, and compound words, as well as syllabication and accent. Dictionaries can also be used for word identification. The dictionary respelling that appears in parentheses after the word supplies the word's pronunciation, but the reader has to know how to use the dictionary's pronunciation key to interpret the respellings appropriately.

Children need to learn to use all of the word recognition skills. Because they will need different skills for different situations, they must also learn to use the skills appropriately.

An overall strategy for decoding unfamiliar words is useful. The following five-step strategy is a good one to teach: (1) use context clues; (2) try the sound of the initial consonant, vowel, or blend in addition to context clues; (3) check for structure clues; (4) use phonics generalizations to sound out as much of the word as necessary; and (5) consult the dictionary.

Test Yourself   *True or False*

_____ 1. It is wise to teach only a single approach to word attack.

_____ 2. All word recognition strategies are learned with equal ease by all children.

_____ 3. Sight words are words that readers recognize immediately without needing to resort to analysis.

_____ 4. The English language is noted for the regularity of sound-symbol associations in its written words.

_____ 5. Teaching a small store of sight words can be the first step in implementing an analytic approach to phonics instruction.

_____ 6. Early choices for sight words to be taught should be words that are extremely useful and meaningful.

_____ 7. Games with complex rules are good ones to use for practice with sight words.

_____ 8. Most practice with sight words should involve the words in context.

_____ 9. If teachers teach phonics well, they do not need to bother with other word recognition strategies.

_____ 10. Consonant letters are more consistent in the sounds they represent than vowel letters are.

_____ 11. Phonics generalizations often have numerous exceptions.

_____ 12. It is impossible to teach too many phonics rules, since these rules are extremely valuable in decoding unfamiliar words.

_____ 13. In a word that has only one vowel letter at the end, the vowel letter usually represents its long sound.

_____ 14. It is wise to teach only one phonics generalization at a time.

_____ 15. Structural analysis skills include the ability to recognize prefixes and suffixes.

_____ 16. The addition of a prefix to a root word can change the word's meaning.

_____ 17. Inflectional endings can change verb tenses.

_____ 18. The apostrophe in a contraction indicates possession or ownership.

_____ 19. Every syllable contains a vowel sound.

_____ 20. There is only one vowel letter in each syllable.

_____ 21. Open syllables end in consonant sounds.

_____ 22. The vowel sound in an open accented syllable is usually long.

_____ 23. The schwa sound is often found in unaccented syllables.

_____ 24. When dividing words into syllables, we treat consonant blends and consonant digraphs as units and do not divide them.

_____ 25. Prefixes and suffixes generally form separate syllables.

_____ 26. Prefixes and suffixes are usually accented.

_____ 27. Picture clues are the most useful word recognition clues for sixth-grade students.

_____ 28. A comparison or contrast found in printed material may offer a clue to the identity of an unfamiliar word.

_____ 29. Context clues used by themselves provide only educated guesses about the identities of unfamiliar words.

_____ 30. Children should be expected to memorize the diacritical markings used in their dictionaries.

_____ 31. Accent marks indicate which syllables are stressed.

_____ 32. Some words have more than one accented syllable.

_____ 33. Writing new words is helpful to some learners in building sight vocabulary.

_____ 34. The language experience approach is good for developing sight vocabulary.

_____ 35. One method of teaching sight words is best for all students.

Multiple Choice

_____ 1. In the word *myth,* the *y*
    a. has the characteristics of a vowel.
    b. is always silent.
    c. has the characteristics of a consonant.

_____ 2. When it occurs in the initial position in a syllable, the letter *w*
    a. stands for a vowel sound.
    b. is always silent.
    c. stands for a consonant sound.

_____ 3. In the word *strong,* the letters *str*
    a. represent a consonant blend.
    b. are silent.
    c. represent a single sound.

_____ 4. Consonant digraphs
    a. represent two blended speech sounds.
    b. represent a single speech sound.
    c. are always silent.

_____ 5. The word *sheep* is made up of
    a. five sounds.
    b. four sounds.
    c. three sounds.

_____ 6. In the word *boat,* the *oa* is a
    a. vowel digraph.
    b. diphthong.
    c. blend.

_____ 7. In the word *boy,* the *oy* is a
    a. vowel digraph.
    b. consonant digraph.
    c. diphthong.

_____ 8. The word *diphthong* contains
    a. three consonant blends.
    b. three consonant digraphs.
    c. a consonant digraph and two consonant blends.

_____ 9. In the word *know,* the *ow* is a
    a. diphthong.
    b. vowel digraph.
    c. consonant blend.

_____ 10. In the word *his,* the letter *s* has the sound usually associated with the letter(s)

   a. *s.*

   b. *z.*

   c. *sh.*

_____ 11. Which type of accent mark indicates the heaviest emphasis?

   a. Primary

   b. Secondary

   c. Tertiary

Self-Improvement Opportunities

1. Compare the *Dolch List of 220 Service Words* and the *Dolch List of 95 Picture Words* with the words found in the preprimers and primers of a contemporary basal reading series. Are the words on the Dolch lists still high-usage words, even though the lists were compiled many years ago?

2. Plan exercises for presenting the words on a basic sight word list in context; many of these are function words and have meanings that are hard for children to conceptualize. For example, *for* and *which* produce no easy images, but a child would understand the following sentences:

   I brought this *for* you.

   Which one is mine?

   Try your exercises in a classroom if you have the opportunity.

3. React to the following statement: "Going back to teaching basic phonics skills will cure all of our country's reading ills."

4. Make arrangements to observe a phonics lesson in which the teacher uses the synthetic approach and another lesson in which the teacher uses the analytic approach. Evaluate the two approaches. Be sure to evaluate the methods rather than the instructors.

5. Look up references related to the controversy over the value of teaching syllabication as part of a word recognition program. Prepare a paper on this topic.

6. React to the following statement: "I do not believe in teaching children to use context clues. It just produces a group of guessers."

7. Compile a list of words whose pronunciation depends on the context. Plan a lesson for presenting some of these words to a group of youngsters in the grade level of your choice.

8. Compare the dictionary pronunciations of the following words in old and new dictionaries and in dictionaries published by different companies. Analyze the differences among diacritical markings. Use the words *gypsy, ready, lecture, away, ask, believe, baker,* and *care.*

9. Locate a popular picture book and examine it for examples of phonic and structural analysis elements that you could teach effectively from it. Plan a lesson to teach one or more skills with the book as a basis for the instruction.

10. Start a collection of rhymes, riddles, and poems that you can use to promote auditory discrimination skills.

11. Curtis and McCart (1992) suggest fun ways to promote word recognition skills with adolescents who are poor readers. Locate their article and evaluate the games and techniques they suggest. Try out these games and techniques with students, if possible, and report on their effectiveness to your classmates.

12. Lewkowicz (1994) suggests a game to improve phonemic awareness for kindergartners or first graders. Locate her article and try this activity with a group of young children. Report your results to your classmates.

Key Vocabulary

Pay close attention to these terms when they appear in the chapter.

analogies

antonyms

appositive

categorization

context clues

etymology

euphemism

figurative language

homographs

homonyms

hyperbole

metaphor

morphemes

personification

schema

semantic feature analysis

semantic maps

simile

synonyms

word webs

Meaning Vocabulary

Setting Objectives

When you finish reading this chapter, you should be able to

1. Discuss some factors involved in vocabulary development.
2. Name and describe several techniques of vocabulary instruction.
3. Identify some special types of words and explain how they can cause problems for children.

Figure 4.1 *Chapter 4 Organization*

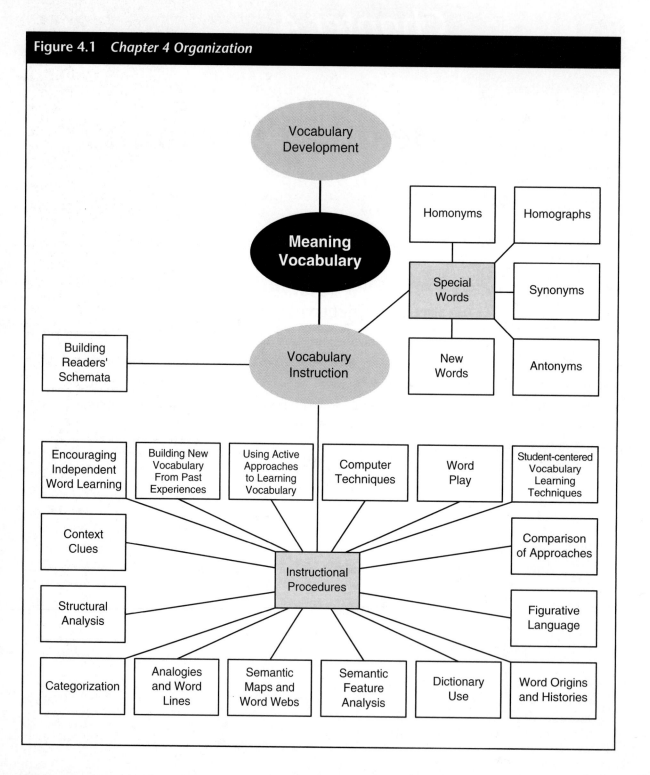

Meaning vocabulary (words for which meanings are understood) is essentially the set of labels for the clusters of concepts that people have learned through experience. These clusters of concepts, or knowledge structures, are called *schemata*. (Schemata are also discussed in detail in Chapter 5.) Because students must call on their existing schemata in order to comprehend, meaning vocabulary development is an important component of comprehension (Jones, 1982). Therefore, direct instruction in word meanings is a valuable part of reading instruction. Research indicates that preteaching new vocabulary terms can result in significant gains in comprehension (Roser and Juel, 1982; Carney et al., 1984) and that long-term vocabulary instruction, in which words are taught and reinforced over a period of time, enhances comprehension of materials containing those words (Beck, Perfetti, and McKeown, 1982; McKeown et al., 1983; Robinson et al., 1990).

In Chapter 3 we examined the importance of decoding words and developing a sight vocabulary, but these abilities have little value if students do not understand the words. Children's sight vocabularies should be built from words they already comprehend, words that are a part of their meaning vocabularies. This chapter focuses on the development of extensive meaning vocabularies and the difficulties that certain types of words may present to youngsters.

Vocabulary Development

It is difficult to pinpoint the age at which children learn the precise meanings of words. Early in the language development process, they learn to differentiate between antonyms (opposites), making more discriminating responses as they grow older. Sometimes they overgeneralize about word meanings: a very young child who learns the word *car,* for example, may apply it to any motor vehicle, making no discrimination among cars, trucks, vans, and other kinds of vehicles. Some children as old as nine years have trouble distinguishing between the meanings of *ask* and *tell*, and some children as old as ten years have not yet differentiated between the words *brother* and *boy* and the words *sister* and *girl* (McConaughy, 1978). As children mature, they learn more about choosing specific words.

Children increase their vocabularies at a rapid rate during the elementary school years. Vocabulary building is a complex process involving many kinds of words: words with *multiple meanings* (The candy is *sweet.* Mary has a *sweet* disposition.); words with *abstract definitions* (*Justice* must be served.); homonyms (She will take the *plane* to Lexington. He has on *plain* trousers.); homographs (I will *read* the newspapers. I have *read* the magazine.); synonyms (Marty was *sad* about leaving. Marty was *unhappy* about leaving.); and antonyms (Bill is a *slow* runner. Mary is a *fast* runner.). Children must also acquire meanings for a number of relational terms, such as *same/different, more/less, taller/shorter, older/younger, higher/lower,* and so on. In content area instruction, students must deal with *technical vocabulary* (words whose only meanings are specific to the content areas, for example, *photosynthesis*) and *specialized vocabulary* (words with general meanings as well as specialized meanings that are specific to the content area, for example, *pitch* in the area of music). Content area materials also abound with special *symbols* and *abbreviations* that children must master in order to read the materials successfully.

SELF-CHECK: OBJECTIVE 1   What are some factors to consider in vocabulary development? (See Self-Improvement Opportunity 4.)

Vocabulary Instruction

Children learn much vocabulary by listening to the conversations of those around them. Therefore, a language-rich environment promotes vocabulary acquisition (Anderson and Nagy, 1991). Teachers can provide such environments in their classrooms. They can greatly influence children's vocabulary development simply by being good models of vocabulary use. For example, when teachers read aloud or give explanations to the class, they should discuss any new words used and encourage the children to use them. Teachers should not "talk down" to children but should use appropriate terminology in describing things to them and participating in discussions with them.

Learning new vocabulary may just involve acquisition of a new label for a concept that is already known. In this case, the teacher's task is simple. The teacher provides the new term (such as *journey*) and tells the children it means the same thing as a familiar term (such as *trip*) (Armbruster and Nagy, 1992).

Most teachers recognize the importance of vocabulary instruction as a part of reading and language arts classes. The importance of teaching word meanings and encouraging variety in word choice and exactness in expressing thoughts is generally accepted. Teachers therefore usually give attention to many aspects of vocabulary instruction—such as structural analysis; use of context clues; and use of reference books, such as dictionaries and thesauruses—during language classes. During these lessons, teachers also need to help the children understand the real-world purpose for building vocabulary: a rich vocabulary helps us to communicate effectively. The more words we know and use appropriately, the better we are able to communicate our knowledge and our feelings to others.

Vocabulary instruction should take place throughout the day, however, not just during the language arts or reading period. Vocabulary knowledge is important in all subject areas covered in the curriculum. Children need to develop their vocabularies in every subject area so that the specialized or technical words they encounter are not barriers to learning. Nelson-Herber (1986) suggests intensive direct teaching of vocabulary in specific content areas to help students read the content materials successfully. She endorses building from the known to the new, helping students understand the interrelationships among words in concept clusters (groups of related concepts), and encouraging students to use new words in reading, writing, and speaking. Construction of word meaning by the students from context, experience, and reasoning is basic to her approach. At times the

reading-writing connection

students work in cooperative groups on vocabulary exercises, and they are involved with vocabulary learning before, during, and after reading of assigned material. The techniques described in this chapter and the ideas presented in Chapter 10 will help teachers plan effectively for vocabulary instruction in various content areas.

Choosing words to teach can be a problem for teachers. Blachowicz and Lee (1991) suggest choosing these terms from classroom reading materials. The terms should be central to the selections in which they appear. The teacher should activate prior knowledge related to the words before the reading begins and have students use the new vocabulary in postreading discussion. Words that students still *reading-writing connection* do not understand well need further attention and elaboration. The students might use the words in retellings, dramatizations, or writings based on the story or selection for further experiences.

Teachers can approach vocabulary instruction in a variety of ways, but some vocabulary instructional techniques appear to be more effective than others. The most desirable instructional techniques are those that

1. Assist students in integrating the new words with their background knowledge.

2. Assist students in developing elaborated (expanded) word knowledge.

3. Actively involve students in learning new words.

4. Help students acquire strategies for independent vocabulary development.

5. Provide repetition of the words to build ready accessibility of their meanings.

6. Have students engage in meaningful use of the words (Carr and Wixson, 1986; Nagy, 1988; Blachowicz and Lee, 1991; Beck and McKeown, 1991).

We will now look at several common methods of vocabulary development.

Building Readers' Schemata

Vocabulary terms are labels for *schemata*, or the clusters of concepts each person develops through experience. Sometimes children cannot understand the terms they encounter in books because they do not know the concepts to which the terms refer. In this case, concept or schemata development involving the use of direct and vicarious experiences is necessary. Blachowicz (1985) affirms the importance of building a conceptual base for word learning.

A good technique for concept development is to offer as concrete an experience for the concept as possible. The class should then discuss the attributes of the concept. The teacher should give examples and nonexamples of the concept, pointing out the attributes that distinguish examples from nonexamples. Next, the students should try to identify other examples and nonexamples that the teacher supplies and give their reasons. Finally, the students should suggest additional examples and nonexamples. This sequence is closely related, although not identical, to that suggested by Graves and Prenn (1986).

For example, to develop the concept of *banjo,* the teacher could bring a banjo to class. The teacher would show it to the students, play it for them (or get someone to do so), and let them touch it and pluck or strum the strings. A discussion of its attributes would follow. The children might decide that a banjo has a circular body and a long neck, that it has a tightly stretched cover over the body, that it has strings, and that one can play music on it. The teacher might show the children pictures or real examples of a variety of banjos, some with five and some with four strings, and some with enclosed backs and some with open backs. Then the teacher might show the children a guitar, pointing out the differences in construction (different shape, different material forming the front of the instrument, different number of strings, etc.). The teacher might also show several other instruments, at first following the same procedure, then letting the students identify how they are different from and similar to banjos. The students can provide their own examples of banjos by bringing in pictures or actual instruments. They will note that, although there may be some variation in size and appearance, the essential attributes are present. They can also name and bring pictures or actual examples of instruments that are not banjos, such as harps, mandolins, or violins, and explain why these instruments do not fit the concept.

Concrete experiences for abstract concepts are difficult to provide, but the teacher can use approximations. For example, to develop the concept of *freedom,* the teacher can say, "You may play with any of the play equipment in the room for the next ten minutes, or you may choose not to play at all." After ten minutes have passed, the teacher can tell the class that they were given the freedom to choose their activity; that is, they were not kept from doing what they chose to

Children can demonstrate action words to show understanding of their meanings.
(© *Sybil Shelton/Peter Arnold*)

do. The teacher may then offer several examples of freedom. One might be the freedom to choose friends. No one else tells the children who their friends have to be; they choose based on their own desires. The teacher should also offer several nonexamples of freedom, perhaps pointing out that during a game players are restrained by a set of rules and do not have the freedom to do anything they want to do. Then the teacher should ask the students to give examples of freedom and explain why these examples are appropriate. A student may suggest that the freedom we have in this country to say what we think about our leaders is a good example, because we are not punished for voicing our views. After several examples, the students will be asked for nonexamples. They may suggest that people in jail do not have freedom, because they cannot go where they wish or do what they wish. After students have offered a number of nonexamples, the teacher may ask them to be alert for examples and nonexamples of freedom in their everyday activities and to report their findings to the class. Some may discover that being "grounded" by their parents is a good nonexample of freedom.

Thelen (1986) indicates that meaningful learning is enhanced by teaching general concepts before specific concepts. In this way, the children have the schemata they need to incorporate new facts they encounter. Using this approach, the teacher presents the concept of *dog* before the concept of *poodle,* and the children thus have a prior pool of information to which they can relate the new information about *poodle.* Isabel Beck has stated that ownership of a word, or the ability to relate the word to an existing schema, is necessary for meaningful learning. In other words, students need to relate the word to information they already know. Semantic mapping and semantic feature analysis (discussed later in this chapter) are two particularly good methods for accomplishing this goal.

Firsthand experiences, such as field trips and demonstrations, can help students associate words with real situations. These experiences can be preceded and followed up by discussion of the new concepts, and written accounts of the experiences can help students gain control of the new vocabulary. For example, a field trip to a data-processing facility can be preceded by a discussion of the work that is done in the facility (generating bills, producing payroll checks, etc.). During the field trip, each activity the students witness can be explained as they watch. This explanation should include the proper terms for the data-processing equipment, processes, and personnel. After the trip, the students can discuss computers, keyboards, monitors, printers, printouts, word processing, operators, programmers, and other things and people to which they were exposed. They can make graphic displays of the new terms (see the sections on semantic maps and word webs), classify the new terms (see the section on categorization), make comparison charts for the words (see the section on semantic feature analysis), analyze the structure of the words (see the section on structural analysis), or manipulate the new terms in some other way. They may write individual summaries of the experience or participate in writing a class summary. They may wish to use reference books to expand their knowledge about some of the new things they have seen. All of these activities will build both the children's concepts and their vocabularies, thereby enhancing their comprehension of material containing this vocabulary.

reading-writing connection

Teachers can help students relate their personal experiences to new words by having them put personal connections on vocabulary word cards (Carr, 1985). For example, a student might connect the personal reaction "Mother's Thanksgiving dinner" with the adjective *elaborate* and write this personal reaction on the word card for *elaborate,* along with other notes about the word.

Vicarious experiences can also help to build concepts and vocabulary. Audio-visual aids, such as pictures, films, filmstrips, records, and videotapes, can be used to illustrate words that students have encountered in reading and provide other words for discussion. Books such as thesauruses, children's dictionaries, and trade books about words—for example, *Words from the Myths* by Isaac Asimov (Boston: Houghton Mifflin, 1961)—are also useful sources of information about words.

Storytelling and story reading are good ways to provide vicarious experiences. Studies by Roe (1985, 1986) and Pigg (1986) showed that a seven-week program of daily one-hour storytelling/story reading sessions with language follow-up activities could improve vocabulary skills of kindergarten, first-grade, and second-grade students. Students in the experimental groups in these studies produced more words in stories, more different words, and more multisyllabic words than students in the control groups did. Language follow-up activities included creative dramatics, creative writing (or dictation), retelling stories with the flannel board, and illustrating scenes from the stories and describing them to the teacher. The following Classroom Scenario is drawn from one of Roe's experiences.

**Classroom
Scenario**

Using Literature Selections to Develop Vocabulary

Dr. Roe (1985), a visiting teacher, was presenting the song "The Old Woman Who Swallowed a Fly" in a first-grade class. After she sang the line "How absurd to swallow a bird," she asked the students, "What does *absurd* mean?" None of them knew.

Dr. Roe told them that *absurd* meant *silly* or *ridiculous*. Then she asked them, "Would it be silly for a woman to swallow a bird?"

The children answered, "Yes," in unison.

"Would it be absurd for me to wear a flowerpot on my head to teach the class?" she then asked.

Again the children answered, "Yes!"

"What are some other absurd things that you can think of?" Dr. Roe finally asked.

Each child gave a reply. If the reply showed understanding of the term, Dr. Roe provided positive reinforcement. If it did not show understanding of the term, her questioning led the child to see why the thing mentioned was not absurd, and the child was given another chance to answer.

Weeks later, when these children encountered the word again in the story *Horton Hatches the Egg*, they remembered its meaning.

Analysis of Scenario
The children encountered a word in the context of a familiar song. The word's meaning was unclear to them, so the teacher supplied both a definition and other examples of the concept behind the term. To ensure that the children really understood the term, the teacher asked them to supply their own examples. This activity helped the children make the word their own through active involvement with it.

Instructional Procedures

A great number of procedures are available for vocabulary development. Although they vary widely, many of them have produced good results, and teachers should be familiar with a variety of approaches. A number of the programs described here combine several approaches, and good teachers will also use combinations of approaches in their classrooms. Graves and Prenn (1986) point out that "there is no one best method of teaching words . . . various methods have both their costs and their benefits and will be very appropriate and effective in some circumstances and less appropriate and effective in others" (p. 597).

literature-centered reading

The findings from a vast amount of research on vocabulary instruction indicate that "extensive reading can increase vocabulary knowledge, but direct instruction that engages students in construction of word meaning, using context and prior knowledge, is effective for learning specific vocabulary and for improving comprehension of related materials" (Nelson-Herber, 1986, p. 627). McKeown and colleagues (1985) also offer support for this assessment.

Some research findings indicate that "vocabulary instruction improves comprehension only when both definitions and context are given, and has the largest effect when a number of different activities or examples using the word in context are used" (Stahl, 1986, p. 663). Techniques requiring students to think deeply about a term and its relationships to other terms are most effective. Class discussion seems to make students think more deeply about words as they make connections between their prior knowledge and new information. Multiple presentations of information about a word's meaning and multiple exposures to the word in varying contexts both benefit comprehension. In addition, the more time spent on vocabulary instruction, the better the results. Vocabulary programs that extend over a long period of time give students a chance to encounter the words in a number of contexts and to make use of them in their own language (Stahl, 1986).

Some teachers use commercial materials for vocabulary instruction. Commercial materials for vocabulary development should focus on the thorough exploration of word meanings. Presentation of each word in context can help specify the intended meaning among a number of possible meanings. Word meanings should be related to the students' own experiences through discussion. Then students should use the words in some way to demonstrate their understanding of the meanings. Multiple experiences with each word are necessary for complete learning, so the number of words presented should not be overwhelming. Spaced reviews of the words will enhance retention of the word meanings.

We will now look at a number of carefully researched techniques and the studies related to them. Then we will describe several common methods of vocabulary development. Each method has possibilities for enhancing students' word knowledge.

Using Active Approaches to Learning Vocabulary

Beck and McKeown (1983) described a program of vocabulary instruction that emphasized relating vocabulary to students' preexisting word knowledge and experiences. Students generated their own context for the terms being taught by answering questions about the words (for example, the teacher might say, "Tell about something you might want to *eavesdrop* on" [p. 624]). The program also helped students to further their word knowledge by introducing new words in global semantic categories, such as *people* or *places,* and by requiring the students to work with the relationships among words. The children were asked to differentiate among critical features of words and to generalize from one word to similar ones. They were also asked to complete analogies involving the words and to pantomime words. These activities were in keeping with the second and third suggestions about vocabulary instruction presented in the list on page 163; the students were active participants in the activities described rather than passive observers. They discussed words, generated meanings, and applied meanings. To ensure thorough learning of the words, students were given a number of exposures to each word in a variety of contexts. The final aspect of Beck and McKeown's program was development of rapid responses to words by using timed activities, some of which were somewhat gamelike. These activities, which certainly kept the students actively involved, probably increased their interest as well.

The children involved in Beck and McKeown's program learned the words taught, developed speed and accuracy in making semantic decisions, showed comprehension on stories containing the target words superior to that of a control group, and evidently learned more than the specific words taught, as indicated by the size of their gains on a standardized measure of reading comprehension and vocabulary.

A closely related procedure, developed by Blachowicz (1986), also helps teachers focus on vocabulary instruction. First, teachers activate what the students know about the target words in the reading selection, using either exclusion brainstorming (in which students exclude unrelated words from a list of possible associated words) or knowledge rating (in which students indicate their degree of familiarity with the words). Then the teachers can elicit predictions about "connections between words or between words and the topic and structure of the selection" (p. 644), emphasizing the words' roles in semantic networks.

(Word webs or semantic feature analysis, discussed later in this chapter, may be used.) Next, the students are asked to construct tentative definitions of the words. They read the text to test these definitions, refining them as they discover additional information. Finally, the students use the words in other reading and writing tasks to make them their own.

Blachowicz (1985, p. 877) points out that "the harder one works to process stimuli . . . the better one's retention." Blachowicz's approach causes the students to work harder by predicting and constructing definitions rather than merely memorizing the material presented. Students seem to retain more information when they have learned it using active tasks than when they have learned it using passive tasks such as memorization.

Another active way to clarify word meanings by associating situations with them is dramatization of words. This technique provides a vicarious (indirect) experience that is more effective than mere verbal explanations of terms. Under some circumstances, dramatization of words has proved to be more effective than use of context clues, structural analysis, or dictionaries (Duffelmeyer, 1980; Duffelmeyer and Duffelmeyer, 1979).

reading-writing connection

Davis (1990) has pairs of students construct "concept cards" for new vocabulary terms. On the cards they list definitions, synonyms, and examples for the terms. She has the students supplement their own knowledge by consulting dictionaries and thesauruses. Then she has them discuss the various connotations of the synonyms provided. Following the discussion, the class is divided into teams that compete to supply the most definitions, synonyms, or examples for words from the cards.

Cudd and Roberts (1993/1994) use sentence expansion activities to work on vocabulary. They create sentence stems composed of syntactic structures and vocabulary the children have encountered in classroom reading materials. Then they display the stems on the board and lead a discussion of them. Students supply endings for the sentences and then read the completed sentences. Students

reading-writing connection

write their sentences based on the stems, working with peer-editing partners. Then they illustrate one or two of their sentences. In this way, students become actively involved in using the target vocabulary.

Petrick (1992) suggests the use of manipulatives to explain or demonstrate content area vocabulary. Teachers can use tape measures to show the meanings of certain lengths (*foot, yard,* etc.), use cotton balls and water to demonstrate *absorption,* or use a rubber band to demonstrate the concept of *elasticity.*

Stahl and Kapinus (1991) found a technique called Possible Sentences to be effective in teaching content area vocabulary. In this activity, the teacher chooses six to eight difficult words and four to six familiar words that are important to the selection. The teacher writes these words on the board and may offer a definition of each one. Students are asked to supply possible sentences for these terms that include at least two of the words. This causes them to think about the relationships among the terms. When all words are represented in the possible sentences, the students read the selection. After reading, each possible sentence is discussed and either accepted as true or changed to make it true. This technique requires much active processing of the vocabulary.

literature-centered reading

Iwicki (1992) and her colleagues found that they could enhance vocabulary learning through an activity called Vocabulary Connections. They put the vocabulary terms and definitions on wall charts and then ask students to relate situations in the literature selection they are currently reading to each word and also relate situations in previously read books to the word. For example, "The word *pandemonium* introduced in *Welcome Home, Jelly Bean* (Shyer, 1988) can be related to events in *The Witches* (Dahl, 1983) and *The Black Stallion* (Farley, 1941)" (Iwicki, 1992, p. 736). This activity can be motivational and can encourage use of higher-level thinking skills.

Primary-grade children can be asked to illustrate new vocabulary words to show their understanding. Then the children's illustrations can be shown to a small group of other class members, who try to identify the word being illustrated in each picture and record it on their papers. Finally, each artist tells which word each of his or her pictures represented. The group members discuss the reasons for their choices, and each artist may need to explain the reason for the chosen illustration. This procedure gets the children very actively involved with words (Baroni, 1987). The discussion time allows students to expand their knowledge of the vocabulary by adding new ideas gained from classmates, and it allows opportunities to amend erroneous impressions.

Building New Vocabulary from Past Experiences

Duffelmeyer (1985) urges teaching word meaning from an experience base. He believes that, without such teaching, students may acquire a store of words for which they have only a shell of meaning without substance. Duffelmeyer suggests four techniques to link word meaning and experience: use of synonyms and examples, use of positive and negative instances of the concepts, use of examples and definitions, and use of definitions together with sentence completion. His techniques are all teacher directed and involve verbal interaction between the teacher and the students.

Duffelmeyer's four techniques may be used in the following ways. In each case, the teacher shows the students the target word, pronounces it for them, and then has them pronounce it.

1. When using synonyms and examples for a target word (*difficult*), the teacher tells the students that another word for *difficult* is *hard* and that, if a task is *difficult,* it is hard to do. The teacher may then ask the children to name *difficult* tasks and tell why the tasks are difficult. Next, the teacher shows the students a sentence containing the word *difficult*. (It is *difficult* to do well on a test if you do not study for it.) The teacher asks why this is a true statement, and the children suggest answers.

2. When using positive and negative instances for a target word (*rude*), the teacher gives a simple definition for the word (*not polite*). Then the teacher asks the students, "If a person holds the door open for someone who has

both hands full of packages, is that person being rude?" The children should decide that this is not a rude act. Then the teacher may ask, "If a person interrupts someone who is speaking, is that person being rude?" The children should decide that this is a rude act. Finally, the teacher may ask the children if they have ever seen anyone do something that was rude. They may offer several examples.

3. When using examples and definitions for a target word (*generous*), the teacher writes on the chalkboard a paragraph containing the word in context and a contextual definition. For *generous,* a teacher in the upper grades might write:

    The president of the company was *generous* when he was asked to contribute to charities. His employees, following his example, gave freely also.

    Next, the teacher asks the students to read the paragraph and tell what they think *generous* means. The teacher then asks the students to give other examples of this concept.

4. When using definition together with sentence completion, the teacher gives the students duplicated sheets containing simple definitions of several words to be taught and sentence fragments containing each word. One entry might be

    1. crust: the hard outer covering of something—The crust of the earth is the part _____.

    Before the students begin to complete the sentences, the class discusses the meaning of *crust* and ways to complete that sentence. Then they fill in the blank with an answer and discuss the word further. For example, the teacher might ask: "What other things besides the earth have crusts?" This question should elicit much discussion. The other words on the pages are handled in the same way.

All four of Duffelmeyer's strategies are effective methods of vocabulary instruction that are congruent with the suggestions for good vocabulary instruction discussed earlier. More detail about these approaches and other examples of their use in teaching can be found in *The Reading Teacher* (Duffelmeyer, 1985).

Kaplan and Tuchman (1980) suggest an additional technique that can help children relate their past experiences to new vocabulary. In this approach, the teacher selects a concept word related to something currently being studied, writes it on the board, and gives the children a specified time within which to write down related words. Then the children share their word lists. If the children do not respond well under time pressure, the teacher can write related words on the board as the children call them out.

Encouraging Independent Word Learning

Instruction that gradually moves the responsibility for determining new word meanings from the teacher to the student helps students become independent learners. Teachers can guide students to use context clues to define words independently by using a four-part procedure. First, students are given categorization tasks. Second, they practice determining meanings from complete contexts. Third, they practice determining meaning in incomplete contexts. Finally, they practice defining new vocabulary by means of context clues (Carr and Wixson, 1986).

Context Clues

In Chapter 3, we discussed the use of *context clues* to help children recognize words that are familiar in speech but not in print. Context clues can also key the meaning of an unfamiliar word by directly defining the word, providing an *appositive*, or comparing or contrasting the word with a known word. For example:

> A *democracy* is a government run by the people being governed. (definition)

> He made an effort to alleviate, or relieve, the child's pain until the doctor arrived. (appositive)

> Rather than encountering hostile natives, as they had expected, many settlers found the natives to be *amicable*. (contrast)

Context can also offer clues in sentences other than the one in which the new word appears, so children should be encouraged to read surrounding sentences for clues to meaning. Sometimes an entire paragraph embodies the explanation of a term, as in the following example:

> I've told you before that measles are contagious! When Johnny had the measles, Beatrice played with him one afternoon, and soon Beatrice broke out with them. Joey caught them from her, and now you tell me you have been to Joey's house. I imagine you'll be sorry when you break out with the measles and have to miss the party on Saturday.

When introducing new words in context, teachers should use sentences that students can relate to their own experiences and that have only one unfamiliar word each. It is best not to use the new word at the very beginning of the sentence, since the children will not have had any of the facilitating context before they encounter it (Duffelmeyer, 1982).

Teachers can use a "think-aloud" strategy to help students see how to use context clues. Here are some sample activities that make use of this strategy.

After several example "think-aloud" activities in which the teacher models the use of context clues, the teacher can ask student volunteers to "think aloud" the context clues to specific words. Students may work in pairs on a context clues worksheet and verbalize their context usage strategies to each other. Finally, the students should work alone to determine meanings from context clues.

Blachowicz (1993) suggests a procedure called *C(2)QU* to teach context use. The steps are as follows:

Model Activities

Intermediate-Level Lesson on Context Clues

Write one of the sentences mentioned previously on the board or display it using a transparency. Say: "Rather than encountering hostile natives, as they had expected, many settlers found the natives to be amicable. I wonder what *amicable* means? Let's see; the sentence says '*Rather than* encountering hostile natives.' That means the natives weren't hostile. *Hostile* means *unfriendly*; so maybe *amicable* means *friendly*."

Model Activities

Primary-Level Lesson on Context Clues

Write the sentence "David wants to keep his new shirt, but Mark wants to exchange his for another color" on the board or show it to the children on a transparency. Then read the sentence aloud and say: "I wonder what *exchange* means? Let's see; the sentence says that David wants to keep his shirt, but Mark wants to exchange his. It also mentions another color of shirt. The *but* means that Mark wants to do something different from keeping his shirt. When I get something and don't like the color, I take it back and swap it for another color. Maybe that is what Mark wants to do. I guess *exchange* means *swap*."

C1: *Context.*   A broad, meaningful context is provided for an unfamiliar word. Students hypothesize about the meaning.

C2: *Context.*   More explicit context is provided. Students orally analyze their original hypotheses.

Q: *Question.*   Students are asked a question involving the meaning of the word. They discuss the meaning.

U: *Use.*   Students are asked to use the word appropriately in oral or written sentences.

This procedure requires active participation by students, which should result in more effective learning.

Context clues are available in both text and illustrations in many trade books, such as *The Amazing Bone* by William Steig (Farrar, Straus & Giroux, 1976). *A Gaggle of Geese*, by Eve Merriam (Knopf, 1960), puts collective terminology for groups into an interesting context (Howell, 1987). Teaching use of context clues in these meaningful settings encourages students to use such clues in their independent reading.

Some researchers have found that use of closed-caption television programs to provide readers with both auditory and visual context was effective with below-average readers and bilingual students (Koskinen et al., 1993; Neuman and Koskinen, 1992). They found that such programs provided readers with print to read in a motivational format. Words could be discussed while the students were viewing video images. Later they could be read from handouts prepared with sentences drawn from the captioned video and finally from magazines and books on

reading-writing connection

the same topic. They could also be used in written retellings of the viewed episode. Although the match between the audio and the captions seen was not exact, the captions were presented at a rapid rate for poor readers (about 120 words per minute), and the captions were in all capital letters, the results teachers obtained were impressive. Some televisions need a TeleCaption decoder to permit viewing of captions; others have built-in decoders. Videotaping the programs allows repetition of the reading for different purposes and use of small segments (only a few minutes each) of video in a lesson. However, copyright laws must be studied to ensure that use is in compliance with these laws.

literature-centered reading

Edwards and Dermott (1989) select difficult words from material about to be assigned, take a quotation using each word in good context from the material, and provide written comments to the students to help them use appropriate context clues or other strategies (primarily structural analysis or dictionary use). The students try to use the clues available to decide on the meanings of the words before reading. Class discussion helps the students to think through the strategy use.

Gipe (1980) expanded a context method (in which students read new words in meaningful contexts) to include having children apply the words based on their own experiences and then studied the effectiveness of this method, compared to three other methods. The other methods were an association method (in which an unknown word is paired with a familiar synonym), a category method

reading-writing connection

(in which students place words in categories), and a dictionary method (in which students look up the word, write a definition, and use the word in a sentence). The expanded context method was found to be the most effective of the four. The application of the new words may have been the most important aspect of the context method that Gipe used. After the students derived the meaning of the word from a variety of contexts, including a definition context, they *applied* the word to their personal experiences in a written response. Thus, the instruction follows the first desirable instructional technique for vocabulary listed earlier in this chapter: assisting students in integrating the new words with their background knowledge.

Teachers need to help students learn *why* and *when* to use context clues (Blachowicz and Zabroske, 1990). Context clues are useful when the context is explicit about word meaning, but they are less useful when the meaning is left unclear. If the clues are too vague, they may actually be misleading (Schwartz, 1988; Schatz and Baldwin, 1986). Furthermore, if the word is not important to understanding the passage, the explicitness of the context is not important. Teachers should model their decision-making processes about the importance of determining the meaning of the word, the usefulness of the context, and the kinds of clues available there through think-alouds. Students need to realize that the meanings they attribute to the words must pass the test inherent in the question "Does this make sense here?" They also need to realize that structural analysis clues may help them decide whether or not a meaning suggested by the context is reasonable.

It is estimated that average ten- to fourteen-year-old students could acquire from 750 to 8,250 new words each year through incidental, rather than directed, contextual learning (Schwartz, 1988; Herman et al., 1987; Nagy, Herman, and Anderson, 1985; Wysocki and Jenkins, 1987). Helping students learn to use context more efficiently should therefore greatly enhance their vocabulary learning.

Activities

1. Using a selection the students are about to read, take an unfamiliar word, put it into a title, and construct several sentences that offer clues to its meaning. Show the title on the overhead projector; then show one sentence at a time, letting the students guess the meaning of the word at each step (Kaplan and Tuchman, 1980).

2. Use a technique called *musical cloze*. First, select a song appropriate for the children and the unit of study. Make deletions in its text: certain parts of speech, words that fit into a particular category, words that show relationships, or something else. Using the original text, have the children practice until they learn the song. Then sing it with the deletions, and ask the children to suggest alternatives for the omitted words or phrases. Write these on the board and sing the song several times, using the children's suggestions in place of the original words. Afterward, lead the students in a discussion of their replacement choices (Mateja, 1982).

Combining contextual and definitional approaches to vocabulary instruction is more effective than using a contextual approach alone. In fact, "it would be hard to justify a contextual approach in which the teacher did not finally provide an adequate definition of the word or help the class arrive at one" (Nagy, 1988, p. 8). In addition, teachers can have students apply context clues fruitfully in conjunction with structure clues, which we will discuss next.

Structural Analysis

Structural analysis, discussed in Chapter 3 as a word recognition skill, can also be used as an aid in discovering meanings of unknown words. Knowing meanings of common affixes and combining them with meanings of familiar root words can help students determine the meanings of many new words. For example, if a child knows the meaning of *joy* and knows that the suffix *-ous* means *full of,* he or she can conclude that the word *joyous* means *full of joy.* Students can often determine meanings of compound words by relating the meanings of the component parts to each other (*watchdog* means a *dog* that *watches*). After some practice, they can be led to see that the component parts of a compound word do not always have the same relationships to each other (*bookcase* means a *case* for *books*).

Children begin to learn about word structure very early. First, they deal with words in their simplest, most basic forms—as *morphemes*, the smallest units of meaning in a language. (The word *cat* is one morpheme.) Then they gradually learn to combine morphemes. If an *s* is added to form the plural, *cats*, the final *s* is also a morpheme, because it changes the word's meaning. There are two classes of morphemes, distinguished by function: *free* morphemes, which have independent meanings and can be used by themselves (*cat, man, son*), and *bound* morphemes, which must be combined with another morpheme to have meaning. Affixes and inflectional endings are bound morphemes; the *-er* in *singer* is an example.

literature-centered reading   Practice activities such as the following can help children see how prefixes and suffixes change meanings of words. *Un-* is the most common prefix appearing in the *Word Frequency Book* (Carroll, Davies, and Richman, 1971; White, Sowell, and Yanagihara, 1989).

Prefix *un-*

Model Activities

Have the students read the book *Fortunately* by Remy Charlip (New York: Scholastic, 1964). Discuss with them the meanings of *fortunately* and *unfortunately*, using the situations from the book to make the discussion concrete and clear. When they have stated that *unfortunately* means *not fortunately* or *the opposite of fortunately*, have them decide what part of the word means *not*. After they identify the *un-* as the part that means *not*, have them name other words they know that begin

with *un-*. Discuss the meanings of these words, pointing out that the prefix means *not* or *the opposite of* in each case in which the remainder of the word forms a root word, but not if the beginning two letters are not a prefix attached to a root word. Ask them to look in their reading assignments for words starting with *un-* in which *un-* is a prefix added to a root word. Have them use their knowledge of the meaning of *un-* to determine the meanings of each of these words.

The teacher may also personalize the study of the prefix *un-* by having the students complete sentences such as the ones in the Model Activity on page 177.

White, Sowell, and Yanagihara (1989) caution teachers that prefixes may have more than one meaning. *Un-, re-, in-,* and *dis-*, the four most frequently used prefixes, have at least two meanings each. *Un-* and *dis-* may each mean either *not* or *do the opposite*. *In-* may mean either *not*, or *in*, or *into*. *Re-* may mean either *again* or *back*. Both the word parts and the context of the word should be considered in determining meanings of prefixed words.

The following Classroom Scenario on page 177 shows another application of structural analysis in the classroom.

Model Activities

Prefix *un-*

Distribute copies of the following list of incomplete sentences. Tell the children that each sentence contains a word with the prefix *un-* added and the same word without the prefix. Explain that the prefix *un-* means *not*. Then ask them to fill in the blanks in the sentences with words or phrases that will make the sentences true. You may wish to give them an example, such as "When I laugh, I am happy, but when I cry, I am unhappy."

1. I am able to _____, but I am unable to _____.

2. The story about_____ is believable, but the one about _____ is unbelievable.

3. I have a _____ that is used and a _____ that is unused.

4. I am available for _____, but I am unavailable for _____.

Classroom Scenario

Use of Structural Analysis Skills

A middle school science textbook presented two theories of the solar system: a geocentric theory and a heliocentric theory. Two diagrams were provided to help the students visualize the two theories, but the diagrams were not labeled. Mrs. Brown, the teacher, asked the students, "Which diagram is related to each theory?"

Matt's hand quickly went up, and he accurately identified the two diagrams.

"How did you decide which was which?" asked Mrs. Brown.

"You told us that *geo-* means *earth*. *Centric* looks like it comes from *center*. This diagram has the earth in the center. So I decided it was geocentric. That would mean the other one was heliocentric. Since the sun is in the center in it, I guess *helio-* means *sun*."

Analysis of Scenario
Mrs. Brown had taught an important science word part the first time it occurred in her class. She had encouraged her students to use their knowledge of word parts to figure out unfamiliar words. Matt followed her suggestions and managed to make decisions about key vocabulary based on his knowledge of word parts.

Peterson and Phelps (1991) use pictures and slogans to help teach the meanings of Latin and Greek word parts. For example, a picture of a rabbit writing would be accompanied by the slogan "Scriptus, the writer." The students also study word cards that contain words derived from the Latin or Greek word parts, such as *prescription* and *scripture*. Students are encouraged to think of other examples and are asked to use the derived words in sentence context.

literature-centered reading

See the Focus on Strategies on Compound Words for an activity that can offer practice in determining meanings of compound words.

Focus on Strategies

Compound Words

Mr. Clay based his lesson on the book *The Seal Mother* by Mordicai Gerstein (Dial, 1986). He introduced the story by saying that it was an old Scottish folktale. He wrote the word *folktale* on the board. Then he asked, "What can you tell me about this word?"

Bobby said, "It is made up of two words: *folk* and *tale*. That makes it a compound word."

"Good, Bobby," Mr. Clay responded. "What does that make you believe this word means?"

"A tale is a story," LaTonya replied.

"That's right," said Mr. Clay. "Can anyone add anything else to what we know about the word's meaning? What does *folk* mean?"

Carl answered tentatively, "A kind of music?"

"There is folk music, just as there are folktales, but we still need a meaning for the word *folk*," Mr. Clay responded.

After he got only shrugs, he explained, "A folktale is a tale, or story, told by the folk, or common people, of a country. Folktales were passed down orally from older people to younger ones over the years. See how both parts of the compound word give something to the meaning?

Listen as I read this story to you. When I finish, we will try to retell the story by listing the main events."

The children listened intently. When he finished the story, Mr. Clay asked them to list the events in the story in order. As they suggested events, he wrote each one on the board. When he had listed all of the events they could remember, they discussed how to put some of the events in the proper order. Mr. Clay erased and moved the sentences around until the children were satisfied.

Then Mr. Clay asked the children, "Did you use any compound words to retell the story?"

Hands shot up all over the room. Mr. Clay called on them one by one, and they pointed out *fisherman, sealskin, without, oilcloth, inside, rayfish, everywhere, grandfather,* and *whenever*. The children who mentioned the words were allowed to go to the board and circle them, identify the two words that made up each compound, and try to define each compound word, using the meanings of the two component words. Other students helped in determining the definitions, and sometimes the dictionary was consulted.

Finally, the children were asked to copy the compound words from the board into their vocabulary study notebooks. "I'm putting three copies of *The Seal Mother* in the reading center for the rest of this week," Mr. Clay said. "When you have time, take your vocabulary notebook to the center and read the book to yourself or with a partner. Each time you find one of our compound words, put a checkmark by the word in your notebook. When you find a compound word that we didn't use in our retelling, copy it into your notebook, and write a definition for it, using the meanings of the two words and the context of the sentence in which you found it. We'll discuss the other words that you found on Friday."

On Friday, the children had found a number of words in the book that they hadn't used in their retelling, including *moonlit, moonlight, everything, wide-eyed, tiptoed, another,* and *into.* A discussion of the words and their meanings followed. Mr. Clay asked how use of some of these words added to the children's understanding of the story.

"*Moonlit* and *moonlight* give you a picture in your mind of the scene," Jared said.

"*Wide-eyed* lets us know how his parents' talk made the boy feel," Marissa added.

"*Tiptoed* showed us how he walked quietly," Tyrone said.

"Watch for compound words in other books that you read, and use the meanings of the two words in each compound to help you with meanings that you don't already know," Mr. Clay told them as he ended the lesson.

Categorization

Categorization is grouping together things or ideas that have common features. Classifying words into categories can be a good way to learn more about word meanings. Young children can begin learning how to place things into categories by grouping concrete objects according to their traits. Once the children have developed some sight vocabulary, it is a relatively small step for them to begin categorizing the words they see in print according to their meanings. Very early in their instruction, children will be able to look at the following list and classify the words into such teacher-supplied categories as "people," "things to play with," "things to eat," and "things to do."

Word List

doll	bicycle	ball
candy	cookie	boy
toy	dig	sing
run	girl	mother
baby	sit	banana

The children may discover that they want to put a word in more than one category. This desire will provide an opportunity for discussion about how a word may fit in two or more places for different reasons. The children should give reasons for all of their placements.

After the children become adept at classifying words into categories supplied by the teacher, they are ready for the more difficult task of generating the categories needed for classifying the words presented. The teacher may give them a list of words such as the following and ask them to place the words in groups of things that are alike and to name the trait the items have in common.

Word List

horse	cow	goose
gosling	mare	filly
colt	gander	bull
stallion	foal	hen
chick	calf	rooster

Children may offer several categories for these words: various families of animals; four-legged and two-legged animals; feathered and furred animals; winged and wingless animals; or male animals, female animals, or animals that might be either sex. They may also come up with a classification that the teacher has not considered. As long as the classification system makes sense and the animals are correctly classified according to the stated system, it should be considered correct. No one way of categorizing is more correct than any other, as long as it is based on groups with common features. Teachers should encourage students to discover various possibilities for classifications.

Discussion of the different classification systems may help to extend the children's concepts about some of the animals on the list, and it may help some children develop concepts related to some of the animals for the first time. The classification system allows them to relate the new knowledge about some of the animals to the knowledge they already have about these animals or others. The usefulness of categorization activities is supported by research indicating that presenting words in semantically related clusters can lead to improvement in students' vocabulary knowledge and reading comprehension (Marzano, 1984).

Bufe (1983) suggests a categorization activity to promote comprehension of stories. It is designed to be used as a prereading strategy. The teacher writes four headings on the chalkboard: "Setting," "Actions," "Characters," and "Words about the Characters." Then the teacher adds words from the story under each category. The children may know some, but not all, of the words. The teacher then presents each list to the children, asking them if there are any words they cannot pronounce, if there are any words they do not know meanings for, and what the words tell them about the story that is about to be read. Pronunciations and meanings are cleared up through discussion, and predictions about the story are made. The predictions may be written in a few sentences. Students can also look for relationships among the words on the four lists.

reading-writing connection

A classification game such as the following provides an interesting way to work on categorization skills.

The ability to classify is a basic skill that applies to many areas of learning. Many of the other activities described in this chapter, including those for analogies, semantic maps, and semantic feature analysis, depend on categorization.

Analogies and Word Lines

Analogies compare two relationships and thereby provide a basis for building word knowledge. Educators may teach analogies by displaying examples of cate-

**Model
Activities**

Classification Game

Divide the children into groups of three or four, and make category sheets like the one shown here for each group. When you give a signal, the children start writing as many words as they can think of that fit in each category; when you signal that time is up, a child from each group reads the group's words to the class. Have the children compare their lists and discuss why they placed particular words in particular categories.

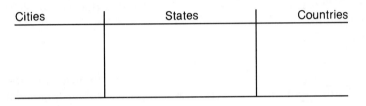

Cities	States	Countries

Other appropriate categories are meats, fruits, and vegetables; mammals, reptiles, and insects; or liquids, solids, and gases.

gories, relationships, and analogies; asking guiding questions about the examples; allowing students to discuss the questions; and applying the ideas that emerge (Bellows, 1980).

Students may need help in grouping items into categories and understanding relationships among items. For example, the teacher might write *nickel, dime,* and *quarter* on the board and ask, "How are these things related? What name could you give the entire group of items?" (Answer: *money.*) Teachers can use pictures instead of words in the primary grades; in either case, they can ask students to apply the skill by naming other things that would fit in the category (*penny* and *dollar*). Or the teacher could write *painter* and *brush* and ask, "What is the relationship between the two items?" (Answer: A *painter* works with a *brush.*) Teachers should remember to simplify their language for discussions with young children and to have students give other examples of the relationship (*dentist* and *drill*). After working through many examples such as these, the students should be ready for examples of simple analogies, such as "Light is to dark as day is to night," "Glove is to hand as sock is to foot," and "Round is to ball as square is to block." Students can discuss how analogies work: "How are the first two things related? How are the second two things related? How are these relationships alike?" They can then complete incomplete analogies, such as "Teacher is to classroom as pilot is to _____." Younger children should do this orally; older ones can understand the standard shorthand form of *come:go::live:die* if they are taught to read the colon (:) as *is to* and (::) as *as* (Bellows, 1980). Once children are familiar with analogies, they can complete activities such as the following in class.

Analogies

Model Activities

Using the following list of incomplete analogies, have students complete the analogies orally or in writing. Have the students explain their reasons for their word choices in either whole-class or small-group discussion.

1. Hot is to cold as weak is to _____.

2. Milk is to drink as potato is to _____.

3. Toe is to foot as finger is to _____.

4. Blue is to blew as red is to _____.

5. Coat is to coats as mouse is to _____.

6. Up is to down as top is to _____.

Teachers may use word lines to show the relationships among words, just as they use number lines for numbers. They can arrange related words on a graduated line that emphasizes their relationships. For young children, they can use pictures and words to match or ask them to locate or produce appropriate pictures. Upper-grade students can be asked to arrange a specified list of words on a word line themselves. Word lines can concretely show antonym, synonym, and degree analogies, as in this example:

reading-writing connection

enormous	large	medium	small	tiny

Analogies that students could develop include "enormous is to large as small is to tiny" (synonym); "enormous is to tiny as large is to small" (antonym); and "large is to medium as medium is to small" (degree). The teacher can have the children make their own word lines and analogies (Macey, 1981).

Dwyer (1988) suggests mapping analogies. Such a map could look like the diagram at the top of page 183.

This map provides the relationship involved, a complete example, two incomplete examples for the students to complete, and one space for an example that comes entirely from the student.

Semantic Maps and Word Webs

Semantic maps can be used to teach related concepts (Johnson and Pearson, 1984; Johnson, Pittelman, and Heimlich, 1986). "Semantic maps are diagrams that help students see how words are related to one another. . . . Students learn the meanings and uses of new words, see old words in a new light, and see relationships among words" (Heimlich and Pittelman, 1986).

To construct a semantic map with a class, the teacher writes on the board or a

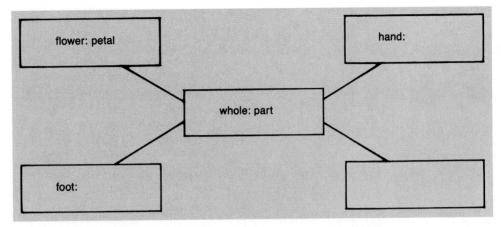

chart a word that represents a concept that is central to the topic under consideration. The teacher asks the students to name words related to this concept. The students' words are listed on the board or chart grouped in broad categories, and the students name the categories. They may also suggest additional categories. A discussion of the central concept, the listed words, the categories, and the interrelationships among the words follows.

The discussion step appears to be the key to the effectiveness of this method, because it allows the students to be actively involved in the learning. After the class has discussed the semantic map, the teacher can give an incomplete semantic map to the children and ask them to fill in the words from the map on the board or chart and add any categories or words that they wish. The children can work on their maps as they do the assigned reading related to the central concept. Further discussion can follow the reading, and more categories and words can be added to the maps. The final discussion and mapping allow the children to recall and graphically organize the information they gained from the reading (Johnson, Pittelman, and Heimlich, 1986; Stahl and Vancil, 1986). Example 4.1 shows a semantic map constructed by one class.

Because a semantic map shows both familiar and new words under labeled categories, the process of constructing one helps students make connections between known and new concepts (Johnson, Pittelman, and Heimlich, 1986). The graphic display makes relationships among terms easier to see.

Research shows that semantic mapping is effective in promoting vocabulary learning; furthermore, it is equally effective with homogeneous small groups and heterogeneous whole classes. The critical element may be the discussion, which allows the teacher to assess the children's background knowledge, clarify concepts, and correct misunderstandings (Stahl and Vancil, 1986).

Schwartz and Raphael (1985) used a modified approach to semantic mapping to help students develop a concept of *definition*. The students learned what types of information are needed for a definition and learned how to use context clues and background knowledge to help them better understand words. Word maps are really graphic representations of definitions. The word maps Schwartz and

reading-writing connection

Example 4.1   *Semantic Map of the Concept* Tennis

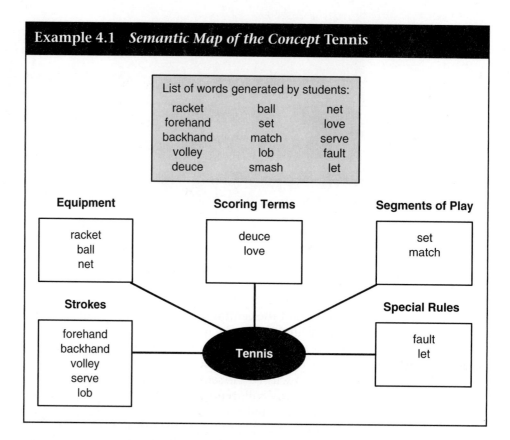

Raphael used contained information about the general class to which the concept belonged, answering the question "What is it?"; the properties of the concept, answering the question "What is it like?"; and examples of the concept (see Example 4.2).

With the basic information contained in such a map, students have enough information to construct definitions. This procedure for understanding the concept of definition is effective from the fourth-grade level through college. The approach used by Schwartz and Raphael started with strong teacher involvement, but control was gradually transferred to the children. Children were led to search the context of a sentence in which the word occurred for the elements of definition needed to map a word. Eventually the teachers provided only partial context for the word, leading the children to go to outside sources, such as dictionaries, for information to complete the maps. Finally, teachers asked the students to write definitions, including all the features previously mapped, without actually mapping the word on paper. This activity helps bring meanings of unknown terms into focus through analogies and examples (Smith, 1990). Schwartz and Raphael (1985) suggest use of it in content area vocabulary instruction.

Word webs are another way to represent the relationships among words

Example 4.2   *Word Map for Definition*

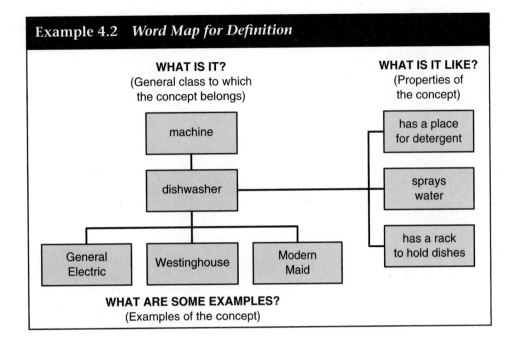

WHAT IS IT?
(General class to which
the concept belongs)

WHAT IS IT LIKE?
(Properties of
the concept)

machine

dishwasher

has a place
for detergent

sprays
water

has a rack
to hold dishes

General
Electric

Westinghouse

Modern
Maid

WHAT ARE SOME EXAMPLES?
(Examples of the concept)

graphically. Students construct these diagrams by connecting related words with lines. The words used for the web may be taken from material students have read in class. Example 4.3 shows such a web, based on the selection "Teaching Snoopy to Dance: Bill Melendez and the Art of Animation," by Valerie Tripp, from the *Houghton Mifflin Reading Series*. The words in parentheses would not be provided to the children; they would be asked to fill in these words, based on the selection they have read, and to check their answers by referring to the selection.

Semantic Feature Analysis

Semantic feature analysis is a technique that can help children understand the uniqueness of a word as well as its relationships to other words (Johnson and Pearson, 1984). To perform such an analysis, the teacher lists in a column on the board or a chart some known words with common properties. Then the children generate a list of features possessed by the various items in the list. A feature only needs to apply to one item to be listed. The teacher writes these features in a row across the top of the board or chart, and the students fill in the cells of the resulting matrix with pluses to indicate the presence of the feature and minuses to indicate its absence.

Example 4.4 shows a partial matrix developed by children for various buildings. "Walls," "doors," and "windows" were other features the children suggested for the matrix; they were omitted from the example only for space considerations. All of these features received a plus for each building, emphasizing the similarities of the terms *jail, garage, museum,* and *church*.

Example 4.3　*Word Web for Basal Reader Selection*

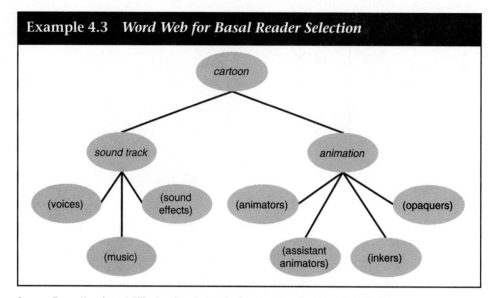

The children discussed the terms as they filled in the matrix. In the places where the question marks occur, the children said, "Sometimes it may have that, but not always. It doesn't have to have it." The group discussion brought out much information about each building listed and served to expand the children's existing schemata.

Students can continue to expand such a matrix after initially filling it out by adding words that share some of the listed features. For example, the children added *grocery store* to the list of buildings in Example 4.4 because it shared the walls, doors, and windows, and they added other features showing the differentiation, such as *food, clerks,* and *shopping carts.*

Johnson and Pearson (1984) suggest that, after experience with these matrices, children may begin to realize that some words have different degrees of the same feature. At this time, the teacher may want to try using a numerical system

Example 4.4　*Semantic Feature Analysis Chart*

	barred windows	exhibits	steeple	cross	cars	lift-up doors	guards	oil stains
jail	+	–	–	–	–	–	+	–
garage	?	–	–	–	+	+	–	+
museum	?	+	–	–	?	–	+	–
church	–	–	+	+	–	–	–	–

of coding, using 0 for *none,* 1 for *some,* 2 for *much,* and 3 for *all.* Under the feature "fear," for example, *scared* might be coded with a 1, whereas *terrified* might be coded with a 3.

Anders and Bos (1986) suggest using semantic feature analysis with vocabulary needed for content area reading assignments. They believe that, because the analysis activates the students' prior knowledge through discussion and relates prior knowledge to new knowledge, students will have increased interest in the reading and therefore will learn more. This technique can be used before, during, and after the reading. A chart can be started in the background-building portion of the lesson, added to or modified by the students as they read the material, and refined further during the follow-up discussion of the material.

Metaphoric or figurative language (nonliteral language) can also be taught through a technique similar to semantic feature analysis (Thompson, 1986). A comparison chart can clarify differences and similarities between concepts that are not literally members of the same category. Finding similarities between essentially dissimilar things helps children understand the comparisons used in metaphoric language. For example, both *eyes* and *stars* might have the characteristic "shining" or "bright," leading to the source of the intended comparison in the expression "her eyes were like stars." (A detailed section on figurative language appears later in this chapter.)

Dictionary Use

The dictionary can be an excellent source for discovering meanings of unfamiliar words, particularly for determining the appropriate meanings of words that have multiple definitions or specific, technical definitions. In some instances, children may be familiar with several common meanings of a word, but not with a word's specialized meaning found in a content area textbook. For example, a child may understand a reference to a *base* in a baseball game but not a discussion of a military *base* (social studies material), a *base* that turns litmus paper blue (science material), or *base* motives of a character (literature). Words that have the greatest number of different meanings, such as *run* or *bank,* are frequently very common.

Dictionaries are not always used properly in schools, however. Teachers should instruct children to consider the context surrounding a word, read the different dictionary definitions, and choose the definition that makes the most sense in the context. Without such instruction, children have a strong tendency to read only the first dictionary definition and to try to force it into the context. The teacher should model the choice of the correct definition for the students so that they can see what the task is. Students will then need to practice the task under teacher supervision.

The following Model Activities, pages 188 and 189, are good to use for practice immediately following instruction in dictionary use and for later independent practice.

Students can also use dictionaries to study *etymology,* the origin and history of words. Dictionaries often give the origin of a word in brackets after the phonetic respelling (although not all dictionaries do this in the same way), and

In order to use the dictionary properly for vocabulary development, students must be instructed to consider a word's context, to read the different definitions, and to choose a definition for the word in its specific context. (© *Ed Lettau/Photo Researchers*)

archaic or obsolete definitions are frequently given and labeled so that students can see how words have changed.

Teaching word meanings through dictionary use has been widely criticized, but it is nevertheless a useful technique for vocabulary development if it is applied properly. Research (e.g., Graves and Prenn, 1986) supports this view.

Model Activities

Appropriate Dictionary Definitions

Write the following sentences on the board. Ask the children to find the dictionary definition of *sharp* that fits each sentence. You may ask them to jot each definition down and have a whole-class or small-group discussion about each one after all meanings have been located, or you may wish to discuss each meaning as it is located. The students may read other definitions for *sharp* in the dictionary and generate sentences for these as well.

1. Katherine's knife was very sharp.

2. There is a sharp curve in the road up ahead.

3. Sam is a sharp businessman. That's why he has been so successful.

4. I hope that when I am seventy my mind is as sharp as my grandmother's is.

5. We are leaving at 2 o'clock sharp.

**Model
Activities**

Multiple Meanings of Words

Give the students a list of sentences drawn from their textbooks that contain words with specialized meanings for that subject. Have them use the dictionary or the textbook's glossary to discover the specialized meanings that fit the context of the sentences. After the students have completed the task independently, go over the sentences with them and discuss reasons for right and wrong responses.

The material you give to the students may look something like this:

Directions: Some words mean different things in your textbooks from what they mean in everyday conversation. In each of the following sentences, find the special meanings for the words and write these meanings on the lines provided.

1. Frederick Smith has decided to *run* for mayor. _____

2. The park was near the *mouth* of the Little Bear River. _____ _____

3. The management of the company was unable to avert a *strike.* _____ _____

4. That song is hard to sing because of the high *pitch* of several notes. _____

5. That number is written in *base* two. _____ _____

Combining a definitional approach to vocabulary instruction with a contextual approach is more effective than using a definitional approach in isolation. Sentences that illustrate meanings and uses of the defined words can help immensely (Nagy, 1988).

Chapter 9 presents information about the mechanics of dictionary use. Chapter 3 discusses using the dictionary for word recognition.

Word Origins and Histories

As mentioned earlier, the study of word origins and histories is called *etymology.* Children in the intermediate grades will enjoy learning about the kinds of changes that have taken place in the English language by studying words and definitions that appear in very old dictionaries and by studying differences between American English and British English. Following is an additional useful source: Funk, Wilfred. *Word Origins & Their Romantic Stories.* Avenal, New Jersey: Outlet Book Company, 1992.

Teachers need to help children understand the different ways words can be formed. *Portmanteau* words are formed by merging the sounds and meanings of two different words (for example, *smog,* from *smoke* and *fog*). *Acronyms* are words formed from the initial letters of a name or by combining initial letters or parts from a series of words (for example, *radar,* from *ra*dio *d*etecting *a*nd *r*anging).

Some words are just shortened forms of other words (for example, *phone,* from *telephone*), and some words are borrowed from other languages (for example, *lasso,* from the Spanish *lazo*). Students should discuss the origins of such terms when they encounter them while reading. In addition, students should try to think of other words that have been formed in a similar manner. The teacher may also wish to contribute other examples from familiar sources.

The teacher can place a "word tree," with limbs labeled *Greek, Latin, Anglo-Saxon, French, Native American, Dutch*, and so forth, on the bulletin board. The class can then put appropriate words on each limb (Gold, 1981). A word tree such as this can be allowed to "grow" as a unit of study on words progresses.

Figurative Language

Figurative language, or nonliteral language, can be a barrier to understanding written selections. Children tend to interpret literally many expressions that have meanings different from the sums of the meanings of the individual words. For example, the expression "the teeth of the wind" does not mean that the wind actually has teeth, nor does "a blanket of fog" mean a conventional blanket. Context clues indicate the meanings of such phrases in the same ways that they cue the meanings of individual words.

Adults often assume children have had exposure to expressions that in fact are unfamiliar to them. Children need substantial help in order to comprehend figurative language. Even basal readers present many of these expressions. Some common figures of speech that cause trouble are

1. *Simile*—a comparison using *like* or *as*

2. *Metaphor*—a direct comparison without the words *like* or *as*

3. *Personification*—giving the attributes of a person to an inanimate object or abstract idea

4. *Hyperbole*—an extreme exaggeration

5. *Euphemism*—substitution of a less offensive term for an unpleasant term or expression

Teaching children to recognize and understand similes is usually not too difficult, because the cue words *like* and *as* help to show the presence of a comparison. Metaphors, however, may cause more serious problems. A metaphor is a comparison between two unlike things that share an attribute (Readence, Baldwin, and Head, 1986). Sometimes children do not realize that the language in metaphors is figurative; sometimes they do not have sufficient background knowledge about one or both of the things being compared; and sometimes they simply have not learned a process for interpreting metaphors.

The two things compared in a metaphor may seem to be incompatible, but readers must think of past experiences with each, searching for a match in attributes that could be the basis of comparison. Visual aids can be helpful in this process. Thompson (1986) suggests a comparison chart like the following.

Comparison Chart

Man	*Mouse*
–	small
–	squeaks
√	alive
–	four legs
√+	timid

–	indicates dissimilarity.
√	indicates similarity.
√+	indicates *important* similarity.

The teacher can "think aloud" about the operation of metaphors and their purposes, asking students questions related to the process being demonstrated. Group discussion of the comparison chart helps to activate students' prior knowledge about the items being compared, and the chart helps make similarities more obvious.

Readence, Baldwin, Rickelman, and Miller (1986) found specific word knowledge to be an important factor in interpreting metaphors. The traditional practice offered in many commercial materials may not be helpful to students in interpreting other metaphors not covered in the material. Readence, Baldwin, and Head (1986, 1987) suggest the following instructional sequence for teaching metaphorical interpretation:

1. The teacher can display a metaphor, such as "Her eyes were stars," together with the more explicit simile, "Her eyes were as bright as stars," and explain that metaphors have missing words that link the things being compared (such as *bright* does). Other sentence pairs can also be shown and explained.

2. Then the students can be asked to find the missing word in a new metaphor, such as "He is a mouse around his boss." They can offer guesses, explaining their reasons aloud.

3. The teacher can explain that people have lists of words related to different topics stored in their minds. Examples can be modeled by the teacher and then produced by the students. At this point, the students can try to select the attribute related to the new metaphor. If there are two incorrect guesses, the attribute *timid* can be supplied and the reason for this choice given. This process can then be repeated with another metaphor.

4. As more metaphors are presented, the teacher can do less modeling, turning over more and more control of the process to the students.

After explaining each type of figurative language, modeling its interpretation, and having students interpret it under supervision, the teacher may provide independent practice activities such as the following ones. Ideally, the teacher should

literature-centered reading

take examples of figurative expressions from literature the children are currently reading and use these expressions in constructing practice activities.

Activities

1. Show students pictures of possible meanings for figurative expressions found in their reading materials, and ask them to accept or reject the accuracy of each picture. Have them look carefully at the context in which the expression was found before answering. (For example, if you illustrate the sentence "She worked like a horse" with a woman pulling a plow, children should reject the picture's accuracy.)

2. Ask children to choose the best explanation of a figurative expression found in their reading materials from a number of possible choices. Encourage them to examine the context before answering. Example: "The sun smiled down at the flowers" means:
   a. The sun was pleased with the flowers.
   b. The sun shone on the flowers.
   c. The sun smiled with its mouth.

3. Give each child a copy of a poem that is filled with figures of speech, and have the class compete to see who can "dig up" all the figures of speech first. You may require students to label all figures of speech properly as to type and to explain them.

4. Have the children participate in an "idioms search," in which they look in all kinds of reading material and try to find as many examples of idioms as they can. Students must define each idiom in a way that corresponds with its usage.

Teachers can also use an activity like the Model Activity on page 193 to illustrate figures of speech.

Student-Centered Vocabulary Learning Techniques

Some vocabulary learning techniques focus on students and their individual needs and interests. Explanations of several of these techniques follow.

Vocabulary Self-Collection Strategy.   Haggard (1986) suggests the following approach for general vocabulary development:

1. Ask each child to bring to class a word that the entire class should learn. (The teacher brings one, too.) Each child should determine the meaning of his or her word from its context, rather than looking it up in the dictionary.

2. Write the words on the board. Let each participant identify his or her word and tell where it was found, the context-derived meaning, and why the class should learn the word. The class should then discuss the meaning of the word, in order to clarify and extend it and to construct a definition on which

**Model
Activities**

Figures of Speech

Display the following cartoon on a transparency:

DENNIS THE MENACE® used by permission of Hank Ketcham and © by Field Enterprises, Inc.

Lead a discussion about the cartoon using the following questions as a guide.

1. What does "been through the mill" really mean, as Dennis's mother used it?

2. What does Dennis think it means?

3. How is the woman likely to react to Dennis's question?

4. How does Dennis's mother probably feel about the question?

5. Can misunderstanding figurative language cause trouble at times? Why do you say so?

Have the children suggest other figurative expressions that could produce misunderstandings. Then, as a follow-up activity, let them draw funny scenes in which the misunderstandings occur.

Also have the children look for other examples in newspaper comics. Ask them to cut out the examples and bring them to school for discussion.

the class agrees. The result may be checked against a dictionary definition, if desired.

3. Narrow the list down to a manageable number, and have the students record

the final list of words and definitions in their vocabulary journals. Some students may want to put eliminated words on their personal lists.

4. Make study assignments for the words.

5. Test the students on the words at the end of the week.

This technique can also be adjusted for use with basal reader assignments or content area assignments. Students can choose words from a basal reader story or, with content area assignments, choose terms that are important for learning the content. Haggard believes the act of choosing words increases students' sensitivity to new words and their enjoyment of learning words.

reading-writing connection **Word Banks or Vocabulary Notebooks.** Students can form their own word banks by writing on index cards words they have learned, their definitions, and sentences showing the words in meaningful contexts. They may also want to illustrate the words or include personal associations or reactions to the words. Students can carry their word banks around and practice the words in spare moments, such as while waiting for the bus or the dentist. In the classroom, the word banks can be used in word games and in classification and other instructional activities.

literature-centered reading Vocabulary notebooks are useful for recording new words found in general reading or words heard in conversations or on radio or television. New words may be alphabetized in the notebooks and defined, illustrated, and processed in much the same way as word bank words.

Both word banks and vocabulary notebooks can help children maintain a record of their increasing vocabularies. Generally, word banks are used in primary grades and notebooks in intermediate grades and above, but there are no set limits for either technique.

Word Play

Word play is an enjoyable way to learn more about words. It can provide multiple exposures to words in different contexts that are important to complete word learning. Gale (1982, p. 220) states, "Children who play with words show a stronger grasp of meaning than those who do not. To create or comprehend a pun, one needs to be aware of the multiple meanings of a word."

The following activities present some other ways that teachers can engage children in word play.

1. Have students write words in ways that express their meanings; for example, they may write *backward* as *drawkcab*, or *up* slanting upward and *down* slanting downward.

2. Ask them silly questions containing new words. Example: "Would you have a terrarium for dinner? Why or why not?"

3. Discuss what puns are and give some examples. Then ask children to make up or find puns to bring to class. Let them explain the play on words to classmates

Activities

who do not understand it. Example: "What is black and white and read all over?" Answer: A newspaper (word play on the homonyms *red* and *read*).

4. Use Hink Pinks, Hinky Pinkies, and Hinkety Pinketies—rhyming definitions for terms with one, two, and three syllables, respectively. Give a definition, tell whether it is a Hink Pink, Hinky Pinky, or Hinkety Pinkety, and let the children guess the expression. Then let the children make up their own terms. Several examples follow.

Hink Pink: Unhappy father—Sad dad

Hinky Pinky: Late group of celebrators—Tardy party

Hinkety Pinkety: Yearly handbook—Annual manual

5. Give the students a list of clues ("means the same as . . . ," "is the opposite of . . . ," and so forth) to words in a reading selection, along with page numbers. Tell them to go on a scavenger hunt for the words and write the words beside the appropriate clues (Criscuolo, 1980).

6. Have students use what Ruddiman (1993) calls the "Vocab Game" to develop students' word knowledge. For this game, have each student bring in a word from real-life reading each week. Have the students try to stump you with their words, while other students try to figure out their classmates' words. In the process, affixes and roots are located, dictionary definitions checked, the contexts in which the words were found shared, synonyms and antonyms discussed, and analogies presented. The class can earn points by stumping you or by figuring out another student's word. Have a recorder keep a record of the information about the words, which you word process and duplicate for the class. Use cloze-type tests (teacher or student constructed) to check the learning of the vocabulary.

7. Students might also enjoy crossword puzzles or hidden-word puzzles that highlight new words in their textbooks or other instructional materials.

Riddles are a very effective form of word play. To use riddles, children must interact verbally with others; to create riddles, they have to organize information and decide on significant details. Riddles can help children move from the literal to the interpretive level of understanding (Gale, 1982). Tyson and Mountain (1982) point out that riddles provide both context clues and high-interest material. Both of these factors promote vocabulary learning.

Riddles can be classified into several categories: those based on homonyms, on rhyming words, on double meanings, and on figurative/literal meanings, for example. (See the section "Special Words" later in this chapter.) An example of a homonym riddle is: "What does a grizzly *bear* take on a trip? Only the *bare* essentials" (Tyson and Mountain, 1982, p. 170).

Riddles work best with children who are at least six years old (Gale, 1982), and they continue to be especially effective with children through eleven years of age. After that, interest in this form of word play wanes.

Computer Techniques

Computers are present in many elementary school classrooms in this age of high technology, and the software available includes many programs for vocabulary development. Although some of them are simply drill-and-practice programs, which are meant to provide practice with word meanings the teacher has already taught, some tutorial programs provide initial instruction in word meanings. (These programs may also include a drill-and-practice component.) Programs focusing on synonyms, antonyms, homonyms, and words with multiple meanings are available, as are programs providing work with classification and analogies.

Since the number of available programs is increasing daily, teachers must select them carefully. Programs vary greatly in pedagogical soundness, technical accuracy, and ease of use; also, some are more appropriate for particular age and ability groups of students. Well-chosen software can provide a teacher with much useful material to supplement a vocabulary program.

reading-writing connection Word-processing programs that have a find-and-replace function can be profitably used in vocabulary instruction. A child may be given a disk that has files containing paragraphs with certain words used repeatedly. The child may use the find-and-replace function to replace all instances of a chosen word with a synonym and then read the paragraph to see if the synonym makes sense in each place it appears. If it does not, the child can delete the synonym in the inappropriate places and choose more appropriate replacements for the original word or actually put the original word back into the file. Then the child can read the file again to see if the words chosen convey the correct meanings and if the variation in word choices makes the paragraph more interesting to read.

A paragraph such as the following one could be a starting place:

> Shonda had to run to the store for her mother because, just before the party, her mother got a run in her pantyhose. Shonda had to listen to her mother run on and on about her run of bad luck that day before she was able to leave the house. When she arrived at the store, she saw her uncle, who told her he had decided to run for office, delaying her progress further. She finally bought the last pair of pantyhose in the store. There must have been a run on them earlier in the day.

Authoring systems (computer programs that allow nonprogrammers to devise computer-assisted instructional materials) can be used to provide vocabulary instruction on words that students need for their content area classes. Wheatley and her colleagues (1993) have successfully developed such materials for remedial college students, and the procedures used could easily be adapted to intermediate-grade instruction. Personalized vocabulary terms can be presented in context with questions requiring student responses. Incorrect responses can lead to tutorial information about context and structural analysis clues. (See Chapter 7 for more about the operation of tutorial computer software.)

Comparison of Approaches

Teachers understandably want to know which approaches to vocabulary instruction are most effective. A few research studies have shed light on this question.
As reported in the section on context clues, Gipe (1980) found that an expanded
context method that included application of the words based on personal experiences was more effective than an association method, a category method, and a
dictionary method. Jiganti and Tindall (1986) compared the effects of a vocabulary program consisting of categorization activities and dramatic interpretations
of new words with those of a dictionary method of instruction. In the dictionary
activity, which was assigned as homework, students were given a list of words to
look up in the dictionary, define, and use in sentences. The classroom program
was more successful and enjoyable than the homework approach. Good readers
learned more than poor readers from the homework approach, but both good
and poor readers benefited from the classroom approach.

Teaching strategies in which the teacher and students work together are generally more effective than those in which students are expected to learn new
words without the teacher's help (Graves and Prenn, 1986). In addition, each
instructional activity related to a word advances the students' mastery of that
word to some degree, but many encounters may be necessary before complete
mastery is achieved. Furthermore, active involvement with the vocabulary to be
learned can be very beneficial. These facts lead to the conclusion that a combination of approaches may be advisable.

SELF-CHECK: OBJECTIVE 2   What are some techniques that can be used for vocabulary
instruction? Which ones appear to be the best, according to the guidelines in this chapter?
(See Self-Improvement Opportunities 1, 2, 5, 6, 7, and 8.)

Special Words

Special types of words, such as those discussed in the following sections, need to
be given careful attention.

Homonyms

Homonyms (also known as *homophones*) can cause trouble for young readers
because they are spelled differently but pronounced the same way. Some common homonyms are found in the following sentences.

I want to *be* a doctor.
That *bee* almost stung me.

She has *two* brothers.
Will you go *to* the show with me?
I have *too* much work to do.

I can *hear* the bird singing.
Maurice, you sit over *here*.

That is the only *course* they could take.
The jacket was made from *coarse* material.

Mark has a *red* scarf.
Have you *read* that book?

I *ate* all of my supper.
We have *eight* dollars to spend.

literature-centered reading

Fred Gwynne's *A King Who Rained* (Windmill, 1970) and *A Chocolate Moose for Dinner* (Windmill/Dutton, 1976) both have homonyms in their titles, as well as throughout their texts (Howell, 1987). Pettersen (1988) suggests letting the students look for homonyms in all of their reading materials. Students can construct lists of homonym pairs that mean something to them because they discovered the qualifying words for at least one word in each pair themselves. This paragraph is a good one to use as a starter for such an exercise, if readers want to try it for themselves. (Hint: *all-awl* is a good start.) Expanding Pettersen's activity to require the use of each homonym in a meaningful sentence is a way to keep the focus on meaning.

reading-writing connection

Activities

1. Have children play a card game to work on meanings of homonyms. Print homonyms on cards and let the children take turns drawing from each other, as in the game of Old Maid. A child who has a pair of homonyms can put them down if he or she gives a correct sentence using each word. The child who claims the most pairs wins.

2. Have students web homonyms in the following way:

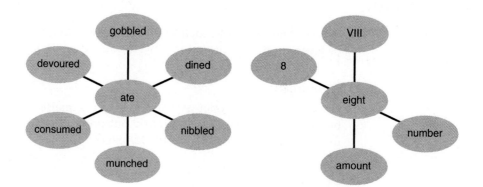

Homographs

Homographs are words that have identical spellings but not the same meanings. Their pronunciations may or may not be the same. Readers must use context clues to identify the correct pronunciations, parts of speech, and meanings of homographs. Examples include:

I will *read* my newspaper. (pronounced *rēd)*
I have *read* my newspaper. (pronounced *rĕd)*

I have a *contract* signed by the president. (noun: pronounced *con' trakt;* means a document)
I didn't know it would *contract* as it cooled. (verb: pronounced *cən/trakt';* means to reduce in size)

The books by Fred Gwynne mentioned in the section on homonyms are also rich sources of homographs.

Synonyms

Synonyms are words that have the same or very similar meanings. Work with synonyms can help expand children's vocabularies.

Study of the sports page of the newspaper for ways that writers express the ideas of *win* and *lose* can be a good way to introduce synonyms. The teacher should take this opportunity to show the students the different shadings of meaning that synonyms may have. For example, the headlines "Cats Maul Dogs" and "Cats Squeak By Dogs" both mean that the Cats beat the Dogs, but one indicates a win by a large margin, whereas the other indicates a close game. In addition, some synonyms are on varying levels of formality (for example, *dog* and *pooch*) (Breen, 1989).

literature-centered reading

Sylvester and the Magic Pebble by William Steig (Simon & Schuster, 1969) offers several good opportunities for discussion of synonyms used in describing the rain's cessation, the lion's movement, and the lion's feelings. In *Alexander and the Terrible, Horrible, No Good, Very Bad Day* by Judith Viorst (Atheneum, 1972), the synonyms are right there in the title, ready for discussion (Howell, 1987). Ideas for other activities follow.

Activities

1. Provide a stimulus word and have the students find as many synonyms as they can. Discuss the small differences in meaning of some words suggested as synonyms. For example, ask: "Would you rather be called *pretty* or *beautiful?* Why?"

2. Use an activity like the Model Activity on page 200 as a basis for discussion of synonyms.

Antonyms

Antonyms are two words that have opposite meanings. Their meanings are not merely different; they are balanced against each other on a particular feature. In the continuum *cold, cool, tepid, warm,* and *hot,* for example, *cold* is the opposite of *hot,* being as close to the extreme in a negative direction as *hot* is in a positive direction. Thus, *cold* and *hot* are antonyms. *Tepid* and *hot* are different, but not opposites. *Cool* and *warm* are also antonyms. Similarly, *buy* and *sell* are antonyms

**Model
Activities**

Synonyms

Have the students rewrite sentences like the ones shown here (preferably sentences drawn from books they are currently reading), substituting a synonym for each word in italics.

1. Gretchen had a *big* dog.

2. We *hurried* to the scene of the fire.

3. Will you *ask* him about the job?

4. I have *almost* enough money to buy the bicycle.

5. Curtis made an *error* on his paper.

6. Suzanne is a *fast* runner.

7. It was a *frightening* experience.

8. Marty was *sad* about leaving.

---

because one is the reverse of the other. But *buy* and *give* are not antonyms, because no exchange of money is involved in the giving. The words are different, but not opposite. Powell (1986) points out that the use of opposition (citing antonyms) in defining terms can help to set the extremities of a word's meaning and provide its shadings and nuances. Research has shown that synonym production is helped by antonym production, but the reverse has not been shown to be true. Therefore, work with antonyms may enhance success in synonym exercises.

literature-centered reading

Frog and Toad Are Friends by Arnold Lobel (Harper & Row, 1970) provides students with examples of antonyms to discuss in an interesting context (Howell, 1987). Teachers may wish to locate other trade books that could be used for meaningful exposures to antonyms.

New Words

literature-centered reading

reading-writing connection

New words are constantly being coined to meet the changing needs of society and are possible sources of difficulty. Have students search for such words in their reading and television viewing and then compile a dictionary of words so new that they are not yet in standard dictionaries. The class may have to discuss these words to derive an accurate definition for each one, considering all the contexts in which the students have heard or seen it (Koeller and Khan, 1981). These new words may have been formed from Latin and Greek word elements, from current slang, or by shortening or combining older words (Richek, 1988).

SELF-CHECK: OBJECTIVE 3   What are some special types of words that may cause comprehension problems for children? What types of problems may they cause? (See Self-Improvement Opportunity 3.)

Summary

Acquiring a meaning vocabulary involves developing labels for the schemata, or organized knowledge structures, that a person possesses. Because vocabulary is an important component of reading comprehension, direct instruction in vocabulary can enhance reading achievement. Although pinpointing the age at which children learn the precise meanings of words is difficult, children generally make more discriminating responses about word meanings as they grow older, and vocabulary generally grows with increasing age.

There are many ways to approach vocabulary instruction. The best techniques link new terms to the children's background knowledge, help them expand their word knowledge, actively involve them in learning, help them become independent in acquiring vocabulary, provide repetition of the words, and have them use the words meaningfully. Techniques that cause children to work harder to learn words tend to aid retention. Teachers may need to spend time on schema development before working with specific vocabulary terms.

Vocabulary development should be emphasized throughout the day, not just in reading and language classes; children can learn much vocabulary from the teacher's modeling vocabulary use. Context clues, structural analysis, categorization, analogies and word lines, semantic maps and word webs, semantic feature analysis, dictionary use, study of word origins and histories, study of figurative language, a number of student-centered learning techniques, word play, and computer techniques can be helpful in vocabulary instruction.

Some special types of words can cause comprehension problems for children. They include homonyms, homographs, synonyms, antonyms, and newly coined words.

Test Yourself   *True or False*

_____ 1. Context clues are of little help in determining the meanings of unfamiliar words, although they are useful for recognizing familiar ones.

_____ 2. Structural analysis can help in determining meanings of new words containing familiar prefixes, suffixes, and root words.

_____ 3. When looking up a word in the dictionary to determine its meaning, a child needs to read only the first definition listed.

_____ 4. Homonyms are words that have identical, or almost identical, meanings.

_____ 5. Antonyms are words that have opposite meanings.

_____ 6. Word play is one good approach to building vocabulary.

_____ 7. Children sometimes make overgeneralizations in dealing with word meanings.

_____ 8. The development of vocabulary is essentially a child's development of labels for his or her schemata.

_____ 9. Work with analogies bolsters word knowledge.

_____ 10. Semantic mapping involves systematically deleting words from a printed passage.

_____ 11. Instruction in vocabulary that helps students relate new terms to their background knowledge is helpful.

_____ 12. Active involvement in vocabulary activities has little effect on vocabulary learning.

_____ 13. Pantomiming word meanings is one technique to produce active involvement in word learning.

_____ 14. Children should have multiple exposures to words they are expected to learn.

_____ 15. Working hard to learn words results in better retention.

_____ 16. There is no one best way to teach words.

_____ 17. Both concrete and vicarious experiences can help to build concepts.

_____ 18. Vocabulary instruction should receive attention during content area classes.

_____ 19. "Think-aloud" strategies can help students see how to use context clues.

_____ 20. Although use of categorization activities is motivational, according to current research findings it is not an effective approach.

_____ 21. Semantic mapping can help students develop a concept of definition.

_____ 22. Semantic feature analysis is the same thing as structural analysis.

_____ 23. Semantic feature analysis can help students see the uniqueness of each word studied.

_____ 24. The study of word origins is called *etymology*.

_____ 25. Word banks can help students maintain a record of their increasing vocabularies.

_____ 26. At present no computer programs are available for vocabulary development.

_____ 27. A word-processing program can facilitate certain types of vocabulary instruction.

_____ 28. Children instinctively understand figures of speech; therefore, figurative language presents them with no special problems.

Self-Improvement Opportunities

1. Plan a dictionary exercise that requires children to locate the meaning of a word that fits the context surrounding that word.

2. In a chapter of a textbook for a content area such as science, social studies, math, language arts, or health, locate examples of difficult words whose meanings are made clear through context clues. Decide which kind of clue each example involves.

3. Construct a board game that requires the players to respond with synonyms and antonyms when they land on certain spaces or draw certain cards. Demonstrate the game with your classmates role-playing elementary students. Alternatively, use the game with children in an actual classroom setting.

4. Ask four six-year-olds, four seven-year-olds, four eight-year-olds, and four nine-year-olds the meanings of *ask* and *tell* and of *brother* and *boy*. Discuss your findings with your classmates. Were there differences in knowledge of precise meanings among the children? Was there a trend in these differences?

5. Plan a lesson designed to teach the concept of *justice* to a group of sixth graders.

6. Identify important vocabulary terms in a textbook chapter. Decide which terms could be defined, or partially defined, through structural analysis. Share your findings with your classmates.

7. Develop a semantic map based on a content area topic with a group of intermediate-grade children. After they have done a reading assignment on the topic, revise the map with them.

8. Locate some commercial computer software designed for some aspect of vocabulary development. Try out the program and evaluate it on the basis of pedagogical soundness, ease of use for teachers and students, and appropriateness for the age or ability level of students you are teaching (or are preparing to teach). Write an analysis of the program, and share your findings with your classmates.

9. Analyze the framework for use of context clues presented by Sinatra and Dowd (*Journal of Reading*, November 1991, pp. 224–229). Describe how it could be helpful for planning instruction in the use of context clues.

10. Collect examples of figurative language from a variety of sources, and use them to develop a lesson on interpreting figurative language.

Chapter 5

Key Vocabulary

Pay close attention to these terms when they appear in the chapter.

anticipation guide

cloze procedure

InQuest

knowledge-based processing

metacognition

reciprocal teaching

relative clause

schema (and schemata)

semantic webbing

story grammar

story mapping

text-based processing

Comprehension: Part 1

Setting Objectives

When you finish this chapter, you should be able to

1. Explain how schema theory relates to reading comprehension.
2. Explain how a reader's purpose and other aspects of the rest of the situation in which reading takes place affect comprehension.
3. Describe some characteristics of text that affect comprehension.
4. Discuss some prereading, during-reading, and postreading activities that can enhance comprehension.

Figure 5.1 *Chapter 5 Organization*

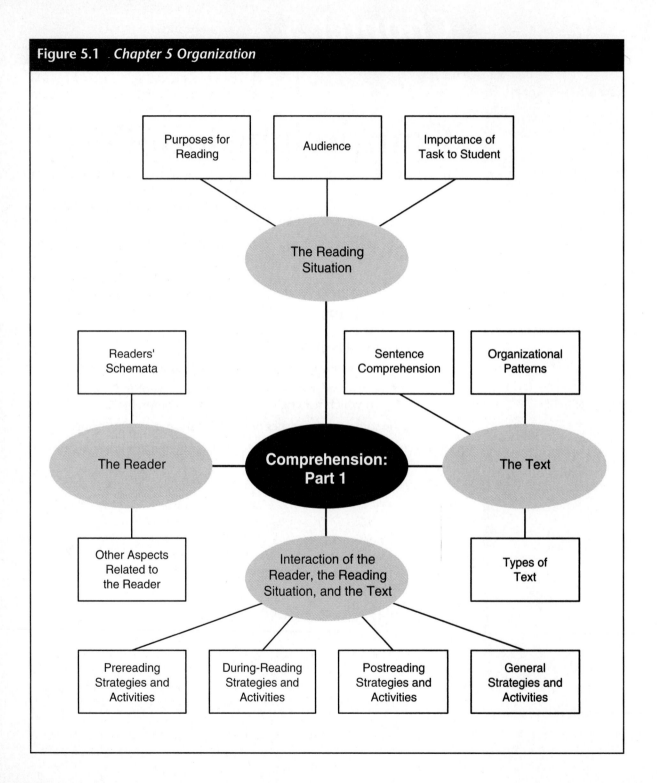

206

The objective of all readers is, or should be, comprehension of what they read. Shanklin and Rhodes (1989) see comprehension as an evolving process, often beginning before a book is opened, changing as the material is read, and continuing to change even after the book is completed. This developmental nature of comprehension is enhanced when the child interacts with others about aspects of the material after it has been read. Therefore, classroom interaction related to reading materials is important to comprehension development and should be planned carefully.

This chapter discusses the importance to comprehension of the interaction among the reader, the reading situation, and the text. It explores the importance of readers' schemata, readers' purposes for reading, audience for reading, and characteristics of the text to be read. It also presents strategies to be used before, during, and after reading.

As Pearson and Johnson (1978) point out, "reading comprehension is at once a unitary process and a set of discrete processes" (p. 227). We discuss the individual processes separately; yet teachers must not lose sight of the fact that there are many overlaps and interrelationships among the processes. Close relationships even exist between comprehension and decoding. Research has shown that good comprehenders are able to decode quickly and accurately (Eads, 1981; "A Talk with Marilyn Adams," 1991). Thus, developing decoding strategies to the automatic stage is important. Teachers should always keep in mind, however, that use of decoding strategies is merely a means of accessing the meaning of the written material. When good decoders have problems with comprehension, they need help in developing language proficiency and listening comprehension. This can be accomplished partly by increased reading at levels that currently yield good comprehension and partly by vocabulary and comprehension strategy instruction (Dymock, 1993).

Comprehension strategy instruction should make use of the students' own textbooks. The teacher should tell the students the strategy they are going to learn and how it will help them in their reading. Then the teacher should describe the strategy, model it, provide teacher-guided practice with it, and provide cooperative and independent practice opportunities (Roe, 1992).

This chapter is a logical continuation of Chapter 4, "Meaning Vocabulary," because vocabulary knowledge is a vital component of comprehension. Therefore, these chapters cannot truly be considered separately and are divided here only for convenience of presentation. Similarly, the coverage of the types of comprehension in Chapter 6 is a continuation of the topic that is separated for ease of treatment.

Example 5.1 shows the relationships among the ideas presented in this chapter and in Chapter 6. Readers approach a text with much background knowledge (many schemata) concerning their world, and they use this knowledge along with the text to construct the meanings represented by the printed material that meet their purposes for reading. To access the information supplied by the text, they must use word recognition strategies (covered in Chapter 3) and comprehension strategies (covered in Chapter 4, this chapter, and Chapter 6). They combine

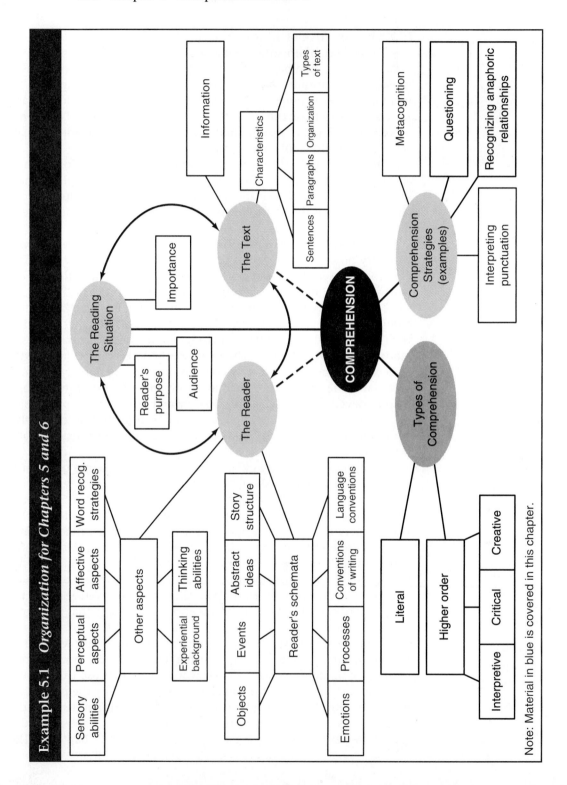

Example 5.1   *Organization for Chapters 5 and 6*

Note: Material in blue is covered in this chapter.

their existing knowledge with new information supplied by the text in order to achieve understanding of the material.

The Reader

This section discusses factors related to readers that affect their comprehension, including their schemata, sensory and perceptual abilities, thinking abilities, word recognition strategies, and affective aspects, such as attitudes, self-concepts, and interests.

Readers' Schemata

Educators have long believed that if a reader has not been exposed to a writer's language patterns or to the objects and concepts to which the writer refers, the reader's comprehension will at best be incomplete. This belief is supported by theories holding that reading comprehension involves relating textual information to preexisting knowledge structures, or *schemata* (Pearson et al., 1979). These schemata represent a person's organized clusters of concepts related to objects, places, actions, or events. Each schema a person has represents what the person knows about a particular concept and the interrelationships among the known pieces of information. For example, a schema for *car* may include a person's knowledge about the car's construction, its appearance, and its operation, as well as many other facts about it. Two people may have quite different schemata for the same basic concept; for example, a race-car driver's schema for *car* (or, to be more exact, his or her cluster of schemata about cars) will differ from that of a seven-year-old child.

Types of Schemata

People may have schemata for objects, events, abstract ideas, story structure, processes, emotions, roles, conventions of writing, and so forth. In fact, "schemata can represent knowledge at all levels—from ideologies and cultural truths . . . to knowledge about what patterns of excitations are associated with what letters of the alphabet" (Rumelhart, 1981, p. 13). Each schema a person has is incomplete, as though it contained empty slots that could be filled with information collected from new experiences. Reading of informational material is aided by the existing schemata and also fills in some of the empty slots in them (Durkin, 1981b).

Students need schemata of a variety of types to be successful readers. They must have concepts about the arrangement of print on a page, about the purpose of printed material (to convey ideas), and about the relationship of spoken language to written language. They need to be familiar with vocabulary and sentence patterns not generally found in oral language and with the different writing styles associated with various literary genres (Roney, 1984).

A *story schema* is a set of expectations about the internal structure of stories (Mandler and Johnson, 1977; Rand, 1984). Readers find well-structured stories easier to recall and summarize than unstructured passages. Possession of a story schema appears to have a positive effect on recall, and good readers seem to have a better grasp of text structure than poor readers. Having children retell stories is a good way to discover their grasp of a story schema (Rand, 1984).

literature-centered reading

Rand (1984) hypothesized that having many experiences with well-formed stories helps children develop a story schema. Storytelling and story reading appear to be excellent ways to develop children's schemata related to stories or other materials they will be expected to read. Hearing a variety of stories with standard structures helps children develop a story schema that allows them to anticipate or predict what will happen next. This ability enables children to become more involved in stories they read and better able to make and confirm or reject predictions—a process that fosters comprehension—effectively. The sentence structures in the stories told and read to children expose them to patterns they will encounter when they read literature on their own and will help make these patterns more understandable (Nessel, 1985; Pigg, 1986; Roe, 1985; Roe, 1986). Other ways to help develop children's story schemata include direct teaching of story structure and story grammars, covered later in this chapter in the section "Story Grammar Activities."

Perhaps the most important concept children need to have in their "reading schema" is the understanding that reading can be fun and can help them do things. They also need extensive background knowledge about the nature of the reading task and general background knowledge on the topics about which they are reading (Roney, 1984). Often children do not comprehend well because they know very little about their world (Cunningham, 1982b).

Research Findings about Schemata

Many research studies have supported schema theory. Anderson and colleagues, for example, discovered that recall and comprehension of passages with two possible interpretations (in one case, wrestling versus a prison break; in another, card playing versus a music rehearsal) were closely related to the readers' background knowledge and/or the testing environment (Pearson et al., 1979). Bransford and Johnson discovered that recall of obscure passages increased if a statement of the passage's topic or a picture related to the passage was provided.

Studies have shown that the provision of background information on a topic before reading is likely to enhance reading comprehension, especially inferential comprehension (Pearson et al., 1979; Stevens, 1982). These findings indicate that teachers should plan experiences that will give children background information to help them understand written material they are expected to read and to help them choose appropriate schemata to apply to the reading. When children have trouble using their experiential backgrounds to assist in reading comprehension, teachers need to find out whether the children lack the necessary schemata or whether they possess the needed schemata, but cannot use them effectively when

Story reading is an excellent way to develop children's schemata related to stories or other materials that they will be expected to read. (© *Bill Paxson/Courtesy of Des Moines Public Schools*)

reading (Jones, 1982). If the children lack the schemata, the teacher should plan direct and vicarious experiences to build them, such as examining and discussing pictures that reveal information about the subject, introducing new terminology related to the subject, and taking field trips or watching demonstrations. An obvious way to obtain background information about some topics is to read about them in other books (Crafton, 1982). Poor readers, in particular, frequently need more help with concept development than teachers provide. They need more discussion time before reading (Bristow, 1985). If children already know about the subject, letting them share their knowledge, preview the material to be read, and predict what might happen can encourage them to draw on their existing schemata (Jones, 1982).

Readers vary in the relative degrees to which they emphasize two processes of comprehension (Spiro, 1979). *Text-based processes* are those in which the reader is primarily trying to extract information from the text. *Knowledge-based processes* are those in which the reader primarily brings prior knowledge and experiences to bear on the interpretation of the material. For example, consider this text: "The children were gathered around a table on which sat a beautiful cake with *Happy Birthday* written on it. Mrs. Jones said, 'Now, Maria, make a wish and blow out the candles.'" Readers must use a text-based process to answer the question

literature-centered reading

"What was written on the cake?" because the information is directly stated in the material. They must use a knowledge-based process to answer the question "Whose birthday was it?" Prior experience will provide them with the answer, "Maria," because they have consistently seen candles blown out by the child who is celebrating the birthday at parties they have attended. Of course, before they use the knowledge-based process, they must use a text-based process to discover that Maria was told to blow out the candles.

Skilled readers may employ one type of process more than the other when the situation allows them to do this without affecting their comprehension. Less able readers may tend to rely too heavily on one type of processing in all situations, resulting in poorer comprehension. Unfortunately, some students have the idea that knowledge-based processing is not an appropriate reading activity, so they fail to use knowledge they have.

Rystrom presents a good argument that reading cannot be exclusively knowledge-based, or "top-down": if it were, two people reading the same material would rarely arrive at the same conclusions, and the probability that a person could learn anything from written material would be slight. Rystrom has an equally convincing argument that reading is not exclusively text-based, or "bottom-up": if it were, all people who read a written selection would agree about its meaning. It is far more likely that reading is interactive, involving both information supplied by the text and information brought to the text by the reader, which combine to produce a person's understanding of the material (Strange, 1980). (See Chapter 1 for a detailed discussion of this idea.) Example 5.2 illustrates this process.

If reading performance results from interaction between information in the text and information the reader possesses, anything that increases a reader's background knowledge may also enhance reading performance. In general, students at schools with broad curricular scopes have been found to score higher on inferential reading comprehension than students at schools with narrow curricular scopes (Singer, McNeil, and Furse, 1984). Increased exposure to social studies, science, art, music, mathematics, and other content areas should therefore enhance reading achievement.

Helping Students Use Their Schemata

Background knowledge that students possess needs to be activated through discussion or by other means, just as related concepts students do not possess need to be developed before reading begins. Children need to realize that what they already know can help them understand the topics discussed in their reading materials (Wilson, 1983). Some techniques that may be used for schema activation include the prediction strategies in a Directed Reading-Thinking Activity (described in Chapters 7 and 10), the preview step of the SQ3R study method (described in Chapter 9), and the purpose questions of the Directed Reading Activity (described in Chapter 7).

Another good way to help children learn to activate schemata is for the teacher to "think aloud" for the students, modeling the activation of schemata

Example 5.2 *Flow of Information During Reading*

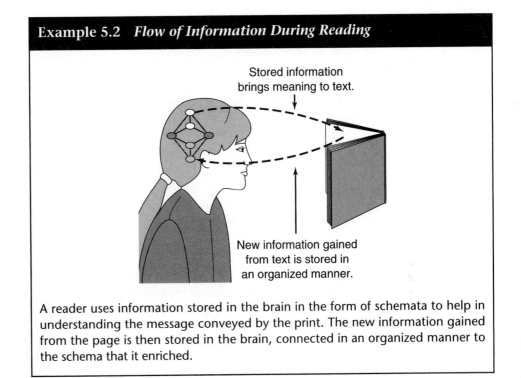

Stored information brings meaning to text.

New information gained from text is stored in an organized manner.

A reader uses information stored in the brain in the form of schemata to help in understanding the message conveyed by the print. The new information gained from the page is then stored in the brain, connected in an organized manner to the schema that it enriched.

for a passage while reading (Bristow, 1985). Knowledge about a topic cannot be activated, however, if no knowledge is possessed (Cunningham, 1982).

Teachers should make sure the material students are asked to read is not too difficult for them. When students read material that is too difficult, they cannot use their background knowledge to help them comprehend material they do not understand (Wilson, 1983). Difficult materials tend to work against students' use of meaning-seeking activities because they cause students to focus too much on decoding and not enough on comprehension.

Other Aspects Related to the Reader

The discussion in Chapter 1 of the many aspects of the reading process includes a number of aspects related to the reader that affect comprehension. Experiential background is the basis for readers' schemata, which were discussed in detail earlier. Other aspects of readers discussed in Chapter 1 under aspects of the reading process include their sensory and perceptual abilities, their thinking abilities, and affective aspects, such as self-concepts, attitudes, and interests. Readers' attitudes and interests affect motivation to read, and readers who are not motivated to read are not likely to give the reading task the degree of attention needed to result in high levels of comprehension. Facility with word recognition strategies also enhances comprehension because it releases the students' attention from the word recognition task and allows the students to apply it to the task of comprehension (Irwin, 1991).

SELF-CHECK: OBJECTIVE 1   What aspects of schema theory have direct application to the teaching of reading? (See Self-Improvement Opportunity 1.)

The Reading Situation

The reading situation includes purposes for the reading, both self-constructed and teacher-directed; the audience for the reading; and the importance the reading task has for the individual.

Purposes for Reading

All of the reading children do should be purposeful, because children who read with a purpose tend to *comprehend* what they read better than those who have no purpose. This result may occur because the children are attending to the material, rather than just calling words. For this reason teachers should set purposes for youngsters by providing them with pertinent objectives for the reading or by helping them set their own purposes by deciding on their own objectives. Objectives may include reading for enjoyment; to perfect oral reading performance or use of a particular strategy; to update knowledge about a topic, to link new information to that already known; to obtain information for an oral or written report; to confirm or reject predictions; to perform an experiment or apply information gained from the text in some other way; to learn about the structure of a text; or to answer specific questions (Blanton et al., 1990; Irwin, 1991).

Teacher-constructed purpose questions can help students focus on important information in the selection and should replace such assignments as "Read Chapter 7 for tomorrow." Providing specific purposes avoids presenting children with the insurmountable task of remembering everything they read and allows them to know that they are reading to determine main ideas, locate details, understand vocabulary terms, or meet some other well-defined goal. As a result, they can apply themselves to a specific, manageable task. However, if teachers always use the same types of purpose questions and do not guide children to set their own purposes, children may not develop the ability to read for a variety of purposes. Purpose-setting activities can help students activate their existing schemata about the topic of the material.

Cunningham and Wall (1994, p. 481) suggest always setting a purpose for student reading that is either "(a) a clear and precise statement of what the students are to focus on while they read or (b) a clear preview of the task they will be asked to perform after reading." This allows students to use the purpose to help them choose reading strategies. Cunningham and Wall suggest making purposes more specific for more difficult texts to guide the students to the important and challenging content.

Blanton and colleagues (1990) recommend setting a single purpose for reading, rather than multiple purposes, for maximum effectiveness. A single purpose may be especially effective for poor readers because it can help to avoid cognitive confusion from the overload of multiple purposes. The purpose should be one that is sustained throughout the entire selection, not met after reading only a small portion of the material; in other words, the purposes should be fairly broad in scope. Purposes should be formed carefully, because poor ones can actually misdirect the students' attention by focusing on information that is not essential to the passage and slighting important information. Purposes should help readers differentiate between relevant and irrelevant information.

When teachers set purposes for reading, they may then "think aloud" how the purpose was developed, thus modeling the purpose-setting procedure for later independent use by students. Even when teachers set purposes for students initially, responsibility for setting purposes should gradually shift from the teacher to the students. Students are capable of setting their own purposes, and they will be more committed to purposes they have set than to ones set by the teacher. Having students predict what will happen in a story or what information will be presented in an informational selection is a step in helping students set themselves the purpose of reading to find out if their predictions are accurate. Such purposes engage the students in the reading more than teacher-generated ones. The Directed Reading-Thinking Activity, described further in Chapters 7 and 10, encourages such personal purpose setting through predictions on the part of the students. Fielding and colleagues (1990) found that prediction questions were more effective than traditional basal reader questions if the predictions were compared with the actual text after reading (Pearson and Fielding, 1991). Therefore, teachers should be sure to follow up on predictions if this type of purpose is used.

Purposes should be discussed immediately after the reading is completed. Neglecting this procedure may cause students to ignore the purposes and merely try to pronounce all the words in the selection.

Basal reader manuals tend to offer a variety of types of purpose questions. However, teachers sometimes do not make use of these ready-made questions, or they may paraphrase them. Researchers have found that teachers' questions sometimes tend to be literal ones, focusing on trivial facts, and they are often poorly formed (Shake and Allington, 1985). If teachers are going to use self-constructed questions, they should give careful thought to the desired outcomes of the reading and the types of purpose questions most likely to lead to these outcomes.

Prereading questions should focus on predicting and relating text to prior knowledge. Students should be asked about the details that relate to problems, goals, attempts to solve problems, characters' reactions, resolutions, and themes (Pearson, 1985). (More about this type of questioning appears in the section "Story Grammar as a Basis for Questioning" in Chapter 6.)

Even when teachers do not provide purpose questions, children are often

guided in the way they approach their reading assignments by the types of questions that teachers have used in the past on tests, using this knowledge to set
their own purposes for reading. If a teacher tends to ask for factual recall of small
details in test questions, children will concentrate on such details and perhaps
overlook the main ideas entirely. In class discussion, the teacher may be bewil-
dered by the fact that the children know many things that happened in a story
without knowing what the basic theme was. Teachers need to be aware that their
testing procedures affect the purposes for which children read content material
in their classrooms.

SELF-CHECK: OBJECTIVE 2   What are some important considerations in setting purposes
for students' reading assignments?

Audience

The audience for the reading may consist of only the reader, reading alone for
personal or teacher-directed purposes. In this case, the reader is free to use his or
her available reading strategies as needed to meet the purposes. The degree to
which the reader has accepted the purposes as valid will affect his or her comprehension of the material.

Sometimes the audience for the reading is the teacher. Mosenthal (1979)
found that third- and sixth-grade students resolved contradictions in text differently when their audience was the teacher than when their audience was younger
children. Third graders restructured text more to reduce contradictions for the
younger children, whereas sixth graders restructured text more for the teacher.
(Mosenthal and Na, 1980b; Mosenthal, 1984). Better readers and poorer readers
may respond to the teacher as an audience differently because the teacher may
encourage more use of a variety of strategies by students in higher reading groups
than by those in lower ones. Teachers have been found to focus more on word
recognition concerns with lower groups and more on meaning with higher
groups (Irwin, 1991), a tendency that could be detrimental to the students in
lower groups. Anderson and colleagues (1983) found that a meaning focus was
more effective than a word recognition focus with both poor and good readers.

Sometimes the audience is other children. In school, a common audience is
the reading group. Some children may comprehend less well when reading to
perform in a reading group than when reading independently. They may even
react differently to different groups of children, for example, younger students as
opposed to students of their own age. Teachers should be aware of this possibility
and assess reading comprehension in a variety of settings.

Importance of Task to Student

The degree to which students embrace the purposes for reading the material will
affect the attention they give to the task and the perseverance with which they

attempt it. The risk factor will have an additional effect on the results of the reading. Mosenthal and Na (1980a) found that students performed differently on reading tasks in high-risk situations, such as tests, than in low-risk situations, such as normal classroom lessons. In high-risk situations, low-ability and average-ability students tended to reproduce the text, whereas high-ability students tended to reproduce and embellish it. In low-risk situations, the students tended to respond according to their typical verbal interaction patterns with the teacher (Mosenthal and Na, 1980b).

The Text

Reading a text involves dealing with its specific characteristics and deriving information from it using word recognition and comprehension strategies. Texts are made up of words, sentences, paragraphs, and whole selections. Since vocabulary is one of the most important factors affecting comprehension, Chapter 4 was devoted to vocabulary instruction. Sentence difficulty and organizational patterns are other text characteristics. Although some suggestions in this section focus on comprehension of sentences or paragraphs, comprehension is a unitary act, and eventually all the procedures discussed here must work together for the reader to achieve comprehension of the whole selection.

People who choose texts and supplementary material for children must be aware of the difficulty of the material they choose, especially when students will use it independently. The directions provided for students and the instructional language used in such materials should be of high quality. The language of the directions should be clearer than the language of the exercises (Spiegel, 1990).

Sentence Comprehension

Children may find complicated sentences difficult to understand, so they need to know ways to derive sentence meanings. Research has shown that systematic instruction in sentence comprehension increases reading comprehension. For example, Weaver had students arrange cut-up sentences in the correct order by finding the action word first and then asking *who, what, where,* and *why* questions (Durkin, 1978–1979). This activity may work especially well when the sentences are drawn from literature selections the teacher has shared with the students. Another approach is to have children discover the essential parts of sentences by writing them in telegram form, as illustrated in the Model Activity on page 218.

Teachers should help children learn that sentences can be stated in different ways without changing their meanings. For example, some sentence parts can be moved around without affecting the meaning of the sentence, as in these two sentences:

On a pole in front of the school, the flag was flying.

The flag was flying on a pole in front of the school.

literature-centered reading

reading-writing connection

Model Activities

Telegram Sentences

Write a sentence like this one on the chalkboard: "The angry dog chased me down the street." Tell the children that you want to tell what happened in the fewest words possible because, when you send a telegram, each word used costs money. Then think aloud about the sentence: "Who did something in this sentence? Oh, the dog did. My sentence needs to include the dog. . . . What action did he perform? He chased. I'll need that action word, too. 'Dog chased. . . .' That doesn't make a complete thought, though. I'll have to tell whom he chased. He chased me. Now I have a complete message that leaves out the extra details. My telegram is: 'Dog chased me.'"

Then let the students write a telegram based on some story they have read or heard. For example, have them write the telegram that Little Red Riding Hood might have sent to her mother after the woodcutter rescued her and her grandmother. This telegram might contain several pared-down sentences.

On the other hand, teachers should acknowledge that moving sentence parts *can* affect the meaning. For example, the following two sentences have distinctly different meanings:

> Carla helped Teresa.

> Teresa helped Carla.

Sentence Difficulty Factors

A number of types of sentences, including those with relative clauses, other complex sentences, those with missing words, those in the passive voice, and those expressing negation, have been found to be difficult for children to comprehend. Children understand material better when the syntax is like their oral language patterns, but the text in some primary-grade reading material is syntactically more complex than the students' oral language.

Relative clauses are among the syntactic patterns that do not appear regularly in young children's speech. Relative clauses either restrict the information in the main clause by adding information or simply add extra information. Both types may be troublesome. In the example "The man *who called my name* was my father," the relative clause indicates the specific man to designate as "my father." "My father, who is a doctor, visited me today" is another example of a sentence with a relative clause. (Kachuck, 1981).

Teachers should ask questions that assess children's understanding of particular syntactic patterns in the reading material and, when misunderstanding is evident, they should point out the clues that can help children discover the correct meanings (Kachuck, 1981). Teachers may find it necessary to read aloud sentences from assigned passages to children and explain the functions of the relative clauses found in the sentences. Then they may give other examples of sentences with relative clauses and ask the children to explain the meanings of these clauses. Feedback on correctness or incorrectness and further explanation should be given at this point. Finally, teachers should provide children with independent practice activities to help them set the new skill in memory.

Students who need more work with relative clauses can be asked to turn two-clause sentences into two sentences (Kachuck, 1981). Teachers can model this activity also, as in the earlier example: "The man called my name. The man was my father." Supervised student practice with feedback and independent practice can follow, using progressively more difficult sentences. Students can move from this activity into sentence combining, which we will examine next. Finally, they should apply their understanding in reading whole passages (Kachuck, 1981). Until they have used the skill in interpreting connected discourse, it is impossible to be sure they have mastered it.

Sentence combining involves giving students two or more short sentences and asking them to combine the information into a single sentence. Such activities bring out the important fact that there are always multiple ways of expressing an idea in English (Pearson and Camperell, 1981). See the following Model Activity.

Model Activities

Sentence Combining

Write on the board the sentences to be combined and then model possible combinations. The following sentences might be used:

Joe has a bicycle.
It is red.

Show several ways to combine the two sentences, including "Joe has a red bicycle," "Joe's bicycle is red," "Joe has a bicycle that is red," and "The bicycle that Joe has is red." Point out that all of these ways of stating the sentence combine the information from both single sentences. (The first construction is the one the children are most likely to produce, but they need to see the other possibilities so that they will not perceive the task as a closed one.)

Model several other examples for the children. Then divide them into small groups to try to complete several examples that you provide on the chalkboard. Let the group members share their combinations when all are finished. Finally, give the children some examples to do independently. Hold a whole-class discussion of the results, with students giving their reasoning for their combinations.

Discussion of a number of sentence combinations may bring out much about the children's syntactic knowledge. Wilkinson and Patty (1993) have found that students can learn to attend to elements of text related to connectives through sentence-combining practice, but not just through reading texts written by other students during sentence-combining practice activities.

Reading and writing specific sentence patterns is beneficial to students' literacy development. Reading patterned books not only helps the children read successfully because of their predictability, but also provides models for their writing efforts (Boyle and Peregoy, 1990).

Punctuation

Punctuation can greatly affect the meaning a sentence conveys; it represents pauses and pitch changes that would occur if the passage were read aloud. While punctuation marks represent the inflections in speech imperfectly, they greatly aid in turning written language into oral language.

Periods, question marks, and exclamation points all signal pauses between sentences and also alter the meaning:

He's a crook. (Making a statement)

He's a crook? (Asking a question)

He's a crook! (Showing surprise or dismay at the discovery)

Commas and dashes indicate pauses within sentences and are often used to set off explanatory material from the main body of the sentence. Commas are also used to separate items in a series or to separate main clauses joined by coordinate conjunctions.

To help students see how punctuation can affect the meaning of the material, use sentences such as the following:

Mother said, "Joe could do it."
Mother said, "Joe could do it?"
"Mother," said Joe, "could do it."

We had ice cream and cake.
We had ice, cream, and cake.
We had ice cream and cake?

Discuss the differences in meaning among the sentences in each set, highlighting the function of each punctuation mark.

Underlining and italics, which are frequently used to indicate that a word or group of words is to be stressed, are also clues to underlying meaning. Here are several stress patterns for a single sentence:

Pat ate one snail.
Pat *ate* one snail.
Pat ate *one* snail.
Pat ate one *snail.*

In the first pattern, the stress immediately indicates that Pat, and no one else, ate the snail. In the second variation, stressing the word *ate* shows that the act of eating the snail was of great importance. In the third variation, the writer indicates that only one snail was eaten. The last variation implies that eating a snail was unusual and that *snail* is more important than the other words in the sentence.

Teachers need to be sure that children are aware of the aids to comprehension that punctuation provides and that they practice interpreting punctuation marks. One possible practice activity follows:

literature-centered reading

> To spark interest in reading a class novel and make students more aware of mechanical elements such as quotation marks, periods, and commas, have students read the novel in parts (as in a play) with a narrator. (Carr, 1991)

SELF-CHECK: OBJECTIVE 3   Explain how children can discover essential parts of sentences by writing them in telegram form. Discuss the effect of punctuation marks on the meanings of sentences.

Organizational Patterns

The internal organization of paragraphs in informational material can have a variety of patterns (for example, listing, chronological order, comparison and contrast, and cause and effect). In addition, paragraphs of each of these types also generally have an underlying organization that consists of the main idea plus supporting details. Whole selections contain these same organizational patterns

---

Model Activities

Chronological Order Paragraphs

Write the following paragraph on the chalkboard:

> Jonah wanted to make a peanut butter sandwich. First, he gathered the necessary materials —peanut butter, bread, and knife. Then he took two slices of bread out of the package and opened the peanut butter jar. Next, he dipped the knife into the peanut butter, scooping up some. Then he spread the peanut butter on one of the slices of bread. Finally, he placed the other slice of bread on the peanut butter he had spread, and he had a sandwich.

Discuss the features of this paragraph, pointing out the functions of the sequence words, such as *first, then, next,* and *finally.* Make a list on the board, showing the sequence of events, numbering the events appropriately, or numbering them directly above their positions in the paragraph. Next, using another passage of the same type, preferably from a literature or content area selection that the students have already read, have them discover the sequence under your direction. Sequence words should also receive attention during this discussion. Then have the students detect sequence in other paragraphs from literature or content area selections that you have duplicated for independent practice. Discuss these independent practice paragraphs in class after the students have completed the exercises. Finally, alert students to watch for sequence as they do their daily reading.

**Model
Activities**

Cause-and-Effect Paragraphs

Write the following paragraph on the chalkboard:

> Jean lifted the box and started for the door. Because she could not see where her feet were landing, she tripped on her brother's fire truck.

Discuss the cause-and-effect relationship presented in this paragraph by saying: "The effect is the thing that happened, and the cause is the reason for the effect. The thing that happened in this paragraph was that Jean tripped on the fire truck. The cause was that she could not see where her feet were landing. The word *because* helps me to see that cause."

Then lead class discussions related to the cause-and-effect paragraph pattern by using other cause-and-effect paragraphs with different key words (such as *since* or *as a result of*) or with no key words at all. These examples should preferably be chosen from the children's classroom reading materials.

---

and others, notably a topical pattern such as the one used in this textbook. Students' comprehension of informational material can be increased if they learn these organizational patterns. The Model Activities in this section show two examples of teaching procedures for paragraph patterns. Similar exercises may be constructed with longer selections as well, preferably ones drawn from books available for the children to read.

literature-centered reading

SELF-CHECK: OBJECTIVE 3   How can teachers help children understand organizational patterns in written materials? (See Self-Improvement Opportunity 2.)

Types of Text

Narrative (storylike) selections generally consist of a series of narrative paragraphs that present the unfolding of a plot. They have a number of elements (setting, characters, theme, and so on) that have been described in story grammars (discussed later in this chapter). Although they are usually arranged in chronological order, paragraphs may be flashbacks, or narrations of events from an earlier time, to provide readers with the background information they need to understand the current situation.

Expository (explanatory) selections are composed of a variety of types of paragraphs, usually beginning with one or more introductory paragraphs and composed primarily of a series of topical paragraphs, with transition paragraphs to indicate shifts from one line of thought to another and illustrative paragraphs to provide examples to clarify the ideas. These selections generally conclude with summary paragraphs.

Teaching students to make use of paragraphs that have specific functions can be beneficial. For example, students can be alerted to the fact that *introductory paragraphs* inform the reader about the topics a selection will cover. These paragraphs usually occur at the beginnings of whole selections or at major subdivisions of lengthy readings.

If children are searching for a discussion of a particular topic, they can check the introductory paragraph(s) of a selection to determine whether or not they need to read the entire selection. (The introductory sections that open each chapter in this book are suitable for use in this manner.) Introductory paragraphs can also help readers establish a proper mental set for the material to follow; they may offer a framework for categorizing the facts readers will encounter in the selection.

Summary paragraphs occur at the ends of whole selections or major subdivisions and summarize what has gone before, stating the main points of the selection in a concise manner and omitting explanatory material and supporting details. They offer a tool for rapid review of the material. Students should be encouraged to use these paragraphs to check their memories for the important points in the selection.

To carry the reader through the author's presentation of an idea or a process, the topical paragraphs within an expository selection are logically arranged in one of the organizational patterns discussed earlier in this chapter. The writer's purpose will dictate the order in which he or she arranges the material—for example, chronologically or in a cause-and-effect arrangement. A history textbook may present the causes of the Civil War and lead the reader to see that the war was the effect of these causes. At times, a writer may use more than one form of organization in a single selection, such as combining chronological order and cause-and-effect organization in history materials.

One way to work on recognition of text patterns is to write examples of text patterns on index cards and give them to small, cooperative groups of students to sort into the patterns represented. Discussion of the reasons for the classifications

literature-centered reading takes place in a whole-class setting. Students move from this activity to locating the patterns in their content textbooks (Kuta, 1992).

Text patterns may be a particular problem for students with learning disabilities. Although these students may be mainstreamed in science and social studies classes, research indicates they may be much less sensitive to text structure than are students without learning disabilities. For them, instruction in text structure should progress from easiest to hardest to learn, starting with sequence, followed by enumeration, and building up to description and, finally, comparison/contrast (Schumm, 1992; Englert and Thomas, 1987).

Regardless of the approach, attention needs to be given to text structure. Pearson and Fielding (1991, p. 832) state, "It appears that any sort of systematic attention to clues that reveal how authors attempt to relate ideas to one another or any sort of systematic attempt to impose structure upon a text . . . facilitates comprehension as well as both short-term and long-term memory for the text."

Chapter 10 discusses various text patterns in more detail.

Interaction of the Reader, the Reading Situation, and the Text

Factors related to the reader, the reading situation, and the text all interact as the student reads in instructional settings. To encourage comprehension of whole selections, teachers usually incorporate prereading, during-reading, and postreading activities into lessons. Some techniques are more general and include activities for more than one of these lesson parts. Example 5.3 shows some techniques applicable to various parts of a lesson.

Prereading Strategies and Activities

Prereading activities are often intended to activate students' problem-solving behavior and their motivation to examine the material (Tierney and Cunningham, 1984). The making of predictions in the Directed Reading-Thinking Activity described in Chapter 7 is a good example of this type of activity. Use of purpose questions as described earlier in this chapter is another example. The following activities can also serve to activate schemata related to the subject or type of text to be read to enhance comprehension of the material, and they can actually be used to build background for topics covered by the reading material.

Previews

Story previews, which contain information related to story content, can benefit comprehension. Research has shown that having students read story previews designed partially to build background knowledge about the stories increases students' learning from the selections impressively and that story previews can help students make inferences when they read. The previews help children to activate their prior knowledge and to focus their attention before reading (Tierney and Cunningham, 1984).

Anticipation Guides

Anticipation guides can be useful prereading devices. Designed to stimulate thinking, they consist of declarative statements, some of which may not be true, related to the material about to be read. Before the children read the story, they respond to the statements according to their own experiences and discuss them (Wiesendanger, 1985). The value of anticipation guides can be extended into the postreading part of the lesson by repeating the process after reading, considering the input from the reading, resulting in a combination anticipation/reaction guide. (See the next Classroom Scenario for an example of an anticipation/reaction guide.) Following is an anticipation guide for the story *The Little Red Hen.*

literature-centered reading

Example 5.3   *Interaction of Reader, Reading Situation, and Text*

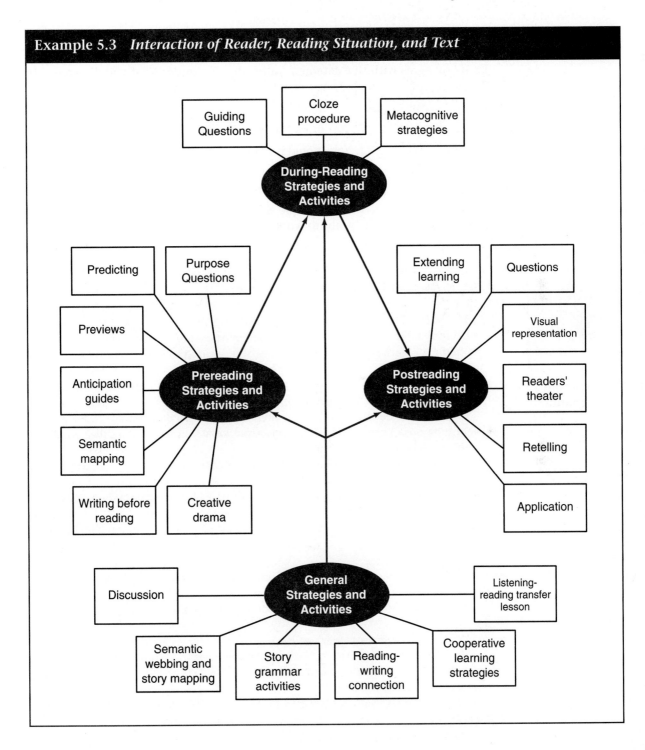

Anticipation Guide

Directions: Read each statement below and make a checkmark on the line under *Yes* if you agree with the statement or on the line under *No* if you disagree with the statement.

Yes   *No*

———————   ———————   1. You should have to work for your rewards.

———————   ———————   2. You should be generous to others with your possessions.

———————   ———————   3. It is important to cooperate to get work done in the fastest and easiest way.

———————   ———————   4. Some people should work to support others who do not want to work.

Classroom Scenario

Use of Anticipation/Reaction Guide

Ms. Bucholtz's sixth-grade class had been studying the many cultures that make up the United States culture. To introduce the Chinese culture to a group of children who had no Chinese-American classmates, she decided to have them read *Child of the Owl* by Laurence Yep, a book for which she had a classroom set. She had prepared an anticipation/reaction guide that was designed to help them banish stereotypes and see the commonalities among all people.

Ms. Bucholtz began the lesson by holding up the book. She said, "Look at the cover of the book I have just given to you. From what you see on the cover, what do you think the book will be about?"

Blake said, "Maybe it will be about a baby owl."

Krystal looked at him disdainfully and said, "Oh, don't be silly. The picture is of a Chinese girl and an owl necklace. She's in front of a Chinese store. I think it's about her getting that necklace."

Ms. Bucholtz looked at Krystal and said, "Your prediction is reasonable, but you shouldn't say someone else's is silly. We don't have enough information yet to know if live owls will be in the story."

"I'm sorry, Blake," Krystal said. "Sometimes the cover does fool you, and it almost looks like an owl is flying behind her."

"That looks like a ghost owl. It looks spooky," said DeRon. "Maybe this is a ghost story."

"Yep sounds Chinese," Marie said.

"It is," Pete replied. "This guy wrote *Dragonwings* too, and it was great. It was about Chinese who came to America. I guess this one will be too, but the main character will be a girl in this one."

"You'll have to read the book to see if your predictions are right," said Ms. Bucholtz, "but first I want you to turn over that paper I put on your desk."

The children turned over the following anticipation/reaction guide:

Anticipation/Reaction Guide

Directions: As you read *Child of the Owl* by Laurence Yep, you will find out some things about Chinese and Chinese-American people and some things about people in general. Before you read the book, write *Yes, No,* or *Sometimes* on the line under the word *Before* to show what you believe to be true at this time. After you read the book, write *Yes, No,* or *Sometimes* on the line under the word *After* to show what you believe then.

Before   *After*

_____   _____   1. Chinese-Americans can speak Chinese.

_____   _____   2. Chinese-Americans can write Chinese.

_____   _____   3. Chinese-Americans live in Chinatowns.

_____   _____   4. Chinese-Americans are very close to family members and take care of them when they need help.

_____   _____   5. Chinese-Americans live just like other Americans.

_____   _____   6. Chinese-Americans are wealthy.

_____   _____   7. All it takes to fit in in Chinatown is to look Chinese.

_____   _____   8. Chinese owls are supposed to be evil.

_____   _____   9. Chinese-Americans eat with chopsticks, instead of forks and knives.

_____   _____   10. People can hurt people whom they care about.

_____   _____   11. The way people look and act on the outside is the way they are inside.

_____   _____   12. Chinese-Americans have feelings that are like other Americans' feelings.

_____   _____   13. People make sacrifices for people whom they love.

_____   _____   14. Chinese-Americans have been treated fairly since they came to this country.

"Bryan, read the directions for us," Ms. Bucholtz requested.

Bryan read the directions.

Then Ms. Bucholtz said, "Please follow the directions and fill in the *Before* column now. Then break into your cooperative groups and discuss the reasons for your answers with your classmates. When all of you have discussed your answers, you may begin reading. A few minutes before the period ends today, I'll stop you and let you discuss your predictions with your group and set new ones if your old ones no longer seem likely. You'll be reading this book all week. We'll discuss and revise predictions every day and jot down our new predictions. When you finish reading, fill in the *After* column on your guide. You may want to look back in the book for evidence for your responses to share later. When your entire group is finished, discuss those responses with your classmates. Then we'll talk about the guide as a whole class. Happy reading!"

The children quickly read and completed the guide, but their small-group discussions were filled with uncertainty about the items that specified Chinese-Americans, since none of the children knew any. Statements such as the following were heard: "Of course, a person who looked Chinese would fit in in Chinatown. I'd stick out like a sore thumb, though." "The Chinese in that book I read weren't wealthy, but that was a long time ago." "Sure, they do; they always have chopsticks in Chinese restaurants." "They can speak Chinese, because we can speak American." They were quick to support the answers they had given for more general categories with statements such as the following: "Mr. Woolly looks mean, but he gives us candy when we are in his store." "But Mr. Lynn looks nice, and he is super." "Guess that means 'Sometimes,' right?" "Yeah, 'Sometimes.'" "My Mom bought me a boom box with her new dress money because she felt sorry for me." "My brother spent *all* of his paycheck to buy flowers for this girl he is crazy about, even though he couldn't go to the ballgame with his friends after he did it."

Predictions were quickly revised after the day's reading, and they continued to be revised every day.

On Friday, the children independently filled out the *After* column on the guide, some of them mumbling about how wrong they had been. Their discussions of the responses in their small groups were lively, with reading from the text to support many points. Some of the comments were as follows: "*Casey* couldn't even speak Chinese." "Her Uncle Phil and his family were wealthy, but her grandmother wasn't. So 'Sometimes.'" "Look at how different Gilbert was than he seemed to be." (This was followed by the reading of several example passages.) The whole-class discussion was rich, featuring comments such as the following: "People are a lot alike in how they feel, even if they look different on the outside." "I felt like she did when her grandmother was in the hospital when my Dad got hurt on the job." "Gilbert is like my cousin. He wants to act cool, too."

Ms. Bucholtz ended the focus on the book by inviting the children to read individually other books about the Chinese or Chinese-American culture for comparisons and contrasts with this book next week.

Analysis of Scenario

Ms. Bucholtz began the lessons by eliciting from the students predictions, based on the book cover, that activated the schemata they had for the story. Then she gave them an anticipation/reaction guide that elicited further predictions and led them to commit their predictions to paper. The small-group discussions of the predictions and adjustment of predictions throughout the week kept the students involved in the reading. Returning to the anticipation/reaction guide at the end caused them to revise predictions based on the reading. They were encouraged to be ready to defend their answers with evidence.

Semantic Mapping

Semantic mapping is a good prereading strategy because it introduces important vocabulary that students will encounter in the passage and activates their schemata related to the topic of the reading assignment. This makes it possible for them to connect new information in the assignment to their prior knowledge. The procedure may also motivate them to read the selection (Johnson et al., 1986). Semantic mapping is discussed in Chapter 4.

reading-writing connection

Writing Before Reading

Hamann and her colleagues (1991) found that having students write about relevant personal experiences before they read a selection resulted in more on-task behavior, more sophisticated responses to characters, and more positive reactions to the selections. This helped the students become more involved with their reading.

Creative Drama

literature-centered reading

Creative drama may be used *before* a story is read to enhance comprehension. The teacher may describe the situation developed in the story and let the children act out their own solutions. Then they can read the story to see how their solutions compared with the actual story. The teacher can take the parts of various characters to help move the drama along and to pose questions related to setting, characters, emotions, and critical analysis (Flynn and Carr, 1994).

During-Reading Strategies and Activities

Some strategies and activities can be used during reading to promote comprehension.

Metacognitive Strategies

Recently much attention has been given to students' use of metacognitive strategies during reading. Certainly, effective use of metacognitive techniques has a positive effect on comprehension. Since learning metacognitive strategies enhances study skills, this topic will be covered in detail in Chapter 9. Some information related to the use of metacognitive skills during reading as an aid to comprehension is included here to show the interrelationships of these two aspects of reading.

Metacognition refers to a person's knowledge of the intellectual functioning of his or her own mind and that person's conscious efforts to monitor or control this functioning. It involves analyzing the way thinking takes place. In reading tasks, the reader who displays metacognition selects skills and reading techniques that fit the particular reading task (Babbs and Moe, 1983).

Part of the metacognitive process is deciding what type of task is needed to achieve understanding. The reader needs to ask:

1. Is the answer I need stated directly? (If so, the reader looks for the author's exact words for an answer.)

2. Does the text imply the answer by giving strong clues that help determine it? (If so, the reader searches for clues related to the question and reasons about the information provided to determine an answer.)

3. Does the answer have to come from my own knowledge and ideas as they relate to the story? (If so, the reader relates what he or she knows and thinks about the topic to the information given and includes both sources of information in the reasoning process in order to come to a decision about an answer.)

(See Poindexter and Prescott [1986] for a specific application.)

Teacher modeling is a good way to teach metacognitive strategies. When modeling cognitive activities, teachers need to help students see their reasoning. It is not possible, however, to reduce the mental processes associated with strategic reading to a fixed set of steps, because "what an expert reader does when encountering an unknown affixed word in one text situation may differ from what is done when an unknown affixed word is met in another textual situation" (Duffy et al., 1988, p. 765). Poor readers often do not grasp the need for variation from situation to situation.

Teachers can help poor readers become more strategic through direct instruction in which they model reasoning processes for the students to help them understand how reading works. Teachers may then ask the students to explain how they made sense of material they have read, and they may provide additional help if the students' responses indicate the need (Herrmann, 1988). Teaching students to combine the two metacognitive strategies of self-questioning and prediction can result in better comprehension scores for middle school students reading below grade level than using only a self-questioning strategy or traditional vocabulary instruction. This may be because the combination strategy causes them to monitor the information more actively as they read to confirm predictions (Nolan, 1991).

Good readers monitor their comprehension constantly and take steps to correct situations when they fail to comprehend. They may reread passages or adjust their reading techniques or rates. Poor readers, on the other hand, often fail to monitor their understanding of the text. They make fewer spontaneous corrections in oral reading than good readers do and also correct miscues that affect meaning less frequently than do good readers. They seem to regard reading as a decoding process, whereas good readers see it as a comprehension-seeking process (Bristow, 1985).

Studies have shown that gifted students tend to be more efficient in the use of strategies, learn new strategies more easily, are more apt to transfer them to new situations, and are better at discussing their understanding of their cognitive processes than average students. There are indications that gifted students, like other students, can benefit from metacognitive instruction (Borkowski and Kurtz, 1987; Cheng, 1993).

Baumann and his colleagues (1993) advocate using *think-alouds* to enhance children's comprehension monitoring: "Think alouds involve the overt, verbal expression of the normally covert mental processes readers engage in when constructing meaning from texts" (p. 185). Baumann and colleagues used think-alouds to model for the students the asking of questions about the material, accessing prior knowledge about the topic, asking if the selection is making sense, making predictions and verifying them, making inferences, retelling what they have already read, and rereading or reading further to clear up confusion. They had the students use think-alouds as they applied the strategies to their reading. At times, the students were divided into small groups or pairs to apply the think-alouds, and this collaborative activity appeared to be especially helpful. Interest was built by comparing the students as readers to reporters: they interview writers as they read, just as reporters interview people. The instructional format used was to tell the students *what* the strategy was, *why* it was important and helpful for them to know, *how* it functions, and *when* it should be used (Baumann and Schmitt, 1986).

**Focus on
Strategies**

Think-Aloud Session

Mr. Barr's fourth-grade class was beginning a unit on elderly people. He had assembled a number of books featuring elderly characters for the unit study. The books covered a wide range of reading levels, and some presented complex or unfamiliar concepts. Mr. Barr wanted to encourage students to use their metacognitive skills as they read from this collection of books. He decided to use one book, *The Hundred Penny Box* by Sharon Bell Mathis, for which he had a class set, to model his own metacognitive processes when reading texts.

First he read the title, author's name, and illustrators' names from the book cover. "I'll bet this will be a good book," he said. "I've read other books by this author, and they were good books. These illustrators are always good too. I loved their illustrations in *Why Mosquitoes Buzz in People's Ears*. Let's see what this book is likely to be about. The picture shows a little boy looking into a box and either getting a penny out or putting one in, while an elderly woman sits in a chair in the background. That box must be the one mentioned in the title. I guess it has a hundred pennies in it. I wonder if they belong to the boy or to the woman, and I wonder if the woman is his grandmother. Maybe she has saved the pennies for him. I'll have to read to find out."

Opening the book to the first page of text, Mr. Barr remarked about the facing page, "I liked the picture on the front better than this one. This one looks a little depressing. I wonder if the book is going to be sad."

Then Mr. Barr read the first paragraph of the text aloud and said, "If Michael is sitting on the bed 'that used to be his' in the room with his great-great-aunt, he probably had to let her have his room. She must have moved in with his family. I wonder how he felt about giving up his bed? . . . Great-great-aunt. . . . A great-aunt is the sister of a grandparent, so a great-great-aunt must be the sister of a great-grandparent. Aunt Dew must be pretty old."

Mr. Barr read the next paragraph and said, "I guess the hundred penny box is Aunt Dew's, and she lets Michael play with it sometimes. . . . Sometimes she would forget who Michael was. I had an elderly uncle who forgot who we were sometimes. He called me by my daddy's name. . . . I wonder what the song has to do with forgetting."

After he read the third and fourth paragraphs, he said, "She called him by his daddy's name too. I think it irritated Michael's mother."

Mr. Barr continued to model his thinking for the children for several more pages. Then he said, "So far it seems that Michael's mother is frustrated with trying to take care of Aunt Dew, but Michael likes to get her to play with him with the box. I think that there is going to be trouble between Michael's mother and Aunt Dew, and I think it will have something to do with that box. I'll have to read on if I want to find out."

Then Mr. Barr asked for a volunteer to read and think aloud about the next part. After reading the second paragraph on page 14, Susan said in alarm, "Is Michael stealing the box? He didn't seem like he would steal from his aunt. I don't think that's it. I'll read on to see."

Several paragraphs later, Susan exclaimed, "Oh, no! His mother is going to burn the box!"

After the next paragraph, Susan said, "But Michael won't let her have it. Is he protecting it from her, or does he want it for himself? I think he's protecting it."

After the next paragraph, Susan said with more assurance, "He *is* protecting it. But I can't believe his mother burned someone else's things up. He's been helping Aunt Dew hide some of her other stuff. Maybe he was going to hide the box. But, if he was, why did he go in the kitchen with it? I'm confused. I'll have to read more."

Mr. Barr stopped her there. He asked her to make a prediction about what would happen next, and she replied, "I think he will run away with the box and save it."

Then Mr. Barr told the class to break up into pre-established groups of four and complete reading the book aloud, taking turns reading and thinking aloud about it as they read. At the end of each person's turn (about two pages each time), that person would summarize the situation and make a prediction about what would happen next.

Impatient to read on, the children quickly formed their groups and began to read. The book was short enough to be completed that day.

The next day the children were reminded of the questioning, predicting, connecting to prior knowledge, and summarizing that they had done in the think-alouds the day before. Mr. Barr encouraged them to continue to do these things silently as they read their individually chosen selections for that day.

Englot-Mash (1991) helps students learn to tie strategies together in a usable manner by presenting them with the flow chart in Example 5.4.

This chart helps the students to think about their fix-up strategies in a concrete way.

Palincsar and Brown (1986) suggest *reciprocal teaching* as a means to promote comprehension and comprehension monitoring. In this technique, the teacher and the students take turns being the "teacher." The "teacher" leads the discussion of material the students are reading. The participants have four common goals: "predicting, question generating, summarizing, and clarifying" (p. 772).

1. Predictions made by the students provide them with a purpose for reading: to test their predictions. Text features such as headings and subheadings help students form predictions.

2. Generating questions provides a basis for self-testing and interaction with others in the group.

3. Summarizing, which can be a joint effort, helps students to integrate the information presented.

4. Clarifying calls attention to reasons the material may be hard to understand. Students are encouraged to reread or ask for help when their need for clarification becomes obvious.

When using reciprocal teaching, the teacher must explain to the students each component strategy and the reason for it. Instruction in each strategy is important. At first, the teacher leads the discussion, modeling the strategies for the children. The children add their predictions, clarifications, and comments on the teacher's summaries and respond to the teacher's questions. Gradually the responsibility for the process is transferred from the teacher to the students. The teacher participates, but the students take on the "teacher" role, too. The interactive aspect of this procedure is very important. Rosenshine and Meister (1994) reviewed research on reciprocal teaching and concluded that such instruction should be incorporated into ongoing practice.

Reciprocal teaching can help poor readers understand how to study and learn from text strategically. The teacher performs each activity on a section of text. Then a student tries to perform the task as the teacher monitors the process. The teacher modifies the task to simplify it if the student has trouble (Herrmann, 1988). This modification of the task is particularly important for poor readers.

Richards and Gipe (1992) describe another very active during-reading strategy. They suggest asking students to consider after each paragraph an idea they know about, appreciate, or understand and an idea they dislike, dispute, or don't understand. They must also give reasons for these reactions. They may share their responses with other students as they go or record them to share after the entire selection has been read. For each paragraph, students may also indicate a connection with their own experiences by telling what the paragraph reminds them of. All of these activities help students connect their knowledge to the text and expand comprehension.

Example 5.4 *Strategy Use*

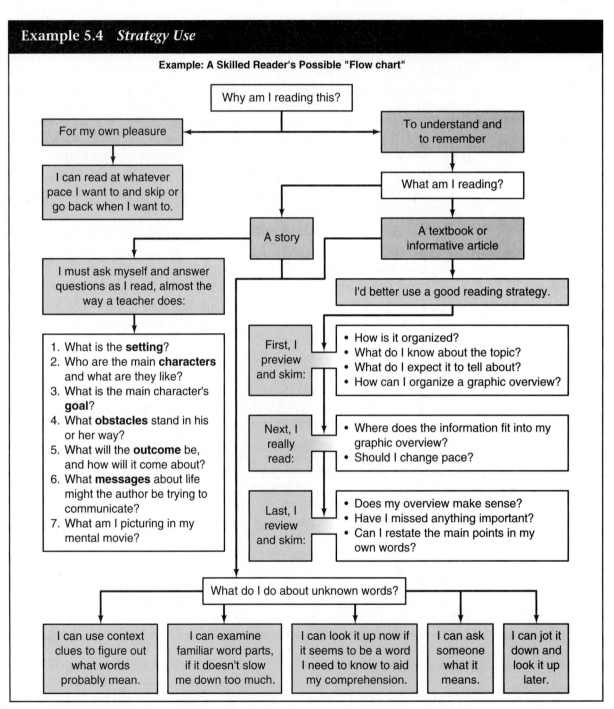

Example: A Skilled Reader's Possible "Flow chart"

Why am I reading this?

For my own pleasure

To understand and to remember

I can read at whatever pace I want to and skip or go back when I want to.

What am I reading?

A story

A textbook or informative article

I must ask myself and answer questions as I read, almost the way a teacher does:

I'd better use a good reading strategy.

1. What is the **setting**?
2. Who are the main **characters** and what are they like?
3. What is the main character's **goal**?
4. What **obstacles** stand in his or her way?
5. What will the **outcome** be, and how will it come about?
6. What **messages** about life might the author be trying to communicate?
7. What am I picturing in my mental movie?

First, I preview and skim:

- How is it organized?
- What do I know about the topic?
- What do I expect it to tell about?
- How can I organize a graphic overview?

Next, I really read:

- Where does the information fit into my graphic overview?
- Should I change pace?

Last, I review and skim:

- Does my overview make sense?
- Have I missed anything important?
- Can I restate the main points in my own words?

What do I do about unknown words?

| I can use context clues to figure out what words probably mean. | I can examine familiar word parts, if it doesn't slow me down too much. | I can look it up now if it seems to be a word I need to know to aid my comprehension. | I can ask someone what it means. | I can jot it down and look it up later. |

Source: Christine Englot-Mash. "Tying Together Reading Strategies," *Journal of Reading,* 35 (October 1991), 151. Reprinted with permission of the International Reading Association.

The following Classroom Scenario shows how one child used her metacognitive skills.

**Classroom
Scenario**

Metacognition

As Ina Maxwell works at her desk one January morning, a student comes by to share a discovery about her reading. The girl is currently reading *Dark Hour of Noon*.

"*Dark Hour of Noon* reminds me of *Number the Stars*, that book we read last fall," she says. "In *Number the Stars,* the Nazis came and told the Jews to move to camps. They took butter and other foods. The Nazis were killing Jews. Adolf Hitler was in charge of the Germans."

Analysis of Scenario
Ms. Maxwell encourages her students to make connections with life experiences and previous reading material as they read. Her encouragement and openness to students' comments lead students to share these connections with her, even when they are unsolicited.

Guiding Questions

During reading, guiding questions are often used to enhance comprehension. Research indicates that questions posed by the teacher when students are reading seem to facilitate comprehension (Tierney and Cunningham, 1984). Some authorities have suggested that extensive use of self-questioning while reading also will facilitate comprehension. Teaching students to turn each factual statement they need to remember into a *why* question that they attempt to answer enhances their learning of the factual information. (For example: "Why did Davy Crockett leave Tennessee to fight at the Alamo?") Better answers to the *why* questions result in better memory for the facts (Menke and Pressley, 1994).

Wong (1985) concluded that it is the cognitive processes activated by self-questioning, such as making inferences and attending to narrative structure, rather than the questioning itself, that are important to comprehension. Yopp (1988) believes that the fact that self-questioning requires active involvement is an important aspect of its effect on comprehension. Questioning techniques are covered in detail in Chapter 6.

Shoop (1986) describes the Investigative Questioning Procedure (*InQuest*), a comprehension strategy that encourages reader interaction with text. In this technique, which combines student questioning with creative drama, the teacher stops the reading at a critical point in the story. One student takes the role of a major character, and other students take the roles of investigative reporters "on the scene." The reporters ask the character interpretive and evaluative questions about story events. More than one character may be interviewed to delve into different viewpoints. Then the children resume reading, although the teacher may interrupt their reading several more times for other "news conferences." When first introducing the procedure, the teacher may occasionally participate as a story character or a reporter, in order to model the processes involved. The class should evaluate the process when the entire story has been covered.

InQuest lets students monitor comprehension. They actively keep up with "what is known." Before this procedure can be effective, however, students must have had some training in generating questions. One means to accomplish this training is to give students opportunities to view and evaluate actual questioning sessions on news shows. They need to learn to ask questions that produce information, evaluations, and predictions and they need to ask a variety of types of questions and to use *why* questions judiciously to elicit in-depth responses.

Cloze Procedure

The *cloze procedure* is sometimes used as a strategy for teaching comprehension. In using the cloze procedure, the teacher deletes some information from a passage and asks students to fill it in as they read, drawing on their knowledge of syntax, semantics, and graphic clues. Cloze tasks can involve deletions of letters, word parts, whole words, phrases, clauses, or whole sentences. In macrocloze activities, entire story parts are deleted. The deletions are generally made for specific purposes to focus on particular skills. When a whole word is deleted and a standard-sized blank is left, the readers must use semantic and syntactic clues to decide on a replacement. If the blanks vary in length according to word length, word recognition skill also can be incorporated. If a short underline is provided for each letter, additional clues become available, and the task of exact replacement becomes easier. However, the discussion of alternatives when standard-sized blanks are used can be extremely beneficial in developing comprehension skills.

Although either random or regularly spaced deletions can lead students to make predictions and confirm predictions based on their language knowledge, such systems of deletion will not focus on a particular skill. Discussion of alternative answers is very important with any deletion pattern used in cloze instruction, but some cloze tasks provide more varied possibilities than do others (Schoenfeld, 1980; Valmont, 1983). Teachers should always elicit reasons for particular choices and give positive reinforcement for good reasoning.

In preparing a cloze passage designed for teaching, rather than testing, teachers should leave the initial and final sentences of the selection intact and delete no more than 10 percent of the words. They can choose passages of any length. Cloze lessons can focus on any specific comprehension skill, such as relating pronouns to their referents, but they should be used only after the teacher has given instruction concerning the skill (Schoenfeld, 1980).

When multiple-choice answers are provided for completing passages, the task is not a true cloze procedure, but is referred to as a *maze* procedure. Maze techniques are probably less effective in encouraging learners to use their linguistic resources (Valmont, 1983). However, they may simplify the task for readers who need scaffolding and may prepare students for participating in cloze activities.

Postreading Strategies and Activities

Postreading strategies help students integrate new information into existing schemata. They also allow students to elaborate upon the learning that has taken place.

Extending Learning

In postreading activities, children should be given an opportunity to decide what further information they would like to have about the topic and where they can find out more (Crafton, 1982). They may read about the topic and share their findings with the class.

Questions

Whereas prereading questions may focus children's learning more than postreading questions do, research indicates that postreading questions may facilitate learning for all information in the text. There appears to be an advantage to using higher-level, application-type, and structurally important questions. Children obtain greater gains from postreading questions if feedback on answers is provided, especially feedback on incorrect answers (Tierney and Cunningham, 1984).

Visual Representation

After reading, students may be asked to sketch or paint what they learned from the text or what it made them think about and then share their sketches with a group, explaining how the sketches relate to the text. The sharing can extend the comprehension of all participants (Shanklin, 1989).

reading-writing connection   Readers' Theater

Readers' theater is another way to enhance comprehension of text. In this approach, after the students read a story, it is transformed into a readers' theater script. The students then take specific parts and practice reading the script together. Finally, they read the script for an audience (Shanklin, 1989).

Retelling

Talking about reading material has been shown to have a positive effect on reading comprehension. Therefore, an appropriate comprehension enhancement technique is *retelling* of the important aspects of the material read. To retell a story or selection, the reader must organize the material for the presentation. Students are generally paired with partners for this activity. After silent reading of a section from the text, one child retells what has been read, while the other listens. Tellers and listeners alternate. This technique has been used with fourth graders, resulting in better comprehension than did producing illustrations or answering questions about the text.

Teachers should introduce the retelling technique by explaining that it will help the children become better storytellers, in the case of presentation of narrative retellings, and help them see how well they understand the reading selections. They should model a good retelling for the students, provide guided practice, and then allow independent practice. Prereading and postreading discussions of the story frequently help students improve the retelling. The teacher may wish to tape retellings and play them back to allow students to identify their strengths and weaknesses. Short, well-constructed materials should be chosen when the procedure is first used (Koskinen et al., 1988; Morrow, 1989).

Children can retell stories for teachers, classmates, or younger children in the school, or they can retell stories into a tape recorder. Story retellings can be done unaided or with the assistance of the pictures in the book. Retellings can also be done with flannel boards, with props (for example, stuffed animals), as chalk talks, or as sound stories in which sound effects are added to the telling of the story. These retellings make children more familiar with the use of "book language" (Morrow, 1989).

Application

A good postreading activity for use with content area selections that explain how to do something (for example, how to work a certain type of math problem or how to perform a science experiment) is to have the students perform the task, applying the information that was read. Postreading activities that are often appropriate for social studies reading are constructing time lines of events included in the reading selection and constructing maps of areas discussed. Many of the activities described in the section "Creative Reading" in Chapter 6 are good postreading activities that ask the students to go beyond the material just read and create something new based on the reading.

General Strategies and Activities

Some types of strategies are useful throughout the reading process. Several of these are discussed next.

Discussion

Goldenberg (1992/1993) advocates what he calls "instructional conversations." Basically these are highly interactive discussions among the teacher and the students. Students focus on a topic chosen by the teacher and are gently guided by the teacher's questions and probing for elaboration and for text support for their positions, but they are not dominated by the teacher. Students are encouraged to use their background knowledge to contribute to the discussion, and, in some cases, the teacher provides needed background information that the students do not have. Sometimes the teacher offers direct teaching of a needed skill or concept.

The discussions generally center on questions for which a number of correct answers may exist. The teacher encourages participation from the students, but does not determine the order of speaking. Ideas are built on previously shared ones, and the teacher is responsive to students' contributions. Students are provided with a positive climate for attempting to construct meaning.

reading-writing connection

Recording points that students make on the board, in a list or on a semantic map, can be helpful. Having students write about the topic after the discussion can show what they have learned.

literature-centered reading

Another way to foster student discussion is through use of informational storybooks, which present facts through fictional situations. These books were found to enhance discussion more than books that were all fiction or all factual (Leal, 1993). The children discussed these books more, made more predictions about them, and connected more outside information to them.

Semantic Webbing and Story Mapping

Semantic webbing is a way of organizing terms into categories and showing their relationships through visual displays that can help students integrate concepts. Each web consists of a core question, strands, strand supports, and strand ties. The teacher chooses a core question, which becomes the center of the web, to which the entire web is related. The students' answers are web strands; facts and inferences taken from the story and students' experiences are the strand supports; and the relationships of the strands to one another are strand ties (Freedman and Reynolds, 1980).

Example 5.5 shows a semantic web based on *Prince Caspian* by C. S. Lewis. This web was developed by Winter Howard, a sixth grader. Before constructing webs like this one, the children in Winter's class read a portion of the book to a point where the hero found himself in a difficult situation. At this point the teacher, Natalie Knox, asked the children to predict what would happen next. The core question ("What will the Old Narnians do with or to Prince Caspian?") focuses on this prediction. Students answered the question individually, and their answers became web strands (for example, "Nikabrik will try to kill Caspian"). Support for strands was drawn from the story and from students' experiences. Then the strands were related through strand ties (shown with broken lines in the example). The webs were then used as a basis for reading the end of the story to see what really happened.

literature-centered reading

Instruction in story structure can benefit reading comprehension, since mental representations of story structures can aid comprehension (Fitzgerald, 1989; Gordon and Pearson, 1983; Davis and McPherson, 1989). A *story map* is "a graphic representation of all or part of the elements of a story and the relationships between them" (Davis and McPherson, 1989, p. 232). In addition to representing plots, settings, characterizations, and themes of stories visually, these maps (sometimes called *literature webs*) can emphasize the authors' writing patterns in predictable books. They "provide an instructional scaffolding for prediction, discussion, and language extension activities using children's trade books" (Reutzel and Fawson, 1989, p. 208).

Example 5.5   *Semantic Web*

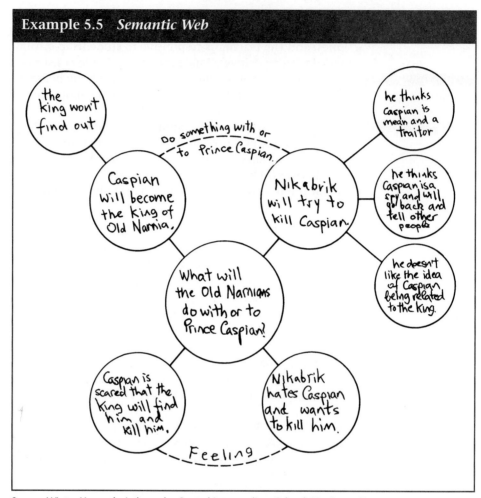

Source: Winter Howard, sixth grade, Central Intermediate School, Harriman, Tennessee.

Some webs are based on plot structure or story grammar, but some are more like structured overviews. One way to construct story maps is to put the theme in the center and arrange main events or settings sequentially in a second level of circles. Circles with characters, events, and actions may be connected to these second-level circles, and each may have additional circles attached to them, arranged in a clockwise order. Teaching readers to fill in story structure components on story maps while reading is beneficial to the students' comprehension (Davis and McPherson, 1989). Primary-grade students can learn about basic story elements from story mapping, first with pictures and later with written phrases (Felber, 1989; Munson, 1989). Example 5.6 shows an example of mapping of just the characters in a story by a first grader.

Story maps resemble semantic maps or webs. They help readers perceive the

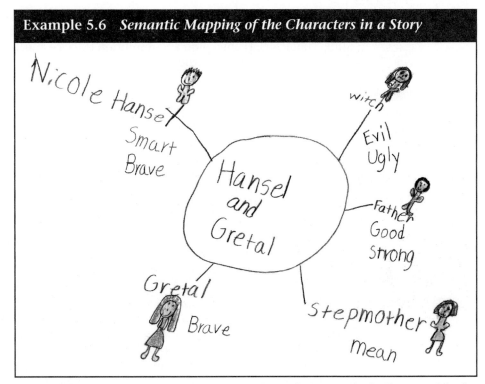

Example 5.6 *Semantic Mapping of the Characters in a Story*

Source: Tiffany Nicole Reagan, Bethany Vincent Frady's first grade, Mary V. Wheeler Elementary School, Pikeville, Tennessee.

way their reading material is organized. They can be used as advance organizers for a story that is about to be read or as a means to focus postreading discussion. When the story map is used as an advance organizer, the students may try to predict the contents of the story from it and then read to confirm or reject their predictions. Students may also refer to the map as reading progresses to help them keep their thoughts organized. After reading, the students can try to reconstruct the map from memory or can simply discuss it and its relationship to the story events. Using maps can help improve comprehension of both narrative and expository text (Reutzel, 1985).

Story Grammar Activities

reading-writing connection

literature-centered reading

A *story schema* is a person's mental representation of story structures and the way they are related. Knowledge of such structures appears to facilitate both comprehension and recall of stories. Children's written stories can serve as a source for understanding their concepts of story, and their retellings of stories also reveal story knowledge (Golden, 1984).

A *story grammar* provides rules that define these story structures. Jean Mandler and Nancy Johnson developed a story grammar that includes six major structures: setting, beginning, reaction, attempt, outcome, and ending (Whaley, 1981). In a simplified version of Perry Thorndyke's story grammar, the structures are setting, characters, theme, plot, and resolution (McGee and Tompkins, 1981). Teachers may be able to help students develop a concept of story by using these or other story grammars.

literature-centered reading

Teachers can use many activities to develop the concept of story. For instance, they can read stories and talk about the structure in terms children understand (folktales and fairy tales make good choices because they have easily identifiable parts), or they can have children retell stories. Reading or listening to stories and predicting what comes next is a good activity, as is discussion of the predicted parts. Teachers may give students stories in which whole sections are left out, indicated by blank lines in place of the material (macrocloze activity), and ask students to supply the missing material and then discuss the appropriateness of their answers. By dividing a story into different categories and scrambling the parts, teachers can give students the opportunity to rearrange the parts to form a good story. Or they can give the children all of the sentences in the story on strips of paper and ask them to put together the ones that fit together (Whaley, 1981).

reading-writing connection

reading-writing connection

An enjoyable activity for working on the concept of story has each student start by writing a setting for a story. Then each paper is passed to a classmate, who adds a beginning and passes the paper to another classmate. Reactions, attempts, outcomes, and endings, respectively, are added as the papers are passed to each successive student. When the stories are complete, they are read aloud to the class (Spiegel and Fitzgerald, 1986).

Fowler (1982) suggests the use of *story frames* to provide a structure for organizing a reader's understandings about the material. Frames are sequences of blanks linked by transition words that reflect a line of thought. Frames like the ones in Example 5.7 can be used with a variety of selections.

The frames can be the basis for the postreading class discussion of a story. Because the frames are open ended, the discussion will include much varied input. The teacher should stress that the information used in subsequent blanks should relate logically to the material that came before it. Students may use frames independently after the process has been modeled and practiced in class, and the class may also discuss the results. This technique is especially useful with primary-grade students and remedial reading students (Fowler, 1982).

Teaching story parts to less able fourth graders and clarifying temporal and causal relationships among the parts aided both literal and inferential comprehension of stories (Spiegel and Fitzgerald, 1986). Similarly, instruction in story parts and causal relationships among them resulted in improved story comprehension for students with learning disabilities (Varnhagen and Goldman, 1986).

reading-writing connection

In both cases instruction involved production of story elements, an example of positive use of the reading-writing connection.

literature-centered reading

Norton (1992) suggests acting out stories through creative drama, drawing plot diagrams, identifying the plot structures of wordless books, and writing stories based on wordless books as ways to work with younger students' understanding of plot structures. Acting out nursery rhymes that have logical sequences (for

reading-writing connection

Example 5.7 *Story Frames*

Figure 1
Story summary with one character included

Our story is about _____. _____ is an important character in our story. _____ tried to_____. The story ends when _____.

Figure 2
Important idea or plot

In this story the problem starts when _____. After that, _____. Next, _____ _____. Then, _____. The problem is finally solved when _____. The story ends _____.

Figure 3
Setting

This story takes place _____. I know this because the author uses the words "_____." Other clues that show when the story takes place are _____ _____.

Figure 4
Character analysis

_____is an important character in our story._____ is important because _____. Once, he/she _____. Another time, _____. I think that _____ is _____because _____
      (character's name)   (character trait)
_____.

Figure 5
Character comparison

_____ and _____ are two characters in our story. _____ is _____ while
   (character's name)   (trait)
_____ is _____. For
   (other character)   (trait)
instance, _____ tries to _____ and _____ tries to _____. _____learns a lesson when_____ _____.

Source: Reprinted with permission of Gerald L. Fowler and the International Reading Association.

Creative dramatics has proven to be superior to discussion and drawing for developing story comprehension for kindergartners and first graders. (© *Elizabeth Crews/Stock Boston*)

example, "Little Miss Muffett") allows students to identify characters, action, and sequence in a simplified setting. By asking the students to try to act out the story in a different order, the teacher can show them how changing the order of events destroys the story.

Creative dramatics has proven to be superior to discussion and drawing for developing story comprehension for kindergartners and first graders (Galda, 1982; Pellegrini and Galda, 1982). Other studies have shown that dramatics can activate schemata, improve readiness, enhance vocabulary development, encourage use of metacognitive strategies, and improve oral reading skills of students in kindergarten through junior high school. The active reconstruction of a story through drama focuses children's minds on the characters, setting, and plot of a story. Interpretation conflicts can be resolved through discussion. Stories with a lot of dialogue are good for use with drama. As students read these stories, they must use their knowledge of such print features as quotation marks to interpret what each speaker is saying (Miller and Mason, 1983; Bidwell, 1992).

Older students also benefit from drawing plot diagrams and relating these diagrams to characterizations and themes. The plot diagram of *Mufaro's Beautiful Daughter* (Steptoe, 1987) in Example 5.8 shows how the plot relates to the charac-

Example 5.8 *Plot Diagram of* **Mufaro's Beautiful Daughter**

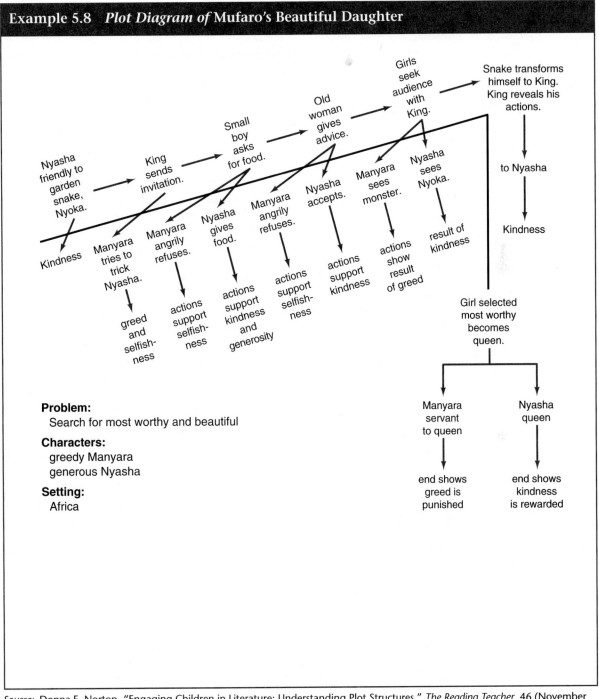

Problem:
Search for most worthy and beautiful

Characters:
greedy Manyara
generous Nyasha

Setting:
Africa

Source: Donna E. Norton, "Engaging Children in Literature: Understanding Plot Structures," *The Reading Teacher*, 46 (November 1992), p. 256. Reprinted with permission of the International Reading Association.

ters of the two daughters and to the overall theme that kindness and generosity are good and will be rewarded, whereas greed and selfishness are bad and will be punished (Norton, 1992).

Teachers can improve understanding of story features such as plots, themes, characters, and setting, by using movies, a medium in which students generally have high interest. For example, they can list types of plots that movies may have and let the students match movies to plots (Sawyer 1994). This understanding can then be transferred to stories in books through parallel techniques.

literature-centered reading

To provide independent practice for beginning readers and prereaders, teachers can videotape stories, giving an introduction to each story and the story structure to be studied. The children should receive directions for listening that focus attention on that structure, as well as directions for follow-up activities such as drawing pictures of characters, setting, or resolution; choosing pictures related to theme from several provided by the teacher; and arranging pictures that relate the plot in sequence. To ensure that the procedures are clear, the entire group should do the activity under the teacher's direction the first time the tapes are used (McGee and Tompkins, 1981).

Settings may serve simply as backdrops for stories, or they may be integral to the narrative, influencing characters, action, and theme. Use of sensory imagery helps to make the setting clear. Pictures in the book also enhance the effect of the words in the text in clarifying setting (Watson, 1991).

Characterization is another story aspect that generally needs attention. Having students create a collage of words describing a character's traits, drawn from both text and pictures and superimposed on a drawing of the character, can help focus students' attention on characterization (Golden et al., 1992).

To help children comprehend stories that start and end at the same place, with a series of events in between, the *circle story* can be effective (Jett-Simpson, 1981; Smith and Bean, 1983). The teacher draws a circle on a large sheet of paper and divides it into a number of pie-shaped sections corresponding to the number of events in the story. The teacher reads the story to the children, who then decide which events need to be pictured in each section of the circle. Circle story completion can be done in small groups, with each child responsible for illustrating a different event. If the paper is large enough, all of the children can work at the same time.

Even though there is much interest among educators in the use of story grammars, questions about this technique remain. Results of studies on the effectiveness of story grammar instruction in increasing reading comprehension have been contradictory (Dreher and Singer, 1980; Greenewald and Rossing, 1986; Sebesta et al., 1982; Spiegel and Fitzgerald, 1986). Some have shown positive effects, and others have shown no benefits. It must be remembered that story grammars describe only a limited set of relatively short, simple stories, ones derived from a fairy tale or folktale tradition, and are unable to describe stories that have characters with simultaneously competing goals (Fitzgerald, 1989; Mandler, 1984; Schmitt and O'Brien, 1986).

reading-writing connection

Reading-Writing Connection

Composition and comprehension both involve planning, composing, and revising. Although these steps may seem clear in composition, their equivalents in reading may be less obvious. Teachers may need to think of the prereading activities related to background building, schema activation, and prediction as the planning phase in comprehension; developing tentative meanings while reading as the composing phase; and revising the meanings when new information is acquired as the revision phase.

Many writing activities that accompany comprehension instruction are composition activities (Pearson, 1985). Writing story predictions based on questioning or prereading word webs is an example of writing in the prereading phase. Note taking during reading may be in the form of outlines or series of summary statements (another obvious link between reading and writing activities). Macrocloze activities related to story grammars and the use of story frames are other ways to use writing to enhance reading. Interpretive reading activities, such as rewriting sentences containing figurative expressions into literal forms and rewriting sentences containing pronouns by using their referents instead, are composition activities. Many writing activities are a part of creative reading instruction. Several of these activities are mentioned in Chapter 8 and the section on creative reading in Chapter 6.

literature-centered reading

A *character journal* involves writing diary entries from the viewpoint of a character in a story. Students can be asked to write a diary entry for each chapter in a book. The entries are written in the first-person voice. Students are encouraged to write as the character might have written, without concern for mechanics and spelling. Personal comments not in the voice of the character can be allowed, but they should be put in parentheses or brackets to set them apart from regular entries. Teacher responses to the entries can help encourage the students and reassure them about their competence. When students are asked to compose diary entries for characters in the literature they are reading, they become more intensely involved in the reading. To accomplish this, the students must get inside the character's head and experience the events through his or her eyes. This perspective produces improved comprehension (Hancock, 1993).

Writing comments about reading may be facilitated through use of a computer. Bernhardt (1994) suggests putting a reading passage on the computer and allowing students to interact with it by breaking it into meaningful or difficult chunks. Then they mark, number, or reorder these chunks and intersperse their own comments and questions in the text. Comments are written in all capital letters so that they stand out from the original text. The active involvement with the text can promote better understanding.

More on the reading-writing connection appears in Chapters 1, 7, 8, and 10.

Cooperative Learning Strategies

Cooperative learning helps students activate their prior knowledge and learn from the prior knowledge of their classmates, keeps them actively engaged in

Composition and comprehension both involve planning, composing, and revising.
(© *Elizabeth Crews*)

reading-writing connection

learning, and enhances attention. Brainstorming of words related to a key vocabulary word can be done in small groups. Ideas can be recorded and shared with the group as a whole. Ideas of the entire class can be summarized at the end of the discussion. Semantic mapping can be done in a similar manner, and comparisons and contrasts of objects or ideas can be graphically developed and shared. The groups can make categorized lists of what they know about the topic before they read about it and again after they read. Before reading, the group can develop questions to be answered during the reading. One helpful activity that can be done during reading is the completion of partially filled-in outline forms

reading-writing connection

by the members of each group. When the reading is finished, different group members can paraphrase sections of the text, and group summaries can be written or shared orally in the group. Mnemonic devices can be developed to help group members remember the material, and inferences can be made about the material. Each group may develop a test on the material for another group to take and discuss with the group that developed it (Uttero, 1988).

literature-centered reading

Cooperative groups work well for helping students understand characterization in a story. After students have read a selection, the teacher can give each group a character to describe. He or she can instruct the children to first web the characters' characteristics and evidence from the story and then write character descriptions based on the web (Avery and Avery, 1994).

Heymsfeld (1991) has children work in cooperative groups, assigning reciprocal teaching roles to the participants (predictor, questioner, clarifier, and summarizer) and adds a recorder. (See the section on metacognitive strategies in this chapter for more information on reciprocal teaching.)

literature-centered reading

Angeletti (1991) has students share their opinions about characters and events in books and back up the opinions with facts from the books. First, the teacher models the procedure; then there is guided individual practice; and, finally, the students work in student-formed small-groups. They use opinion question cards to guide and stimulate the small-group activity. This process teaches the needed technique. Thereafter, there is teacher modeling, silent read-

reading-writing connection

ing, oral sharing in small groups, and individual written responses to the reading in each language arts period. Question types other than opinion (comparison/ contrast, inference, conclusions, characters, author's style, author's purpose, type of literature) are included in the lessons, at first one type at a time. Later students

reading-writing connection

chose from all types. Combining question types in written responses is also modeled by the teacher and then practiced by the students.

Listening-Reading Transfer Lesson

A listening-reading transfer lesson can also be useful in improving comprehension skills. In such a lesson, the teacher asks students to listen to a selection and respond to a purpose (such as determining sequence of events) that he or she has set. As the class discusses the story sequence, the teacher provides guidance, helps children explain how they made their decisions, and, if necessary, rereads the material, to resolve controversies. Then the children read a different selection for the same purpose, and a similar follow-up discussion is conducted. Teachers can use this type of lesson with any comprehension skill (Cunningham, 1982).

SELF-CHECK: OBJECTIVE 4   Describe some good prereading, during-reading, and postreading activities for promoting comprehension. (See Self-Improvement Opportunities 3 and 4.)

Summary

The central factor in reading is comprehension. Since reading is an interactive process that involves the information brought to the text by readers, the information supplied by the text, and the reading situation, good comprehension depends on many factors. Among them are readers' backgrounds of experience, sensory and perceptual abilities, thinking abilities, and word recognition strategies, as well as their purposes for reading, their audience for the reading, the importance of the reading to them, and their facility with various comprehension strategies that will help them unlock the meanings within the text. Children's schemata, built through background experiences, aid comprehension of printed material and are themselves modified by input from this material.

Having a purpose for reading enhances comprehension. Teachers should learn how to set good purposes for children's reading assignments and discover how to help them learn to set their own purposes.

The audience for reading affects the reading strategies used. The audience may be the reader himself or herself, the teacher, or other children.

The importance the reading has for the reader is also a factor. High-risk reading for a test may be done differently from low-risk reading in the classroom setting.

Features of the text itself also affect comprehension. Sentences that are complex, contain relative clauses, are in the passive voice, have missing words, or express negation may need special attention because students may have difficulty comprehending them. The meaning conveyed by punctuation in sentences should receive attention. Students also need help in understanding the functions of paragraphs and the organizational patterns of paragraphs and whole selections.

Prereading, during-reading, and postreading activities can foster children's comprehension of reading selections. Prereading activities such as previews, anticipation guides, semantic mapping, writing before reading, and creative drama can be helpful. Metacognitive strategies, questioning, and the cloze procedure are among the techniques that can be used during reading. Postreading activities usually involve extending knowledge about the topic, questioning, making visual representations, using readers' theater, retelling, and application of concepts. Some activities—such as semantic webbing and story mapping, story grammar and story frame activities, other story structure techniques, writing activities related to reading, cooperative learning strategies, and listening-reading transfer lessons—may be involved in prereading, during-reading, and postreading activities at various times.

Test Yourself *True or False*

_____ 1. Each schema that a person has represents what the person knows about a particular concept and the interrelationships among the known pieces of information.

_____ 2. Anything that increases a reader's background knowledge may also increase comprehension.

_____ 3. Previews for stories that build background related to the stories have a positive effect on comprehension.

_____ 4. Punctuation marks are clues to pauses and pitch changes.

_____ 5. Character journals are journals filled with character sketches.

_____ 6. Comprehension-monitoring techniques are metacognitive strategies.

_____ 7. Punctuation marks do not function as clues to sentence meaning.

_____ 8. Reading comprehension involves relating textual information to preexisting knowledge structures.

_____ 9. Comprehension strategies should be taught in a way that emphasizes their application when students are actually reading connected discourse.

_____ 10. Less able readers may rely too heavily on either text-based or knowledge-based processing.

_____ 11. Richard Rystrom argues that reading is exclusively a top-down process.

_____ 12. InQuest combines student questioning with creative drama.

_____ 13. Story grammar activities can increase children's understanding of story structure and serve as a basis for questioning.

_____ 14. Relative clauses cause few comprehension problems for children.

_____ 15. Semantic webbing involves systematically deleting words from a printed passage.

_____ 16. Think-alouds are useless in teaching metacognitive strategies.

Self-Improvement Opportunities

1. Choose a short selection about an uncommon subject. Question your classmates to find out how complete their schemata on this topic are. Give them copies of the selection to read. Discuss the reading difficulties some of them had because of inadequate prior knowledge.

2. Construct a time line for a chapter in a social studies text that has a chronological-order organizational pattern. Describe to your classmates how you could use the time line with children to teach this organizational pattern.

3. Write an anticipation guide for a well-known folktale. Discuss the guide in class.

4. Construct a story map for a story. Display the map in class, and let your classmates try to predict the contents of the story from it.

5. Read Margaret Egan's article "Capitalizing on the Reader's Strengths: An Activity Using Schema" (_Journal of Reading_, 37 [May 1994], 636–640), and try the check activity "Travail in Nova Scotia" with a group of middle or upper elementary students. Report the results to your class.

6. Read Egan's article, cited in number 5, and compose a check story to use with students in a specific grade. Try your story with such students and report results.

Chapter 6

Key Vocabulary

Pay close attention to these terms when they appear in the chapter.

anaphora

creative reading

critical reading

ellipsis

idiom

interpretive reading

literal comprehension

propaganda techniques

schema (and schemata)

story grammar

topic sentence

visualization

In addition, when you read the section on propaganda techniques, pay close attention to the terms used there.

Comprehension: Part 2

Setting Objectives

When you finish reading this chapter, you should be able to

1. Describe ways to promote reading for literal meanings.
2. Explain the importance of being able to make inferences.
3. Discuss some of the things a critical reader must know.
4. Explain what *creative reading* means.
5. Explain how to construct questions for discussions and assessments.

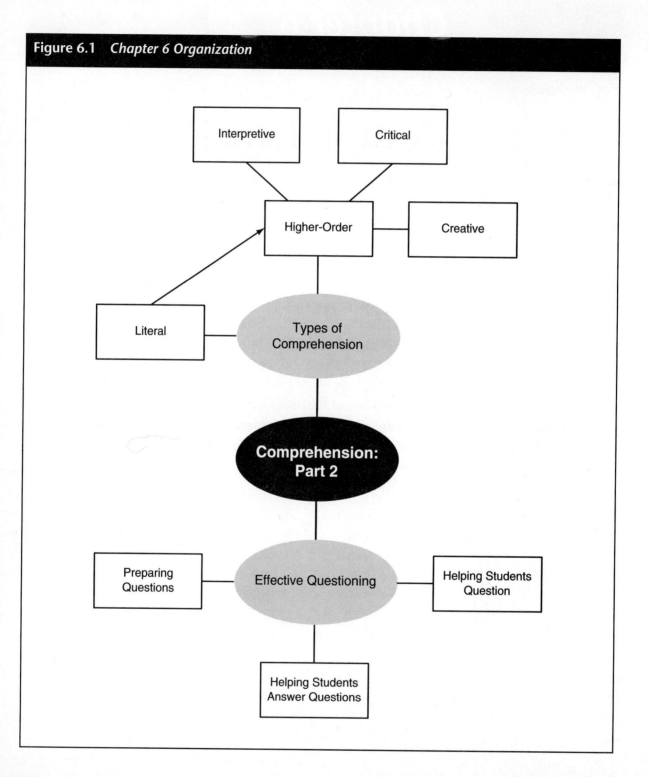

Figure 6.1 *Chapter 6 Organization*

Interpretive

Critical

Higher-Order

Creative

Literal

Types of Comprehension

Comprehension: Part 2

Preparing Questions

Effective Questioning

Helping Students Question

Helping Students Answer Questions

This chapter examines two types of comprehension: literal and higher-order. It describes approaches for developing each type. In addition, it explains questioning techniques that can be used to guide reading, enhance comprehension and retention, and assess comprehension, including three important related activities: preparing questions, helping students answer questions, and helping students question. Example 6.1 shows the relationships among the ideas presented in this chapter and those in Chapter 5.

Studies in the late 1970s and early 1980s called attention to the small amount of time devoted to instruction in reading comprehension in classrooms and the inadequacies of teacher's manuals for basal reading series in providing effective suggestions for teaching comprehension (Durkin, 1978/1979; Durkin, 1981a). These findings alerted educators to the need for teachers to be well informed about comprehension instruction in order to help their students effectively.

Types of Comprehension

Readers employ different types of comprehension in order to understand fully what they read. To take in ideas that are directly stated is *literal comprehension*; this is the most basic type. Higher-order comprehension includes interpretive, critical, and creative comprehension. To read between the lines is *interpretive reading*; to read for evaluation is *critical reading*; and to read beyond the lines is *creative reading*. Example 6.2 shows these types of comprehension and their elements.

Perhaps because literal comprehension is the easiest to deal with in the classroom, teachers have given it a disproportionate amount of attention; but children need to achieve higher-order reading comprehension to become informed and effective citizens.

Literal Comprehension

Reading for literal comprehension, or acquiring information that is directly stated in a selection, is important in and of itself and is also a prerequisite for higher-level comprehension. Recognizing *stated* information is the basis of literal comprehension. The specific, explicitly stated parts of a paragraph or passage that contain the basic information are the details on which main ideas, cause-and-effect relationships, inferences, and so on are built. For example, in the sentence "The man wore a red hat," the fact that a red hat was being worn is one detail that readers can note. To locate details effectively, students may need some direction about the types of details signaled by specific questions. For example, a *who* question asks for the name or identification of a person, or sometimes an animal; a *what* question asks for a thing or an event; a *where* question asks for a place; a *when* question asks for a time; a *how* question asks for the way something is or was accomplished; and a *why* question asks for the reason for something. After discussing these question words and their meanings, the teacher can model for

Example 6.1　*Chapter Organization for Chapters 5 and 6*

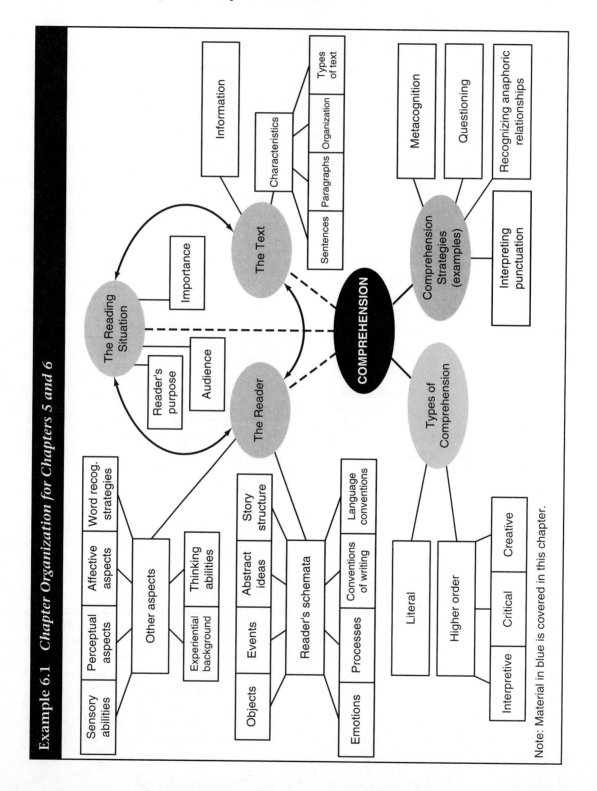

Note: Material in blue is covered in this chapter.

Example 6.2   Types of Comprehension

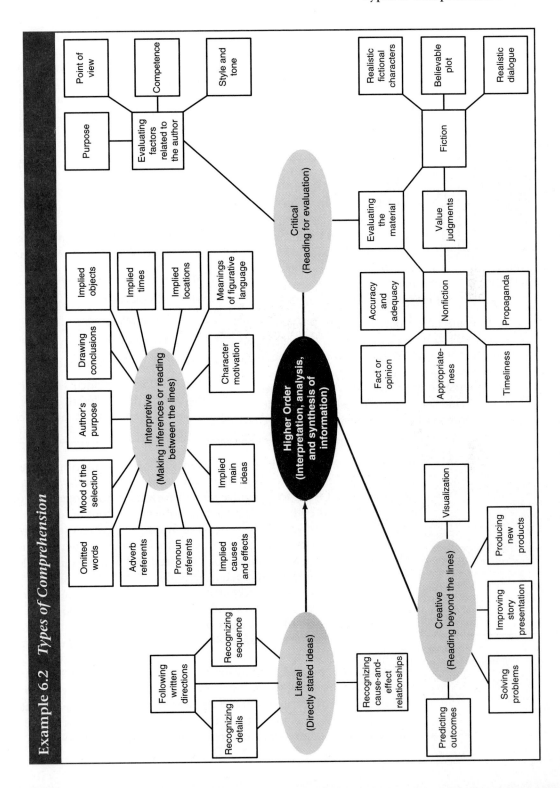

the students the locations of answers to each type of question in a passage displayed on the chalkboard or a transparency. Then the students can participate in an activity such as the following one to practice the skill. Newspaper articles are good for practice of this sort, since lead paragraphs tend to include information about *who, what, where, when, why,* and *how.* The teacher should provide feedback on the correctness of responses as soon as possible after the students complete the activity.

Model Activities

Locating Details in a Newspaper Story

Have the students read the following newspaper article and answer the questions in small groups, making sure that every group member agrees to each answer chosen.

Jane and John Stone, owners of Stone's Grocery, had $100 stolen from them as they left the store last night at eleven o'clock. The robber stepped from behind a shrub outside the door of the grocery store and pulled a gun from his pocket, saying, "Hand over that cash sack!" Stone handed the robber the sack of money he had just removed from the cash register, and the man turned and fled, leaving both Mr. and Mrs. Stone unharmed.

1. Who was involved in this event?
2. What took place?
3. Where did it take place?
4. When did it take place?
5. How or why did it take place?

Have a whole-class discussion of the article, with members from the different groups giving their groups' answers and reasons for their answers.

Sequence, the order in which events in a paragraph or passage occur, is signaled by time-order words such as *now, before, when, while, yet, after,* and so on. Children must learn to recognize straightforward chronological sequence, as well as flashbacks and other devices that describe events "out of order."

Teachers must model the process of finding the correct sequence of events in a passage before expecting students to locate such sequences independently. Helpful time-order words should be discussed and pointed out in selections. Then students need to engage in practice activities related to this skill.

The ability to read and follow directions is a prerequisite for virtually all successful schoolwork. It involves understanding details and sequence.

The teacher should take a set of directions for performing a task and model following these directions carefully, reading the directions aloud as each step is completed and commenting on the meaning of each instruction. Then he or she should follow the directions again, leaving out a vital step. Class discussion about the results of not following directions carefully should follow. After several modeling episodes, the teacher should consistently refer children to written directions instead of telling them how to do everything orally. Children can be asked to read the directions silently and then repeat them in their own words.

Recognizing and understanding a cause-and-effect relationship in a written passage is an important reading skill. It is considered a literal skill when the relationship is explicitly stated ("Bill stayed out *because* he was ill"); it is considered an interpretive skill if the relationship is implied.

Following are some activities for developing literal comprehension.

Activities

1. After students have read a paragraph, preferably from a book they have chosen to read, ask them questions whose answers are directly stated in the paragraph, as shown in the following example. Have them show where they found the answers in the paragraph.

    Tom's favorite toy was his dump truck. Although Tom was usually a generous boy, he never offered to let anyone else play with the truck. He had had the truck for three years, and it was still as good as new. Tom was afraid that other children would be careless with his toy.

    1. a. What was Tom's favorite toy?

        b. What was the condition of Tom's toy?

        c. How long had Tom had his favorite toy?

2. Give the children a set of directions for a task that they need to complete, and have them number the important details (or steps), as has been done in the following example. Go through one or more examples before you ask them to work alone.

    To make a good bowl of chili, first (1) sauté the onions for about ten minutes. Then (2) add the ground beef and brown it. (3) Stir the mixture frequently so that it will not burn. Finally, (4) add the tomatoes, tomato sauce, Mexican-style beans, salt, pepper, and chili powder. (5) Cook over low heat for forty-five minutes to one hour.

3. Make some copies of a menu. After showing students how to locate items and prices, ask them to read it and answer specific questions such as these:

    a. What is the price of a soft drink?
    b. Can you order a baked potato separately? If so, under what heading is it found?
    c. What else do you get when you order a rib steak?
    d. How many desserts are available?

4. Using a description like the following one and reading each step aloud, draw an object on the board. Then give the children a written description of another object and ask them to draw it.

The flower has five oval petals. The petals are red. The center, at which the petals meet, is brown. The flower has a long green stem. At the bottom of the stem are overlapping blade-shaped leaves, which are half as tall as the stem.

5. Display (by writing on the board or by showing a transparency) a paragraph from a book the students have read that contains a cause-and-effect relationship. Model the process of locating the cause and the effect. Point out clue words, such as *because,* if they are present, but make sure the children know they cannot always expect such clues to be present. Then show the children another paragraph from the same book or another one. State the cause of the action, and have them identify the effect. Discuss the children's responses. A paragraph similar to the following one could be used for instruction.

Bobby, Jill, Leon, and Peggy were playing softball in Bobby's yard. Peggy was up at bat and hit the ball squarely in the direction of Bobby's bedroom window. As the group watched in horror, the softball crashed through the window, shattering the glass.

Question: What happened when the softball hit the window?

6. Use the procedure described in activity 5, but describe the effect and have the children identify the cause. Using the same paragraph as an example, the question would be "What caused the window to break?"

7. Use a game of Twenty Questions to focus attention on details. Have a child mentally choose an object (or have a group huddle and choose one secretly), and have classmates try to discover what the object is by asking detail questions. Then give the children real stories to read and list details from, or give them stories from which some important details have been deleted to show them how missing details can affect understanding (Flippo and Smith, 1990).

8. Have the children read a selection such as the folktale "Lazy Jack." Then list the events in the story out of sequence, and show students how to reorder them. Using another selection, like that in the Model Activity "Placing Story Events in Order," ask the children to list the events in sequence. (Use shorter selections for younger children.)

9. Discuss with the children the functions of such key words as *first*, *next*, *last*, and *finally*. Then give them a paragraph containing these words, and ask them to underline the words that help to show the order of events.

10. Prepare handouts with uncolored pictures. Have the children color the pictures according to written directions such as "Color the girl's sweater red. Color her skirt gray. Color her hair brown."

11. Use an activity similar to the Model Activity "Following Directions" on page 262.

12. Teach the children the meanings of words commonly encountered in written directions, such as *underline, circle, divide, color, example, left, right, below, over,* and *match.*

13. Write directions for a project, and have the students complete the steps (Baker, 1982). Construction and cooking projects, as well as science experiments and magic tricks, can be used. Discussion can center on the results that occur if the correct sequence is not followed. Directions can be cut apart, scrambled, and reconstructed to show comprehension of the necessary sequence.

Model Activities

Placing Story Events in Order

Discuss the meaning of sequence with the children. Give an example of the sequence in a very familiar story such as "The Three Little Pigs." Then ask the children to read the following story and place the list of events in order.

We were all excited on Friday morning because we were going to go to the circus. We had trouble concentrating on eating breakfast, but Mother wouldn't allow us to leave the table before we were finished.

Immediately after breakfast, we piled into the station wagon. Everyone was talking at once and bouncing around on the seats as Dad started the car and backed out of the driveway. We were making so much noise and moving around so much that Dad didn't hear or see the truck turn the corner. The truck driver honked his horn, but it was too late. Dad backed right into the side of the truck.

The angry driver jumped out of his truck, but when he saw the crowd of us in the station wagon, he calmed down. He and Dad talked to each other for awhile, staring at the damaged side of the truck occasionally. Then they went into the house to report the accident to the police.

Mother recovered from the shock and told us to get out of the car. "We'll have a long wait before we will be able to leave," she said.

Story Events

The family got into the station wagon.

The truck driver honked his horn.

The family ate breakfast.

Dad backed out of the driveway.

Dad and the truck driver talked.

Mother told the children to get out of the car.

Dad backed into the side of the truck.

Dad and the truck driver went into the house.

The driver jumped out of his truck.

After everyone has finished the exercise independently, discuss the children's results in class. Be sure to have the children give the reasons for their decisions.

**Model
Activities**

Following Directions

Give the students handouts with the following information printed on them.

Directions: Read all the items before you begin to carry out each instruction. Work as quickly as you can; you have five minutes to finish this activity.

1. Write your name at the top of the paper.

2. Turn the paper over and add 15 and 25. Write the answer you get on this line:_____.

3. Stand up and clap your hands three times.

4. Count the number of times the word *the* is written on this page. Put the answer on this line: _____.

5. Go to the board and write your name.

6. Count the people in this room. Put the answer under your name at the top of the page.

7. Now that you have read all of the directions, take your paper to the teacher. It should have no marks on it.

After the children have finished the exercise, hold a discussion about why some of them made marks on the paper that they should not have made. Emphasize the importance of reading and following directions carefully to avoid errors.

SELF-CHECK: OBJECTIVE 1 Describe a procedure for developing children's literal comprehension of information in printed material. (See Self-Improvement Opportunities 1 and 2.)

Higher-Order Comprehension

Higher-order reading comprehension goes beyond literal understanding of a text. It is based on the higher-order thinking processes of interpretation, analysis, and synthesis of information.

Knowledge is necessary to higher-order thinking, but students do not always use the knowledge they possess to think inferentially, critically, and creatively (Beck, 1989). They may have the background knowledge needed for comprehending a text but may fail to use it, or they may have misconceptions about certain topics that are more detrimental to comprehension than no background knowledge at all. All groups of students, regardless of socioeconomic level or ethnic origin, vary in background knowledge. Semantic mapping accompanied by group discussion can help students with little individual knowledge about a topic pool their information and expand their knowledge (Maria, 1989).

Making *predictions* about reading material is an important higher-order reading skill. Predicting what will happen in a story or other reading selection engages students' interest and leads them to organize their thinking. A hypothesis-testing process is initiated in which students make predictions and then read to confirm or reject them. If the predictions must be rejected, the students revise them. In all cases, they must be ready to explain why they made the predictions and why they believe the predictions can be accepted or must be rejected.

Students need to realize that *any* evidence that refutes a prediction is enough to show the prediction is not valid, but even a great deal of supporting evidence in favor of a prediction may not conclusively prove that it is true. They also need to realize that just because a prediction has not been refuted at one point in the reading does not mean that evidence to refute it will not appear later. People often tend to overlook refuting evidence while noticing confirming evidence, and students must be taught to avoid doing this. By refuting unsupportable predictions, students reduce uncertainty about the story's outcome. Teachers should ask students if their predictions have been proven wrong yet and ask other, similar questions to encourage them to search for refuting evidence (Garrison and Hoskisson, 1989).

Asking for predictions when the text offers clues about what will happen helps make students aware of the usefulness of text information in making inferences. Asking for predictions when there are no text clues about what will happen encourages creative thinking on the part of the children. Both types of prediction activities are good to include in lessons over time (Beck, 1989).

Interpretive Reading

Interpretive reading is reading between the lines or *making inferences*. It is the process of deriving ideas that are implied rather than directly stated. Interpretive reading includes making inferences about main ideas of passages, cause-and-effect relationships that are not directly stated, referents of pronouns, referents of adverbs, and omitted words. It also includes detecting the mood of a passage, detecting the author's purpose in writing a selection, drawing conclusions, and interpreting figurative language.

No text is ever fully explicit. Some relationships among events, motivations of characters, and other factors are left out, with the expectation that readers will figure them out on their own. Readers, therefore, must play an active role in constructing the meanings represented by the text. They must infer the implied information by combining the information in the text with their background knowledge of the world. Stories that require more inferences are more difficult to read (Carr, 1983; Pearson, 1985).

Lange (1981) has pointed out that "readers make inferences consistent with their schemata" (p. 443), but it is important to realize that children have less prior knowledge than adults do and do not always make inferences spontaneously, even when they possess the necessary background knowledge.

Even very young children can, during their daily activities, make inferences by connecting new information to information they already possess, but they do not necessarily apply this skill to reading without teacher direction. Active involvement with the printed message enhances students' abilities to make inferences related to it.

literature-centered reading   Comparing events in students' own lives with events that might occur in stories they are about to read is one way to help them see the thinking processes they should use when they read. Even poor readers show the ability to make inferences about the material they are reading when such a procedure is used

(Hansen and Hubbard, 1984). Having young children listen to one another's experiences related to a story, listen to one another's predictions about the story, and write down their own experiences and predictions can enhance their ability to make inferences about the story (Hansen, 1981b). In addition, providing practice in answering inferential questions is an effective method for helping the children improve in this skill (Hansen, 1981a; McCormick and Hill, 1984).

McIntosh (1985) suggests that teachers should ask first graders to make inferences based only on pieces of information located close together in the text. When the information is not adjacent in the text, the teacher can use guiding questions to lead students to it. This type of instruction helps students become aware of the need to search actively for the meanings of written passages. Older children grow in their ability to make inferences, possibly because of their increased knowledge of the world.

Students are expected to make inferences about a number of things: locations, people who act in certain ways, time, actions, devices or instruments, categories, objects, causes and/or effects, solutions to problems, and feelings. To make these inferences, they can relate important vocabulary in the reading material to their backgrounds of experience. First, the teacher should explain how important words in a passage can help in making a particular inference about the passage. Then the teacher should have students practice and apply this procedure. During the application phase, students are asked to make an inference based on the first sentence and then retain, modify, or reject it as each subsequent sentence is read (Johnson and Johnson, 1986). Such instruction is needed because some students will make hypotheses about the reading material but will fail to modify them when additional information shows them to be incorrect. Instead, they may distort subsequent information in an attempt to make it conform to their original hypotheses. These children may have problems with passages that present one idea and follow it with a contrasting idea or passages that present an idea and subsequently refute it. They may also have difficulty with passages that give examples of a topic, followed by a topic statement, or with passages that give no topic statement (Kimmel and MacGinitie, 1985).

Using a passage that contains a word with multiple meanings, asking for possible meanings for the word based on initial sentences, and then reading to confirm or disprove these predictions about meanings can be a good way to help

literature-centered reading

students learn to revise hypotheses when reading. Reading stories written from unusual points of view can also help; for example, *The True Story of the 3 Little Pigs*, as told to Jon Scieszka (Viking Kestrel), is written from the wolf's point of view (Kimmel and MacGinitie, 1985).

Pearson (1985) succinctly describes a method related to teaching inference skills that was developed by Gordon and Pearson (1983): "(1) ask the inference question, (2) answer it, (3) find clues in the text to support the inference, and (4) tell how to get from the clues to the answer (i.e., give a 'line of reasoning')" (Pearson, 1985, p. 731). First, the teacher models all four steps; then the teacher performs steps 1 and 2, while requiring the students to complete steps 3 and 4; then the teacher performs steps 1 and 3, requiring the students to complete steps 2 and 4; and finally the teacher asks the question (step 1) and the students perform all the other steps. The responsibility for the task is thus gradually transferred from teacher to students. This is an excellent procedure and can be used for other skills as well.

Interpreting anaphora is another task that requires students to make inferences. *Anaphora* refers to the use of one word or phrase to replace another one (Irwin, 1991). Examples are using pronouns in place of nouns (*he* for a noun like *Bill*), using adverbs for nouns or noun phrases (*here* for a phrase like *in the kitchen*), letting adjectives stand for the nouns that would have followed them (*several* for *several people*), using a superordinate term to stand for a subordinate one (*reptile* for *rattlesnake*), using an inclusive term to stand for an extended section of text (*This* for *a disturbance in the neighborhood* presented in an earlier sentence), and letting referents in another sentence or clause represent deleted items (*I will too*, following *Mom will bake brownies for the sale. Bake brownies for the sale* is "understood").

At some point, teachers will probably need to address in class all forms of anaphora, but the approaches used can be similar. Modeling of the thought processes used is important. Since children frequently have trouble identifying the noun to which a pronoun refers, they need practice in deciding to whom or

Readers employ literal comprehension as well as higher-order comprehension (interpretive comprehension, critical reading, creative reading) to understand fully what they read. (© *Richard S. Orton/The Picture Cube*)

to what pronouns refer. The Classroom Scenario on pronoun referents in the next section offers ideas for instruction about and practice with pronouns. Some other forms of anaphora are discussed in subsequent sections.

Pronoun Referents.   A piece of writing seldom, if ever, explicitly states the connection between a pronoun and its referent (an anaphoric relationship), so the task of determining the referent is an inferential one. Students recall structures in which the referent is a noun or a noun phrase more easily after reading than structures in which the referent is a clause or a sentence (Barnitz, 1979).

> Mark wanted an ice cream cone but did not have enough money for it. (noun phrase referent)
>
> Mike plays the guitar for fun, but he does not do it often. (sentence referent)

Similarly, children find it easier to remember structures in which the pronoun follows its referent than ones in which the pronoun comes first (Barnitz, 1979).

> Because it was pretty, Marcia wanted the blouse.
>
> Marcia wanted the blouse because it was pretty.

literature-centered reading   Teachers should give attention to the structures just described. They should use stories or content selections the students are currently reading and explain the connections between the pronouns and referents in a number of examples before asking students to make the relationships themselves. See the following Classroom Scenario for an example of such a procedure.

Classroom Scenario

Pronoun Referents

Mr. Stevens wrote the following sentence on the chalkboard: "Joan put the license plate on her bicycle." Then he read it to the class. After reading the sentence, he modeled the process involved in determining the referent in the sentence by saying, "*Her* is a pronoun that stands for a noun (or, with younger children, 'a person, place, or thing'). The noun usually comes before the pronoun that stands for it. The two nouns in this sentence that come before *her* are *Joan* and *plate*. *Her* indicates a woman or a girl. A plate isn't a woman or a girl, so *her* probably stands for *Joan*."

Then he wrote this second sentence on the chalkboard: "Since the book was old, it was hard to replace." He asked the children to determine the referent for *it* in this sentence in the way he had determined the referent for *her* in the other sentence.

Ronnie said, "*It* refers to *book*."

Mr. Stevens asked Ronnie, "How did you know?"

"You told us that *it* refers to a thing, and the book is the only thing mentioned in the sentence," Ronnie responded.

"That's good thinking," Mr. Stevens replied, as he wrote a new sentence on the board for further guided practice. After another student successfully dealt with this sentence, Mr. Stevens gave the students a handout that included several paragraphs from a book they were reading in class. Each paragraph included pronouns and referents. He asked the students to draw an arrow from each pronoun to its referent and be ready to explain their choices later in the day in small-group sessions.

Analysis of Scenario
Mr. Stevens followed a good instructional plan by first modeling the skill of determining pronoun referents, then offering the students guided practice in which they were asked to support their responses with reasons, and finally having students practice independently using other sentences chosen from material they were currently reading.

After all of the sentence structures with pronouns have been considered separately, the teacher should use activities such as the following one to provide practice in integrating learning.

Model Activities

Anaphoric Cloze—Pronoun Referents

Give students passages duplicated from their classroom reading materials in which you have deleted either the pronouns or the referents. Ask the students to fill in the correct words in the blanks. They may be allowed to work on the task cooperatively in pairs or in groups. For less advanced readers, you may provide choices from which the students select the correct words (Irwin, 1991).

Adverb Referents.   At times adverbs refer to other words or groups of words without an explicitly stated relationship. Teachers can explain these relationships, using examples such as the following, and then let children practice making the connections independently.

I'll stay at home, and you come here after you finish. (The adverb *here* refers to *home*.)

I enjoy the swimming pool, even if you do not like to go there. (The adverb *there* refers to *swimming pool*.)

Omitted Words.   Sometimes words are omitted and said to be "understood," a structure known as *ellipsis*. Ellipsis can cause problems for some students, so again teachers should provide examples, explain the structure, and then give children practice in interpreting sentences.

> Are you going to the library? Yes, I am. (In the second sentence, the words *going to the library* are understood.)

> Who is going with you? Bobby. (The words *is going with me* are understood.)

> I have my books. Where are yours? (Here the second sentence is a shortened form of *Where are your books?*)

After this structure has been thoroughly discussed, students may practice by restating the sentences, filling in the deleted words.

Main Ideas.   The main idea of a paragraph is the central thought around which the whole paragraph is organized. It is often, but not always, expressed in a *topic sentence* in expository writing; in narrative writing, even fewer topic sentences will be found.

To understand written selections fully and to summarize long selections, children must be able to determine the main ideas in their reading materials. Teachers should provide them with opportunities to practice recognizing main ideas and help them to realize the following facts:

1. A topic sentence often states the main idea of the paragraph.

2. The topic sentence is often, though not always, the first sentence in the paragraph; sometimes it appears at the end or in the middle.

3. Not all paragraphs have topic sentences.

4. The main idea is supported by all of the details in a well-written paragraph.

5. When the main idea is not directly stated, readers can determine it by discovering the topic to which all the stated details are related.

6. The main idea of a whole selection may be determined by examining the main ideas of the individual paragraphs and deciding to what topic they are all related.

The teacher should model the thought process students need to follow in deciding on the main idea of a selection before asking them to try this task independently. For paragraphs with topic sentences, the teacher can show students that the topic sentence is the main idea and that the other sentences in the paragraph relate to it by taking a paragraph, locating the topic sentence, and showing the relationship of each of the other sentences to the topic sentence. Then the teacher can give the students paragraphs and ask them to underline the topic sentences and tell how each of the other sentences relates to each topic sentence.

Activities such as those illustrated in the following Focus on Strategies and described in the Model Activity on pages 270–271 can give pupils practice in locating main ideas in paragraphs.

**Focus on
Strategies**

Finding Main Ideas

Mrs. Braswell wrote the following paragraph on the chalkboard:

Edward Fong is a good family man. He is well educated, and he keeps his knowledge of governmental processes current. He has served our city well as a mayor for the past two years, exhibiting his outstanding skills as an administrator. Edward Fong has qualities that make him an excellent choice as our party's candidate for governor.

She said: "I am going to try to locate the topic sentence, the one to which all of the other sentences are related. The topic sentence provides one type of main idea for the paragraph. . . . Now, let's see, is it the first sentence? No. None of the other sentences appear to support his being a good family man. . . . Is it the second sentence? No. It isn't supported by the first sentence. . . . Is it the third sentence? No. It may be supported by the second sentence, but not by the others. . . . Is it the fourth sentence? Yes, I think it is. A candidate for governor would do well to be a good family man, be well educated and knowledgeable about government, and have experience as a city administrator. All the other sentences support the last one, which is broad enough in its meaning to include the ideas expressed in the other sentences."

After this demonstration, Mrs. Braswell let one student "think aloud" the reasoning behind his or her choice of a topic sentence for another paragraph. Finally, she had students work on this process in pairs, "thinking aloud" to each other.

A topic merely identifies the subject matter; a main idea also includes the type of information given about the topic. For example, a topic of a paragraph or selection might be "football," whereas the main idea might be "There are several different ways to score in football."

Duffelmeyer and Duffelmeyer (1991) suggest the use of gamelike activities to show students that a topic and a statement about the topic combine to make a main idea statement. They encourage following these activities with modeling of the writing of details to support the main idea statements formed, followed by guided practice for the students in performing this task.

reading-writing connection

To give students a concrete analogy for main ideas and details, a teacher can use a familiar object such as a bicycle. The bicycle can be identified as the main idea, and the handlebars, seat, pedals, gears, wheels, and chain can represent the supporting details that together make up the main idea.

Finding the main idea in whole selections of nonfiction generally is a categorizing process in which the topic is located and the information given about the topic is then examined (Moldofsky, 1983). In fiction, however, there is not a "topic" but a central problem, which is rarely stated explicitly.

Individual teachers mean different things when they request main ideas from students, and, when students are asked to give the main idea of a passage, some produce topics, some topic sentences, and some brief summaries. A description of the task expected, however, may be all students need to lead them to produce the desired response (Moore and Cunningham, 1984).

In many selections, readers must infer the main idea from related details. Even in selections in which the main idea is directly stated, readers generally must make inferences about which sentence states the main idea. The teacher can help develop students' readiness to make such inferences by asking them to locate the main ideas of pictures first. Then the teacher can ask them to listen for main ideas as he or she reads to them. Finally, the teacher can have them look for main ideas of passages they read.

Showing students how to infer unstated main ideas is a more difficult process than showing them how to decide which stated sentence represents the main idea. In the following Model Activity, the teacher could compare each of the possible choices to the details in the selection, rejecting those that fail to encompass the details. As students practice and become more proficient at identifying implied main ideas, the teacher should omit the choices and ask them to state the main idea in their own words (Moore and Readence, 1980). Teachers can also increase passage length as the children gain proficiency, beginning with paragraphs that have directly stated topic sentences, moving to paragraphs that do not have directly stated topic sentences, and finally moving gradually to entire *literature-centered reading* selections. Because of their obvious morals, Aesop's fables are good for teaching implied main ideas. The teacher can give students a fable and ask them to state the moral, then compare the actual morals to the ones stated, discuss any variations, and examine reasoning processes. Children may have fun using Arnold Lobel's *Fables* (Harper & Row, 1980) with this activity as well.

Model Activities

Inferring Unstated Main Ideas

Model the generation of a main idea for a paragraph from one of the students' textbooks that has an unstated main idea. Be sure to show how each sentence in the paragraph supports the main idea you generated. Then display a copy of the following paragraph (or a similar one from one of their textbooks) and main idea choices on the chalkboard or a transparency.

The mayor of this town has always conducted his political campaigns as name-calling battles.

Never once has he approached the basic issues of a campaign. Nevertheless, he builds himself up as a great statesman, ignoring the irregularities that have been discovered during his terms of office. Do you want a person like this to be reelected?

The main idea of this selection is:

1. The current mayor is not a good person to reelect to office.

2. The mayor doesn't say nice things about his opponents.

3. The mayor is a crook.

4. The mayor should be reelected.

Say: "In this selection, the main idea is implied but not directly stated. Choose the correct main idea from the list of possible ones. Try to use a thinking process similar to the one I used in the example that I gave for you. Be ready to explain the reason for your choice to your classmates."

Eventually the students should be given a paragraph and asked to construct a main idea statement with no choices provided.

Finding main ideas in fiction is a somewhat different process. To help students learn to locate a central problem in a fictional work, the teacher should first activate their schemata for problems and solutions, perhaps by talking about background experiences or stories previously read. Then the class may identify and categorize types of problems. Finally, the teacher should model the process of identifying a central story problem with a familiar, brief story. Pauses during reading to hypothesize about the central problem and to confirm or modify hypotheses can show the students how to search for the thing the central character wants, needs, or feels—the thing that provides the story's problem. The teacher should let the children see how the story's events affect the hypotheses they have made. Events of a story may be listed on the board to be analyzed for the needs or desires of the main character (Moldofsky, 1983).

literature-centered reading

Activities

1. Gather old newspapers and cardboard for mounting. Cut from the newspapers a number of articles that you think will interest the children, and separate the text of each article from its headline. Mount each article and title on cardboard. The children's task is to read each article and locate the most suitable headline for it. To make the task easier, have them begin by matching captions to pictures, use very short articles, or use articles that are completely different in subject matter. Have the children discuss the reasons for their choices. Make the activity self-checking by coding articles and headlines. To follow up, you might use these ideas: (a) have children make pictures and captions to share in the reading center, or (b) have them try to match advertisements to pictures or captions to cartoons.

2. Collect newspaper articles and cut off headlines. Then have students construct titles using the information in the lead paragraph. Show them how to do this before you ask them to work on the task alone.

Cause and Effect.   Sometimes a reader needs to infer a cause or an effect that has been implied in the material. Cause-and-effect relationships can be taught using cause-and-effect chains in real life and in novels (Ollmann, 1989). Brainstorming out loud about causes and effects may help children develop more skill in this area. The teacher can ask: "What could be the effect when a person falls into the lake? What could be the cause of a crying baby?" Then the teacher should elicit the reasoning behind children's answers. The following Classroom Scenario describes a practice activity for this skill.

literature-centered reading

Classroom Scenario

Inferring Cause-and-Effect Relationships

Mrs. Taylor stacked three books on the edge of her desk as the children watched. Then she said, "Cover your eyes or put your heads down on your desks so that you can't see the books anymore. Don't peek."

When all eyes were covered, Mrs. Taylor knocked the books off of the desk. Then she said, "You can open your eyes now."

The children opened their eyes and saw the books on the floor.

"What caused the books to be on the floor?" Mrs. Taylor asked.

Rob immediately responded, "You knocked them off."

"How do you know that I knocked them off?" Mrs. Taylor persisted. "You didn't see me do it."

"Nobody except you was up there," Rob replied.

"How do you know that I didn't just lay them gently on the floor?" the teacher then asked.

"Because they made such a loud noise," Rob answered. "If you had put them down gently, there wouldn't have been much noise."

"Excellent thinking, Rob!" said Mrs. Taylor. "You used clues to figure out something that you didn't actually see. When you read, you can use that skill, too. Sometimes the author leaves clues about what he wants you to know, but he doesn't come right out and say it. You have to use clues he gives and 'read between the lines' to find out what happened. We're going to try doing that right now."

Mrs. Taylor passed out a handout with the following paragraphs on it. She said, "Read the following paragraphs and answer the question."

Jody refused to go to bed when the babysitter told her it was time. "This is a special occasion," she said. "Mom and Dad said I could stay up two hours later tonight."

Reluctantly, the babysitter allowed Jody to sit through two more hour-long TV shows. Although her eyelids drooped, she stubbornly stayed up until the end of the second show.

This morning Jody found it hard to get out of bed. All day there was evidence that she was not very alert. "What is wrong with me?" she wondered.

Question: What caused Jody to feel the way she did today?

When everyone had finished reading and had answered the question independently, Mrs. Taylor had one child answer the question aloud. The other children verified the answer, and several pointed out the clues in the material that helped them to decide on the answer.

Analysis of Scenario

Mrs. Taylor used a concrete experience to show the children how they made inferences about experiences every day. Then she had them try to apply the same kind of thinking to a reading experience, analyzing their thinking and pointing out the clues they used, so that classmates who were having trouble with the skill could see how they processed the information.

Detecting Mood.   Certain words and ways of using words tend to set a mood for a story, poem, or other literary work. Teachers should have children discuss how certain words trigger certain moods—for example, *ghostly, deserted, haunted,* and *howling* convey a scary mood; *lilting, sparkling, shining,* and *laughing* project a happy mood; *downcast, sobbing,* and *dejected* indicate a sad mood. They should model for the children the process of locating mood words in a paragraph and using these words to determine the mood of the paragraph. Then they can give the children copies of selections in which they have underlined words that set the mood and let them decide what the mood is, based on the underlined words. Finally, teachers can give the students a passage such as the one provided in the following Classroom Scenario and tell them to underline the words that set the mood. After the students complete the practice activity, they should discuss the mood that the words established.

`literature-centered reading`

**Classroom
Scenario**

Detecting Mood

Mrs. Vaden read the following excerpt from *Homesick: My Own Story* by Jean Fritz (Dell, 1982, p. 138) to her class.

> By the time we were at the bottom of the hill and had parked beside the house, my grandmother, my grandfather, and Aunt Margaret were all outside, looking exactly the way they had in the calendar picture. I ran right into my grandmother's arms as if I'd been doing this everyday.
> "Welcome home! Oh, welcome home!" my grandmother cried.
> I hadn't known it but this was exactly what I'd wanted her to say. I needed to hear it said out loud. I was home.

Mrs. Vaden said, "In this passage, the mood of happiness is effectively developed by describing the girl running into her grandmother's arms, the cries of 'welcome' from her grandmother, and the statement 'I was home.' All these things combine to help us feel the happy mood. Some authors carefully choose words to help readers feel the mood they want to share. Read the paragraph on the board, decide what mood the author wanted to set, and be ready to tell the class which words helped you to decide about the mood."

The following paragraph was on the board:

> Jay turned dejectedly away from the busy scene made by the movers as they carried his family's furniture from the house. "We're going away forever," he thought sadly. "I'll never see my friends again." And a tear rolled slowly down Jay's cheek, further smudging his unhappy face.

Steve raised his hand. When the teacher called on him, he said, "The mood is sad."

"That's right," Mrs. Vaden responded. "What clues did you use to decide that?"

"*Sadly, tear,* and *unhappy,*" he replied.

Sharon chimed in, "I see another one. *Dejected* is a sad word, too."

"Very good," said Mrs. Vaden. "You both found clues to the mood of this paragraph. Next, we will look for the mood as we begin to read our story for this week. Jot down the clue words as you find them to help you decide on the mood."

Analysis of Scenario

Mrs. Vaden first showed the children how she decided about the mood of a passage in a literature selection with which they were familiar. Then she gave them an opportunity to determine the mood for another selection, under her supervision. Finally, she asked them to apply the skill in further purposeful reading activities.

Detecting the Author's Purpose. Writers always have a purpose for writing: to inform, to entertain, to persuade, or to accomplish something else. Teachers should encourage their students to ask, "Why was this written?" by presenting them with a series of stories and explaining the purpose of each one, then giving them other stories and asking them to identify the purposes. The class should discuss reasons for the answers. The following Model Activity gives students practice in detecting purpose.

literature-centered reading

Detecting the Author's Purpose

Model Activities

Display the following list of reading selections on the board, or display the actual books. Ask the children to consider the selections and decide for each selection whether the author was trying to inform, entertain, or persuade.

This Is the Way It Works: A Collection of Machines by Robert Gardner. New York: Doubleday, 1980.

Sure Hands, Strong Heart: The Life of Daniel Hale Williams by Lillie Patterson. Champaign, Ill.: Garrard, 1981.

The Good, the Bad, and the Goofy by Jon Scieszka. New York: The Trumpet Club, 1992.

A Book of Puzzlements: Play and Invention with Language by Herbert Kohl. New York: Schocken, 1981.

"Put Safety First." A pamphlet.

After each child has had time to make a decision about each selection, ask volunteers to share their responses and the reasons for each one. Clear up any misconceptions through discussion.

Drawing Conclusions. To draw conclusions, a reader must put together information gathered from several sources or places within the same source. Students may develop readiness for this skill by studying pictures and drawing conclusions from them. Answering questions like the following may also help. The teacher should model the process before having the students attempt it.

1. What is taking place here?

2. What happened just before this picture was taken?

3. What are the people in the picture preparing to do?

Cartoons may be used to good advantage in developing this comprehension skill. The teacher can show the students a cartoon like the one below and ask a question that leads them to draw a conclusion, such as "What kind of news does Dennis have for his father?" Putting together the ideas that an event happened today and that Dennis's father needs to be relaxed to hear about it enables students to conclude that Dennis was involved in some mischief or accident that is likely to upset his father. The teacher can model the necessary thinking process by pointing out each clue and relating it to personal knowledge about how parents react. Then students can practice on other cartoons.

DENNIS the MENACE

"LET ME KNOW WHEN YOU'RE RELAXED ENOUGH TO HEAR ABOUT SOMETHIN' THAT HAPPENED TODAY."

DENNIS THE MENACE® used by permission of Hank Ketcham and © by Field Enterprises, Inc.

literature-centered reading

In the early grades, riddles such as "I have a face and two hands. I go tick-tock. What am I?" offer good practice in drawing conclusions. Commercial riddle books, which allow readers to answer riddles and explain the reasoning behind their answers, may also be used for developing this skill.

Another way to help children draw conclusions is to ask questions about sentences that imply certain information. For example, the teacher can write on the chalkboard, "The two men in white uniforms removed a stretcher from the back of their vehicle." Then the teacher can ask: "What kind of vehicle were these men driving? What are your reasons for your answers?" Even though the sentence does not directly state that the vehicle is an ambulance, the details lead to this conclusion. With help, children can become adept at detecting such clues to implied meanings. The following Model Activity offers practice with this activity.

**Model
Activities**

Drawing Conclusions

Divide the children into small cooperative groups. Give each group a copy of a handout containing the following two paragraphs. Tell the children: "Read each paragraph and answer the question that follows it. After each person in your group has finished, discuss the answers with the members of your group and explain why you answered as you did. Modify your answers if you believe your thinking was wrong originally. Be ready to share your decisions with the rest of the class."

Ray went through the line, piling his plate high with food. He then carried his plate over to a table, where a server was waiting to find out what he wanted to drink. Where was Ray?

_____

_____

Cindy awoke with pleasure, remembering where she was. She hurried to dress so that she could help feed the chickens and watch her uncle milk the cows. Then she would go down to the field, catch Ginger, and take a ride through the woods. Where was Cindy?

_____

_____

Hold a whole-class discussion in which representatives from each small group share their groups' answers.

To draw conclusions about characters' motives in stories, children must have some knowledge about how people react in social situations. This knowledge comes from their backgrounds of experience. Teachers' questions can encourage inferences by requiring students to consider events from the viewpoints of different characters; to think about the characters' likely thoughts, feelings, and motives; and to anticipate consequences of the actions of various characters (Moss and Oden, 1983).

Interpreting Figurative Language. Interpreting figurative language is an inferential task. Idioms abound in the English language. An *idiom* is a phrase that has a meaning different from its literal meaning. A person who "pays through the nose," for example, does not make use of that body part but does pay a great deal. Idioms make language more difficult to comprehend, but they also add color and interest (Bromley, 1984).

Eustolia Perez found that third-grade Mexican-American children benefited from oral language activities that included practice with idioms (Bromley, 1984).

Nonnative students often lack the backgrounds of experience with the culture to help them interpret idioms. They may be confused over the idea that a word or phrase has different meanings in different contexts.

literature-centered reading

It may be helpful to teach idioms by defining and explaining them when they occur in reading materials or in oral activities. Studying the origins of the expressions may also be helpful. After an idiom's meaning has been clarified, stu-

reading-writing connection

dents need to use it in class activities. They may rewrite sentences to include newly learned idioms or replace these idioms with more literal language. Deaton (1992) found that doing writing that makes use of idioms can help students better understand the meanings. Illustrating idioms is another helpful activity. Stu-

reading-writing connection

dents can also listen for idioms in class discussion or try using them. Creative writing about possible origins of idioms may elicit interest in discovering their real origins (Bromley, 1984).

literature-centered reading

One of the best ways to teach figurative language, as well as all interpretive reading strategies and skills, is through think-alouds. The following Focus on Strategies below includes excerpts from a think-aloud used by a primary-grade classroom teacher in which she emphasized the figurative language in the selection and shows how she followed up the think-aloud to focus attention specifically on personification.

More extensive coverage of figurative expressions appears in Chapter 4. That discussion identifies different types of figures of speech and offers teaching suggestions.

SELF-CHECK: OBJECTIVE 2   Explain why children need to know how to make inferences.

**Focus on
Strategies**

Figurative Language Instruction

Evelyn Forbes was reading aloud from the story "The Big Green Umbrella" by Elizabeth Coatsworth while the students followed along in their books. As she read the paragraph of text that said that "the umbrella seemed to grow tired of keeping the rain off the Thomases on rainy days and standing in the dark corner. . . . It had heard the talk of the winds . . . whispering of raindrops, which had seen all the world. . . . the umbrella acted," she stopped and inserted her thoughts about the text. "Wind can't really talk, and raindrops can't whisper," she mused. "Umbrellas can't grow, hear, or act. People do. Why is the author making the umbrella have the characteristics of a person?" At this point she paused and discussed personification with the students, connecting it to previous reading they had done. After the discussion, she drew the following diagram on the board and had the children suggest the characteristics given to the umbrella that were characteristics of a person. She wrote these characteristics on the raindrops falling from the umbrella.

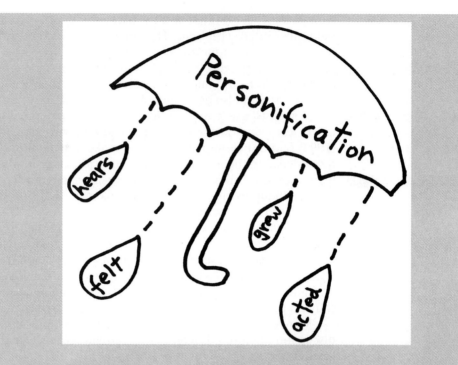

Reading further, Mrs. Forbes came to the statement that "it soared upward like a kite" and "turned head-over-heels like a child at play." She repeated the similes and said, "These words paint a picture in my head of kites flying in a blue sky while children turn somersaults in the grass. What pictures are in your heads?" Then she called the children's attention to the use of *like* to compare the umbrella with things that she knew about that she could picture.

Later in the paragraph, the umbrella was said to be "dancing and bowing above the river," and the children were able to apply their knowledge of personification once more. Mrs. Forbes stopped reading after a few more paragraphs in which the story characters have speculated about the plight of the umbrella. She said, "Mr. Thomas is wrong about the umbrella. What do you think is going to happen?" The students' predictions ended the lesson for that day, leaving them eager for reading time the next day, when they would discover whether or not their predictions were right.

Critical Reading

Critical reading is evaluating written material—comparing the ideas discovered in the material with known standards and drawing conclusions about their accuracy, appropriateness, and timeliness. The critical reader must be an active reader, questioning, searching for facts, and suspending judgment until he or she has considered all the material. Critical reading depends on both literal and interpretive comprehension, and grasping implied ideas is especially important.

People must read critically to make intelligent decisions based on the material they read, such as which political candidate to support, which products to buy, which movies to attend, which television programs to watch, and so on. Since children face many of these decisions early in life, they should receive early instruction in critical reading.

Teachers can begin promoting critical reading in the first grade, or even kindergarten, by encouraging critical thinking. When reading a story to the class, they can ask, "Do you think this story is real or make-believe? Why do you think so?" If the children have difficulty in answering, questions such as "Could the things in this story really have happened? Do you know of any children who can fly? Have you ever heard of any *real* children who can fly? Have you ever heard of anyone who stayed the same age all of the time? Do all people grow up after enough years have passed?" can be helpful. By asking "Can animals really talk? Have you ever heard an animal talk?" teachers can help children understand how to judge the reality or fantasy in a story.

Critical thinking can also be promoted at an early stage through critical reading of pictures. If children are shown pictures that contain inaccuracies (for example, a car with a square wheel), they can identify the mistakes. Children's magazines often contain activities of this type, and illustrators of books often inadvertently include incorrect content. After the children have read (or have been read) a story containing such a picture, ask them to identify what is wrong in the picture, according to the story.

Critical listening instruction and critical reading instruction have been effective with students in grades one through six, regardless of whether or not they have already mastered basic decoding skills, and such instruction is appropriate for remedial, as well as developmental, readers. Instruction in critical listening has been shown to improve critical reading and general reading comprehension for remedial readers in grades four through six (Boodt, 1984).

reading-writing connection Critical reading is closely related to revision in writing. Both activities require critical thinking. Students must evaluate their own writing to improve it, just as they evaluate the writing of others as they read.

Group thinking conferences can help students become better critical readers. In these small-group conferences, students read their own written materials aloud. After a piece has been read, the teacher motivates discussion by asking what the piece was about, what the students liked about it, and what questions or suggestions the students might have for the author. The students revise their **literature-centered reading** own pieces after the group conferences. The same type of conference can be held about a published text by a professional author. This process gives student writers insight into what readers expect of writers. If students fail to respond in ways that alert their classmates to missing or inappropriate aspects of the written pieces, the teacher can ask questions aimed at helping them make these discoveries (Fitzgerald, 1989).

To foster critical reading skills in the classroom, teachers can encourage pupils to read with a questioning attitude and can lead them to ask questions such as the following when they are reading nonfiction:

1. Why did the author write this material?

2. Does the author know what he or she is writing about? Is he or she likely to be biased? Why or why not?

3. Is the material up to date?

4. Is the author approaching the material logically or emotionally? What emotional words does he or she use?

5. Is the author employing any undesirable propaganda techniques? If so, which ones? How does he or she use them?

Fiction can also be read critically, but the questions that apply are a little different.

1. Could this story really have happened?

2. Are the characters believable within the setting furnished by the story? Are they consistent in their actions?

3. Is the dialogue realistic?

4. Did the plot hold your interest? What was it that kept your interest?

5. Was the ending reasonable or believable? Why or why not?

6. Was the title well chosen? Why or why not?

literature-centered reading | Reading groups may be used for discussion of the material, whether all of the children have read the same selection or some of them have read different selections on a common topic or from a common genre. The children compose questions to be discussed by the group, with the group making the decision about which questions to consider. When questions have been selected, the children prepare for the group meeting by reading and/or rereading material to answer the questions, taking notes about their findings, and marking (with paper markers) passages in the book that support their answers. The group discussions that ensue are just that: children discuss without holding up their hands for a turn or being called on. They respond to the comments and questions of the other group members (Reardon, 1988). In this activity, analysis of the material is meaningful to the students: they decide what is significant in the material, and they relate the material to matters of importance to them, for example, how the author's use of language affects the story.

Careful questioning by the teacher to extend limited and stereotyped depictions of people in reading materials can help children develop expertise in critical reading. Children must be encouraged to relate their personal experiences to the materials. Children can examine stereotyped language in relation to stories in which it occurs, and teachers can point out the problems caused by looking at people and ideas in a stereotyped way (Zimet, 1983). For example, some books give the impression that certain nationalities have particular personality characteristics, but it should be easy to demonstrate that not all people of that nationality are alike, just as not all Americans are alike.

Critical thinking is often important to the interpretation of humor (Whitmer,

1986). Therefore, humorous literature can be an enjoyable vehicle for teaching critical reading skills. It is especially good for determining the author's purpose (often to entertain, but sometimes also to convince through humor) and for evaluating content (especially distinguishing fact from fantasy and recognizing assumptions).

Many excellent books for children are filled with themes of honesty and dishonesty, sharing and selfishness, courage and cowardliness, and many others. Discussion of these themes in the context of the stories' characters, with consideration of alternatives available to them and of the appropriateness or inappropriateness of their actions, can build skill in critical reading (McMillan and Gentile, 1988). The students can be asked to compare the actions of the characters to standards of behavior set by the law, the school, parents, and so forth.

Resnick (1987) points out that "[h]igher order thinking often yields multiple solutions, each with costs and benefits, rather than unique solutions" and that "[h]igher order thinking involves imposing meaning, finding structure in apparent disorder" (p. 3). Literature analysis can help students become skillful in performing these tasks. One critical reading activity is to have children evaluate the evidence that Chicken Little had that the sky was falling and decide whether or not the other animals were right to just take her word for it. They can also be asked if the Little Red Hen used good strategies to elicit help from the other animals and what else she might have done (Beck, 1989).

`literature-centered reading`

To analyze characterization in literature selections, students must be able to make inferences about characters. Norton (1992) believes teachers need to model the process of making inferences about characters for the students. They can read examples from a text, pause and verbalize a question that requires an inference, and answer the question, using supporting data from the text and making their reasoning process clear to the students. They can tell how their prior knowledge and beliefs affected the answer. Then students can be asked to attempt these same steps. Norton suggests the story *Shiloh* (Naylor, 1991) as a good one for helping students learn to make inferences about characters.

Norton (1992, p. 65) says that students must understand that making inferences involves going beyond the information stated in the text and that "they must use clues from the text to hypothesize about a character's emotions, beliefs, actions, hopes, and fears. Students must also be aware that authors develop characters through dialogue, narration, thoughts, and actions." This activity leads directly into character analysis.

Commeyras (1989) suggests the use of literature selections and a grid developed by Ashby-Davis (1986) to help students learn about character analysis. Example 6.3 shows a completed grid based on the character of Tom Sawyer. Such a grid leads students to collect evidence about a character, interpret the evidence, and make a generalization about the evidence after all of it has been collected. Looking for commonalities and discrepancies in the data and considering the amount of evidence available for a conclusion drawn are important to good critical analysis. When readers draw evidence from reactions of other characters in the story, they must evaluate the credibility of the sources before accepting the evidence.

Example 6.3   *Sample Grid on* Tom Sawyer

	External clues	Student's interpretation

(1) Frequent kinds of statements made by this character

A. Fibs   A. Tom gets his way.

B. Commands   B. Tom is confident.

My summary of these interpretations of statements:

Tom is bold and daring.

(2) Frequent actions of the character

A. Mischievous   A. Tom likes to fool around.

B. Heroic   B. Tom isn't afraid.

My summary of these interpretations of actions:

Tom's good deeds are more important than his misbehavior.

(3) Frequent ways of thinking by this character:

A. He schemes.   A. Tom finds solutions.

B. He's optimistic.   B. Tom has confidence.

My summary of these interpretations of thought:

Tom is smart.

(4) What do others frequently say to the character:

A. What have you done?   A. Tom is unpredictable.

B. This is fun!   B. Tom has good ideas.

Summary of my interpretations of these statements:

Tom is independent in his actions.

(5) What do others do to this character:

A. They get mad at him.   A. Tom upsets people.

B. They follow his lead.   B. Tom gets respect.

Summary of my interpretation:

Tom gets to people one way or another.

(6) What do others say about the character:

A. He's stubborn.   A. Tom doesn't give up.

B. He's brave.   B. Tom helps others.

Summary of my interpretation:

Tom isn't all good or all bad.

My final generalization concerning the personality of Tom Sawyer:

Tom Sawyer is a boy who gets into trouble,
but ends up doing the right thing in the end.

Source: Michelle Commeyras, "Using Literature to Teach Critical Thinking," *Journal of Reading,* 32 (May 1989), 703–707. Reprinted with permission of Michelle Commeyras and the International Reading Association.

Gauthier (1992) recommends having students fill out character charts to enhance critical thinking. In this activity, the teacher chooses a short book in which characters are involved in good and bad events and prepares a character chart for it. The columns in the chart are headed *Characters, Good, Bad,* and *Notes.* The *Good* and *Bad* columns are for good and bad events each character encounters. All characters in the story are listed in order of appearance. The teacher reads the story fairly slowly, and the students fill in their charts. During a rereading of the story, the teacher pauses at various points to allow the children to tell how they have classified events and give reasons for their classifications.

Santino (1991) suggests having students compare different versions of folktales with Venn diagrams and comparison charts to improve comprehension and see commonalities in stories from different cultures. Example 6.4 shows a comparison of a Russian folktale with an Appalachian one.

Teachers can also encourage students to think critically by having them compare film versions of stories with the text versions. Analysis of the dramatic interpretation of a story can also provide students with a model of creative response to the narrative (Duncan, 1993).

If the children have adequate schemata for understanding the text, it is better to have them read the text before seeing the film. Sometimes the children may be exposed to the story on film, but only a portion of the text version may be used in instruction. Then some students may be motivated to finish the text on their own. Most film versions are necessarily abbreviated versions. However, seeing an abbreviated presentation of a story that provides a knowledge of its basic structure may provide needed support for disabled readers, giving them confidence to attempt to read the text (Duncan, 1993).

reading-writing connection   Students can use Venn diagrams to show how characters were alike and different in film and text versions of stories. They can also write film reviews, including notes about how true the film was to the book. *Sarah, Plain and Tall; Where the Red Fern Grows;* and *The Secret Garden* are books that have good film versions available for comparison.

Commeyras (1993) suggests using Dialogical-Thinking Reading Lessons (D-TRLs) to promote critical thinking among students. She explains, "D-TRLs encourage students to (a) return to the text to verify or clarify information; (b) consider multiple interpretations; (c) identify reasons to support interpretations; and (d) evaluate the acceptability and relevance of competing or alternative interpretations" (p. 487).

A story that contains an issue that can be considered from more than one perspective is chosen for the D-TRL. During the reading phase of the D-TRL, the reading may be guided or independent, depending on the students' capabilities. During the discussion phase, the central question is introduced, along with two hypothetical conclusions about the answer. The children are invited to take one of the positions or announce that they are undecided. This helps to engage students in the search for information. Then the students search the text for support for each conclusion. The teacher lists all suggestions on the board. After reasons have been listed, the students should evaluate each one. Criteria for evaluation should include: (1) Is the reason based on verifiable information (either from the

Example 6.4 *Comparison of Folktales*

Comparison of Two Stories

	Hardy Hardhead	Fool of the World and the Flying Ship
QUEST	To break enchantment and marry King's daughter	Provide flying ship to Czar and marry Czar's daughter
CHARACTERS	Two older brothers (Tom & Will) favored by parents Younger brother (Jack) – thought to be foolish Old Man ← Tom and Will didn't share / Jack shared food / Gave Jack a flying ship and money (Take in everyone) [1]Hardy Hardhead [2]Eatwell [3]Drinkwell [4]Runwell [5]Harkwell [6]Seewell [7]Shootwell	Two older brothers favored by parents Younger brother – Fool of the World Old Man ← Fool shared food / Showed Fool how to get flying ship (Take in everyone) [4]Man with bread [5]Man walking around lake [3]Man on one leg (other tied to head) [1]Man listening to all that is being done in the world [2]Man with gun [6]Man with wood on shoulders [7]Man with sack of straw
ACTION	Each person Jack picked up helped Jack win a bet with the witch.	Each person the Fool picked up helped him perform a seemingly impossible task for the Czar.
RESOLUTION	Jack paid back old man and kept ship. Enchantment on King's girl was broken.	Fool married princess. They fell in love with each other.

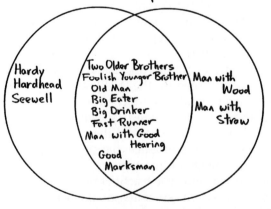

text, prior knowledge, or logic)? (2) Is the reason relevant to the conclusion? Then the students attempt to draw final conclusions from the entire discussion. Some may believe they were correct initially; some may still be undecided; and some may have changed their positions, based on the evidence brought out in the discussion. After students can do all of this well, they can generate their own hypothetical conclusions in subsequent lessons and, eventually, their own central questions.

literature-centered reading

Evaluating Factors Related to the Author.   Krieger (1990) found that middle-school students were not aware of the authors of the material they read and the devices the authors used (flashbacks, foreshadowing, and so forth) for special purposes. She read to these students, modeling her thinking processes concerning why the author included certain details as she read. She asked them to make predictions about what might happen next from clues left by the author. Outside assignments based on the material read allowed for further thinking about the story or the author by the students; students might be asked to keep listening journals with reactions to the stories, for example. Through this listening experience, Krieger opens the students' minds to the ways authors express ideas, making it more likely that they will be able to read stories with understanding later.

reading-writing connection

McKeown and her colleagues (1993) have developed a technique called Questioning the Author to help children access ideas in a text. They point out that someone wrote the ideas in the text and that some people do not write as clearly as others. Students are invited to figure out the ideas behind the author's words, determine the author's reasons for presenting the particular information and decide whether the author has presented the ideas clearly. Then students are asked to state confusing material in a clearer way. Teachers should model this process for students before asking them to do it independently.

The mature critical reader must consider and evaluate factors related to the person who wrote the material, taking into account the following four categories.

Author's purpose. The critical reader will try to determine whether the author wrote the material to inform, to entertain, to persuade, or for some other purpose. This is an interpretive reading skill.

Author's point of view. The critical reader will want to know if the writer belonged to a group, lived in an area, or held a strong view that would tend to bias any opinions about a subject in one way or another. Two accounts of the Revolutionary War might be very different if one author was from Canada and the other from the United States.

reading-writing connection

Students can learn more about point of view by writing letters or essays about issues from different points of view. For example, they might take the point of view of an elementary school student, a concerned parent, or a principal when a school dress code is being considered.

In having students make decisions about author bias, teachers can use a laboratory balance and a bag of marbles. Students can put marbles on one side of the balance for positive statements and on the other side for negative ones and thus have a concrete representation of the bias (Henk, 1988).

Author's style and tone. The author's style is the manner in which he or she uses vocabulary (vividness, precision, inclusion of emotional words, use of figurative language) and sentence structure (the order within the language). Special attention should be given to use of *figurative language,* language that is not meant to be taken literally, and use of emotional words, which do much to sway the reader toward or away from a point of view or attitude. Note the effects of these two sentences:

Author 1:   Next we heard the *heart-rending* cry of the wounded tiger.

Author 2:   When the tiger was shot, it let out a *vicious* roar.

Teachers should be aware of undesirable aspects of the style or tone of some writers of material for youngsters. A condescending tone, for example, will be quickly sensed and resented.

Author's competence. The reliability of written material is affected by the author's competence to write about the subject in question. If background information shows that a star football player has written an article on the nation's foreign policy, intermediate-grade youngsters will have little trouble determining that the reliability of the statements in this article is likely to be lower than the reliability of a similar article written by an experienced diplomat.

To determine an author's competence, students should consider his or her education and experience, referring to books such as *Current Biography* (H. W. Wilson, 1993) and *Sixth Book of Junior Authors and Illustrators* (H. W. Wilson, 1989) or to book jacket flaps to find such information. Teachers can give students a topic and ask them to name people who might write about it. Students can discuss which people might be most qualified, or they can compare two authors of books on the same subject and decide which one is better qualified. Students who are knowledgeable about a topic and others who are not can write reports on that topic, while the remaining students predict which people are likely to have the most accurate reports. The students can follow up with a comparison for accuracy (Ross, 1981).

Evaluating the Material.   Besides comprehending the material literally, the critical reader needs to be able to determine and evaluate the following factors.

Timeliness. The critical reader will wish to check the date the material was published, because the timeliness of an article or a book can make a crucial difference in a rapidly changing world. An outdated social studies book, for example, may show incorrect boundaries for countries or fail to show some countries that now exist; similarly, an outdated science book may refer to a disease as incurable when a cure has recently been found. A history book with a 1985 copyright date would contain no information about Operation Desert Storm.

Accuracy and adequacy. Nonfiction material should be approached with this question in mind: "Are the statements presented here true?" The importance of a good background of experience becomes evident in this situation. A reader who has had previous experience with the material will have a basis of comparison not available to one lacking such experience. A person with only a little knowledge of a particular field can often spot such indications of inadequacy as exaggerated statements, one-sided presentations, and opinion offered as fact. Obviously, readers can check reference books to see if the statements in the material are supported elsewhere.

Appropriateness. Critical readers must be able to determine whether the material is suitable for their purposes. A book or an article can be completely accurate and not be applicable to the problem or topic under consideration. For example, a child looking for information for a paper entitled "Cherokee Ceremonies" needs to realize that an article on the invention of the Cherokee alphabet is irrelevant to the task at hand.

reading-writing connection

Reissman (1992) has students read the Bill of Rights and, in small groups, paraphrase each amendment. The groups critique one another's paraphrases. They clip stories from the newspaper that relate to the amendments and form a collage from them. Another group reads the articles and explains their relationship to the Bill of Rights. The team that made the collage judges the accuracy of the responses.

thematic learning

Inquiry Charts can be constructed in order to promote use of critical reading strategies (Hoffman, 1992). First, the class identifies a topic and formulates the questions that will be the basis of the inquiry. The teacher records these on a large I-Chart (See Example 6.5 for a sample I-Chart). Materials, such as textbook selections, trade books, encyclopedia articles, and magazine articles, that pertain to the topic are also collected and listed on the I-Chart as they are used.

literature-centered reading

Next, the teacher questions the students to discover their prior knowledge about the topic and enters their responses, whether correct or incorrect, on the I-Chart under the identified questions. Information the students have that is not related to the identified questions is recorded under "Other Interesting Facts and Figures." If students have other questions that have not been identified, these are listed under "New Questions." Then the students read the source material independently or in a group, or the teacher reads it to them. Each source is discussed, and decisions are made about the appropriateness of the information in answering the identified questions. Information pertinent to the questions is recorded in the proper spaces. More "Interesting Facts" and "New Questions" may also be added.

literature-centered reading

reading-writing connection

After all sources have been read and information from them recorded, the students write summary statements to answer each question, considering the information from all of the sources. They also summarize the "Interesting Facts." Then the students compare what they had listed as prior knowledge with the newly acquired information and note the differences, clarifying any misconceptions previously held. Unanswered "New Questions" are researched further by individuals or small groups, who must decide about appropriate sources for the information, and findings are reported to the class.

Differentiation of fact from opinion. This skill is vital for good critical reading.

People often unquestioningly accept as fact anything they see in print, even though printed material is often composed of statements of opinion. Some authors intermingle facts and opinions, giving little indication that they are presenting anything but pure fact. Also, many readers are not alert to clues that signal opinions. By pointing out these clues and providing practice in discrimination, teachers can promote the ability to discriminate between facts and opinions.

Example 6.5   *I-Chart*

I - CHART
GUIDING QUESTIONS

TOPIC: Columbus	1. Why did Columbus sail?	2. What did he find?	3. What important things did he do when he got there?	4. How was Columbus regarded by others?	Other Interesting Facts & Figures	New Questions
WHAT WE KNOW	to prove the world was round	America	... not sure	He was a hero	He sailed in 1492. He was Spanish	Did he have a family?
SOURCES 1. *Meet Christopher Columbus, de Kay New York: Random House, 1989*	He was trying to find a new route to the Indies	He found friendly Indians... some pieces of gold... different islands. He found America	He named the islands. He claimed the land for Queen Isabella and King Ferdinand. He brought back gold for Isabella	At the beginning people regarded him as a normal person. Later, when he got back, they thought he was a great man.	C.C. had asked the King of Portugal for ships. He was turned down. When he came back he landed in Portugal and was taken to the King. The King was mad that he didn't help him.	Whatever happened to his son?
2. *The World Book Encyclopedia. World Book Childcraft, Inc. 1979*	to find riches... and a shorter route to the Indies. He wanted to be known as a great sailor and explorer.	He found America. Indians... new islands.	He named the islands. He captured some Indians as slaves. He became the governor.	He was an "understanding... dreamy" person. It sounds like he had a lot of friends	In other books I've read he wasn't very popular. He had 2 sons, not 1. Six brothers and a sister. He was born in Italy.	Whatever happened to his sons?
3. *Where do You Think You're Going Christopher Columbus? Jean Fritz. New York: G.P. Putnam's Sons, 1980*	Because he liked to travel and explore they said they would give a big reward for finding a new route to the Indies	He found Indians... Some small hunks of gold	He talked to the Indians. He asked for directions to the Palace of the Khan. He named the islands	Before he went he was wealthy because he had married a rich woman. He was famous after he sailed, but a couple of years later, everyone forgot about him.	Columbus sounded greedy in this book. He said he saw land first and claimed the prize money. He claimed that all of this was God's work.	Was he really cruel to the Indians? Whatever happened to the slaves he brought back to Spain?
SUMMARY	To find a new route to the Indies... He hoped to find riches and become famous as an explorer. He already knew the world was round.	He found America and the Indians living there. He found a little gold.	He claimed the new land for Spain. He named the islands. He met with the Indians. He took some back to Spain as slaves. He became Governor.	Before he sailed he was normal... a dreamer. After he came back he was famous and a hero. He seemed greedy. Everyone forgot about him after a while.	He claimed he was doing God's work. His family supported him. He tried to get money for his voyage from lots of people. He was born an Italian.	Find out more about his family and what happened to them. Was he cruel to the Indians? What happened to the slaves?

Source: James V. Hoffman. "Critical Reading/Thinking across the Curriculum: Using I-Charts to Support Learning." *Language Arts,* February 1992. Copyright 1992 by the National Council of Teachers of English. Reprinted with permission.

Some readers have trouble reading critically because they lack a clear idea of what constitutes a fact. Facts are statements that can be verified through direct observation, consultation of official records of past events, or scientific experimentation. The statement "General Lee surrendered to General Grant at Appomattox" is a fact that can be verified by checking historical records. For various reasons, opinions cannot be directly verified. For example, the statement "She is the most beautiful girl in the world" is unverifiable and is therefore an opinion. Even if every girl in the world could be assembled for comparison, people's standards of beauty differ and a scale of relative beauty would be impossible to construct.

Knowledge of key words that signal opinions, such as *believe, think, seems, may, appears, probably, likely,* and *possibly,* can be extremely helpful to readers. Teachers often find that pointing out such indicators to children and giving the children practice in locating them is highly beneficial.

Children must also understand that not all opinions are of equal value, since some have been based on facts, whereas others are unsupported. Critical readers try to determine the relative merit of opinions as well as to separate the opinions from the facts.

Newspaper editorials offer one good way for children to practice distinguishing fact from opinion, especially in the intermediate grades. Students can underline each sentence in the editorial with colored pencils, one color for facts and another for opinions. They can then be encouraged to discuss which opinions are best supported by facts.

Furleigh (1991) has students read and analyze an editorial for the subject or main idea, the writer's opinion about the subject, and their own opinions about the subject. The teacher or peers then evaluate the answers each student provides. When peers do the evaluations, the evaluations become additional practice sessions for them.

literature-centered reading   Activities similar to the Model Activity on page 290 may also be used to help children make this difficult differentiation.

Recognition of propaganda techniques. Elementary school children, like adults, are constantly deluged with writing that attempts to influence their thinking and actions. Some of these materials may be used for good purposes and some for bad ones. For example, most people would consider propaganda designed to persuade people to protect their health as "good" and propaganda intended to persuade people to do things that are harmful to their health as "bad." Since *propaganda techniques* are often used to sway people toward or away from a cause or point of view, children should be made aware of these techniques so that they can avoid being unduly influenced by them.

The Institute for Propaganda Awareness has identified seven undesirable propaganda techniques that good critical readers should know about:

1. Name calling—using derogatory labels (*yellow, reactionary, troublemaker*) to create negative reactions toward a person without providing evidence to support such impressions.

**Model
Activities**

Fact and Opinion

Give the students copies of the following paragraph, which opens the book *Homesick: My Own Story* by Jean Fritz (Dell, 1982, p. 9):

> In my father's study there was a large globe with all the countries of the world running around it. I could put my finger on the exact spot where I was and had been ever since I'd been born. And I was on the wrong side of the globe. I was in China in a city named Hankow, a dot on a crooked line that seemed to break the country right in two. The line was really the Yangtse River, but who would know by looking at a map what the Yangtse River really was?

Ask students to read this opening paragraph carefully, underlining any part or parts that are statements of opinion. Ask them to decide what they can tell about the main character from both the facts and the opinions revealed in this opening paragraph. Then have them decide how the located opinion or opinions are likely to affect the story about to be read.

Let the students share their reactions to this opening passage before they begin to read the book. After they have finished reading the book, have them discuss whether or not their initial reactions were accurate.

2. Glittering generalities—using vague phrases to influence a point of view without providing necessary specifics.

3. Transfer technique—associating a respected organization or symbol with a particular person, project, product, or idea, thus transferring that respect to the person or thing being promoted.

4. Plain-folks talk—relating a person (for example, a politician) or a proposed program to the "common people" in order to gain their support.

5. Testimonial technique—using a highly popular or respected person to endorse a product or proposal.

6. Bandwagon technique—playing on the urge to do what others are doing by giving the impression that everyone else is participating in a particular activity.

7. Card stacking—telling only one side of a story by ignoring information that favors the opposing point of view.

Teachers should describe propaganda techniques to the class and model the process of locating these techniques in printed materials such as advertisements. Then the children should practice this skill.

Children can learn to detect propaganda techniques by analyzing newspaper and magazine advertisements, printed political campaign material, and requests for donations to various organizations. A technique called ALERT can help students critically analyze commercial messages. The technique can be used for print, audio, or video commercial messages, but this discussion will focus on print messages. Lessons focusing on audio (radio) and video (television) messages could conceivably be used as preparation for examining print messages, since problems with decoding would not arise, but ultimately children need to focus on reading advertising critically. Teachers can use advertisements for easily obtainable, inexpensive materials for this activity. The steps in this procedure are as follows:

1. *A*—Advance organizer. The teacher tells the children that they are to read certain advertisements to find repeated or "loaded" words, the product being promoted, and special effects (for example, pictures, well-known characters, and so on) used in the copy.

2. *L*—Listen/Learn. The children read to identify the information they were alerted to by the advance organizer.

3. *E*—Examine/Explain. The children evaluate the message in the advertisement, aided by teacher-posed questions to stimulate appropriate thinking (for example, "Were any persuasive statements made?").

4. *R*—Restate/Read. The children put the meaning of the advertisement into their own words. They may either do this independently or the group may dictate to a scribe (the teacher or another student). Students locate key words, phrases related to the product, the product's name, and the advertiser's claims about the product. These can be marked on the paraphrased text or listed on the chalkboard.

5. *T*—Think/Test/Talk. Students plan and perform product tests to help them evaluate the claims in the advertisements (Allen et al., 1988).

Making value judgments. Readers need to be able to determine whether the actions of both fictional and real-life characters are reasonable or unreasonable. To help children develop this ability, teachers may ask questions such as the following:

literature-centered reading

Was the Little Red Hen justified in eating all the bread she made, refusing to share with the other animals? Why or why not?

Was it a good thing for Heidi to save bread from the Sessmans' table to take back to the grandmother? Why or why not?

Readers draw on their schemata related to right and wrong actions in order to complete this type of activity. Because of their varying schemata, not all children will answer in the same way.

Activities like the following ones can be used to provide children with practice in critical reading strategies.

Activities

1. Have a propaganda hunt. Label boxes with the names of the seven propaganda techniques listed earlier. Then ask children to find examples of these techniques in a variety of sources and drop their examples into the boxes. As a class activity, evaluate each example for appropriateness to the category in which it was placed.

2. Use computer simulation programs for practice in making critical judgments. These programs provide simulated models of real-life experiences with which students can experiment in a risk-free manner.

3. Ask students to compare two biographies of a well-known person by answering questions such as "How do they differ in their treatment of the subject? Is either of the authors likely to be biased for or against the subject? Are there contradictory statements in the two works? If so, which one seems most likely to be correct? Could the truth be different from both accounts?"

4. Have students compare editorials from two newspapers with different viewpoints or from different areas. Have them decide why differences exist and which stand, if either, is more reasonable, based on facts.

5. Ask students to examine newspaper stories for typographical errors and to determine whether or not each typographical error changed the message of the article.

6. Have the class interpret political cartoons from various newspapers.

7. Ask students to examine the headlines of news stories and decide whether or not the headlines fit the stories.

8. Using a list of optional topics—school policies, parental restrictions, and so forth—ask students to write editorials, first presenting facts, then their opinions, and finally their reasons for the opinions (Rabin, 1981).

9. Locate old science or geography books containing statements that are no longer true, and use them to show the importance of using current sources. Let students compare old and new books to find the differences (new material included, "facts" that have changed, etc.), and discuss what types of material are most and least likely to be dependent on recent copyright dates for accuracy (Ross, 1981).

10. Have students become acquainted with the typical viewpoint of a particular writer or newspaper and then predict the position that writer or newspaper will take on an issue. Later, have them check to discover the accuracy of their predictions (Ross, 1981).

reading-writing connection

11. Direct students to write material that will persuade their classmates to do something. Then examine the results for the techniques they used.

12. Discuss the nutritional aspects of sugar and chemical food additives and the foods that contain them. Then have students examine the ingredient lists from popular snacks, asking themselves what food value various snacks have, according to their labels (Neville, 1982).

SELF-CHECK: OBJECTIVE 3   What do critical readers need to know about the authors of the selections they are reading?

React to this statement: "I know it is correct because it is here in this book in black and white."

Name seven commonly used propaganda techniques. Give an example of each.

(See Self-Improvement Opportunities 1 and 3.)

Creative Reading

Creative reading involves going beyond the material presented by the author. Like critical reading, creative reading requires readers to think as they read, and it also requires them to use their imaginations. Such reading results in the production of new ideas.

Teachers must carefully nurture creative reading, trying not to ask only questions that have absolute answers, since such questions may discourage the diverse processes characteristic of creative reading. To go beyond the material in the text, readers must make use of their background schemata, combining this prior knowledge with ideas from the text to produce a new response based on, but not completely dictated by, the text. Creative readers must be skilled in the following areas.

Predicting Outcomes.   Predicting outcomes, discussed earlier as a good purpose-setting technique, is a creative reading skill. In order to predict outcomes, readers must put together available information and note trends, then project the trends into the future, making decisions about what events might logically follow. A creative reader is constantly predicting what will happen next in a story, reacting to the events he or she is reading about and drawing conclusions about their results.

An enjoyable way to work on this skill is to have students read one of the action comic strips in the newspaper for several weeks and then predict what will happen next, based on their knowledge of what has occurred until that time. The teacher can record these predictions on paper and file them; later, students can compare the actual ending of the adventure with their predictions. The teacher should be sure students can present reasons to justify what they predict. When judging their theories, the teacher should point out that some predictions may seem as good a way to end the story as the one the comic strip artist used. Other predictions may not make sense, based on the evidence, and reasons for this should be made clear.

literature-centered reading   Another way to work on prediction is to stop students at particular points in their reading of a literature selection and let them predict what will happen next.

In the story "Stone Soup," for example, the teacher would stop before the first townsperson contributed food to the soup and ask what the students think will happen next. A similar pause and request for a prediction after the point in the story at which the first contribution was made to the soup will then be appropriate.

To help students acquire the skill of reading creatively, teachers should model the thought process involved. After the students practice on various texts, the teacher can ask them to explain their reasons for thinking as they did. Some questions they might answer for *Heidi,* for example, are as follows:

What would have happened in the book if Peter had not pushed Klara's wheelchair down the side of the mountain?

What would have happened if Herr Sessman had refused to send Heidi back to the Alm, even though the doctor advised it?

Visualization.   *Visualization* is seeing pictures in the mind, and readers draw on their existing schemata to accomplish this. By vividly visualizing the events depicted by the author's words, creative readers allow themselves to become a part of the story; they see the colors, hear the sounds, feel the textures, taste the flavors, and smell the odors the writer describes. They will find that they are living the story as they read. By doing this, they will enjoy the story more and understand it more deeply.

Guided imagery has been shown to enhance comprehension, but training in visualization may be less effective with very young children, who may not be able to form images on command, than with third- through sixth-grade students (Tierney and Cunningham, 1984). It can be used before reading, during reading, or after reading. Students can be told to see pictures in their minds as they read silently. This can help them with later recall of events read. Guided imagery activities before reading a story can help readers draw on their past experiences to visualize events, places, and things in a story. Creating such images before reading has been shown to result in better literal comprehension than is produced by creating the images after reading (Harp, 1988; Fredericks, 1986).

Dee Mundell suggests four steps for helping children develop techniques for visualization. First, teachers should lead students to visualize concrete objects after they have seen and closely examined them in the classroom. Then teachers can ask children to visualize objects or experiences outside the classroom. They can draw concrete objects they visualize and compare their drawings to the actual objects later. Next, teachers can read high-imagery stories to the children, letting individuals share their mental images with the group and having small groups illustrate the stories after the reading. Finally, teachers should encourage students to visualize as they read independently (Fredericks, 1986).

Open-ended questions can aid development of imagery (Fredericks, 1986). For example, if a child says she sees a house, the teacher can ask, "What does it look like?" If she replies that it is white with green trim, the teacher may ask, "What is the yard like?"

Literature-centered reading

Following are activities that encourage visualization.

Activities

1. Give students copies of a paragraph from a children's book that vividly describes a scene or a situation, and have them illustrate the scene or situation in a painting or a three-dimensional art project.

2. Using a paragraph or statement that contains almost no description, ask students questions about details they would need in order to picture the scene in their minds. An example follows.

    The dog ran toward Jane and Susan. Jane held out her hands toward it and smiled.

    Questions: What kind of dog was it? How big was it? Why was it running toward the girls? What happened when the dog reached the girls? Where did this action take place? Was the dog on a leash, behind a fence, or running free?

3. Have the children dramatize a story they have read, such as the folktale "Caps for Sale."

4. Have students draw cartoon sequences that depict a story's events. Discuss the accuracy of the pictures in representing these events. Ask the students to imagine the cartoon sequences in their heads. Have them use their mental images to answer comprehension questions (Rasinski, 1988).

5. Have students write vivid descriptions of pictures they are shown. Then have them share and discuss the descriptions (Rasinski, 1988).

6. Compare the characters, action, and scenery in a movie with mental images formed from reading a book or story (Rasinski, 1988).

Solving Problems.   Creative readers relate the things they read to their own personal problems, sometimes applying the solution of a problem they encounter in a story to a different situation. For instance, after reading the chapter in *Tom Sawyer* in which Tom tricks his friends into painting a fence for him, a child may use a similar ruse to persuade a sibling to take over his or her chores or homework.

literature-centered reading

To work on developing this problem-solving skill, teachers need to use books in which different types of problems are solved, choosing an appropriate one to read or to let the children read. Then the teacher can ask the children questions such as the following:

1. What problem did the character(s) in the story face?

2. How was the problem handled?

3. Was the solution a good one?

THE FAMILY CIRCUS。   **By Bil Keane**

"I like reading. It turns on pictures in
your head."

Reprinted with special permission of King Features Syndicate, Inc.

4. What other possible solutions can you think of?

5. Would you prefer the solution in the book or one of the others?

Literature selections abound with characters trying to solve problems in efficient and inefficient ways. Children can analyze these problem-solving situations. Problems in a story can be identified as they occur. Discussion of the situation can take place at each problem occurrence. Some element of the story can be changed, and the children can then be asked how the character would have handled the new situation (Beck, 1989). *Encyclopedia Brown* and *Nate the Great* mysteries offer good problem-solving opportunities for children in intermediate and primary grades, respectively (Flynn, 1989). Any of the *Amelia Bedelia* books would also work well for this activity.

Bransford and Stein's IDEAL approach to problem solving is good to use in conjunction with cooperative learning techniques (Bransford and Stein, 1984; Flynn, 1989). The *I* stands for *identifying* the problem, the *D* for *defining* the problem more clearly, the *E* for *exploration* of the problem, the *A* for *acting* on ideas, and the *L* for *looking* for the effects. Cooperative learning techniques encourage the development of problem-solving skills through discussion, negotiation, clarification of ideas, and evaluation of the ideas of classmates. These activities lead to meeting group and individual goals.

In a game called "Here Comes the Judge," students wrote about problem situations that would require courtroom resolutions. One member of the group role-played the part of the judge; other group members played the parts of lawyers, defendants, and witnesses. The judge had to weigh the evidence presented and make the final decision (Flynn, 1989).

Improving Story Presentation.   Creative readers may be able to see how a story could be improved to make it more interesting. For example, excessive description may cause a story to move too slowly, and certain parts could be deleted or changed to be more concise. Another story may lack sufficient description to allow students to picture the setting and characters well enough to become involved. In this case, the teacher should ask them to add descriptive passages that make visualization easier. Perhaps one child believes that a story would be better with more dialogue and may write scenes for the characters, to replace third-person narration. Another child may think a story needs a more gripping opening paragraph. The possibilities for skill development are numerous, but the teacher must remember that this skill is extremely advanced and may be mastered only by the best readers in the elementary grades, although many others will attain it before their school years are over.

reading-writing connection

Producing New Creations.   Art, drama, and dance can be useful in elaborating on what students read. By creating a new ending for a story, adding a new character, changing some aspect of a character, or adding an additional adventure within the framework of the existing story, students approach reading creatively. Following are some possible activities; some of them involve responding to literature through writing. (More on the reading-writing connection appears in Chapter 8.)

reading-writing connection

literature-centered reading

Activities

1. Ask students to illustrate a story they have read, using a series of pictures or three-dimensional scenes.

2. Have students write plays or poems based on works of fiction they have read and enjoyed.

3. Have the students write prose narratives based on a poem they have read.

4. After the children have read several stories of a certain type (such as *Just So Stories*), ask each of them to write an original story of the same type.

5. Have the students transfer the story of Heidi to the Rocky Mountains or to Appalachia.

SELF-CHECK: OBJECTIVE 4   Define *creative reading* and discuss some of the things creative readers must be able to do.

Effective Questioning

Whether teachers prepare only test questions or both purpose and test questions, all teachers use both written and oral questions as a part of class activities. Regardless of when they are used, questions have been found to foster increased comprehension, apparently because readers give more time to the material related to answering them (Durkin, 1981b). Research indicates that simply asking more inference questions during and after reading stories results in improved inferential comprehension (Hansen, 1981a; Hansen and Pearson, 1983; Pearson, 1985). Thus, the types of questions that teachers ask about selections affect the type of information that students recall about selections, and students remember best information about which they have been directly questioned (Wixson, 1983). For this reason, teachers need to understand thoroughly the process of preparing questions.

Farrar (1983) believes that oral questioning for comprehension should be carried out differently from written questioning. Whereas written questions need to be clear, concise, and complete, oral questions are part of complex social interactions and may need to be stated differently, so that they will be less threatening. Questions stated in less threatening ways encourage responses. Hints and chains of questions that bring out needed background information and lead to successful answers to complex questions reduce the threat of questioning. Other educators believe that, instead of merely questioning students about literature, teachers should have conversations about it with students. They should not turn the conversations into inquisitions. The teacher can enter the conversations and discussions as a member of the group (Harp, 1989). This approach opens the way to questions that ask for information the questioner really wants, rather than questions that merely check comprehension.

Farrar (1984a) asserts that the phrasing of questions should depend on the amount of challenge individual children need. Questions can be phrased differently and still address the same content. The phrasing can make questions easier or harder to answer and can require simple or complex answers. It may take several questions requiring simple responses to elicit all the information obtainable from one question that requires a complex response.

Another related problem is some children's lack of familiarity with the question-answer-feedback sequence often used for instructional purposes. Some children have not been exposed to this language pattern at home and find it strange and confusing that the teacher is asking for information he or she already knows. Teachers may need to actively teach the question-answer-feedback strategy in oral and written situations so that students will respond appropriately (Farrar, 1984b). Teacher modeling of the answers to questions is helpful. In the process, the teacher can explain how to interpret the question, how and where to find the information, and how to construct the answer after the information is located (Armbruster, 1992).

Preparing Questions

Teachers often ask questions that are devised on the spur of the moment. This practice no doubt results from the pressure of the many different tasks a teacher must perform during the day, but it is a poor one for at least two reasons. First, questions developed hastily, without close attention to the material involved, tend to be detail questions ("What color was the car? Where were they going?"), since detail questions are much easier to construct than most other types. But detail questions fail to measure more than simple recall. Second, many hastily constructed questions tend to be poorly worded, vague in intent, and misleading to students. Example 6.6 shows some options on which to base questioning.

Example 6.6   *Options for Questioning*

Questions Based on Comprehension Factors

1. Main idea—identify central theme or idea of selection
2. Detail—identify directly stated facts
3. Vocabulary—define words to fit the context of the selection
4. Sequence—identify order of events in selection
5. Inference—infer information implied by the author
6. Evaluation—judge ideas presented, based on a standard
7. Creative response—go beyond the material and create new ideas based on the material read

Questions Based on Source of Answers

1. Textually explicit—answers directly stated in the text
2. Textually implicit—answers implied by the text that require inferences on the part of the reader
3. Scriptually implicit—answers come from the reader's background knowledge

Questions Based on Story Grammar

1. Setting—when and where story took place and who was involved
2. Initiating event—event that started story sequence
3. Reaction—main character's reaction to the initiating event
4. Action—main character's actions caused by the initiating event and subsequent events
5. Consequence—result of main character's actions

Questions Based on Comprehension Factors

One basis for planning questioning strategies is to try to construct specific types of questions to tap different types of comprehension and different factors related to comprehension. Seven major types of questions are generally useful in guiding reading: main idea, detail, vocabulary, sequence, inference, evaluation, and creative response.

Main Idea Questions.   Main idea questions ask the children to identify the central theme of the selection. These questions may give children some direction toward the nature of the answer. The question "What caused Susie to act so excited?" could direct readers toward the main idea of a passage in which Susie was very excited because she had a secret. An example of a question that offers no clues to the main idea is "What is a sentence that explains what this selection is about?" Main idea questions help children to become aware of the relationships among details.

Detail Questions.   Detail questions ask for bits of information covered by the material. They ask for information such as "Who was coming to play with Maria? What was Betty bringing with her? What happened to Betty on the way to Maria's house? When did Betty finally arrive? Where had Betty left her bicycle?" Whereas it is important for students to assimilate the information these questions cover, very little depth of comprehension is necessary to answer them all correctly. Therefore, even though these questions are easy to construct, they should not constitute the bulk of the questions the teacher asks.

Vocabulary Questions.   Vocabulary questions check children's understanding of word meanings, generally as used in a particular selection. For discussion purposes, a teacher might ask children to produce as many meanings of a specific word as they can, but purpose questions and test questions should ask for the meaning of a word as it is used in the selection being read.

Sequence Questions.   Sequence questions check the child's knowledge of the order in which events occurred in the story. The question "What did Alex and Robbie do when their parents left the house?" is not a sequence question, since children are free to list the events in any order they choose. The question "What three things did Alex and Robbie do, in order, when their parents left the house?" requires children to display their grasp of the sequence of events.

Inference Questions.   Inference questions ask for information that is implied but not directly stated in the material. These questions require some reading between the lines. The following is an example.

> Margie and Jan were sitting on the couch listening to Michael Bolton CDs. Their father walked in and announced, "I hear that Michael Bolton is giving a concert at the Municipal Auditorium next week." Both girls jumped up and ran toward their father. "Can we go? Can we go?" they begged.

Question: Do you think Margie and Jan liked to hear Michael Bolton sing? Why or why not?

The types of questions that teachers ask about selections affect the type of information that students recall about selections, and students remember best information about which they have been directly questioned. (© *Joel Gordon*)

Evaluation Questions. Evaluation questions require children to make judgments about the material. Although these judgments are inferences, they depend on more than the information implied or stated by the story; the children must have enough experience related to the situations involved to establish standards for comparison. An example of an evaluation question is "Was the method Kim used to rescue Dana wise? Why or why not?" These questions are excellent for open-ended class discussion but hard to grade as test questions.

Creative Response Questions. Creative response questions ask children to go beyond the material and create new ideas based on the ideas they have read. Questions requiring creative response are also good for class discussions. As a means of testing comprehension of a passage, however, they are not desirable, since almost any response could be considered correct. Examples of creative response questions include "If the story stopped after Jimmy lost his money, what ending would you write for it?" and "If Meg had not gone to school that day, what do you think might have happened?"

Other Categorizations of Question Types

Pearson and Johnson (1978) suggest three question types. They label questions as *textually explicit* when they have answers that are directly stated in the text, *textually implicit* when they have implied answers (but the text contains clues for making the necessary inference), and *scriptually implicit* when the reader must answer them from his or her background knowledge.

The reader's own characteristics interact with the text and the question to determine the actual demands of the question-answering task. A reader's interest, background knowledge, and reading skill affect the difficulty and type of question for each reader. The structure of a question may lead a teacher to expect a textually explicit response, whereas the student's background may cause him or her to give a scriptually implicit response (Wixson, 1983). For example, if the text tells readers how to construct a kite, a child who has actually made a kite before reading the material may answer the question on the basis of direct experience, rather than from information presented in the text.

Inability to take the perspective of another person can affect comprehension. Students who can take the perspective of another person do better on scriptually implicit questions than those who cannot (Gardner and Smith, 1987).

Story Grammar as a Basis for Questioning

Another basis for questioning deserves attention: use of story grammar. A story is a series of events that are related to one another in particular ways. As people hear and read many stories, they develop expectations, sometimes called *story schemata,* about the types of things they will encounter; these help them organize information. Related story schemata are described by *a story grammar.* As Sadow (1982) suggests, questions based on a story grammar may help children develop story schemata. The questions should be chosen to reflect the logical sequence of events.

David Rumelhart proposed a simple story grammar that "describes a story as consisting of a setting and one or more episodes" (Sadow, 1982, p. 519). The setting includes the main characters and the time and location of the events, and each episode contains an initiating event, the main character's reaction to it, an action of the main character caused by this reaction, and a consequence of the action, which may act as an initiating event for a subsequent episode. (Sometimes some of the elements of an episode are not directly stated.) Sadow suggests the following five generic questions as appropriate types to ask about a story:

1. Where and when did the events in the story take place, and who was involved in them? (setting)

2. What started the chain of events in the story? (initiating event)

3. What was the main character's reaction to this event? (reaction)

4. What did the main character do about it? (action)

5. What happened as a result of what the main character did? (consequence) (p. 520)

Such questions can help students see the underlying order of ideas in a story, but of course teachers should reword them to fit the story and the particular children. For example, Question 1 can be broken into three questions (*where, when, who*), and the teacher can provide appropriate focus by using words or phrases from the story. After students address these story grammar questions, which establish the essential facts, they should answer questions that help them relate the story to their experiences and knowledge (Sadow, 1982).

Marshall (1983) has also suggested using story grammar as a basis for developing comprehension questions and for evaluating student retellings, which can sometimes be used instead of questions. A checklist for story retellings can indicate if story parts were included and whether they were included with or without prompts. In Marshall's questioning scheme, *theme* questions are similar to main idea questions and ask about the major point or moral of the story. As in Sadow's questioning scheme, *setting* questions are *where* and *when* questions. *Character* questions ask about the main character and/or other characters. *Initiating events* questions often ask about a problem faced by a particular character. *Attempts* questions ask what a character did about a situation or what he or she will do. *Resolution* questions ask how a character solved the problem or what the reader would do to solve the problem. *Reaction* questions focus on what a character felt, the reasons for a character's actions or feelings, or the feelings of the reader.

Guidelines for Preparation

Some guidelines for preparing questions may be useful to teachers who wish to improve their questioning techniques. The following suggestions may help teachers avoid some pitfalls that other educators have detected:

1. In trying to determine overall comprehension skills, ask a variety of questions designed to reflect different types of comprehension. *Avoid overloading the evaluation with a single type of question.*

2. Don't ask questions about obscure or insignificant portions of the selection. Such questions may make a test harder, but they don't convey realistic indications of comprehension. *"Hard" tests and "good" tests are not necessarily synonymous.*

3. Avoid ambiguous or tricky questions. *If a question has two or more possible interpretations, more than one answer for it has to be acceptable.*

4. Questions that a person who has not read the material can answer correctly offer you no valuable information about comprehension. *Avoid useless questions.*

5. Don't ask questions in language that is more difficult than the language of the selection the question is about. *Sometimes you can word questions in a way that prevents a child who knows the answer from responding appropriately.*

6. Make sure the answers to sequence questions require knowledge of the *order* of events. *Don't confuse questions that simply ask for lists with sequence questions.*

7. Don't ask for unsupported opinions when you are testing for comprehension. Have children give support for their opinions, by asking, "Why do you think that?" or "What in the story made you think that?" *If you ask for an unsupported opinion, any answer will be correct.*

8. Don't ask for opinions if you want facts. *Ask for the type of information you want to receive.*

9. Avoid questions that give away information. Instead of asking, "What makes you believe the boy was angry?" ask, "How do you think the boy felt? Why?" *Questions may lead students to the answers by supplying too much information.*

10. If a question can be answered with a *yes* or a *no*, or if a choice of answers is offered, the child has a chance to answer the question correctly without having to read the selection at all. *Avoid questions that offer choices.*

11. Use precise terms in phrasing questions related to reading. *Ask students to compare or contrast, to predict, or to draw conclusions about the reading* (Smith, 1989).

Helping Students Answer Questions

Raphael and Pearson (1982) taught students three types of Question-Answer Relationships (QARs). QAR instruction encourages students to consider both information in the text and their own background knowledge when answering questions (Raphael, 1986). The relationship for questions with answers directly stated in the text in one sentence was called "Right There." The students looked for the words in the question and read the sentence containing those words to locate the answer. The relationship for questions with an answer in the story that required information from multiple sentences or paragraphs was called "Think and Search," and the relationship for questions for which answers had to come from the reader's own knowledge was called "On My Own" (Raphael and Pearson, 1982). Modeling the decision about question-answer relationships and correct answers based on them was an important part of the teaching. Supervised practice following the modeling, with immediate feedback on student responses, was also important. The practice involved gradually increased passage lengths, progressing from simpler to more difficult tasks (Raphael, 1982). Learning the three types of QARs enhanced students' success in answering questions. The training appeared to help average- and low-ability students most (Raphael, 1984). Primary-grade children needed more repetition to learn QARs than intermediate-grade children did (Raphael, 1986).

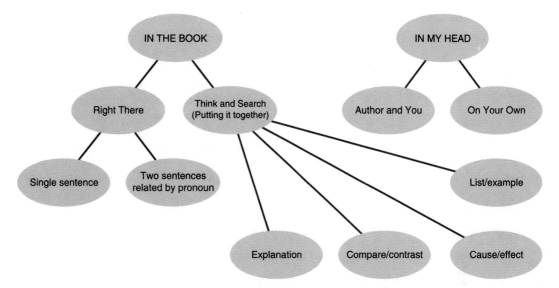

Source: Reprinted with permission of Taffy E. Raphael and the International Reading Association.

Raphael (1986) subsequently modified QAR instruction to include four categories, clustered under two headings. The following diagram illustrates this modification.

In the modified scheme, the "In My Head" category is divided into questions that involve both the text information and the reader's background of experiences (Author and You) and those that can be answered from the reader's experience without information from the story (On My Own) (Raphael 1986).

Discussing the use of the QAR categorization to plan questioning strategies, Raphael (1986) states:

> Questions asked prior to reading are usually On My Own QARs. They are designed to help students think about what they already know and how it relates to the upcoming story or content text. In creating guided reading questions, it is important to balance text-based and inference questions. For these, Think and Search QARs should dominate, since they require integration of information and should build to the asking of Author and You QARs. Finally, for extension activities, teachers will want to create primarily On My Own or Author and You QARs, focusing again on students' background information as it pertains to the text. (p. 521)

Helping Students Question

Active readers constantly question the text. As they construct meaning, they ask themselves, "Does this make sense?" Many authorities advocate teaching the reader to generate questions throughout the reading process to enhance comprehension, and such training has proven to be effective. Students who are trained to ask literal questions about material being read have learned to discriminate questions from nonquestions and good literal questions from poor ones. After they practiced the production of good literal questions for paragraphs and then for stories that they read to answer the questions, their comprehension improved (Cohen, 1983). Other students who were taught (through modeling, with gradual phasing out of teacher involvement) to generate their own questions based on a story grammar also had enhanced comprehension (Nolte and Singer, 1985). Bristow (1985) believes that provision of interspersed questions in the text to provide a transition from teacher questioning to self-questioning may be helpful.

Kitagawa (1982, p. 43) encouraged children to become questioners by asking questions that had to be answered by a question, such as "What question did the author mainly answer in the passage we just read?" She also encouraged them to develop questions they wished to have answered through educational activities, such as field trips, and to construct preview questions, based on titles and pictures, for reading selections. Students were asked what questions they would ask the author of a selection or a character, if they could, and they were asked to predict the questions that would be answered next in the selection.

The Reciprocal Questioning (ReQuest) procedure, developed by Manzo (1969), seems a promising way to improve reading comprehension as well as help children develop questioning techniques. ReQuest is a one-to-one teaching technique that encourages children to formulate questions about the reading material. Following is a condensed outline of the procedure:

1. Both child and teacher have copies of the selection to be read.

2. Both silently read the first sentence. The child may ask the teacher as many questions as he or she wishes about that sentence. The child is told to try to ask the kinds of questions the teacher might ask, in the way the teacher might ask them.

3. The teacher answers the questions but requires the child to rephrase those questions he or she cannot answer because of their poor syntax or incorrect logic.

4. After the teacher has answered all of the child's questions, both read the second sentence, and the teacher asks as many questions as he or she believes will profitably add to the child's understanding of the content.

5. After reading the second sentence, the teacher requires the child to integrate the ideas from both sentences.

6. As the reading progresses, the teacher periodically asks the child to verify his or her responses.

Throughout this interaction, the teacher constantly encourages the child to imitate the teacher's questioning behavior, reinforcing such behavior by saying, "That's a good question" or by giving the fullest possible reply.

This procedure continues until the child can read all of the words in the first paragraph, can demonstrate literal understanding of what he or she read, and can formulate a reasonable purpose, stated as a question, for completing the remainder of the selection.

SELF-CHECK: OBJECTIVE 5   Name seven types of questions that are useful in guiding reading and checking comprehension.
List five of the eleven guidelines for question preparation mentioned in this section that you believe are most important.
(See Self-Improvement Opportunity 4.)

Summary

This chapter examines types of reading comprehension. Literal comprehension results from reading for directly stated ideas. Higher-order comprehension goes beyond literal comprehension to include interpretive, critical, and creative reading. Interpretive reading is reading for implied ideas; critical reading is reading for evaluation; and creative reading is reading beyond the lines. Teachers can generally teach strategies in all of these areas most effectively through explanation and modeling, guided student practice, and independent student practice.

Questioning techniques are important to instruction because teachers use questions to provide purposes for reading, elicit and focus discussion, and check comprehension of material read. Questions may be based on comprehension factors or story structure. Students may need to be taught how to approach answering questions. Self-questioning by the reader is also a valuable comprehension and comprehension-monitoring technique. Teachers can help students develop the skill of self-questioning.

Test Yourself   *True or False*

_____   1. Literal comprehension involves acquiring information that is directly stated in a selection.

_____   2. Students must attend to details when they follow directions.

_____   3. Critical reading is reading for evaluation.

_____   4. Critical reading strategies are easier to teach than literal reading strategies.

_____   5. Higher-order comprehension may involve determining the author's purpose.

_____ 6. Critical readers are not interested in copyright dates of material they read.

_____ 7. An inference is an idea that is implied in the material, rather than being directly stated.

_____ 8. Elementary school children are too young to be able to recognize propaganda techniques.

_____ 9. A bandwagon approach takes advantage of the desires of people to conform to the crowd.

_____ 10. Critical thinking skills should first be given attention in the intermediate grades.

_____ 11. Critical readers read with a questioning attitude.

_____ 12. Creative reading involves going beyond the material presented by the author.

_____ 13. Teachers should give little class time to creative reading because it is not practical.

_____ 14. In composing comprehension questions for testing purposes, teachers should use several types of questions.

_____ 15. A good test is a hard test, and vice versa.

_____ 16. Listing questions and sequence questions are the same thing.

_____ 17. The main idea of a paragraph is always stated in the form of a topic sentence.

_____ 18. Children make inferences that are consistent with their schemata.

_____ 19. Some children have difficulty determining referents of pronouns and adverbs.

_____ 20. Young children are unable to make inferences.

Self-Improvement Opportunities

1. Use old newspapers to devise teaching materials for
   a. finding main ideas.
   b. locating propaganda techniques.
   c. distinguishing fact from opinion.
   d. recognizing sequence.
2. Make a board game based on a favorite children's book for a grade of your choice.

3. Make a file of examples of each propaganda technique listed in the chapter. File ideas for teaching activities, games, bulletin boards, and so on, and show your files to your classmates, sharing with them the possible instructional uses of your file.

4. Using the seven question types based on comprehension factors that are described in this chapter, make up questions about the content of this chapter or of another chapter in this book. Bring the questions to class, and ask classmates to respond.

Chapter 7

Key Vocabulary

Pay close attention to these terms when they appear in the chapter.

computer-assisted instruction

computer-managed instruction

directed reading activity

directed reading-thinking activity

eclectic approaches

individualized reading approach

interest inventory

language experience approach

linguistics

literature-based approaches

minimally contrasting spelling patterns

programmed instruction

trade books

word bank

Major Approaches and Materials for Reading Instruction

Setting Objectives

When you finish reading this chapter, you should be able to

1. Discuss the characteristics of different types of published reading series.

2. Compare and contrast a directed reading activity with a directed reading-thinking activity.

3. Discuss the characteristics of literature-based approaches to reading instruction.

4. Explain the rationale behind the language experience approach.

5. Discuss the place of computers in reading instructional programs.

6. Discuss how a teacher might use elements of several approaches in a single classroom.

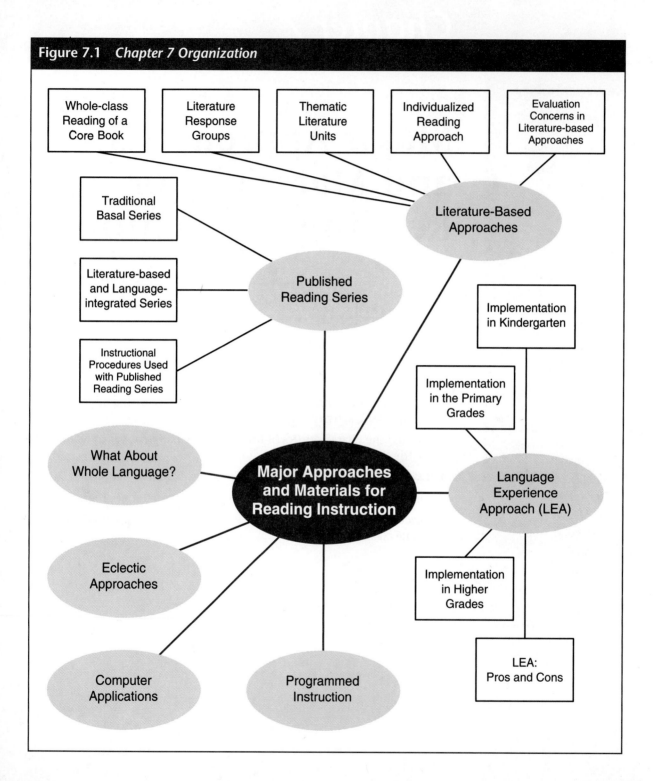

Figure 7.1 *Chapter 7 Organization*

Whole-class Reading of a Core Book

Literature Response Groups

Thematic Literature Units

Individualized Reading Approach

Evaluation Concerns in Literature-based Approaches

Literature-Based Approaches

Traditional Basal Series

Literature-based and Language-integrated Series

Published Reading Series

Instructional Procedures Used with Published Reading Series

Implementation in Kindergarten

Implementation in the Primary Grades

What About Whole Language?

Major Approaches and Materials for Reading Instruction

Language Experience Approach (LEA)

Eclectic Approaches

Implementation in Higher Grades

Computer Applications

Programmed Instruction

LEA: Pros and Cons

O ver the years, educators have developed many approaches to teaching reading. This chapter discusses some of the more widely accepted approaches. These approaches are not mutually exclusive; many teachers use more than one method simultaneously. They often select the best techniques and materials from a number of approaches to meet the varied needs of individual students in their classrooms. We take the position that no one approach is best for all students or all teachers. Therefore, we attempt to acquaint teachers with the characteristics of different approaches so that they will be able to choose intelligently the procedures to be used in their classrooms.

Just as there are many approaches, there are many types of materials that can be used for reading instruction, varying from chalkboards and charts to published reading series, library books, and computers. All are tools to help teachers present reading instruction effectively.

Because whole language is a philosophy (see Chapter 1), we do not present it as an approach in this chapter. Some of the approaches given here, however, are consistent with the whole language philosophy, and teachers can use most instructional materials holistically.

Published Reading Series

Many schools depend on published reading series for materials to support reading instruction. For many years, the published reading series have been like the traditional basal series described here. These series have been evolving over time. Recently, publishers have been moving toward more literature-based and language-integrated series as they try to take into account both the criticisms of the traditional series and the current theory and research in reading.

Traditional Basal Series

For many years, basal reader series have been the most widely used materials for teaching reading in the elementary schools of the United States. They begin with prereading materials and provide materials for development and practice of reading strategies in each grade. These series generally have consisted of one or more readiness books, some preprimers, a primer, a first reader, and one or two readers for each successive grade level through grade six or eight.

In addition to the student books, basal reader series include teacher's manuals with detailed lesson plans to help teachers use the readers effectively. Teachers who follow these plans use what is called a *directed reading activity (DRA)*, described later in this chapter. Basal reader series also include workbooks and/or blackline duplicating masters of skill sheets that children can use to practice skills and strategies they have previously learned in class. Workbooks are not designed to teach the skills and strategies and should not be used for this purpose. Many publishing companies offer other supplementary materials to be used in conjunction with basal series, such as "big books" (chart-sized replicas of books); student

literature-centered reading

journals; read-aloud libraries for the teacher; unit tests; puppets to go with some early stories; computer management, reinforcement, and/or enrichment activities; and various other items. Big books are important tools in holistic teaching. They are discussed in detail in Chapter 2.

literature-centered reading   Basal reading series are quite useful for elementary school teachers. They provide anthologies of stories, content area selections, poems, plays, and so on that can be the basis for enriching classroom reading activities. Many of these pieces are whole selections or excerpts from high-quality literature. The new basals contain much literature because the publishers are trying to provide material that teachers want (Cullinan, 1992). Many newer basal reading programs are presenting integrated, thematic approaches to reading, but not all of these programs provide teachers with theme-level goals and objectives. Many of the cross-curricular activities have weak relations to the theme and the other curricular areas and therefore lack sufficient focus and connections, although they are improvements on previous basal units (Lipson et al., 1993).

The teacher's manuals offer many valuable suggestions for teaching reading lessons and thus can save much lesson preparation time. Such suggestions are becoming less skill driven and more language oriented in many series and offer positive guidance for teachers, helping them to include all aspects of reading (word recognition, comprehension, oral reading, silent reading, reading for information, and reading for enjoyment) in their reading lessons. Manuals allow for systematic teaching and reteaching of skills and strategies and systematic review. They also offer ways to monitor the success of the instruction (Wiggins, 1994).

As Wiggins (1994) points out, when a basal reading program is used, teachers have an idea of what the students have been taught in past years. This can aid in curricular planning.

Some educators do not view all of these characteristics favorably. To them, the fact that the anthologies provide identical materials for groups of children appears to negate student choice, although much student choice can still take place in classrooms in which basals are used, if teachers provide opportunities for choice. For example, students can choose certain stories to read and discuss in their reading groups, leaving other stories to be used for independent or partner reading or not to be read at all.

For some educators, the carefully graded materials and controlled vocabularies of basals evoke the image of "dumbed-down" (overly simplified) text that has received so much media attention. Many publishers today, however, seem to be considering factors other than readability formulas to aid in placement, and vocabulary control may be more often accomplished by using traditional stories with repetitive lines and predictable formats than by changing the stories to fit vocabulary goals.

Some educators believe the detailed lesson plans offered in the basals tie teachers down to a specific lesson sequence and release them from exercising personal judgment. This outcome is possible, of course, but it need not be the case. Teachers may choose from among the offered suggestions those that fit their needs and discard the ones that do not. If, however, teachers try to do everything suggested, they may use valuable time for activities that are inappropriate for some groups of children, leaving inadequate time for appropriate ones. Teachers should not use basal readers from front to back in their entirety without considering the special needs of the children in their classes. A teacher might use one set of activities from the basal one year and a different set the next year to accommodate the different needs of the two classes.

The systematic teaching of skills and strategies will not appeal to educators who believe that there is no particular skill sequence that should be followed and that skill instruction should arise out of observed needs. Even those who believe these things, however, may find some of the teaching suggestions in basals useful for adaptation to specific situations when the need for a skill or strategy is evident.

literature-centered reading

Authors of basal readers are continually working to improve them. To provide stories with high quality, limited vocabulary, and extensive repetition, they include unaltered folktales in some of the early readers. They also include other good literature, often without adaptation, as well as more content area material. Unlike the language in earlier basal readers, the language in today's basal readers is more natural and conversational. They have diversified characters, including people of various racial and ethnic groups, elderly people, and people with disabilities, and depict them in less stereotyped ways than in the past. Women are portrayed in roles other than the traditional ones.

reading-writing connection

Some educators have complained that basal reader workbook pages often fail to relate directly to the story in the reader and give insufficient attention to higher-level comprehension skills. Therefore, teachers may wish to have students write responses to the selections in reading logs and let students discuss the selections in literature response groups or use a variety of other literary response activities, such as drama, art, and storytelling, rather than depending on workbook activities that are unrelated to the stories or that cover comprehension superficially.

Although some educators have rejected basal readers, based on shortcomings that typified much different reading series than the ones available today, McCallum (1988) warns teachers to avoid "throwing out the basals with the bath water." He points out the efforts that basal publishers have made to put many research findings about reading to practice in basal lessons within the context of the pressures classroom teachers face. He applauds the fact that basal readers address considerations from diagnosis to reading appreciation and that they offer suggestions for both instructional techniques and guided practice. He recognizes, as do others, that continued revisions of the series are needed to continue improving the offerings. Teachers must be prepared to analyze the content of basal programs, make use of the good materials when they are appropriate to the particular classroom contexts, and choose not to use inappropriate suggestions. They should make their instructional needs known to publishers. Publishers have been responsive to user reactions in the past and are likely to continue to be responsive.

Hoffman and McCarthey (1995) report that studies of the first grade materials of old and new basals of five companies show that the new materials are very different from the old ones. The new materials have less vocabulary control, more diversity of genre, minimal adaptations, higher literary quality, increased predictability, and decreased decodability. These findings are encouraging.

Uses and Misuses of Basal Materials

Much of the criticism of basal readers has focused on less than desirable uses of the materials. Teachers have a responsibility to plan the use of all materials in their classrooms, including the basal readers, regardless of the presence or absence of guiding suggestions accompanying the materials.

If teachers perceive basals as *total* reading programs, they may fail to provide the variety of experiences children need for a balanced program. Basals can never provide all of the reading situations a student needs to encounter.

Many teachers form basal reading groups based on achievement. They place the best readers in the top group, the average readers in a middle group or groups, and the poorest readers in the lowest group. In this way, these teachers believe they can provide all of the children with basal materials that are appropriate for their reading levels. In actuality, however, the match of materials with children is not always good. Forell (1985) has pointed out that good readers are often placed in comfortable reading materials in which word recognition problems are not frequent and attention can be given to meaning, using context clues to advantage. Poor readers, however, are often placed in "challenging" material that causes frustration and is not conducive to comprehension, because so much attention is needed for word recognition—an arrangement that denies them a chance for fluent reading. All readers should be given material that is comfortable enough to allow reasonable application of comprehension skills. Teachers may be reluctant to place students in materials at as low a level as they need in order to allow this to happen, but doing so can be beneficial in the long run.

Wiggins (1994) suggests a different way to use the basal that could alleviate the problems created by some current grouping practices. He recommends teaching core basal reader lessons with the whole class and forming small groups for follow-up activities. The composition of the small groups would be flexible, clustering students with common weaknesses and strengths, and would be based on the needs for that particular day. All students would start at the beginning of the on-grade-level book, and instruction, rather than materials, would be adjusted. Although vocabulary would be introduced, prior knowledge assessed, purposes developed for reading, and discussions of reading held in a whole-class setting, differentiated reinforcement activities would be provided in small groups, according to the specific needs. Some small groups might be teacher-directed; others might be cooperative. Center work could also provide reinforcement. The reading center might involve independent reading, shared reading, peer tutoring, or cooperative learning activities.

Blanton, Moorman, and Wood (1986) suggest that teachers use direct instruction in basal reader skill lessons in the following way:

1. Assess the students' background knowledge related to the skill.

2. Explain the skill in detail, including when it is needed and why it is important.

3. Have the students try to explain the skill in their own words.

4. Model the use of the skill for the students and then provide them with guided practice with the skill.

5. Have students apply the skill in regular reading materials, with the teacher monitoring and providing instruction as needed.

6. Lead the students in discussion of real-world encounters with the skill. For example, they might decide that reading recipes makes extensive use of the skill of detecting sequence.

The basal reader series can be seen as a continuum from the rigidly controlled and teacher-directed materials of yesterday to the more open-ended, diverse, and student-centered materials of today. (© *Carol Palmer/The Picture Cube*)

Some of these steps may already be included in basal manual instructions. Teachers can add the other steps for more complete skills lessons.

Some educators have expressed concern that teachers do not allow students to do a sufficient amount of contextual reading (as opposed to reading isolated words and sentences). Although some studies (for example, Gambrell, 1984) have reinforced this concern, it is not necessarily a fault of the basal, but of the implementation of the lessons. Teachers need to provide much time for actual reading of connected text, if reading programs are to be successful, regardless of the approach used.

There is no reason for teachers to use basal readers *only* as indicated in the manual (Weiss, 1987; Fuhler, 1990; Reutzel, 1986). Weiss (1987) points out possible variations from following suggestions in teacher's manuals exactly. She suggests that teachers read the selection and decide what should be done before, during, and after reading, allowing the children input into the lesson. Students may be asked to illustrate scenes from the story, write questions to be answered by other class members, write other adventures for story characters, read books by the author of the story or books related to the story, or engage in many other activities that encourage active participation and interaction with the selection. Fuhler (1990) also encourages teachers to pick and choose from basal materials according to the children's needs.

reading-writing connection

literature-centered reading

Educators have expressed considerable concern about the misuse of workbooks that accompany basal readers; some teachers use them to keep children busy while they meet with other children or do paperwork. Wiggins (1994) decries the fact that some teachers assign all pages sequentially to all students, regardless of appropriateness to the individual child's needs. It is important to note that the fault here is with the teachers' procedures and not with the workbooks. Workbook activities should always be purposeful, and teachers should never assign workbook pages simply to keep students occupied. Teachers should also grade and return completed workbook assignments promptly, since children need to have correct responses reinforced immediately and need to be informed about incorrect responses so that they will not continue to make them.

There are ways by which teachers can increase the effectiveness of their use of workbooks. One possibility is to use the every-pupil-response technique, having all students respond to instructions at the same time. When students are to respond orally to the exercises, the teacher can ask a question and then call on a specific child to answer. By giving the question before calling on a specific student, the teacher encourages all the children to listen to and consider the question, since they do not know who will be asked to respond (Schachter, 1981).

In summary, teachers do not have to follow all suggestions in the manuals—or, indeed, *any* of the suggestions—in order to use basal materials to provide children with a variety of reading materials that would not otherwise be available in many schools. Likewise, they are not limited to using only the suggestions in the manuals. The manner in which basal materials are used, not the basals themselves, has often been the main concern about basal programs.

Types of Basal Reading Programs

Although the preceding discussion of basal reading programs contained some generalizations about them, the intention is not to imply that all basal reader series are alike. On the contrary, these series differ in basic philosophies, order of presentation of strategies and skills, degree and type of vocabulary control, types of selections, and number and types of practice activities provided. Some supplement workbook/skill sheet material with student journals that call for more varied responses. Most are eclectic in approach, but some emphasize a single method, such as a linguistic or an intensive phonics approach.

Linguistics is the scientific study of human speech. Linguistic scientists (also called *linguists*), such as Leonard Bloomfield, have provided principles that have affected development of reading instructional materials. Some of these principles have been applied to many of the basal reading series. Several series have been based specifically on Bloomfield's ideas and have incorporated a number of his beliefs, including the following:

1. Beginning readers should be presented with material that uses only a single sound for a letter at a time. Other sounds for the letter should not be presented until the first association is mastered.

2. Irregularly spelled words should be avoided in beginning reading material, although some (for example, *a* and *the*) must be used to construct sentences that have relatively normal patterns.

3. Word-attack skills should be taught by presenting *minimally contrasting spelling patterns,* words that vary by a single letter. For example, one lesson might contain the words *can, tan, man, ban, fan, ran,* and *pan.* This exposure to minimally contrasting patterns is designed to help the child understand the difference a certain letter makes in the pronunciation of a word.

4. Sounds should not be isolated from words, however, because when sounds are pronounced outside the environment of a word, they are distorted. This is particularly true of isolated consonant sounds; *buh, duh,* and *puh* are sounds incorrectly associated with the letters *b, d,* and *p.*

These materials emphasize reading orally. Reading is looked on as turning writing back into spoken language. (See Bloomfield and Barnhart [1961], for a discussion of Bloomfield's approach.)

Series that focus on intensive phonics use a synthetic phonics approach to phonics instruction. (See Chapter 3 for a description of this approach.) The materials often look similar to the ones found in a linguistic series, but the sounds are not isolated from the words in a linguistic approach, whereas they are taught in isolation and then blended into words in a synthetic phonics approach.

Teachers should be aware of the differences among basal series. Before a school system adopts a basal series, teachers should examine many series and select the one that best fits their own student population and supports their philosophy regarding reading instruction.

Changes Occurring in Basal Reader Programs

Despite the variations in philosophy and presentation described in the previous section, traditional basal reader programs have focused primarily on reading instruction, rather than on the integration of language skills. Generally they have contained much specially written material and/or many adapted stories in order to fit grade-level readability standards. All lessons have tended to be teacher directed, with little time allocated for independent reading by the students. Generally only one teaching procedure has been suggested, although enough enrichment suggestions were often included to give teachers some choice in individualizing their class presentations. The series' skill instruction and practice components have often included mainly work with isolated words, sentences, and paragraphs, and they have often had numerous skill activities to be completed in each lesson.

literature-centered reading   Many current series have moved away from this traditional mold. More are offering integrated reading and language instruction, providing literature selections or excerpts that have not been modified heavily (or at all), and offering practice activities that go beyond worksheets alone. They are often explicitly giving the teacher greater decision-making power in using the materials and are frequently including more independent student activities. Publishers are incorporating the newer techniques to different degrees. One of the most common variations among series lies in the approaches taken to the skill instruction and practice. Most publishers have tried to retain the positive features of their previous programs, while offering more literature and integrated activities. The offerings of basal reader series, finally, can be seen as a continuum from the rigidly controlled and teacher-directed materials of yesterday to the more open-ended, diverse, and student-centered materials of today. Some publishers have moved so far in the new directions that they now refer to their materials as *literature-based* and *language-integrated* series to reflect the newer philosophy.

Literature-Based and Language-Integrated Series

literature-centered reading   One of the most widely heralded moves recently made by educational publishers is the creation of *literature-based* reading series. These programs offer quality literature selections for students to read, often in their entirety and without adaptation. In addition, some series are integrating instruction involving all the
reading-writing connection   language arts, including listening, speaking, and writing activities to accompany the literature selections that make the lessons true communication experiences. Example 7.1 shows excerpts from a literature-based series selection.

The story presented is the fourth one in a thematic unit of five related stories about "Experiences." The major outcome expected from the unit is that the "students read, understand, and share personal narratives" (p. 173B). Page 173E shows an overview of how the theme is taught in relation to *Barrio Boy*. Pages 174B–174D offer information about prereading activities, theme goals, and ongoing theme activities. Pages 205J–205K offer teachers a variety of activities from

Example 7.1   *Literature-Based Series Example*

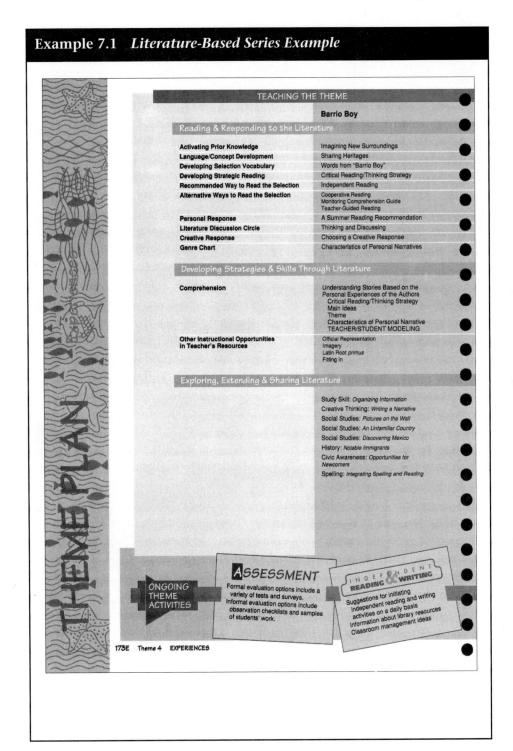

THEME PLAN

TEACHING THE THEME

Barrio Boy

Reading & Responding to the Literature

Activating Prior Knowledge	Imagining New Surroundings
Language/Concept Development	Sharing Heritages
Developing Selection Vocabulary	Words from "Barrio Boy"
Developing Strategic Reading	Critical Reading/Thinking Strategy
Recommended Way to Read the Selection	Independent Reading
Alternative Ways to Read the Selection	Cooperative Reading
	Monitoring Comprehension Guide
	Teacher-Guided Reading
Personal Response	A Summer Reading Recommendation
Literature Discussion Circle	Thinking and Discussing
Creative Response	Choosing a Creative Response
Genre Chart	Characteristics of Personal Narratives

Developing Strategies & Skills Through Literature

Comprehension	Understanding Stories Based on the Personal Experiences of the Authors
	Critical Reading/Thinking Strategy
	Main Ideas
	Theme
	Characteristics of Personal Narrative
	TEACHER/STUDENT MODELING
Other Instructional Opportunities in Teacher's Resources	Official Representation
	Imagery
	Latin Root *primus*
	Fitting In

Exploring, Extending & Sharing Literature

Study Skill: *Organizing Information*

Creative Thinking: *Writing a Narrative*

Social Studies: *Pictures on the Wall*

Social Studies: *An Unfamiliar Country*

Social Studies: *Discovering Mexico*

History: *Notable Immigrants*

Civic Awareness: *Opportunities for Newcomers*

Spelling: *Integrating Spelling and Reading*

ONGOING THEME ACTIVITIES

ASSESSMENT
Formal evaluation options include a variety of tests and surveys. Informal evaluation options include observation checklists and samples of students' work.

INDEPENDENT READING & WRITING
Suggestions for initiating independent reading and writing activities on a daily basis. Information about library resources. Classroom management ideas.

173E   Theme 4   EXPERIENCES

Example 7.1 *Literature-Based Series Example (cont.)*

DISCUSSING EXPERIENCES

■ Anthology, pages 172-173, or Theme Poster 4

ACTIVATING PRIOR KNOWLEDGE Use the Anthology or the Theme Poster to engage students in a discussion of memorable experiences in their lives and of personal narrative as a type of writing. You may wish to ask the following questions:

• What events in your life might make good stories?
• What stories have you heard other people tell that involve particularly memorable characters or unusual events?

Home-School Connection
PARENT RESOURCES

■ Newsletter 4

PREVIEWING THE LITERATURE

■ Anthology, pages 172-239

BUILDING BACKGROUND Have students turn to pages 172-173. Point out the title and the genre label. Explain that in this theme students will be reading five personal narratives (stories about things that have happened in the authors' lives).

Have students read the table of contents on page 174. Then have them preview each story. The following can be used to initiate a discussion.

• Do you think "The Figgerin' of Aunt Wilma" will be humorous or serious? Why?
• What kinds of experiences do you think Gary Soto tells about in "Summer School"?
• What kind of information might you expect to learn about the Reverend Martin Luther King, Jr., in a personal narrative written by his daughter?
• What might have seemed strange or confusing to Ernesto Galarza when he first came to the United States from Mexico?
• How do you think Jean Fritz felt about coming to the United States in 1927?

Example 7.1   *Literature-Based Series Example (cont.)*

Ongoing Theme Activities

The following three major projects or activities extend across the theme. They are designed to manage students' time meaningfully and creatively.

Introduce now or anytime during the theme.

INDEPENDENT READING & WRITING

- Teacher's Book, pages 238C-238D
- Journal, page 68

- Writing Center Poster 4–creative writing experiences
- Additional theme reading and writing activities

Refer to Teacher's Book pages 238C-238D for suggestions on how to help students start planning their independent reading and writing projects.

A Theme PROJECT

- Teacher's Book, pages 238E-238F
- Theme Project booklet, Journal pages 89-94

The Theme Project, "Making a Time Capsule," requires students to work in a group to plan, organize, and conduct research. After students have developed a group work plan, encourage them to set up daily and weekly work schedules. Detailed suggestions for guiding students through the Theme Project appear on Teacher's Book pages 238E-238F.

- Independent or cooperative activity

THE Writing Center

- Teacher's Book, pages 238G-238H
- The Writing Center booklet, Journal pages 95-98

The Writing Center Project, "Writing an Autobiographical Incident," is a process-writing activity involving the prewriting, drafting, revising, proofreading, and publishing stages. Guide students in planning and scheduling their work. Detailed suggestions for each stage of the project appear on Teacher's Book pages 238G-238H.

- Independent or cooperative activity

Theme 4 EXPERIENCES 174D

Example 7.1 *Literature-Based Series Example (cont.)*

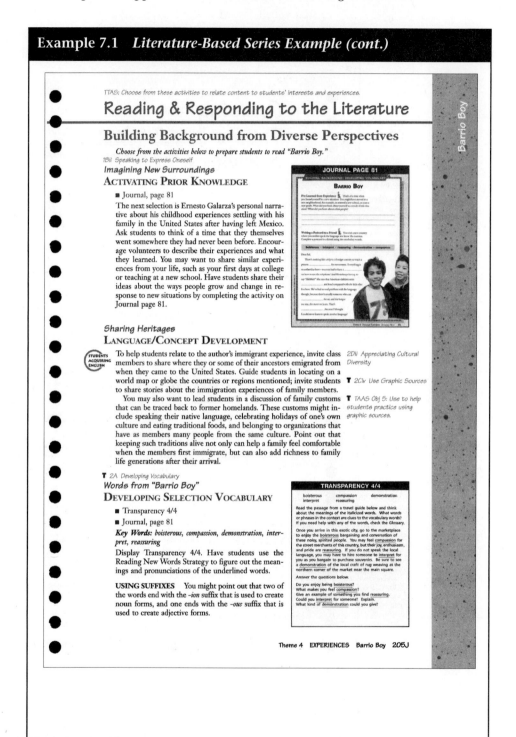

TTAS: Choose from these activities to relate content to students' interests and experiences.

Reading & Responding to the Literature

Building Background from Diverse Perspectives

Choose from the activities below to prepare students to read "Barrio Boy."

1Bii Speaking to Express Oneself

Imagining New Surroundings
ACTIVATING PRIOR KNOWLEDGE

■ Journal, page 81

The next selection is Ernesto Galarza's personal narrative about his childhood experiences settling with his family in the United States after having left Mexico. Ask students to think of a time that they themselves went somewhere they had never been before. Encourage volunteers to describe their experiences and what they learned. You may want to share similar experiences from your life, such as your first days at college or teaching at a new school. Have students share their ideas about the ways people grow and change in response to new situations by completing the activity on Journal page 81.

Sharing Heritages
LANGUAGE/CONCEPT DEVELOPMENT

(STUDENTS ACQUIRING ENGLISH) To help students relate to the author's immigrant experience, invite class members to share where they or some of their ancestors emigrated from when they came to the United States. Guide students in locating on a world map or globe the countries or regions mentioned; invite students to share stories about the immigration experiences of family members.

You may also want to lead students in a discussion of family customs that can be traced back to former homelands. These customs might include speaking their native language, celebrating holidays of one's own culture and eating traditional foods, and belonging to organizations that have as members many people from the same culture. Point out that keeping such traditions alive not only can help a family feel comfortable when the members first immigrate, but can also add richness to family life generations after their arrival.

2Dii Appreciating Cultural Diversity

▼ *2Civ Use Graphic Sources*

▼ *TAAS Obj 5: Use to help students practice using graphic sources.*

▼ *2A Developing Vocabulary*

Words from "Barrio Boy"
DEVELOPING SELECTION VOCABULARY

■ Transparency 4/4
■ Journal, page 81

Key Words: boisterous, compassion, demonstration, interpret, reassuring

Display Transparency 4/4. Have students use the Reading New Words Strategy to figure out the meanings and pronunciations of the underlined words.

USING SUFFIXES You might point out that two of the words end with the *-ion* suffix that is used to create noun forms, and one ends with the *-ous* suffix that is used to create adjective forms.

Example 7.1   *Literature-Based Series Example (cont.)*

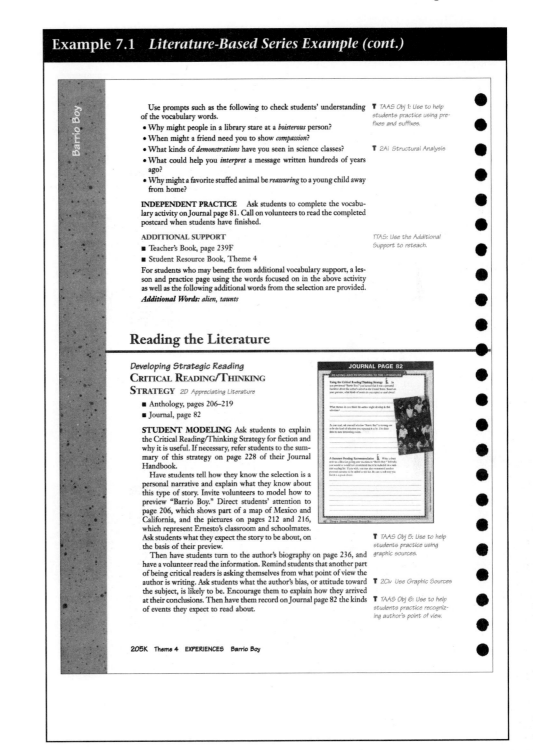

Use prompts such as the following to check students' understanding of the vocabulary words.

- Why might people in a library stare at a *boisterous* person?
- When might a friend need you to show *compassion*?
- What kinds of *demonstrations* have you seen in science classes?
- What could help you *interpret* a message written hundreds of years ago?
- Why might a favorite stuffed animal be *reassuring* to a young child away from home?

TAAS Obj 1: Use to help students practice using prefixes and suffixes.

2Ai Structural Analysis

INDEPENDENT PRACTICE   Ask students to complete the vocabulary activity on Journal page 81. Call on volunteers to read the completed postcard when students have finished.

ADDITIONAL SUPPORT

- Teacher's Book, page 239F
- Student Resource Book, Theme 4

For students who may benefit from additional vocabulary support, a lesson and practice page using the words focused on in the above activity as well as the following additional words from the selection are provided.

Additional Words: alien, taunts

TTAS: Use the Additional Support to reteach.

Reading the Literature

Developing Strategic Reading
CRITICAL READING/THINKING
STRATEGY   *2D Appreciating Literature*

- Anthology, pages 206–219
- Journal, page 82

STUDENT MODELING   Ask students to explain the Critical Reading/Thinking Strategy for fiction and why it is useful. If necessary, refer students to the summary of this strategy on page 228 of their Journal Handbook.

Have students tell how they know the selection is a personal narrative and explain what they know about this type of story. Invite volunteers to model how to preview "Barrio Boy." Direct students' attention to page 206, which shows part of a map of Mexico and California, and the pictures on pages 212 and 216, which represent Ernesto's classroom and schoolmates. Ask students what they expect the story to be about, on the basis of their preview.

Then have students turn to the author's biography on page 236, and have a volunteer read the information. Remind students that another part of being critical readers is asking themselves from what point of view the author is writing. Ask students what the author's bias, or attitude toward the subject, is likely to be. Encourage them to explain how they arrived at their conclusions. Then have them record on Journal page 82 the kinds of events they expect to read about.

TAAS Obj 5: Use to help students practice using graphic sources.

2Civ Use Graphic Sources

TAAS Obj 6: Use to help students practice recognizing author's point of view.

205K   Theme 4   EXPERIENCES   Barrio Boy

Example 7.1 *Literature-Based Series Example (cont.)*

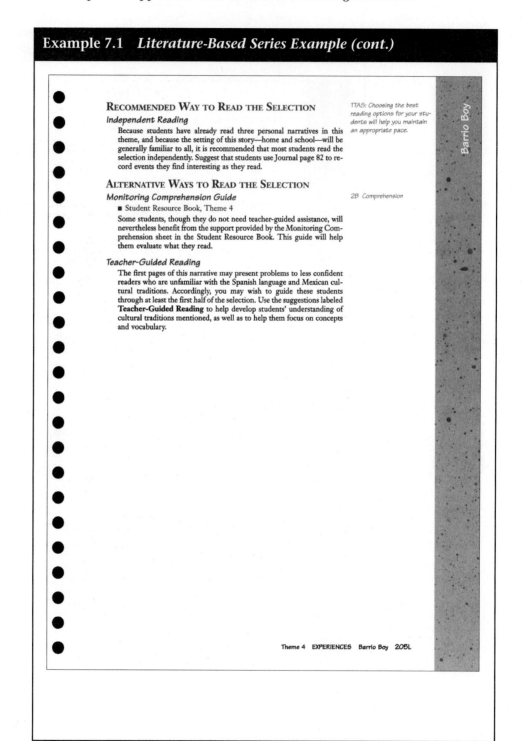

RECOMMENDED WAY TO READ THE SELECTION

Independent Reading

Because students have already read three personal narratives in this theme, and because the setting of this story—home and school—will be generally familiar to all, it is recommended that most students read the selection independently. Suggest that students use Journal page 82 to record events they find interesting as they read.

TTAS: Choosing the best reading options for your students will help you maintain an appropriate pace.

ALTERNATIVE WAYS TO READ THE SELECTION

Monitoring Comprehension Guide

■ Student Resource Book, Theme 4

2B Comprehension

Some students, though they do not need teacher-guided assistance, will nevertheless benefit from the support provided by the Monitoring Comprehension sheet in the Student Resource Book. This guide will help them evaluate what they read.

Teacher-Guided Reading

The first pages of this narrative may present problems to less confident readers who are unfamiliar with the Spanish language and Mexican cultural traditions. Accordingly, you may wish to guide these students through at least the first half of the selection. Use the suggestions labeled **Teacher-Guided Reading** to help develop students' understanding of cultural traditions mentioned, as well as to help them focus on concepts and vocabulary.

Barrio Boy

Theme 4   EXPERIENCES   Barrio Boy   205L

Example 7.1 *Literature-Based Series Example (cont.)*

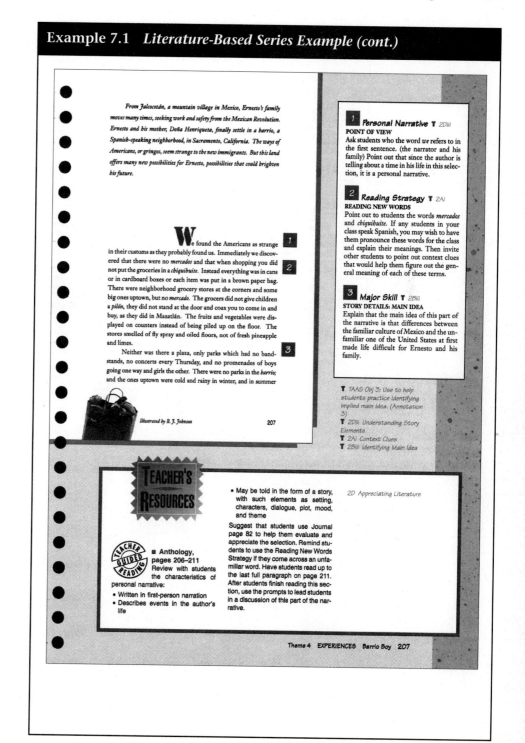

From Jalcocotán, a mountain village in Mexico, Ernesto's family moves many times, seeking work and safety from the Mexican Revolution. Ernesto and his mother, Doña Henriqueta, finally settle in a barrio, a Spanish-speaking neighborhood, in Sacramento, California. The ways of Americans, or gringos, seem strange to the new immigrants. But this land offers many new possibilities for Ernesto, possibilities that could brighten his future.

We found the Americans as strange in their customs as they probably found us. Immediately we discovered that there were no *mercados* and that when shopping you did not put the groceries in a *chiquihuite*. Instead everything was in cans or in cardboard boxes or each item was put in a brown paper bag. There were neighborhood grocery stores at the corners and some big ones uptown, but no *mercado*. The grocers did not give children a *pilón*, they did not stand at the door and coax you to come in and buy, as they did in Mazatlán. The fruits and vegetables were displayed on counters instead of being piled up on the floor. The stores smelled of fly spray and oiled floors, not of fresh pineapple and limes.

Neither was there a plaza, only parks which had no bandstands, no concerts every Thursday, and no promenades of boys going one way and girls the other. There were no parks in the *barrio*; and the ones uptown were cold and rainy in winter, and in summer

Illustrated by B. J. Johnson   207

1 **Personal Narrative** ▼ 2Diii
POINT OF VIEW
Ask students who the word *we* refers to in the first sentence. (the narrator and his family) Point out that since the author is telling about a time in his life in this selection, it is a personal narrative.

2 **Reading Strategy** ▼ 2Ai
READING NEW WORDS
Point out to students the words *mercados* and *chiquihuite*. If any students in your class speak Spanish, you may wish to have them pronounce these words for the class and explain their meanings. Then invite other students to point out context clues that would help them figure out the general meaning of each of these terms.

3 **Major Skill** ▼ 2Biii
STORY DETAILS: MAIN IDEA
Explain that the main idea of this part of the narrative is that differences between the familiar culture of Mexico and the unfamiliar one of the United States at first made life difficult for Ernesto and his family.

▼ *TAAS Obj 3: Use to help students practice identifying implied main idea. (Annotation 3)*
▼ *2Diii Understanding Story Elements*
▼ *2Ai Context Clues*
▼ *2Biii Identifying Main Idea*

TEACHER'S RESOURCES

■ **Anthology,** pages 206–211
Review with students the characteristics of personal narrative:
• Written in first-person narration
• Describes events in the author's life

• May be told in the form of a story, with such elements as setting, characters, dialogue, plot, mood, and theme

2D Appreciating Literature

Suggest that students use Journal page 82 to help them evaluate and appreciate the selection. Remind students to use the Reading New Words Strategy if they come across an unfamiliar word. Have students read up to the last full paragraph on page 211. After students finish reading this section, use the prompts to lead students in a discussion of this part of the narrative.

Theme 4 EXPERIENCES Barrio Boy **207**

Example 7.1 *Literature-Based Series Example (cont.)*

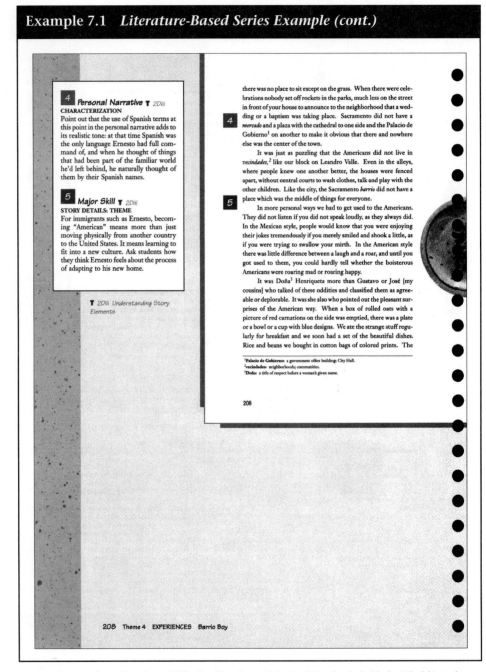

4 *Personal Narrative* ▼ *2Diii*
CHARACTERIZATION
Point out that the use of Spanish terms at this point in the personal narrative adds to its realistic tone: at that time Spanish was the only language Ernesto had full command of, and when he thought of things that had been part of the familiar world he'd left behind, he naturally thought of them by their Spanish names.

5 *Major Skill* ▼ *2Diii*
STORY DETAILS: THEME
For immigrants such as Ernesto, becoming "American" means more than just moving physically from another country to the United States. It means learning to fit into a new culture. Ask students how they think Ernesto feels about the process of adapting to his new home.

▼ *2Diii Understanding Story Elements*

there was no place to sit except on the grass. When there were celebrations nobody set off rockets in the parks, much less on the street in front of your house to announce to the neighborhood that a wedding or a baptism was taking place. Sacramento did not have a *mercado* and a plaza with the cathedral to one side and the Palacio de Gobierno[1] on another to make it obvious that there and nowhere else was the center of the town.

It was just as puzzling that the Americans did not live in *vecindades*,[2] like our block on Leandro Valle. Even in the alleys, where people knew one another better, the houses were fenced apart, without central courts to wash clothes, talk and play with the other children. Like the city, the Sacramento *barrio* did not have a place which was the middle of things for everyone.

In more personal ways we had to get used to the Americans. They did not listen if you did not speak loudly, as they always did. In the Mexican style, people would know that you were enjoying their jokes tremendously if you merely smiled and shook a little, as if you were trying to swallow your mirth. In the American style there was little difference between a laugh and a roar, and until you got used to them, you could hardly tell whether the boisterous Americans were roaring mad or roaring happy.

It was Doña[3] Henriqueta more than Gustavo or José [my cousins] who talked of these oddities and classified them as agreeable or deplorable. It was she also who pointed out the pleasant surprises of the American way. When a box of rolled oats with a picture of red carnations on the side was emptied, there was a plate or a bowl or a cup with blue designs. We ate the strange stuff regularly for breakfast and we soon had a set of the beautiful dishes. Rice and beans we bought in cotton bags of colored prints. The

[1]**Palacio de Gobierno:** a government office building; City Hall.
[2]**vecindades:** neighborhoods; communities.
[3]**Doña:** a title of respect before a woman's given name.

208

208 Theme 4 EXPERIENCES Barrio Boy

which to choose when introducing the story. Pages 205K–205L give ideas for reading strategically and ways to read the story. This range of choices encourages teachers to make independent decisions about the lesson, based on the characteristics of their individual classes. The story pages from the student book are found on pages 207–219 of this teacher's manual, reduced in size, with instructional notes and resources included on the sides and bottoms of the pages. Pages 207–208 of this material are reproduced here to show how the various parts of the story are connected to instructional suggestions for the teacher. Other lesson pages contain suggestions for student responses to *Barrio Boy*, including discussion ideas, ideas for creative response, writing activities, oral rereading, and ideas for exploration of language; suggestions for developing comprehension strategies and skills through the literature; and ideas for exploring, extending, and sharing the story. Teachers are encouraged to select from the suggested activities and different ways of reading the selection the ones that meet the needs and interests of the students in the particular class.

SELF-CHECK: OBJECTIVE 1   Discuss the characteristics of different types of published reading series. Explain how published reading series have changed over the years. (See Self-Improvement Opportunities 1, 7, 8, and 9.)

Instructional Procedures Used with Published Reading Series

A number of instructional procedures can be used with published reading series. Some are built into the manuals included in the series, and some can be easily adapted to use with these materials.

Directed Reading Activity (DRA)

The *directed reading activity (DRA)* is a teaching strategy used to extend and strengthen a child's reading abilities. It can be used with a story from a published reading series or with any other reading selection, including content area materials or trade books. The DRA is the strategy that is generally built into basal reading series' teacher's manuals. Following are five components often included in the DRA:

1. *Motivation and development of background.* The teacher attempts to interest students in reading about the topic by helping them associate the subject matter with their own experiences or by using audiovisual aids to arouse interest in unfamiliar areas. It may not be necessary to work on motivation for all stories.

    At this point, the teacher can determine whether the children have the backgrounds of experience and language needed for understanding the story, and, if necessary, he or she can develop new concepts and vocabulary before they read the story.

2. *Directed story reading (silent and oral).* Before children read the story silently, the teacher provides them with purpose questions (or a study guide) or helps them to set their own purposes (by questioning or predicting) to direct their reading (on a section-by-section basis at lower grade levels). Following the silent reading, the teacher may ask children to read aloud their answers to the purpose or study-guide questions, read aloud to prove or reject their predictions, or read orally for a new purpose. Oral reading is not always included in upper-grade lessons. This section of the lesson is designed to aid children's comprehension and retention of the material.

3. *Strategy- or skill-building activities.* At some point during the lesson, the teacher provides direct instruction in one or more word recognition or comprehension strategies or skills.

4. *Follow-up practice.* Children practice strategies and skills they have already been taught, frequently by doing workbook exercises.

5. *Enrichment activities.* These activities may connect the story with art, music, or creative writing or may lead the children to read additional material on the same topic or by the same author. Creative drama is often included as an enrichment activity, linking the reading with speaking and listening.

Although the steps may vary from series to series, most basal reading lessons have parts that correspond to this list of components. Directed reading of a story generally involves the teacher asking questions and the children reading to find the answers, or the teacher asking the children to make predictions and read to confirm or reject them. Traditional basal readers tend to give the teacher responsibility for purpose setting. Literature-based and language-integrated series, in contrast, have moved toward giving students more responsibility for purpose setting and stress the making and confirming of predictions.

Adaptations of the DRA.   Rearranging a basal reading lesson so that the activities labeled *enrichment activities* are completed before, rather than after the story is read, can produce better results than presentation in the traditional order. These activities help the students build and integrate background knowledge (Reutzel, 1985; Prince and Mancus, 1987; Thames and Readence, 1988; Pearson and Fielding, 1991).

Comprehension monitoring (metacognitive activities) can be made a natural part of a DRA by using student *predictions*, rather than teacher questions, as the purpose-setting vehicle for the lessons, using the title, pictures, and children's background information about the general topic that has been activated as a basis for the predictions. The predictions are revised as necessary as the children read the material, much as is done in a directed reading-thinking activity, discussed in the next section. *Self-questioning* before and during the reading is encouraged. In addition, stops at logical story breaks can be made to allow *summarization* of main points as a check for continuing comprehension. Summarization of the entire selection can follow completion of the reading. The students may ask classmates questions they have generated about story features (Schmitt and Baumann,

1986). Some basal series incorporate some of these activities into their teacher's manual suggestions, and the newer literature-based and language-integrated readers tend to use the predicting and confirming techniques regularly.

SELF-CHECK: OBJECTIVE 2   What are the parts of a directed reading activity? (See Self-Improvement Opportunity 2.)

The Directed Reading-Thinking Activity (DRTA)

One alternative to the DRA is the *directed reading-thinking activity (DRTA)*. The DRTA fits into a whole language philosophy better than does the DRA because it focuses on student control instead of primarily teacher guidance of the reading. The DRTA is a general plan for directing children's reading of either stories in published reading series, trade books, or content area selections and for encouraging children to think as they read and to make predictions and check their accuracy. Stauffer (1968) offers some background for understanding the DRTA:

> Children are by nature curious and inquiring, and they will be so in school if they are permitted to inquire. It is possible to direct the reading-thinking process in such a way that children will be encouraged to think when reading—to speculate, to search, to evaluate, and to use. (p. 348)

Stauffer (1969) further points out that teachers can motivate students' effort and concentration by involving them intellectually and encouraging them to formulate questions and hypotheses, to process information, and to evaluate tentative solutions. The DRTA is directed toward accomplishing these goals. The teacher observes the children as they read, in order to diagnose difficulties and offer help (kidwatching time). Perhaps because the student is interacting with the material during reading, the DRTA is extremely useful for improving children's comprehension of selections. After the reading, skill-building activities take place.

The lesson plan in Example 7.2 illustrates the steps in the directed reading-thinking activity. It is designed for use with the reading selection *Barrio Boy,* excerpted in Example 7.1. The strategy and skill-building activities in the basal teacher's manual can be used with this instructional procedure.

Making predictions about what will occur in a text encourages children to think about the text's message. In making predictions, students use their background knowledge about the topic and their knowledge of text organizational patterns. This step provides purposes for reading: trying to confirm one or more predictions from others in the group and to confirm or reject their own. It also encourages students to apply metacognitive skills as they think through their lines of reasoning. When students are unable to make predictions as requested, the teacher can model his or her thinking in making a prediction, using a think-aloud, or provide several possible predictions for the student to choose from and ask for the reason a particular one is chosen. The teacher should accept all predictions and encourage the students to reflect on their accuracy later. If students are new at making predictions, the teacher can use highly predictable materials, such as folktales, to encourage success. It may help to have the students summarize what has happened before making predictions (Johnston, 1993).

Example 7.2   *DRTA Plan for a Reading Selection from a Published Series*

[Note: Page numbers mentioned in this DRTA plan refer to pages in the selection excerpted in Example 7.1. Not all of the story is reproduced there, but it can be found in *Beyond the Reef*.]

Step 1: Making Predictions From Title Clues

Write the title of the story or chapter to be studied on the chalkboard, and have a child read it. For this selection, write "Barrio Boy." Ask the children, "What do you think this story will be about?" Give them time to consider the question thoroughly, and let each child have an opportunity to make predictions. All student predictions should be accepted, regardless of how reasonable or unreasonable they may seem, but the teacher should not make any predictions during this discussion period.

Step 2: Making Predictions From Picture Clues

Have the students open their books to the beginning of the selection. Ask them to examine carefully the picture on the first page. After they have examined it, ask them to revise the predictions they made earlier, based on the additional information in the picture.

Step 3: Reading the Material

Have the students read the italicized paragraph that introduces the story on page 207 to check the accuracy of their predictions.

Step 4: Assessing the Accuracy of Predictions and Adjusting Predictions

When all of the children have read the italicized paragraph, lead a discussion by asking such questions as "Who correctly predicted what the story was going to be about?" Ask the children who believe they were right to read orally to the class the parts of the paragraph that support their predictions. Children who were wrong can tell why they believe they were wrong. Let them revise their predictions, if necessary, and then ask them, "Now what do you think the story will tell about Ernesto's and his mother's experiences?"

Example 7.2 *(cont.)*

Step 5: Repeating the Procedure Until All Parts of the Lesson Have Been Covered

Have the children read pages 207–211 (end of the second complete paragraph) to check the accuracy of their predictions. Have them read selected parts orally to justify the predictions they think were correct and tell why they believe other predictions were incorrect. Have them revise or adjust their predictions, based on their reading. Then pose the question "What do you think will happen when Ernesto enrolls in school?" and have them read pages 211–213 (end of second paragraph) to check their predictions. After a discussion of the accuracy of the predictions and revisions of predictions, ask them, "How do you think Ernesto will adjust to school? Do you think he will have problems? If so, what kinds? Will he overcome the problems?" Have them read to the end of the story to check their predictions for the final time.

In preparing a DRTA, the teacher should select points at which to pause so that the children can make predictions. These points should probably be ones where the story line changes, points of high suspense, or other logical spots, and there should be no more than four or five stops in a story (Haggard, 1988). During pauses, the teacher may use one or more open-ended questions to elicit student predictions about the next part of the story (Blachowicz, 1983). Smyers (1987) suggests that at each stopping point the students should be asked to write questions, particularly prediction-eliciting questions. She believes this activity involves the students in the story even more completely, keeps the faster readers from becoming bored while the slower readers finish reading the section, and frees the teacher from having to formulate all the prediction-eliciting questions. This procedure also helps to balance the student-teacher exchanges in class, increasing the students' share. (See Chapter 10 for an example of the DRTA applied to a content area lesson.)

SELF-CHECK: OBJECTIVE 2   What are the steps in a DRTA? (See Self-Improvement Opportunity 6.)

Literature-Based Approaches

literature-centered reading

Currently educators are recognizing the value of using quality literature as a basis for reading instruction. Using literature in this way is congruent with a whole language philosophy, although some whole language advocates regard some literature-based approaches to reading instruction as too structured. Many types of literature are useful for this purpose. Wordless picture books, for example, provide materials for the emerging literacy of young children. These children can learn to follow a plot without having to decode words, and they can learn to provide their own interpretations of the author's ideas. Patterned books can provide another level of literary exposure for beginning readers. Books of all types may be read aloud to students or be made available in reading corners for students to read independently. Activities such as retelling stories with or without flannel boards, writing reactions to books, and conversing about books with the teacher and other students may take place.

reading-writing connection

A literature-based approach places emphasis on connecting the stories to the children's personal background knowledge, analyzing stories and selections for particular elements, and monitoring students' understanding of the reading materials. The writers' styles can be studied and used as models for children's personal writing. Essential reading skills and strategies can be taught within the context of the material the children are actively involved in reading. (Aiex, 1988; Fuhler, 1990).

Obviously, given these priorities, the foundation of a literature-based program must be *trade books,* that is, books not written primarily for instructional purposes. Most teachers have always made use of trade books for children in their classrooms. They have read aloud to the children from these books, urged students to read the books in the classroom reading center or to check them out from the school library for recreational reading, and used them as supplements to basal instruction. In a literature-based program that is built on a whole language perspective, the teacher uses knowledge of students' backgrounds and attempts to "hook" them on reading selections. He or she has a clear instructional plan and clear goals and expectations for students. The students' strategy use is monitored by both teacher and students, who share in responsibility for learning (Ruddell, 1992).

Teachers who wish to choose trade books for their programs may consult lists of award-winning books (for example, Caldecott and Newbery Award winners) and other selection aids (see Chapter 8). School librarians and children themselves are other excellent sources of ideas. Teachers should take care to include multicultural literature in their selection process, because exposure to it can be important for students (Rasinski and Padak, 1990). See the appendix to Chapter 13 on multiethnic literature for a listing of useful books.

Teachers may obtain books from the school library, purchase books with classroom funds for the classroom library, or obtain books through commercial book clubs. Some of these clubs offer free books for the classroom when certain numbers are purchased by individual students. Parents may also donate to the classroom library books that are no longer wanted at home.

Literature-based programs may be conducted in a number of ways, and combinations of these approaches are common in most literature-based classrooms. Four such approaches are whole-class reading of a core book, use of literature response groups with multiple copies of several books, use of thematic literature units, and individualized reading approaches (Henke, 1988; Zarillo, 1989; Hiebert and Colt, 1989). Each of these approaches will be discussed in turn. A common adjunct to all of them is Sustained Silent Reading (SSR), in which students and teachers alike are allowed time to read materials of their own choice without interruption (Tunnell and Jacobs, 1989). Hilbert (1992/1993) suggests holding student-led discussion groups every five to eight weeks to allow children to share and compare the plots, themes, and characters of books they have read during SSR. Later, groups may report their decisions to the whole class. Reading may also be shared through puppet shows, puppet displays, or posters. SSR is described in detail in Chapter 8.

Literature-based instruction has been successful with a wide range of students. Zuker (1993) found that a literature-based whole language teaching/learning philosophy applied in classes with students who had language and learning disabilities resulted in positive gains in listening, speaking, reading, and writing.

On the other hand, Scharer and Detwiler (1992) point out some concerns regarding literature-based instruction. When it is used, teachers find it hard to be sure all needed strategies and skills are being covered, hard to know how to assess progress, and hard to know how to handle the poorer readers. Certainly teachers need to be well prepared as language teachers to use the approaches effectively.

Whole-Class Reading of a Core Book

Generally, core books used for whole-class reading are acquired in classroom sets so that every student has a personal copy. Teachers usually select these books for the quality of the material and sometimes because they fit into the overall classroom curriculum by relating to studies in other curricular areas, such as social studies and science. It is a further advantage if the teacher personally likes the book, for the teacher's attitude is communicated to the children as the reading progresses. It is important that the books selected provide something significant to talk about (Egawa, 1990).

Before a book is presented to the class, there may be prereading activities in which the students share personal experiences related to the book's content and activate information they possess about the topics or themes covered in it. (See Chapter 5 for information about techniques for schema activation.) The teacher may also present a minilesson on some literary element that is important in the book, such as characterization or flashbacks (Atwell, 1987). Purposes for listening to or reading the material are often set by having students predict what will happen in the story, based on the title and possibly on the picture on the book's cover or the first page of the story. At other times, purposes may be set by having students generate questions about the story that they expect to answer from reading. Occasionally the teacher may suggest some purpose question that will focus the readers on a key element in the book, such as "How is the setting of the story important to its plot?"

Sometimes the teacher first presents the book to the students by reading aloud part or all of it, depending on the students' reading abilities and the difficulty of the book. A chapter book may be read in installments over a period of days. After the teacher's oral reading, silent reading of the book by the students generally follows. At other times, the students may read the book silently first. Sometimes some students may present the book or a portion of it in a readers' theater as an introduction for other students.

At strategic points in the initial reading or independent rereading, there are usually pauses for small-group or whole-class discussion of the material. If predictions were made initially, these discussions may focus on the predictions, which can be evaluated, retained for the time being, altered slightly, or changed completely, based on the new information. The discussion may also focus on the purpose questions that were generated or on students' personal reactions to the story. To guide these discussions, the teacher may design questions that help the children to relate the story to their own experiences and to think critically and creatively about the material.

reading-writing connection

Between reading sessions, students may write reactions to the story in literature logs. The literature logs may be written just for the individual students, to help them think through what they are reading; or they may be dialogue logs, addressed to the teacher or a buddy. If the logs are a part of a written dialogue with the teacher, the teacher must respond to each entry with his or her own reaction to the story and/or to the student's reaction. Students should be free to write any honest response to the material without concern for negative teacher reaction. For example, a student who is bored by the story should feel free to say so in the log. Thus, the teacher's comments should be encouraging, thought provoking, and nonjudgmental. The teacher should not be looking for predetermined responses, but should respond with genuine interest in the students' comments (Wollman-Bonilla, 1989; Fuhler, 1994). Students should be encouraged to link the reading material with personal experiences. The teacher should model such entries for students by sharing his or her personal log entries orally. Students should also be encouraged to note phrases and expressions that appealed to them, statements expressing personal confusion, and predictions about what will happen next. Many different learning goals may be met through this student-teacher interaction (Flitterman-King, 1988; McWhirter, 1990). An example of one type of literature log is presented in Example 7.3 on page 337. Another type is presented in Chapter 8.

reading-writing connection

Follow-up activities should be used after the book has been read to extend the children's understanding and help them elaborate on the ideas they gained from the shared book. These activities often involve writing, for example, composing another episode for the characters in the story, another story of the same genre, or a character sketch of a favorite character. Retelling the story in various ways is a good follow-up activity, especially for young children. They may simply retell the story to a partner, who may ask questions about missing events or ideas; they may retell the story using a flannel board and appropriate pieces; or they may act out the story through creative dramatics or puppetry. Illustrating the story sequence or selected parts of the story is a good follow-up activity that causes the students to reflect on the story and provides the teacher with insight into the students' degrees of comprehension of the story. The students may construct group

Example 7.3 *Literature Log*

EIGHT COUSINS   Read to 53
10-8-86
      Each time I read this book it seems to get easier to read.
I guess it is because I'm getting used to the proper English used.
I enjoy it a lot and feel so carried off when I read it. So far the
story is very good and I just want to always know whats going
to happen next.
                                                        Anita

Anita,
      I haven't read *Eight Cousins*, but I sure would like to after
reading your enthusiastic responses. I must confess that Louisa
May Alcott is one author I've never read. I think I'll read *Eight
Cousins* and give her a try.
      Can you discover what or how the author is creating such
a wonderful feeling for you?
                                                        Mrs. H.

Source: Jill Dillard, "Lit Logs: A Reading and Writing Activity for the Library/Media Center and the Classroom." Reprinted with permission of the author and the Ohio Educational Library/Media Association's *Ohio Media Spectrum* journal, from the Winter 1989 issue, Vol. 41, No. 4, p. 39.

or individual story maps after the reading. The maps can be displayed in the classroom or shared during discussions or oral presentations. Students may apply information learned in the story (for example, how to do origami), or they may read related materials because of aroused interest in the topic.

reading-writing connection

Teachers have made many individual modifications of the procedures for close reading of a book by a class. Shaw (1988) had fifth graders keep narrative journals in which they wrote after reading each chapter of their book, taking the perspective of the main character to relate that character's adventures. Through this activity, they learned much about summarizing and the first-person narrative form. Journal writing is a powerful way to reflect and discover insights about material read. It encourages active reading and gives the teacher a glimpse of the students' personal transactions with the story (Fuhler, 1994).

Cairney (1987) had students make character "mug sheets" for examining the personality traits of the characters in their readings. For each character, the students could include such items as name, alias, age, address, description, special features, major goals in life, and unusual or interesting habits. The teacher should model the completion of one or more mug sheets on familiar characters (for example, Gilly Hopkins) before asking students to complete the sheets individually or in cooperative groups.

Wertheim (1988) created a personal teaching guide for the novels she had her students read by listing difficult vocabulary at the beginning of each chapter; underlining important vocabulary in the text; writing discussion questions on the pages to which they pertained (coded as literal, inferential, and critical); writing other, more inclusive, questions at ends of chapters; and listing follow-up activities at the end of the book. This plan appears to be very practical and efficient.

Example 7.4 describes one way to do close reading of a core book. This example is not intended to prescribe a procedure; many variations are possible.

Example 7.4 *Whole-Class Reading of a Core Book*

In this lesson, the teacher has chosen the book *Patchwork Quilt* because of the way it shows relationships among the characters. This book is good for use with younger readers; for older readers, teachers would probably choose chapter books, with the discussion times coming at the ends of chapters.

The teacher opens with a minilesson on character development, leading the children to see how authors reveal characterization through the things the character says and does, the things other characters say about the character, and the ways they react to him or her.

Next, the teacher asks the students to brainstorm their personal associations for the words *Grandma*, *Quilt*, and *Masterpiece*. Webs of these associations are written on the board or on a chart.

Now the teacher invites the children to predict what the story will be about. They write down their predictions or share them orally with partners or the whole group. The teacher tells the children that as they read the story they should look for clues that will either confirm or disprove their predictions, and they should also look for the characteristics of the characters (noticing what is said about and to them, what they say, and what they do).

The teacher may ask the students to read just the first two pages of the story and stop to discuss these questions with others at their tables:

What is the relationship between Tanya and her grandmother like?

Do you have a relationship like that with some older person?

Now students may read the rest of the story, with the number of pages read each time varying with the maturity of the students. Some possible stopping points and questions for discussion in the small groups include the following.

After two more pages:

Did Tanya's mother understand why Grandma wanted to make the quilt?

How did the reaction of Tanya's mother to the quilt make Grandma feel? How could you tell?

Example 7.4   *Whole-Class Reading of a Core Book (cont.)*

After five more pages:

What did Grandma mean when she said, "A quilt won't forget. It can tell your life story."?

Can a quilt really tell stories? If so, how?

Did Mama find out what Grandma meant about the quilt telling stories? How do you know?

After four more pages:

When Grandma got sick, why didn't she tell the others at first?

How did she feel about leaving her quilt unfinished? How could you tell?

Why did each person who worked on the quilt do what he or she did?

Would you have wanted to work on it if you had been one of them? Why or why not?

After the next page:

Was Tanya right to take squares out of Grandma's old quilt without asking permission? Why did she do it? What will Grandma think of it?

After the story is finished:

How did Grandma feel about her quilt pieces going into the quilt?

What did she say and do that makes you believe that?

Why did they give Tanya the quilt?

How will Tanya feel about this quilt when she is older?

Do you have anything that you feel that way about?

Follow-up activities for after the reading may include some of the following:

1. Find another book that tells about a relationship between a child and a grandparent or another older person. Compare and contrast the stories.

2. Design a get-well card that Tanya might have made for her grandmother when she was sick.

3. Write a diary entry that Tanya might have made on the third day after she saw how sick her grandmother was. Have Tanya tell her diary how she felt about her grandmother's illness.

4. Pick a character and describe him or her. List his or her characteristics and why you did or did not like him or her.

5. Make a small patchwork quilt for the classroom. (Students provide material scraps for it. The children design the quilt pattern after looking at books about quilts and pictures of quilts, then cut out the pieces, and sew them together.) The quilting may be done by a volunteer parent or group of parents, or a resource person may show quilts and demonstrate quilting.

Literature Response Groups

reading-writing connection

In literature response groups, the teacher chooses several books for which multiple copies are available, introduces each one, lets children choose which book to read, presents the books to the children if they are unable to read them independently first, holds discussions about the books, may have students respond in logs, and lets the children help decide about ways to share the experience of the books (Egawa, 1990). In these groups, students initiate and sustain discussion topics, connect literature selections to their lives, compare literature selections and authors with each other, note authors' styles, and consider authors' intents. The structured book choices lead them to try books in a variety of genres and by a variety of authors (Keegan and Shrake, 1991; Samway et al., 1991).

reading-writing connection

Reading response journals allow the collection of reactions to the reading throughout the reading process, not just at the end, and can be the basis for small-group discussions. Supportive comments by the teacher can encourage students to react honestly to the material and persevere in the reading. Sometimes students may need encouragement to be more specific in their entries (Hancock, 1992; Raphael et al., 1992; Fuhler, 1994).

Moore (1991) had teachers in a graduate methods course take part in electronic dialogue journals with fifth-grade students (using computers and modems). The partners discussed the book *Superfudge* by Judy Blume. The teachers modeled good discussions of characters and setting through their entries, and the quality of students' entries improved. Both groups enjoyed the interaction.

Hancock (1992) believes awareness of typical response patterns in literature response journals can help teachers encourage extensions of response types. Some possible response types involve interaction with the characters, empathy with the characters, prediction and validation of predictions, personal experiences that relate to the reading, and philosophical reflections. Since spelling and grammar are not checked in any way, the students feel freer to communicate.

This approach is described in more detail in Chapter 8.

Thematic Literature Units

thematic learning

Thematic literature units center around a theme, such as homes, families, survival, taking care of our earth, wild animals, pets, specific geographic regions (for example, South America), or specific groups of people (for example, Japanese); a genre, such as biography, science fiction, or folktales; or an author, such as Cynthia Voigt, Judith Viorst, or Maurice Sendak. Themes can help teachers and learners focus on meaning making. A theme offers a *focus* for instruction and activities, making it easier for students to see the reason for classroom activities, acquire an integrated knowledge base, and achieve depth and breadth of learning. The variety of materials used allows for these accomplishments (Lipson et al., 1993).

There are other values as well. The reflection involved in studying themes can enhance metacognition, but perhaps the biggest advantage of thematic teaching is the promotion of positive attitudes toward reading and writing. The range of topics covered and the opportunity for self-selection promote student interest and positive attitudes. Another advantage is that time is less fragmented in a classroom in which the teacher uses thematic units. The number of subjects to be taught is reduced by embedding one subject in another one (Lipson et al., 1993).

Evans (1994) describes a bilingual thematic unit on fear, composed of scary stories from English and Spanish cultures. The focus can be on understanding fear and overcoming it. Since fear is a universal emotion, its use as a topic allows for cultural comparisons of literary treatments of the topic. *Great Scary Imaginings* (Humanities Software) is a computer program that could be used with such a unit. It is designed to go with Mercer Mayer's *There's a Nightmare in My Closet* (The Dial Press, 1968). It contains a database of activities to encourage the children to write about the story with a compatible word-processing program. Other print books, such as Mayer's *You're the Scaredy Cat* (Four Winds Press, 1974) or his *Terrible Troll* (The Dial Press, 1968) can be used for a unit on scary things along with the computer program *Monsters & Make-Believe* (Pelican). This is a talking word processor with graphics capabilities that allow students to create pictures of monsters using various body parts supplied by the program (Wepner, 1993).

White and Lawrence (1992) describe building a thematic unit on the literature selection *Why Mosquitoes Buzz in People's Ears* by Verna Aardema. Related readings and activities were chosen to complement and elaborate on this selection.

The teacher collects a variety of related books (a *textset*) for the children to read during the unit. The organization of the unit provides the mental set for the children to see connections among the literature selections (Roser, Hoffman, and Farest, 1990; Lipson et al., 1993). Roser and colleagues (1992) incorporated literature comparison charts (which they called *language charts*) into thematic units to facilitate the making of connections among the stories. The charts seemed to enhance the students' reactions to the literature.

Textsets are books that have the same author, theme, topic, genre, or some other characteristic. They can set the stage for critical thinking by students as they look for connections. Textsets encourage discussion and varied interpretations (Heine, 1991). A textset on Katherine Paterson's books might include *Bridge to Terabithia, Lyddie, The Great Gilly Hopkins, Jacob Have I Loved*, and *The Sign of the Chrysanthemum*. Textsets are available for computers on CD-ROM, as well. *Stories and More* (IBM) is a primary-level, literature-based, read-aloud program. It provides voice-supported reading as well as interactive computer activities for some of the stories (Wepner, 1992). Obviously, use of textsets allows small-group discussion in which students can compare and contrast a variety of related books and write in response journals about the relationships they have discovered.

reading-writing connection

Thematic units are often opened with prereading activities for developing background, such as those mentioned earlier for the core book, in which children discuss what they already know about the focus of the unit. Students may brainstorm terms they associate with the theme, and these terms may be organized into a semantic web. (See Chapters 4, 5, and 8 for more on semantic webs and literature webs.)

The teacher may read aloud one or more books that fit the focus of the unit before allowing students to form small groups to read from multiple copies of other related books. One fifth-grade teacher read aloud *Lincoln: A Photobiography* at the beginning of a unit on biography and let the students form small groups to read such books as *What's the Big Idea, Ben Franklin?*; *Eleanor Roosevelt: First Lady of the World*; *A Weed Is a Flower: The Life of George Washington Carver*; and others for which she had secured multiple copies. Single copies of other biographies were also available for independent reading, as well as short biographies in basal readers, anthologies, and periodicals (Zarrillo, 1989).

Some unit activities should be designed for whole-group participation (for example, the read-alouds), some for small-group participation (for example, activities related to the multiple-copy books), and some for independent work (for example, literature logs about books read individually). Many books need to be available in single and multiple copies to meet the varied needs of the students and to allow students who work quickly to choose additional books to read.

The teacher may read aloud to the entire class the selection or selections chosen to open the unit. Some selections may be presented through videotapes or audiotapes. Each reading should be accompanied by or followed by discussion of the material, writing in literature logs, and other activities, such as those listed for follow-up activities in the section on whole-class reading of a core book.

reading-writing connection

The teacher may then give book talks about the books that are available in multiple copies to help children make decisions about the groups in which they will work. Students should have choices regarding these books, although it may be necessary to let them give their top three choices and be assigned a book from these choices because of the limited number of copies available for each book. Book talks may also be given for some of the single-copy books. In addition, as students finish reading certain books, they may give book talks to entice their classmates to read these books.

Whole-group activities are likely to include minilessons related to the reading that the children are doing. These minilessons may focus on literary elements or reading strategies.

When small groups meet about the books they are reading in common, activities such as those described in the section "Literature Response Groups" in Chapter 8 can be used. As small-group and independent reading progresses, students may continue to build on the webs they started during the introductory activities. At the end of the unit, culminating activities may include comparing and contrasting the books read and some elements of the books, such as characters, settings, plots, and themes; construction of time lines related to the unit theme; creative dramatics based on readings; writing related to the theme; and so on. For example, students may cooperatively write a story with the same theme that appears in the books they have read in the unit (Marzano, 1990).

reading-writing connection

Some commercial materials are available to help teachers plan activities for thematic literature units. *Bookshelf, Stage 1* (Scholastic) contains six copies each of eighteen different books. Thirteen themes and a variety of genres are included. The kit also contains big books, audiocassettes, and a teacher's resource book. The resource book provides a wide choice of suggestions for using each literature selection. Spiegel (1990) recommends this set of materials for young readers because of its many positive attributes. She recommends *Reading Beyond the Basics Plus* (Perfection Form) for grades four through six. This is a set of resource books for ten high-quality children's novels. Each one provides a variety of activity choices for use with one of the novels.

Example 7.5 shows one type of thematic literature unit plan.

Individualized Reading Approach

The *individualized reading approach* encourages children to move at their own paces through reading material they have chosen, rather than requiring them to move through teacher-prescribed material at the same pace as other children placed in the same group for reading instruction. With the individualized reading approach, which is designed to encourage independent reading, each child receives assistance in improving performance when need for such assistance becomes apparent.

Characteristics of an individualized reading approach include the following:

1. *Self-selection.* Children are allowed to choose material they are interested in reading. Each child may choose a different book. The teacher may offer suggestions or give help if it is requested, but the decision ultimately rests with the child. Thus, an individualized reading approach has built-in motivation: children want to read the material because they have chosen it themselves.

2. *Self-pacing.* Each child reads the material at his or her own pace. Slower students are not rushed through material in order to keep up with the faster ones, and faster children are not held back until others have caught up with them.

3. *Strategy and skill instruction.* The teacher helps students, either on an individual basis or in groups, develop their word recognition and comprehension strategies and skills as needed.

4. *Recordkeeping.* The teacher keeps records of each child's progress. He or she must know the levels of a child's reading performance to know which books the child can read independently, which are too difficult or frustrating, and which can be read with the teacher's assistance. The teacher must also be aware of a student's reading strengths and weaknesses and should keep a record of the strategies and skills help the child has received. Each child should keep records of books read, new words encountered, and new strategies learned.

5. *Student-teacher conferences.* One or two times a week, the teacher schedules a conference with each child, varying from three to fifteen minutes depending on the purpose.

Example 7.5 *Thematic Literature Unit Plan*

Pam Petty, a second-grade teacher at Carthage Elementary School in Carthage, Tennessee, developed a thematic unit around the reading of *Freckle Juice* by Judy Blume (Dell, 1971).

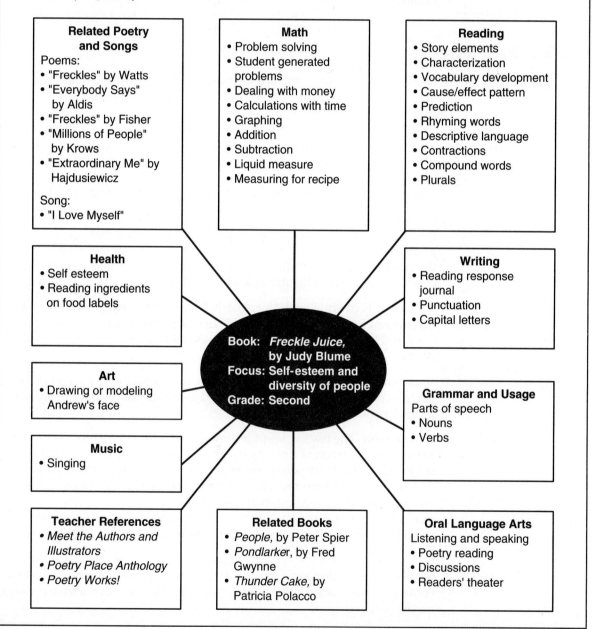

Related Poetry and Songs
Poems:
- "Freckles" by Watts
- "Everybody Says" by Aldis
- "Freckles" by Fisher
- "Millions of People" by Krows
- "Extraordinary Me" by Hajdusiewicz

Song:
- "I Love Myself"

Math
- Problem solving
- Student generated problems
- Dealing with money
- Calculations with time
- Graphing
- Addition
- Subtraction
- Liquid measure
- Measuring for recipe

Reading
- Story elements
- Characterization
- Vocabulary development
- Cause/effect pattern
- Prediction
- Rhyming words
- Descriptive language
- Contractions
- Compound words
- Plurals

Health
- Self esteem
- Reading ingredients on food labels

Writing
- Reading response journal
- Punctuation
- Capital letters

Art
- Drawing or modeling Andrew's face

Book: *Freckle Juice,* by Judy Blume
Focus: Self-esteem and diversity of people
Grade: Second

Grammar and Usage
Parts of speech
- Nouns
- Verbs

Music
- Singing

Teacher References
- *Meet the Authors and Illustrators*
- *Poetry Place Anthology*
- *Poetry Works!*

Related Books
- *People,* by Peter Spier
- *Pondlarker,* by Fred Gwynne
- *Thunder Cake,* by Patricia Polacco

Oral Language Arts
Listening and speaking
- Poetry reading
- Discussions
- Readers' theater

Example 7.5   *Thematic Literature Unit Plan (cont.)*

Pam's unit plan also uses other literature selections as it focuses on self-esteem and diversity among people. It has cross-curricular connections with a number of content areas: listening/speaking, reading, writing, health, math, art, and music, as shown in the diagram.

The unit covers ten days of instruction, as follows:

Day 1

The children are introduced to Judy Blume, the author. The teacher shares information gleaned from Scholastic's *Meet the Authors and Illustrators* by Deborah Kovacs and James Preller. Other books by Judy Blume are displayed. The children examine the book for information such as title, author, copyright date, and publisher. They are asked to look at the cover picture and the picture at the beginning of Chapter 1 and make predictions based on the title and pictures.

Day 2

The students read Chapter 1. They keep a word log of "neat" words and unknown words found in the chapter. In the search for "neat" words, students look for interesting language usage. (This activity is repeated for each chapter.) The class begins to construct a story map on the board. The teacher diagrams the elements of the story as the students dictate. The students use the map to fill in data about the story on a story-frame handout that asks for main characters, setting, problem, and solution. They copy the map on the board onto the back of their story-frame handout.

The poems "Freckles" by Mabel Watts, "Everybody Says" by Dorothy Aldis, and "Freckles" by Alieen Fisher (found in *Poetry Place Anthology*, Scholastic, 1983) are used for choral reading. Then they are examined for rhyming words, plurals, nouns, verbs, and contractions. The words in the poems are used to stimulate brainstorming about other words that share the same characteristics.

The students begin a reading response journal in which they respond each day to the reading. They also discuss their entries in small groups.

For each chapter (Chapter 1 on this day), on a cause-and-effect chart, one main action is chosen as the cause and entered on the left side of the chart, and the result or effect of this action is entered on the right side.

Day 3

The students read Chapter 2. They read the poem "Millions of People" by Jane W. Krows (*Poetry Place Anthology*), which is useful for promoting self-esteem. They also examine the poem for plurals, nouns, and rhyming words. The teacher may also use the poem for vocabulary development.

Example 7.5   *Thematic Literature Unit Plan (cont.)*

The students sing "I Love Myself" (Affective Enterprises).

The students do creative writing on "The Best Things about Me" or "What I Would Like to Change about Myself (and Why)," or they design flyers advertising Freckle Juice for sale.

Day 4

The students read Chapter 3. They examine a designated book page and categorize the nouns found into persons, places, or things. The categories are listed on the board, and discussion follows.

The teacher reads aloud the book *People* by Peter Spier (Doubleday, 1980). This book shows global diversity among people.

The children write original recipes for curls, blue eyes, height, or other traits.

Day 5

The students take one card per character and list that character's name, description, and traits on one side of the card. They draw a picture of the character on the back. Students hold up character cards to respond to questions in class.

For art, the students draw Andrew's face or make it out of clay and glue on popcorn or other materials for freckles.

Day 6

The students read Chapter 4. They do choral reading of the poem "Extraordinary Me" by Babs Bell Hajdusiewicz (*Poetry Works!*, Modern Curriculum Press, 1990). The students use the descriptive language to draw a picture of the person. Then they compare their pictures with the one on the poem chart.

The students make lists of words to describe themselves. Classmates read the lists and try to guess who was being described.

Day 7

The students read Chapter 5. They finish the story map and story frame.

The students go back through the book and do a scavenger hunt to find and list contractions and compound words (individually, in pairs, or in groups). Discussion and comparison of lists follow. They also participate in a game in which the teacher reads sentences from the book aloud. The students use game markers to select the appropriate punctuation or capitalization needed for each sentence from a handout provided by the teacher.

The teacher gives the students a handout with a boy's face on it, laminating

Example 7.5   *Thematic Literature Unit Plan (cont.)*

film, and markers. The students listen to the teacher read descriptions of three story events: being embarrassed at school, drawing blue spots on face, and being sad and sick after drinking juice. The students color laminating film and hold it on the boy's picture to show which event is being read about.

Day 8

The students do math problems related to Andrew's allowance and saving to buy the juice, problems related to telling time (connected with events in the story), problems about adding or multiplying quantities of liquid (quarts of freckle juice), and problems related to making and reading graphs. The teacher reads *Pondlarker* by Fred Gwynne to the students to further stimulate discussion of self-esteem.

Day 9

Students use the list of contractions found in the story on Day 7 to make flip cards containing the contractions and their component words.

The students retell the story or perform it through readers' theater.

The teacher reads *Thunder Cake* by Patricia Polacco to the children. This book involves both self-esteem and a recipe.

Day 10

The teacher shows students cans and boxes of food or juice and tells them to write down the expected ingredients for Thunder Cake. Then the class follows the recipe for Thunder Cake and compares the actual list of ingredients to the students' expected list. The students discuss "surprise" ingredients (such as tomatoes).

6. *Sharing activities.* The teacher plans some time each week for the children to share books they have read individually. The children may share with the entire class or with a small group. Sharing can sometimes take the form of book auctions in which the children bid with play money on the opportunity to read a book next. The "auctioneer" tries to interest the students in bidding by telling about the book (Bagford, 1985).

7. *Independent work.* The children do a great deal of independent work at their seats, rather than spending most of the assigned reading period in a group with the teacher. Better readers and older children can benefit more from time spent in individualized reading than can poorer readers and younger students, who need more teacher direction (Bagford, 1985).

Since exposure to different types of literature can help children build schemata for these types and should thus increase their efficiency in processing texts, the individualized reading approach is congruent with schema theory (Hacker, 1980). In addition, the variety of material students read provides them with vicarious experiences that help build other schemata and thus enhance future comprehension. Children encounter words in a variety of meaningful contexts, thus extending their vocabulary knowledge (Bagford, 1985).

Individualized reading helps students realize that reading is enjoyable. At the same time, reading books at comfortable reading levels develops fluency and can contribute to improved reading rates (Bagford, 1985).

To set up an individualized reading program, a teacher must have available a large supply of books, magazines, newspapers, and other reading materials—at least three to five books per child, covering a variety of reading levels and many different interest areas. This collection will need to be supplemented continuously after the program begins, for many children will quickly read all the books that are appropriate for them. Sources of books were mentioned earlier in this section on literature-based approaches.

The teacher should have read a large number of the books available to the children, since doing so makes it much easier to check the students' comprehension. Starting a file of comprehension questions and answers for books being used in the program is a good idea; these questions will be available year after year and will help refresh the teacher's memory of the books.

The teacher will also find it convenient to have a file of strategy- and skill-developing activities, covering the entire spectrum of word recognition and comprehension strategies and skills and a wide range of difficulty levels.

When starting an individualized program, the teacher should determine the children's reading levels and interests in order to choose books for the program that cover a sufficiently broad range of topics and difficulty levels. Informal reading inventories that provide information about a child's levels of performance (discussed at length in Chapter 11) yield a great deal of useful information, as do *interest inventories* that contain questions like the ones shown in Example 7.6. The teacher must administer such inventories orally to primary-level children.

Before initiating an individualized program, the teacher can plan routines to follow in the classroom, considering questions such as: (1) How are books to be checked out? (2) How will conferences be set up? (3) What should children who are working independently at their desks do when they need assistance? The room arrangement can also be planned in advance to allow for good traffic flow. If books are categorized and located in a number of places instead of bunched together in a single location, students will have less trouble finding them, and the potential noise level in the room will be lower.

The teacher may find that having a file folder for each child helps in organizing and recordkeeping. Each file folder can contain both checklists on which to record strategy and skill strengths and weaknesses and a form noting conference dates and instructional help given. Students can keep their own records in file folders that are accessible to both them and the teacher. These records will take

Example 7.6   *Interest Inventory*

1. What do you like to do after school?
2. What television programs do you enjoy most?
3. What are your hobbies?
4. Where would you like to go on a trip?
5. What sports do you like best?
6. What school subjects do you like best?
7. What types of stories do you like to hear someone read to you?
8. What types of stories do you like to read on your own?

different forms, depending on the maturity of the children. A primary-level record might look like the following one.

Name of Book	Author	Evaluation (Circle One)		
		Good	O.K.	Bad
		Good	O.K.	Bad
		Good	O.K.	Bad
		Good	O.K.	Bad

An intermediate-level record might look like this one.

Name of Book	Author	Comments

A form that children at all levels could use might look like this one.

New Words from Reading		
Word	Pronunciation	Definition

Student-teacher conferences serve a variety of purposes, including the following:

1. *To help with book choices.* Teachers should spend some time showing children how to choose appropriate books. Teachers can encourage them to read one or two pages of the books they think might appeal to them and consider the number of unfamiliar words they encounter. If there are more than five unfamiliar words per page, the book might be too difficult, whereas if there are no unfamiliar words, the child should consider the possibility that he or she could read more difficult material. A teacher who has given an interest inventory can suggest potentially interesting books to students who find it hard to make a choice. Student-written book reviews may also be provided for students who are having trouble deciding about books. Students can learn to write good reviews by examining models of written reviews and receiving assistance from the teacher or librarian (Jenks and Roberts, 1990).

`reading-writing connection`

2. *To check comprehension.* Conferences help determine how well the children are comprehending the books and other materials they are reading. Much of the time, the teacher and students may have authentic discussions about issues in the book during the conferences. Sometimes, however, the teacher may ask a student to retell all or part of the story or ask a variety of types of comprehension questions. (See Chapter 6 for information on question types.)

3. *To check word recognition strategies and oral reading skills.* The teacher can ask a child to read orally, observing his or her methods of attacking unfamiliar words and using oral reading skills, such as appropriate phrasing and good oral expression.

4. *To give strategy and skill assistance.* If a child is the only one in the room who needs help with a particular strategy or skill, the teacher can help that child on a one-to-one basis during a conference.

5. *To plan for sharing.* Some conferences are designed to help children prepare for sharing their reading experiences with others. If a child wishes to read a portion of a book to the class, the teacher might use a conference to listen to the child practice audience reading and to give help with the presentation.

There is nothing contradictory about using group instruction in an individualized reading program. A teacher can group children with similar skill difficulties to give help. The important thing is to be sure that all children get the instruction they need when they need it and are not forced to sit through instruction they do not need.

In an individualized reading program, each child is expected to be involved in independent silent reading a great deal of the time. This time should not be interrupted by noisy surroundings or non-task-oriented activities. The teacher should make the rules for the reading time very clear and indicate acceptable activities, such as taking part in student-teacher conferences, selecting a book, reading silently, giving or receiving specific reading assistance, taking part in a reading group, completing a strategy or skill-development practice activity, or keeping records concerned with reading activity.

Individualizing a reading program is a huge undertaking, but such a program can be introduced gradually in two ways:

1. *Use part of the time.* Introduce the individualized program one day a week while using the basal program the other four days. Then increase time spent in the individualized program one day at a time over a period of weeks until all five days of the week are devoted to it.

2. *Use part of the class.* Introduce the program to one reading group at a time while the remaining groups continue the basal program. If the children are grouped by achievement, the top group will be a good first choice because they are likely to have more independent work habits and will probably learn the routines more quickly than the other children would. After one group has become familiar with the approach, other groups can be introduced to it, until the entire class is participating in the individualized reading program.

The main advantages of an individualized reading approach follow.

1. Children have built-in motivation to read books they have chosen themselves.

2. Children are not compared negatively with one another because every child has a different book and the books are primarily trade books, which have no visible grade designations.

3. Each child has an opportunity to learn to read at his or her own rate.

4. Student-teacher conferences create a great deal of personal contact between the teacher and students.

Characteristics of this approach that some educators have considered to be disadvantages are the following:

1. The teacher must amass and continually replenish a large quantity of reading material.

2. The need to schedule many individual conferences and small-group meetings can create time difficulties.

3. An enormous amount of bookkeeping is necessary.

4. The program lacks a sequential approach to strategy and skill development.

**Focus on
Strategies**

Individualized Reading Approach

Mr. Neal is sitting at a table with Paul, a student who has been reading the book *Maniac McGee*. They are having a lively discussion about which characters in the story value reading and how they show that they do. Mr. Neal is able to tell from this discussion how well Paul has comprehended aspects of the book, but he is also engaged in a valid discussion of the content about which he has a personal opinion with a boy who has his own opinion, feels free to share it, and knows how to use events from the book to back up his ideas.

In the meantime, most of the other class members are reading from self-selected books at their desks or on the carpeted area of the reading center. When Megan has problems with a word in her book, she quietly leans over and asks for assistance from her assigned buddy, Tracy. When Tracy fails to be of help, Megan lists the word, page, and paragraph and reads on in her book.

Trey, who has a great deal of trouble sustaining independent reading over a period of time, is sitting at the computer, reading from a book on CD-ROM that allows him to click on words he doesn't know to obtain both pronunciations and definitions. With this assistance, Trey is able to remain focused on his reading for the entire period.

Jason and Joshua are sitting close together discussing the mock interview they plan to use during the book-sharing time on Friday. Both have read *Hatchet* and have decided to share with the rest of the class by having Jason play a reporter and Joshua play Brian. They are intently listing interview questions and answers to use for this purpose.

As Mr. Neal finishes the conference with Paul, he asks who needs some help. Megan and Mark hold up their hands, and Mr. Neal moves to their desks to offer assistance. Then he returns to the conference table and calls Michael, who is scheduled for the next conference, to come up. Michael has been having difficulty with word recognition skills, and Mr. Neal asks him to read orally from some new material in the book he is currently reading in order to assess the particular difficulties that he is having.

After Michael's conference, Mr. Neal will meet with a small group of students who need help in making inferences when they read. He will model the process for them and have them engage in some directed practice activities.

Each student in Mr. Neal's class has self-selected material to read when he or she is not involved in a teacher-student conference, a peer-planning session, or a needs-group session. The students know the procedures to use when they have trouble, and they know they can receive individual attention during conferences or at intervals during class time if they follow accepted procedures. The fact that they have chosen their reading material heightens their motivation to read it and makes student engagement more likely.

Evaluation Concerns in Literature-Based Approaches

Because literature-based approaches lack the built-in assessment tools found in basal readers, some teachers worry about ways to address accountability when they use such an approach. Fuhler (1990) suggests a portfolio approach to students' evaluation in which work samples and challenging projects are included. She uses checklists of important reading behaviors and writes anecdotal records about progress, based on weekly individual conferences. Other evaluation tools are book talks presented by the children and dialogue journal entries, in which the teacher and student write their opinions of books. The records that students and teachers keep of books read and strategies mastered are also very helpful in evaluation. Teachers may wish to use *The Whole Language Evaluation Book* (Goodman et al., 1989) to help them plan evaluation strategies. (See also the discussion in Chapter 11.)

SELF-CHECK: OBJECTIVE 3   Name and describe four types of literature-based reading approaches. (See Self-Improvement Opportunities 4 and 11.)

Language Experience Approach (LEA)

The *language experience approach* interrelates the different language arts and uses the children's experiences as the basis for reading materials. The rationale for this approach has been stated very concisely by one of its leading proponents, R. V. Allen:

reading-writing connection

What I can think about, I can talk about.

What I can say, I can write—or someone can write for me.

What I write, I can read.

I can read what I write, and what other people can write for me to read. (1973, p. 158)

This approach to reading is obviously not new, although its implementation has changed over the years. Today the experience charts used in the approach may be either group or individual compositions; stories about field trips, school activities, or personal experiences outside school; or charts that contain directions, special words, observations, job assignments, questions to be answered, imaginative stories or poems, or class rules. Current applications are often found in whole language classrooms, since this approach allows the children control over the content and language used in the stories.

Because the stories used in the language experience approach are developed by the children, they are motivational, and because they use the language of the children, the reading material is meaningful to the children. Frequently, basal reader stories are not meaningful to many children because the language or content is unfamiliar. The language experience approach has been used effectively with students who speak English as a second language, providing material for reading instruction that they can understand (Moustafa and Penrose, 1985; Moustafa, 1987).

A child's background may be limited, but every child has experiences that can be converted into stories. In addition, the teacher can plan interesting firsthand experiences that can result in reading material that is meaningful for all students.

The language experience approach is consistent with schema theory. Because it uses the child's experiences as the basis for written language, the child necessarily has adequate schemata to comprehend the material and can thus develop a schema for reading that includes the idea that written words have meaning (Hacker, 1980). The language patterns found in stories composed by children are often much more mature than those found in basal readers, since children use compound and complex sentences and a wide vocabulary. Nevertheless, children seem to find their own language patterns much easier to read than those in basal readers, probably because clues in a familiar context are easier to use. In fact, students often pick up the long, unusual words in experience stories faster than many of the short service words, probably because the distinctive configurations of these words contribute to recognition.

With the language experience approach, reading grows out of natural, ongoing activities. Children can see the relationships between reading and their oral language. This approach helps them to visualize reading as "talk written down" and offers good opportunities for developing the concepts of *writing, word,* and *sentence.* During the language experience process, children see the transformation from oral language to print take place, including directionality, spacing between words, and punctuation and capitalization. Framing the individual language units with the hands also helps to illustrate their meanings (Blass, Jurenka, and Zirzow, 1981). Another benefit is that observations made during dictation and reading of a language experience story and during the follow-up activities can provide the teacher with diagnostic insights into children's reading difficulties (Waugh, 1993).

Implementation in Kindergarten

Chapter 2 describes the use of language experience charts in kindergarten and also provides an example of a chart. At this level, teachers often use the charts to emphasize that oral language can be recorded and reconstructed, rather than focusing on having the children read the charts. Others, such as Karnowski (1989), involve kindergarten students in activities more like those described for the primary grades in the next section. Karnowski's approach uses the language experience approach with process writing, having the children choose their topics for writing from among their previous experiences. Discussion and sometimes dramatic play and/or drawing precede the writing of the story. The initial dictation of the story is revised and edited according to the children's direction, to show that first drafts are not the only drafts. The teacher reads and rereads charts before the children read them independently. Then the teacher uses the charts to teach vocabulary, decoding, and comprehension skills. Of course, the charts are "published" for reading by the children and their peers. This approach fits perfectly with the current belief in emergent literacy.

Individual stories may be solicited by asking the children to write something they want the class to know, a kind of written show-and-tell. The writing should include invented spellings such as the ones described in Chapter 2 (Coate and Castle, 1989).

Those children who have started to recognize many words may move into a program similar to the one described next for use in the primary grades.

Implementation in the Primary Grades

Implementation of the language experience approach with a group of primary-grade students may take a number of forms, but the following steps are common:

1. Participating in a common experience
2. Discussing the experience
3. Cooperative writing of the story on a chart, the board, or a computer
4. Participating in extension activities related to the story

reading-writing connection

reading-writing connection

After the children have participated in a common experience and have talked it over thoroughly, they are ready to compose a group experience story. First, the teacher may ask for suggestions for a title, allowing the students to select their favorite by voting. Then the teacher records the title on the chalkboard or a transparency. Each child offers details to add to the story, which the teacher also records. She or he may write "Joan said" by Joan's contribution or may simply write the sentence, calling attention to capitalization and punctuation while doing so. After recording each idea, the teacher reads it aloud. After all contributions have been recorded, the teacher reads the entire story to the class, sweeping his or her hand under each line to emphasize the left-to-right progression. Then the teacher asks the class to read the story with him or her as he or she moves a hand under the words. Under cover of the group, no child will stand out if he or she does not know a word.

If the children have had numerous experiences with this type of activity, the teacher may proceed to other activities involving the story. If this is a very early reading experience for the group, the teacher will probably stop at this point until the next day. On the second day, the class can be divided into three or four groups with which the teacher can work separately. To begin each group session, the teacher rereads the story to the children, using a master chart made the day before. Then the group rereads it with him or her. Next, a volunteer may read the story with the teacher, filling in the words he or she knows while the teacher supplies the rest. After each child in the group has had a chance to read, the teacher asks students to find certain words on the chart. The teacher may also show the children sentence strips (also prepared the day before) and have them match these strips with the lines on the chart, either letting volunteers reconstruct the entire chart from the sentence strips or using this as a learning-center activity to be completed individually while other groups are meeting. Group charts can be useful in developing many skills and are commonly used for lessons in word endings, compound words, long and short vowels, rhyming words, initial consonants, capitalization, punctuation, and other areas.

If the teacher makes a copy of the story for each student, it is possible to underline on that copy the words that the student recognizes while reading the story. The teacher may then make word cards of these words, which serve as the beginnings of the children's *word banks*. (Word cards containing the words a child has used in stories can eventually be used to practice sight vocabulary, work on word recognition skills, and develop comprehension skills.) As a group of students finishes meeting with the teacher, the students may be given the opportunity to illustrate their stories individually.

reading-writing connection

After this first attempt, students will write most experience stories in small groups, sometimes working on a story together and sometimes producing and sharing individual stories. At times, some children may dictate their stories to helpers from higher grades. Some teachers use tape recorders for dictation.

When students are dictating individual stories, the teacher should accept stories of any length (Mallon and Berglund, 1984). Some children will be ready to produce longer stories sooner than others. When children dictate very brief stories, however, the teacher can ask questions to prompt them to expand the narratives (Reimer, 1983). If a student suggests an irrelevant sentence, the teacher may wish to question the student about its appropriateness for the story before recording it. If a child rambles through a lengthy description, the teacher may ask, "How do you want that written down for your story?" This question may result in a more focused response (Mallon and Berglund, 1984).

Class stories do not always have to be in the same format. They may take the form of reports, newspaper articles, descriptive essays, or letters, or they can be creative in content while using a particular writing style to which the children have been exposed. For example, after reading predictable books to the children, the teacher can encourage the children to produce the same kind of story. The repetition and predictability in the stories make sharing these child-developed books with classmates a profitable way to provide extensive practice in reading familiar words and language structures (Reimer, 1983). Storytelling can act as the stimulus for the children to tell and write stories that are related in some way (Nelson, 1989).

It is important that teachers use the children's own language in language experience stories, even if the children's language does not fit the teacher's idea of basic words and sentence patterns for reading. If they do not do so, students are not likely to reap the full benefits of this approach.

Computers can be useful in a language experience lesson. The teacher can type into the computer student-dictated material and modify it as the students direct. When using the computer in this way, the children should be directly facing a large monitor, with the teacher sitting at an angle to the monitor. This arrangement gives the students who are composing the story an unobstructed view (Smith, 1985). The students may use one beginning and develop different endings, then print out the various versions for comparison. The teacher can give students individual printed copies to illustrate and/or expand (Grabe and Grabe, 1985).

Another way to use the computer that takes advantage of its graphics capabilities is to provide a sequence of pictures that tell a story and let the students dictate a title and a story to fit the pictures. The teacher can enter the dictated material into the computer, and the children can read their stories from the computer screen. Then the teacher can print the story and pictures for them (Grabe and Grabe, 1985).

At some point the students may be able to enter their stories into the computer themselves. Several word-processing programs are easy enough for even primary students to learn to use. *Magic Slate II* (Sunburst Communications) has twenty-, forty-, and eighty-column versions and can accommodate users as young as first graders as well as adult users. *The Bank Street Writer III Student Edition* (Scholastic) is designed for use in grades two through twelve. IBM's *Listen to Learn* goes beyond simple word processing; it "talks" through a speech synthesizer. Text can be displayed on the computer monitor and spoken simultaneously, or the children can type in text and listen as it is spoken. This program can help children build sight vocabulary, among other skills, and, like the other programs listed here, can be used very effectively with the language experience approach.

Children can write stories on the computer most effectively when several students work together. One child can decide what to write and enter the text, while one or more "advisers" offer help with mechanics, spelling, grammar, or computer operation (Starshine and Fortson, 1984); or the group of children can collectively decide what to say, taking turns entering sentences as they are composed.

Sharing stories, whether orally or in written form, is very important, since group members will soon see that certain words occur over and over again and that they can read the stories their classmates write. The experience stories written by the group as a whole may be gathered into a booklet under a general title chosen by the group, and individuals may also bind their stories into booklets. Children will enjoy reading one another's booklets, and a collection of their own stories provides both a record of their activities and evidence of their growth in reading and writing.

In one school a multicultural group of first graders wrote language experience stories, illustrated them, made them into books, and set up a classroom library. The books were given library pockets and checkout cards and were cataloged and shelved as they might be in a regular library. Children assumed jobs as reference librarians, check-out librarians, check-in librarians, and so forth. Both older and younger children in the school were scheduled for visits to use the library, which was operated for six days, and the student librarians learned a great deal during the project (Powers, 1981).

As time passes and the children learn to write and spell, they may wish to write experience stories by themselves, asking the teacher or turning to their word banks or dictionaries for help in spelling. Teachers should allow children to use invented spellings when they are writing, since they can go back and correct spelling and rewrite the story in a neater form later if others are to read it.

reading-writing connection

Rereading and editing require children to make judgments about syntax, semantics, and the topic and about whether or not others will understand the written account. These activities provide ways to emphasize comprehension when using language experience stories. At first this should be done with extensive teacher guidance; later children can work more independently (Sulzby, 1980). The Classroom Scenario below presents the language experience approach in a primary-grade classroom.

Word banks offer many opportunities for instructional activities. When children have accumulated a sufficient number of word cards in their word banks, they can use them to compose new stories or to play word-matching or visual and auditory discrimination games. To develop comprehension skills, a teacher can use classification games, asking questions such as "How many of you have a color word? A word that shows action? A word that names a place?" When each student has as many as ten word cards, the children can begin to alphabetize them by the first letter, which gives them a practical reason to learn alphabetical order. They can also develop picture dictionaries representing the words on their cards, or they can search for their words in newspapers and magazines. After they recognize that their words appear in books, they will realize they can read the books. The uses for word banks seem to be limited only by the teachers' and children's imaginations.

**Classroom
Scenario**

Language Experience Approach

A lifelike raccoon puppet was shown to the children in a first-grade classroom. The presenter introduced the puppet as Rocky Raccoon and proceeded to tell them about his personality, including his preferences (for example, Rocky Road ice cream and rock music). The children looked at Rocky, touched his fur, and discussed him thoroughly. Then they dictated the following story:

Rocky Raccoon

Rocky is beautiful. Rocky is soft. Rocky is funny. Rocky is a nice raccoon. Rocky can do tricks. Rocky is cuddly. Rocky is fluffy.

The presenter read the story to the class and allowed them to read it with her. Then she posed this question: "Does your story sound like the ones that you have been listening to your teacher read to you?"

After thinking about it, the children said it did not sound like the books they had heard being read. The presenter then asked them, "What could you do to the story to make it sound more like the stories in books?"

Several children said, "Not repeat *Rocky* so many times. Use longer sentences. Put stuff from sentences together."

Step by step, the presenter questioned them about which *Rocky* mentions to change and what to change them to and which sentences went together and how they should be combined. The children's revisions were recorded one at a time, and the story was reread each time to see if they liked it better. They also decided to add a sentence. The final version that met with their approval went like this:

Rocky Raccoon

Rocky is beautiful. He is soft. He is funny. Rocky is a nice raccoon. He can do tricks. He is cuddly and fluffy. Rocky looks like he is wearing a mask.

Analysis of Scenario
This activity was the children's first experience with revising their own writing. They liked the fact that they could change the writing around to make it sound better to them. Even though they did not end up with classic literature, they had taken a step in their literacy development.

Implementation in Higher Grades

The language experience approach has many applications above the primary grades. These applications are often in content area instruction: writing the results of scientific experiments; comparing and contrasting people, things, or events; writing directions for performing a task; and so forth.

Many computer applications lend themselves to upper-grade activities, for they allow children to enter their stories easily and provide ease of revision without the drudgery of recopying. A good computer application is the production of a newspaper based on experiences around the school. Programs are available that make the production of a nice-looking newspaper relatively easy for children. Children can be reporters, who initially enter the stories into the computer; editors, who edit the work of the reporters; and "typesetters," who format the edited material (Mason, 1984).

Text structures found in content area textbooks, such as comparison-and-contrast patterns, can initially be taught through language experience activities. Then students will be more likely to understand these structures when they encounter them in content materials. First, the teacher can present children with two items and ask them how these items are alike. Then the teacher can ask how the items are different. The class can construct a chart of these likenesses and differences during the discussion. After the discussion, the children can dictate a language experience story based on the information listed on their chart. The teacher can encourage them to write first about likenesses and then about differences. Practice activities with the completed story may include matching the two parts of a contrast, for example, matching "a marble is round," with "a jack has points." Parts of the story can be scrambled, and then the story can be rearranged with the comparisons and contrasts lined up appropriately (Kinney, 1985).

Heller (1988) has pointed out that direct teaching of story structure during language experience activities that are used with older remedial learners can be helpful. She also emphasizes the inclusion of revision and editing as natural extensions of experience story writing.

LEA: Pros and Cons

The language experience approach offers something for children regardless of the modes through which they learn best because it incorporates all modes. For instance, the learners use the auditory mode when stories are dictated or read aloud, the kinesthetic (motor) mode when they write stories, and the visual mode when they read stories.

reading-writing connection

The language experience approach promotes a good self-concept. It shows children that what they have to say is important enough to write down and that others are interested in it. It also promotes close contact between teachers and students. Finally, this approach has been highly successful as a remedial technique in the upper grades, allowing remedial readers to read material that interests them rather than lower-level materials that they quickly recognize as being designed for younger children.

Of course, the LEA also has some potential disadvantages. These are as follows:

1. Some educators view the lack of sequential development of reading skills, caused by the unstructured nature of the approach, as a disadvantage. However, there is no one correct sequence for presenting reading skills. Children learn from a variety of programs that provide different skill sequences.

2. Some educators regard the lack of systematic repetition of new words and the lack of vocabulary control in general as drawbacks.

3. The stories may lack literary quality.

4. Making charts is a very time-consuming process.

5. If this approach is used to the exclusion of other methods of reading instruction, at some point the limitations of the children's backgrounds of experience may keep them from developing in reading as they should. The LEA, however, is rarely used in isolation.

SELF-CHECK: OBJECTIVE 4 What is the rationale behind the language experience approach? What are some of the LEA's advantages and disadvantages? (See Self-Improvement Opportunity 3.)

Programmed Instruction

Programmed instruction is sometimes used to offer individualized instruction. Programmed materials instruct in small, sequential steps, each of which is referred to as a *frame*. The student is required to respond in some way to each frame and is instantly informed of the correctness of his or her response (given immediate reinforcement). Because the instruction is presented to an individual child, rather than to a group, each child moves through the material at his or her own pace, thereby benefiting from some individualization. Branching programs provide an even greater degree of individualization by offering review material to children who respond incorrectly to frames, thereby indicating that they have not mastered the skills being presented.

Programmed instruction can also provide follow-up reinforcement for instruction presented by the teacher, freeing the teacher from many drill activities and allowing him or her more time to spend on complex teaching tasks. The programmed materials are designed to be self-instructional and do not require direct teacher supervision.

On the other hand, programmed instruction does not lend itself to teaching many complex comprehension skills, such as those involving analysis and interpretation, nor does it promote flexibility of reading rate. It also does not encourage student-to-student interaction (Wood, 1989). Word analysis and vocabulary-building skills are most prominently treated in programmed materials, so teachers may wish to use other materials (for example, basal texts) or techniques (for example, semantic webbing) to present and provide practice in the complex comprehension skills. Materials used with programmed instruction may consist of print materials such as programmed texts, or they may exist in electronic format, presented on computers.

Computer Applications

Computers are found more frequently in classrooms today than they were in the past, although they are still not available in large enough quantities to offer every elementary school student substantial computer time each day. Computers are valuable tools for the reading teacher. Through software available for computer-assisted instruction (CAI), computer-managed instruction (CMI), word processing, database applications, and literature presentation, teachers can plan many meaningful learning experiences for students. Because of the interactive characteristics of the computer—it can provide immediate responses to input from student users—teachers find it is a good tool for individualizing instruction. Because of its ability to patiently repeat instructions without showing irritation or judging students negatively, it is also useful for remedial instruction. Word-processing programs allow teachers and students alike to easily revise and edit their written products, which can then be printed in neat form to be read by class members.

reading-writing connection

Database programs allow the categorization, storage, and orderly retrieval of data collected during research reading. Newer programs present literature in an interactive format, allowing students to hear stories or individual words from stories read, to see animated scenes from the story, to obtain definitions of words, or to accomplish other interactive tasks.

Many computers are now capable of reading texts aloud, using synthetic speech. This enhances the utility of computer programs for young children and readers with disabilities. Computers can also provide larger print for visually impaired readers, and the color and typeface of print shown on the monitor can

be changed. In *Wiggleworks: Scholastic Beginning Literacy System*, a program that presents established children's books on CD-ROM, students can record a sentence in their own voices, enter the sentence into the computer, have the computer read what has been entered in synthetic speech, and replay their recorded speech at any point for comparison. This capability allows self-monitoring of students' writing (Rose and Meyer, 1994; Mike, 1994).

Today's multimedia programs let students input text with the keyboard, draw onscreen or on paper and scan the material into the computer, use predrawn pictures and backgrounds, record sounds to include in documents, or select sounds

Software available for microcomputers enables students either to practice skills they already have learned, or to interact with the computer to write stories or solve problems. (© *Elizabeth Crews/Stock Boston*)

from prerecorded ones. This helps students with varied learning styles to approach composition more easily (Rose and Meyer, 1994).

There are two broad categories of computer use for individualizing instruction: *computer-assisted instruction* (CAI), in which a computer administers a programmed instructional sequence to a student, and *computer-managed instruction* (CMI), in which the computer takes care of such tasks as recordkeeping, diagnosis, and prescription of individualized assignments. These two approaches are often available in a single coordinated package.

Drill-and-practice programs, which consist of practice lessons on skills students have previously been taught, are the simplest types of computer applications and the ones most commonly found in classrooms. With drill-and-practice programs, students receive material in a programmed sequence (as described in the section "Programmed Instruction") and receive immediate feedback on the correctness of their answers. Some programs give students more than one opportunity to respond to an item before telling them the correct answer.

Practice is important for developing accuracy in and automaticity of reading skills. Computer drill-and-practice programs can provide repetition without the impatience teachers sometimes manifest. When the goal is developing accuracy, the computer can be used to present a few exercises accompanied by clear, immediate feedback, particularly for incorrect answers. After children have attained accuracy, the teacher can have them practice using computer programs with larger numbers of exercises, sometimes emphasizing speed, that are accompanied by less extensive feedback. Some drill-and-practice programs recirculate missed items for further practice, without requiring the teacher to plan or execute such repetition (Balajthy, 1984). These programs can conserve a teacher's time while providing individualized instruction. The interactive nature of CAI makes this drill more interesting and helps keep the learner engaged in the activity (Esbensen, 1981).

Game characteristics can add interest to computer drills. With or without the game format, computers have the capability to provide graphics that increase the appeal of the programs (Balajthy, 1984). The visual and auditory support given to the written word is beneficial, as is the provision of a massive information retrieval base (Herriott, 1982).

In *tutorial programs*, the computer actually presents instruction, then follows it with practice activities. Depending on the correct and incorrect responses a student gives as the program progresses, he or she may be branched to a remedial sequence of instruction, taken back through the initial instruction, directed through the typical sequence for the instruction, or skipped ahead in the program to avoid unnecessary practice. Some programs do not give students direct control over the sequence; others allow them to request review, remedial help, or additional practice.

Programs may be self-paced or computer-paced. Self-paced programs allow students to move at their own rates through the material, thereby providing more attention to individual differences than computer-paced programs, which progress through the material at a predetermined rate (Balajthy, 1984). Sometimes the programs are self-paced on a page-by-page basis; the student presses "Return" when he or she wants to continue. Other programs are designed to allow the student to choose a pace for the entire program when the study session starts.

Programs can also be linear or branching. Linear programs take all students through the same sequence of material, although they generally allow the students to progress at their own rates. Branching programs, on the other hand, adjust the instructional sequence according to each student's performance. Branching programs are obviously more helpful for individualizing instruction.

reading-writing connection

Word processing on the computer allows children to experiment with language and to control their own learning processes (Heffron, 1986). As described in the section "The Language Experience Approach," word processing can ease the tasks of writing and revising for both the teacher and the students. Butler and Cox (1992) found that when first graders are allowed to work in pairs to compose stories on a computer, they discuss language usage, spelling, and punctuation, as well as the mechanics of computer use. They reread what they have written frequently as a springboard to adding new text, as both contribute to the story line. The full facilitative effects of word processing on the quality of student writing may not be evident until students become proficient in the use of the program and the equipment (Owston, Murphy, and Wideman, 1992; Schumm and Saumell, 1993).

Database programs are also being used for reading activities in today's classrooms. When using databases, students perform such tasks as reading and following directions, taking notes, gathering and categorizing data, summarizing, posing questions, predicting outcomes, making comparisons and contrasts using collected information, using reference materials, identifying key words for efficient data access, and testing hypotheses. All of these activities require them to be active, purposeful readers (Layton and Irwin, 1989).

The heart of a CAI system is the software, the programs that actually provide the instruction. These programs vary in quality depending on the programmers; the computer can only carry out the instructions its developers have given it. Teachers should try out software before purchasing it, if possible, because some pedagogically unsound educational software is being sold. Teachers need to ask themselves questions such as the following about programs they are considering purchasing:

1. Is the material instructionally sound?

2. Is the program easy for the learner to use?

3. Does use of the program accomplish something that is needed in this classroom?

To be instructionally sound, the program should present accurate information in a reasonable sequence with an appropriate amount of student interaction. It should not reward incorrect answers with clever messages or graphics, while not doing this for correct answers. It should be easy to use, providing clear instructions about what to do to advance material on the screen, to respond to questions (Should students use a letter or an entire typed-out answer to respond to a multiple-choice question? Should they touch the screen on or beside the correct answer?), and to receive help when needed. Erroneous keystrokes should not "dump" a student out of the program but allow him or her to recover in a clear and easy way.

Even good programs are not useful if they do not accomplish something that needs to be done. Only the teacher can decide whether or not a program does that.

Programs that are currently available come in all levels of complexity and involve the use of many different skills. Some examples follow:

1. *Snooper Troops* (Spinnaker Software Corporation) presents students with mysteries to be solved by collecting and following clues and testing hypotheses (Dudley-Marling, 1985). This material is obviously good for developing higher-order comprehension skills.

2. *The Cave of Time* (Bantam Software) is one of a number of interactive fiction stories based on Bantam Books' *Choose Your Own Adventure* series ("What's in Store Software Guide," 1986). It causes students to use higher-order comprehension skills as they create an adventure.

3. *Jack and the Beanstalk: An Animated Storybook* (Tom Snyder Productions) is referred to as "lapware." This means it was designed for a child and an adult to experience together. The adult reads the story aloud from the computer, while the child presses a computer key to turn each page. At points in the story, the child has to decide what will happen next. The adult explains the options to the child, and the child makes a decision and presses the key related to the desired option. This story version is a space-age adaptation of the familiar story. The child can produce several variations on the story by choosing different options. Thus, the story is flexible enough to be used multiple times. The child is in charge of the story and can return to the previous choices or decide on new ones (Holzberg, 1989).

4. *The New Talking Stickybear Alphabet* (Optimum Resource, Inc.) offers three activities. In the Alphabet game, when the user presses a letter key, Stickybear says the letter and a word beginning with it. Both upper- and lower-case examples of the letter appear on the screen, along with the word that Stickybear says and an animated picture. In Letter Hunt, Stickybear tells the user to press a particular letter, and a picture that begins with the letter appears when a correct response is given. The letter itself appears when an incorrect response is given, with a request for the child to try again. In Fast Letters, the user presses a letter key and Stickybear says the letter, which is also displayed on the screen (Perry, 1989).

5. *The Newsroom* (Springboard) is a desktop publishing program that allows students to construct newspapers. This experience exposes them to practice in a number of language skills (Balajthy and Link, 1988).

6. *Super Solvers Midnight Rescue!* (The Learning Company) is a game designed to help build reading comprehension. Students must read letters, diaries, newsletters, and excerpts from classics to collect clues and solve a mystery. The program features animation and sound effects (Larson, 1994).

Some teachers wonder if there is a place for computers in whole language and literature-based classrooms. DeGroff (1989, 1990) and many others say there is. Whole language and literature-oriented teachers often make use of computer programs, such as the interactive fiction examples just cited, that are more open-ended than the drill-and-practice programs. Especially popular are such programs as *The Semantic Mapper* (Kuchinskas and Radencich, 1986), a student utility program that facilitates the construction of semantic maps; *The Literary Mapper* (Kuchinskas and Radencich, 1990), a literature-based version of *The Semantic Mapper* in which character, setting, and action maps are already developed to allow students to begin quickly formulating ideas about salient story elements; *Language Experience Recorder Plus (LER+)*, a word processor with primary print that uses a speech synthesizer to speak what students record; and *Super Story Tree* (Bracket, 1989), a program with graphics, fonts, sound, and music that students can use to create interactive branching stories (Wepner, 1990). Other useful programs for these teachers are *Success with Reading* (Balsam and Hammer, 1985), which ties in trade book reading with onscreen activities, and *The Comprehension Connection* (Reinking, 1987), a program that offers onscreen "help" options with each passage. In addition, the following software can be used extensively in literature-based and whole language classrooms (Wepner, 1990; Wepner, 1992; Lee, 1994; Larson, 1994): *The Children's Writing and Publishing Center* (The Learning Company, 1989); *Kid Works 2* (Davidson & Associates), a talking word-processing program with icons for nouns, verbs, and adjectives and a paint option for creating illustrations; *Story Book Weaver* (MECC), a story-writing program with a wealth of objects to use in illustrating the stories; *Creative Writer* (Microsoft Corp.), a creative writing and desktop publishing program; *Great Beginnings* (Teacher Support Software), a talking word processing-program with graphics and stimulus words related to four themes; *The Scholastic Process Writer* (Scholastic), which offers a word processor, a computer-based writing coach, and postwriting tools; and *Magic Slate II* (Sunburst Communications), a word processor adaptable to a number of age levels of students through its twenty-, forty-, and eighty-column versions. *Author! Author!* (Mindplay) is a program that allows children to write scripts for plays and create stages with movable graphics of characters and props (Wepner, 1993).

Two software packages are available for use with Judith Viorst's *Alexander and the Terrible, Horrible, No Good, Very Bad Day* (Macmillan, 1972): *Alexander and the Terrible, Horrible, No Good, Very Bad Day* (Sunburst Communications) and *Terrible Days I* (Humanities Software). Both of these programs can be used with *Magic Slate II: 40-Column* (Sunburst Communications) (Wepner, 1993).

Database software, such as *Appleworks*, can be used to help students organize data for writing reports, and much writing is exchanged among classrooms when

literature-centered reading

reading-writing connection

literature-centered reading

reading-writing connection

literature-centered reading

reading-writing connection

networks and electronic mail systems, such as *QUILL* (D. C. Heath), are available (Newman, 1989; DeGroff, 1990). Interactive telecommunications involves transmissions of text typed on a computer with a modem through telephone lines. A telecommunications software program allows a user to dial the number of a receiver's computer, transfer information, and disconnect the call. Use of such experiences has resulted in more extensive writing and improved attitudes and performance in reading and writing among middle-grade students (Riel, 1989; Moore, 1991). Newman (1989) found similar advantages for older students in length of text produced, attitudes toward writing, and language development (Moore, 1991).

When pairs of students are allowed to work together at the computer, the language interactions are rich, whether the students are reading an interactive fiction story, using a simulation program, or writing a story together. The computer screen appears to be a stimulus for interaction as children pass by or wait for turns (DeGroff, 1990; Cochran-Smith, 1988). The computer offers opportunities for reading meaningful material, such as messages, directions, stories, and informational articles, some of which have been written by the students (DeGroff, 1990).

Some computer-based programs for teaching reading employ a multisensory approach. The IBM *Writing to Read* program, for example, attempts to teach reading through an approach that involves tactile, visual, and auditory senses (Heffron, 1986). This is an expensive program that includes five types of workstations, only two of which involve computers (Slavin, 1990).

Using new hypertext and hypermedia applications can also result in multisensory experiences. With hypermedia, a variety of media can be viewed and/or heard in an order chosen by the user (Dillner, 1993/1994). *Hypertext* refers to information that is linked in a nonsequential manner. *Hypermedia* refers to "a mixture of technologies controlled by hypertext. Hypermedia can include information from any number of video and audio sources (e.g., music, text, animation, film, graphics, speech, newsreels, still images)" (Blanchard and Rottenberg, 1990, p. 657). Hypertext allows enhancements to text that assist comprehension; with hypertext and hypermedia applications, for example, a student can use a mouse pointer and click when the cursor is over boldfaced words in the material. This may display a glossary text that may define the word, provide a picture, and/or read the word aloud. Hypertext applications may also provide graphic organizers or interspersed questions. They may offer options for taking notes as the reading progresses and printing out notes for review or as a basis for developing essays. Although some applications of hypertext to reading are currently available, most require large random access memories and hard disk drives. Hypermedia applications may require laserdiscs/videodiscs/compact discs and players, as well as high-resolution color monitors. Some examples of reading applications include *The Manhole* and *Cosmic Osmo* (Activision, 1989) and *A Country Christmas* (B&B Soundwords, 1989). All include text, graphics, and sound effects. The first two also include speech (Anderson-Inman et al., 1994; Blanchard and Rottenberg, 1990).

reading-writing connection

reading-writing connection

Multimedia software allows students to "expand classroom publishing to include colorful graphics, moving images, sound effects . . . , music, and written and spoken words (D'Ignazio, 1991, p. 250). Such possibilities make high-interest projects possible. For example, *The Bank Street Writer for the Macintosh* (Scholastic Software) offers multiple fonts and has a hypertext function with buttons that allow students to provide additional explanations about their text, create data-bases of information about their subjects, or create sounds for their products. A graphic gallery, spelling checker, and thesaurus come with the package, and other Macintosh graphics can be imported. *Pelican Press* (Toucan), also for the Macintosh, is an easy-to-learn publishing program that allows students to create signs, posters, cards, banners, and calendars. *Bulletin Board Maker* (Pelican), for the Apple, allows students to make posters, signs, announcements, and newsletters (Wepner, 1993).

Reviews in periodicals such as *Electronic Learning* and *The Computing Teacher,* as well as those in *The Reading Teacher,* can be helpful. The Minnesota Educational Computing Consortium (MECC), a large distributor of educational software with an extensive catalog of offerings, may also be a useful resource.

Some teachers use authoring software or programming languages to produce their own programs. This option is extremely time consuming, especially if programming languages are used, but authoring systems demand less computer expertise, and teachers can learn to use them in a shorter time frame to produce computer-based courseware. Some are fairly user friendly, containing menus, prompts, and help options. These systems guide the user through the development process step by step. They provide outlines for lessons that the user fills in with text, questions, answers, feedback, and prompts, for example. The better systems are fairly expensive, but the interested teacher may wish to investigate such options (Isaak and Joseph, 1989). Teachers should not feel pressured to construct courseware in order to use the computer. Much commercial material is available, and evaluation skills may be more valuable than development skills.

Computer-managed instruction can help teachers keep track of student performance and guide their learning activities. Some systems, for example, provide tests on specific objectives that are computer scored. The computer then matches the student's deficiencies to available instructional materials, suggests instructional sequences for the teacher to use, or assigns material directly to the student. The computer may also perform tasks such as averaging grades on a series of tests, thereby removing quite a bit of burdensome recordkeeping from the teacher's shoulders (Hedges, 1981; Coburn et al., 1982).

Management systems are built into some individual CAI programs. They allow the teacher to see how well children perform, and sometimes they indicate which items were answered incorrectly. The management systems in some programs tell students when to move on to more difficult levels of the program or when to drop back to easier ones. Some of these management systems, however, do not save results from session to session but erase data when the computer's power is turned off (Balajthy, 1984).

The computer generation is indeed here. Children are not intimidated by

reading-writing connection

computers, and teachers need to keep in step. The use of computers holds much promise for education, but the technology is changing rapidly, so teachers need to stay current.

SELF-CHECK: OBJECTIVE 5   What kinds of questions should teachers ask about the computer software they plan to purchase for reading instruction? (See Self-Improvement Opportunities 5 and 10.)

Eclectic Approaches

Eclectic approaches combine the desirable aspects of a number of different methods rather than strictly adhering to a single one. Teachers often take an eclectic approach in choosing instructional materials and techniques to fit their unique situations and provide a variety of reading experiences for children. The following examples are only possibilities, and teachers should remember that the only limitations are school resources and their own imaginations.

literature-centered reading

1. Language experience stories can be based on characters, events, or ideas in either trade books or basal stories. The teacher can plan an experience related to the story, lead a discussion of the experience, and record the students' dictated account. If an experience such as this is used prior to reading the book or basal story, it can help to activate the children's schemata related to the story. It will also probably involve use of some of the same vocabulary in the story, providing an introduction to this vocabulary in context. The story may also be used as a basis for skills instruction suggested in the basal reader (Jones and Nessel, 1985).

reading-writing connection

2. Grabe (1981) also suggests having the teacher supplement the basal reader approach by having children write "books about the book": they dictate stories about the basal selection using the new vocabulary. This approach has been found to enhance comprehension and vocabulary skills. In a classroom with two reading periods each day, the teacher may use the basal reader during the first period and the language experience approach during the second, relating the experience story to the basal story and thereby helping the children gain additional practice with much of the same vocabulary.

literature-centered reading

3. In one school district's effort to allow teachers to go beyond the basal, some teachers used basal readers for up to 50 percent of the reading time. The remainder of the time was spent on shared reading of trade books. Teachers could not use the basal more than 50 percent of the time, but they were free to use the trade books for their reading instruction for the entire time, if they so chose. This practice allowed the teachers a wide range of choice and control over decisions about reading instruction in their own classrooms. In some classrooms, the basal stories were simply used as they fit into thematic units being taught (Henke, 1988).

thematic learning

literature-centered reading

reading-writing connection

4. In a class in which whole-class reading of a core book is taking place, language experience stories can be written, based on material from the particular book being read. For example, if the core book is *The Cay* by Theodore Taylor (Avon, 1969), the experience might be to try to weave a mat while blindfolded. The students could write a story about the experience and, in the process, develop a better understanding of the difficulty Phillip had when Timothy asked him to weave a mat, even though he was blind.

reading-writing connection

5. Computer-assisted instruction can be used with any approach. The use of the word-processing function of the computer makes the computer a natural tool for implementation of the language experience approach. Children who tend to produce only short stories because of difficulties in writing are freed to write more extensively with the ease of editing the computer offers.

literature-centered reading

6. Teachers can use the individualized reading approach for two or three days each week and the basal program for the rest of the week, or they can alternate weeks with the individualized reading approach and the basal. They may supplement either or both with occasional language experience activities, either on or off of the computer.

reading-writing connection

thematic learning

reading-writing connection

7. Teachers can use a thematic literature unit approach to reading instruction, making use of pertinent basal reader stories as they are available and using language experience activities as appropriate to the planned curriculum. They may use database software to store information about the unit on the computer in an organized way, and they may use word-processing software to produce written reports about aspects of the theme.

**Classroom
Scenario**

An Eclectic Approach

Ms. Gray, a teacher who embraces an eclectic approach to reading instruction, is working with one reading group in a corner of the room during her scheduled reading time. At the same time, children from another reading group are illustrating a language experience story that they wrote on the previous day. As they finish their illustrations, pairs of children from this group are forming sentences with their word-bank words. Several other children are busy reading self-selected library books at their seats.

Three children have returned to the room from the library and have seated themselves together to discuss some research reading they have been doing on space travel. One of them is holding the printout from a database query she had made during the library trip.

In another corner of the room, two girls are reading an interactive text story on a microcomputer, discussing each decision and coming to a consensus about it before indicating their choices through keyboard commands.

> **Analysis of Scenario**
> In this classroom, all of the students are busy at reading tasks, but the tasks involve many different approaches to reading instruction. The teacher has chosen activities that fit the children's individual instructional needs.

SELF-CHECK: OBJECTIVE 6   Discuss how you might choose to use the elements of several different approaches in your classroom.

What About Whole Language?

Some readers may be wondering why whole language is not featured as a section of this chapter. As mentioned at the beginning of the chapter, we have not included it in this way because whole language is not an *approach* to reading instruction. Rather, it is a curricular philosophy, or belief system, as described in Chapter 1.

Many of the approaches mentioned in this chapter are frequently used by whole language teachers: the language experience approach, use of thematic literature units, use of literature response groups, some variations of whole-class reading of a core book, the individualized reading approach, and some computer applications.

Some educators even say that teachers can use a whole language philosophy and blend the instructional activities with systematic direct instruction (Spiegel, 1992; Yatvin, 1991). Spiegel (1992) sees direct instruction as teaching children strategies to be used flexibly to meet reading needs and suggests blending the best of whole language and systematic direct instruction in reading strategies to assist all children in reaching their full literacy potential. Strategies may be taught and then practiced using authentic materials, rather than worksheets or other forms of isolated drill. This position will likely be heavily debated for some time to come.

Summary

Basal reader series are the most widely used materials for teaching reading in elementary schools in this country. Basal readers have been improved in recent years and provide teachers with anthologies of reading materials, detailed teacher's manuals, and many supplementary materials. Some published series are being called literature-based and/or language-integrated series because of their greater focus on quality literature selections and integration of other types of language activities with the reading. Many new series are also giving teachers and students more decision-making power and control over the lessons. Literature-based and language-integrated series focus on more prediction making by the students and more instructional options for the teacher than are found in traditional basal reader manuals.

The directed reading activity (DRA) is the teaching strategy presented in traditional basal manuals. This strategy can be used with other reading materials as well. Teachers can use the *enrichment activities* of the DRA before the story to help build and integrate background. Comprehension monitoring can also be made a natural part of a DRA. An alternative to the DRA is the directed reading-thinking activity (DRTA).

Literature-based reading approaches include whole-class reading of a core book, literature response groups reading several books for which there are multiple copies, thematic literature units, and the individualized reading approach. Whole-class reading of a core book, thematic literature units, and the individualized reading approach all include use of minilessons. Thematic literature units center around a theme, a genre, or an author. All of these approaches include various types of responses to literature. The individualized reading approach allows children to move at their own paces through reading material that they have chosen. Student-teacher conferences help the teacher monitor progress and build rapport with the students. Sharing activities allow group interaction.

The language experience approach interrelates the different language arts and uses children's experiences as the basis for reading materials. This approach has many advantages: it incorporates the visual, auditory, and kinesthetic modes of learning; it promotes a positive self-concept and fosters close contact between teachers and students; and it serves as an effective remedial technique in the upper grades. This approach can be introduced in kindergarten, but it continues to have applications for all students in higher grades, especially in conjunction with content area activities.

Some approaches have been particularly designed to help individualize instruction. Among these are programmed instruction and computer approaches, in addition to the individualized reading approach. Programmed instruction is administered through materials that present information in small, sequential steps. The student responds at each step and receives immediate feedback about the correctness of the response. Students are allowed to learn at their own paces. Computer approaches include computer-assisted instruction (CAI) and computer-managed instruction (CMI), in which the computer takes care of such tasks as recordkeeping, diagnosis, and prescription of individualized assignments. Drill-and-practice programs, tutorial programs, interactive fiction programs, game-type simulation programs, database programs, and word-processing programs are some of the computer-based instructional materials available. Many computer applications have been found to be appropriate for use in whole language classrooms. Computer-managed instruction can help teachers keep track of student performance and guide learning activities.

An eclectic approach combines desirable aspects of a number of different methods. The only limitation to possible combinations is the teacher's imagination.

Whole language has not been treated extensively in this chapter because it is a philosophy, rather than an approach. However, many of the approaches described in this chapter are congruent with a whole language philosophy. Chapters 1, 2, and 8 also present much information related to this philosophy.

Test Yourself   *True or False*

_____ 1. All published reading series are alike.

_____ 2. Teacher's manuals in basal reading series generally provide detailed lesson plans for teaching each story in a basal reader.

_____ 3. Basal reader workbooks are designed to teach reading skills and do not require teacher intervention.

_____ 4. Workbook activities are useful only for keeping children busy while the teacher is engaged in other activities.

_____ 5. Published literature-based reading series have moved toward offering teachers more decision-making opportunities than traditional basal readers generally offered.

_____ 6. The language experience approach (LEA) uses child-created material for reading instruction.

_____ 7. A word bank is a collection of words that the teacher believes children should learn.

_____ 8. The language experience approach promotes a better self-concept in many children.

_____ 9. The individualized reading approach utilizes self-selection and self-pacing.

_____ 10. The individualized reading approach involves no direct skills instruction.

_____ 11. Student-teacher conferences are an integral part of the individualized reading approach.

_____ 12. When literature-based reading programs are used, children interact with texts in meaningful ways.

_____ 13. Close reading of core books, discussion, and writing related to the reading take place in literature-based classrooms.

_____ 14. Thematic literature units involve the reading of a single book by all class members and writing of a book report on the book.

_____ 15. Programmed instruction presents instructional material in small, sequential steps.

_____ 16. An eclectic approach combines features from a number of different approaches.

_____ 17. Sometimes computers are useful in diagnosing students' reading difficulties and prescribing corrective programs.

_____ 18. The language experience approach is not consistent with schema theory.

_____ 19. Drill-and-practice programs are among the rarest and most complex CAI programs.

_____ 20. Open-ended computer applications, such as word-processing and database programs, do not fit in whole language classrooms as well as do drill-and-practice programs.

_____ 21. The directed reading-thinking activity is a good alternative to the directed reading activity to provide a more student-centered experience.

_____ 22. Word processing on the microcomputer is useful for writing language experience stories.

_____ 23. The language experience approach is not useful above first grade.

_____ 24. Whole language instruction is a well-defined approach to teaching reading, complete with standard activities and materials.

Self-Improvement Opportunities

1. Visit an elementary school classroom and discuss the instructional materials used in the reading program with the teacher(s).

2. Visit a school and watch an experienced teacher use a DRA.

3. Develop a language experience chart with a group of children. Use it to teach one or more reading strategies.

4. Plan an individualized reading approach for a specific group of children. Explain what materials will be used (include reading levels and interest areas of the materials) and where they will be obtained. Outline the recordkeeping procedures; explain how conferences will be scheduled and the uses to which they will be put; and describe the routines children will follow for selecting books, checking out books, and receiving help while reading.

5. Look into the possibility of utilizing CAI in the reading program of a school near you. Find out what computer programs that fit into the current reading program are available. Decide what equipment would be needed to use these programs. Investigate the cost of the equipment and programs.

6. Develop a directed reading-thinking activity (DRTA) for a trade book. Then try it out in an elementary school classroom or present it to a group of your peers in a reading or content methods course.

7. Choose a basal reader for a grade level you might teach. Examine it for variety of writing types (narrative, expository, poetry). Make a chart showing the frequency of the various types. Note also the frequency of different types of content (language skills, social studies, science, art, mathematics, music, and so on). Report your results to the class.

8. Choose a computer program that could be used as a part of the reading program in a grade level of your choice. Answer the three questions listed on page 364 in reference to the program, considering "this classroom" in Question 3 to refer to the grade level you chose. Write a narrative that tells why you would or would not recommend the program, considering all the factors presented in the section on computers in this chapter.

9. Plan a thematic literature unit for a grade level of your choice. Think about ways that you can actively involve the children with the books. Share your plan with your classmates.

Chapter 8

Key Vocabulary

Pay close attention to these terms when they appear in the chapter.

Caldecott Award

community of authors

desktop publishing

genre

journal

literature response
  groups

Newbery Award

ownership

readers' theater

reading and writing
  workshops

selection aid

Sustained Silent
  Reading (SSR)

thematic unit

webbing

whole language

writing process

Language and Literature: Holistic Learning

Setting Objectives

When you finish reading this chapter, you should be able to

1. Discuss some basic principles of whole language.

2. Explain the importance of integrating the language arts and of integrating language across the curriculum.

3. Identify some relationships between reading and writing.

4. Understand how to implement the writing process and list the major steps in this process.

5. Discuss procedures for using journals and for implementing writing and reading workshops.

6. Design a classroom environment conducive to reading and writing.

7. Select appropriate literature of good quality and high interest and read or tell stories expressively.

8. Discuss a variety of ways to respond to literature.

9. Identify ways to use children's literature in different areas of the curriculum and to create thematic units.

Figure 8.1 *Chapter 8 Organization*

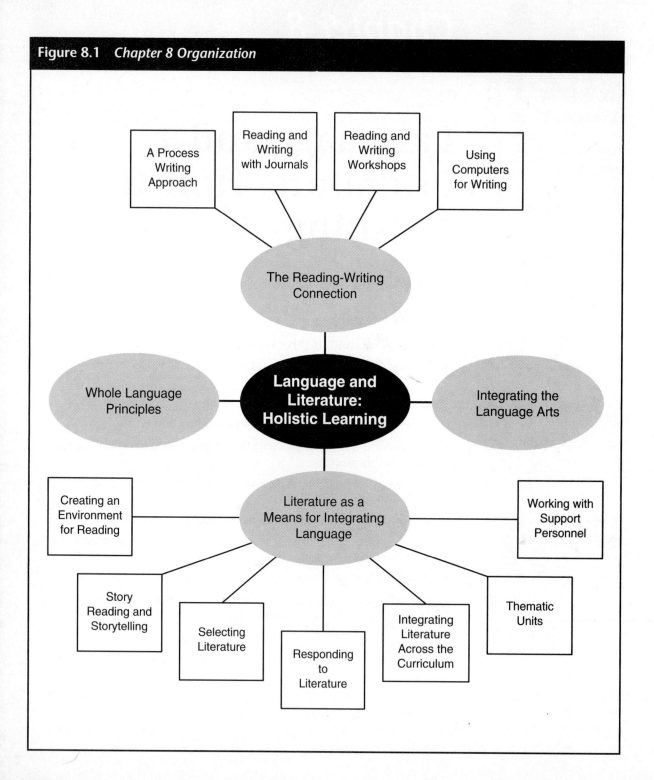

A Process Writing Approach

Reading and Writing with Journals

Reading and Writing Workshops

Using Computers for Writing

The Reading-Writing Connection

Whole Language Principles

Language and Literature: Holistic Learning

Integrating the Language Arts

Creating an Environment for Reading

Literature as a Means for Integrating Language

Working with Support Personnel

Story Reading and Storytelling

Selecting Literature

Responding to Literature

Integrating Literature Across the Curriculum

Thematic Units

Many of the concepts and teaching strategies presented in this chapter—and indeed, throughout the text—are based on the whole language philosophy, described in Chapters 1 and 7. This chapter opens with a brief discussion of some whole language principles, which are the basis for many of the strategies and procedures that follow. The chapter also presents reasons for connecting the language arts, particularly reading and writing, and discusses the value of literature for integrating the curriculum. Reading-writing connections are demonstrated through discussions of process writing, journal writing, and reading and writing workshops. The chapter also supports the concept of student-centered learning, which enables students to make choices, take risks, and assume responsibility for their learning.

The second part of the chapter focuses on the use of literature to integrate the curriculum. It provides ideas for enabling the teacher to create a classroom environment where children can learn within a community of authors who understand and support one another's efforts and can experience a sense of ownership in their reading and writing. That section also offers suggestions for selecting appropriate literature for children, as well as for helping children choose books for themselves. Many ways to respond to literature, including literature response groups, oral interpretation, drama, written expression, art, and music, are presented. Trade books may be used in all areas of the curriculum, and suggestions are given for creating thematic units focusing on specific books, genres, themes, and authors.

Whole Language Principles

The term *whole language* means different things to different people, but most educators agree on certain basic tenets. Many of these tenets, or guiding principles, and strategies for implementing them are found throughout this book, particularly in this chapter. They include the following:

thematic learning
reading-writing connection

- *Learning is integrated.* Students learn more effectively when they can see connections and relationships among ideas and subjects than when they learn bits and pieces of information in isolation.

reading-writing connection

- *Whole language tasks are authentic.* Authentic activities relate to real-world tasks such as writing letters and reading for information. When students can see the purpose and meaning of the work they do, they understand why it is important to do it.

- *Learning is social.* The purpose of language is to communicate with others. Students therefore learn to use language by sharing ideas, working cooperatively, and becoming part of a community of learners.

- *Whole language classrooms are learner centered.* To feel a commitment to learning language, students need to be actively involved in the learning process by accepting such responsibilities as making choices, taking part in negotiating decisions regarding procedures and curriculum, and self-evaluation.

literature-centered reading

- *Literature is an integral part of the whole language curriculum.* Since a widely accepted premise is that children learn to read by reading, classrooms should offer a wide variety of books and related materials. Good books can be used across the curriculum as sources of information and pleasure.

SELF-CHECK: OBJECTIVE 1   What are some principles to follow when implementing the whole language philosophy? (See Self-Improvement Opportunity 1.)

Integrating the Language Arts

reading-writing connection

The integration of reading, writing, listening, and speaking in the classroom is not a new idea; indeed, curriculum designers have advocated it from time to time for decades (Jensen and Roser, 1990). In many classrooms, however, the practice of scheduling a specific amount of time for spelling, handwriting, reading groups, grammar, and so forth has prevailed. Such segmentation of the language arts interferes with children's natural, purposeful use of language in real situations, and it may result in their failure to apply what they already know about oral language to reading and writing.

For the classroom teacher, integration may mean setting aside a large block of time for language arts. This time period allows for flexible scheduling and freedom to fully develop special projects. Integration means coordinating activities so that children can see the natural connections among the various forms of language as they work to achieve goals. During this extended time period, children may engage in a variety of language activities, such as pursuing research projects, responding creatively to stories, preparing a school newspaper, or working at a poetry center. With a little guidance from the teacher, they become aware of the interrelationships among the language arts. They see, for instance, how the stories they read can serve as models for the stories they want to write, how the information they need for writing reports can be found by using research materials, or why good handwriting and correct spelling are important for publishing their own books.

Although a time period may be allocated for language arts instruction, integrated language experiences extend throughout the day into every area of the curriculum. For example, reading, writing, speaking, and listening are essential for learning about ideas that have changed history and science concepts that have resulted in new discoveries. In the following activities, the teacher provides integrated language arts lessons by reading a story or a book and then allowing the students to pursue their natural curiosity. During these lessons, children become involved in listening, speaking, reading, writing, and problem solving.

Investigation that meets the children's "need to know" spans the language arts without regard for time periods set aside for discrete language subjects. As a result, children are likely to view language learning as a meaningful, worthwhile effort instead of a series of purposeless exercises. The following Model Activities have literature as their focus.

literature-centered reading

Integrated Language Lesson in a Primary Class

Model Activities

After reading Eric Carle's *The Very Hungry Caterpillar*, encourage discussion by saying to the children: "Let's think about this story. Could a caterpillar really eat so much? How does the caterpillar change in this story? How can a caterpillar stay on a leaf without falling off?" The children respond eagerly and raise questions of their own. Then say: "You're raising good questions. Where can we find out some answers?" Lead the children to suggest looking in books about caterpillars, observing real caterpillars, and asking the science teacher. Say to the children: "When you discover some answers, we can write our own stories about caterpillars and put them in a book."

Integrated Language Arts Lesson in an Intermediate Class

Model Activities

After reading Katherine Paterson's *Park's Quest* to the class, ask: "What do you think the title means? What is a quest?" If the students wish to pursue various aspects of the book, form groups to investigate topics that interest them. These topics may lead to such activities as a debate over the United States' involvement in the Vietnam War, a student-made book that connects the quest of King Arthur with that of Park, a diary in which students write from Park's perspective after each day on the farm, a report on the causes and effects of a stroke on a person's health, and an annotated bibliography of books about the Vietnam War.

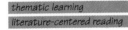

thematic learning
literature-centered reading

The Focus on Strategies shows how a single book can become a theme for learning in many areas. As seen here, the teacher may introduce a book that so intrigues the students that they assume an active role in developing meaningful related activities. They contribute their own ideas so that their investigation is truly learner centered rather than teacher directed.

Focus on Strategies

Developing a Literature-Based, Student-Centered Theme That Integrates the Language Arts

Ms. Brison introduced Chris Van Allsburg's *The Wretched Stone* to her students by asking them to listen for clues that tell what the stone represents. This story was one of her favorites, and she hoped the students would like it too. When she finished reading it aloud, the students eagerly raised their hands to tell what they thought the stone really was. Isaac, the class scientist, thought it was malachite, and Katrina knew it must be a mirror (not a bad guess!). Others thought it was an object from outer space.

The students begged Ms. Brison to reread the story, and she agreed to do so if they would listen again for clues. This time Janis solemnly said, "I believe it's a television because that's how television makes some people act." The others quickly agreed as they noted the similarities between a television set and the stone in the story.

Still fascinated, the students wanted to know more about the story, so Ms. Brison asked them what they would like to do with it. Mike suggested finding other books by Chris Van Allsburg to read, and Beth wanted to learn more about the way sailors lived and worked long ago. Tim said he could teach a group how to make sailor's knots, and Molly said they could write logs as if they were sailors on the ship.

Ms. Brison recorded the ideas on the chalkboard, then placed each idea at the top of a piece of chart paper. She wrote *Other* at the top of one chart to allow the students to come up with other creative responses. She told the students to think about what they would like to do and then sign up to work on a topic. Those responsible for finding other books by Van Allsburg first checked the school library and the neighborhood branch library. Tim's dad took him to the downtown library, where he found *The Widow's Broom*. Susie knew someone who had a copy of *The Stranger* that she was able to borrow, and Ms. Brison located *Two Bad Ants* at the Teacher Center. Each day she read a different story until the children became quite familiar with Van Allsburg's style. "His books always have something mysterious in them," Jack said. "Yes," Connie continued, "and they start like it's for real, and then something happens that makes you know it has to be fantasy."

As their projects neared completion, the students decided to put their work at a center so that they could see what others were doing. The students who signed up to research the lives of sailors years ago collected books about sailing, took notes, and compiled an illustrated informational book that told of the hardships of sea travel—the food sailors ate, the length of their journeys, weather signs, the consequences of storms at sea, and the stars they used to chart their courses. Some students, intrigued by pirates on the high seas, found stories and legends about pirates, particularly Blackbeard. Another group dramatized the story for the class next door, and students who had read *Jumanji* decided to make their own board game with penalties and rewards. Van Allsburg's detailed illustrations intrigued many children, who compared his black-and-white drawings in earlier books with the colored ones in more recent books.

"I guess I didn't have to wonder if the students would like *The Wretched Stone*," Ms. Brison thought. "I can't believe how enthusiastic they were, and all I really had to do was introduce the book. They took it from there."

Ms. Brison realized that, while the students were having fun investigating Chris Van Allsburg, they were actually learning a great deal about language and literature. She got out her curriculum guide and checked off several language skills for her grade level: making inferences, differentiating reality from fantasy, recognizing an author's style, locating information, and using reference materials. Of course, there were other skills as well.

This had been a truly integrated language arts theme: the thoughtful listening as the students tried to identify the elements of mystery, the well-supported points they made while defending their views about Van Allsburg's use of fantasy, the reading of related storybooks and reference materials, and the incredible informational book they wrote that portrayed the harsh life at sea. Perhaps the logs they wrote as sailors impressed Ms. Brison most of all. The students had used such vivid descriptive words to express their feelings as they moved from being lively, active sailors to entranced viewers of the stone.

Ms. Brison chuckled to herself as she realized how her teaching had changed over the years. Instead of planning a theme herself and providing all the resource materials, she had students accepting this responsibility with a little guidance from her. Instead of learning discrete skills and using workbooks, the students were using authentic language strategies that had evolved from an intriguing book. Not a bad arrangement, she thought, as she glanced over the books on her shelf and pulled out Lynne Cherry's *The Great Kapok Tree*. I wonder what they will do with this one!

SELF-CHECK: OBJECTIVES 2 AND 9   Think of a favorite children's book. How might children become involved in an integrated language lesson with that book? (See Self-Improvement Opportunities 12 and 15.)

The Reading-Writing Connection

reading-writing connection   In recent years, many educators have viewed both reading and writing as composing processes (Butler and Turbill, 1987; Flood and Lapp, 1987; Squire, 1983). Based on prior knowledge, attitudes, and experiences, the reader constructs meaning from text and the writer composes meaningful text. Both reading and writing require the use of similar thinking skills, such as analyzing, selecting and organizing, inferencing, evaluating, problem solving, and making comparisons. Tierney and Shanahan (1991, p. 275) state that "reading and writing, to be understood and appreciated fully, should be viewed together, learned together, and used together."

Reading and writing tend to reinforce each other. According to Smith (1983), children must learn to read like writers in order to write like writers. By carefully observing an author's use of dialogue while reading a story, for instance, a child begins to learn how to create dialogue when writing a story. Or, in trying to write a description of the setting for a piece of writing, a child reads and rereads the setting from another selection to get ideas.

Table 8.1 shows examples of links between reading and writing (based on Butler and Turbill, 1987; Hornsby, Sukarna, and Parry, 1986). Stotsky (1983) warns, however, that although similarities exist in the ways in which reading and writing are learned, research shows there are sufficient differences to warrant attention to each independently, as well as in combination.

Table 8.1   Links Between Reader and Writer

Reader	Writer
Brings, uses prior knowledge about topic	Brings, uses prior knowledge about topic
Reconstructs another's meaning	Constructs own meaning
Predicts what comes next	Predicts what should come next
Has expectations for text based on experiences	Has expectations for how text might develop
Modifies comprehension of text as reading continues	Develops and changes meaning while writing
Engages in "draft reading"—skimming, making sense	Engages in "draft writing"—getting ideas, writing notes
Rereads to clarify	Rewrites to clarify
Uses writer's cues to help make sense of reading	Uses writing conventions to assist reader
Responds by talking, doing, and/or writing	Gets response from readers

Reading and writing are both developmental processes, and the relationships between them change as children advance in school (Flood and Lapp, 1987; Shanahan, 1988). What is learned and how it is learned differs over time, with spelling/word recognition dominating the early years and a reading comprehension/writing vocabulary and organization dimension prevailing for more advanced readers (Shanahan, 1988).

Educators have explored many ways of implementing the linkage between reading and writing in purposeful ways. Teachers and children have used message boards, or centrally located bulletin boards, for sending and receiving messages (Boyd, 1985; Harste, Short, and Burke, 1988), and some students correspond with other students through pen-pal programs. Several types of young authors' programs exist for various purposes, including encouraging children to write illustrated bound books and to share their writing with other authors outside their schools (Harris-Sharples, Kearns, and Miller, 1989). Following are some class activities for combining writing with reading.

Activities

1. Let the students write a class newspaper on one of these themes: (a) news stories that are modern adaptations of fairy tales and Mother Goose rhymes, (b) a newspaper written at the same time and place as the setting of the book the teacher is reading to the class, or (c) a literary digest of news about books. Children may compose advertisements for favorite books to place in the newspaper.

2. Encourage students to write a radio or television script based on a story they have read. (First, they should read some plays to become familiar with directions for staging and appropriate writing style for dialogue.)

3. When students write reports or stories, let them read what they have written to their peers in order to get critical reactions. As a result, they may want to make some revisions.

4. Arrange for students to write to pen pals from other regions of the country. As they correspond, they are likely to become interested in those geographical areas, so provide resource materials for them to read about their pen-pals' homes.

5. Hold a young authors' conference in which children display and read from books they have published. The conference could take place among classes within a single school, or it could be districtwide.

6. As children become involved in a thematic unit, let them find places to write for information. They will need to describe their needs and ask for appropriate resource material. When they receive the material, they will need to read it to be able to decide how to use it for their projects.

SELF-CHECK: OBJECTIVE 3   What are some ways reading and writing are similar? (See Self-Improvement Opportunity 2.)

A Process Writing Approach

A *process writing approach* is a child-centered approach to writing in which children create their own pieces of writing based on their choice of topic, their awareness of audience, and their development of ideas from initial stages through revisions to final publication. The process is ongoing, with writing in some form generally occurring every day and with pieces in various stages of development.

Two important concepts are basic to process writing. The first of these is a sense of *ownership,* in which the writer feels complete responsibility for the piece, from choice of topic to types of revisions to form of publication. The other is *community of authors,* a supportive and cooperative relationship among students and between students and teacher in which writers explore possible topics, try out ideas, and struggle together to create satisfying pieces of writing (Kirby, Latta, and Vinz, 1988; Lamme, 1989).

reading-writing connection

Cross-grade process writing programs provide opportunities for older students to act as literary advisors and/or attentive audiences for younger children and for younger children to act as audiences for older writers. One of the authors of this text (Roe) conducted a program in which fifth graders from Austin Hamby's class served as partners for Ann Norris's second graders, as described in the following Classroom Scenario.

Classroom Scenario

Cross-Grade Process Writing

During the second–fifth grade partnership at Crossville Elementary School, the fifth graders were preparing to give their completed books to their second-grade partners. It was their first attempt at process writing, and most of them were somewhat amazed at how well their stories had developed with input from classmates and teachers during conferences. One boy said, "This is a good story. I'd really like to keep it for myself." Nevertheless, he gave his book to his partner, who was delighted with it and told the story to anyone who would listen. A couple of times fifth graders excitedly showed the program director their writing, saying, "Look what I wrote for my partner! It wasn't part of an assignment; I just wanted to do it."

Analysis of Scenario
Awareness of their audience for the stories caused students to devote much attention to the development process. The students were much more concerned about revising their stories to improve them and copying them neatly for their partners than they had been about polishing stories that were written before the project began. The fifth graders produced whole books for their young partners, complete with title pages, copyright dates, dedications, and "about the author" sections. Writing for authentic purposes obviously made a difference in the quality of these students' writing.[1]

Stages of the Writing Process

The *writing process* consists of the following major stages: prewriting, drafting, revising, editing, and publishing and/or sharing. These stages may be used at any grade level, although, of course, first graders' writing will be very simple, and their bookmaking will require a great deal of guidance from the teacher. In fact, in some cases the teacher may write stories from student dictation. As children progress through the grades, they will be capable of producing more complex, more carefully edited works. The stages of the writing process may be briefly described as follows.

Prewriting.   The author prepares for writing by talking, drawing, reading, and thinking about the piece and by organizing ideas and developing a plan.

Drafting.   The author sets ideas on paper without regard for neatness or mechanics.

Revising.   After getting suggestions from others, the author may wish to make some changes in the initial draft. These changes may include adding dialogue, deleting repetitious parts, adding depth to a character, clarifying meaning, providing needed information, or changing the ending of the story.

---

[1] Betty D. Roe, *Report on Non-Instructional Assignment* (Cookeville, Tenn.: Tennessee Technological University, 1990).

Editing.   With careful proofreading and the help of peers and the teacher, the author corrects spelling and mechanics.

Sharing and Publishing.   After careful revisions, the authors are eager to share finished pieces with real audiences. Pages can be fastened with brads, taped together, sewn, or professionally bound. Finished books may be kept in the classroom or taken to the school library, fitted with pockets, and checked out.

SELF-CHECK: OBJECTIVE 4   What are the basic steps in the writing process? (See Self-Improvement Opportunity 3.)

Reading and Writing with Journals

reading-writing connection

Students do journal writing to reflect on and record their thoughts and ideas. Writers control the content by choosing their subjects and recording information as they please, without concern for correctness of form or mechanics. Writers also determine the audience, for sometimes journals or designated pages within them are personal, and other times they are meant to be shared. Journals may be spiral notebooks or simply papers stapled together with student-decorated construction-paper covers. Students must have time for journal writing, preferably on a daily basis, so that they can think about what they want to write. A child of any age can do journal writing, with younger children using invented spellings and pictures to express their ideas.

Dialogue journals are interactive, with the teacher or other reader responding to the student's writing. The responder should never correct the student's writing but can model proper spelling and writing conventions in the response. The reader may ask for elaboration or clarification, or may simply comment on what the student has written. Most important, however, is that the dialogue be an honest exchange of ideas and serve as a means of communication. As a responder, the teacher begins to understand the problems, concerns, and needs of students.

To introduce students to journal writing, the teacher might discuss diary writing and read books written in letter or journal form, such as Joan Blos's *A Gathering of Days: A New England Girl's Journal, 1830–32* or Beverly Cleary's *Dear Mr. Henshaw*. The teacher should write in a journal along with the children to model the importance of recording thoughts and ideas. If students have trouble finding topics, the teacher might offer such suggestions as an important event, a perplexing problem, or a really good friend. Writers should understand that journals are a place where they can complain, ask questions, or express their true feelings.

Journal writing can take various forms. Reading or literary journals enable students to write responses to what they have read and receive the teacher's supportive feedback as a guide for further reading (Wollman-Bonilla, 1989). In buddy journals (see Example 8.1), student pairs "converse" in writing on a continuing basis, thus engaging in a meaningful writing and reading exchange (Bromley, 1989). In some classes, students meet in small groups to share entries on designated days (Harste, Short, and Burke, 1988).

Example 8.1 *Buddy Journal Entries*

> Fri, 16, Feb, 1990
>
> Erin,
>   You are a very good reader. You are going to be a better reader if you keep practicing.
>   do you like school? What is your favorite subject? My favorite subject is spelling.
>
>   Your partner,
>   Lesley Ann Richards

> Wed. 21, 1990
>
> Lesley,
>   I do not like school very much. My favorite subject is scisce.
>   do you like school?
>
>   Your Partner,
>   Erin Young

Source: Leslie Ann Richards and Erin Young, Crossville Elementary School, Crossville, Tennessee.

SELF-CHECK: OBJECTIVE 5   How does journal writing help a student improve reading and writing abilities? (See Self-Improvement Opportunities 3 and 4.)

Writing and Reading Workshops

Reading and writing workshops provide opportunities for teachers to teach specific strategies directly during brief minilessons and for students to spend most of their time actually reading and writing. These workshops operate in the manner described here.

Writing workshops consist of four steps: a minilesson, a status-of-the-class report, the actual writing workshop, and sharing time (Atwell, 1987). The minilesson lasts only a few minutes and deals with issues related to following procedures, writing realistic dialogue, using mechanics correctly, starting with good leads, or similar ones. The status-of-the-class check is made as the teacher calls each student's name and records what the student will be doing during the workshop. The writing workshop, when most students write and/or confer, consumes most of the class time. Group share occurs during the last few minutes when students share their writing, try out ideas, and respond to one another's writing.

Although formats differ, most reading workshops operate in a similar manner, beginning with a minilesson that might be about an author or a genre. After the teacher records student-selected tasks on the status-of-the-class record sheet, students spend most of their time with self-selected reading and responses. During this time, the teacher may hold conferences with some of the students. Before the end of class, students spend five to ten minutes sharing their activities, books, or projects with one another (Atwell, 1985, 1987; Reutzel and Cooter, 1991).

The following Classroom Scenario, taken from Holly Martin's sixth-grade class, illustrates what happens during a typical writing workshop.

Classroom Scenario

Writing Workshop

Holly Martin begins by asking the students to recall what their four options are during writing workshop. They reply that they can read, write, think, and write in journals. She reminds them that good writers "take the time" and "make the effort," and then says she will be asking some of them to conference with her during class. She asks them to brainstorm what to write, and they respond with letters to pen pals in other schools, Writer's Showcase, poetry to submit to a magazine, and essays for special friends. After checking with students about what they plan to do, she lets them pursue their writing. Some move to the alcove where trade books are shelved, select their books, and sprawl on the floor to read them. Others pick up their writing folders to begin work on a piece. Still others begin writing in their journals. Holly calls on one student, and he discusses with her some problems he is having in completing his story. She asks a few questions that lead him to consider some options, takes notes on what occurred, and then moves on to the next student. As the class continues, students move about, finding the materials they need, talking quietly with other students, and continuing their writing.

Analysis of Scenario
These students understand their purposes for writing (to correspond with pen pals, enter contests, write newspaper articles, etc.) and are free to make choices about what they need to do to meet their objectives.

Using Computers for Writing

In many schools, students are fortunate enough to have access to computers, either in the classroom or in a computer lab. A word-processing program for the computer enables students to enter rough drafts quickly, revise frequently, and print a final copy. Students can revise by inserting or deleting material and moving chunks of text, and they can edit by correcting spelling and mechanics. Once students learn basic commands, they realize the ease of using word processing for all stages of writing.

Children can use computers to enhance their understanding of how authors think and feel and their awareness of authors' writing styles. Wepner (1993) recommends introducing students to books written by the same author, such as those by Mercer Mayer, Judith Viorst, and Betsy Byars, with the software from such companies as Broderbund, Humanities, IBM, Sunburst, and Scholastic. These programs allow students to listen to and watch stories; interact with each page; retell stories in unique ways by using various fonts, print sizes, and backgrounds; and fill in speech bubbles to let characters speak to one another.

Lively responses to literature are likely to occur in classrooms with nurturing environments that provide an abundance of fine-quality books, adequate time for selecting and reading, introductions of new books, daily reading aloud, book discussions, and creative experiences with literature. (*Elizabeth Crews/Stock Boston*)

According to Balajthy and Link (1988), *desktop publishing* is an application of computers that invites student-teacher collaboration for creating class newspapers and magazines. They describe a school in which fifth and sixth graders create a class newspaper by first choosing a theme and then breaking the theme into categories. Student reporters conduct interviews or do research, then plan the layout. Students work in pairs during the writing process, first making handwritten rough drafts and then using keyboarding skills to enter stories into the computer. They complete their newspaper by using the computer to check spelling and style, modifying stories to fit space limitations, selecting appropriate graphics, and writing headlines.

In a summary of research on the effectiveness of using word processors in the classroom, Balajthy (1989) makes the following points:

1. Use of word processors motivates students to write greater amounts of text than they would using pen and paper.

2. When they use word processors, students revise more and use a greater variety of revision strategies than they do with pen or pencil.

3. Because the monitor presents a limited display of written text, teachers may suggest that students refer to hard copy in making revisions.

4. Students edit more carefully and produce fewer errors with word processors than when writing by hand.

5. Word processing alone may not automatically improve writing ability, but it can if it is used along with prompting, instruction, and feedback.

6. Use of word processors is popular with teachers because it motivates students to write and allows them to revise easily. Also, teachers know that computer literacy is important for their students' future careers.

Literature as a Means for Integrating Language

literature-centered reading — The fortunate child who comes from a literate home environment already knows, from many experiences with lap reading and bedtime stories, the delights that books hold. Family storybook reading promotes language and literacy skills, develops values in meaningful ways, builds a knowledge base, helps the child understand story construction, and provides opportunities to think about and discuss stories (Taylor and Strickland, 1986). As this child enters school, more books are encountered through listening, sharing, and reading, and books become bridges that link home and school. The less fortunate child, however, may have no such link, and the teacher must introduce this child to literature by providing daily story times and access to a wide variety of books. For children from either background, literature can be the basis for learning to read and write and for developing positive attitudes toward further language learning.

Creating an Environment for Reading

Lively and interesting responses to literature are likely to occur in classrooms with "nurturing environments" (Hickman, 1984, p. 381). Such environments provide many of the following features: an abundance of high-quality books in both the classroom and school libraries; adequate time for selecting and reading books; introductions of new books; daily reading aloud; book discussions in whole classes, with small groups, and between individuals; use of correct literary terminology; and creative and long-term experiences with literature.

The classroom environment is supportive and free from the risks that inhibit honest expression. Children feel a sense of ownership in the reading they do by choosing the books they want to read and deciding where and how to read them, how to respond, and how their own related work is to be displayed or published.

reading-writing connection They may sit in an author's chair to read their own writing or favorite stories by professional authors to their friends.

Children have purposes and opportunities for reading and writing throughout the day and across all areas of the curriculum. Teachers read aloud daily to students from various forms of children's literature and provide a variety of good books for classroom library shelves. They set up writing centers with activities that encourage children to make written responses to books, being sure to allow time for such reading and writing to take place. They integrate trade books with all curricular areas and suggest activities that require thoughtful reactions to literature. Writing materials, including lined and unlined paper, pencils with erasers, colored pens for revising and editing, and folders for completed work, are readily available.

In this kind of classroom, teachers encourage children to read by arranging portable, freestanding bulletin boards and chalkboards, sets of shelves, and other furniture to create nooks and crannies for reading. They provide carpet scraps and

literature-centered reading cushions that allow children to read comfortably and privately. Bookshelves and containers filled with books should be within easy reach. Backs of furniture become spaces for showing children's works and placing inviting displays about books. Working together, teacher and students can design bulletin boards and arrange displays that center around a theme (e.g., transportation, the Westward Movement, President's Day, books of fantasy) or books by a popular author. (See Example 8.2 for a sample bulletin board.) Some starting points for book displays are suggested next.

Madeline, by Ludwig Bemelmans. Use a French flag, a model of the Eiffel Tower, and a poster of Paris from a travel agency.

White Snow, Bright Snow, by Alvin Tresselt. Include a display of student-made white paper snowflakes on a dark background and marshmallow snowmen standing in detergent snowflakes.

The Story of Johnny Appleseed, by Aliki. Display a map of Johnny Appleseed's travels, along with an apple, seeds from an apple, and apple blossoms (if in season).

Example 8.2   *Bulletin-Board Display*

For this bulletin board, use a carpet scrap, a puff of cotton for a cloud, and some book jackets to accompany the artwork.

A Gathering of Days: A New England Girl's Journal, 1830–32, by Joan Blos. Use a map of New England and a looseleaf notebook for students to record imaginary events that could have happened to them if they had been Catherine's friends.

Charlotte's Web, by E. B. White. Make a three-dimensional diorama from a small carton with the top and one side cut off. Set up a scene with the word TERRIFIC woven into a fishnet web, a pipe-cleaner spider, a model of a pig, and some straw. Place some books about spiders nearby.

Place book jackets or photocopies of book covers around a wall map of the world with strands of yarn that reach from the book jacket to the place on the map that is the setting for the book. Examples include Katherine Paterson's *Jacob Have I Loved* for Chesapeake Bay, Lois Lowry's *Number the Stars* for Denmark, Jean Craighead George's *Julie of the Wolves* for the Arctic tundra, and Paula Fox's *Lily and the Lost Boy* for Greece (see Example 8.3).

Sustained Silent Reading (SSR), or Drop Everything and Read (DEAR), occurs in classrooms where children are given time, a wide selection of books, and encouragement to read. The teacher sets aside a period of time each day, usually from fifteen to thirty minutes, for silent reading. SSR can be used by a single classroom or by the entire school (students and staff). The teacher also reads to model the value of reading even for adults. Since there is no formal reporting or assessment at the conclusion of SSR periods, students feel no pressure as they read. SSR can

Example 8.3   *Display of Books with Settings Around the World*

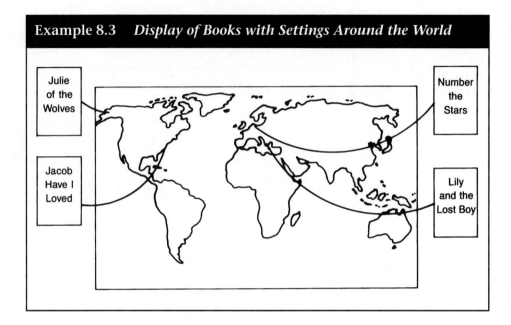

be effective with kindergartners and first graders, but it consists mostly of looking at books and pretend reading, and it tends to be noisier (with children reading aloud to themselves) and of shorter duration (five to ten minutes) (Kaisen, 1987; McCracken and McCracken, 1986).

SELF-CHECK: OBJECTIVE 6   Identify several ways to make the classroom environment inviting to young readers. (See Self-Improvement Opportunity 14.)

Story Reading and Storytelling

literature-centered reading

Reading aloud to children of all ages fulfills many purposes. Good oral reading by the teacher serves as a model and allows students to experience literature they might not be able or inclined to read for themselves. It can whet their appetites to read more on their own, since an exciting chapter or section of a book often stimulates children to read the entire book themselves. Besides providing exposure to specific books, reading to children can introduce them to creative and colorful use of language in prose and poetry, present new vocabulary and concepts, and acquaint them with the variety of language patterns found in written communication.

Just before reading aloud to the class, the teacher might ask students to listen to how the author uses a lead sentence to create interest in the story or uses dialogue to develop characterization. During the story, the teacher can stop occasionally to point out a literary technique or to ask students to close their eyes and visualize a descriptive passage. After completing the story or chapter, the teacher

might ask students what they specifically liked or disliked about the way the author wrote. When the teacher points out such features to the class, students learn to evaluate material, thus making them more critical readers and improving their writing abilities as well. The following Classroom Scenario shows how one teacher reads aloud to her third graders.

Classroom Scenario

Reading Aloud to Students

Kim Yunker calls her students to a corner of the classroom that has been set up to resemble a room in pioneer days. She asks a child to turn off the lights while she lights a kerosene lamp. Seated in a rocker, she chooses a book from many that relate to the unit theme, "Little House in the Big Woods." She introduces Cynthia Rylant's *When I Was Young in the Mountains* and then begins reading aloud. Occasionally she interjects questions such as "What is okra?" and "What do you think a johnny house is?" After she finishes the book, she asks questions about life in pioneer days, and the children browse quietly through some of the other books. As the children leave, they return to illustrating spelling words related to the unit (e.g., *maple, wagon, slate*) or building a fort from Lincoln Logs.

Analysis of Scenario
In Kim Yunker's class, story reading is integrated with the unit so that children are able to make connections between the stories and the work they are doing in other subjects.

Research supports the benefits of reading aloud to students. In *Becoming a Nation of Readers,* Anderson and colleagues (1985) conclude, "The single most important activity for building the knowledge required for eventual success in reading is reading aloud to children" (p. 23). In addition, Michener (1988) finds research support for the following benefits of reading aloud to students:

1. Helps them get off to a better start in reading.

2. Improves their listening skills.

3. Increases their ability to read independently.

4. Expands their vocabularies.

5. Improves their reading comprehension.

6. Helps them to become better speakers.

7. Improves their abilities as writers.

8. Improves the quantity and quality of independent reading.

Teachers should read in natural tones and with expression, providing time for sharing the illustrations, exploring key words and phrases, and evaluating reactions. The best stories to read aloud are those that children cannot easily read by themselves, that the teacher personally likes and is thoroughly familiar with, and that possess the qualities characteristic of the best literature. Although teachers typically choose fiction, Doiron (1994) recommends reading nonfiction as well for a balanced reading program. Jim Trelease's *The New Read-Aloud Handbook* (1989) is an excellent source of information about how and what to read aloud to children.

Similarly, teacher storytelling acquaints children with literature and provides good listening experiences. With no book between the storyteller and the audience, listeners focus on each word and gesture. They visualize the story to suit themselves because there are no illustrations (Nessel, 1985), and they develop their imaginations and move toward higher levels of thinking (Aiex, 1988). Folktales are especially good for telling because they were told and told again long before they were captured in print.

reading-writing connection

Students as storytellers develop fluency and expression in oral language. By preparing and telling stories, they also develop poise and build self-esteem. As storytellers, students must be aware of pitch, volume, timing, and gesture, as well as the responsiveness of the audience. A logical progression is for students to move from hearing, reading, and telling stories to writing original stories, which are often based on literary patterns they already know (Peck, 1989).

SELF-CHECK: OBJECTIVE 7   Identify several benefits of story reading and storytelling. How should a teacher prepare for story reading and storytelling? (See Self-Improvement Opportunities 5 and 6.)

Selecting Literature

From the thousands of books published annually for children, teachers and media specialists must select good-quality literature that they think children will want to read. Making such decisions is a challenge and a responsibility. Teachers can assess children's personal reading interests by simply asking them to list three things that interest them or by administering an interest inventory such as the one found in Chapter 7.

Many *selection aids,* or references that identify and evaluate publications, are available to help teachers and librarians select literature for specific purposes. Among the most comprehensive are *The Children's Catalog* (1991) and *The Elementary School Library Collection: A Guide to Books and Other Media, Phases 1, 2, 3* (1992). Both of these reference works contain author, title, and subject indexes, along with annotations of the books listed.

Another useful source in selecting children's books is a listing of Newbery and Caldecott Award winners. The John Newbery Award is presented annually to the author whose book is selected by a special committee as the year's most distinguished contribution to American literature for children. Excellence in illustration is the criterion used in granting the annual Randolph Caldecott Award.

Some educators advocate classics, quality books that have endured for a generation or more, as the foundation for reading. Not all classics are popular with students, however, so it is important to choose appropriate works and avoid those that may discourage students from reading. In a study of fifth and sixth graders, Wilson and Abrahamson (1988) found that children disliked many of the older classics, finding *Robinson Crusoe,* for example, "boring," "too hard to read," "too long," and using "too many hard words." The students chose for their favorites *Charlotte's Web; The Borrowers; The Lion, the Witch, and the Wardrobe;* and *Little House in the Big Woods.*

Another consideration in choosing books is their social significance in relation to human values, cultural pluralism, and aesthetic standards (Norton, 1991). For minority children, multicultural literature based on familiar traditions and values can be a mirror that reflects and validates their own cultural experiences. For mainstream children, such books can be revealing windows into less familiar cultures (Cox and Galda, 1990).

Despite adult critics' recommendations, many children prefer to make their own choices. Each year since the 1974–1975 school year, the International Reading Association–Children's Book Council Joint Committee has published an annotated list of "Children's Choices," which appears in the October issue of *The Reading Teacher.* Each list is compiled by approximately 10,000 children who, working in teams, read new books and vote for their favorites. Since children are the ultimate critics of their literature, teachers and librarians should consider their choices seriously when purchasing and recommending books.

In helping children select books, teachers need to know both the books that are available and their children's needs and interests. Teachers can guide children's choices by helping them locate books on special topics, sampling new books to pique their interest, allowing time for children to browse in the library, and suggesting titles on occasion. Regardless of this assistance, however, most children will value the freedom to choose their own books.

Selecting appropriate poetry for children is especially difficult. Poorly chosen poems can prejudice children against poetry, whereas a suitable poem will amuse, inspire, emotionally move, or intellectually interest them. Children prefer poems with rhyme, rhythm, humor, and narration; works by Shel Silverstein (*Where the Sidewalk Ends, Light in the Attic*) and Jack Prelutsky (*The New Kid on the Block, Something Big Has Been Here*) are natural favorites. The humor they use comes from alliteration, plays on words, or highly exaggerated situations, as in "Sarah Cynthia Sylvia Stout Who Would Not Take the Garbage Out" (from *Where the Sidewalk Ends*). Kupiter and Wilson (1993) contend, however, that teachers must sensitively cultivate an interest in poetry that goes beyond Silverstein and Prelutsky; they must build bridges from these popular poems to the rich array of diverse poetry waiting to be tapped.

Many teachers prefer paperback books, because multiple copies of one book cost the same as a single library edition, allowing teachers to order enough for small groups of children to read and use in follow-up activities and discussions. Paperback books are often available at special reduced rates through book clubs such as Scholastic, Troll, and Trumpet.

Many good children's magazines are available for different reading levels and different areas of interest. These periodicals are excellent classroom resources and offer several benefits for the reading program: (1) the material is current and relevant; (2) the reading range varies in levels of difficulty and content presented; (3) several genres usually appear in a single issue; (4) language activities, such as crossword puzzles, contests, and children's writings, are often included; (5) the illustrations and photographs are excellent and can improve comprehension; and (6) their low cost makes them easily accessible (Seminoff, 1986). Classroom subscriptions to two or three favorites will enrich the reading program. Some popular choices are listed in Appendix B to this chapter, and a more complete listing is available in Stoll's *Magazines for Kids and Teens* (1994).

To build a classroom library, the ingenious teacher will consider many sources in seeking quality literature. Some possibilities include

- Writing small grants
- Buying carefully selected books at garage and flea market sales
- Using bonus points from book clubs
- Spending money from appropriate school funds
- Using book fund allotments to buy trade books instead of workbooks and textbooks
- Rebinding books discarded by the public library
- Requesting books from friends whose children have outgrown them
- Asking students to contribute a book instead of giving the teacher a Christmas gift
- Rotating book collections with other teachers
- Borrowing books from students' home library collections

SELF-CHECK: OBJECTIVE 7   Identify several considerations in providing children with good-quality literature that meets their needs and interests. (See Self-Improvement Opportunities 7, 8, 9, and 10.)

Responding to Literature

When students encounter books they enjoy, they are eager to respond to them. The teacher should provide opportunities for a variety of responses and let the children themselves decide what is appropriate so that they feel a sense of ownership. Teachers should realize that interpretations of literature may vary from student to student; thus, they should "be prepared to expect, respect, and accept a wide variety of student responses" (Sweet, 1993, p. 8). For students who are uncertain about ways to respond, the teacher can offer suggestions and model procedures. Two things the teacher should avoid, however, are (1) letting a response project become so immense that it overshadows the literature and (2) giving students worksheets on which answers are graded as right or wrong.

Literature Response Groups

An organized way of responding to literature is through *literature response groups* or literature circles (Bell, 1990; Gilles, 1989; Harste, Short, and Burke, 1988; Strickland et al., 1989; Zogby, 1990). These groups give students opportunities to read and respond to good literature, engage in high-level thinking about books, and do extensive and intensive reading.

Groups are formed after the teacher and students have established rapport so that they feel comfortable exchanging thoughts and ideas. Usually there are three or four groups in a class, each consisting of four to eight members. Groups generally meet daily or two or three times a week, with each group lasting about two to three weeks. On days when groups do not meet, the teacher may teach mini-lessons, provide opportunities for students to read other types of materials, have selective oral reading, hold reading or writing workshops, or offer other reading-related activities. Exact procedures for groups vary, but the following practices are typical:

1. Have available multiple copies of several good books. Briefly introduce them to the students, and ask the students to write their names and their first and second choices on slips of paper. Form groups based on student selections, not achievement levels.

> reading-writing connection

2. Explain literature logs, in which students are to write their reflections about what they read (see Example 8.4).

3. Have students meet in groups, look through their books, decide how far to read each time (it must be a reasonable "chunk"), and begin reading. With younger children, read the book to them and then place the book, along with a tape, at the listening center.

> reading-writing connection

4. During group sessions, have a student leader conduct the activities, which may consist of silent reading, writing in and sharing literature logs, asking open-ended questions, discussing what was read, and doing extension activities.

5. Encourage students to create extension projects individually, in pairs, or as a group. Examples include reading a similar book or a book by the same author, creating a drama, and writing an epilogue for the story.

6. Have students evaluate their own performances by using a checklist similar to the following one. Discuss the evaluation with each student, item by item.

    _____ Used reading time wisely.

    _____ Completed assigned number of pages each time group met.

    _____ Participated in discussion.

    _____ Listened to others attentively.

Example 8.4   *Literature Log*

Part 1

Amaroq, the Wolf

NAME: Katie Smith
DATE: September 11

TITLE OF BOOK: Julie of the wolves
PAGE STARTED: 20
PAGE STOPPED: 45

RETELL:

Miyax is still looking for food. No matter what she will not give up. Now she is communicating with the wolves. She talks and acts like them.

Jello, one of the wolves, brings food back from the hunt and Miyax gets offered some.

COMMENTS:

- p. 20 How many wolves? Have I missed missed something?
- p. 22 Does Miyax think the wolves can understand her? Can they?
- p. 23 Eelie? Excitement = Eelie?
- p. 24 Why does she try to make the wolves get food for her when she has an ulo?
- p. 25 Sunny Night?
- p. 27 "learn about her family" Does that mean her wolf family?

REACTION:

Exciting!

_____ Wrote something in literature log each time.

_____ Helped plan and carry out extension activity.

7. Keep your own checklist for each student. Use one form for each group each time groups meet. (See Chapter 11 for a teacher's checklist for literature response groups.)

Although students feel a sense of ownership in their selection of books and freedom of expression, the teacher plays a vital role in ensuring that groups operate effectively. By giving clear directions and setting examples, the teacher enables students to conduct their groups independently. After modeling log entries and discussion questions and responses, the teacher helps students move beyond literal comments and simple retellings to insightful observations. By observing difficulties students are having, the teacher offers minilessons on reading strategies that are based on what the students are reading. The teacher cannot be part of every group each day, but should participate actively in each group by reading, writing, and discussing. When an operational problem arises, the teacher searches for a better way, thus keeping procedures flexible so that they meet students' current needs.

Oral Interpretation of Literature

Fluent oral reading with intonation and phrasing that accurately reflect the mood and tone of the story or poem is another way to respond to literature. Oral reading is more difficult than silent reading because, in order to convey the author's message to an audience, the reader must pronounce words correctly, phrase appropriately, enunciate distinctly, use proper intonation, and pace the reading appropriately. To accomplish these goals, the oral reader should have an opportunity to read silently first to become acquainted with the author's style of writing, determine the author's message, and check the correct pronunciation of unfamiliar words. If the passage is particularly difficult, the reader may need to practice it aloud to ensure proper phrasing and intonation.

Oral reading skills require special attention. The teacher may demonstrate good and poor oral reading, let the children analyze these performances, and then help students draw up a list of standards or guidelines like the following:

1. Be sure you can pronounce each word correctly before you read your selection to an audience. If you are not sure of a pronunciation, check the dictionary or ask for help.

2. Say each word clearly and distinctly. Don't run words together, and take care not to leave out word parts or add parts to words.

3. Pause in the right places. Pay attention to punctuation clues.

4. Emphasize important words. Help the audience understand the meaning of the selection by the way you read it. Read slowly enough to allow for adequate expression, and speak loudly enough to be easily heard.

5. Prepare carefully before you read to an audience.

When well-rehearsed oral reading occurs, there should be one or more people with whom the reader is attempting to communicate through reading. Audience members should not have access to the book from which the performer is reading so they cannot follow the reading with their eyes. Instead, they should listen to the reader to grasp the author's meaning or, if the reader is reading to prove a point, to agree or disagree. The reader must attempt to hold the audience's attention through oral interpretation of the author's words. A stumbling performance will lead to a restless, impatient audience and a poor listening situation.

Some examples of purposes for audience reading include

1. Confirming an answer to a question by reading the portion of the selection in which the answer is found.

2. Reading aloud the part of an assigned story that is funniest or saddest or that tells about a particular person, thing, or event.

3. Reading a news story in which the class should be interested or background information for a topic of discussion from a reference or trade book.

4. Making announcements or issuing invitations.

5. Sharing a part of a published story, a poem (poems are written to be read aloud), or an experience story that the reader has enjoyed.

6. Participating in choral reading or readers' theater.

7. Reading aloud directions for a group activity, such as performing an experiment, making a model, or playing a game.

8. Participating in a class read-aloud program. Spend about forty-five minutes each week on an oral reading session in which students take turns reading aloud for a few minutes from favorite trade books.

9. Sharing riddles, jokes, and tongue twisters to entertain classmates.

10. Reading stories aloud to children in lower grades.

11. Reading the part of a character in a play or the narration for a play or other dramatic presentation.

Books by Paul Fleischman contain poems for two voices that invite students or groups of students to collaborate in reading aloud. Sometimes passages are to be read singly and sometimes in unison, but students must read expressively and fluently to achieve the proper effect. *Joyful Noise* contains poems about insects that think and act as humans; *I Am Phoenix* consists of poems that celebrate a variety of birds.

Responses Through Drama

The dramatic process includes activities such as

1. Pantomiming story situations

2. Characterizing objects or persons

3. Improvising situations and dramatizing stories

4. Reading and creating plays (and using aids, such as puppets)

5. Performing readers' theater

6. Reading/speaking choral verse

Through the ages, communication has taken place through body actions. Movement stories or poems delight children, and *pantomiming* is one way to dramatize through movement. Beginning with simple activities such as pretending to be a toad under a mushroom, pantomimes can progress to include several children. Since young children usually know some nursery rhymes when they enter school, these rhymes can be used for pantomime. It's fun to be Jack or Jill running up the hill, Little Bo Peep looking for her sheep, or the scary spider chasing Miss Muffet away from her tuffet. Fables (such as Aesop's) are also good for a group to act out, as are folktales like *Little Red Riding Hood*.

Teachers can focus on *characterization* (being an animal or another person) by asking children to interpret the giant in *Jack and the Beanstalk*. How does he walk? What kind of person is he? How old is he? What should his facial expressions be like? What is his relationship with the other characters in the story?

Acting without a script is called *improvisation* or *creative dramatics*. Children who participate in this form of drama must have the main points of a story firmly in mind and understand the roles of the characters. Usually the teacher reads a favorite story to the students and tells them in advance that they may act it out. Children volunteer to play different parts and interpret the story as they understand it. Children at the primary level may dramatize such stories as *The Three Billy Goats Gruff* or *The Three Bears,* and intermediate students may act out scenes from *Rip Van Winkle* or Katherine Paterson's *The Great Gilly Hopkins.*

Puppets—either simple hand puppets the children have made, in which the head is moved by the index finger and the arms by the third finger and thumb, or rod puppets, controlled by one or more dowel rods to which the puppet is attached—are very useful for presenting plays. Puppets may be constructed from paper sacks, Styrofoam, rubber balls, papier-mâché, old socks, fruits or vegetables, sticks, and so on. Tape-recording the script as the children read it (or act it out) and then playing it during the puppet performance may help some children concentrate on hand movements until they can coordinate both speaking and manipulating the puppets.

In *readers' theater*, students read aloud in dramatic style from scripts. No sets, costumes, or props are necessary, and the emphasis is on interpretive oral reading (Cullinan and Galda, 1994; Savage, 1994). The readers must understand their characters fully in order to interpret their roles in the story. The performers should rehearse their parts, perhaps adding sound effects or background music where appropriate, and then perform their story for an audience.

SELF-CHECK: OBJECTIVE 8   What are several ways children can respond to literature through drama? Consider ways you might want to use drama in your classroom. (See Self-Improvement Opportunity 11.)

Responses Through Written Expression

Traditional written book reports in which students merely summarize plots of stories have in many cases been replaced by more creative, naturalistic responses to literature. Students are encouraged to react thoughtfully to what they read by writing in literature logs or critically reviewing books on note cards that are filed for other students to read. In one class, students place minireviews of favorite books they want to recommend on a bulletin board. Example 8.5 is a sample of a child's recommendation.

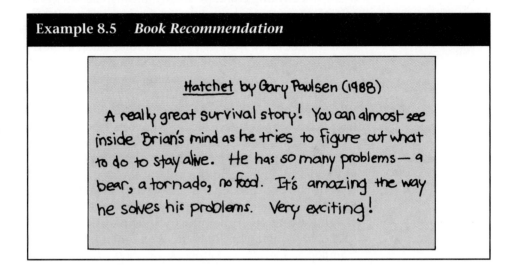

Example 8.5   *Book Recommendation*

> <u>Hatchet</u> by Gary Paulsen (1988)
>
> A really great survival story! You can almost see inside Brian's mind as he tries to figure out what to do to stay alive. He has so many problems— a bear, a tornado, no food. It's amazing the way he solves his problems. Very exciting!

Several ideas for activities that combine reading and writing were presented earlier in this chapter. Here are some additional activities that focus on written responses to literature.

Activities

1. Ask students to collect as many Newbery Award books and Honor books (runners-up to Award books) as they can find, read several of them, and ask their friends to read others. After making up and filling out an evaluation checklist for each book, including such criteria as characterization, author's style, authenticity of setting, and plot development, they may add to the checklist comments about the merit of each book.

2. Let each student make an original book jacket for a favorite book by illustrating the cover, writing a brief biographical sketch of the author on one flap, and writing a "blurb" to make the book sound appealing on the other flap.

3. Have each student choose a favorite character from literature, such as Pippi Longstocking or Curious George, and write a story about an imaginary visit to the school or a day spent in her or his company.

4. Let each student read a biography of a famous person from history and write a story about what would happen if that person lived today—for example, how he or she would bring peace to the world, solve medical problems, or protect the environment. The popular *Lincoln: A Photobiography*, by Russell Freedman, would be a good choice.

5. Choose an environmental book, such as Chris Van Allsburg's *Just a Dream*, and have students discuss the issues. Ask them each to choose one issue that especially concerns them and write letters to their congressperson describing the issue and recommending solutions.

6. Read Byrd Baylor's *I'm in Charge of Celebrations,* and discuss the meaning of *celebration* as used in this book. Then ask the children to keep journals of their own special celebration days over a period of two or three months. Students may wish to share their celebrations by reading from their journals.

7. Read to the class several books by a single author, such as Robert Munsch. Ask the students to discuss in groups the special features of Munsch's books, record their findings, and then share their observations with the rest of the class.

8. Read Mem Fox's *Wilfred Gordon McDonald Partridge* or a similar book about elderly people to the class, and discuss both the contributions and special needs of older people. Ask each child to identify an elderly person to whom he or she can write a letter or send a story. Help the children follow through with their plans.

Responses Through Art and Music

Many children who have difficulty expressing themselves with words prefer to respond to literature in other ways (Hoyt, 1992). Art and music offer creative options for these children.

Through exposure to well-illustrated picture books, children learn to appreciate the artists' work and begin to see themselves as illustrators capable of creating their own art (Galda and Short, 1993). They can interpret stories through many art media, including clay, paint, papier-mâché, scraps of felt and ribbon, colored pencils and pens, and three-dimensional objects. Using such media, they create collages and montages, dioramas and puppet figures, mobiles and stabiles, and illustrations for their own storybooks (Russell, 1994).

More picture books of children's story songs and singing games are available than ever before, and these books help children connect the words they sing with the words they see in print (Beaty, 1994). Some examples are

The Wheels on the Bus by Maryann Kovalski (Boston: Little, Brown, 1987). An action song with movements and sounds that accompany the wheels, wipers, horns, and so forth.

Old McDonald Had a Farm by Glen Rounds (New York: Holiday House, 1989). A familiar song with repetitive phrases such as "With a MOO-MOO here" and a chorus of "EE-AY, EE-AY, OH."

Abiyoyo by Pete Seeger; Michael Hays, illustrator (New York: Macmillan, 1986). A story song based on a South African lullaby in which a little boy and his father make a monster disappear.

By picturing the instruments and simulating the sounds of a marching band, Lois Ehlert's *THUMP, THUMP, Rat-a-Tat-Tat* (Singapore: Harper & Row, 1989) can provide the stimulus for creating a rhythm band.

SELF-CHECK: OBJECTIVE 8   Recall some books that were your favorites when you were a child. What types of responses to literature would be appropriate to use with these books? (See Self-Improvement Opportunities 11 and 13.)

Integrating Literature Across the Curriculum

For students who find textbooks difficult or dull, supplementary trade books from a variety of genres offer a viable option for learning content area material.

In social studies, award-winning trade books can be found for nearly every period of history. Elizabeth Speare's *The Bronze Bow* is a novel about a boy who encounters Jesus in Rome; Marguerite De Angeli's *The Door in the Wall* treats the situation of a crippled boy in fourteenth-century England; *The Courage of Sarah Noble,* by Alice Dalgliesh, describes a young girl who must face the difficulties of living in Connecticut in early pioneer days; *The Sign of the Beaver,* by Elizabeth Speare, is the story of a boy's struggle to survive in the Maine wilderness in the 1700s; Carol Brink's *Caddie Woodlawn* brings the reader into the excitement of living on the Wisconsin frontier during the last half of the nineteenth century; Paula Fox's *The Slave Dancer* tells about a boy who becomes involved in the slave trade with Africa during pre–Civil War days; and Patricia MacLachlan's *Sarah, Plain and Tall* unites a woman from the East with a motherless family on a prairie farm during pioneer days. Biographies of famous people who lived during different historical periods also add spice to textbook accounts.

Teachers can use trade books to develop mathematical concepts as well. Starting with simple counting books such as the vividly illustrated *Brian Wildsmith's 1, 2, 3's,* teachers can use books to expand concepts dealing with shapes, comparative size, and ordinal numbers. Through the humorous and provocative situations in Rod Clement's *Counting on Frank,* the reader begins to think like a mathematician—experimenting, calculating, and estimating. Two books by David Schwartz, *How Much Is a Million?* and *If You Made a Million,* use ridiculous situations to help the reader conceptualize the enormity of large numbers like one million.

Vocabulary lessons are lively and fun when the class uses trade books for word play and for learning interesting features of words (Blatt, 1978; Burke,

1978). In the Amelia Bedelia books by Peggy Parish, Amelia takes everything literally, with disastrous results: her sponge cake is made of sponges! Fred Gwynne's *A Chocolate Moose for Dinner* illustrates figurative expressions and words with multiple meanings as a child might visualize them. William Steig's *CDB* uses letters of the alphabet to represent words for silly sayings.

An area of special concern today is the environment, which is well represented in children's literature (Galda, 1991; Galda and MacGregor, 1992; Pierce and Short, 1994). Lynne Cherry's beautifully illustrated *A River Ran Wild: An Environmental History* documents the story of the Nashua River—its pollution and revitalization—and her *The Great Kapok Tree* relates how the animals of a Brazilian rain forest convince a man not to cut down their home. Jeannie Baker has also written two thought-provoking environmental books: *Window*, which shows how a wilderness evolves into a crowded city, and *Where the Forest Meets the Sea*, in which a boy explores a prehistoric rain forest and ponders its future. In Chris Van Allsburg's *Just a Dream*, Walter's dream helps him realize the importance of caring for the environment.

The following list of activities combines various types of responses to literature. The value of using different forms of literature to integrate the curriculum becomes obvious as students study history by reading biographies of famous people, learn geography by comparing viewpoints of books about different countries, see relationships by examining concept books, understand current issues by reading books about the environment, gain insights into literature by discussing character development and story conflicts, and so on.

Activities

1. When more than one student reads the same book, try the following suggestions: dramatize a scene from the story; set up a puppet show and tape-record the voices of the characters; or compare views about character development, conflicts in the story, and the ending of the book.

2. For biographies, have students discuss the childhoods of famous people, what influences caused them to become famous, and what struggles they faced to accomplish their goals.

3. When students have read biographies of creative people, ask them to include examples of the subjects' famous works in their reviews: playing a recording by a well-known composer, showing an art print by a painter, or displaying a product of an inventor.

4. For books about travel, let students read several books about the same country and compare points of view or give an illustrated lecture on the country by locating it on the map and showing postcards and other travel materials.

5. For realistic fiction, encourage students to identify the problems of the characters and how they are solved, relate the situation in the book to the students' own environments, or propose alternate solutions for the characters' problems.

6. From a selection of reference books, informational books, and historical fiction, ask students to study a particular period in history. Have them develop a project, such as a dramatization or a panel discussion, based on their impressions of this era.

7. Divide the class into groups and ask each group to select a broad topic such as animals, holidays, or nature. Borrow several poetry anthologies from the library and ask each group to portray the topic in poetry, perhaps by tape-recording poems, making a poetry booklet, or pantomiming poems as they are read aloud.

8. Arrange a panel discussion in which several students who have read different books by the same author talk about similarities and differences in the books along with the writer's strengths and weaknesses, general philosophy, and change in style over time.

SELF-CHECK: OBJECTIVE 9 Suggest some ways you can use trade books to enrich teaching in the content areas. (See Self-Improvement Opportunities 12 and 15.)

Thematic Units

thematic learning

Thematic units can be used within literature-centered instruction as an effective means of both integrating literature across the curriculum and extending knowledge. (See also the discussions of thematic units in Chapters 7, 10, and 12.) Four ways to develop themes are around a book, a topic, a genre, and an author. Example 8.6 is a graphic portrayal of a literature web with Faith Ringgold's *Tar Beach*, a Caldecott Honor Book that tells of Cassie Lightfoot's dream to be free. A web for Lois Lowry's *Number the Stars*, a Newbery Award winner, is shown in Example 8.7. This book deals with a Danish girl's heroic efforts to smuggle Jews to safety during World War II. Both books offer rich opportunities to integrate the curriculum.

Webbing is a technique that connects a central topic, or in these cases a book, to related ideas. A web is a framework that cuts across curricular areas. Emphasizing that no two webs are alike, Huck, Hepler, and Hickman (1993) recommend webbing as a plan for literature study that grows out of students' interests and the strengths of the books. During the process of creating a web, teachers become aware of the many directions in which books can lead children. Although the teacher uses the web as an overall plan, students contribute their own ideas as the theme unfolds so that the study becomes learner centered. Bromley's *Webbing with Literature* (1991) suggests further ideas for using literature webs.

Also endorsing the use of webbing, Norton (1993) suggests a procedure for developing a unit. The first step is to identify a theme that can be enriched with literature. Then the teacher and students construct a web with subtopics that become the subjects of study for groups of students. They locate books and other resources that will help them investigate their subjects, then share their findings creatively with the rest of the class. Example 8.8 shows another way to develop a

Example 8.6   *Literature Web*

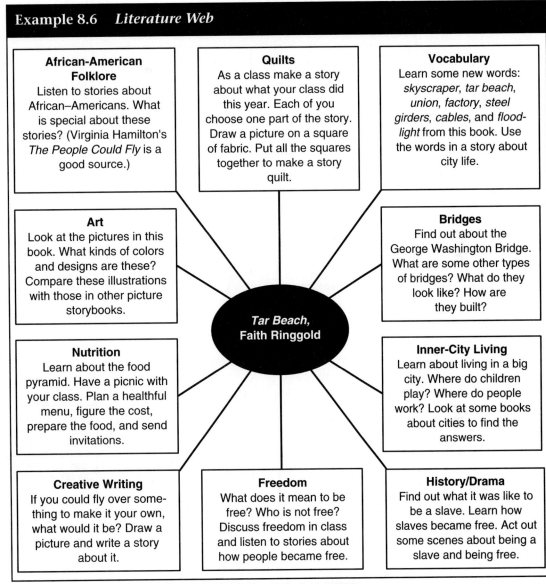

African-American Folklore
Listen to stories about African–Americans. What is special about these stories? (Virginia Hamilton's *The People Could Fly* is a good source.)

Quilts
As a class make a story about what your class did this year. Each of you choose one part of the story. Draw a picture on a square of fabric. Put all the squares together to make a story quilt.

Vocabulary
Learn some new words: *skyscraper, tar beach, union, factory, steel girders, cables,* and *floodlight* from this book. Use the words in a story about city life.

Art
Look at the pictures in this book. What kinds of colors and designs are these? Compare these illustrations with those in other picture storybooks.

Bridges
Find out about the George Washington Bridge. What are some other types of bridges? What do they look like? How are they built?

***Tar Beach,* Faith Ringgold**

Nutrition
Learn about the food pyramid. Have a picnic with your class. Plan a healthful menu, figure the cost, prepare the food, and send invitations.

Inner-City Living
Learn about living in a big city. Where do children play? Where do people work? Look at some books about cities to find the answers.

Creative Writing
If you could fly over something to make it your own, what would it be? Draw a picture and write a story about it.

Freedom
What does it mean to be free? Who is not free? Discuss freedom in class and listen to stories about how people became free.

History/Drama
Find out what it was like to be a slave. Learn how slaves became free. Act out some scenes about being a slave and being free.

Source: Web based on *Tar Beach* by Faith Ringgold. New York: Crown, 1991.

literature-based, learner-centered thematic unit that is based on the K-W-L procedure (Ogle, 1989) described in Chapter 10. The theme is immigrants.

Some commercially prepared resources, such as the *Inquiring into the Theme* series published by Perfection Learning, are available for developing or supplementing literature-based thematic studies. Software packages to support curriculum integration are also available (Wepner, 1992). These packages feature

Example 8.7   *Literature Web*

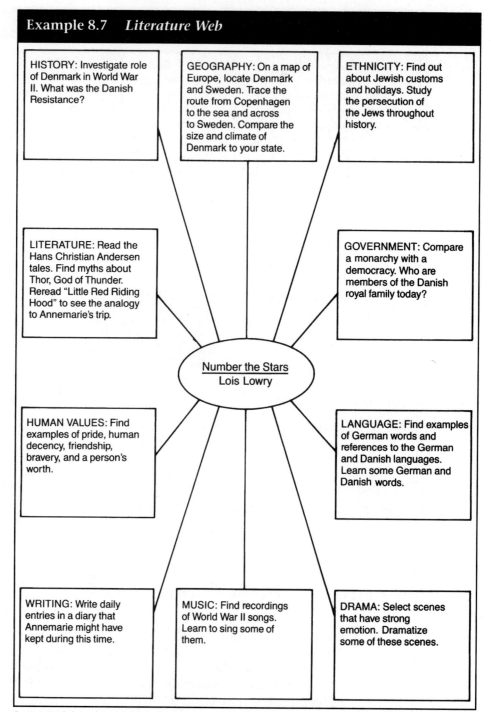

HISTORY: Investigate role of Denmark in World War II. What was the Danish Resistance?

GEOGRAPHY: On a map of Europe, locate Denmark and Sweden. Trace the route from Copenhagen to the sea and across to Sweden. Compare the size and climate of Denmark to your state.

ETHNICITY: Find out about Jewish customs and holidays. Study the persecution of the Jews throughout history.

LITERATURE: Read the Hans Christian Andersen tales. Find myths about Thor, God of Thunder. Reread "Little Red Riding Hood" to see the analogy to Annemarie's trip.

GOVERNMENT: Compare a monarchy with a democracy. Who are members of the Danish royal family today?

Number the Stars
Lois Lowry

HUMAN VALUES: Find examples of pride, human decency, friendship, bravery, and a person's worth.

LANGUAGE: Find examples of German words and references to the German and Danish languages. Learn some German and Danish words.

WRITING: Write daily entries in a diary that Annemarie might have kept during this time.

MUSIC: Find recordings of World War II songs. Learn to sing some of them.

DRAMA: Select scenes that have strong emotion. Dramatize some of these scenes.

Source: Web based on *Number the Stars* by Lois Lowry. Boston: Houghton Mifflin, 1989.

Media specialists, librarians, parents, and other members of the community can work with teachers to encourage language learning and reading of literature. (© *Jean Claude-Lejeune/ Stock Boston*)

imaginative, interactive adventure stories (e.g., *Animal Rescue*); opportunities to become production artists and script writers for plays (e.g., *Puppet Plays*); music programs for listening to or creating melodies (e.g., *Kidstime* and *The Treehouse*); and ways to create varieties of theme-related puppets (e.g., *Puppetmaker*).

Any *genre*, or classification of literature, can be a focus for study (Tompkins and McGee, 1993). In Example 8.9 the genre is folktales. Other viable genres are poetry, historical fiction, biography, and fantasy, each of which may be divided into subtopics. For instance, types of fantasy that may be studied are (1) modern literary tales based on folktales, (2) fantastic stories, which are basically realistic but contain elements of fantasy, (3) science fiction, or (4) high fantasy with heroes and heroines who confront evil for the sake of humanity.

A fourth type of thematic unit is based on a popular children's author. Knowing something about the real person behind their favorite books and *how* and *why* stories were written helps children develop author awareness and appreciation (Savage, 1994). Good choices of authors are Eric Carle, Tomie DePaola, Steven Kellogg, and Leo Lionni for younger children and Katherine Paterson, Gary Paulsen, Beverly Cleary, and Lois Lowry for older ones. Most children's libraries contain references on children's authors, such as the *Sixth Book of Junior Authors and Illustrators* (1989), published by the H. W. Wilson Company.

Example 8.8   *Thematic Unit: Immigrants*

Topic: Immigrants (adapted from the curriculum framework theme of multicultural studies)

Goal: To understand how immigrants adjust to a new environment

Initiating Activity: Read Allen Say's Caldecott winner *Grandfather's Journey* (Houghton Mifflin, 1993), the story of the author's grandfather, who lived in both Japan and the United States. Follow the reading with a discussion of how it feels to belong to two countries, and introduce the word *immigrant.*

What We Know: Ask the children what they know about immigrants. They respond by saying:

People come to the United States from all over the world.

Many of them speak different languages.

They have different customs.

What We Want to Learn: Ask the children what they want to learn. They respond by saying:

How do immigrants get to be citizens?

How do they feel about leaving their homes?

What are some problems they face in a new land?

How We Can Find Out: Ask the children how they will find the answers. They respond by saying:

Read books about people who are immigrants.

Invite an immigrant to speak to the class.

Ask our families where we came from.

Resource Materials: With your help and that of the librarian, the children collect trade books and reference sources to learn about immigrants. Some of their favorites are

Immigrant Kids by Russell Freedman (New York: Scholastic, 1980). Photographs tell the story of immigrant children at home, school, work, and play.

The Lotus Seed by Sherry Garland (Orlando: Harcourt Brace Jovanovich, 1993). A Vietnamese family flees its homeland to escape a war and takes along a precious lotus seed.

Molly's Pilgrim by Barbara Cohen (New York: Lothrop, 1983). A Jewish girl takes a doll to school dressed as her mother was dressed when she left Russia.

Refugees by Carole Seymour-Jones (New York: New Discovery Books, 1992). People who believe they must leave their country face problems in the new land.

Example 8.8   *Thematic Unit: Immigrants (cont.)*

How My Family Lives in America by Susan Kuklin (New York: Bradbury, 1992). Children of parents born in other countries tell what makes their families special.

Activities: The children

1. inquire about their family backgrounds and find books about their own cultures.
2. use reference books to discover how immigrants become U.S. citizens.
3. read independently each day from a theme-related book.
4. make displays of books that feature different cultures.
5. write travel diaries of their journeys to the new land.
6. discuss which prized possessions they would take with them.
7. choose one nationality that represents many of the children and divide into groups to study the contributions of that culture (prominent people, inventions and discoveries, songs and dances, folklore, games, foods, vocabulary words, and customs).
8. meet in groups to prepare projects on these topics.
9. write a play about emigrating to the United States based on experiences and feelings understood from books read.

Culminating Activity: The children invite another class to attend their play, view their book displays, and observe or participate in their group projects.

What We Learned: Ask the children what they learned. They will give many answers, including these:

About our own heritages

Contributions of different nationalities

Some of the problems immigrants face

Example 8.10 is a thematic unit based on Judy Blume, a popular children's author. Students may use it independently or in cooperation with other students at a literature center. It is an integrated language arts unit in which students become involved in reading, writing, listening, and speaking as they pursue activities related to Judy Blume and her books. In addition, students must use thinking skills and creative responses, analyze personal feelings and understand problems that others may be experiencing, and build an appreciation of literature by studying elements of literature (e.g., theme and characterization) and by learning about the author. Students will need multiple copies of several of Blume's books.

reading-writing connection

Example 8.9 *Thematic Unit on Folklore*

1. Let children read and compare folktale variants, beginning with the Brothers Grimm tales and moving toward contemporary versions. (Reference source: Household Stories [New York: McGraw-Hill, 1966]).

2. Encourage children to tell stories, repeating familiar favorites or creating new tales.

3. Read and/or tell classic folktales to the students.

4. Provide opportunities for discovering word origins and literary allusions, especially in myths (e.g., echo, Pandora's box, Mercury, Atlas).

5. Let children dramatize folktales using puppets, pantomime, readers' theater, and creative dramatics.

6. Encourage children to write creatively. Have them
   a. study the characteristics of a fable (brevity, animal characters, a moral) and create new fables.
   b. write modern versions of fairy tales.
   c. make up a ballad based on folklore and set it to music.
   d. make up original *pourquoi* tales, such as "Why the Rabbit Has Long Ears."
   e. write new endings for folktales after changing major events in the stories, such as having the First Little Pig build his house out of stone and the Third Little Pig build his house out of spaghetti.
   f. select a newspaper story, find a moral for it (e.g., "theft doesn't pay"), and write a fable about this moral.

7. Help students find out how folktales were originally communicated and how they came to be written.

8. Invite storytellers for children to hear. Ask students to interview the storytellers about techniques and about the origins of the tales they tell.

9. Encourage students to compare similarities in characters and motifs of folktales from around the world (e.g., the Jackal in India, the Weasel in Africa, and Brer Rabbit in the United States).

10. Have students locate the origins of various versions of folktales on a map.

11. Ask students to compare the artwork used to illustrate folktales (e.g., the illustrations in Walt Disney's version of *Snow White and the Seven Dwarfs* with Nancy Burkert's illustrations).

12. Provide tapes of music and dance based on folktales, such as selections from Stephen Sondheim's *Into the Woods*.

13. Ask students to consider the moral values depicted in folklore and compare them with values in today's literature.

14. Have students create a time line that shows the approximate times when various types of folklore originated.

Example 8.10   *A Thematic Unit on an Author: Judy Blume and Her Books*

Directions: Read several Judy Blume books and think about them. Then read the activities at the literature center, and choose two or more from each category. Keep your work in a file folder at the center. You may wish to work with other readers.

A. About the Author

1. Write a letter to Judy Blume in care of the publisher, and ask her
   a. Why did you become a writer?
   b. Are the characters real people?
   c. How do you know so much about how we feel?
   d. Whatever you would like to know.

2. Name a theme that you would like Judy Blume to write about next.
   a. Write a paragraph suggesting a story line.
   b. Describe what you think the main character would be like.

3. Find out all you can about Judy Blume. Consult magazine articles, books about authors, and information on book jackets. Then
   a. design a bulletin board display using book jackets, a picture of Judy Blume, and interesting facts about her life.
   b. make an illustrated booklet containing reviews of her books and information about her background as a writer.
   c. prepare a presentation about Judy Blume and her books to give to another class.

4. Prepare a mock interview with Judy Blume for radio or television. After you have rehearsed it, present it to the class.

5. Plan a panel discussion or debate with other Blume readers about whether or not authors should write on the kinds of themes Judy Blume chooses.

6. Listen and react critically to others as they make presentations or debate issues. Write or discuss your reactions.

B. About the Books

1. Make a collage of magazine pictures related to the themes in Judy Blume's books.

2. Choose favorite scenes from Blume's books. Find others who have read the same books, and act out the scenes for your class.

3. Write diary entries for five consecutive days in the life of one of the characters.

4. Identify the theme for each book you read. Then relate these themes to yourself and to people you know.

5. Predict what the characters in the books you have read will be doing in five or ten years.

6. Think about the characters, and choose one to be your friend. Give reasons for your choice. Is there someone you would not like for a friend? If so, why?

7. Should Judy Blume's books be translated into other languages for boys and girls in other countries to read? Why or why not?

8. Create a television commercial to advertise one or more of Blume's books. You may want to include a musical jingle.

9. Could one of Blume's books be made into a television series? Consider possible story lines and audience reactions.

10. Make riddles of character descriptions for others to guess.

11. Make and play a game of Concentration using book titles and character names from Judy Blume's books.

12. Choose one book that several of you have read, and talk about all the emotions or feelings that are discussed in the book. Make a list.

C. About Specific Books

1. *Freckle Juice* (New York: Four Winds Press, 1971)
   a. Make up your own recipe for freckle juice.
   b. How would you like to change your appearance? What difference would it make? How important is appearance?

2. *Then Again, Maybe I Won't* (Scarsdale, N.Y.: Bradbury Press, 1971).
   a. How would you feel if you suddenly became rich? Poor?
   b. React to Tony's feelings about his physical development. In your opinion, are his feelings realistic? Why or why not?

3. *Blubber* (Scarsdale, N.Y.: Bradbury Press, 1974).
   a. Write a page in Blubber's diary expressing her feelings about being fat.
   b. Suggest ways that Blubber could have defended herself.

4. *Are You There God? It's Me, Margaret* (Scarsdale, N.Y.: Bradbury Press, 1970).
   a. What kind of relationship does Margaret have with God? How does her relationship compare with yours?
   b. What were some of the problems Margaret had in moving to a new place? Make a list of the problems you might face if you moved.

5. Participate in a literature response group based on one of Judy Blume's books.

SELF-CHECK: OBJECTIVE 9   What are four ways to focus a thematic unit centered around literature? What is a literature web? (See Self-Improvement Opportunities 12 and 15.)

Working with Support Personnel

literature-centered reading Teachers and librarians should work together to use the library's resources both to reinforce subject matter and encourage students to read for pleasure. Teachers work with librarians by suggesting books and materials that will complement units of study and relate to the interests of their students. Librarians cooperate with teachers by introducing new books, presenting stories to the class, and showing students how to use the library.

Parents and the community should also be part of a school's literature program. If they realize the value of literature in their children's reading program, parents can encourage them to read for pleasure. Parent-teacher organizations can sponsor programs to review children's books and magazines that may be unfamiliar to parents and to suggest ways parents can provide a home atmosphere that promotes interest in reading. Parents or members of the community might also like to join children during an SSR or storytelling session; some non-school personnel may be excellent storytellers or have books they are willing to contribute. The school, the home, and the community can work together to encourage language learning and love of literature.

Summary

Some basic principles of whole language are that learning is integrated, tasks are authentic, learning is social, classrooms are learner centered, and literature is an integral part of the curriculum. Applications of these principles are found throughout the text.

Instead of separating the language arts into discrete time periods, teachers should integrate instruction in reading, writing, listening, and speaking. When children learn language as an integrated whole, they are likely to view reading and writing as meaningful events.

Many similarities exist between reading and writing. Both are composing processes in which meaning is constructed. Teachers can use this natural connection by guiding children into activities that call for both reading and writing. Process writing is a child-centered approach to writing that consists of five steps: prewriting, drafting, revising, editing, and publishing. Journal writing and reading enable students to record their ideas and, in many cases, read responses from their teacher. Writing and reading workshops provide minilessons and large blocks of time for students to concentrate on actual writing and reading. Computers enable students to edit their compositions easily and do desktop publishing.

Literature is useful for integrating language. Story reading and storytelling provide multiple benefits by enticing children to read and providing them with knowledge. Teachers should consider both literary merit and children's interests when helping children choose books, and they should establish environments with an abundance of interesting books and attractive displays that create interest in reading.

Children respond to literature in many ways, including literature response groups, oral reading, drama, written expression, art and music, and other types of activities. Literature spans the curriculum by offering a wide variety of books on various subjects, and teachers can make literature the core of thematic units. These units may focus on books, themes, genres, or authors. Support personnel from the media center, home, and community contribute to the school's language and literature program.

Test Yourself *True or False*

———— 1. Ideally, the language arts should be integrated throughout the curriculum.

———— 2. Reading and writing are both composing processes.

———— 3. The *writing process* refers to the way children use punctuation, grammar, and spelling.

———— 4. Children generally prefer poems with thoughtful, serious themes.

———— 5. During the drafting stage, students must be careful to observe correct use of spelling and mechanics.

———— 6. Children must work alone when doing revisions.

———— 7. In dialogue journals, usually the student writes some thoughts and the teacher responds in writing.

———— 8. Journal writing is a good opportunity for teachers to correct students' handwriting, spelling, and grammar.

———— 9. In writing and reading workshops, students complete workbook exercises.

———— 10. Elementary students are capable of using word processors to write and edit compositions.

———— 11. Literature can be an effective way to integrate the language arts across the curriculum.

———— 12. The major purpose of teaching literature is to enable children to know the titles and authors of children's books.

———— 13. When reading aloud, teachers should speak in natural tones and with expression.

———— 14. Selection aids are people who advise librarians about which books to order.

———— 15. The Newbery Award is given for excellence in illustration.

———— 16. Many good children's magazines are being published.

———— 17. Silent reading is more difficult than oral reading.

———— 18. Performers in readers' theater memorize their parts.

_____ 19. Literature response groups require the use of multiple copies of the same book.

_____ 20. When writing responses to literature, a child's first priority should be the mechanics of writing.

_____ 21. There is no need for teachers to read aloud to children after children learn to read for themselves.

_____ 22. Award-winning trade books can be found for nearly every period in history.

_____ 23. A literature web may have a book at the center with related subjects radiating from it.

_____ 24. Parents, media specialists, and the community should join to support the reading program.

Self-Improvement Opportunities

1. For each of the whole language principles given in this chapter, find a specific strategy for implementing the principle. You may use this text, other references, or classroom observations for sources of information.

2. Read three selections from recent research about the connections between reading and writing. Write a brief summary of each selection and a conclusion based on all three selections.

3. Locate a classroom in which a teacher is using journal writing, process writing, word processing, or a reading or writing workshop with the students. Observe how the teacher organizes and manages the activity and what the children are doing. If possible, ask a child to explain the activity to you. Take notes on your findings, and share them in a group during class.

4. Keep a journal in which you reflect on your college class or the class you are teaching for a period of four weeks or longer. Your instructor may wish to respond, or you may find another student who will respond.

5. Select a read-aloud story for an age level of your choice. Then share it with a small group of children or your peers. Tape and evaluate your reading.

6. Choose a grade level you would like to teach, and make a list of books you would like to read aloud to your class.

7. Ask children to name their favorite books, and see if some books are named by several children. Administer an interest inventory to a group of children to find out their reading interests. (See Chapter 7 for a sample interest inventory.)

8. Ask a child to evaluate a book by answering questions you have prepared. Then see if your own evaluation agrees with the child's analysis.

9. Find a selection aid or children's book catalog, and analyze its usefulness in helping you choose appropriate books for an elementary classroom.

10. Find copies of children's magazines, and choose two or three that you would like for your classroom. Write a brief review of each.

11. Select a story with strong characterization to adapt for a readers' theater production. Get together with other students and write a script based on the story that elementary children could use.

12. Think of some ways to use children's literature to enrich each area of the curriculum. Then choose one subject and find five books you could use to supplement the textbook.

13. Find a group of children to work with you, and help them respond to a book through music or art.

14. Make a drawing of a creatively designed classroom with nooks and crannies for reading and writing. Consider availability of materials and resources.

15. Develop a literature web from one of your favorite children's books.

Chapter Appendix A

Children's Books Cited In Chapter 8

Aliki. *The Story of Johnny Appleseed.* Englewood Cliffs, N.J.: Prentice–Hall, 1963.

Ashbjornsen, Peter Christian, and Jorgen E. Moe. *The Three Billy Goats Gruff.* New York: Harcourt, Brace and World, 1957.

Baker, Jeannie. *Where the Forest Meets the Sea.* London: Walker Books, 1987.

Baker, Jeannie. *Window.* New York: Greenwillow, 1991.

Baylor, Byrd. *I'm in Charge of Celebrations.* New York: Scribner's, 1986.

Bemelmans, Ludwig. *Madeline.* New York: Viking, 1962.

Blos, Joan W. *A Gathering of Days: A New England Girl's Journal,* 1830–32. New York: Scribner's, 1979.

Blume, Judy. *It's Not the End of the World.* Scarsdale, N.Y.: Bradbury, 1972.

Branley, Franklyn M. *Think Metric!* New York: Crowell, 1973.

Brink, Carol. *Caddie Woodlawn.* New York: Macmillan, 1936.

Burkert, Nancy. *Snow White and the Seven Dwarfs.* New York: Farrar, 1973.

Carle, Eric. *The Very Hungry Caterpillar.* New York: Crowell, 1971.

Cherry, Lynne. *The Great Kapok Tree.* San Diego: Harcourt Brace Jovanovich, 1990.

Cherry, Lynne. *A River Ran Wild: An Environmental History.* San Diego: Harcourt Brace Jovanovich, 1992.

Clark, Rod. *Counting on Frank.* New South Wales, Australia: Collins/Angus and Robertson, 1990.

Cleary, Beverly. *Dear Mr. Henshaw.* New York: Morrow, 1983.

Cleary, Beverly. *Ramona Quimby, Age 8.* New York: Morrow, 1981.

Dalgliesh, Alice. *The Courage of Sarah Noble.* New York: Charles Scribner's Sons, 1954.

Daugherty, James. *Daniel Boone.* New York: Viking, 1932.

De Angeli, Marguerite. *The Door in the Wall.* New York: Doubleday, 1949.

Feuerlecht, Robert Strauss. *The Legends of Paul Bunyan.* New York: Macmillan, 1966.

Fleischman, Paul. *Joyful Noise.* New York: Harper & Row, 1988.

Fleischman, Paul. *I Am Phoenix.* New York: Harper & Row, 1988.

Fox, Mem. *Wilfred Gordon McDonald Partridge.* Brooklyn: Kane/Miller, 1985.

Fox, Paula. *Lily and the Lost Boy.* New York: Yearling, 1987.

Fox, Paula. *The Slave Dancer.* Scarsdale, N.Y.: Bradbury, 1974.

Freedman, Russell. *Lincoln: A Photobiography.* New York: Clarion, 1987.

Galdone, Paul. *The Gingerbread Boy.* New York: Seabury, 1973.

George, Jean. *Julie of the Wolves.* New York: Harper & Row, 1973.

Gwynne, Fred. *A Chocolate Moose for Dinner.* New York: Dutton, 1973.

Hanlon, Emily. *How a Horse Grew Hoarse on the Site Where He Sighted a Bare Bear.* New York: Delacorte, 1976.

Irving, Washington. *Rip Van Winkle and the Legend of Sleepy Hollow.* New York: Macmillan, 1965 (from *The Sketch Book,* 1819).

Kipling, Rudyard. *Just So Stories.* New York: Doubleday, 1972.

Lewis, C. S. *The Lion, the Witch, and the Wardrobe.* New York: Macmillan, 1950.

Lowry, Lois. *Number the Stars.* Boston: Houghton Mifflin, 1989.

MacLachlan, Patricia. *Sarah, Plain and Tall.* New York: Harper & Row, 1985.

Norton, Mary. *The Borrowers.* San Diego: Harcourt Brace Jovanovich, 1952.

Parish, Peggy. *Amelia Bedelia.* New York: Harper & Row, 1963.

Parish, Peggy. *Teach Us, Amelia Bedelia.* New York: Greenwillow, 1977.

Paterson, Katherine. *The Great Gilly Hopkins*. New York: Crowell, 1979.
Paterson, Katherine. *Jacob Have I Loved*. New York: Crowell, 1981.
Paterson, Katherine. *Park's Quest*. New York: Puffin, 1989.
Paulsen, Gary. *Hatchet*. New York: Bradbury, 1987.
Prelutsky, Jack. *The New Kid on the Block*. New York: Greenwillow, 1984.
Prelutsky, Jack. *Something Big Has Been Here*. New York: Greenwillow, 1990.
Rylant, Cynthia. *When I Was Young in the Mountains*. New York: Dutton, 1983.
Schwartz, David M. *How Much Is a Million?* New York: Scholastic, 1985.
Schwartz, David M. *If You Made a Million*. New York: Scholastic, 1985.
Sendak, Maurice. *In the Night Kitchen*. New York: Harper & Row, 1970.
Sendak, Maurice. *Where the Wild Things Are*. New York: Harper & Row, 1964.
Silverstein, Shel. *The Light in the Attic*. New York: Harper & Row, 1981.
Silverstein, Shel. *Where the Sidewalk Ends*. New York: Harper & Row, 1974.
Speare, Elizabeth. *The Bronze Bow*. Boston: Houghton Mifflin, 1961.
Speare, Elizabeth. *The Sign of the Beaver*. Boston: Houghton Mifflin, 1983.
Steig, William. *CDB*. New York: Simon & Schuster, 1968.
Tresselt, Alvin. *White Snow, Bright Snow*. New York: Lothrop, 1947.
Udry, Janice. *A Tree Is Nice*. New York: Harper & Row, 1957.
Van Allsburg, Chris. *Jumanji*. Boston: Houghton Mifflin, 1981.
Van Allsburg, Chris. *Just a Dream*. Boston: Houghton Mifflin, 1990.
Van Allsburg, Chris. *Two Bad Ants*. Boston: Houghton Mifflin: 1988.
Van Allsburg, Chris. *The Stranger*. Boston: Houghton Mifflin: 1986.
Van Allsburg, Chris. *The Widow's Broom*. Boston: Houghton Mifflin: 1992.
Van Allsburg, Chris. *The Wretched Stone*. Boston: Houghton Mifflin: 1991.
White, E. B. *Charlotte's Web*. New York: Harper & Row, 1952.
Wilder, Laura Ingalls. *Little House in the Big Woods*. New York: Harper & Row, 1932.
Wildsmith, Brian. *Brian Wildsmith's 1, 2, 3's*. New York: Franklin Watts, 1965.

Chapter Appendix B

Children's Periodicals

Boys' Life (1325 Walnut Hill Lane, P.O. Box 15079, Irving, TX 75015–2079). Age range 7–17. Boys in Scouting, general interest.

Chickadee (Young Naturalist Foundation, 255 Great Arrow Ave., Buffalo, NY 14207–3082). Age range 3–9. Science and nature.

Child Life (P.O. Box 71333, Red Oak, IA 51591–0133). Age range 7–9. Safety, health, fitness, nutrition; general interest.

Children's Digest (P.O. Box 7133, Red Oak, IA 51591). Age range preteen. Fitness, sports, general interest.

Children's Playmate (P.O. Box 7133, Red Oak, IA 51591). Age range 6–8. Safety, health, and nutrition; general interest.

Cobblestone (Cobblestone Publishing Co., 7 School Street, Peterborough, NH 03458). Age range 8–15. American history.

Creative Kids (Prufrock Press, P.O. Box 8813, Waco, TX 76714–8813). Ages 8–14. Literature.

Cricket: The Magazine for Children (P.O. Box 593, Mt. Morris, Ill. 61054–0593). Ages 7–14. Fiction, nonfiction, and art.

Faces (7 School Street, Peterborough, NH 03458). Age range 8–14. World cultures.

Highlights for Children (P.O. Box 269, Columbus, OH 43272–0002). Age range 2–12. General interest.

Humpty Dumpty's Magazine (P.O. Box 10003, Des Moines, IA 50340). Age range 4–6. General interest, health.

Jack and Jill (P.O. Box 10003, Des Moines, IA 50340). Age range 7–10. Health and fitness; general interest.

Ladybug, the Magazine for Young Children. (P.O. Box 593, Mt. Morris, IL 61054–0593). Age range 2–7. General interest.

National Geographic World (P.O. Box 2330, Washington, DC 20013–2330). Age range 8–14. Natural history, science, outdoor adventures, young achievers.

Odyssey (Cobblestone Publishing, 7 School St., Peterborough, NH 03458). Age range 8–14. Astronomy and space science.

Owl (Young Naturalist Foundation, 255 Great Arrow Ave., Buffalo, NY 14207). Age range 8+. Science, nature, and environment.

Ranger Rick (National Wildlife Federation, 8925 Leesburg Pike, Vienna, VA 22184–0001). Age range 6–12. Nature, environment, outdoors.

Scholastic Magazines (several options) (2931 E. McCarty St., P.O. Box 3710, Jefferson City, MO 65102–3710). Ages 6–18. Language arts, math, current events, home economics, and social studies.

Stone Soup: The Magazine for Children. (Children's Art Foundation, P.O. Box 83, Santa Cruz, CA 95063). Age range 6–13. Writing and art by children.

3–2–1 Contact (Box 51177, Boulder, CO 80322). Age range 8–12. Science, nature, and technology.

Your Big Backyard (National Wildlife Federation, 8925 Leesburg Pike, Vienna, VA 22184). Age range 3–5. Nature and conservation.

Zillions—The Consumer Reports for Kids (P.O. Box 51777, Boulder, CO 80321–1777). Age range 8–14. Consumer education.

Chapter 9

Key Vocabulary

Pay close attention to these terms when they appear in the chapter.

bar graphs

circle or pie graphs

database

guide words

legend

line graphs

metacognition

picture graphs

reading rate

reading/study
techniques

scale

SQRQCQ

SQ3R

Reading/Study Techniques

Setting Objectives

When you finish reading this chapter, you should be able to

1. Discuss the features of the SQ3R study method.

2. Explain the importance of developing flexible reading habits.

3. Name some skills a child needs in order to locate information in books, libraries or media centers, or computer databases.

4. Describe how to help a child learn to take good notes, make a good outline, and write a good summary.

5. Discuss the metacognitive strategies children need.

6. Explain how to teach a child to use graphic aids in textbooks.

Figure 9.1   *Chapter 9 Organization*

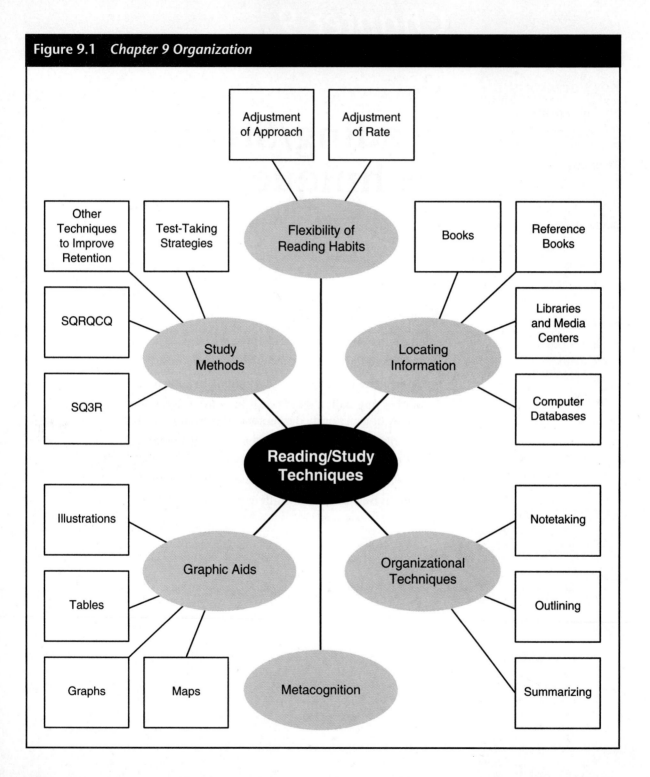

*R*eading/study techniques are strategies that enhance comprehension and retention of information in printed material and thus help children cope successfully with reading assignments in content area classes and with the informational reading they will need to do throughout their lives. Students need to develop the ability to use good study methods that can help them retain material they read, the ability to take tests effectively, flexibility of reading habits, the ability to locate and organize information effectively, and the ability to use metacognitive strategies when studying. They also need to learn the skills necessary to derive information from graphic aids (maps, graphs, tables, and illustrations) in content area reading materials.

Teaching study techniques is not exclusively the job of the intermediate-grade teacher, although the need for such instruction is more obvious at this level than at the primary level. Primary-grade teachers must lay the foundation for this instruction and make the children aware of the need for study skills. They can do this in a number of ways. They can have the children begin to keep assignment books in which to record all school assignments with related instructions and due dates. Teachers can introduce children to such activities as making free-form outlines related to stories they have heard or read and occasionally writing group

Although reference books such as encyclopedias, dictionaries, almanacs, and atlases can be helpful tools, teachers should use caution in assigning work from these books because their readability is often high. (*Mimi Forsyth/Monkmeyer Press Photo Service*)

experience charts in outline form. They can also let the children see them using indexes and tables of contents of books to find needed information, encourage the children to watch them use the card catalog to help locate books, and read aloud information related to content area study from a variety of reference books. Primary teachers can begin actual study skill instruction in the use of some parts of books (tables of contents, glossaries), dictionary use (alphabetical order, use of picture dictionaries), library use (location of the easy-to-read books, check-in and check-out procedures), map reading (titles, directional indicators, legends), graph reading (picture graphs, circle graphs, simple bar graphs), and picture reading.

Since some children are ready for more advanced techniques (such as note taking) much sooner than others, intermediate-grade teachers should determine the readiness of individual children for instruction in study techniques and offer instruction to fit their capabilities. Those children who are ready for more advanced techniques should be helped to develop these strategies as early as possible, because study techniques help children succeed in all subjects.

Teachers may present study techniques during a content class when the need arises or during a reading class, but they should be sure the strategies are applied to content soon after the reading class. Children will retain study techniques longer if they apply them, and they will see these skills as useful tools, rather than busywork exercises. They are more likely to apply their new knowledge if they practice the techniques in the context in which they will use them. Therefore, a teacher may find it very effective to set aside time during a content class to teach a study strategy that students will need to use immediately in that class.

Study Methods

Study methods are techniques that help students study written material in a way that enhances comprehension and retention. Unlike the directed reading activities (DRAs) found in teacher's manuals in basal reading series, study methods are student directed, rather than teacher directed. (See Chapter 7 for a description of a DRA.)

SQ3R

Probably the best-known study method is Robinson's *SQ3R* method: Survey, Question, Read, Recite, Review (Robinson, 1961). For this method, the steps given to the students are as follows:

- *Survey*. As you approach a reading assignment you should notice the chapter title and main headings, read the introductory and summary paragraphs, and inspect any visual aids such as maps, graphs, or illustrations. This initial survey provides a framework for organizing the facts you later derive from the reading.

- *Question*. Formulate a list of questions you expect to be answered in the reading. The headings may give you some clues.

- *Read*. Read the selection in order to answer the questions you have formulated. Since this is purposeful reading, making brief notes may be helpful.

- *Recite*. After reading the selection, try to answer each of the questions you formulated earlier without looking back at the material.

- *Review*. Reread to verify or correct your recited answers and to make sure that you have the main points of the selection in mind and that you understand the relationships among the various points.

reading-writing connection

Using a study method such as SQ3R will help a student remember content material better than simply reading the material would. Consequently, it is worthwhile to take time in class to show students how to go through the various steps. Teachers should have group practice sessions on SQ3R, or on any study method, before expecting the children to perform the steps independently.

Material chosen for SQ3R instruction should be content material on which the students should normally use the method. The teacher should ask all the students to survey the selection together, reading aloud the title and main headings and the introductory and summary paragraphs, and discussing the visual aids, in the first practice session.

The step that needs most explanation by the teacher is the Question step. The teacher can show children how to take a heading, such as "Brazil's Exports," and turn it into a question: "What are Brazil's exports?" This question should be answered in the section, and trying to find the answer provides a good purpose for reading. A chapter heading, such as "The Westward Movement," may elicit a variety of possible questions: "What is the Westward Movement?" "When did it take place?" "Where did it take place?" "Why did it take place?" "Who was involved?" The teacher can encourage children to generate questions like these in a class discussion during initial practice sessions.

After they have formulated questions, students read to find the answers. The teacher might make brief notes on the chalkboard to model behavior the children can follow. Then he or she can have students practice the Recite step by asking each child to respond orally to one of the purpose questions, with the book closed. During the Review step, the children reread to check all the answers they have just heard.

In subsequent practice sessions, the teacher can merely alert the children to perform each step and have them all perform the step silently at the same time. It will probably take several practice sessions before the steps are thoroughly set in the students' memories.

SQ3R is probably the best-known study method, but it is not the only one. Another useful method is explained in the following section.

SELF-CHECK: OBJECTIVE 1   Describe the SQ3R study method.

SQRQCQ

Another method that seems simple enough to use with good results at the elementary level is one developed especially for use with mathematics materials: SQRQCQ (Fay, 1965). *SQRQCQ* stands for Survey, Question, Read, Question, Compute, Question. This approach may be beneficial because youngsters frequently have great difficulty reading statement problems in mathematics textbooks. For this method, the steps given to the students are as follows:

- *Survey*. Read through the problem quickly to gain an idea of its general nature.

- *Question*. Ask, "What is being asked in the problem?"

- *Read*. Read the problem carefully, paying attention to specific details and relationships.

- *Question*. Make a decision about the mathematical operations to be carried out and, in some cases, the order in which they are to be performed.

- *Compute*. Do the computations you decided on in the preceding step.

- *Question*. Decide whether or not the answer seems to be correct, asking, "Is this a reasonable answer? Have I accurately performed the computations?"

As with SQ3R, the teacher should have the whole class practice the SQRQCQ method before expecting students to use it independently. Teaching the method takes little extra time, since it is a good way to manage mathematics instruction. (You may wish to refer to this section again as you read the section in Chapter 10 on mathematics materials.)

Other Techniques to Improve Retention

In addition to providing students with a good study method, a teacher can improve their ability to retain content material by following these suggestions:

1. Conduct discussions about all assigned reading material. Talking about ideas they have read helps to fix these ideas in students' memories.

2. Teach students to read assignments critically. Have them constantly evaluate the material they read, and avoid giving them the idea that something is true "because the book says so" by encouraging them to challenge any statement in the book if they can find evidence to the contrary. The active involvement with the material that is necessary in critical reading aids retention. (See Chapter 6 for a thorough discussion of critical reading.)

3. Encourage students to apply the ideas about which they have read. For example, after reading about parliamentary procedure, students can conduct a club meeting; after reading about a simple science experiment, they can actually conduct the experiment. Children learn those things they have applied in real life better than those about which they have only read.

4. Always be certain that students have in mind a purpose for reading before beginning each reading assignment, since this increases their ability to retain material. You may supply them with purpose questions or encourage them to state their own purposes. (Information about purpose questions is found in Chapters 5 and 6.)

5. Use audiovisual aids to reinforce concepts presented in the reading material.

6. Read background material to students to give them a frame of reference to which they can relate the ideas they read.

7. Prepare study guides for content area assignments. Study guides (duplicated sheets prepared by the teacher) help children retain their content area concepts by setting purposes for reading and providing appropriate frameworks for organizing material. (Study guides receive extensive attention in Chapter 10.)

8. Teach students to look for the author's organization. Have them outline the material or construct a diagram of the organizational pattern.

9. Encourage children to picture the ideas the author is describing. Visualizing information will help them remember it longer. Some children will find it helpful to draw, graph, or chart the ideas they visualize. Semantic webs are particularly useful. (See Chapter 10 for a description of the use of webs with content material.)

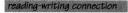 10. Teach note-taking procedures and encourage note taking. Writing down information often helps children retain it.

11. After children have read the material, have them summarize it in their own words in either written or oral form.

12. Have children use spaced practice (a number of short practice sessions extended over a period of time) rather than massed practice (one long practice session) for material you wish them to retain over a long period of time.

13. Encourage *overlearning* (continuing to practice a skill for a while after it has been initially mastered) of material you wish students to retain for long periods of time.

14. When appropriate, teach some simple mnemonic devices (short phrases or verses used as memory aids)—for example, "there is a rat in the middle of separate."

15. Offer positive reinforcement for correct responses to questions during discussion and review sessions.

16. Encourage students to look for words and ideas that are mentioned repeatedly, because they are likely to be important ones.

17. Encourage students to study more difficult and less interesting material when they are most alert (Memory and Yoder, 1988).

18. Teach students to ask and answer *why* questions about each factual statement in an informational passage (Menke and Pressley, 1994).

Test-Taking Strategies

Students need to retain what they have read in order to do well on tests, but sometimes students who know the material fail to do as well as they could because they lack good test-taking strategies. Students may study in the same way for essay tests and objective tests, for example. Helping them understand how to study for and take different types of tests can improve their performances.

Teachers can help students prepare for taking essay tests by helping them understand the meanings of certain words, such as *compare, contrast, describe,* and *explain,* that frequently appear in essay questions. The teacher can state a potential question using one of these terms and then model the answer to the question, explaining what is important to include in the answer. If a contrast is requested, the differences in the two things or ideas should be explained. If a comparison is requested, likenesses should be included.

Preparation for objective tests can include learning important terms and their definitions, studying for types of questions that have been asked in the past, and learning to use mnemonic devices to help in memorizing lists. Teachers should encourage students to use all of these techniques.

Teachers can also encourage students to consider the words *always, never,* and *not* carefully when answering true-false questions, since these words have a powerful effect on the meaning. They can make sure students realize that if any part of a true-false statement is false, the answer must be false. They can also caution students to read and consider all answers to a multiple-choice question before choosing an answer.

Children can also be helped to perform better on standardized tests through focused instruction. Teachers should discuss with the children the purpose of the tests and the special rules that apply during testing well before the standardized tests are to be given. They should provide practice in completing test items within specified time limits. A practice test with directions, time limits, and item formats as similar as possible to those of the actual test should be given to familiarize the children with the overall testing environment. The teacher can help the children view the test as a game in which they are trying to get as many correct answers as possible. After the practice test, the children can ask the teacher about any problems they experienced (Stewart and Green, 1983).

Children need to learn to follow the directions for testing exactly, including those related to recording answers. They should learn to answer first those items they can answer quickly and to check answers if they have time left. They need to realize the importance of reading all answers before choosing the best one and to understand that they should guess rather than leave an answer blank if there is not a severe penalty for guessing.

Flexibility of Reading Habits

Flexible readers adjust their approaches and rates to fit the materials they are reading. Good readers continually adjust their reading approaches and rates without being aware of it.

Adjustment of Approach

literature-centered reading

Flexible readers approach printed material according to their *purposes for reading* and the *type of material*. For example, they may read poetry aloud to savor the beauty of the words, or they may read novels for relaxation in a leisurely fashion, giving attention to descriptive passages that evoke visual imagery and taking time to think about the characters and their traits. If they are reading novels simply to be able to converse with friends about the story lines, they may read less carefully, wishing only to discover the novels' main ideas and basic plots.

Flexible readers approach informational reading with the goal of separating the important facts from the unimportant ones and paying careful attention in order to retain what they need from the material. Rereading is often necessary if the material contains a high density of facts or very difficult concepts and interrelationships. With such material, reading every word may be highly important, whereas it is less important with material containing few facts or less difficult concepts. Flexible readers approach material for which they have little background with greater concentration than material for which their background is extensive.

Some reading purposes do not demand the reading of every word in a passage. Sometimes *skimming* (reading selectively to pick up main ideas and general impressions about the material) or *scanning* (moving the eyes rapidly over the selection to locate a specific bit of information, such as a name or a date) is sufficient. Skimming is the process used in the Survey step of SQ3R, when students are trying to orient themselves to the organization and general focus of the material. Scanning is useful when searching for names in telephone books or entries in dictionaries or indexes.

Adjustment of Rate

Children often make the mistake of trying to read everything at the same rate. Some of them read short stories as slowly and carefully as they read science experiments, and they will probably never enjoy recreational reading because they have to work so hard and it takes them so long to read a story. Other children read everything rapidly, often failing to grasp essential details in content area reading assignments even though they complete the reading. Reading rate should not be considered as separate from comprehension. The optimum rate for reading a particular piece is the fastest rate at which the reader maintains an acceptable level of comprehension.

Students will use study time more efficiently if they are taught to vary their rates to fit the reading *purposes* and *materials*. A student should read light fiction for enjoyment much faster than a mathematics problem that must be solved. When reading to find isolated facts such as names and dates, the student will do better to scan a page rapidly for key words than to read every word of the material. When reading to determine main ideas or organization of a selection, he or she will find skimming more practical than reading each word of the selection.

The following activity illustrates one way to help pupils fit their reading rates to reading materials.

Model Activities

Adjusting Reading Rates

Ask students questions such as these:

1. What rate would be best for reading a science experiment?

   a. Fast

   b. Moderate

   c. Slow

2. Which of these materials could you read the fastest and still meet your purpose?

   a. A television schedule

   b. A newspaper article

   c. A science textbook

Follow up answers with the question "Why?" If students do not choose "slow" as the answer to the first question, analyze the reason they give and point out any problems, making it clear to them that every step in a science experiment must be done accurately and in the proper sequence or the experiment will not work. To ensure that they understand all details and follow the proper sequence, students must read slowly enough not to overlook any detail and may even have to reread to be absolutely accurate.

If children do not answer, "a television schedule," for the second question, ask what purpose they would have in reading such a schedule. When they reply, "to find what is on at a particular time" or "to find out when a certain program is on," point out that it is possible to scan for this information and that scanning is the fastest type of reading. They might intend to locate specific facts in a newspaper or a science textbook, but the format of a television schedule facilitates scanning, and it would probably be faster to read, even if the purposes for reading each type of material were similar.

Another way to help children fit appropriate rates to materials is to give them various types of materials and purposes, allow them to try different rates, and then encourage them to discuss the effectiveness of different rates for different purposes and materials. This will be particularly helpful if regular classroom materials are used for the practice. Emphasis on increasing reading speed is best left until children have well-developed basic word recognition and comprehension skills. By the time they reach the intermediate grades, some will be ready for help in increasing their reading rates. It is important to remember that speed without comprehension is useless, so the teacher must be sure students maintain comprehension levels as they keep working to increase their reading rates.

Students whose basic skills are good enough to qualify them for rate improvement exercises need to realize that they can save time when doing some functional reading and that they can read more recreationally in the same amount of time they currently use if they increase their reading rates (Bergquist, 1984). Some techniques teachers can use with students to help them increase their reading rates include the following.

Activities

1. To encourage students to try consciously to increase their reading rates, time their reading for three minutes. At the end of that period, have the students count the total words read, divide by three, and record the resulting number as their rate in average words per minute. To ensure that they are focusing on understanding, follow the timed reading with a comprehension check. The students can graph the results of these timed readings over a period of time, along with the comprehension results. Ideally, students will see their rates increase without a decrease in comprehension. If the children's comprehension does decrease, encourage them to slow down enough to regain an appropriate comprehension level.

2. To help children cut down on unnecessary regressions (going back to reread), have them use markers to move down the page, covering the lines just read.

3. To help decrease children's anxiety about comprehension that could impede their progress, give them easy material for practice in building their reading rates.

SELF-CHECK: OBJECTIVE 2   Explain the reasons that children should learn to read different materials at different rates. (See Self-Improvement Opportunity 1.)

Locating Information

To engage in many study activities, students need to be able to locate the necessary reading material. A teacher can help by pointing out the location aids in textbooks, reference books, and libraries and by showing them how to access databases.

Books

Most books offer students several special features that are helpful for locating needed information, including prefaces, tables of contents, indexes, appendices, glossaries, footnotes, and bibliographies. Teachers should not assume that children can adjust from the basal reader or trade book format to the format of content subject books without assistance. Basal readers have a great deal of narrative (storylike) material that, unlike most content material, is not packed with facts to be learned. When the trade books used in a program are primarily fiction, they will also be narrative in format. Although most basals have a table of contents and a glossary, they contain fewer of the special features just mentioned than do content textbooks; and, although some nonfiction trade books have tables of contents and/or glossaries, not all do. Therefore, teachers should present content textbooks to children carefully.

Preface/Introduction

When presenting a new textbook to students in the intermediate or upper grades, the teacher can ask them to read the preface or introduction to get an idea of why the book was written and of the manner in which the author or authors plan to present the material. Children should be aware that the prefaces and introductions of books they plan to use for reference can give them valuable information.

Table of Contents

On the day a new textbook is distributed, the teacher can also lead students in an examination of its table of contents. Even primary-level students can learn that the table of contents lists the topics the book discusses and the pages on which they appear, making it unnecessary to look through the entire book to find a specific section. The teacher can help students discover information about their new textbooks by asking questions such as the following:

What topics are covered in this book?

What is the first topic discussed?

On what page does the discussion about _____ begin? (This question can be repeated several times with different topics inserted in the blank.)

Indexes

Students in the intermediate and upper grades should become familiar with indexes. They should understand that an index is an alphabetical list of items and names mentioned in a book and the pages where these items or names appear, and that some books contain one general index and some contain subject and author indexes as well as other specialized ones (for example, a first-line index in a music or poetry book). Most indexes contain both main headings and subheadings, and students should be given opportunities to practice using these headings to locate information within their books. The teacher can lead children to examine the index of a book to make inferences about topics that the author considers to be important, based on the amount of space devoted to them. The following Focus on Strategies shows use of the index to locate information.

Focus on Strategies

Using the Index to Locate Information

Several children in Ms. Rand's class needed to find out how to check addition problems the day before, but had trouble locating the part of the book they wanted and spent too much time on the task. Ms. Rand noticed that none of the children used the index to find the pages. When she questioned a couple of them, she found out that they had only a hazy concept that the index was in the back of the book, and they didn't know how to use it.

The next day, Ms. Rand set out to remedy this situation. "Turn to page 315 of your math books," she told her class. "Tell me what you find there."

Here is a portion of what the children found:

Sample Index

Addition
    checking, 50–54
    meaning of, 4
    on number line, 10–16, 25–26
    number sentences, 18–19
    regrouping in, 80–91, 103–104
Checking
    addition, 50–54
    subtraction, 120–125
Circle, 204–206
Counting, 2–4
Difference, 111–112
Dollar, 35
Dozen, 42
Graph, 300–306
    bar, 303–306
    picture, 300–303

"It's called the *index*," Tommy replied, as he located the page.

"Right, Tommy," said Ms. Rand. "The index is a part of the book that can help you find information that you need to locate in the book. It lists the topics in the book in alphabetical order, and after the topic it has the pages on which the topic is discussed in the book. For example, in your index, information about graphs is found on pages 300 through 306. The dash shows that all the pages in between 300 and 306 are about graphs too. If it had been written this way—(*She writes on chalkboard.*) 300, 306—that would mean the information would just be on those two pages. Who can tell me which pages talk about circles?"

"Pages 204 and 206," Tamara said.

"What about page 205?" asked Ms. Rand.

Ramon broke in: "It is about circles, too. You said the dash meant all of the pages between the ones listed."

"Oh, yeah," agreed Tamara, "205 is part of it, too."

"Very good," Ms. Rand replied. "Now look under the listing for Graph, and notice that there are some words indented there. These are types of graphs, and the particular types are listed with their own page numbers. When there is a list of indented terms under the main term, those terms are related to the main term, but they are there to help you find more specific topics. If I wanted to find out about bar graphs, I could look on pages 303 through 306. I wouldn't have to look at the other pages about graphs, because bar graphs wouldn't be discussed there. What if I wanted to read about picture graphs?"

"You would read pages 300 through 303," Penny replied.

"Right! And what if I wanted to find out about regrouping in addition?" Ms. Rand asked.

"Pages 80 through 104," said Morgan.

"All of them?" asked Ms. Rand.

"Well, there are dashes," Morgan replied.

"What else do you see besides the dashes?" Ms. Rand asked.

"There is a comma between the 91 and the 103," Morgan reported.

"What do you think that tells you?" Ms. Rand asked.

"I guess that 92 through 102 don't have anything about regrouping on them," Morgan answered hesitantly.

"Good thinking," Ms. Rand replied. "You are getting that punctuation figured out."

Then she told the class, "Now get in your math work groups and see if you can answer the questions on this sheet about the index in your math text."

The sheet contained the following questions:

1. On what pages would you look to find out how to check addition problems? Under what main topics and subheadings do you have to look to discover these page numbers?

2. On what page will you find *dollar* mentioned?

3. On what pages would you look to find out how to add using a number line? What main heading did you look under to discover this? What subheading did you look under?

4. Is there information about addition on a number line on pages 10 and 16? Is information about this topic on any other pages?

After the small groups had all reached agreement on the answers, the whole class discussed the items to ensure that everyone had been successful in understanding the process.

At the end of the lesson, Ms. Rand said, "Find the meaning of *addition* and read it to me."

Mark did so.

"Did you look in the index to find the page number?" she asked.

"Yes, I did," Mark said proudly.

"Do you think you found it more quickly by looking in the index than you would have by turning through the book to find it?"

"Yes," Mark replied.

"When you need to look things up in your textbooks, remember that the index can be helpful to you," Ms. Rand reminded the group as the lesson ended.

In using an index, thinking skills become important when the word being sought is not listed. Readers must then think of synonyms for the word or another form of the word that might be listed. Brainstorming possibilities for alternative listings for a variety of terms could be a helpful class activity to prepare students to be flexible when such situations occur.

Appendices

Students can also be shown that the appendices of books contain supplementary information that may be helpful to them, for example, bibliographies or tabular material. There are times when children need to use this material, but they will not be likely to use it if they do not know where to find it.

Glossaries

Primary-grade children can be shown that glossaries, which are often included in their textbooks, are similar to dictionaries but include only the words presented in the book in which they are found. Textbooks often contain glossaries of technical terms that can greatly aid students in understanding the book's content. The skills necessary for proper use of a glossary are the same as those needed for using a dictionary. (See Chapters 3 and 4 for discussions of dictionary use.)

Footnotes and Bibliographies

Footnotes and bibliographies refer students to other sources of information about the subject being discussed in a book, and teachers should encourage students to turn to these sources for clarification, for additional information on a topic for a report, or simply for their own satisfaction.

The bibliography, which appears at the end of a chapter or at the end of the entire textbook, is generally a list of references that the author consulted when researching the subject or that contain additional information. In some cases, bibliographies list books by a particular author or appropriate selections for particular groups.

Reference Books

Elementary school children often need to find information in such reference books as encyclopedias, dictionaries, almanacs, and atlases. Unfortunately, many students reach high school still unable to use such aids effectively. Though some skills related to the use of reference books can be taught in the primary grades (for example, use of picture dictionaries), the bulk of the responsibility for teaching use of reference books rests with the intermediate-grade teacher.

Important skills for effective use of reference books include the following:

General
1. Knowledge of alphabetical order and understanding that encyclopedias, dictionaries, and some atlases are arranged in alphabetical order

2. Ability to use guide words, knowledge of their location on a page, and understanding that they represent the first and last entry words on a dictionary or encyclopedia page

3. Ability to determine key words under which related information can be found.

Encyclopedias
1. Ability to use cross-references

2. Ability to determine which volume of a set of encyclopedias will contain the information needed

Dictionaries
1. Ability to use pronunciation keys

2. Ability to choose from several possible word meanings the one that most closely fits the context in which a word is found

Atlases
1. Ability to interpret the legend of a map

2. Ability to interpret the scale of a map

3. Ability to locate directions on maps

Because encyclopedias, almanacs, and atlases are often written at much higher readability levels than other materials used in the classroom, teachers must use caution when assigning work in these reference books. Children are not likely to profit from looking up material in books that are too hard for them to read; when asked to do so, they tend to copy the material word for word without trying to understand it.

However, teachers should keep in mind the difference between *assigning* students to use a particular reference work and letting the students *choose* to use any work that interests them. Readers can handle much more difficult levels of high-interest material than of low-interest material. Therefore, a student who is intensely interested in the subject matter of an encyclopedia article may be able to glean much information from it, even if his or her usual reading level for school materials is lower. For this reason, teachers should never forbid students to try to use material that *may be* too difficult for them. They should, however, avoid *forcing* students to struggle with material that is clearly beyond their range of understanding.

Many skills related to the use of an atlas are included in the section on map reading in this chapter. Some factors related to dictionary and encyclopedia use are discussed in the following sections.

Dictionaries

Before a child can use a dictionary for any of its major functions, he or she must be able to locate a designated word with some ease. Three important skills are necessary to do this: using alphabetical order, using guide words, and locating variants and derivatives.

Using Alphabetical Order.   Since the words in a dictionary are arranged in alphabetical order, children must learn to use alphabetical order to find the words they seek. Beginning with the first letter of the word, they gradually learn alphabetization by the first two or three letters, discovering that sometimes it is necessary to work through every letter in a word in the process.

The following Model Activities provide three ideas for developing and strengthening students' knowledge of alphabetical order.

Model Activities

Alphabetical Game

Talk about the fact that at school and in other situations, people are often lined up or seated according to alphabetical order, based on their names. Discuss the advantages of being able to locate easily their positions in such an arrangement. Then divide the class into two teams and line players up in alphabetical order by name. In the first round of the game, have students take turns answering when you call a letter of the alphabet by responding with the next letter of the alphabet. Give the player's team a point for a correct answer, and deduct a point for an incorrect answer. After an incorrect answer, give the other team an opportunity to answer correctly on the same letter. In the second round, the team member must answer with the preceding letter of the alphabet; in the third round, he or she must give the two letters that immediately precede and follow the letter you call. The same activity can be carried out in class without using teams.

Model Activities

Alphabetical Order

On the front side of each of twelve file cards, write the words in the following list. On the reverse side, write the letters. Make an answer key and place it in an envelope marked "Answer Key." Set the cards up at a learning center. Tape the answer key envelope to one side of the center. Have the children follow the directions given after the list below. (As you can see, this message is a seasonal one, but the activity can be redesigned for any number of cards with whatever message you choose.)

1.	able—H	7.	noticeable—E
2.	accept—A	8.	noticed—W
3.	apple—P	9.	powerful—Y
4.	heart—P	10.	puppy—E
5.	height—Y	11.	steak—A
6.	monster—N	12.	streak—R

Directions: Place the words printed on the file cards in alphabetical order. When you have done so, arrange the cards on your desk in left-to-right order, with card 1 displaying the word that comes first in the alphabet. Place them as shown here.

Order for Cards

1 2 3 4 5

6 7 8

9 10 11 12

Now turn the cards over. If you have alphabetized the cards correctly, they will spell out a message for you. If you do not find a message on the backs of the cards, turn the cards over and study them carefully to see which ones are not in alphabetical order. Rearrange the cards correctly and look for the message again. Look for the correct arrangement in the answer key, if you find yourself unable to work this puzzle correctly.

**Model
Activities**

Alphabetizing for a Picture Dictionary

Have first graders who are studying a science or social studies topic make a picture dictionary of words related to the topic that they encounter. For example, if the class is studying animals in science, the children might construct a picture dictionary that includes *bears, deer, lions, tigers, elephants,* and so on. The teacher can list each animal that enters the study on the board, and a child can find a picture of the animal, write the word on a page for the picture dictionary, and illustrate the page. The students can also write or dictate a factual statement about each animal. After a number of pages have been constructed, a small group of students can alphabetize them and place them in a looseleaf notebook. As more animals are studied, pages can be added for each one, constructed by one child and alphabetized in the class picture dictionary by another one. Of course, throughout the study, all students can use the picture dictionary for spelling help or just to browse.

Using Guide Words.   Children need to learn that the guide words at the top of a dictionary page tell them the first and last words on that page. If they are proficient in using alphabetical order, they should be able to decide whether or not a word will be found on a certain page by checking to see if the word falls alphabetically between the two guide words.

Following are some suggested activities for students' work with guide words in the dictionary.

Activities

1. If each child has a copy of the same dictionary, use that dictionary for this activity; otherwise, use the glossary in the back of a textbook. Tell the children to turn to a certain page and read the guide words. Then ask them to locate the first guide word where it appears as an entry word on the page and tell where it is found. Follow the same procedure with the second guide word. Direct the students to repeat this activity with a number of pages. Then ask them to explain what guide words tell dictionary users.

2. Write two guide words on the board. Have each child write as many words as possible that would be found on a dictionary page with those guide words. Set a time limit. The child with the most correct words can be declared the winner, but this doesn't have to be a competitive activity.

Here is another suggestion for practice with guide words.

Model Activities

Guide Words

Divide the group into two or more teams. Write the word pair *BRACE—BUBBLE* on the chalkboard or a chart. Ask the children to pretend that these words are the guide words for a page of the dictionary. Explain that you would expect the word *brick* to be on this page because *bri* comes after *bra* and *r* comes before *u*. Then write words, one at a time, from the following list on the board below the word pair. Let each team in turn tell you if the word would be found on the page with the designated guide words. Ask them to tell why they answered as they did. The team gets a point if the members can answer the questions correctly. The next team gets a chance to answer if they cannot. The reason for the answer is the most important part of the response.

1. beaker	11. bring
2. boil	12. brother
3. break	13. broke
4. braid	14. bracelet
5. bud	15. bunny
6. buy	16. bribe
7. brave	17. branch
8. border	18. bridge
9. bypass	19. brake
10. brag	20. barber

Variation: Write four guide words and the two dictionary pages on which they appear on the chalkboard or a chart. For example, you could write

Page 300 *RAINBOW—RAPID*

Page 301 *RAPPORT—RAVEN*

Write the words from the following list below the two sets of guide words, one at a time. Ask each team in turn to indicate on which page the displayed word would be found, or if the word would be found on neither page. Have them tell why they answered as they did. (Of course, you would model the decision-making process for them, as described earlier, before the activity starts.) If the team answers the questions about a word correctly, it is awarded a point. If the team answers incorrectly, the next team gets a chance to answer.

1. rare	8. ratio
2. ramble	9. range
3. ranch	10. raw
4. rabbit	11. rank
5. rash	12. raincoat
6. razor	13. race
7. rave	14. raise

Locating Variants and Derivatives.   Variants and derivatives are sometimes entered alphabetically in a dictionary, but more often they are either not listed or are listed in conjunction with their root words. If they are not listed, the reader must find the pronunciation of the root word and combine the sounds of the added parts with that pronunciation. This procedure requires advanced skills in word analysis and blending.

Here are two ideas for exercises in locating variants and derivatives in the dictionary.

Determining the Correct Entry Word

Model Activities

As the students are reading a story that contains many words with affixes, call their attention to the affixed words as they occur in the text. Tell the students that, if they wanted to look up the words in the dictionary, they might not be able to find them listed separately. These words have prefixes, suffixes, and inflectional endings added to root words, so students might need to locate their root words to find them. Choose one word from the text, perhaps *happily*. Point to the word, and say: "I recognize the -*ly* ending here. The rest of the word is almost like *happy*. The *y* was changed to *i* when the ending was added. So the root word is *happy*." Repeat this procedure for one or two other words from the text.

Later, as a follow-up activity, write on the board the list of words presented below. Then, for each word, ask the students to find the root word and tell about the other word parts that made the root word hard to find. They may also discuss the spelling changes made in the root word when endings were added.

1. directness
2. commonly
3. earliness
4. opposed
5. undeniable
6. gnarled
7. customs
8. cuter
9. joyfully
10. computable
11. comradeship
12. concentrating

Locating Variants and Derivatives

Model Activities

Have the students, working in small cooperative groups, make lists of words with prefixes, suffixes, and/or inflectional endings from a book they have been reading. When they have assembled their lists, see that each student has a dictionary. Have the group leader give a signal to the group members to begin looking up the words. The first one to locate each target word gives the group a predetermined signal that he or she has found the word. The other group members stop searching, leaving their fingers in their dictionaries in case the signaler was in error. The signaler reads the entry word under which the word was found and shares the meaning of the entry word and the affixed word. The group rules on the accuracy of the finding. If the signaler was incorrect, the leader tells the group to continue the search. If the signaler was correct, the leader starts the search for another word. If a variant is not listed, the group decides together what the base word probably is and then asks for verification from the teacher, presenting the reasons for the decision. The teacher may wish to circulate among the groups and give individual assistance to children who are having difficulty.

Some dictionaries are available on computer diskettes or compact disk, read-only memory format (CD-ROM). The *Random House Webster's School & Office Dictionary* (WordPerfect Main Street), available on diskette, provides definitions, spellings, pronunciations, and idioms. It even allows the user to find words through their definitions: "By looking up *flock* AND *geese*, for example, the dictionary will return the word *gaggle*" (Johnson, 1994, p. 22). The *Macmillan Dictionary for Children* (Simon & Schuster Interactive) is available on CD-ROM and features interactive multimedia. It is appropriate for children ages six to twelve. Users can hear words pronounced when they click on them with the mouse; they can hear 400 sound effects related to the words; and they can play three word games. There are color illustrations for many words, in addition to the standard definitions, sentences using the words, syllabic breakdowns, spellings, pronunciations, and plural forms (Johnson, 1994). The *American Heritage Dictionary of the English Language,* Third Edition, is also available on CD-ROM with an extensive illustration program (Houghton Mifflin 1994). Other aspects of dictionary use are discussed in Chapters 3 and 4.

Encyclopedia Use

Since encyclopedias vary in content and arrangement, students should be exposed to several different sets. Besides asking them to compare encyclopedias on an overall basis, noting such things as type of index used, number of volumes, and publication date, teachers should have them compare the entries on a specified list of topics. The Model Activity on page 446 can provide children with instruction and practice in the use of the encyclopedia as they work on a thematic unit on the Revolutionary War.

thematic learning

Encyclopedia articles are often very difficult for many intermediate-grade readers to comprehend. This difficulty makes putting the information they find into their own words harder. Yonan (1982) suggests using a topic with a low difficulty level and high interest for first attempts at encyclopedia reports. Then the teacher can have the students take a viewpoint that makes word-for-word copying hard. For example, they can take the viewpoint of an animal they are researching and write in the first person. The students and teacher can construct a list of things the students should look for about their topics, and the students can list what they already know about each category of information. Next, the children can read the captions for the graphic aids in the encyclopedia article to gather information. Then they can skim the written material to gather main ideas. Finally, they should read the material carefully and put it into their own words. They should be encouraged to choose interesting facts for their reports and to consult other sources to check their facts and obtain additional ideas.

Electronic encyclopedias have become widely available and are located in some school settings. These encyclopedias are available in a compact disk, read-only memory (CD-ROM) format that is accessed by a computer. Some of these encyclopedias have text, pictures, sound, and animation. They can be searched through use of key words and phrases, alphabetical title searches, and topical searches. They are motivational and easy to use (Rickelman et al., 1991). Four currently available encyclopedias are *My First Encyclopedia* (Knowledge Adventure), recommended for ages three to six; *Random House Kid's Encyclopedia* (Knowledge Adventure), recommended for ages seven to twelve; *Compton's*

Model Activities

Encyclopedia Skills

Have students find the correct volume for each of the following topics, without opening the volume:

Revolutionary War

George Washington

Declaration of Independence

Muskets

British Parliament

Battle of Bunker Hill

Have them check their choices by actually looking up the terms. If they fail to find a term in the volume where they expected to find it, ask them to think of other places to look. Let them check these possibilities also. Continue the process until each term has been located. Here is a possible dialogue between teacher and student:

Teacher: In which volume of the encyclopedia would you find a discussion of George Washington?

Student: In Volume 23.

Teacher: Why did you choose Volume 23?

Student: Because *W* is in Volume 23.

Teacher: Why didn't you choose Volume 7 for the Gs?

Student: Because people are listed under their last names.

Teacher: Look up the term and check to see if your decision was correct.

Student: It was. I found "George Washington" on page 58.

Teacher: Very good. Now tell me where you would find a description of the Battle of Bunker Hill.

Student: In Volume 2 under "Battle."

Teacher: Check your decision by looking it up.

Student: It's not here. It must be under "Bunker."

Teacher: Good idea.

Student: Here it is. It's under "Bunker Hill, Battle of."

Interactive Encyclopedia (Compton's NewMedia), recommended for fifth graders to adults, and the *Encarta*, which is written for ages nine to fifteen. These encyclopedias require equipment that is expensive enough to be unavailable in many individual classrooms, but schools should be able to provide them in the library or media center (Wepner, Seminoff, and Blanchard, 1995; Krushenisky, 1993; Melnick, 1991).

Other Reference Materials

thematic learning

Children are often asked to use materials other than books, such as newspapers, magazines, catalogues, transportation schedules, and pamphlets and brochures, as reference sources. For a thematic unit on pollution, for example, students might search through newspapers, magazines, and government pamphlets for stories and information about pollution and groups that are trying to do some-

literature-centered reading

thing about it, in addition to using trade books related to this problem. Similarly, a class studying Alaska might look in the newspaper to find out about the current weather in Alaska; in encyclopedias for information about weather patterns, clothing worn in different areas and/or seasons, geographical data, and points of interest; in travel brochures for methods of transportation to and within the state and prices for such transportation from various locations; in airline brochures for travel schedules; in magazines for feature stories about Alaska; and in catalogues to locate appropriate clothing for a trip to a particular part of Alaska in a certain

literature-centered reading

month. All of these sources would supplement information gathered from non-fiction and fiction trade books about Alaska. To benefit fully from such information, students must be able to use these varying reference sources effectively.

To help youngsters learn to locate information in newspapers, teachers can alert them to the function of headlines and teach them how to use the newspaper's index. Teachers also should devote some class time to explaining journalistic terms, which can help children better understand the material in the newspaper, and to explaining the functions of news stories, editorials, columns,

thematic learning

and feature stories. Some of this instruction could actually be a part of a thematic unit on the newspaper. Children are often fascinated by the procedures involved in publishing a newspaper and the techniques used to design and produce a good newspaper. Activities such as the following would be appropriate.

Activities

1. During class discussion, explain the meanings of any of the following terms and abbreviations with which the children are not familiar: *AP, byline, dateline, editorial.*

2. Use activities found in Chapters 6 and 10 concerning types of stories, columns, features, and advertisements in the newspaper.

3. Develop activities similar to the Model Activity on page 448, on using the newspaper's index. Always model the skill to be practiced before expecting the students to perform it independently. Whenever possible, use real newspapers as a basis for activities similar to the one shown.

thematic learning

Other instruction could take place as an integral part of other units being used in the classroom. For example, before the students search the newspaper for information on pollution for the unit mentioned earlier, the teacher could introduce activities related to developing the concept of *main idea* (see Chapter 6) to sensitize youngsters to the function of headlines. This could help make their newspaper searches more efficient and meaningful.

In helping children to obtain information from magazines, teachers can call attention to the table of contents and give the children practice in using it, just as they do with textbooks. Distinguishing between informational and fictional materials is important in reading magazines, as is analyzing advertisements to detect propaganda. Chapter 6 contains activities related to these critical reading skills.

Model Activities

Using a Newspaper's Index

Hand out copies of the following newspaper index, or write the example on the board or a chart.

Index

Classified Ads	B-5-10
Comics	B-11-12
Crossword	B-11
Editorials	A-2-3
Entertainment	B-3-4
Finance	A-4-7
Horoscope	A-8
Humor columns	A-8-9
Obituaries	A-11

Have a class discussion based on the following questions:

1. Where in the newspaper would you find information about the stock market? Why would you look there?

2. In what section would you look to find a movie that you would like to see or to find the television schedule? How did you know to look there?

3. On what page is the crossword puzzle found? How did you know?

4. How many pages have comics on them? How did you know?

5. Where would you look to find out which people have died recently? How did you know to look there?

To obtain information from catalogues, children again need to be able to use indexes. Activities suggested in this chapter for using indexes in newspapers and textbooks can be profitably used here also. The ability to read charts giving information about sizes and about shipping and handling charges may also be important in reading catalogues. Teachers can use activities like the Model Activity on *thematic learning* page 449 to provide students with practice in reading charts in catalogues. This could be used in connection with the unit on Alaska mentioned earlier, in which the children may be figuring how much it would cost them to outfit themselves for the trip.

A variety of transportation schedules, pamphlets, and brochures may be used as reference sources in social studies activities. Since their formats may vary greatly, teachers will need to provide practice in reading the specific materials they intend to use in their classes.

Libraries and Media Centers

For whole language and literature-based classrooms, as well as for more traditional ones, school libraries or media centers are key locations. Teachers and librarians/media specialists should work together as teams to develop the skills that students need to use libraries effectively. (The librarian/media specialist will

Model Activities

Reading Charts in Catalogues

Hand out a copy of the following chart, or display it on the board. This chart describes shipping and handling charges assessed by one company.

Shipping and Handling Charges

If your order is:

up to $6.99, add $.90

$7.00 to $10.99, add $1.30

$11.00 to $14.99, add $1.70

$15.00 to $18.99, add $2.10

Use the following questions to lead a discussion of reading the chart. Model your thinking in answering the first question before you ask the children to answer the others and tell how they obtained their answers.

1. Your order comes to $8.70. What are the shipping and handling charges? For what amount should you write your check?_____

2. Your order comes to $14.99. What are the shipping and handling charges?_____

3. Your order is only $.90. What are the shipping and handling charges?_____

hereafter be referred to as *librarian* for the sake of easy reference, but the expanded role this person plays in dealing with multimedia should be kept in mind.)

Librarians can be helpful in many ways. They can show students the locations of books and journals, card catalogs, and reference materials (such as dictionaries, encyclopedias, atlases, and the *Reader's Guide to Periodical Literature*) in the library; explain the procedures for checking books in and out; and describe the rules and regulations regarding behavior in the library. Demonstrations of the use of the card catalog and the *Readers' Guide* and explanations of the arrangement of books under the Dewey Decimal System, which is the system most often used in elementary school libraries, are also worthwhile. Prominently displayed posters can remind children to observe check-out procedures and library rules. Currently, librarians are more frequently using library periods, not only to help children locate and select books, but also to share literature with them (Walmsley, 1992).

Librarians may also introduce students to book reviews that can guide them in their selection of materials. The children can also be guided to write reviews that they can share with other students (Jenks and Roberts, 1990).

By familiarizing children with reasons for using the library and explaining to them why they may need to use such aids as manual and computerized card catalogs, the Dewey Decimal System, and the *Reader's Guide,* teachers can prepare students for a visit to the library. While they are still in the classroom, the children can learn that cards in the manual card catalog are arranged alphabetically and that the card catalog contains subject, author, and title cards. Sample cards of

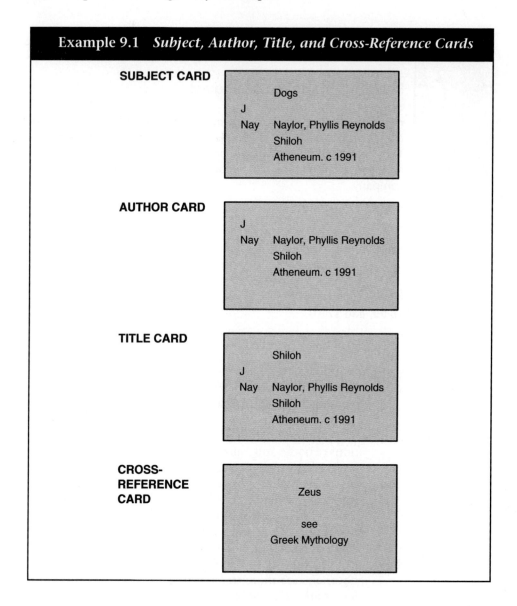

Example 9.1 *Subject, Author, Title, and Cross-Reference Cards*

SUBJECT CARD

	Dogs
J	
Nay	Naylor, Phyllis Reynolds
	Shiloh
	Atheneum. c 1991

AUTHOR CARD

J	
Nay	Naylor, Phyllis Reynolds
	Shiloh
	Atheneum. c 1991

TITLE CARD

	Shiloh
J	
Nay	Naylor, Phyllis Reynolds
	Shiloh
	Atheneum. c 1991

CROSS-REFERENCE CARD

Zeus

see

Greek Mythology

each type, similar to those shown in Example 9.1, can be drawn on posters and placed on the bulletin board. In addition, fifth and sixth graders will benefit from a lesson that explains the use of cross-reference cards (also shown in Example 9.1).

The teacher may want to construct a model of a card-catalog drawer and have the children practice using it. Children may enjoy constructing the three main types of cards for several books they have read and then alphabetizing these cards to make a miniature card catalog.

If the school has a computerized card catalog, students will be able to search for books by title, author, and subject, just as they do with the manual card catalog. They can choose the type of search they need, type in the key words necessary for the search, and view a list of the available books on the monitor. For example, in Example 9.2 the student chose an author search, then typed in *Cherry*. The author search, shown at the top of the example, showed three books written or illustrated by Lynne Cherry. The student chose number *2* from this list and received the full record display for *A River Ran Wild: An Environmental History*.

Here are two other suggestions for practice with library skills:

1. The teacher can send the children on a scavenger hunt that requires using the library by dividing the class into teams and giving the teams statements to complete or questions to answer. (Example: The author of *The Secret Garden* is _____ .)

2. The teacher can give students questions and ask them to show on a map of the library where they would go to find the answers (Muller and Savage, 1982).

Spiegel (1990) recommends *Looking It Up* (Fearon Teacher Aids, 1989) as a resource for teaching library skills to children in grades two through five. This reproducible workbook contains eight units on a variety of topics related to library skills. The Classroom Scenario on locating information shows how one class puts their research skills to work.

thematic learning

**Classroom
Scenario**

Locating Information

Students in a fifth-grade classroom are about to begin a study of World War II. They have formed into groups, each of which will research a different topic related to the war. One group is going to research transportation methods for troops.

When the children in Keith's group meet, Keith says, "First we need to know the different types of transportation that were used. I think we can find that in the encyclopedia under 'World War II.' Who would like to check that out?"

"I will," replies Elaine. "I'll look in all of the different encyclopedias and see if they all have the same information or if they have different stuff. That will help us when we divide up jobs later."

"Good," Keith says. "Then we can make a list of the types of transportation, and each one of us can look up one or two of them and get more details. We can use the dictionary for a basic definition and the encyclopedia for more details on the type of transportation we are looking for, like 'jeeps.' Where else will we get information?"

"We can check the card catalog," Tammy suggests. "The subject cards on 'World War II' and things like 'jeeps' would give us some leads."

"I have a book at home on airplanes," Randy says. "Some of them were from World War II. Can I draw some for our report?"

"Great!" Keith says. "We need some visuals for our report, and you are better at drawing than the rest of us. We'll want some drawings of those planes and tanks and probably some other stuff. We'll all be on the lookout for examples that you can use for models. I'll also ask my Great Uncle Joe about it. He was in the Army in World War II."

Analysis of Scenario

These students have received instruction that made them aware of places to find information for class studies, and they are putting that information to use as they work in their research group. Randy does not have ideas about where to find things in the library, but he recognizes that he has a valuable personal resource and offers it for the study. The children have been taught that there are sources of information other than school materials, and they freely plan to use personal books and even primary sources.

literature-centered reading

reading-writing connection

The librarian is an important ally for the teacher as thematic units are planned, for no unit will be successful if the needed reading materials are not available in a reasonable supply. Both books and other media are needed for these units, and the books need to be on a variety of levels. The librarian is also a valuable helper as children search the library for this related material as the unit progresses. Librarians have useful input for teachers and students alike about books that are good for reading aloud, for sustained silent reading, and for reference sources. Cooperative planning between teachers and librarians can ensure that what goes on in the library and in the classroom are connected (Lamme and Ledbetter, 1990; Hughes, 1993). Schools in which a whole language philosophy is embraced have children moving in and out of the library all the time. The library is used as "an extension of the classroom" (Hughes, 1993, p. 294). Children use the library to find books, to read, to write and to interact with classmates about books. Many use it to do research on questions they need to answer, and their research is specific and of personal interest. Children use location aids in books more adeptly and at an earlier age than they did before the advent of whole language instruction (Hughes, 1993).

Computer Databases

In today's schools, students need to be able to locate and retrieve information from computer *databases,* in addition to performing more traditional activities. "A database is an organized collection of information which can be electronically searched and sorted according to its various categories" (Layton and Irwin, 1989, p. 724). Each database is somewhat like a filing cabinet or several filing cabinets, with separate file folders for the different articles in the database. The information is categorized and indexed for easy retrieval. Users may create their own databases or use existing ones, such as *Fiction Finder* (ESSi), *BookBrain* (Oryx), or

Example 9.2 *Computerized Card Catalog Output*

| | Author Search | Thu Mar 16 6:00 PM |

1. Cherry, Lynne, Ill.   Item No.: 3ACPL000236885
   Chipmunk song/by Joanne Ryder; pictures by Lynne Cherry.
   Call Number: E RYD   Date: c1987   Type: BK

2. Cherry, Lynne.   Item No.: 5ACPL000005272
   A river ran wild: an environmental history/Lynne Cherry.
   Call Number: J 974.4 CHE   Date: c1992   Type: BK

3. Cherry, Lynne, Ill.   Item No.: 3ACPL000234724
   When I'm sleepy/by Jane R. Howard; illustrated by Lynne Cherry.
   Call Number: E HOW   Date: c1985   Type: BK

4. Cherry, Sheldon H.   Item No.: 12334
   Planning ahead for pregnancy: health, fitness, and fertility/Sheldon...
   Call Number: 618.24 C   Date: 1987   Type: BK

5. Cherryh, C. J.   Item No.: 7CANE000000471
   Chanur's legacy
   Call Number: F CHE   Date: Type: NEO

"*" – Indicates All Copies Are Out
Enter A Number For The Full Record Display

) Scroll Up/Down   F9) Help   Esc) End Search

TITLE:	A river ran wild: an environmental history/Lynne Cherry.
COPIES:	2 – 2 Available For Loan
CALL NUMBER:	J 974.4 CHE
SYSTEM NO.:	8054
AUTHOR:	Cherry, Lynne.
EDITION:	1st ed.
PLACE OF PUB:	San Diego:
PUBLISHER:	Harcourt Brace Jovanovich,
DATE OF PUB:	c1992
DESCRIPTION:	[34 p.]: col. ill., col. maps; 24 x 29 cm.
NOTES:	"A Gulliver Green book."
NOTES:	An environmental history of the Nashua River, from its discovery by Indians through the polluting years of the Industrial Revolution to the ambitious clean-up that revitalized it.
SUBJECT:	WATER QUALITY — NASHUA RIVER (MASS. AND N.H.) — HISTORY — JUVENILE LITERATURE.
SUBJECT:	MAN — INFLUENCE ON NATURE — NASHUA RIVER (MASS. AND N.H.) — HISTORY — JUVENILE LITERATURE.
SUBJECT:	INDIANS OF NORTH AMERICA — NASHUA RIVER (MASS. AND N.H.) — HISTORY — JUVENILE LITERATURE.
SUBJECT:	MAN — INFLUENCE ON NATURE.
SUBJECT:	NASHUA RIVER (MASS. AND N.H.) — HISTORY — JUVENILE LITERATURE
SUBJECT:	NASHUA RIVER VALLEY (MASS. AND N.H.) — HISTORY — JUVENILE LITERATURE.
SUBJECT:	NASHUA RIVER (MASS. AND N.H.) — HISTORY.
LC CARD NBR:	91–012892 /AC
ISBN:	0152005420 :
LOCATION:	ACL*
COPY NO.:	1–2

USA Profile (Active Learning Systems). Using databases, students pose questions, decide on key words to access the data, read, follow directions, collect and categorize data, summarize material, and make comparisons and contrasts (Layton and Irwin, 1989). The electronic encyclopedias discussed earlier are examples of databases that are available in some schools. In addition, many databases can be accessed through such online services as Telnet and Internet. For example, computer users can access LOCIS (Library of Congress Information System) through these two services ("Open to Suggestion," 1994).

Smith (1991) found that HyperCard allowed students to create large databases with text, attractive graphics, and pleasing controls. Smith's students made a "Fantastic Fiction" HyperCard stack on which they shared their reactions to books they had read. They also developed stacks recreating the Algonquin myth "Why the Lynx Has a Short Tail" and a stack about the causes, battles, and results of the War of 1812.

SELF-CHECK: OBJECTIVE 3 What special features of books can help students locate desired information? Describe each feature briefly.
Name several types of reference books and enumerate special skills needed to use each one.
Describe three types of cards used in a card catalog. (See Self-Improvement Opportunities 2, 3, and 4.)

Organizational Techniques

reading-writing connection When engaging in such activities as writing reports, elementary school students need to organize the ideas they encounter in their reading. Too often teachers at the elementary level give little attention to organizational techniques such as note taking, outlining, and summarizing, and too many students enter secondary school without knowing how to perform these tasks.

Note Taking

Teachers may present note-taking techniques in a functional setting when children are preparing written reports on materials they have read. Children should be taught

1. To include key words and phrases in their notes.

2. To include enough of the context to make the notes understandable after a period of time has elapsed.

3. To include a bibliographical reference (source) with each note.

4. To copy direct quotations exactly.

5. To indicate carefully which notes are direct quotations and which are reworded.

Key words—the words that carry the important information in a sentence—are generally nouns and verbs, but they may include important modifiers. Example 9.3 shows a sample paragraph and a possible set of notes based on this paragraph.

Example 9.3 *Sample Paragraph and Notes*

A restaurant is not as easy a business to run as it may appear to be to some people, since the problem of obtaining good help is ever-present. Cooks, dishwashers, and servers are necessary personnel. Cooks must be able to prepare the food offered by the restaurant. Dishwashers need to be dependable and thorough. Servers need to be able to carry out their duties politely and efficiently. Poorly prepared food, inadequately cleaned dishes, and rude help can be the downfall of a restaurant, so restaurant owners and managers must hire with care.

SAMPLE NOTE CARD

Problem for restaurant owner or manager — good help: good cooks; dependable, thorough dishwashers; polite, efficient servers. Hire with care.

After reading the paragraph shown in Example 9.3, the note taker first thinks, "What kind of information is given here?" The answer, "Problem for restaurant owner or manager—good help," is the first note. Then the note taker searches for key words to describe the kind of help needed. For example, cooks who "are able to prepare the food offered by the restaurant" can be described as "good cooks"—ten words condensed into two that carry the idea. In the case of the nouns *dishwasher* and *servers,* descriptive words related to them are added; condensation of phrases is not necessary (although the *and*s between the adjectives may be left out) because the key words needed are found directly in the selection. The last part of the paragraph can be summed up in the warning "Hire with care." It is easy to see that key-word notes carry the message of the passage in a very condensed or abbreviated form.

A teacher can go through an example like this one with the children, telling them what key words to choose and why, and then provide another example, letting the children decide as a group which key words to write down and having them give reasons for their choices. Finally, each child can do a selection individually. After completing the individual note taking, the children can compare their notes and discuss reasons for choices.

Students can take notes in outline form, in sentences, or in paragraphs. Beginners may even benefit from taking notes in the form of semantic webs or maps. (See Chapters 4, 5, and 10 for elaboration of these techniques.)

Example 9.4 shows several sample note cards.

Example 9.4 *Sample Note Cards*

1st REFERENCE FROM SOURCE

> Goertzen, Valerie Woodring. "Folk Music." *The World Book Encyclopedia*, 1994, VII, pp. 321-322.
>
> Folk songs are passed along from person to person and gradually change in form through the years.

SOURCE PREVIOUSLY USED

> Goertzen, p. 321.
>
> "Ballads have a stanza form, in which a melody is repeated for each of the verses. There may also be a refrain that is sung several times during the song."

INCOMPLETE SENTENCES

> Goertzen, pp. 321-322.
>
> Kinds of folk music: ballads, work songs, union songs, spirituals, dance songs, game songs, nonsense songs, American Indian "power" songs, call and response songs.

Outlining

Teachers can lead children to understand that outlining is writing down information from the material they read in a way that shows the relationships among the main ideas and the supporting details, although, of course, the children must already know how to recognize main ideas and details. Two types of outlines that are important for children to understand are the *sentence* outline, in which each point is a complete sentence, and the *topic* outline, which is composed of key words and phrases. Since choosing key words and phrases is in itself a difficult task for many youngsters, it is wise to present sentence outlines first.

The first step in forming an outline is to extract the main ideas from the material and to list these ideas beside Roman numerals in the order in which they occur. Supporting details are listed beside capital letters below the main idea they support and are slightly indented to indicate their subordination. Details that are subordinate to the main details designated by capital letters are indented still further and preceded by Arabic numerals. The next level of subordination is indicated by lower-case letters, although elementary students will rarely need to make an outline that goes beyond the level of Arabic numerals.

A model outline form like the one shown in Example 9.5 may help students understand how to write an outline in proper form.

Example 9.5 *Sample Outline*

TITLE
I. Main idea
  A. Detail supporting I
  B. Detail supporting I
    1. Detail supporting B
    2. Detail supporting B
      a. Detail supporting 2
      b. Detail supporting 2
    3. Detail supporting B
  C. Detail supporting I
II. Main idea
  A. Detail supporting II
  B. Detail supporting II
  C. Detail supporting II

The teacher can supply students with partially completed outlines of chapters in their content textbooks and ask them to fill in the missing parts, gradually leaving out more and more details until the students are doing the complete outline alone. To develop students' readiness for outlining, the teacher can use the Model Activity on page 458.

This activity can be used as a first step in teaching the concept of outlining to first and second graders. The next step might be to have the students make free-form outlines, or story webs, in which they use words, lines, and arrows to arrange key words and phrases from the story in a way that shows their relationships. Simple, very familiar stories allow children to concentrate on arranging the terms logically rather than on locating the details. Example 9.6 shows a web based on the familiar story "The Three Little Pigs." (See Chapter 5 for more information on webbing or mapping stories.)

Teacher modeling of web construction should come first. Then one or more story webs may be constructed cooperatively by the whole class. The teacher may need to provide the key words and phrases in early experiences with webbing. The children can then cooperatively develop webs in small groups with help from the teacher's probing questions about connecting lines, directions of arrows, and

Model Activities

Readiness for Outlining

1. Provide the children with a set of items to be categorized.

2. Ask them to place the items in categories. More than one arrangement may be possible; let them try several.

3. Provide the children with a blank outline form of this type:

4. Have the children fill in the outline.

Example:

a. Provide plastic animals: horse, cow, chicken, pig, elephant, lion, sea gull, rooster, tiger.

b. Give them time to categorize.

c. Provide this outline:

d. Possible solution:

Animals

Farm   Wild

Wings   No wings   Wings   No wings

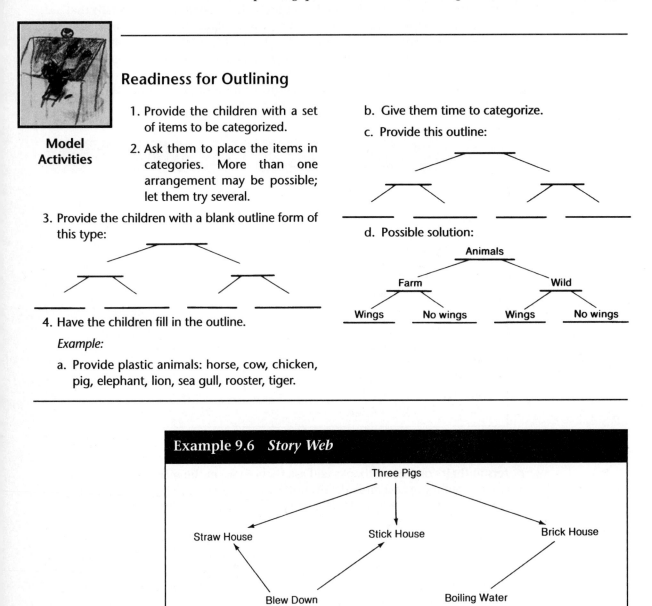

Example 9.6 *Story Web*

Three Pigs

Straw House   Stick House   Brick House

Blew Down   Boiling Water

Wolf

positions of phrases. The children may also ask the teacher questions about their decisions. As they develop proficiency with the task, the teacher can allow them to choose key words and phrases themselves, at first with assistance and then independently. After mastering this step, the children can move on to forming webs without assistance (Hansell, 1978).

Children can obtain outlining practice by outlining material the teacher has entered into a computer file. The children can move phrases and headings around with a word-processing program and create an outline in relatively painless fashion.

Summarizing

In a summary, a student is expected to restate what the author has said in a more concise form. Main ideas of a selection should be preserved, but illustrative material and statements that merely elaborate on the main idea should not be included.

Children should be led to see that, when making summaries, they should delete trivial and redundant material. Superordinate terms can be used to replace lists of similar items or actions (for example, *people* for *men, women, and children*). Steps in an action may be replaced by a superordinate action (*baked a cake* for *took flour, butter, . . . and then placed it in an oven*). Each paragraph can be represented with its topic sentence or implied main idea sentence (Brown and Day, 1983; Brown, Day, and Jones, 1983; Recht, 1984).

The teacher should model the deletion of nonessential material when constructing summaries and then should have students practice this activity under supervision. Choosing superordinate terms and actions and choosing or constructing topic sentences should also be modeled and practiced. Easy material should be used for beginning instruction, and paragraphs should be used before proceeding to longer passages (Recht, 1984).

One possible way the teacher can build children's experience with summarizing is to give them a long passage to read and three or four summaries of the passage. The teacher can let the students examine the summaries and decide which one is best and why each of the others was not satisfactory. The teacher can help in this exploration process by asking appropriate questions if the students appear confused about what to consider. For example, the teacher may ask, "Does this sentence tell something different, or is it just an example?" After the children have been successful in differentiating between the satisfactory and unsatisfactory summaries, the teacher can refer them to a passage in one of their textbooks, along with several possible summaries, and have them choose the best summary and tell why they did not choose each of the others.

In addition, the Model Activities on page 460 can provide practice with summarizing.

Valeri-Gold (1989, p. 53) suggests that the teacher show the children how a summary is like a mathematical problem. The equation would be "Summary =

Author's main point + Supporting details." This analogy may help some students remember what to include in their summaries.

SELF-CHECK: OBJECTIVE 4 Three types of organizational techniques have been discussed in this section. Name and explain the function of each.

Model Activities

Writing Headlines

Give the children copies of news stories without headlines, like the following one, and let them provide headlines that contain the main ideas of the stories.

Coopersville's pollution index has increased to a highly undesirable level this year. Chemists reveal that on a scale of 100, Coopersville's pollution is 95, compared to 75 for the average U.S. urban area. This report merely verifies what most residents of Coopersville have known for a long time— Coopersville exists under a cloud of smog.

Have the students compare and discuss their answers.

Model Activities

Single-Sentence Summaries

Have the children read a short passage like the following one and try to summarize its content in a single sentence.

Sometimes your hair makes a noise when you comb it. The noise is really made by static electricity. Static electricity collects in one place. Then it jumps to another place. Rub your feet on a rug. Now touch something. What happens? Static electricity collects on your body, but it can jump from your finger to other places. Sometimes you can see a spark and hear a noise.

Have students compare their answers and revise them as they discuss the merits of different answers.

Metacognition

Metacognitive strategies (strategies involving the ability to examine one's intellectual functioning) are important in reading for meaning and in reading for retention. Comprehension monitoring and taking steps to ensure comprehension when deficiencies are discovered are associated with reading for meaning. Students who monitor their comprehension and use fix-up strategies such as rereading, self-questioning, retelling, predicting and verifying, and reading further while withholding judgment are more likely to comprehend and retain the information read. Recognizing important ideas, checking mastery of the information read, and developing effective strategies for study are metacognitive techniques involved in reading for retention (Paris, Wasik, and Turner, 1991; Baumann, Jones, and Seifert-Kessell, 1993; Baker and Brown, 1984).

Metacognition involves knowing what is already known, knowing when understanding of new material has been accomplished, knowing how the understanding was reached, and knowing why something is or is not known. Children have shown some awareness of these aspects of learning (Guthrie, 1983).

Research indicates that comprehension monitoring is a developmental skill that is not fully developed until adolescence. Ann Brown and Sandra Smiley discovered that low-ability students did not always benefit from monitoring strategies. These strategies may be beneficial only if students possess the background and understanding to use them effectively. With attention to students' levels of maturity, however, aspects of comprehension monitoring can be taught. It is important for teachers to guide students toward actually using these strategies, rather than just teaching them *about* the strategies (Meir, 1984).

To help children develop metacognitive strategies, the teacher must convince them of the need to become active learners. Children need to learn to set goals for their reading tasks, to plan how they will meet their goals, to monitor their success in meeting their goals, and to remedy the situation when they do not meet their goals.

To plan ways to meet their goals, children need to know certain techniques, such as relating new information to their background knowledge, previewing material to be read, paraphrasing ideas presented, and identifying the organizational pattern or patterns of the text. Students should learn the value of periodically questioning themselves about the ideas in the material to see if they are meeting their goals (Babbs and Moe, 1983). They need to learn to ask if the information they have read makes sense. If it does not make sense, they need to learn to ask why it does not make sense. They should decide if they have a problem with decoding a word, understanding what a word means, understanding what a sentence is saying, understanding how a sentence relates to the rest of the passage, or grasping the focus or purpose of the passage (Wilson, 1983). If they have not met their goals because they did not recognize certain words, they need to use context clues, structural analysis, phonics, and possibly the dictionary. If word meaning is the problem, they can again use any of these techniques (except phonics). If sentence structure or sentence relationships are the problem, they can try identifying key words, breaking down sentences into separate meaning units, locating antecedents for pronouns, and other such techniques.

Teachers should teach specific strategies for students to use when they do not comprehend material. Moderately difficult material should be used for this instruction so that they will have some actual comprehension problems to confront, although it should not be too difficult to be useful. Teachers should present background information before the children read, so that they have the information needed to apply comprehension strategies. Teachers need to encourage children to make guesses in their efforts to comprehend the text (Fitzgerald, 1983).

The teacher can model strategies for monitoring comprehension by reading a passage aloud and "thinking aloud" about his or her own monitoring behaviors and hypotheses. Noting things that are currently known and unknown and modifying these notes as more information is added can be helpful. Students should be drawn into the process in subsequent lessons by using the "think-aloud" strategy. Eventually they need to apply the monitoring strategy independently (Fitzgerald, 1983). "Think alouds require a reader to stop periodically, reflect on how a text is being processed and understood, and relate orally what reading strategies are being employed" (Baumann, Jones, and Seifert-Kessell, 1993, p. 185). Teacher modeling and student practice of think-alouds can help students learn metacognitive strategies. Students have to be told what each strategy is and why it is important. Then modeling by the teacher through think-alouds and guided and independent practice by the students are needed (Baumann, Jones, and Seifert-Kessell, 1993).

Teachers can ask students to read difficult passages and then ask questions about them. The children write their answers and indicate their degree of confidence in the answers. Incorrect answers should have low confidence ratings and correct answers should have high ratings in order to indicate good comprehension monitoring (Fitzgerald, 1983).

Blachowicz and Zabroske (1990) suggest a metacognitive approach to developing context-use strategies for middle school at-risk readers. Its three components are letting students know *why* and *when* to use context through modeling, giving students an idea of what kinds of clues the context may provide by having teachers and students work together to build inductively a list of types of context clues found in materials, and giving students a strategy for locating and using the clues. The students were told to look at the target word and at the words before and after it; to connect what they knew with what the author said; to predict the possible meaning of the material; and to decide whether they understood, needed to try again, or needed to consult an expert or reference.

Miholic (1994) has developed an inventory to encourage students to think about what they do as they read. The results of such an inventory also provide teachers with insights into students' strategy use.

More information on metacognition appears in Chapter 5.

SELF-CHECK: OBJECTIVE 5   What can teachers do to help children develop metacognitive skills?

Graphic Aids

Textbooks contain numerous reading aids that children often disregard because they have had no training in how to use them. We have already discussed glossaries, footnotes, bibliographies, and appendices in this chapter, but we also need to consider graphic aids such as maps, graphs, tables, and illustrations.

Fry (1981) believes that teachers should give more attention to the development of graphical literacy—the ability to read maps, graphs, pictures, and diagrams. Teachers should explain how these aids function, model their use for the students, and provide students with supervised practice in extracting information from them. Actually making graphic aids is also a good technique to help students develop their communication abilities.

Maps

Many maps appear in social studies textbooks, and they are also sometimes found in science, mathematics, and literature books. As early as the first grade, children can begin developing skills in map reading, which they will use increasingly as they progress through school and maps appear with greater frequency in reading materials. If they do not comprehend the maps, children will find it more difficult to understand the concepts presented in narrative material.

A first step in map reading is to examine the title (for example, "Annual Rainfall in the United States") to determine what area is being represented and what type of information is being given about the area. The teacher should emphasize the importance of determining the information conveyed by the title before moving on to a more detailed study of the map. The next step is to teach children how to determine directions. By helping them to locate directional indicators on maps and to use these indicators to identify the four cardinal directions, the teacher makes children aware that north is not always at the top nor south at the bottom of a map, although many maps are constructed in this manner.

Interpreting the map's *legend* is the next reading task. The legend contains an explanation of each symbol used on the map, and, unless a reader can interpret these symbols, he or she will be unable to understand the information the map contains.

Learning to apply a map's *scale* is fairly difficult. Because it would be highly impractical to draw a map to the actual size of the area represented (for instance, the United States), maps show areas greatly reduced in size. The scale shows the relationship of a given distance on the map to the same distance on the earth.

Upper-elementary school students can be helped to understand about latitude and longitude, the Tropic of Cancer and the Tropic of Capricorn, the north and south poles, and the equator. Students should also become acquainted with map terms such as *hemisphere, peninsula, continent, isthmus, gulf, bay,* and many others.

Each time children look at a map of an area, the teacher should encourage them to relate it to a map of a larger area—for example, to relate a map of Tennessee to a map of the United States. This points out the position of Tennessee within the entire United States.

Thematic maps show the distribution of a particular phenomenon over a specific geographic area. They include maps that focus on weather, land elevation, population distribution, or political boundaries, for example. Each of these types of maps needs special instructional attention if students are to benefit sufficiently from reading them. Students also need practice thinking critically about the information that maps can provide (Mosenthal and Kirsch, 1990). For example, the teacher may provide students with a map of the United States in the early 1800s that shows waterways, bodies of water, and population distributions and ask the students to draw conclusions about the population distributions. The effect of the bodies of water should be evident to the children.

Some suggestions for teaching map-reading skills follow. These skills are best taught when the students need to read maps for a purpose in one or more of their classes. Map skills should be immediately applied to these authentic materials after instruction takes place.

Activities

1. In teaching children about directions on maps, give them pictures of directional indicators that are tilted in various ways, with north indicated on each one. Model the location of other directions, based on the knowledge of where north is, for one of the indicators. Then let the students fill in *S, E,* and *W* (for *south, east,* and *west*) on each of the other indicators.

2. To teach children to apply a map's scale, help them construct a map of their classroom to a specified scale. Provide step-by-step guidance.

3. Model the use of a map's legend. Then have the children practice using the map's legend by asking them questions such as the following:
   Where is there a railroad on this map?
   Where is the state capital located?
   Where do you see a symbol for a college?
   Are there any national monuments in this area? If so, where are they?

4. Let the children show that they understand terms such as *gulf* and *peninsula* by locating these features on a map.

5. Give the children a map of their county or city, and let them locate their homes on the map.

6. Use the MAP (Make-A-Place) activity, originated by L. B. James, to develop map-reading skills (Hayes, 1992). In it, each student draws a map of an imaginary place. As this task proceeds, students find out names for the earth's surface features, discover how the earth's surface features are represented on maps, and learn the important features of maps, such as directional indicators and legends. They also learn how these features affect land use and cultural development.

7. Give the children maps such as the one presented in Example 9.7, and have them answer questions about them.

Example 9.7 *Sample Map and Questions: Number of American Indians by Counties of the U.S., 1970*

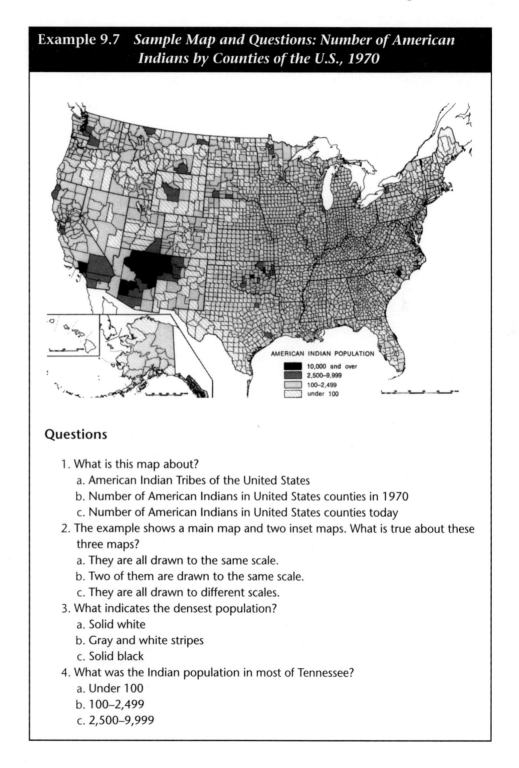

AMERICAN INDIAN POPULATION

- 10,000 and over
- 2,500–9,999
- 100–2,499
- under 100

Questions

1. What is this map about?
   a. American Indian Tribes of the United States
   b. Number of American Indians in United States counties in 1970
   c. Number of American Indians in United States counties today
2. The example shows a main map and two inset maps. What is true about these three maps?
   a. They are all drawn to the same scale.
   b. Two of them are drawn to the same scale.
   c. They are all drawn to different scales.
3. What indicates the densest population?
   a. Solid white
   b. Gray and white stripes
   c. Solid black
4. What was the Indian population in most of Tennessee?
   a. Under 100
   b. 100–2,499
   c. 2,500–9,999

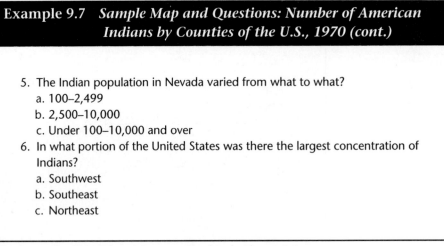

Map Source: Rand McNally and Company. Reprinted with permission.

Graphs

Graphs often appear in social studies, science, and mathematics books to clarify written explanations. Four basic types of graphs are described as follows and illustrated in Example 9.8.

1. *Picture* graphs express quantities through pictures.

2. *Circle* or *pie* graphs show relationships of individual parts to the whole.

3. *Bar* graphs use vertical or horizontal bars to compare quantities. (Vertical bar graphs are easier to read than horizontal ones.)

4. *Line* graphs show changes in amounts.

Students can learn to discover from the graph's title what comparison is being made or information is being given (for example, time spent in various activities during the day or populations of various counties in a state), to interpret the legend of a picture graph, and to derive needed information accurately from a graph.

One of the best ways to help children learn to read graphs is to have them construct meaningful graphs (Hadaway and Young, 1994). Following are some examples of graph construction activities:

1. A picture graph showing the number of festival tickets sold by each class. One picture of a ticket could equal five tickets.

2. A circle graph showing the percentage of each day that a child spends sleeping, eating, studying, and playing.

3. A bar graph showing the number of books read by class members each week for six weeks.

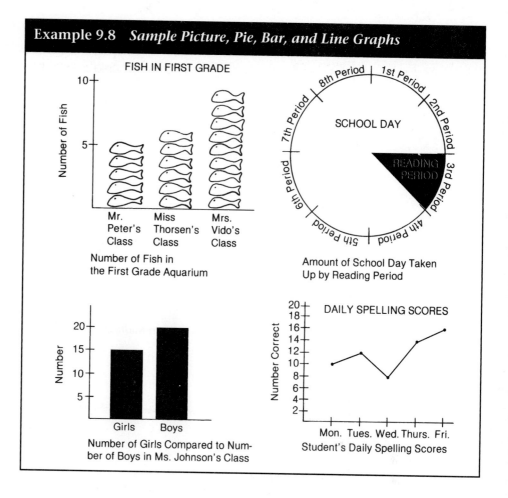

Example 9.8   *Sample Picture, Pie, Bar, and Line Graphs*

FISH IN FIRST GRADE

Number of Fish in
the First Grade Aquarium

Amount of School Day Taken
Up by Reading Period

Number of Girls Compared to Number of Boys in Ms. Johnson's Class

Student's Daily Spelling Scores

4. A line graph showing the weekly arithmetic or spelling test scores of one child over a six-week period.

A teacher should also construct graphs like the one shown in Example 9.9, a good type to use when the students are studying the results of a current election, and model the location of information in the graphs. Then the teacher can ask the children to answer questions about the graphs.

Tables

Tables, which may appear in reading materials of all subject areas, may present a problem because children have trouble extracting specific facts from a large mass of available information. The great amount of information provided in the small amount of space on tables can confuse children unless the teacher provides a procedure for reading tables.

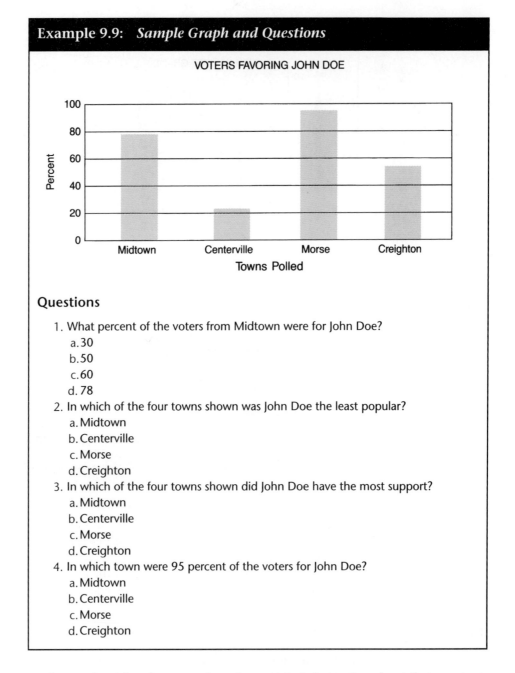

Example 9.9: *Sample Graph and Questions*

VOTERS FAVORING JOHN DOE

Questions

1. What percent of the voters from Midtown were for John Doe?
   a. 30
   b. 50
   c. 60
   d. 78
2. In which of the four towns shown was John Doe the least popular?
   a. Midtown
   b. Centerville
   c. Morse
   d. Creighton
3. In which of the four towns shown did John Doe have the most support?
   a. Midtown
   b. Centerville
   c. Morse
   d. Creighton
4. In which town were 95 percent of the voters for John Doe?
   a. Midtown
   b. Centerville
   c. Morse
   d. Creighton

Just as the titles of maps and graphs contain information about their content, so do the titles of tables. In addition, since tables are arranged in columns and rows, the headings can provide information. To discover specific information, students must locate the intersection of an appropriate column with an appropriate row. The teacher can model reading tables, verbalizing the mental processes involved in locating the information. Then the children can be asked to read a table, such as the multiplication table shown in Example 9.10, and answer related questions. Some sample questions are provided.

Example 9.10 *Sample Table and Questions*

Multiplication Table

	1	2	3	4	5	6	7	8	9
1	1	2	3	4	5	6	7	8	9
2	2	4	6	8	10	12	14	16	18
3	3	6	9	12	15	18	21	24	27
4	4	8	12	16	20	24	28	32	36
5	5	10	15	20	25	30	35	40	45
6	6	12	18	24	30	36	42	48	54
7	7	14	21	28	35	42	49	56	63
8	8	16	24	32	40	48	56	64	72
9	9	18	27	36	45	54	63	72	81

Questions

1. What is the product of 5 × 6?
2. What is the product of 9 × 3?
3. Is the product of 5 × 4 the same as the product of 4 × 5?
4. Which number is greater: the product of 3 × 8 or the product of 4 × 7?
5. When a number is multiplied by 1, what will the product always be?
6. Why is 24 where the 4 row and the 6 column meet?
7. How do the numbers in the 2 row compare with the numbers in the 4 row?

Organization skills that are important for elementary school students to learn include note taking, outlining, and summarizing. (© *Elizabeth Crews*)

Illustrations

Various types of illustrations, ranging from photographs to schematic diagrams, are found in textbooks. Too often children see illustrations merely as space fillers, reducing the amount of reading they will have to do on a page. As a result, they tend to pay little attention to illustrations even though illustrations are a very good source of information. A picture of a jungle, for example, may add considerably to a child's understanding of that term; a picture of an Arabian nomad may illuminate the term *Bedouin* in a history class. Diagrams of bones within the body can show a child things that cannot readily be observed firsthand.

SELF-CHECK: OBJECTIVE 6   Name the four types of graphic aids discussed in this section, and briefly discuss the type of information each one offers. (See Self-Improvement Opportunities 5, 6, and 7.)

Summary

Reading/study techniques enhance students' comprehension and retention of printed material. Study methods, such as SQ3R and SQRQCQ, can help students retain material that they read. A number of other techniques can also help children with retention.

Developing test-taking strategies can allow students to show teachers more accurately what they have learned. Students need strategies for taking objective and essay tests, and they need special strategies for standardized testing situations.

Flexible reading habits can help children study more effectively. Children need to be able to adjust their approaches to the reading and adjust their reading rates.

Children need to learn strategies for locating information in library books and textbooks, using the important parts of the books; in reference books, such as dictionaries and encyclopedias; in the library; and in computer databases. They also need to learn how to organize the information when they find it and to learn how to monitor their comprehension and retention of material (metacognition).

In addition, students need to know how to obtain information from the graphic aids found in textbooks. They must be able to read and understand maps, graphs, tables, and illustrations.

Test Yourself   *True or False*

_____   1. SQ3R stands for Stimulate, Question, Read, Reason, React.

_____   2. SQ3R is a study method useful in reading social studies and science materials.

_____ 3. SQRQCQ is a study method designed for use with mathematics textbooks.

_____ 4. Students remember material better if they are given opportunities to discuss it.

_____ 5. Study guides are of little help to retention.

_____ 6. Writing information often helps children to fix it in their memories.

_____ 7. Massed practice is preferable to spaced practice for encouraging long-term retention.

_____ 8. Students should read all reading materials at the same speed.

_____ 9. Rereading is often necessary for materials that contain a high density of facts.

_____ 10. Many content area textbooks offer glossaries of technical terms as reading aids.

_____ 11. Index practice is most effective when children use their own textbooks rather than a worksheet index that has no obvious function.

_____ 12. Children need to be able to use subject, author, and title cards found in the card catalog.

_____ 13. Elementary school students have no need to learn how to take notes, since they are not asked to use this skill until secondary school.

_____ 14. Subordination in outlines is indicated by lettering, numbering, and indentation.

_____ 15. The legend of a map tells the history of the area represented.

_____ 16. North is always located at the top of a map.

_____ 17. A good way to help children develop an understanding of graphs is to help them construct their own meaningful graphs.

_____ 18. Children may use newspapers, magazines, catalogues, and brochures as reference sources.

_____ 19. Teachers do not need to teach journalistic terms to elementary-level youngsters; this is a higher-level activity.

_____ 20. Using catalogues requires the ability to read charts.

_____ 21. Key words are the words that carry the important information in a sentence.

_____ 22. The ability to recognize main ideas is a prerequisite skill for outlining.

_____ 23. Guide words indicate the first two words on a dictionary page.

_____ 24. When making summaries, redundant material should be retained.

_____ 25. Some children fail to do well on essay tests because they do not understand terms like *compare* and *contrast*.

_____ 26. Children need to practice under standardized testing conditions so that they will be familiar with the testing situation when they take a standardized test.

_____ 27. Comprehension monitoring is a skill that can be fully developed in first grade.

_____ 28. Rereading can be a useful metacognitive strategy.

Self-Improvement Opportunities

1. Using materials of widely varying types, develop a procedure to help elementary students learn to be flexible in their rates of reading.

2. Choose a content area textbook at the elementary level, and plan procedures to familiarize children with the parts of the book and the reading aids the book offers.

3. Collect materials that youngsters can use as supplementary reference sources (newspapers, magazines, catalogues, brochures, etc.), and develop several short lessons to help the children read these materials effectively.

4. Visit an elementary school library and listen to the librarian explaining the reference materials and library procedures to students. Evaluate the presentation and decide how you might change it if you were responsible for it.

5. Collect a variety of types of maps, and decide which features of each type will need most explanation for children.

6. Make a variety of types of graphs into a display that you could use in a unit on reading graphs.

7. Collect pictures and diagrams that present information. Ask several children to study these pictures and extract as much information from them as possible. Then analyze the results.

8. Choose a textbook from a subject area and grade level of your choice. Examine closely the material on twenty consecutive pages, and list the study skills needed to obtain information from these pages effectively.

Chapter 10

Key Vocabulary

Pay close attention to these terms when they appear in the chapter.

cloze test

concept-text-application (CTA) approach

content area textbook

Directed Reading-Thinking Activity (DRTA)

expository passage organizer (EPO)

expository style

figurative language

frustration level

guided reading procedure (GRP)

independent level

instructional level

K-W-L teaching model

language arts

language experience approach (LEA)

narrative style

question-only strategy

readability

study guide

Reading in the Content Areas

Setting Objectives

When you finish reading this chapter, you should be able to

1. Use a cloze test to determine the difficulty of written materials.

2. Identify some readability formulas that you can use to assess the difficulty of written materials.

3. Describe several general techniques for helping students read content area materials.

4. Describe some procedures and materials that are helpful in presenting material in language arts, social studies, mathematics, and science and health books.

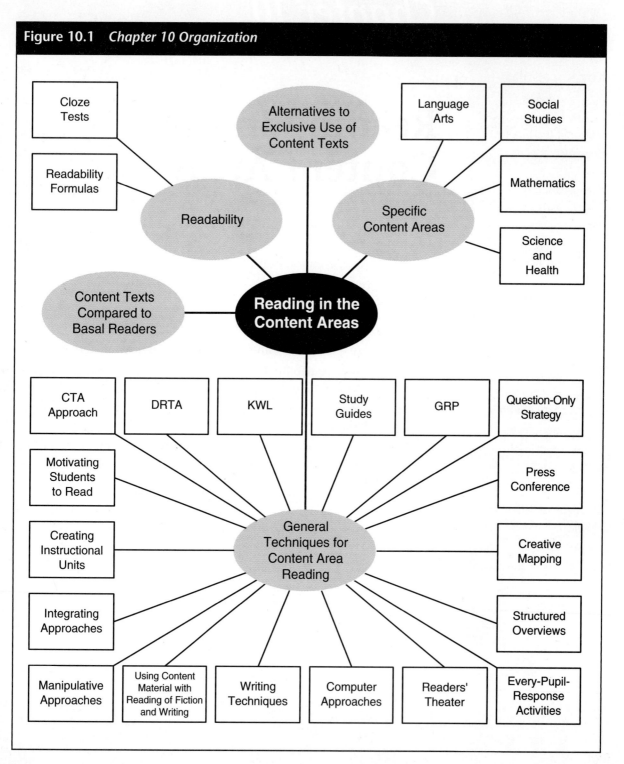

Figure 10.1 *Chapter 10 Organization*

Cloze Tests

Readability Formulas

Alternatives to Exclusive Use of Content Texts

Language Arts

Social Studies

Mathematics

Readability

Specific Content Areas

Science and Health

Content Texts Compared to Basal Readers

Reading in the Content Areas

CTA Approach

DRTA

KWL

Study Guides

GRP

Question-Only Strategy

Motivating Students to Read

Press Conference

Creating Instructional Units

General Techniques for Content Area Reading

Creative Mapping

Integrating Approaches

Structured Overviews

Manipulative Approaches

Using Content Material with Reading of Fiction and Writing

Writing Techniques

Computer Approaches

Readers' Theater

Every-Pupil-Response Activities

Reading in content area textbooks, such as those for social studies, science, mathematics, and other curricular areas, is often difficult for students. Content textbooks contain *expository* (explanatory) material that can be harder for children to read than *narrative* (story) material. They also contain many new concepts (Olson and Gee, 1991).

To read well in content area textbooks, children need good general reading strategies, including word recognition and comprehension, and reading/study strategies. If they cannot recognize the words they encounter, they will be unable to take in the information from the material. Without good literal, interpretive, critical, and creative reading comprehension strategies, they will not understand the textbook's message. And if they lack good reading/study strategies, they will be less likely to comprehend and retain the material.

Reading strategies are often initially acquired in reading class. Because content area books present special reading problems, however, teachers should be aware that simply offering their students instruction in basal readers during reading class, even though today's basal readers contain more content-oriented text, is not sufficient if the children are to read well in content area texts and nonfiction trade books. These trade books (library books, or nontextbook material) are used to supplement the curriculum in some classes and as the core of the curriculum in others. Special help with content area reading, at the time children are expected to do such reading, is important, for this is when children most effectively learn how to apply the strategies and techniques. Classrooms in which the teachers integrate learning activities across the curriculum (as in whole language classrooms), rather than scheduling separate periods for language, science, social studies, and so on, will offer opportunities throughout the day to help children read and comprehend the expository texts generally used in content areas.

Because of the special challenges posed by reading in content area textbooks, teachers often use concrete manipulatives (such as maps and pictures) to develop concepts, require retellings of text material, and have students summarize the material to check understanding. The teachers encourage students to visualize information and brainstorm about the topics, and they often provide narratives on the same topic and use audio or computer materials to aid comprehension. Semantic mapping of the main topic, use of the K-W-L procedure, and use of expository paragraph frames are other good techniques (Olson and Gee, 1991).

This chapter examines several content areas—language arts, social studies, mathematics, and science and health—along with their specific reading difficulties and activities to promote readiness and good comprehension. In addition, it presents general content area reading strategies to use in conjunction with the many strategies already described in Chapters 5 and 6 as comprehension aids in reading content area material.

Content Texts Compared to Basal Readers

Large portions of basal readers are written in a narrative style that describes the actions of people in particular situations. They do not present the density of ideas typical of content textbooks, which are generally written in an expository style, with heavy concentrations of facts. Children find narrative material easier to read than expository material. Basal reader selections often have entertaining plots that children can read for enjoyment. Content selections rarely offer this enticement.

Many children are unfamiliar with the organizational structures of expository texts. Therefore, students are left without a predictable structure to use when they are asked to read such materials (Beck and McKeown, 1991).

Students must give attention to each sentence in a content book, for nearly every one will carry important information that they must acquire before they can understand later passages. This is rarely true of basal readers, in which each selection is generally a discrete entity.

literature-centered reading

Not only are content textbooks (with the exception of many literature books) generally more difficult to read than basal readers, but in content areas teachers and students use many supplementary materials, some of which have been prepared as trade books, not textbooks. Whereas basal readers often have planned repetition of key words to encourage their acquisition, content area texts present many new concepts and vocabulary terms with little planned repetition. All of the content areas have specialized and technical vocabularies that students must acquire. Generally, basal readers contain little specialized or technical vocabulary. (See Chapter 4 for a discussion of specialized and technical vocabulary.)

Content textbooks contain a large number of graphic aids that students must interpret, whereas basal readers contain much smaller numbers of these aids. The illustrations in basal readers above first-grade level are included primarily for interest value, but those in content books are designed to help clarify concepts and need to be studied carefully.

Research studies have found comprehension of some content textbooks difficult because they lack unity, obvious purpose, and interest; have high readability levels for the grades at which they are placed; provide only superficial coverage of many topics; and have difficult organizations and writing styles (Holbrook, 1985; Moss, 1991). They also sometimes contain dated information because of infrequent adoptions of new texts (Moss, 1991).

Whereas content area textbooks have abundant headings that signal the organization of the selection, few such headings are used in basal readers, and the ones that are used are less informative than those in the content books. In reading content books, children should be helped to see that in many cases the headings outline the material for them, indicating main ideas and supporting details.

Readability

The teacher's first step in helping children to read content material is to be aware of the level of difficulty of the textbook assignments they make. Teachers must adjust their expectations for each student according to that student's reading ability, so that no child is assigned work in a book on his or her *frustration level*—that is, the level at which the material is so difficult that it will immediately be frustrating and the student will be unable to comprehend it. Trying to read from a book that is too hard for them can prevent students from learning the content. If children are forced to try to read a book at this difficulty level, they may develop negative attitudes toward the subject, the teacher, and even school in general. Students will probably learn best from printed material that is written on their *independent levels*, or the levels at which they read with ease and comprehension. They can also learn from textbooks written on their *instructional levels*, or the levels at which they read with understanding when given sufficient help by the teacher. (See Chapter 11 for further discussion of independent, instructional, and frustration levels.)

Cloze Tests

One way for the teacher to estimate the suitability of a textbook for students is to construct and administer a *cloze test*. The procedure for doing this follows:

1. Select a passage of approximately 250 consecutive words from the textbook. The passage should be one the students have not read, or tried to read, before.

2. Type the passage, leaving the first sentence intact and deleting every fifth word thereafter. In place of deleted words, substitute blanks of uniform length.

3. Give students the passage and tell them to fill in the blanks. Allow them all the time they need.

4. Score the test by counting as correct only the exact words that were in the original text. Determine each student's percentage of correct answers. If a student had less than 44 percent of the answers correct, the material is probably at his or her frustration level and is therefore too difficult. Thus, you should offer alternative ways of learning the material. If the student had from 44 to 57 percent of the answers correct, the material is probably at that student's instructional level, and he or she will be able to learn from the text if you provide careful guidance in the reading by developing readiness, helping with new concepts and unfamiliar vocabulary, and providing reading purposes to aid comprehension. If the student had more than 57 percent of the answers correct, the material is probably at that student's independent level, and he or she should be able to benefit from the material when reading it independently (Bormuth, 1968).

A teacher using the percentages given here must count *only* exact words as correct, since the percentages were derived using only exact words. Synonyms must be counted as incorrect, along with obviously wrong answers and unfilled blanks.

Because all the material in a given textbook is unlikely to be written on the same level, teachers should choose several samples for a cloze test from several places in the book in order to determine the book's suitability for a particular child.

Example 10.1 shows a cloze passage for a social studies textbook. This passage contains 283 words. No words have been deleted from the first sentence in order to give the student an opportunity to develop an appropriate mental set for the material that follows, and the entire paragraph in which the fiftieth blank occurs has been included in order to complete the thought that was in progress. A score of fewer than 22 correct responses indicates that the material is too difficult; a score of 22 to 28 indicates that the child can manage the material if the teacher gives assistance; and a score of more than 28 indicates that the child can read the material independently.

Some authorities prefer cloze tests to informal reading inventories, or IRIs (see Chapter 11 for a discussion of IRIs), for matching textbooks to students because these tests put the child in direct contact with the author's language without having the teacher as a mediator (through the written questions). Frequently a child can understand the text but not the teacher's questions related to it, which can cause the teacher to underestimate the child's comprehension of the material. On the other hand, some children react with frustration to cloze materials; these children would fare better if tested with an IRI.

Example 10.1 *Cloze Passage*

Directions: Read the following passage and fill in each blank with a word that makes sense in the sentence.

The first battle in July 1861 began like a holiday outing. Union supporters

packed picnic _____ and followed soldiers from _____, D.C., into Virginia.
              (1)   (2)

Newspaper _____ also came to get _____ story.
          (3)   (4)

Armies from the _____ and the South met _____ a stream called Bull
                (5)   (6)

_____, about 25 miles from _____, D.C. At first Confederates _____ the
(7)   (8)   (9)

Union soldiers back. _____ the Confederates attacked. Fierce _____ broke
                     (10)   (11)

out, and the _____ army won the battle.
             (12)

_____ Battle of Bull Run _____ the North that it _____ not win the war
(13)   (14)   (15)

_____. Congress passed laws calling _____ troops to serve three _____.
(16)   (17)   (18)

President Lincoln's generals had _____ plan to save the _____. The Union's
                                 (19)   (20)

"anaconda plan" _____ named for the snake _____ squeezes its prey to
                (21)   (22)

Example 10.1 *Cloze Passage (cont.)*

_____ . The Union planned to _____ the strength out of _____ South by a
(23)   (24)   (25)

blockade, _____ closing of southern ocean _____ . Union ships would stop
(26)   (27)

_____ and keep Southerners from _____ money by selling cotton _____
(28)   (29)   (30)

other countries.

Under the _____ plan, Union ships would _____ control of the Mississippi
(31)   (32)

_____ . Confederate states would then _____ unable to send boats _____
(33)   (34)   (35)

supplies and soldiers to _____ Confederate states. Finally, Union _____ would
(36)   (37)

try to capture _____ , the Confederate capital.
(38)

The _____ also had plans. One _____ to destroy Union ships. _____
(39)   (40)   (41)

1862, the South sent _____ iron-sided steamship, *Merrimack*, up _____ James
(42)   (43)

River. (The South _____ the ship the *Virginia*.) _____ *Merrimack* was far
(44)   (45)

stronger _____ the Union's wooden ships. _____ Union ships fired at
(46)   (47)

_____ , the cannonballs could not _____ the ship's sides.
(48)   (49)

The _____ day, the Union sent its own iron ship, the *Monitor*, to attack the
(50)

Merrimack. The two ships battled, with no clear winner.

Answers: (1) lunches (2) Washington (3) reporters (4) the (5) North (6) near
(7) Run (8) Washington (9) held (10) Then (11) fighting (12) Confederate (13) The
(14) showed (15) would (16) easily (17) for (18) years (19) a (20) Union (21) was
(22) that (23) death (24) squeeze (25) the (26) or (27) ports (28) supplies
(29) earning (30) to (31) anaconda (32) take (33) River (34) be (35) with (36)
other (37) forces (38) Richmond (39) South (40) was (41) In (42) its (43) the
(44) renamed (45) The (46) than (47) When (48) it (49) pierce (50) next

Children should have experience with cloze-type exercises before teachers use this procedure to help match students with the appropriate levels of textbooks. If they have not had such experiences, they may not perform as well as they otherwise would.

After determining each student's ability to benefit from the class textbook, the teacher has the information needed to make instructional decisions. Those students who are on the independent level will be able to read textbook assignments and prepare for class discussion independently and will often be able to set their own purpose questions to direct their reading. Those who are at an instructional level will need to have the teacher introduce material carefully, build concepts and vocabulary gradually, and assign purpose questions. Those who are at a frustration level on the material will need to be introduced to the subject and, in order to understand the concepts and information involved, be given either (1) some simpler materials with a lower readability level than that of the text, such as trade books, or (2) selections written by the teacher on an appropriately low level.

All students can participate together in discussing the material, and the teacher can record significant contributions on the board in the same way as in recording a language experience story. (Detailed discussions of the language experience approach appear later in this chapter and in Chapter 7.) When the teacher asks students to read the contributions from the board at the end of the discussion period, even poor readers may be able to read fairly difficult contributions because they have heard the sentences being dictated and have seen them being written down. Before the next class, the teacher can duplicate the class summary for each student to use in reviewing for tests. During study periods, he or she can help the children who are at their frustration levels to reread the notes, emphasizing the new words and concepts.

literature-centered reading

Readability Formulas

Standardized tests are one way to obtain information about students' reading achievement levels. Teachers should remember, however, that a standardized test score is not necessarily a reliable measure of a child's reading ability in a content textbook, because these tests are generally not built on passages that are comparable in style and writing patterns to those in content materials. Informal tests based on actual content materials may be better indicators of the difficulty of content material for particular students.

When teachers have determined the students' reading levels with standardized instruments, they can obtain an approximate idea of whether a textbook is appropriate by testing it with a standard measure of readability. Among widely used readability formulas, the *Spache Readability Formula* is designed for primary-grade books (Spache, 1966), the *Dale-Chall Readability Formula* is designed for materials from the fourth-grade through college levels (Dale and Chall, 1948), and the *Fry Readability Graph* (Fry, 1977) can be used on material at all levels.

Because readability formulas are strictly text based, they do not give information related to the interactive nature of reading. For example, they cannot gauge a reader's background knowledge about the topic, motivation to read the material, or interest in the topic, although these are important factors in determining the difficulty of a text for a particular child. In addition, they cannot separate reasonable prose from a series of unconnected words (Rush, 1985). They cannot measure the effects of an author's writing style or the complexity of concepts presented, and they do not consider the format of the material (typeface and type size, spacing, amount of white space on the page, and so on). For these reasons, no formula offers more than an approximation of level of difficulty for material. Formulas do, however, generally give reliable information about the relative difficulty levels of textbook passages and other printed materials, and this information can be extremely helpful to teachers. Example 10.2 shows a quick way to estimate readability.

Computer programs designed to test readability can ease the burden of making calculations by hand. Such programs are available for several formulas (Judd, 1981), including Dale-Chall and Fry (Balajthy, 1986; Rude, 1986). A number of grammar and style checkers, such as *Grammatik* (Reference Software International), run several other formulas.

Research shows not only that many content area textbooks are written at much higher readability levels than are basal readers for the corresponding grades, but also that subject matter textbooks often vary in difficulty from chapter to chapter. If teachers are aware of various levels of difficulty within a text, they can adjust teaching methods to help students gain the most from each portion of the book, perhaps by teaching easier chapters earlier in the year and more difficult chapters later on. Of course, this technique is not advisable for teaching material in which the concepts in an early, difficult chapter are necessary for understanding a later, easier chapter.

A good way to decrease the readability levels of content passages for students is to teach the content vocabulary thoroughly before the material containing that vocabulary is assigned to be read. The more unfamiliar content vocabulary is a major factor in the higher difficulty levels of many content area materials.

SELF-CHECK: OBJECTIVES 1 AND 2   Describe how to use a cloze test to estimate the suitability of a textbook for a child or group of children.
Name two widely used readability formulas.
(See Self-Improvement Opportunity 1.)

Alternatives to Exclusive Use of Content Texts

literature-centered reading   Some students find textbooks difficult to read or are unmotivated to read them because they find them dull and dry. For such students, supplementary trade books offer one viable option for learning content area material (Moss, 1991). Many children experience their first serious difficulties with reading as they begin reading textbooks, but the continued use of high-interest trade books along with textbooks may ease the transition. In selecting and using appropriate trade books, teachers should follow certain steps: identify concepts for further development;

Example 10.2 *Graph for Estimating Readability*

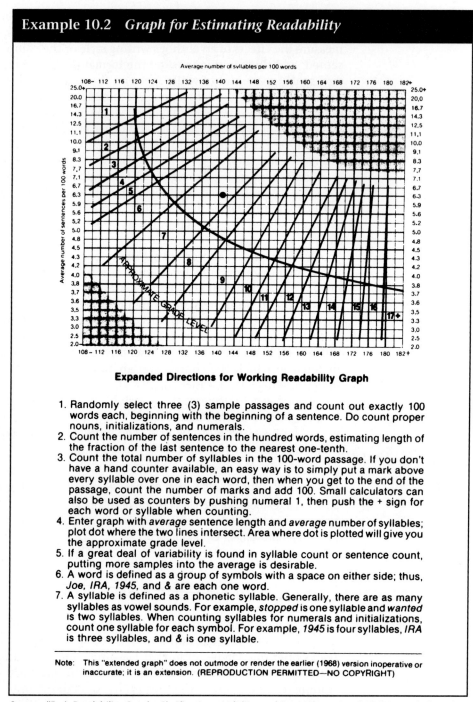

Average number of syllables per 100 words

Expanded Directions for Working Readability Graph

1. Randomly select three (3) sample passages and count out exactly 100 words each, beginning with the beginning of a sentence. Do count proper nouns, initializations, and numerals.
2. Count the number of sentences in the hundred words, estimating length of the fraction of the last sentence to the nearest one-tenth.
3. Count the total number of syllables in the 100-word passage. If you don't have a hand counter available, an easy way is to simply put a mark above every syllable over one in each word, then when you get to the end of the passage, count the number of marks and add 100. Small calculators can also be used as counters by pushing numeral 1, then push the + sign for each word or syllable when counting.
4. Enter graph with *average* sentence length and *average* number of syllables; plot dot where the two lines intersect. Area where dot is plotted will give you the approximate grade level.
5. If a great deal of variability is found in syllable count or sentence count, putting more samples into the average is desirable.
6. A word is defined as a group of symbols with a space on either side; thus, *Joe, IRA, 1945,* and *&* are each one word.
7. A syllable is defined as a phonetic syllable. Generally, there are as many syllables as vowel sounds. For example, *stopped* is one syllable and *wanted* is two syllables. When counting syllables for numerals and initializations, count one syllable for each symbol. For example, *1945* is four syllables, *IRA* is three syllables, and *&* is one syllable.

Note: This "extended graph" does not outmode or render the earlier (1968) version inoperative or inaccurate; it is an extension. (REPRODUCTION PERMITTED—NO COPYRIGHT)

Source: "Fry's Readability Graph: Clarifications, Validity, and Extension to Level 17," *Journal of Reading,* 21 (December 1977), 249.

locate suitable trade books to help teach these concepts; present books to students by reading them aloud or making copies available for independent reading prior to textbook assignments; use trade books during and after reading of the text to extend concept acquisition; and provide follow-up activities in the forms of creative writing, drama, and interviewing (Brozo and Tomlinson, 1986).

By using nonfiction trade books to enhance the study of topics in the students' textbooks, regardless of whether or not the students have trouble reading the textbooks, teachers can help students learn more about the content. This practice is common in whole language classrooms, as well as many others. Trade books can be chosen to coincide with students' reading levels, easing one typical problem. These books can be visually appealing to students and, therefore, can arouse their interest. They can also cover a topic in greater depth than the length limits of a textbook would allow, and they frequently have very coherent organizational patterns. Newer books ensure access to timely information (Moss, 1991).

General Techniques for Content Area Reading

reading-writing connection

When working with students who are reading in the content areas, teachers should do many of the things suggested in earlier chapters for directing the reading of any material, such as developing vocabulary knowledge, activating background knowledge about the topic, and providing purposes for reading. They should also suggest use of a study method, such as SQ3R or another appropriate one, encourage note taking, and provide suggestions to promote retention of the material. (Information about these activities appears in Chapters 4, 5, 6, and 9.) Teachers may also use a number of other techniques to help their students read in content areas more effectively. This section discusses several approaches.

Motivating Students to Read

Mathison (1989) has found that teachers can stimulate interest in reading content area materials in a number of ways. Two strategies are using analogies to help give new ideas familiar connections and telling personal anecdotes that can help personalize reading material. For example, study of arteries and veins in a sixth-grade class could be motivated by drawing an analogy to roads leading into the downtown area; or, in a study of a particular climate, the teacher might share a personal anecdote about a camping trip in such a climate. Teachers should examine each reading assignment for possibilities for motivational introductions.

Stories can help children see the connections that exist among people across time and from different places because of common needs people share. The participation in storytelling sessions helps the students develop shared experiences that create bonds among classmates (Combs and Beach, 1994). Such bonds allow the students to cooperate more freely as they work toward common goals in the classroom.

Concept-Text-Application (CTA) Approach

The *concept-text-application (CTA)* approach is similar to the Directed Reading Activity. It involves organizing lessons to help elementary school students understand expository text (Wong and Au, 1985). The phases in the CTA approach are as follows:

1. *C—Concept assessment/development phase.* This phase consists of a prereading discussion in which the children's background knowledge about the topic is assessed and new concepts and terms needed for comprehension of the text may be developed.

2. *T—Text phase.* In this phase, the teacher introduces the reading selection and sets purposes for reading. The class reads the text silently in segments, with guided discussion following the reading of each segment. During discussion, information brought out in the first two phases is organized graphically on the chalkboard.

3. *A—Application phase.* In this phase, the teacher plans postreading activities to encourage the children to use the knowledge they have gained. This phase generally involves discussion that may include summarizing and synthesizing information, and students may be asked to evaluate and respond creatively to the material. Additional research and reports can be included.

Directed Reading-Thinking Activity (DRTA)

The *Directed Reading-Thinking Activity (DRTA)* can be used to direct children's reading of either basal reader stories or content area selections. (A complete discussion of the DRTA is found in Chapter 7.) As Harp (1989) points out, in this activity students predict, read, and prove predictions as the teacher asks them what they think, why they think that, and how they can prove their points.

The lesson plan in Example 10.3 illustrates the steps in a sample DRTA. It is designed for use with a chapter entitled "Exploring and Settling the New Lands" from *The Country* by Gertrude Stephens Brown with Ernest W. Tiegs and Fay Adams (Lexington, Mass.: Ginn and Company, 1983, pp. 122–139). The plan could also include activities for vocabulary or concept development. The words *nomadic, moccasins, stockade, wagon train, jerky, timber line,* and *compromise* may need attention. In addition, information about the Native American tribes mentioned—the Shoshoni, the Mandans, and the Nez Percés—could be useful background-building material. Questions for reflecting on the reading and related activities for extending the learning experience appear at the end of the selection.

Keith Thomas has developed the *Directed Inquiry Activity (DIA)*, which is based on the Directed Reading-Thinking Activity, for study reading in content areas. Here the children preview a part of the reading assignment and predict responses to the questions *who, what, when, where, how,* and *why,* which are recorded on the chalkboard. Following class discussion of the ideas, students read to confirm or alter their predictions. The predictions provide purposes for reading and, along with discussion, provide the mental set needed for approaching reading (Manzo, 1980).

Example 10.3 *Social Studies Lesson Plan Using the DRTA*

Step 1: **Making predictions from title clues** Write the title of the chapter to be studied on the chalkboard, and have a child read it. Ask the children, "What do you think this chapter will cover?" or "What do you think this section will tell about exploring and settling new lands?" Give them time to consider the question thoroughly, and let each child have an opportunity to make predictions. Then write the subheading of the first subsection, "A Shoshoni Girl Grows Up," on the chalkboard, and allow the children to adjust predictions or make further predictions. Accept all predictions, regardless of how reasonable or unreasonable they seem, and refrain from stating your own predictions during this discussion period.

Step 2: **Making predictions from picture clues** Have the students open their books to the beginning of the selection. Ask them to examine carefully the pictures and the map shown in this selection. After they have examined the illustrations, ask them to revise the predictions they made earlier.

Step 3: **Reading the material** Ask the children to read the selection to check their predictions. They may read this material in nine segments, corresponding to the nine subdivisions with main headings or paragraph headings, or they may read it in two segments, corresponding to the main headings alone. After reading each segment, they move to Step 4.

Step 4: **Assessing the accuracy of predictions and adjusting predictions** When the children have read the first assigned segment, lead a discussion by asking such questions as "Who correctly predicted what this section would tell?" Ask the children who believe they were right to read orally to the class the parts of the selection that support their predictions. Children who were wrong can tell why they believe they were wrong. Then have the children adjust their predictions on the basis of what they have just read and the heading of the second segment. Some children may keep former predictions that still seem to be appropriate; others may discard predictions that no longer appear to be accurate and form new predictions, based on the new input.

Step 5: **Repeating the procedure until all parts of the lesson have been covered** At each stopping place, the procedure in Step 4 is repeated.

K-W-L Teaching Model

Ogle (1986, 1989) has devised what she calls the *K-W-L teaching model* for expository text. The *K* stands for "What I *Know*," the *W* for "What I *Want* to Learn," and the *L* for "What I *Learned*." In the first step the teacher and the students discuss what the group already knows about the topic of the reading material. The teacher may ask the students where they learned what they know or how they could verify the information. Students may also be asked to think of categories of information that they expect to find in the material they are about to read. The second step involves class discussion of what the students want to learn. The teacher may point out disagreements about the things that the students think

reading-writing connection

they already know and may call attention to gaps in their knowledge. Then each student writes down personal questions to be answered by the reading. Students then read the material. After they have finished reading, they record what they have learned from the reading. If the reading did not answer all of their personal questions, students can be directed to other sources for the answers.

Example 10.4 is an example of a K-W-L study sheet that was filled out by a fourth-grade girl who was working with teacher Gail Hyder.

Study Guides

Study guides, duplicated sheets prepared by the teacher and distributed to the children, help guide reading in content fields and alleviate those difficulties that interfere with understanding. They help students read expository material more effectively. They can set purposes for reading, as well as provide aids for interpreting material through suggestions about how to apply reading strategies. These guides also serve as vehicles for group discussions and cooperative learning activities. Mikel (1993) believes that teaching content subjects through use of cooperative learning groups increases the students' learning. There are many kinds of study guides, and the nature of the material and the reason for reading it can help teachers determine which kind to use.

Content-process guides, as shown in Example 10.5, focus on both the content and process aspects of reading. The study guide in Example 10.5 directs students' reading in the following way. First, the overview question offers an overall purpose for the reading, helping students read the material with the appropriate mental set. The first item after the overview question gives students content purposes for reading the first section. Notice that the questions are phrased to elicit thought about the information in the passage. Following the purposes are two questions about vocabulary meanings. The students are encouraged to use their skills in structural analysis to help them understand the vocabulary presented. This is process guidance. The second item offers purposes for reading the second main section. Notice that it specifies the groups under consideration. It is followed by a vocabulary question and a process suggestion to use context clues.

Example 10.4 *Completed K-W-L Sheet*

K - W - L   Welcome to the Green House by: Jane Yolen

What I Know	What I Want to Know	What I Learned
a lot of animal live there.	What kind of animal live there.	butter flys, snakes, frogs, bats, fish, bees,
Plant live there.	What kind of plants grow there.	wild pigs, tamarin toucan, herons, Ocelot, Hizards,
A Green house is very hot.	How hot it is in there.	huming birds, sloth.
		<u>flowers</u> crimson, orchid trees, vines lianas, very hot A wet house,

Source: Stephanie Hunsucker, fourth grade, Crossville, Tennessee.

Example 10.5 *Sample Selection and Study Guide*

[Note: The material in this passage is part of a discussion of the Seven Years' War.]

The Proclamation of 1763   With the French defeat, many colonists eagerly prepared to move across the Appalachian Mountains. However, the British were worried. They knew that new settlements would anger the Iroquois, Delaware, Shawnee, and other Indian tribes who already lived there. To prevent fighting, the British issued the Proclamation of 1763. This act saved all land west of the Appalachians for Indians. Colonists could not settle there.

The Proclamation upset many colonists. Earlier, the French had blocked new settlements. The French had been defeated. Now, though, the British also stopped people from moving west. Many colonists wondered why they had fought the war.

Example 10.5   *Sample Selection and Study Guide (cont.)*

The Cost of Victory   Colonial anger at Britain's Proclamation of 1763 was just one hardship the war caused. The British, the Indians, and the colonists each faced new troubles.

In Britain, the war had caused the government to borrow money. Between 1754 and 1763, the money Britain owed doubled. The country needed money to pay back its many loans.

Britain also had to pay the 10,000 soldiers it sent to North America. These troops were needed to protect the large new British empire. Britain now had to spend three times as much to defend its American empire as it did before the war.

For many Indian tribes, the war brought a loss of power. They could no longer use the French to help them against the British. And even 10,000 British soldiers could not stop settlers from moving onto Indian lands.

In the colonies, the war caused great suffering. Boston, a city of about 2,200 families, lost 700 men during the war. These deaths left many widows and orphans who needed help just to buy food.

Study Guide

Overview Question: What were the effects of the war on the people of America and Great Britain?

1. Read the section titled "The Proclamation of 1763" to find out what effect this action had on the colonists. Were the colonists pleased with the effect? How can you tell?

   What is a settlement? What is a proclamation? If you don't know, locate the root words to help you figure this out.

2. Read the section titled "The Cost of Victory" to discover other hardships the war caused. Look for hardships faced by the British, the Indian tribes, and the people of the colonies.

   What is a synonym for *hardship*? Look for a context clue to this word's meaning.

Source: From *America Will Be* in *Houghton Mifflin Social Studies* by Armento, et al. Copyright 1994 by Houghton Mifflin Company. Reprinted by permission of Houghton Mifflin Company. All rights reserved.

Pattern guides are study guides that stress the relationship among the organizational structure, the reading/thinking skills needed for comprehension, and the important concepts in the material. The first step in constructing such a guide is to identify the important concepts in the material. Then information about each concept must be located within the selection, and the author's organizational pattern must be identified. The teacher then integrates the identified concepts, the writing pattern, and the skills necessary for reading the material with understanding in a guide that offers as much direction as specific students need—whether it be the section of text in which the information is located; the page number; or the page, paragraph, and line numbers.

These first graders, who are looking at a book about Martin Luther King, illustrate how even young children become involved in content area reading. (© *Joseph Schuyler/ Stock Boston*)

A pattern guide for a selection with a cause-and-effect writing pattern might be constructed in this manner:

1. Identify the reading/thinking process on the upper left portion of the guide and in the directions. Example:

   Cause/Effect
   As you read this material, look for the effects related to the causes listed below.

2. Offer page numbers or page and paragraph numbers for each listed cause.

3. Consider offering some completed items to get the students started and to model the correct responses (Olson and Longnion, 1982).

Conrad (1989) found that her students were able to work more effectively with cause-and-effect relationships if the effects were listed on the left side of the page and the causes on the right side. She believed this was because students tend to want to tell what happened and then add a *because* phrase. Example 10.6 shows a complex cause-and-effect pattern guide that also has an implicit comparison-contrast element, since effects on three populations are compared. This pattern guide is based on the text selection in Example 10.5.

Example 10.6 *Cause-and-Effect Pattern Guide*

| | Effects | | |
Causes	On British	On Indians	On Colonists
Proclamation of 1763	Drew colonists' anger	Land west of Appalachians saved for them	Denied right to settle on land west of Appalachians
Seven Years' War	Needed money to pay back loans Had to pay larger numbers of soldiers	Loss of power Not enough British soldiers to keep settlers off of their lands	Widows and orphans who needed help to buy food

Miller and George (1992) suggest using *expository passage organizers (EPOs)*—reading and writing process study guides—to help students see the structure of expository text, understand how it affects comprehension and retention, and use reading of expository text as a model for writing it. These EPOs get students actively involved with the introduction, body, and conclusion of a text. They identify such text structures as cause/effect, problem/solution, and comparison/contrast, and label the critical components of these structures, for example, the causes and the effects in the cause/effect pattern. EPOs also identify main ideas and supporting details, and they offer models for writing. Example 10.7 shows an Expository Passage Organizer.

Example 10.7 *Expository Passage Organizer*

Sample Expository Passage Organizer (EPO) for a Problem–Solution Text

Instructions:
   A. Complete the following EPO by looking back at the passage.
   B. Correct your EPO by using the completed EPO on the last page of this study guide.

Passage pattern: Problem-solution

Title _____

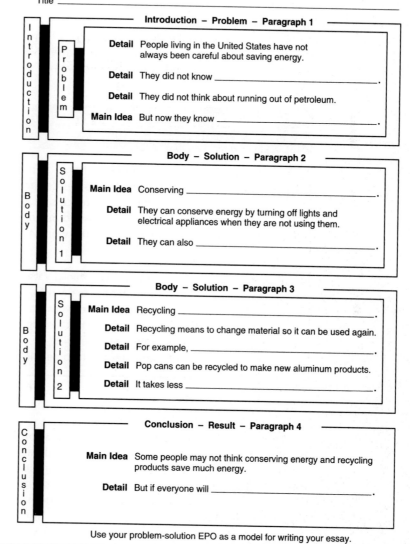

Introduction – Problem – Paragraph 1

Introduction / Problem

Detail   People living in the United States have not always been careful about saving energy.

Detail   They did not know _____ .

Detail   They did not think about running out of petroleum.

Main Idea   But now they know _____ .

Body – Solution – Paragraph 2

Body / Solution 1

Main Idea   Conserving _____ .

Detail   They can conserve energy by turning off lights and electrical appliances when they are not using them.

Detail   They can also _____ .

Body – Solution – Paragraph 3

Body / Solution 2

Main Idea   Recycling _____ .

Detail   Recycling means to change material so it can be used again.

Detail   For example, _____ .

Detail   Pop cans can be recycled to make new aluminum products.

Detail   It takes less _____ .

Conclusion – Result – Paragraph 4

Conclusion

Main Idea   Some people may not think conserving energy and recycling products save much energy.

Detail   But if everyone will _____ .

Use your problem-solution EPO as a model for writing your essay.

Source: Kathleen K. Miller and John E. George. "Expository Passage Organizers: Models for Reading and Writing." *Journal of Reading,* 35 (February 1992), 374. Reprinted with permission of Kathleen K. Miller and the International Reading Association.

Anticipation guides, which are used before reading a selection, require students to react to a series of statements related to the selection to be read. The children can react to the anticipation guide again when they have finished reading to see the differences, if any, between their initial opinions and the correct responses. When the teacher asks for responses both before and after reading, the guide is often referred to as an anticipation/reaction guide.

The statements in an anticipation guide should relate to major concepts and significant details in the reading material. They may reflect common misconceptions about the topic, challenging students' beliefs. They should link students' prior knowledge with text concepts, and they should be general (Duffelmeyer, 1994). The guide may be used in a group setting, with students discussing and justifying their responses (Wood and Mateja, 1983). Example 10.8 shows an anticipation/reaction guide for a selection about computers.

Example 10.8   *Anticipation/Reaction Guide for a Selection about Computers*

Directions: Read each sentence below. If you think the sentence says something that is right, write *yes* on the line that is beside the sentence and below the word *Before*. If you do not think what the sentence says is right, write *no* on the line that is beside the sentence and below the word *Before*. After you read, you will write your *yes* or *no* for each sentence under the word *After*.

Before   **After**

_____ _____   1. A computer can think by itself.
_____ _____   2. A computer has many uses.
_____ _____   3. A computer is useless without a program.
_____ _____   4. People control what a computer can do.
_____ _____   5. All computers are alike.
_____ _____   6. A computer can help people do work.

Duffelmeyer and Baum (1992) suggest extending the anticipation guide by having students decide if the text supported each of their choices and having them indicate why their choices were correct or incorrect by citing evidence from the text. This seems to be a good addition to the procedure.

Study guides should be prepared carefully and used with discrimination. Regardless of whether students cooperate to find the answers to questions on a study guide or work individually, the teacher should be sure the class discusses the questions or items after reading the material. Remember that a study guide will not increase the likelihood that a student will understand a selection if the selection is too difficult for that student to read.

Guided Reading Procedure

Anthony Manzo's *guided reading procedure (GRP)*, designed to help readers improve organizational skills, comprehension, and recall, is appropriate for content area reading at any level. The steps in the procedure follow:

1. Set a purpose for reading a selection of about 500 words, and tell the children to remember all they can. Tell them to close their books when they finish reading.

2. Have the students tell everything they remember from the material, and record this information on the board.

3. Ask students to look at the selection again to correct or add to the information they have already offered.

4. Direct the children to organize the information in an outline (see Chapter 9), semantic web (see Chapter 5), or some other arrangement.

5. Ask synthesizing questions to help students integrate the new material with previously acquired information.

6. Give a test immediately to check on the children's short-term recall.

7. Give another form of the test later to check medium- or long-term recall (Ankney and McClurg, 1981).

Question-Only Strategy

With the *question-only strategy*, the teacher first tells the students the topic for study and explains that they must learn all they can by asking questions about it. Then they will be given a test covering all the ideas the teacher believes are important, whether or not the questions have covered those ideas. The students then ask their questions, and the teacher answers them. Following the questions, a test is given. Later, the students discuss what questions they should have asked, but did not ask, during the questioning step. Finally, they read their texts or use some other means of learning what they did not learn through their questions. The teacher may choose to give a follow-up test after the study (Manzo, 1980).

Press Conference

literature-centered reading

Press Conference is a strategy in which some students take the parts of characters in material that has been read (literature, science, social studies, current events) and others take the parts of reporters interviewing the characters. The interviews must have carefully planned questions, and the interviewers must take detailed notes from which they compose news stories about the interviewees and/or the

reading-writing connection

events in which they have been involved. These stories are taken through a process writing approach, and the final versions are published in a class newspaper (Dever, 1992).

Creative Mapping

Naughton (1993/1994) suggests *creative mapping* to enhance content area reading. Creative mapping combines semantic mapping with pictures to display material in a way that helps students see relationships and also helps them recall it.

First, a picture that represents the topic or main idea is drawn. Then supporting details are arranged on or around the image in an organized manner. Students draw on background knowledge and the text to complete the map.

Structured Overviews

Structured overviews of the vocabulary from a content area reading assignment can help students learn the terms and concepts. At first, the teacher can present an overview on an overhead projector, with students answering questions about how the vocabulary is related to the concepts in the assignment as the overview is developed in front of them, or the overview can be placed on strips on the bulletin board. Later the students can work cooperatively in small groups to form overviews or they can make individual overviews from a chapter they read (Wolfe and Lopez, 1992/1993).

Every-Pupil-Response Activities

reading-writing connection   Gaskins and her colleagues (1994) found that use of *every-pupil-response activities*, such as engaging in written responses to text, facilitated participation in discussion about the text. These responses were not graded, but were used to help students assess their own understanding of the text and sometimes of its organizational structure. Partner discussions followed the writing and in turn were followed by whole-class discussions. The students helped one another to clarify their understandings and to see alternate interpretations.

Teachers reminded the students to support their positions with evidence from the text. Teachers also presented the students with real-life problems to which they could apply information from the text, eliciting enthusiastic small-group discussions. They talked about the strategies that would best fit the solution of the particular problem, why these strategies should help, when they should be used, and how to use them. Teachers modeled strategy use for the students before asking them to participate in guided practice. Strategies could include such activities as use of an index and organization of information. (See Chapter 9 for information about these strategies.)

Readers' Theater

literature-centered reading   Young and Vardell (1993) suggest using *readers' theater* (a dramatic reading of a text in parts by two or more readers) with nonfiction trade books to increase reading-writing connection active involvement with the material and add to enjoyment of it. Books with dialogue are especially easy to adapt to readers' theater scripts. Some other types of text may be rewritten as dialogue, or multiple narrators may be assigned. Prologues may be added to introduce the material in the scripts, and/or postscripts may be added to bring some scripts to a close. Students should have an active part in developing the scripts, making their production as much of a learning experience as the performances. Suggestions of books to use include David M. Schwartz's *How Much Is a Million?* for math; Joanna Cole's books about the magic school bus for science; and Joan Anderson's *The First Thanksgiving Feast*, Russell Freedman's *Buffalo Hunt*, and Jean Fritz's *And Then What Happened, Paul Revere?* for social studies.

Sustained Silent Reading (SSR) for Expository Materials

In regular sustained silent reading periods, children have free choice of materials to read, and they generally choose narrative materials. Joranko (1990) has a separate SSR period for her intermediate-grade students for reading in expository materials, to expose them to these materials in a self-selection situation on a regular basis. This approach should help students become familiar with many expository text structures without the pressure that accompanies assigned reading.

Learning Text Structure

Many students do not use text structure to help them comprehend and retain information from content area textbooks, but research has shown that text structure can be taught (McGee and Richgels, 1985). Systematic attention to clues about the organizational structure of a text and creation of visual representations of the relationships among ideas aid both comprehension and retention (Pearson and Fielding, 1991). Five of the more common expository text structures are cause/effect, comparison/contrast, problem/solution, description, and collection (see Example 10.9). Use of description and use of collection (a series of descriptions about a topic presented together) are more common in elementary-level texts than are the other three types.

reading-writing connection Using graphic organizers (such as webs), teachers can show how passages with the same text structure can have different content. Then they can prepare a graphic organizer for each structure to be taught. Focusing on one structure at a time, they can present students with the graphic organizer for a passage and have them construct a passage based on this organizer (see the section "Webs Plus Writing" in this chapter), which will include appropriate clue words, such as *because, different from,* and so forth. Teachers should emphasize how the clue words help both readers and writers. After revising and refining their passages, students can compare them with the passage on which the graphic organizer was based (McGee and Richgels, 1985).

Example 10.9   *Graphic Representations for Common Expository Text Structures*

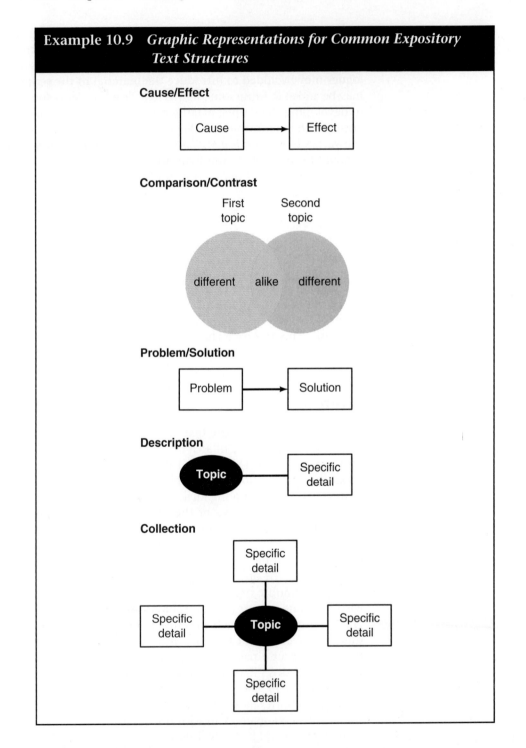

Cause/Effect

Cause → Effect

Comparison/Contrast

First topic   Second topic

different   alike   different

Problem/Solution

Problem → Solution

Description

Topic — Specific detail

Collection

Specific detail

Specific detail — Topic — Specific detail

Specific detail

Hadaway and Young (1994) encourage the use of visual representations to help students grasp organization and content. They suggest the use of index cards to assist in the construction of time lines, especially when multiple sources are used. Venn diagrams can help students see common elements of concepts and can help them visualize similarities and differences to see comparisons and contrasts. Flow charts help students visualize a sequence of events, such as the sequence of steps in a science experiment.

Maps of the content may be used before, during, and/or after students read it. (See Chapter 5 for a discussion and some examples of semantic mapping.) Sometimes the teacher can construct the maps, and at other times students can do so (Flood, 1986). The teacher should also ask appropriate questions before, during, and after reading. (See Chapter 6 for a discussion of questioning techniques.)

reading-writing connection

Another way to work on students' knowledge of text structure is through use of expository paragraph frames. *Expository paragraph frames* are similar to the story frames described in Chapter 5. They provide sentence starters that include signal words or phrases to fit the paragraph organization. The sequential pattern appears to be an easy one for young children to recognize and use (Cudd and Roberts, 1989). The teacher can write a sequential paragraph that uses the cue words for sequence: *first, next, then, finally*. The sentences can be copied on sentence strips, the sequential nature of the material can be discussed in the group, and the students can be asked to arrange the sentences in sequential order in a pocket chart. The children can read the arranged sentences together. Then they can arrange the sentences individually and copy them on their papers in paragraph form. Finally, they can illustrate the information. The teacher can show the children a frame with the signal words and model filling in the frame with responses elicited from students. At this point, the meanings of signal words can be clarified.

Any expository structure can be used with appropriate frames. Cudd and Roberts (1989) suggest the use of two types of reaction frames that are elaborations of enumeration frames. One type leads the children to tie prior knowledge to new information; for example,

Before I started reading about trucks, I knew _____
_____.

In the book I read, I learned that _____.
I also learned _____. The thing that surprised me most was _____.

Cairney (1990) says that these frames provide probes that encourage text recall. Lewis and her colleagues (1994) have found sequential, enumeration, comparison, contrast, and reaction frames to work well. They also have had success with getting children to draw pictures depicting sequential text after they read, but before they write about the material; having them transform the information in the text into a graphic form (for example, a chart or a map); and having them rewrite material in another genre, such as a job advertisement.

Computer Approaches

reading-writing connection

Dowd and Sinatra (1990) point out that there are three kinds of computer software designed to help students learn about text structure. One type models the different text structures, and then has the students write something based on the model. The *Thinking Networks for Reading and Writing* series (Think Network Inc.) is an example of this type of software. Another type includes interactive/prompt tutorials on particular types of discourse. Some of these allow students to write working outlines for papers; and others allow students to process a complete draft, revise it, and edit it. *A Tutorial Approach for the Descriptive Style: Writing a Character Sketch* (Minnesota Educational Computing Corporation) is an example of this type of software for use in middle school classes. The last type lets students use their knowledge of text structure to do real-life activities requiring use of such knowledge, such as writing a class newspaper. *The Children's Writing and Publishing Center* (The Learning Company) is an example of this type. This program does not instruct students in text structure, but it gives them an opportunity to use it.

World Classroom is a global online computer education network over which students can discuss curricular projects for the content areas with peers around the world. There are projects for science, social studies, language arts, and world events. To subscribe to this resource, a teacher needs a modem, communications software, and access to a telephone line (Wepner, 1993).

Mulligan and Gore (1992) recommend *Kids Network* by National Geographic Society and Technical Education Research Center (TERC). It "is a telecommunication based series of programs that enable an interdisciplinary approach to science for Grades 4–6, designed to involve students hands-on in science, geography, computer technology, and telecommunications activities" (pp. 379–380). Students collect and analyze local data and share their findings with students around the world through the central Kids Network computer or electronic bulletin board. This program allows students to do research and analyze and communicate findings, resulting in authentic writing.

reading-writing connection

thematic learning
literature-centered reading

Wepner (1992) has described how Elsie Nigohosian designed a cross-curricular unit on endangered species using books, software, magazines, and musical recordings. Some teachers overlook software when planning thematic units. Wepner (1992) makes other suggestions for using technology with content area units. She points out the value of using the *Colonial Times Database* from the *Bank Street Beginner's Filer* (Sunburst Communications) for information about the thirteen colonies during a thematic study of colonial times, along with books such as *The Secret Soldier: The Story of Deborah Sampson* by Ann McGovern (Four Winds Press, 1975), *And Then What Happened, Paul Revere?* by Jean Fritz (Coward McCann, 1973), and *The Sign of the Beaver* by Elizabeth George Speare (Houghton Mifflin, 1983). Software to use with science units includes Learningways' *Animal Watch: Whales, Earth Watch: Weather Forecasting* and *A Closer Look: The Desert. Math Shop* (Scholastic) simulates shopping in ten shops in a mall. It helps to connect students' mathematics skills to real-life situations.

More user-friendly authoring programs now allow many classroom teachers to develop computer-aided lessons for content area reading (Dillner, 1993/1994). With so many good materials available commercially, however, teachers should not feel that developing their own materials is a necessity.

Writing Techniques

reading-writing connection A number of writing techniques may be used to advantage in helping students learn to read effectively in the content areas. Probably the best known is the language experience approach. Others include feature analysis plus writing, webs plus writing, and keeping learning logs.

Language Experience Approach (LEA)

The *language experience approach (LEA)* is a good basic method to use in content area teaching (Jones and Nessel, 1985). Expository text structure can be taught through the LEA (Kinney, 1985). For example, a teacher who wishes to have students learn the comparison-and-contrast pattern of writing can have them discuss how two objects are alike and different, make a chart showing the likenesses and differences, and dictate a story based on the chart. The teacher can ask first for likenesses and then for differences as the dictation takes place. Then the children can use their own story to locate the two related parts of a contrast and do other activities related to the structure. (This chapter contains several examples of applying the language experience approach to specific content areas to promote learning of the content.)

The *Global Method* is a content-oriented version of the language experience approach (Sullivan, 1986) that is particularly useful for social studies and science classes. Students are encouraged to observe things around them, record their observations (in pictures or writing), and associate what they observe with their past experiences and prior knowledge. Children keep an observation notebook in which they record things observed in school, at home, on trips, or anywhere they happen to go. Then they organize their observations. The teacher leads the children to draw conclusions about word parts in words chosen from their notebooks, thereby allowing them to work with words they can already identify. This enhances students' decoding skill while they are engaged in content learning.

Feature Analysis Plus Writing

A *feature matrix* can be helpful for gathering, comparing, and contrasting information about several items in the same category (Cunningham and Cunningham, 1987). The teacher first reads through the material and selects the members of the category and some features that some, all, or none of them have. Then he or she forms them into a matrix like the one in Example 10.10 and displays the matrix to the class. The students copy the matrix onto their papers and then place pluses in the cells for which they think the category members display the respective features and minuses in the cells for which they think the category members do not display the respective features. If they are unsure about whether or not a specific feature belongs to a category member, they leave the cell blank. Then the students read the assigned material to confirm or revise their original markings and to fill in any empty spaces. They are encouraged to erase and change marks if the information read refutes initial ideas. During class discussion following the reading, the students and teacher complete the class matrix cooperatively. If there is disagreement, students return to the text to find support for their positions. Some points may require library research.

Example 10.10	*Semantic Feature Matrix for Geometric Shapes*				
	Straight lines	Curved lines	Four sides	Three sides	All sides must be equal in length
Triangle Rectangle Circle Square					

The information on the feature matrix can then be used as a basis for writing about the reading material. For instance, in Example 10.10, the teacher can choose one geometric shape and can model the writing of a paragraph about it. Students and teacher can then cooperatively write another paragraph about another shape. Then each student or small group of students may choose other shapes to write about. (Note that the matrix can be expanded to include many more shapes and features.) Using the information from a feature matrix for paragraph writing promotes retention of information covered in the matrix.

Webs Plus Writing

Webs are useful organizers in the content areas (Cunningham and Cunningham, 1987). Before the reading of the content material, the teacher records the information the students think they know about the topic of the chapter in the form of a web like the one shown in Example 10.11.

The students may make individual webs, containing only the points they think are correct. Then they read the material, checking the information on the web and adding the new information they find. In class discussion following the reading, the class web is revised and disagreements are settled by consulting the text. The class can write paragraphs about different strands of the web—for example, about famous leaders from Tennessee.

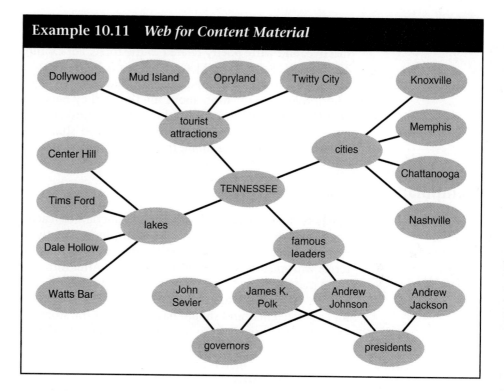

Example 10.11 *Web for Content Material*

Keeping Learning Logs

Using *learning logs* or journals to promote content area learning is a very effective technique. Students can follow the reading or discussion of a content topic with written summaries, comments, or questions related to the reading or class discussion. The content teacher can read the comments and adjust future lessons in response to the degree of understanding or confusion reflected in the logs (Gauthier, 1991).

Using Content Material with Reading of Fiction and Writing

Ollmann (1991) suggests using content material in the prereading phase to prepare students for reading literature that involves content concepts. The prereading of factual material may be accompanied by attention to the strategies needed to read the preliminary factual material that will help students understand the literature selection. Encyclopedia articles, travel magazines and brochures, *National Geographic*, or other material can often provide background information related to the setting or to scientific concepts involved in the stories. When the prereading material is being examined, the teacher can emphasize such strategies as skimming, scanning, use of alphabetical order and guide words, and others in a realistic setting.

Besides reading factual content material, students can read poems and other literature related to the content, think about the content from an aesthetic perspective, and write poetry related to the topic. For example, they can read poems like Heide's "Rocks" and McCord's "This Is My Rock" and Peters's book *The Sun, the Wind, and the Rain* when they are studying geology. Then they can write in descriptive or poetic form about the things they have discovered from the more factual books (McClure and Zitlow, 1991). Long (1993) suggests using acrostic poems, rather than formal written reports to share information gained from researching a topic. She found that they worked well for third graders.

Manipulative Materials

Teachers can use *manipulative* learning materials to teach both content objectives and the reading skills necessary to attain these objectives. An example of manipulative materials would be puzzles that require matching content vocabulary terms with pictures representing the terms. After introducing and demonstrating these materials in whole-class sessions, the teacher should place them in learning centers for students to use independently. The materials should have directions for easy reference, and should have a way for the students to determine the accuracy of their answers or to receive reinforcement. If activities call for divergent thought, reinforcement is usually provided through sharing of a report or project. Activities include matching technical vocabulary terms with illustrations of their meanings in a puzzle format, matching causes with effects, and following directions to produce an art product (Morrow, 1982).

Integrating Approaches

Because no single technique will enable all students to deal with the many demands of content material, a teacher must know many approaches, teach them directly, and let the students know why they help. Children need to be able to pick out an appropriate approach for a particular assignment. "The eight areas to be considered in planning a content lesson are objectives, vocabulary, background and motivation, survey and prediction, purposes for reading, guided reading, synthesis and reorganization, and application" (Gaskins, 1981, p. 324). The ultimate goal is to make students capable of studying effectively on their own.

To begin, the teacher should present to the class some content and process (reading/study strategy) *objectives* for each lesson, then move on to *vocabulary* by presenting and teaching words through context clues or by relating the words to ones the children already know. Next comes a discussion designed to *supply background information, motivate the students, and relate the material to things they already know*. Then the teacher asks the students to *survey the material and predict* what it is going to tell. *Purposes for reading* are set, either through the predictions or by other techniques. The teacher should *guide the reading* through use of a study guide; reading to verify hypotheses; reading to answer *who, what, when, where, how,* and *why* questions; or selective reading to discover important information. Then the teacher should plan activities that guide students to *synthesize and reorganize information*—for example, use the guided reading procedure, construct main-idea statements, take notes, write a content-based language experience story on the material (first in groups, then individually), or make graphic representations of the content (graphs, charts, diagrams). Students need to be given opportunities to *apply* in some way the concepts they have read about (Gaskins, 1981).

Creating Instructional Units

thematic learning

literature-centered reading

Two types of instructional units used in conjunction with content instruction are thematic units, in which the theme is a concept or a topic, and literature-based units across the curriculum, in which a piece of literature is the central factor. Literature should be an integral part of both types. Smith and Johnson (1994) say, "Literature can become the lens through which content is viewed." It puts the content into context and perspective. In all classrooms, but especially in whole language classrooms, reading aloud or Sustained Silent Reading, paired reading and discussion, guided reading, and literature response groups are becoming a part of much content area instruction. The following Classroom Scenario shows students working in a small group on a thematic unit.

**Classroom
Scenario**

Thematic Unit on Survival

The children in Ms. Parker's sixth-grade class had been reading books related to the theme of *survival.* Several of them were seated around a table, preparing to discuss how their books related to the theme.

"In *Julie of the Wolves,* Miyax has to survive by herself on the Alaskan tundra," Tonya began.

"In *Hatchet,* Brian has to survive by himself after his plane crashes in the Canadian wilderness," David said.

"Karana was left alone on an island off the coast of California," Zack said, referring to the main character in *Island of the Blue Dolphins.*

"Well, Phillip wasn't all alone on the Caribbean island in *The Cay* at first, but he did need help because he was blind after the blow to his head," David said. "Timothy, the black man, was really the one who made sure Phillip would survive. He used a lot of survival techniques."

"Let's list the survival techniques the characters used," Bruce said. "We could web them like Ms. Parker had us do with settings last month. We could use headings like 'Food' and 'Clothing.'"

"That's a good idea!" Tonya chimed in. "How about 'Shelter' for another heading?"

"Karana ate abalones and scallops from the sea," Zack said, "and she made herself a fenced-in house and a shelter in a cave."

"That's a good start," said Tonya. "Let's get that down on paper before we go on." She went to the storage shelf and returned with a piece of drawing paper and a black marker. She handed the materials to Bruce, the group member with the best handwriting skills. "Put your ideas and Zack's down before we forget them," she said. "Then we'll add more things from other people."

As Bruce began to write on the drawing paper, several other children began to take notes on their own papers about contributions they wanted to make.

Analysis of Scenario

The children in Ms. Parker's class had worked in discussion groups many times and were ready to participate when they came to the table. Tonya acted the part of a good leader by getting the discussion started and by collecting materials for the webbing and delegating the task of actually constructing the web to another student. Ms. Parker had taught a valuable skill, webbing, in earlier lessons, and these children remembered it and put it to use.

Thematic Content Units

The use of thematic units was discussed as one approach to literature-based reading instruction in Chapter 7. The same concept can apply to teaching content units (Crook and Lehman, 1991). Thematic content units involve linking reading of fiction and nonfiction about a content topic in order to help the children obtain a more complete picture of the topic. As Doiron (1994) points out, facts can be embedded in fiction and narrative structures can be used to convey facts presented in nonfiction. Thus, both types of books are useful, and children need to be able to read both types. Some thematic units are related to a single discipline; some are interdisciplinary, linking content and skills from different disciplines through authentic tasks; and some are integrative, in which the theme is the focus and lines between the disciplines are not evident (Smith and Johnson, 1994). (Students may collaborate with the teacher in theme selection, or the content may be mandated by the school district.) Teachers should choose broad themes that lend themselves to good instructional activities (Lapp and Flood, 1994). A web of the content topic can be elaborated with fiction and nonfiction selections about each subtopic, as shown in Example 10.12.

literature-centered reading

Although Example 10.12 focuses only on trade books, textbooks, magazines, newspapers, films, and software can all be included in the webbing process. Teachers should not overlook the possible value of picture books in content units for the upper grades. These books are often relegated to the primary grades, but many are appropriate for older students, and they add motivation and variety to lessons (Danielson, 1992). Eve Bunting has written a number of books that would be appropriate for these students, although they can be used with younger students, as well. They include *How Many Days to America?* (Clarion, 1988), *Terrible*

Example 10.12 *Thematic Content Unit*

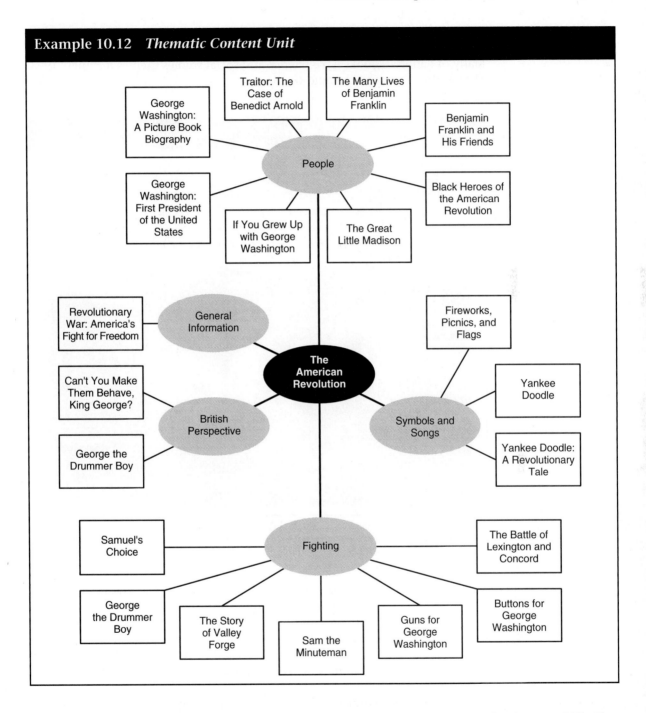

Things (The Jewish Publication Society, 1989), and *The Wall* (Clarion, 1990). Thematically focused alphabet books by Jerry Pallotta, George Ella Lyon, Gisela Jernigan, Abbie Zabar, Malka Drucker, and John Agard are also good. They cover a variety of topics, with many focusing on science and social studies concepts. For example, books by Zabar, Drucker, Red Hawk, and Agard introduce other cultures. Many of Pallotta's books have science and social studies themes (Chaney, 1993; Thompson, 1992). See Example 10.13.

Example 10.13 *Page from Thematic Alphabet Book*

K k

K is for Kulan. Kulans have incredible endurance. People have seen them run without stopping for more than twenty miles. They could easily run a marathon. Kulans are not only found in the desert. They are also found in areas called steppes. A steppe is a huge grassland or plain often found on the edge of a desert.

How many miles are in a marathon? The alphabet is a clue.

Source: Jerry Pallotta, *The Desert Alphabet Book* (Watertown, Mass.: Charlesbridge Publishing, 1994). Copyright © 1994 by Jerry Pallotta. Illustration copyright © 1994 by Mark Astrella. Used with permission by Charlesbridge Publishing.

After resources have been located and organized, the classroom activities to be used in the unit can be planned, with the web as a helpful reference, for it is not a complete plan. Teachers must decide on goals and objectives for their units, because not all concepts presented in all of the sources can possibly be used. Then they must choose instructional procedures and related activities to meet these goals, gather related materials, schedule unit activities, and decide how to assess the outcomes.

literature-centered reading   Thematic units connect information from language arts, science, social studies, math, art, music, and drama. Text sets (sets of books on one topic, by the same author, of the same genre, about the same culture, etc.) are useful in unit instruction. After students read the related texts, they can share and extend their understanding of each text in a different way than would have been possible if they had read only one text. (Harste, Short, and Burke, 1988). Literature focuses can range from such topics as the Holocaust (Zack, 1991) to life long ago contrasted with life today (Rosenbloom, 1991).

To set reading purposes, students can brainstorm questions about a topic. The children learn to read selectively to answer their questions. They can sort their questions into categories, discovering that by doing so they can find answers to more than one question at a time by locating the proper sections of books and becoming aware of the organization of nonfiction. When they share information with the class, they may refer to the text to prove points (Hess, 1991).

Literature-Based Units Across the Curriculum

literature-centered reading

A single piece of literature can be the basis of a unit that will include activities from many curricular areas. Related science, social studies, math, art, and music content may be taught with the piece of literature as the focal point. Language learning can take place along with reading, discussion, and writing done in relation to the literature selection. Example 10.14 shows one such unit for a sixth-grade class.

reading-writing connection

SELF-CHECK: OBJECTIVE 3   Name several general techniques for helping students read content area materials. Describe two of these techniques in detail. (See Self-Improvement Opportunities 2 and 4.)

Specific Content Areas

Special reading difficulties are associated with each of the content areas. It is best to teach skills for handling these difficulties when students need them in order to read their assignments.

Language Arts

The language arts block of the elementary school curriculum involves listening, speaking, reading, and writing instruction. It includes the subjects of reading, literature, and English. Since basal readers that may be used during reading class were discussed in other chapters in this textbook, they will not be considered here. Although literature is treated briefly in this chapter, more thorough coverage is found in Chapter 8.

Literature

literature-centered reading

Ideally, a literature program should encourage students to learn about their literary heritage, expand their imaginations, develop reading preferences, evaluate literature, increase their awareness of language, and grow socially, emotionally, and

Example 10.14   *Literature-Based Unit Across the Curriculum*

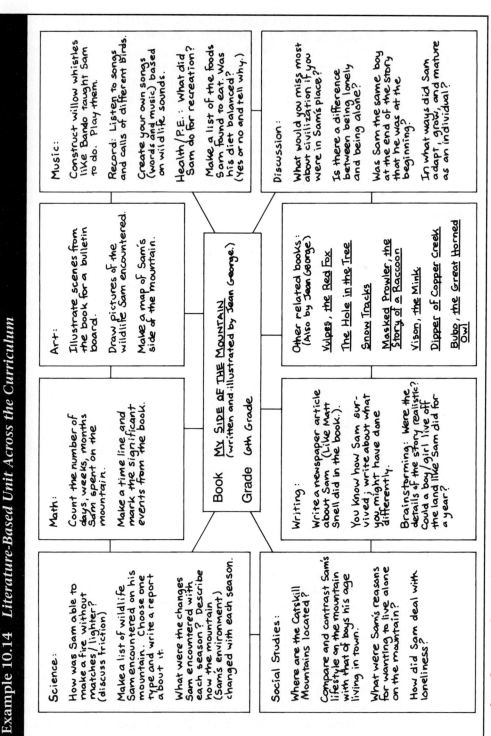

Book   MY SIDE OF THE MOUNTAIN
(written and illustrated by Jean George.)

Grade   6th Grade

Music:

Construct willow whistles like Bando taught Sam to do. Play them.

Record: Listen to songs and calls of different birds.

Create your own songs (words and music) based on wildlife sounds.

Health/P.E.: What did Sam do for recreation?

Make a list of the foods Sam found to eat. Was his diet balanced? (Yes or no and tell why.)

Discussion:

What would you miss most about civilization if you were in Sam's place?

Is there a difference between being lonely and being alone?

Was Sam the same boy at the end of the story that he was at the beginning?

In what ways did Sam adapt, grow, and mature as an individual?

Art:

Illustrate scenes from the book for a bulletin board.

Draw pictures of the wildlife Sam encountered.

Make a map of Sam's side of the mountain.

Other related books: (Also by Jean George)

Vulpes, the Red Fox

The Hole in the Tree

Snow Tracks

Masked Prowler, the Story of a Raccoon

Vison, the Mink

Dipper of Copper Creek

Bubo, the Great Horned Owl

Math:

Count the number of days, weeks, months Sam spent on the mountain.

Make a time line and mark the significant events from the book.

Writing:

Write a newspaper article about Sam (Like Matt Snell did in the book.).

You know how Sam survived; write about what you might have done differently.

Brainstorming: Were the details of the story realistic? Could a boy/girl live off the land like Sam did for a year?

Science:

How was Sam able to make a fire without matches/lighter? (discuss friction)

Make a list of wildlife Sam encountered on his mountain. Choose one type and write a report about it.

What were the changes Sam encountered with each season? Describe how the environment (Sam's environment) changed with each season.

Social Studies:

Where are the Catskill Mountains located?

Compare and contrast Sam's lifestyle on the mountain with that of boys his age living in town.

What were Sam's reasons for wanting to live alone on the mountain?

How did Sam deal with loneliness?

Source: Steve Gunter, graduate student, Tennessee Technological University, Cookeville, Tennessee.

intellectually. These goals can be reached through a well-planned program in which the teacher reads aloud to students daily and provides them with opportunities to read and respond to literature. Teachers may teach literary skills directly through a unit on poetry or a novel, or they may integrate these skills with basal reader and language arts lessons.

Teaching Literature Skills.   When developing literature programs, teachers should plan diversity in children's exposure to literature, rather than allowing students to have only random encounters with books (Stewig, 1980). They can organize instruction by genres (forms or categories), literary elements, or topics in order to vary students' experiences, and they should introduce students to the specialized vocabulary and skills they need to develop an appreciation of literature.

In literature classes, children are asked to read and understand many literary forms, including short stories, novels, plays, poetry, biographies, and autobiographies. One characteristic of all these forms is the frequent occurrence of *figurative* or nonliteral language, which is sometimes a barrier to understanding. Children tend to interpret such language literally. Chapter 4 covers teaching children to deal with figurative expressions.

Literary Elements.   To understand literary passages, children need to be able to recognize and analyze plots, themes, characterization, settings, and authors' styles. The *plot* is the overall plan for the story; the *theme* is the main idea the writer wishes to convey; and *characterization* is the way in which the writer makes the reader aware of the characteristics and motives of each person in the story. The *setting* consists of time and place, and the *style* is the writer's mode of expressing thoughts. Teacher-directed questioning can make students aware of these literary elements and help children understand the interrelationships among them. Following are some points related to major story elements:

1. *Setting.* Teachers should point out how time and place affect the plot, characterization, and mood of a story. Stories must be true to their settings; characters behave differently today from the way they behaved a hundred years ago, and city life involves situations different from those that occur in country life. All of these facts make understanding the setting of a story important. *Madeline* by Ludwig Bemelmans is a good book to use in helping children see the importance of setting (Sharp, 1984).

2. *Characterization.* Children who examine literature with strong characterization find that writers develop their characters through dialogue, actions, interactions with others, and insights into their thoughts and feelings, as well as through description. Looking for these clues will make the children more attuned to the characters and should increase their overall understanding of the piece of literature. Children can also take note of how characters grow and change as the story progresses (Galda, 1989). The characterizations in Cynthia Voigt's *Dicey's Song* make good discussion material. In addition, the children can read *Miss Nelson Is Missing* by Harry Allard and James Marshall and compare and contrast the two identities of Miss Nelson. They

could write dialogue for "Miss Nelson" and "Miss Swamp" and use this dialogue in a puppet show, imitating the way each character would speak, as well as using appropriate lines (Dreher, 1989).

3. *Plot.* Children may analyze short, simple stories to see how writers introduce their stories, develop them through a series of incidents, create interest and suspense, and reach satisfying conclusions. Awareness of the ways plots are developed can increase understanding of narratives. Picture books with predictable plots are good places to start. Mem Fox's *Hattie and the Fox* is a good choice for picture-book plot analysis (Galda, Carr, and Cox, 1989). *Doctor Desoto* by William Steig is another good book for examining plot with children (Sharp, 1984).

4. *Style.* Children should examine written material to analyze the authors' choices of words, sentence patterns, and manners of expression. The styles of writing in Maurice Sendak's *Chicken Soup with Rice,* Cynthia Rylant's *When I Was Young in the Mountains,* and Patricia MacLachlan's *Sarah, Plain and Tall* could be discussed and compared.

5. *Theme.* The concept of *theme* is abstract. Smit (1990) suggests selecting two stories that have the same theme but different settings, plots, and other elements to allow students to see how the same theme can be developed in different ways. She suggests *Why the Chimes Rang* by Raymond MacDonald Alden and *The Grateful Statues,* a Japanese folktale, for helping the students discover the theme of *giving.*

One way that teachers may work on these elements is through journal writing (Au and Scheu, 1989). (See Chapters 7 and 8 for more on journal writing.) The children may be asked to respond to a story by selecting a character from the story and writing a journal entry as though that character were writing it. The entries can be dated according to the time in which the book takes place. The journal writers can leave clues in their entries to the identities of the characters doing the writing. These entries can be shared orally, with the other children trying to decide which character wrote each entry. Such an activity encourages attention to characterization, point of view, and mood (Jossart, 1988).

Webbing literary elements related to a story can help students clarify their concepts of these elements. The teacher can read the story and have the students listen for the elements that need to be added to the web (Norton, 1993).

Literary Forms.   Children's literature consists of a variety of genres or literary forms, including historical and realistic fiction, biographies, poetry, plays, informational books, and fantasy and folklore. Historical fiction, biographies, and informational books are all useful for integrating with content areas, whereas good realistic fiction serves as a model for helping children to understand others and solve problems in their own lives. Poetry encourages children to explore their emotions, and plays offer the pleasure of acting out favorite stories. Both modern fantasy and folklore allow children to escape into worlds of imaginary characters and events. Teachers should use all of these forms in their literature programs, and they can enhance children's understanding of them by reading literature of all forms aloud and pointing out the characteristics of each genre.

Folklore presents many possibilities for introducing different literary forms. Intermediate-grade children especially enjoy tall tales, and they can try to locate the exaggerations in the stories. Another form of folklore is the fable, which is usually characterized by brevity, a moral, and use of animal characters. Students can practice identifying the morals of the fables before they read the ones stated in the books. Myths, *pourquoi* (*why*) tales, some Native American folklore, and Rudyard Kipling's *Just So Stories* provide explanations for universal origins. These stories are excellent for helping children to understand different cultures and become familiar with literary classics.

Teachers can introduce children to poetry by reading them poetry of all kinds and asking them to respond freely and with feeling. The children should then have opportunities to read much poetry for themselves and to participate in choral reading/speaking of poetry. Galda (1989) suggests following the reading of poems to which children respond positively with a focus on rhythm and rhyme, alliteration and onomatopoeia, and metaphors and imagery, to name only a few elements.

Spiegel (1991) suggests *Poetry Please!* (The Magic Library Series, TV Ontario) for introducing children to poetry as a genre. This program is a fifteen-minute video that explores what poetry is through examples and discussion. Stop-tape questions and a read-along activity get students actively involved. A teacher's guide suggests a variety of activities to use with the tape. *Poetry Works!* (Modern Curriculum Press) is a kit for kindergarten through grade three that includes poetry posters and an extensive teacher's guide that provides related poems and activities to be used with each poem. The thematic arrangement of the poems allows easy integration with social studies and science.

reading-writing connection   In a poetry-writing program for fourth and fifth graders in her school, Freeman (1983) identifies a series of activities, beginning with visits by a consultant who reads poetry aloud and directs children's attention to the ideas expressed in the poems. The program continues with attention to basic language patterns and alliterative word games before moving to various poetry forms (such as cinquains and haiku, discussed later). Attention to rhyming forms (couplets and quatrains) and free verse concludes the series of activities.

Play reading is quite different from reading the narrative and expository material discussed previously. Reading plays can help students see the relationship between print and spoken language (Manna, 1984). "A play's script, consisting mostly of dialogue, the sequence of events, and a limited description of the setting, stimulates children to pay close attention to textual details and helps them develop language skills basic to interpretive reading" (p. 712). Bringing the play to life involves many interpretive and creative decisions about the setting, action, and characters. Discussion about the way dialogue should be delivered makes the students sensitive to language styles and usages that fit the context and the characters.

Comparisons of narrative and script versions of the same stories can help students see the differences in the writing styles and help them learn to look for information in the right places (Manna, 1984). Many plays based on children's stories are readily available. Basal readers often include such plays, as do some trade books.

Both creative dramatizations of plays and dramatized reading, such as readers' theater, can be used in elementary classrooms. Tape-recording rehearsals for later evaluation and having children produce their own scripts for plays from narratives they have read are also valuable procedures (Manna, 1984).

reading-writing connection

English

English textbooks cover the areas of listening, speaking, and writing and generally consist of a series of sections of instructional material followed by practice exercises. The technical vocabulary includes such terms as *determiner, noun, pronoun, manuscript, cursive,* and *parliamentary procedure.* The concepts presented in the informational sections are densely packed; each sentence is usually important for understanding, and examples are abundant. Children need to be encouraged to study the examples because they help to clarify the information presented in the narrative portion of the textbook.

Teachers are wise to plan oral activities in class to accompany the listening and speaking portions of the English textbook, since such practice allows students to apply the concepts immediately and helps them retain the material. Similarly, it is wise to ask students to apply the concepts encountered in the writing section as soon as possible in relevant situations to aid retention.

reading-writing connection

Composition instruction can form the basis for reading activities. Children read to obtain information to include in their compositions, and they read to learn different styles of writing. For example, they read poems to absorb the style of writing before attempting to write poetry. Children can also read their own material in order to revise it to enhance clarity or ensure correct use of language conventions. They may read it aloud to peers for constructive criticism, or their peers may read it themselves (Dionisio, 1983).

Much of a student's formal vocabulary instruction takes place in English classes. Trade books can be the basis for vocabulary lessons. Fred Gwynne's *The King Who Rained* offers good examples of figurative expressions and words with multiple meanings that can be used to interest students in word study. Emily Hanlon's *How a Horse Grew Hoarse on the Site Where He Sighted a Bare Bear* offers examples of homonyms in nonsense verses.

Social Studies

In social studies reading, youngsters encounter such technical terms as *democracy, tropics, hemisphere, decade,* and *century,* as well as many words with meanings that differ from their meanings in general conversation. When children first hear that a candidate is going to *run* for office, they may picture a foot race, an illusion that is furthered if they read that a candidate has decided to enter the *race* for governor. If the term *race* is applied to people in their texts, the children may become even more confused. Children who know that you *strike* a match or make a *strike* when bowling may not understand a labor union *strike*. Discussions about the *mouth* of a river could bring unusual pictures to the minds of youngsters. The teacher is responsible for seeing that the students understand the concepts these terms represent.

Social studies materials also present children with maps, charts, and graphs to read. Ways of teaching the use of such reading aids have been suggested in Chapter 9. Social studies materials must be read critically. Students should be taught to check copyright dates to determine timeliness and to be alert for such problems as outdated geography materials that show incorrect boundaries or place names.

Social studies texts in particular have been criticized for being difficult to read, often requiring more reading ability than prospective readers have, and varying four or more years in difficulty from passage to passage. Social studies texts have often been found to assume unrealistic levels of background knowledge on the part of the students and to lack coherence (Stetson and Williams, 1992; Beck and McKeown, 1991), interest, and meaning for them (Guzzetti, Kowalinski, and McGowan, 1992). In social studies texts, the absence of directly stated main ideas in many passages and even in paragraphs can cause comprehension problems (Doyle, 1984).

literature-centered reading   Trade books can be used to enhance the social studies program. They provide causal relationships between concepts and give students a chance to answer their own questions about the content from their reading. Trade books offer opportunities to meet curricular objectives for both reading and social studies simultaneously. Maps in trade books can be used to teach map-reading skills, to locate the places being studied and to identify the features of the land in these places, for example. When using such books, brainstorming about prior knowledge and forming semantic maps can be helpful. Then teachers can have students use think sheets on which they list their questions about a central question posed by the teacher, their ideas about how the questions would be answered, and how the texts answered the questions. They may eventually produce their own question-and-answer books about the topic (Guzzetti, Kowalinski, and McGowan, 1992).

The five fundamental themes in geography are location (where a story takes place and why); place (what the place is like); relationships within places (including human/environmental relationships); movement of people, materials, and ideas (descriptions and consequences); and regions (including how they change) (Norton, 1993; Committee on Geographic Education, 1983; *GEONews Handbook*, 1990). Norton (1993) shows how the books *People of the Breaking Day* by Marcia Sewell (Atheneum, 1990), *Christopher Columbus: Voyager to the Unknown* by Nancy Smiler Levinson (Lodestar, 1990), *Encounter* by Jane Yolen (Harcourt Brace Jovanovich, 1992), and *The Other 1942: Jewish Settlement in the New World* by Norman H. Funkelstein (Scribner's, 1989) can help students learn about these five themes in the context of literature rather than textbook discussions. This treatment, supplemented with other books about the period, offers diverse per-spectives on the geographic concepts being studied.

Picture books can be valuable for presenting many social studies concepts to middle and upper elementary students. These books elaborate on topics that would otherwise get limited attention. Sensitive issues that are ignored in text-books can often be treated effectively in fictional accounts. Children become emotionally involved with other people and historical situations through these books (Farris and Fuhler, 1994).

Fictionalized biographies and diaries used for social studies instruction are excellent for teaching children to evaluate the accuracy and authenticity of mate-rial, since authors have invented dialogue and thoughts for the characters to make the material seem more realistic. Teachers should lead children to see that these stories try to add life to facts but are not completely factual, perhaps by hav-ing them check reference books for accuracy of dates, places, and names. Some-times reading an author's foreword or postscript will offer clues to the fictional aspects of a story; for example, at times only the historical events mentioned are true. Students should also be aware that authors use first-person narrative accounts to make the action seem more personal, but that in reality the supposed speaker is not the person who did the writing. Also, any first-person account offers a limited perspective, because the person speaking cannot know everything that all the characters in the story do or everything that is happening at one time. Teachers should alert students to look for the author's bias and ask them to check to see how much the author depended on actual documents if a bibliography of sources is given (Storey, 1982).

Zarnowski (1988) shared fictionalized biographies with her fourth graders orally, had them read some for themselves, and had them write their own biogra-phies about Benjamin Franklin, about whom they collected much information through reading and listening to their teacher read. The students learned a great deal about both fictionalized biographies and Benjamin Franklin (and some other famous people) through this experience.

Another approach to reading biographical material is to have students choose a famous person; read that person's biography; do additional research on the per-son, using multiple sources; make time lines of events in the person's life; and take on the role of that person in role-playing sessions. Since reading research strategies should be taught in context (McAlcon, 1993), this procedure would provide a fertile ground for such teaching. Such studies can also naturally link social studies with science and language.

Use of biographies can help students think about social issues and individu-als' involvement with them, assessing the importance of events and understand-ing the objective and subjective dimensions of the events. This can lead to lessons on determining fact and opinion (Miller, Clegg, and Vanderhoff, 1992).

Some contemporary biographies are *Thurgood Marshall and Equal Rights* by Seamus Cavan (Millbrook Press, 1993), *Boris Yeltsin: Man of the People* by Eleanor H. Ayer (Dillon Press, 1992), and *Bill Clinton, Our 42nd President* by Robert Civiklik (Millbrook Press, 1993) (Pierce and Short, 1993). Other books containing biographical material include *A Picture Book of Benjamin Franklin* by David A. Adler (Holiday House, 1989) and *True Stories about Abraham Lincoln* by Ruth Belov Gross (Lothrop, Lee, & Shepard, 1990) (Galda and DeGroff, 1990). *Zlata's Diary: A Child's Life in Sarajevo* by Zlata Filipovic (Scholastic, 1994) is another up-to-date source for factual material about a person involved in historical drama.

Children can also be drawn into historical periods and issues through historical fiction. Historical fiction transforms a series of events into an interpretation of these events, providing humanizing details. It can help students understand the times in which historical events occurred. Children are able to become emotionally involved with people from the past. As they identify with the actual historical characters in the books they read, they face conflicting viewpoints that require them to do critical thinking. They read to interpret the moral and ethical issues faced during these events. They see multiple perspectives and can make informed judgments (Johnson and Ebert, 1992; Levstick, 1990). As students study these materials, teachers can read related materials to them to build background. Then the students can do activities such as making time lines based on their readings, marking maps to show where events in the reading occurred, classifying characters as to beliefs or allegiances, producing mock newspapers from the times, illustrating events and places described, writing diaries for characters in the reading, or writing letters to characters with comments and advice (Johnson and Ebert, 1992).

Social studies materials are generally written in a very precise and highly compact expository style in which many ideas are expressed in a few lines of print. Authors may discuss a hundred-year span in a single page or even a single paragraph or may cover complex issues in a few paragraphs, even though whole books could be devoted to these issues. Study guides are recommended for helping students read social studies materials with understanding and purpose.

Social studies materials are organized in a variety of ways, including cause-and-effect relationships, chronological order, comparisons and/or contrasts, and topical order (for example, by regions, such as Asia and North America, or by concepts, such as transportation and communication). The content selection in Example 10.5 is an example of the cause/effect pattern, but it also offers comparisons and contrasts of the effects of the war on different groups. To help children deal with cause-and-effect and chronological order arrangements, teachers can use the ideas found in Chapter 6 for helping students determine such relationships and sequences. Drawing time lines is one good way to work with chronological order, and pattern guides such as the one in Example 10.6 are ways to work on cause/effect or comparison/contrast relationships.

If the teacher points out the organizational pattern of the selection, children approach the reading with an appropriate mental set, which aids greatly in comprehension of the material.

Social studies materials are frequently written in a very impersonal style and may be concerned with unfamiliar people or events that are often remote in time

literature-centered reading

or place. Students may also lack interest in the subject. For these reasons, teachers should use many interesting trade books to personalize the content and to expand on topics that are covered very briefly in the textbook. Biographies of famous people who lived during different historical periods add spice to textbook accounts, and use of literature about different peoples is one way to approach multicultural issues (Rasinski and Padak, 1990; Martinez and Nash, 1990; Pugh and Garcia, 1990). Walker-Dalhouse (1992) believes the use of multiethnic literature can decrease negative stereotyping of people from other cultures. Norton (1990) suggests presenting multicultural literature in a sequence including traditional literature; traditional tales from one area; autobiographies, biographies, and historical nonfiction; historical fiction; and contemporary fiction, biography, and poetry. She makes suggestions for each segment of the sequence with Black and Hispanic literature selections. Hennings (1982) suggests a number of children's storybooks that can be used to teach social studies concepts. Some of them follow.

> Aardema, Verna. *Why Mosquitoes Buzz in People's Ears: A West African Tale.* New York: Dial Press, 1975. (justice)
> Burton, Virginia Lee. *The Little House.* Boston: Houghton Mifflin, 1942. (change)
> Waber, Bernard. *"You Look Ridiculous," Said the Rhinoceros to the Hippopotamus.* Boston: Houghton Mifflin, 1966. (individual differences)

Hennings (1982) also suggests comparing and contrasting similar stories to gain a more complete understanding of the concepts being developed. Use of stories can also promote inferential thinking and reading, since their messages are often implied, rather than directly stated.

Using the Newspaper

The newspaper is a living textbook for social studies through which youngsters learn about tomorrow's history as it is happening today. Different parts of the newspaper require different reading skills, as noted here:

1. *News stories*—identifying main ideas and supporting details (who, what, where, when, why, how), determining sequence, recognizing cause-and-effect relationships, making inferences, drawing conclusions

2. *Editorials*—discriminating between fact and opinion, discovering the author's point of view, detecting author bias and propaganda techniques, making inferences, drawing conclusions

3. *Comics*—interpreting figurative language and idiomatic expressions, recognizing sequence of events, making inferences, detecting cause-and-effect relationships, drawing conclusions, making predictions

4. *Advertisements*—detecting propaganda, making inferences, drawing conclusions, distinguishing between fact and opinion

5. *Entertainment section*—reading charts (TV schedule and the like), evaluating material presented

6. *Weather*—reading maps

Each of these skills is discussed fully in either Chapter 6 or Chapter 9.

Student newspapers such as *Weekly Reader* (Field Publications) are often used in the elementary classroom. *Weekly Reader* has a separate publication for each grade level.

Most regular newspapers vary in difficulty from section to section. A check with a readability formula of available newspapers, especially local ones, will help teachers decide if their students can use the newspapers profitably.

Teachers can begin newspaper study by determining what students already know with an inventory like the one shown in Example 10.15.

Example 10.15 *Newspaper Inventory*

Directions: Answer the following questions about your use of the newspaper.
1. What newspaper(s) come to your home?
2. Do you read a newspaper regularly? How often?
3. What parts of the newspaper do you read? _____ News _____
   Editorials _____ Comics _____ Entertainment section _____
   Features _____ Advertisements _____ Columns _____ Other
   (Give names.) _____
4. How do you locate the part of the newspaper that you want? _____ turn
   each page _____ use the index
5. Where is the index in a newspaper?
6. What do the following terms mean?
   a. AP   d. editorial
   b. byline   e. lead
   c. dateline f. masthead

After administering such an inventory, the teacher can decide where the students need to begin in newspaper study. Some will need an initial orientation to the parts of the newspaper and the information found in each part; some will need help with location skills; and some will need help with newspaper terminology.

Following are several activities to help children read newspapers more effectively.

1. Have students locate the *who, what, where, when, why,* and *how* in news stories.

2. Using news stories with the headlines cut off, have students write their own headlines and compare them with the actual headlines.

3. Have children scan a page for a news story on a particular topic.

4. Give children copies of news stories about the same event from two different newspapers. Then ask them to point out and discuss likenesses and differences.

Activities

5. Using copies of conflicting editorials, have students underline facts in one color and opinions in another color and discuss the results. Also, have them locate emotional language and propaganda techniques in each editorial.

6. Discuss the symbolism and the message conveyed by each of several editorial cartoons. Then ask students to draw their own editorial cartoons.

7. Have students compare an editorial and a news story on the same topic. Discuss differences in approach.

8. Tell students to locate comics that are funny. Then ask them to explain why they are funny.

9. Have students study the entertainment section and decide which movies or plays would be most interesting to them or locate time slots for certain television programs.

10. Encourage children to try to solve crossword puzzles.

11. Have students compare human interest features with straight news stories to discover which type of writing is more objective, which has more descriptive terms, and so on. Have them dramatize appropriate ones.

12. Ask students to search grocery advertisements from several stores for the best buy on a specified item or to study the classified advertisements to decide what job they would most like to have and why. Then ask them to write their own classified ads.

13. Have the youngsters study the display advertisements for examples of propaganda techniques.

14. Ask students to use the index of the paper to tell what page to look on for the television schedule, weather report, and so on.

15. Ask the children to search through the newspaper for typographical errors. Then discuss the effects of these errors on the material in which they appear.

16. Have students search the sports page for synonyms for the terms *won* and *lost*. Ask them why these synonyms are used.

Mathematics

Reading in mathematics poses special difficulties. First is the technical and specialized vocabulary. Young children have to learn terms like *plus, minus, sum,* and *subtraction,* whereas older children encounter such terms as *perimeter* and *diameter.* Words with multiple meanings also appear frequently. Discussions about *planes, figures,* or raising a number to the third *power* can confuse children who know other, more common meanings for these words. Nevertheless, many mathematics terms have root words, prefixes, or suffixes that children can use in determining their meanings. (For example, *triangle* means "three angles.")

To help build math vocabulary, teachers can assign a math word for each day, which students must identify and use in a sentence. One child may "own" the word, wearing a card on which the word is written and giving a presentation on it to the rest of the group, or students may be asked to identify or illustrate math terms written on cards before they are allowed to line up to leave the room. The teacher can ask questions about which terms being studied apply to a particular problem or ask the children to dramatize the problems or meanings of math terms (Kutzman and Krutchinsky, 1981).

Mountain (1993) suggests constructing stories that require the use of math synonyms in context to help students build concepts. Here is an example:

> Mother needed *one yard* of material to make the cover.
> "Mr. Huffer sells the material by the foot," Jamie complained.
> "Then buy *three feet* of material," said Mother. "You're lucky he doesn't sell it by the inch. Then you'd have to remember to get *thirty-six* inches."

Some of the synonyms in the story can be provided and others left out, to be filled in by the students from the context.

Mathematical crossword puzzles provide good practice with specialized vocabulary. The Model Activity on page 522 shows an example.

Difficulties with words are not the only problems children have with math textbooks. They are also required to understand a different symbol system and to read numerals as well as words, which involves understanding place value. Children must be able to interpret such symbols as plus and minus signs, multiplication and division signs, symbols for union and intersection, equal signs and signs indicating inequalities, and many others, as well as abbreviations such as *ft., lb., in., qt., mm, cm,* and so on.

Symbols are often particularly troublesome to children, perhaps partly because some symbols mean other things in other contexts; for example, − means *minus* in math but is a dash or a hyphen in regular print. Matching exercises such as the one described in the Model Activity on page 523 encourage youngsters to learn the meanings of symbols.

To read numbers, students must understand place value. They must note, for example, that the number 312.8 has three places to the left of the decimal point (which they must discriminate from a period), which means that the leftmost numeral indicates a particular number of hundreds, the next numeral tells how many tens, and the next numeral tells how many ones (in this case, three hundreds, one ten, and two ones, or three hundred twelve). To determine the value to the right of the decimal, they must realize that the first place is tenths, the second place is hundredths, and so forth. In this example, there are eight tenths; therefore, the entire number is three hundred twelve and eight tenths. This is obviously a complex procedure, involving not merely reading from left to right but also reading back and forth.

Model Activities

Mathematical Crossword Puzzle

Construct a crossword puzzle based on the key vocabulary in the content material. The following one is based on terminology from the field of mathematics. Place the puzzle in a learning center, including an answer key in an accompanying envelope. Have the students who complete the puzzle check their answers, using the answer key provided for them.

¹P	L	U	²S			³E
O			U			Q
⁴I	N		⁵M	⁶I	N	U	S
N			⁷O	N		A
⁸T	E	N		C		L
		E		H		

Across

1. Two _____ two equals four.
4. Abbreviation for inch
5. Ten _____ one equals nine.
8. In the decimal system base _____ is used.

Down

1. A decimal _____ shows place value.
2. Total
3. The same amount in all containers, or _____ amounts
6. 1/12 of a foot
7. One × _____ = one.

Mathematical sentences also present reading problems. Children must recognize numbers and symbols and translate them into verbal sentences, reading $9 \div 3 = 3$, for example, as "nine divided by three equals three."

Students will need help in reading and analyzing word problems as well. Teachers should arrange such problems according to difficulty and avoid assigning too many at one time (Schell, 1982). Story problems can present special comprehension difficulties. They require the basic comprehension skills (determining main ideas and details, seeing relationships among details, making inferences,

**Model
Activities**

Matching Activity for Symbols

Place the symbols =, ≠, >, <, −, +, and ÷ on separate index cards. Write *equals, is not equal to, is greater than, is less than, minus, plus,* and *divided by* on other individual cards. Shuffle the cards and give them out randomly to students. Then let one student with a symbol card go to the front of the room and hold up his or her card. The student with the matching card should go up to join the first student. If nobody moves, the students with the definition cards all hold them up where the first student can see them and he or she calls the student with the matching card to the front. If the student at the front cannot choose correctly, a student without a card may volunteer to make the match. After the match is made, the pair, or the trio if outside help was used, watches as other matches are made. Then each pair or trio thus formed makes up a math problem using its own symbol for the rest of the class to solve. These problems are written on the chalkboard. All students go to their seats and work the problems on their own papers. Then students who were not involved in constructing the problems volunteer to work them on the board, with the original pairs or trios acting as verifiers.

---

drawing conclusions, analyzing critically, and following directions). Chapter 9 contains a description of the SQRQCQ study method for mathematics, which takes these requirements into account.

Sometimes children find it useful to draw a picture of the situation a problem describes or to manipulate actual objects, and teachers should encourage such approaches to problem solving when they are appropriate. Teachers should watch their students solve word problems and decide where they need the most help: with computation, with problem interpretation (understanding of problems that they are not required to read for themselves), with reading, or with integration of the three skills in order to reach a solution. Small groups of students who need help in different areas of problem solving can be formed (Cunningham and Ballew, 1983).

Since story problems are not written in a narrative style, children often lack the familiarity with the text structure needed for ease of comprehension. The pattern of writing for story problems is procedural, with important details at the beginning and the topic sentence near the end. This pattern fails to offer children an early purpose for their reading (Reutzel, 1983).

Braselton and Decker (1994) suggest that teachers have students think of the word problems as short stories that they could comprehend by using their prior knowledge. They suggest the use of a graphic organizer to help students visualize the steps in problem solution. The use of the organizer can be taught through modeling by the teacher, followed by guided practice and independent practice by the students. Example 10.16 shows an example of such an organizer.

Example 10.16 *Graphic Organizer for Math*

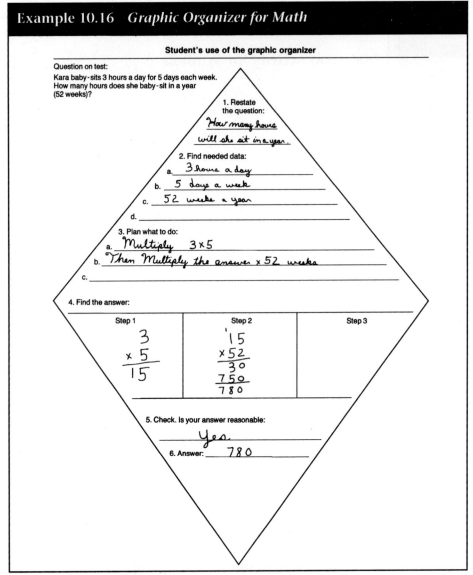

Student's use of the graphic organizer

Question on test:
Kara baby-sits 3 hours a day for 5 days each week.
How many hours does she baby-sit in a year
(52 weeks)?

1. Restate the question:
How many hours will she sit in a year.

2. Find needed data:
a. *3 hours a day*
b. *5 days a week*
c. *52 weeks a year*
d. _____

3. Plan what to do:
a. *Multiply 3 × 5*
b. *Then Multiply the answer × 52 weeks*
c. _____

4. Find the answer:

Step 1	Step 2	Step 3
3 × 5 15	15 × 52 30 750 780	

5. Check. Is your answer reasonable:
Yes.

6. Answer: *780*

Source: Stephania Braselton and Barbara C. Decker, "Using Graphic Organizers to Improve the Reading of Mathematics," *The Reading Teacher*, 48 (November 1994), 279. Reprinted with permission of Stephania Braselton and the International Reading Association.

Collier and Redmond (1974) point out that mathematics material is very concise and abstract in nature and involves complex relationships. A high density of ideas per page appears in this kind of material, and understanding each word is very important, for one word may be the key to understanding an entire section. Yet elementary teachers too often approach a math lesson in terms of developing only computational skill, apparently not realizing that reading skills can be advanced during arithmetic lessons or that arithmetic statement problems would be more comprehensible if attention were given to reading skills.

Hadaway and Young (1994) suggest that children will benefit from creating story problems related to their own experiences after a group language experience approach with classroom-related math problems. A research study showed that students who made up their own math story problems to solve performed better on tests of application skills than did those who practiced textbook word problems. Children are likely to interpret a story problem more successfully if they have constructed a similar problem (Ferguson and Fairburn, 1985). Fortescue (1994, p. 576) says, "To write about a mathematical problem, one must separate the problem into a series of steps that lead to a solution. So, in writing about math problems or activities, students become familiar with analytical writing while gaining and displaying a deeper understanding of the math concept."

Wood (1992) suggests that each student in a group can be given a different computation that involves the same operation, can solve the problem and think aloud or write the solution process, and then can present the solution to the group. Another approach would be to give all students the same problem to solve individually and have them discuss and critique or expand one another's retellings.

Students may also be given a reaction guide composed of statements about the mathematics material that are either true or false and, working in cooperative groupings, they can complete the guide by agreeing or disagreeing with each statement and providing the reason (Wood, 1992).

Fortescue (1994) gave third graders math task cards and asked them to complete the activities on the cards, record the results, and describe what they did during the activity. Each activity and the way to talk and write about it were modeled for the whole group before the activity was completed by the students. The students completed the activities, talked to one another about them, and then wrote about them. They had other students and then the teacher read their descriptions to verify that they were clear. These activities clarified their thinking about math processes.

Teachers can use literature to help them teach mathematical material. Counting books, for example, can provide material for teaching addition and subtraction. Bell (October 1988) suggests the books *Animals One to Ten* by Deborah Manley, and *Anno's Counting House* by Mitsumasa Anno for working with addition and subtraction. An excellent book for developing concepts of large numbers is *How Much Is a Million?* by David M. Schwartz, and a good one for encouraging them to work with division is *The Doorbell Rang* by Pat Hutchins. This book can also be used for addition with younger children. Children's literature can also help students learn to tell time. Bell (November 1988) suggests using *The Scarecrow Clock* by George Mendoze for this purpose and the book *Chicken Soup with Rice* by Maurice Sendak for motivating children to learn to read the calendar. The following Focus on Strategies section shows a mathematics lesson that is based on literature.

**Focus on
Strategies**

Mathematics Lesson Based on Literature

Ms. Barnes opened the class by displaying the book *The Doorbell Rang* by Pat Hutchins. "From the picture on the cover of this book and the title *The Doorbell Rang,* what do you think it will be about?" she asked the children.

"There are lots of people in the picture," Sammy said. "I think a lot of people have come to visit. The doorbell rings every time somebody comes. We have a doorbell that people ring when they come."

"What else does the picture make you think?" Ms. Barnes asked.

"They've tracked up the kitchen," said Monica. "The mom is going to have to clean it up. She'll send them all out."

"Does anybody else have something to add?" Ms. Barnes asked.

"The children don't look happy. Maybe she is running them out," Tasha suggested.

"They are looking out the slot in the door. Maybe the person that just rang the bell is someone they don't like," Jimmy said.

"Or maybe the kids don't want anyone else to come," Don added.

"Listen carefully as I read the story to see if your predictions were right," Ms. Barnes said. "Also listen to see what this book has to do with math."

Ms. Barnes read the story. When she finished, she asked, "Were your predictions right?"

"I was right that lots of people came and the bell rang every time," Sammy said.

"Mom didn't send them out of the kitchen, so Tasha and I were wrong," Monica said.

"I was wrong," Jimmy said. "They acted like they liked the people who came."

"But I'll bet they really didn't want all of those people to come and share the cookies. I think I was right, even though they don't act bad about it," Don said.

"How does all of this fit into a math problem?" asked Ms. Barnes.

"They have to decide how many cookies to give each person," Don replied.

"That's right. Now we are going to see how they figured it all out," Ms. Barnes said as she handed out stacks of plastic chips to each set of math partners in the room.

"Now," she said, "listen carefully and use your chips to answer my questions as I go back through the story."

She read the first two pages. "How many children were there?" she asked.

"Two," the children chorused.

"How many cookies did each one get?" she asked.

"Six," answered the children.

"We need to know how many cookies there were in all," she said. "What do we do to get this answer?"

"We add them," answered Joey.

"Who can write out an addition problem on the board that we have to solve?" she asked.

Benny went to the board and wrote "6 + 6 = ".

"Now solve the problem," she told them.

The children, who had used the chips to solve problems before, worked with their partners to form two rows of six chips each and count them. Soon hands were up all over the room. When all were finished, Ms. Barnes called on Billy, who proudly answered "Twelve."

"Did anyone get any other answer?" she asked. A sea of shaking heads answered her. "Good job," she said. She let Sean go to the board and write the answer to the problem after the equals sign. Then she read further in the book.

"How many children were there after Tom and Hannah came?" she asked. Hands went up immediately, without use of the chips.

Ms. Barnes let Sammy give the answer, "four," and go to the board and write the entire problem and answer: "$2 + 2 = 4$."

"Show with your chips how Sam and Victoria knew that each one would get three cookies," Ms. Barnes directed. The children arranged their chips into four rows of three chips each.

"Now write an addition problem to show how putting these cookies back on the plate would give us the twelve we started with," she told them. Children wrote on their own papers and consulted with their partners before holding up their hands. Ms. Barnes let Laticia write "$3 + 3 + 3 + 3 = 12$" on the board. She asked if everyone agreed, and they did.

She repeated the above procedure for the entrance of Peter and his brother and again for the entrance of Joy and Simon and their four cousins, with the added step of asking how many people were at the door when Joy and Simon came. The children quickly did the addition of two plus four without the aid of chips.

At the end of the lesson, the children counted the cookies on the tray that Grandma brought, added the number to twelve by combining the chips from several sets of partners, and put the total number of chips into twelve rows to see how many each one would have before they let in that last person at the door.

A whole language approach to teaching mathematics would include presenting mathematics content in ways that are like real-life uses—in other words, as a problem-finding social activity that is a tool with which to make sense out of life. Therefore, the mathematics program in a whole language setting would have problems related to students' everyday experiences, and, because students help to shape the curriculum in such classrooms, the problems would be written by teachers and students. First, the teacher would present relevant problems that reflect a particular topic, such as decimals. Students would explore how this topic relates to their background experiences. Then they would construct their own story problems, solve them, and share them with peers, who might give them feedback that would lead to revision. Finally, their problems would be "published" for others to work (Winograd and Higgins, 1994/1995). Language and mathematics strategy lessons would be interwoven as children worked on such tasks as conducting surveys and constructing graphs (Jongsma, 1991).

Donna Strohauer uses a technique called "mathematician's circle" in which students (one at a time) share problems they have generated with a group and invite other students to solve the problems. Answers and explanations of answers follow, and peers of the students presenting the problems are asked to make suggestions about the problems (Winograd and Higgins, 1994/1995).

Graphs, maps, charts, and tables, which often occur in mathematics materials, were discussed in Chapter 9. Students need help with these graphic aids in order to perform well on many mathematical assignments.

Science and Health

Extremely heavy use of technical vocabulary is typical in science and health textbooks, in which students will encounter terms like *lever, extinct, rodent, pollen, stamen, bacteria, inoculation,* and *electron*. Again, some of the words that have technical meanings also have more common meanings, for example, *shot, matter, solution,* and *pitch*. In these classes, as in all content area classes, the teacher is responsible for seeing that students understand the concepts represented by the technical and specialized terms in their subjects. For example, a science teacher might bring in a flower to explain what the *stamens* are and where they are located. Although diagrams are also useful, a diagram is still a step removed from the actual object, and the more concrete an experience students have with a concept, the more likely it is that they will develop a complete understanding of the concept.

Comprehension strategies, such as recognizing main ideas and details, making inferences, drawing conclusions, recognizing cause-and-effect relationships, classifying items, recognizing sequence, and following directions, are important in reading science and health materials, as are critical reading strategies. Students must determine the author's purpose for writing, check the completeness and timeliness of the information presented, and check the accuracy of the material (Casteel and Isom, 1994). Because material can rapidly become outdated, it is very important that students be aware of the copyright dates of these materials. The scientist's inquiring attitude is exactly the same as that of the critical reader. The ability to use such reading aids as maps, tables, charts, and graphs is also necessary.

Armbruster (1992/1993) points out that students need to learn how to read scientific material in order to obtain valid scientific information. She says, "The same skills that make good scientists also make good readers" (p. 347). Casteel and Isom (1994) have clearly illustrated the relationship of literacy processes to understanding of scientific material. The literacy processes form the root system that supports the branches that represent the parts of the scientific method, which in turn support the scientific facts, concepts, laws, and theories of science. (See Example 10.17.)

Science and health materials must be read slowly and deliberately, and rereading may be necessary to fully grasp the information presented (Mallow,

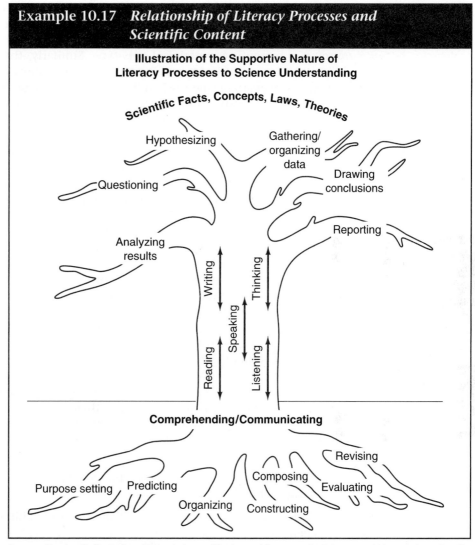

Example 10.17 *Relationship of Literacy Processes and Scientific Content*

Illustration of the Supportive Nature of Literacy Processes to Science Understanding

Source: Carolyn P. Casteel and Bess A. Isom, "Reciprocal Processes in Science and Literacy Learning," *The Reading Teacher*, 47 (April 1994), 540. Reprinted with permission of Carolyn P. Casteel and the International Reading Association.

1991). These materials, like social studies materials, are written in a highly compact, expository style that often involves classification, explanations, and cause-and-effect relationships. The suggestions in Chapter 9 for teaching outlining skills can be especially useful in working with classification, which involves arranging information under main headings and subheadings.

Explanations in science and health materials often describe processes, such as pasteurization of milk, that may be illustrated by pictures, charts, or diagrams designed to clarify the textual material. Teachers might apply the material in

Chapter 9 on reading diagrams and illustrations or the material in Chapter 6 on detecting sequence, since a process is generally explained in sequence. The directed inquiry activity described earlier in this chapter would also be extremely useful in presenting material of this type. Similarly, the suggestions given in Chapter 6 for recognizing cause-and-effect relationships will help children handle this type of arrangement when it occurs in science textbooks.

Science textbooks often contain instructions for performing experiments. Readers must be able to comprehend the purpose of an experiment, read the list of materials to determine what must be assembled in order to perform the experiment, and determine the order of steps to be followed. The suggestions in Chapter 6 on locating main ideas, details, and sequential order and learning to follow directions should be useful when reading material of this nature. Before they perform an experiment, children should attempt to predict the outcome, based on their prior knowledge. Afterward they should compare their predicted results with the actual results, investigating the reasons for differences. Did they perform each step correctly? Can they check special references to find out what actually should have happened?

Because science textbooks are often written at higher difficulty levels than the basal readers for the same grade level, some children will need alternate materials for science instruction. Trade books are available on all levels of difficulty to meet this need.

literature-centered reading

Smardo (1982) suggests the use of children's literature, along with hands-on exploration, to clarify science concepts in early childhood programs. Teachers can use children's trade books that deal with scientific concepts to help students distinguish between real and make-believe situations. Discussion of the books offers children a chance to ask questions, share their opinions and background knowledge, make predictions, and engage in inferential and critical thinking. Smardo suggests books that can be useful for particular scientific concepts, including the following:

Carle, Eric. *Mixed Up Chameleon.* Philadelphia: Thomas Y. Crowell, 1975. (animal changes)

Carle, Eric. *The Very Hungry Caterpillar.* New York: Philomel, 1969. (animal changes)

DeRegniers, Beatrice. *Shadow Book.* New York: Harcourt Brace Jovanovich, 1960. (shadows)

Krauss, Ruth. *Carrot Seed.* New York: Harper & Row, 1945. (growing)

Provensen, Alice, and Martin Provensen. *A Year at Maple Hill Farm.* New York: Atheneum, 1978. (seasons)

Zion, Gene. *Summer Snowman.* New York: Harper & Row, 1955. (melting)

Presenting scientific ideas and common misconceptions in story format, rather than in a straight expository format, as the books cited above do, helps students learn scientific information (Maric and Johnson, 1990; Schumm, 1991).

These students use many diverse reading and study skills in their science class as they follow directions, interpret diagrams, and relate text exposition and description to scientific materials and models. (© *David S. Strickler/The Picture Cube*)

Science informational books, such as Laurence Pringle's *Into the Woods: Exploring the Forest Ecosystem,* help children understand the laws of nature. The color photographs and realistic illustrations found in many science books increase a child's enjoyment and understanding (Norton, 1987). *Tree of Life: The World of the African Baobab* by Barbara Bash and *The Hidden Life of the Desert* by Thomas Wiewandt emphasize the interrelatedness of plant and animal life. Another type of ecosystem is explored in *Life in a Tidal Pool* by Alvin and Virginia Silverstein (Martinez and Nash, 1990). Animal life in general is depicted in Doris

Gove's *A Water Snake's Year*, Miriam Schleiss's *Squirrel Watching*, and Jan Sterling's *Bears* (Galda and MacGregor, 1992).

Endangered species are discussed in *No Dodos: A Counting Book of Endangered Animals* by Amanda Wallwork; *Saving Endangered Mammals: A Field Guide to Some of the Earth's Rarest Animals* by Thane Maynard; *The Endangered Florida Panther* by Margaret Goff Clark; and *On the Brink of Extinction: The California Condor* by Caroline Arnold. *Four Against the Odds: The Struggle to Save Our Environment* by Stephen Krensky and *The Fire Bug Connection* by Jean Craighead George are biographies of environmental activists. *Earthways: Simple Environmental Activities for Children* by Carol Petrash and *What To Do about Pollution* by Anne Shelby contain environmental activities for children (Pierce and Short, 1993/1994). Rule and Atkinson (1994) have analyzed books about ecology to help teachers choose wisely books that show realistic ecology problems, address possible solutions, have positive tones, avoid stereotypes, and are appropriate for the intended audience.

In addition, in some cases teachers can relate either basal reader stories or stories in trade books to science study by making science job cards to be used as follow-up activities to stories. Following is a sample job card:

> What kind of weather do you believe was occurring in the story? Tell why you think this is true. Share your ideas with your reading group. (Whitfield and Hovey, 1981)

reading-writing connection Keeping a science log or journal is a traditional practice for scientists and makes a natural connection to language instruction. Children can enter a short science-related passage in a journal each day. The passage can vary from a single sentence about a nature observation to a complete explanation of an experiment and its results. Students can also write reports on science projects, detailing the procedures and the findings. These reports may be taken through initial drafts and revisions to the finished products (Rubino, 1991).

Science activities that involve direct experiences, such as using manipulative materials, doing experiments, or making observations of phenomena, can be used as the basis for language experience stories or charts that will provide reading material in science (Barrow, Kristo, and Andrew, 1984). The experience is accompanied and/or followed by class discussion, after which the children produce a chart or a story about the experience. They may illustrate the story after they write it, or they may draw their observations first and then write about them. Reading of related concept books, such as the ones just mentioned, may provide children with material to use in expanding their stories.

Having students brainstorm questions about material read in the science text, categorize the questions, and work as cooperative groups to answer them resulted in children interacting with the text as a group and sharing information (Sampson, Sampson, and Linek, 1994/1995). Such active involvement tends to facilitate learning.

reading-writing connection Science centers in the primary grades can involve students in learning vocabulary, recording observational data, illustrating factual material, reconstructing factual materials, listening to and writing stories, and writing nonfiction books. All of these are active ways to learn the material (Piech, 1991).

SELF-CHECK: OBJECTIVE 4   Identify some potential mathematics, social studies, and science and health reading problems, and describe procedures and materials that could help overcome them.
(See Self-Improvement Opportunities 3, 4, 5, and 7.)

Summary

Teachers must be aware that basal reading instruction alone is not likely to prepare children thoroughly to read in the content areas. Students need to learn reading skills that are appropriate to specific subject areas, as well as general techniques that are helpful in reading expository text. Content texts present more reading difficulties than do basal reader materials. They have a greater density of ideas presented, and they lack the narrative style that is most familiar to the children. They may also contain many graphic aids that have to be interpreted.

Teachers need to be aware of the readability levels of the materials they give children to read, and they must adjust their expectations and reading assignments based on the students' reading levels in relation to the readability of available instructional materials. Cloze tests and informal reading inventories can be used to predict how well children can read particular texts. Teachers can also use readability formulas in conjunction with the children's reading test scores to estimate the appropriate materials for specific children. Although readability formulas have the drawback of being completely text based, they can help teachers assess the relative difficulty of material with reasonable accuracy. Computer programs can help teachers apply readability formulas.

Many techniques can be used to help children read content area materials more effectively. Among them are the Directed Reading-Thinking Activity, the guided reading procedure, the question-only strategy, Press Conference, the language experience approach, feature analysis plus writing, keeping learning logs, webbing, creative mapping, structured overviews, every-pupil-response activities, readers' theater, the concept-text-application approach, the K-W-L teaching model, use of study guides, use of manipulative materials, computer approaches, integrated approaches, thematic content units, and literature-based units across the curriculum.

Each content area presents special reading difficulties, such as specialized vocabulary. Reading in literature involves comprehending many literary forms, including short stories, novels, plays, poetry, biographies, and autobiographies. English textbooks cover the areas of listening, speaking, reading, and writing. The techniques presented in these areas need to be practiced through authentic oral and written experiences. Social studies materials abound with graphic aids to be interpreted and require much application of critical reading skills. The newspaper is a good teaching aid for the social studies area. Mathematics has a special symbol system to be learned, but perhaps the greatest difficulty in this content area is the reading of story problems. Children need to learn a procedure for approaching the reading of such problems. Science and health materials contain many graphic aids. They also often include instructions for performing experiments, which must be read carefully to ensure accurate results.

Use of literature selections to work with content area concepts is effective in every content area. In addition, including real-life activities and connections to the students' backgrounds of experiences enhances learning.

Test Yourself *True or False*

_____ 1. Content area textbooks are carefully graded in terms of difficulty and are generally appropriate to the grade levels for which they are designed.

_____ 2. One difficulty encountered in all content areas is specialized vocabulary, especially common words that have additional specialized meanings.

_____ 3. The cloze technique can be used to help determine whether or not a textbook is suitable for a specific child.

_____ 4. All children in the fifth grade can benefit from the use of a single textbook designated for the fifth grade.

_____ 5. Readability formulas are too complicated for classroom teachers to use.

_____ 6. Students often must acquire early concepts and vocabulary in content textbooks before they can understand later content passages.

_____ 7. Offering youngsters instruction in basal readers is sufficient to teach reading skills needed in content area textbooks.

_____ 8. Story problems in mathematics are generally extremely easy to read.

_____ 9. Mathematics materials require a child to learn a new symbol system.

_____ 10. Concrete examples are helpful in building an understanding of new concepts.

_____ 11. Science materials need not be read critically, since they are written by experts in the field.

_____ 12. An expository style of writing is very precise and highly compact.

_____ 13. The cause-and-effect pattern of organization is found in social studies and science and health materials.

_____ 14. Social studies materials frequently have a chronological organization.

_____ 15. All parts of the newspaper require identical reading skills.

_____ 16. The directed inquiry activity involves predictions made by the children.

_____ 17. Study guides may set purposes for reading.

_____ 18. The Directed Reading-Thinking Activity is a general plan for teaching either basal reader stories or content area selections.

_____ 19. Readability formulas take into account the interactive nature of reading.

_____ 20. Expository text structure can be taught through the language experience approach.

_____ 21. Anticipation guides are used before reading a selection and can be the basis for discussion after reading has taken place.

_____ 22. Children's literature can be used to teach social studies and science concepts.

_____ 23. Real-life mathematics problems produced by children are effective teaching tools.

_____ 24. Expository paragraph frames can scaffold children's attempts to write about content area topics.

_____ 25. Passages using math synonyms can help students build concepts.

_____ 26. Use of picture books should be avoided above the third grade.

Self-Improvement Opportunities

1. As a test of your ability to use the *Fry Readability Graph*, turn to the sample selection in Example 10.5 and determine its readability. Check your answer with your classmates' answers. If your answers don't agree, study the procedure again and determine where an error was made.

2. Develop a Directed Reading-Thinking Activity (DRTA) for a content area lesson. Then try it out in an elementary school classroom, or present it to a group of classmates in your reading or content methods course.

3. Develop a lesson for teaching students the multiple meanings of words encountered in science and health, social studies, mathematics, or literature. Try the lesson out in an elementary school classroom, or present it to a group of your peers.

4. Select a passage from a social studies or science textbook. Prepare a study guide for children to use in reading/studying the passage.

5. Develop a bibliography of trade books that youngsters who are unable to read a particular content area textbook could use.

6. Demonstrate to your classmates the usefulness of newspaper reading in your particular content area.

7. Prepare a comparison/contrast chart for some topic in your content area.

Chapter 11

Key Vocabulary

Pay close attention to these terms when they appear in the chapter.

achievement test

anecdotal record

authentic assessment

capacity level

checklist

cloze procedure

criterion-referenced test

frustration level

independent level

informal assessment

informal reading inventory (IRI)

instructional level

kidwatching

miscue

norm-referenced test

performance-based assessment

portfolio

reading miscue inventory (RMI)

rubric

running record

Assessment of Student Progress

Setting Objectives

When you finish reading this chapter, you should be able to

1. Describe some ways in which authentic assessment differs from traditional assessment.

2. Explain the importance of observation and identify some ways to record observations.

3. Evaluate the development of literary interests.

4. Implement portfolio assessment in an elementary classroom.

5. Identify some ways for students to assess their own progress.

6. Construct and interpret informal tests.

7. Recognize and analyze the significance of a reading miscue.

8. Differentiate among informal assessment, criterion-referenced tests, and norm-referenced tests.

9. Identify some features and limitations of norm-referenced tests.

Figure 11.1 *Chapter 11 Organization*

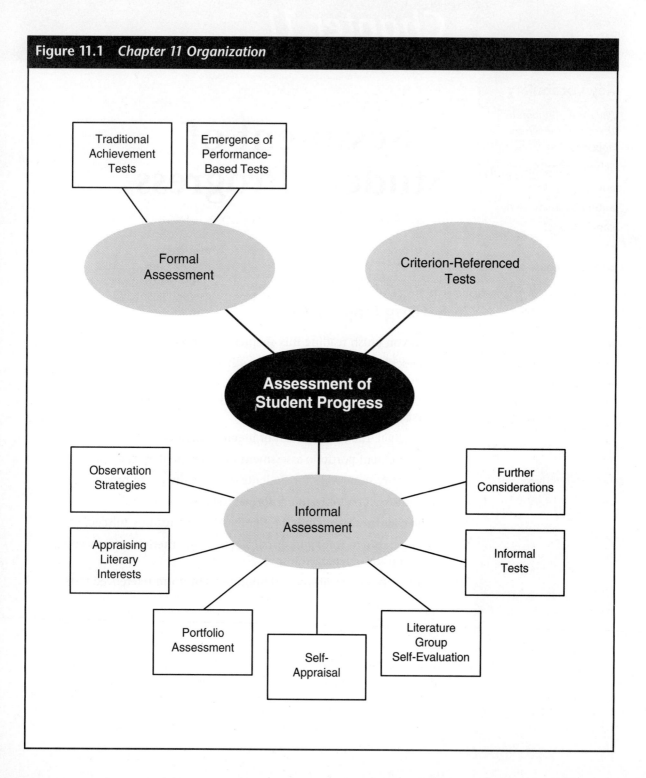

*A**ssessment* is the collection of data, such as test scores and informal records, to measure student achievement, and *evaluation* is the interpretation and analysis of these data. Evaluating student progress is important because it enables the teacher to discover each student's strengths and weaknesses, to plan instruction accordingly, to communicate student progress to parents, and to evaluate the effectiveness of teaching strategies. Assessing student learning is essential for good teaching and should be an integral part of instructional procedures. Although assessment is often simply equated with testing, multiple measures—such as day-to-day observation, student conferences, and samples of students' work—provide a more valid evaluation of a student's capabilities.

The field of assessment is undergoing a great many changes as researchers strive to make procedures correspond more closely to current views about the reading process. This chapter first examines some issues in assessment and several types of informal assessment, many of which reflect the current emphasis on using authentic reading and writing tasks to evaluate student progress. After a brief look at criterion-referenced tests, the chapter concludes with some types of norm-referenced tests, including both traditional achievement tests and emerging performance-based standardized tests.

Movement Toward Authentic Assessment

To bring assessment in line with current views of the reading process, many educators are moving toward authentic, or holistic, assessment. Because it takes place during the teaching-learning process, this type of assessment is an integral part of the curriculum. Authentic assessment does not measure language as a set of fragmented subskills; rather, it treats oral and written language as an integrated whole. Such assessment occurs in the context of functional, relevant learning. Self-evaluation is an important aspect of authentic assessment, for learners must be aware of their own success and growth (K. Goodman 1991).

Although similar, authentic assessment and performance-based assessment differ somewhat. In *authentic assessment,* evaluation is based on the student's performance on a freely chosen task in a real-life situation (Meyer, 1992). According to Hiebert, Valencia, and Afflerbach (1994, p. 9), "The aim of authentic assessment is to assess many different kinds of literacy abilities in contexts that closely resemble the actual situations in which those abilities are used." *Performance-based assessment* measures a student's ability to perform a specific behavior, such as writing a response to a book, when assigned to do this task. Often associated with performance assessment is outcome-based education (OBE), which addresses such desired outcomes for student learners as becoming complex thinkers, effective communicators/producers, and skilled information processors. Because traditional tests that measure only recall or recognition of information are inappropriate for evaluating such outcomes, performance assessment is more likely to be used for evaluating students' ability to apply knowledge and skills to real-life situations (Marzano, 1994).

Ideally, instruction and assessment should merge (Brown and Lytle, 1988; Y. Goodman, 1989). "Evaluation is part of curriculum; it cannot be divorced from classroom organization, from the relationship between teachers and students, from continuous learning experiences and activities" (Y. Goodman, 1989, p. 4). Assessment should be a continuous process in which teachers observe and interact with students in various types of learning activities throughout the day. To provide a match between the strategies students use when they read and the skills that are being assessed, many educators are turning to kidwatching, portfolios, response journals, checklists, and retellings. They are also evaluating debates, collaborative activities, presentations, projects, journals, performances, exhibitions, process writing, and experiments (Sugarman, Allen, and Keller-Cogan, 1993; Wiggins, 1990).

Although many publishers are revising instructional materials and many teachers are implementing procedures based on recent trends in reading comprehension, corresponding changes in standardized tests are just beginning to occur. The reading process can be assessed with both informal procedures and standardized tests, but few standardized tests reflecting the new emphasis on the reading process are currently available for classroom use. Unfortunately, "the reading required on most tests is not much like the reading behavior that our new understanding describes" (Farr, 1992, p. 31). (See Table 11.1 for contrasts between views of reading and assessment practices.)

Shepard (1989) further explains the dichotomy between standardized testing and authentic assessment. Large-scale standardized tests must be objective, formal, time efficient, widely applicable, cost efficient, centrally processed, and presented in a form useful to policymakers. On the other hand, assessment that corresponds with instruction needs to be informal, meaningful to students, capable of providing immediate feedback, and directly related to meaningful instructional tasks.

Teachers who want their students to do well on tests therefore face a dilemma, because most tests still measure skill proficiency instead of the ability to read strategically. Many school systems exert pressure and provide incentives for high test scores; thus, teachers believe they must teach the subskills on the test instead of the more important concepts (Shepard, 1989). In the same vein, Winograd, Paris, and Bridge (1991, p. 109) say, "Misaligned tests force teachers to abandon their curricular goals to prepare students for skill-based tests."

As a result of the trend toward authentic assessment, educators are experimenting with a variety of informal techniques and new approaches to standardized testing (Pikulski, 1989). Instead of being test centered, assessment is becoming teacher and student centered. Instead of teachers assuming full responsibility for assessing progress, students are sharing in the evaluation of their own reading. Instead of focusing on mastery of discrete skills, standardized tests are including passages of continuous text like those students read in natural situations.

SELF-CHECK: OBJECTIVE 1   What are some ways that assessment procedures are changing? (See Self-Improvement Opportunities 4 and 5.)

Table 11.1 *A Set of Contrasts Between New Views of Reading and Current Practices in Assessing Reading*

New views of the reading process tell us that . . .	*Yet when we assess reading comprehension, we . . .*
Prior knowledge is an important determinant of reading comprehension.	Mask any relationship between prior knowledge and reading comprehension by using lots of short passages on lots of topics.
A complete story or text has structural and topical integrity.	Use short texts that seldom approximate the structural and topical integrity of an authentic text.
Inference is an essential part of the process of comprehending units as small as sentences.	Rely on literal comprehension test items.
The diversity in prior knowledge across individuals as well as the varied causal relations in human experiences invite many possible inferences to fit a text or question.	Use multiple choice items with only one correct answer, even when many of the responses might, under certain conditions, be plausible.
The ability to vary reading strategies to fit the text and the situation is one hallmark of an expert reader.	Seldom assess how and when students vary the strategies they use during normal reading, studying, or when the going gets tough.
The ability to synthesize information from various parts of the text and different texts is hallmark of an expert reader.	Rarely go beyond finding the main idea of a paragraph or passage.
The ability to ask good questions of text, as well as to answer them, is hallmark of an expert reader.	Seldom ask students to create or select questions about a selection they may have just read.
All aspects of a reader's experience, including habits that arise from school and home, influence reading comprehension.	Rarely view information on reading habits and attitudes as being as important as information about performance.
Reading involves the orchestration of many skills that complement one another in a variety of ways.	Use tests that fragment reading into isolated skills and report performance on each.
Skilled readers are fluent; their word identification is sufficiently automatic to allow most cognitive resources to be used for comprehension.	Rarely consider fluency as an index of skilled reading.
Learning from text involves the restructuring, application, and flexible use of knowledge in new situations.	Often ask readers to respond to the text's declarative knowledge rather than to apply it to near and far transfer tasks.

Source: Sheila Valencia and P. David Pearson. "Reading Assessment: Time for a Change." *The Reading Teacher*, 40 (April 1987), 726–733. Reprinted with permission of Sheila Valencia and the International Reading Association.

Informal (Nonstandardized) Assessment

In the day-to-day program, the classroom teacher will necessarily depend more on informal assessment devices than on formal assessment instruments. (Formal instruments are commercially available tests that have been standardized against a specific norm or objective.) In simple terms, this means that the effective teacher observes and records individual strengths and weaknesses during the educational process, adjusting instruction to meet individual needs. Informal assessment is based on the following principles (Teale, Hiebert, and Chittenden, 1987):

1. Assessment is an integral part of instruction.

2. Methods of assessment vary and include analyses of students' reading and writing and teacher observations.

3. Assessment covers a variety of skills and knowledge related to different forms of literacy.

4. Systematic assessment occurs regularly.

5. Assessment takes place in many different contexts.

6. Informal assessments resemble regular classroom activities.

7. Assessments are appropriate for children's cultural backgrounds and developmental levels.

The following sections present some types of informal assessment.

Observation Strategies

Test scores provide little help in the moment-to-moment decision making that occurs throughout the school day (Johnston, 1987). Based on informal observations and hunches, however, teachers can modify instructional strategies, clarify explanations, give individual help, use a variety of motivational techniques, adjust classroom management techniques, and provide reinforcement as needed.

Since much student assessment occurs informally, teachers need to interpret their observations with insight and accuracy. Johnston (1987) suggests several characteristics of teachers who successfully evaluate students' literacy development. Expert evaluators recognize patterns of behavior and understand how reading and writing processes develop. They notice, for example, that one child is unable to make reasonable predictions or that another uses invented spellings effectively. Observant teachers listen attentively and perceptively, both at scheduled conferences and during the course of each day. Good observers evaluate as they teach, and they accept the responsibility for assessing children's needs and responding to them, instead of relying only on test data.

Recordkeeping is an essential part of observation, and it may occur in different ways. Some teachers keep a notebook with a separate page to record observations for each child; others jot dated notes on sticky tags or on file cards that they later place in the students' files or portfolios. (See Example 11.1 for a sample observation card.) As they move about the room, teachers may carry clipboards for recording observations. Mickelson (1990) suggests that teachers use class sheets with a square for each name, similar in form to a calendar. As teachers write notes, they stick them on the children's names. At the end of the day or week, there may be many notes for some children and few for others. As children assume more responsibility for directing their own activities, teachers have more time to record observations (Rhodes and Nathenson-Mejia, 1992).

Example 11.1 *Observation Card*

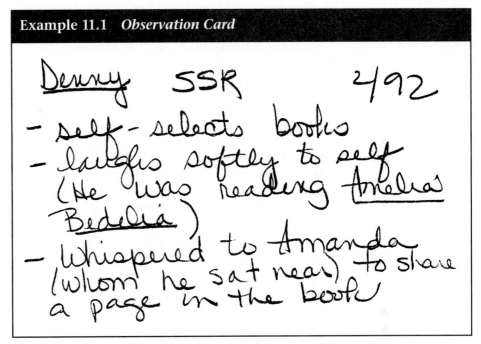

Source: Reprinted by permission from Beverly Mackie, Jere Whitson Elementary School, Cookeville, Tennessee, 1994.

Observation, Interaction, and Analysis

Three aspects of informal teacher evaluation are observation, interaction, and analysis (Goodman, Goodman, and Hood, 1989). During *observation*, the teacher carefully watches the activities of a single child, a group of children, or the whole class in order to evaluate language use and social behaviors. *Interaction* takes place when the teacher raises questions, responds to journal writing, and conferences with children in order to stimulate further language and cognitive growth. During *analysis*, the teacher gets information by listening to a child read or discuss and by examining a child's written work. The teacher then applies knowledge of learning principles to analyze the child's ability to use language.

Kidwatching

Kidwatching, a term introduced by Yetta Goodman (1978), is direct or informal observation of a child in various classroom situations. Based on the premise that language development is a natural process, kidwatching allows teachers to explore two questions: (1) What evidence exists that language development is occurring? and (2) What does a child's unexpected production say about the child's knowledge of language? It is based on three premises (Y. Goodman, 1985):

1. Observers should use a theoretically sound framework to make meaningful and unbiased interpretations of what they see.

2. Observers should watch children in a wide variety of literacy situations.

3. Observers should consider the interactions between children and adults in language learning.

Anecdotal Records

Anecdotal records, written accounts of specific incidents in the classroom, are another option. The teacher records information about a significant language event: the time and place, the students involved, what caused the incident, what happened, and possibly the implications. Such records may be kept of individual students, groups, or the whole class. Their value lies mainly in evaluating progress, instructional planning, informing others (including the students), noting changes in language development, and understanding attitudes and behaviors (*A Kid-Watching Guide,* 1984; Rhodes and Nathenson-Mejia, 1992). Teachers who keep anecdotal records regularly become more sensitive to their students' special interests and needs than they were before they kept such records (Baskwill and Whitman, 1988). A sample anecdotal record might read:

> When Kim Ying was added to our class today, I asked Steve to be his buddy—to help him understand what we do in class, to eat lunch with him, to include him on the playground, etc. I was taking a big chance. Kim knew only a little English, and Steve has such a poor self-concept. Would putting them together work? I watched. Steve stuck to Kim like glue. When Kim was unsure what to do, Steve was there to show him. During free reading time, Steve showed Kim where to find books and recommended *The Very Quiet Cricket*, an easy favorite. Steve took Kim into a corner and helped him read, carefully pointing to the words and pictures. Steve was not only Kim's buddy, but also his tutor. I can see Kim beginning to feel comfortable in our class, and I am amazed at the way Steve's self-concept is blossoming with his new responsibility!

literature-centered reading

Checklists

Some teachers also keep *checklists*, such as the literacy observation checklist in Example 11.2 or the one for oral reading in Example 11.3, which may be based on an audiotape of a child's oral reading. Teachers can make several copies of the checklist for each child, and keep them in individual folders. By filling out the forms periodically and dating each one, teachers have a written record of each child's progress.

Example 11.2 *Literacy Observation Checklist*

Child's name _____ Teacher's name _____

Place a check beside each characteristic that the child exhibits.

Characteristic	Date	Date	Date
1. Uses variety of comprehension strategies.	———	———	———
2. Expresses interest in reading and writing.	———	———	———
3. Reads voluntarily.	———	———	———
4. Applies word recognition skills.	———	———	———
5. Writes coherently.	———	———	———
6. Reads aloud fluently.	———	———	———
7. Expresses ideas well orally.	———	———	———
8. Listens attentively.	———	———	———
9. Enjoys listening to stories.	———	———	———
10. Asks sensible questions.	———	———	———
11. Makes reasonable predictions.	———	———	———
12. Evaluates and monitors own work.	———	———	———
13. Works well independently.	———	———	———
14. Self-corrects errors.	———	———	———
15. Shows willingness to take risks.	———	———	———

Example 11.3 *Oral Reading Checklist*

Child's Name _____ Date _____

Put a check beside each behavior the child exhibits.

1. _____ Reads with appropriate expression and intonation.
2. _____ Reads by phrases and thought units, not word by word.
3. _____ Pauses for commas.
4. _____ Responds to periods, question marks, and exclamation points.
5. _____ Changes tone of voice to indicate different speakers if reading dialogue.
6. _____ Pronounces words distinctly.
7. _____ Reads words correctly.
8. _____ Does not repeat words.
9. _____ Seems to enjoy reading aloud.
10. _____ Reads at an appropriate rate.

An example of using a checklist for evaluation during literature response groups, discussed in Chapters 7 and 8, comes from Natalie Knox's sixth-grade class (see the Classroom Scenario on evaluation in literature response groups). This was Ms. Knox's and the children's first time to use multiple sets of books from quality literature instead of basal readers.

**Classroom
Scenario**

Evaluation of Literature Response Groups

Natalie Knox reminds the students of their responsibilities for reading, discussing, writing in their literature logs, and planning for their next session while they are in their groups. She tries to meet with each group as both a participant and an evaluator. As she joins a group that is reading Lois Lowry's *Number the Stars*, she enters the discussion and also keeps a checklist of each student's status. One day's checklist is shown in Example 11.4.

Analysis of Scenario

As she visits different groups, Natalie is gaining a great deal of information over a period of time about students' interests and enthusiasm, ability to gain insights about characters and plot development, and skill in group interaction. From her observations, Natalie can make judgments about progress in student responses to literature and social interactions. The informal records of her observations can serve as a basis for parent conferences and entries on report cards.

Rubrics

A *rubric* provides specific criteria for describing student performance at different levels of proficiency in different content areas (O'Neil, 1994). Students receive a number of points that represent minimal to high-quality work, depending on the type of response. For example, during group reading, the criterion for a high-quality response that would earn the highest number of points might be "Carries on a meaningful conversation about reading," and the criterion for a minimal response with low or no points might be "Unable to express thoughts or feelings about reading material" (Winograd, 1994, p. 421). In some cases, educators establish criteria for district- or statewide standards and train scorers to be consistent in their grading (Garcia and Verville, 1994).

A well-constructed rubric lets students know in advance what is expected of them and helps teachers grade students' work fairly. When constructing rubrics, teachers may invite students to suggest criteria to include (Batzle, 1992). Then, when students receive their grades, they are more likely to understand them because they can refer to the criteria instead of just getting a letter grade without explanation. Routman (1991) suggests that students evaluate their own progress by completing rubrics periodically. Example 11.5, based on Routman's examples

Example 11.4   *Checklist for Literature Response Groups*

Number the Stars — Meeting #1

Student	Attended	Read to page	Shared # of items	Asked questions clarification	Made predictions &/or connections within the book (or other books)	Made connections to real situations	Responded to others in group	Read from response journal
Kristine Green	✓	60	✓	-Ellen's family?		-Far away relatives	✓	hesitant
Marie Orby	✓	60	✓✓	-May star? -Buttons?	-Sister's death?		✓	excellent
Katie Smith	✓	125	✓✓✓	-Symbols? -Religion?		-Family, friends, religious difference	✓ Missy, Marie	thorough
Missy Bug	✓	65	✓✓	-Peter's involvement?				detailed
Megan Clifton	✓	60	✓✓✓✓	-Symbols?	-Fishing? -Mom's?	-Aunt's death	✓ Marie	-skipped around -sequence?
Next meeting: 11/19 Read to: p. 94								

Example 11.5 *Reading Rubric*

Name: _____ Date: _____

Scoring: 1 (lowest) to 10 (highest)

	Grading Periods					
	1	2	3	4	5	6
1. Reads voluntarily for pleasure.						
2. Makes thoughtful comments during book discussions.						
3. Reads aloud fluently and with expression.						
4. Chooses books wisely for personal reading.						
5. Responds reflectively in writing or other media.						
6. Willingly shares reading with others.						
7. Does an in-depth related project with a selected book.						
8. Completes a reasonable number of books.						
9. Keeps accurate records.						
10. Participates in whole-class reading activities.						

Total score: _____

Six-weeks grade: _____

(pp. 333–340), is an informal way to use a rubric for reading that is useful for classroom grading purposes. By adding the scores, the teacher can arrive at a portion of the six-weeks grade for reading, and the student can see areas of strengths and areas that need improvement.

Conferences and Interviews

Another type of informal assessment occurs when teachers have conferences with children (or interview them) about their attitudes, interests, and progress in reading. Conferences may either be scheduled, or they may happen spontaneously when opportunities arise. Sample questions for teachers to ask include the following:

Do you like reading? Why or why not?

Do you think reading is important? Why or why not?

What books have you read recently? What did you like/dislike about them?

Are you a good reader? Why do you think that?

What do you do when you have a problem understanding what you are reading?

What do you do when you come to a word that you don't know?

Teachers use informal assessment devices to observe and record individual strengths and weaknesses during the educational process, adjusting instruction to meet individual needs. (© *Susan Lapides*)

Through interviews, teachers learn how students make interpretations and construct meaning. They also gain insights into the reasoning behind children's task performances as the children explain their answers (Seda and Pearson, 1991).

Retellings

literature-centered reading   Story retelling, another form of informal assessment, occurs when a student retells a story she or he has heard or read (Goodman, Watson, and Burke, 1987). Retellings can also be done with expository text and material from different genres, such as biographies, fables, and mysteries, so that the reader can explore different types of texts (Johnston, 1992). At first, the teacher encourages the student to retell without offering assistance, but when the student appears to have finished, the teacher may help by asking open-ended questions that will stimulate further retelling. By listening carefully and taking notes, the teacher can learn much about a student's understanding and appreciation of the story. Retellings also benefit students by improving their comprehension, sense of structure, and use of oral language (Fisette, 1993).

SELF-CHECK: OBJECTIVE 2   Briefly describe three ways to record observations. Which one(s) would you prefer to use, and why? (See Self-Improvement Opportunities 2, 6, 7, 8, and 9.)

Appraising Literary Interests

literature-centered reading An observant teacher who takes time to be a sensitive, yet critical, evaluator of each child's progress is probably the best judge of the quality of a child's reactions to literature. The following questions will help the teacher in the evaluation process: Are the children

1. gaining an appreciation of good literature? How do I know?

2. making good use of time in the library and during free reading of books and periodicals?

3. enjoying storytelling, reading aloud, choral reading, and creative drama?

4. getting to know themselves better through literature?

5. increasing their understanding of their own and other cultures through knowledge of the contributions of their own people and people of other lands?

6. becoming sensitive to sounds, rhythms, moods, and feelings as displayed in prose and poetry?

7. maturing in awareness of the structure and forms of literature?

8. enjoying dictating stories, reading aloud to one another, and exchanging books with friends?

9. able to compare books by author's style, characterization, settings, plot development, and so forth?

Teachers can obtain answers to these questions through spontaneous remarks by the child ("Do you know any other good books about space travel?"), through directed conversation with the class ("What books would you like to add to our classroom library?"), and during individual conferences, when children have opportunities to describe books they like and dislike.

Every school day provides countless opportunities for obtaining information: listening to conversations between children, observing their creative activities, studying their library circulation records, and conferring with parents. Time spent looking through and discussing various books in the library with a child will provide the teacher with great insight into the child's reactions.

One excellent device for showing changes in literary taste over a period of time is a *cumulative reading record,* in which children record each book they read, giving the author, title, kind of book, date of report, and a brief statement of how well they liked the book. Gradually, the children can tell more about what they liked and what they disliked about a particular book.

Another device is a *personal reading record,* maintained separately by (or for) each child. This record classifies reading selections by topic such as poetry, fantasy, adventure, mystery, myths and folklore, animals (or more specifically, for example, horses and dogs), biography, other lands, and sports. By focusing on the types of literature the children read, teachers may encourage them to read about new topics and to expand their reading interests.

SELF-CHECK: OBJECTIVE 3   Describe ways to assess development of literary interests. (See Self-Improvement Opportunities 3 and 8.)

Portfolio Assessment

Many teachers—in some cases statewide—are adopting a portfolio approach to assessment. A *portfolio* is a collection of a student's work over a period of time, usually kept in an expandable file folder. It should focus on what a student *can* do. There is no best way to implement portfolio assessment, unless a district mandates procedures, so teachers and students must decide what works for them. Batzle (1992) identifies three possibilities:

1. A *working portfolio,* a collaboration of student-chosen samples, parent comments, and teacher records

2. A *showcase portfolio,* student-selected samples of best work only

3. A *record-keeping portfolio,* records of evaluation and test scores kept by the teacher

Valencia (1990) identifies four guiding principles based on research and classroom practice for implementing a working portfolio approach. Assessment must be authentic, continuous, multidimensional (including a wide range of cognitive processes and literacy activities), and collaborative (involving reflection by both teacher and student).

During the year students indicate their progress in a variety of ways; thus, selective samples of their work can provide an overview of the year's work. In deciding which samples to include in a portfolio, the teacher must first consider the goals of the instructional program (Valencia, 1990; Weaver, 1990). Samples should reflect broad, holistic curricular goals, not narrow tasks. To provide a variety of samples, teachers might use four data-gathering categories as follows (Anthony et al., 1991):

• Observation of process (e.g., anecdotal comments, notes from conferences and interviews, retellings)

• Observation of products (e.g., learning logs, audiotapes, self-assessments, writing folders)

• Classroom measures (e.g., teacher-made tests)

• Decontextualized measures (e.g., standardized test profiles)

Some consistency can be maintained in portfolio contents for purposes of districtwide evaluation by identifying required evidence, which consists of activities, checklists, or projects that relate to goals and are included for all children in a particular grade. In addition, supporting evidence may be included to show the student's unique capabilities (Valencia, 1990).

Since a key component of the portfolio is writing samples, the teacher and the student should know some criteria to apply when evaluating progress in writing.

The following guidelines, used selectively as appropriate for each piece, may be helpful (Bratcher, 1994; *A Kid-Watching Guide*, 1984).

1. *Sense of story*. Does the student show effective use of characterization, setting, plot, theme, and story beginning and ending?

2. *Audience*. Has the writer provided the information that the audience needs to know?

3. *Syntax*. Is the writer using more complex sentence structures than he or she did previously?

4. *Orthographic conventions*. Is there movement from invented spellings to conventional spellings? Has progress been made in standard use of punctuation, spacing and directionality of handwriting, and legibility?

5. *Content concepts*. Is the writer making the main idea clear and providing details to support the main idea? Are gaps in content avoided?

6. *Process concepts*. Does the writer use each step in the writing process successfully?

In most cases, both students and teacher should decide what goes into the portfolio, and the portfolio should be accessible to both for review at all times. Farr (1989) suggests that students should be responsible for organizing and maintaining their portfolios so that they are ready to use as a basis for discussion with the teacher. For the portfolio to be passed along from year to year, it must be manageable in size, so some information must be summarized, some samples sent home at the end of the year, and only meaningful samples kept.

Although it is important for teachers and students to review portfolios together periodically, such reviews can consume considerable time. Teachers should develop rotating schedules in order to have conferences with students at least once a month. The Focus on Strategies illustrates one type of conferencing procedure.

**Focus on
Strategies**

Using Portfolio Assessment

Although this was Mr. Fernandez's first year to use portfolios, he was quickly becoming aware of their usefulness. They were very helpful during parent conferences, because he could show the parents exactly what their children had done during that six-week period—the progress they had made or, in a few cases, the lack of progress. The parents seemed to understand better what their children were doing by looking at their work than by having him try to explain it.

Mr. Fernandez had also found the samples of students' work useful when it was time to give report card grades. He had always believed that grades should be more than averages of test scores, and now he could use their work samples to supplement the test score averages. Quite often, an examination of their work told him they were capable of better work than their tests indicated. If anyone questioned his judgment about his grades, he would be able to show these samples, along with the test scores, to support his evaluation.

Perhaps best of all, most children liked working on their portfolios. They really enjoyed looking back through their papers, recalling different pieces they had worked on and realizing they were getting better. They also liked being able to choose which pieces to include, although sometimes Mr. Fernandez suggested additional pieces.

He had told some of the students that he would meet with them today about their portfolios and asked them to pull their portfolios from the file in the back of the room and have them ready. Now, while they were reading independently, he would begin visiting these children at their seats. Taking along a stool, he seated himself beside Marcus and said quietly, "Marcus, let's see what you've included in your portfolio."

Marcus proudly showed his table of contents, which some of the children had decided to make. Then he turned to the section on his literature log. Marcus confided to Mr. Fernandez, "I really enjoyed reading *Hatchet*. I wanted to include what I wrote about it so I can remember why I liked the book so much." As Mr. Fernandez glanced through Marcus's responses, he could see that Marcus had some remarkable insights about Brian's problem-solving processes as Brian attempted to survive in the wilderness. Marcus had not simply summarized what happened, but had reflected on Brian's survival skills and identified them with his own. "I like the way you refer to Brian's problem-solving skills, Marcus," Mr. Fernandez said. "Can you think how you might learn more about survival skills?".

Leaving Marcus to ponder this question, Mr. Fernandez moved on to Tabitha and asked to see her portfolio. Reluctantly, Tabitha pulled it from her desk and opened it. Her papers were disorganized: math tests were mixed in with writing samples, and some work was undated. Mr. Fernandez asked her what she might do to get her papers ready to show him, and she said she would try to put all the reading and writing papers together. He agreed to return later. It was strange that some children seemed to care so much about their portfolios, whereas others took little interest in them.

Robin was next. She had been waiting for Mr. Fernandez and had her portfolio open. Eagerly, she produced a letter she had just completed about cleaning up the environment. "You know how we've been studying about the environment," Robin said. "I really got excited about doing something when you read us *A River Ran Wild*, so I decided to write a letter and send it to the editor of the *Tribune*. Do you think they'll print it?" As Mr. Fernandez read through the letter, he realized that Robin had picked up ideas from the book that she was applying to Simpson's Pond, the one that had become so polluted that fish couldn't live in it anymore. "This letter has many fine recommendations in it," Mr. Fernandez told Robin. "I think you should send it. Can you find the address?"

Moving on to Jeremy, Mr. Fernandez asked, "Jeremy, did you include your report on reptiles in your portfolio? You seemed really interested in writing about your findings, and I'd like to see what you've done." After shuffling through some papers, Jeremy found the report and showed it to Mr. Fernandez. "You have some good notes here and a rough draft," said Mr. Fernandez. "Where is your finished paper?" Jeremy admitted he hadn't done one, adding that he didn't like to have to write papers over. Reflecting on Jeremy's comment, Mr. Fernandez asked him how he would feel about using the computer to word process his paper. Glancing up, Jeremy said that idea might work. "Writing it on the computer is better because I can make the changes easier. Maybe I'll try that." "Be sure to show it to me when you finish," said Mr. Fernandez. "I'm interested in what you write."

Next, Mr. Fernandez came up to Kurt and asked to see his portfolio. "Show me whatever you like," he told Kurt. Kurt pulled out a review he had written of *Maniac Magee*. As Mr. Fernandez looked at the paper, he noticed that this review was little more than a summary and was carelessly written. He knew Kurt had done much better writing than this sample. "Why did you choose this, Kurt?" he asked. "I don't know," Kurt responded. "I guess I just put any old thing in. I don't see what difference it makes." "It's important that you have a reason to place pieces in your portfolio," said Mr. Fernandez. "Think how you can select your most significant work."

When Mr. Fernandez completed his visits for the morning, he realized how much he had learned about the students' work as they explained their portfolios to him. From Kurt he learned that he would need to help students make judgments about their work so that they could decide which selections merited inclusion in their portfolios. He would need to spend more time with Tabitha. She really needed some help with organizing her portfolio and completing her work. Perhaps Robin would help her; they seemed to get along well, and Robin's portfolio was well organized. He needed to find a way to encourage Jeremy to finish his work. The computer seemed to motivate him this time, but he would need to help Jeremy set goals for completing his work. Robin had surprised him with her enthusiasm about the environment. He needed to encourage her to find ways to extend her interest. Marcus was such an avid reader that his responses to *Hatchet* were no surprise. What Marcus needed was a good supply of books, time to read, and opportunities to respond. Mr. Fernandez realized that periodic portfolio reviews were a fine way to get to know his students better and understand their work.

Next year, Mr. Fernandez thought, he would do a few things differently. He had heard of placing an audiotape in each portfolio and recording the children's oral reading periodically. That would be another way to measure their progress. He also needed a better system of weeding out some of their work; their portfolios would be quite bulky by the end of the year. He would try to get some ideas from teachers who were already using portfolios so that he could make the procedure run smoother next time. "We're off to a good start this year, though," Mr. Fernandez thought, "and next year will be even better."

How can portfolios be used for evaluation? No grades should be given on the portfolios themselves (Farr and Tone, 1994), but portfolio assessment can (1) show what students have learned over a period of time, (2) enable students to develop criteria for judging their own work, (3) relate to real-life learning opportunities that reflect day-to-day thinking, (4) offer guidance for setting individual goals, and (5) enable teachers to evaluate teaching practices and curricula (DeFina, 1992).

SELF-CHECK: OBJECTIVE 4   List as many items as you can that are appropriate for inclusion in a portfolio. What is the value of collecting and organizing these items? (See Self-Improvement Opportunities 4, 5, and 10.)

Self-Appraisal

Assessment should help students develop the ability to judge their own accomplishments—to set their own goals, decide how to achieve those goals, and assess their progress in meeting the goals—in order to experience a sense of ownership in the assessment process (Au, 1990). "Their own evaluation of their work is the most important aspect of evaluation, because when students know what they do well and choose what they want to work on for growth, their own progress is their goal" (Hansen, 1987, p. 90).

Teachers can guide students toward self-assessment in a number of ways (Hansen, 1992; Winograd, Paris, and Bridge, 1991). By sharing audiotapes of oral reading, observation note cards, and checklists, teachers can help students become aware of their strengths and ways they might improve. Through interviews, they can help students focus on their own progress by asking such questions as "How has your reading improved in the last month?" and "What goals would you like to set for yourself in reading and writing?" Discussions based on books recently read can develop students' awareness of whether or not their choices included different genres, were challenging, and reflected varied interests. By including student self-evaluations as part of report card grades, teachers show students that they value their judgments.

Students who display metacognition are aware of how they learn and of their personal strengths and weaknesses in relation to specific learning tasks. They ask themselves questions in order to assess the difficulty of an assignment, the learning strategies they might use, any potential problems, and their likelihood of success. While reading or studying, their self-questioning might proceed as follows:

1. Do I understand exactly what I am supposed to do for this assignment?

2. What am I trying to learn?

3. What do I already know about this subject that will help me understand what I read?

4. What is the most efficient way for me to learn this material?

5. What parts of this chapter may give me problems?

6. What can I do so that I will understand the hard parts?

7. Now that I am finished reading, do I understand what I read?

Students who learn to monitor their reading and studying through generating their own questions are usually more successful than students who do not (Babbs and Moe, 1983; Baker and Brown, 1984; Cohen, 1983).

The self-appraisal form in Example 11.6 is designed primarily for intermediate and middle-school children. It enables them to assess their competency in various reading skills and recognize areas of strength or weakness. Teachers can use the results to understand students' perceptions of their own needs and plan appropriate instruction.

One application for self-appraisal is found in Natalie Knox's literature response groups (see the Classroom Scenario on literature group self-evaluation).

Example 11.6   *Self-Check Exercise*

Directions: Read the following sentences and put a number beside each one.
Put 1 beside the sentence if it is nearly always true.
Put 2 beside the sentence if it is sometimes true.
Put 3 beside the sentence if it is hardly ever true.

_____ I understand what I read.

_____ I can find the main idea of a paragraph.

_____ I think about what I read and what it really means to me.

_____ I can "read between the lines" and understand what the author is trying to say.

_____ I think about what I already know about the subject as I read.

_____ I can figure out new words by reading the rest of the sentence.

_____ I can figure out new words by "sounding them out."

_____ I can use a dictionary to figure out how to pronounce new words.

_____ I can use a dictionary to find word meanings.

_____ I know how to find information in the library.

_____ I can find books I like to read in the library.

_____ I can read aloud easily and with expression.

_____ I know what is important to learn in my textbooks.

_____ I know how to use the indexes in my books.

_____ I know how to study for a test.

_____ I ask myself questions as I read to make sure I understand.

**Classroom
Scenario**

Literature Group Self-Evaluation

The students have completed the book for their literature response group, and it is time to fill out the self-evaluations Natalie has given them (see Example 11.7). After carefully rating themselves, they give themselves grades and justify their grades with reasons. Some of the children wrote as follows:

The grade I think I deserve for this literature group is ___*A*___ because

most of the answers above are number threes. And I love discussing questions and other things about my book.

The grade I think I deserve for this literature group is _____ B _____ because

I think I deserve a B because I sometimes took my vocabulary folder home and left it and then didn't have it.

The grade I think I deserve for this literature group is _____ B _____ because

I did ok but I didn't do perfect a C is rediculous but an A is way too much!

The grade I think I deserve for this literature group is _____ B _____ because

I guess I deserved this grade because sometimes I didn't keep up with litterature responce and reading.

The grade I think I deserve for this literature group is _____ B _____ because

Because I really made disturbances when It was supposed to be quiet reading time   But I do apoligize.

The grade I think I deserve for this literature group is _____ C _____ because

I think I can do better in keeping up with my journal. Mostly, I keep my voice level down and rarely get called down.

Analysis of Scenario

Such self-evaluation encourages children to reflect on their work and to become aware of their strengths and weaknesses. In so doing, they become independent learners.

Example 11.7 *Self-evaluations for Literature Response Groups*

Literature Group Self-Evaluation

Directions: Use the following to rate your performance this six weeks.
  0 = not at all
  1 = some
  2 = adequately
  3 = above average

I, _____, am reading _____.
This is my own self-evaluation.

Reading

  1. Kept up with reading   _____
  2. Used my reading time wisely   _____
  3. Did not disturb others during reading time   _____
  4. Did not take my book without permission   _____

Group Responses

  1. Contributed quality responses   _____
  2. Volunteered responses   _____
  3. Asked legitimate questions   _____
  4. Listened to others in the group   _____
  5. Came to group with things to share   _____
  6. Made predictions concerning events in the book   _____
  7. Made connections to other things in the book   _____
  8. Made connections to real-life situations   _____
  9. Behaved appropriately in group   _____

Response Writing Log

  1. Kept up with entries in my log   _____
  2. Wrote quality responses in my log   _____
  3. Shared entries with the group when asked   _____

The grade I think I deserve for this literature group is _____
because _____
_____

Signature _____ Date _____

SELF-CHECK: OBJECTIVE 5   Why is self-evaluation an important aspect of assessment? How can teachers provide opportunities for students to evaluate themselves? (See Self-Improvement Opportunities 8 and 10.)

Informal Tests

In addition to such informal assessments as observations, checklists, rubrics, and portfolios, teachers may administer informal tests for specific purposes. Teachers may construct these tests or may find them commercially available in manuals or books.

Informal Tests of Specific Content or Skills

Sometimes the classroom teacher needs to administer an informal test to check students' knowledge and understanding of a specific skill or content area. For instance, the teacher might construct a vocabulary test from words students have learned during a unit. An example of another type of test is the Informal Dictionary Inventory shown in Example 11.8, which illustrates how a teacher can check on each student's ability to use the dictionary.

Basal reader programs usually include tests to be used for determining how well students have learned the content of a specific unit of instruction. Workbooks also contain skill tests to be given periodically. In addition, some school systems require teachers to give tests on basic skills. Whenever such tests are given, they should be used for diagnosing students' strengths and weaknesses, deciding if reteaching is needed, and providing direction for future learning experiences.

Cloze Procedure

The cloze procedure, described in Chapter 10, helps the teacher know if a textbook is easy or difficult for a child to read. By filling in words that have been

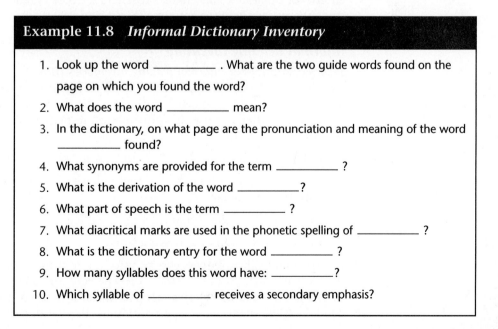

Example 11.8 *Informal Dictionary Inventory*

1. Look up the word _____ . What are the two guide words found on the page on which you found the word?

2. What does the word _____ mean?

3. In the dictionary, on what page are the pronunciation and meaning of the word _____ found?

4. What synonyms are provided for the term _____ ?

5. What is the derivation of the word _____?

6. What part of speech is the term _____ ?

7. What diacritical marks are used in the phonetic spelling of _____ ?

8. What is the dictionary entry for the word _____ ?

9. How many syllables does this word have: _____?

10. Which syllable of _____ receives a secondary emphasis?

deleted from a textbook selection, the student reveals his or her familiarity with the subject and ability to read the text with understanding. Test results give information about the student's independent, instructional, or frustration levels for both narrative and expository material.

Computer Approaches

Computers provide interesting and motivational alternatives to traditional testing (Johnston, 1983; McCarthy, 1994; Schreiner, 1985). Some computer programs automatically place learners in the appropriate branches of programs for text, item type, and level of difficulty according to the child's initial item performance. In this way, diagnosis is continuous because it occurs as students select their answers.

Computer games often require students to read and follow directions. The teacher can assess each child's comprehension by noting responses, such as the number of clues a child needs to get information from the text onscreen.

Teachers can use computers for assessment in several additional ways. Online testing allows students to work at terminals connected to a computer that analyzes their responses. Sometimes computers are used to scan mark-sensitive answer sheets that students have completed while working with test booklets. The computer scores the tests, thus freeing the teacher from this task. Software is also available to help teachers modify test items and entire tests, perform test and item analysis, collect and analyze test scores and student grades, record grades for various assignments, and compute final grades (Kubiszyn and Borich, 1987). With a Macintosh LC and *Grady Profile Portfolio Assessment* software, teachers can gather and review all of a student's written work, as well as samples of oral presentations. *Gradebook Plus* enables teachers to record grades daily and compute a student's average grade at any time (McCarthy, 1994).

Informal Reading Inventory

Teachers administer *informal reading inventories (IRIs)* to get a general idea of a child's strengths and weaknesses in word recognition and comprehension. IRIs help teachers identify specific types of word recognition and comprehension errors so that they can use this information to plan appropriate instruction. An IRI can indicate a child's

1. independent reading level (level to be read "on his or her own").

2. instructional level (that is, the reading level of the material the child can use with teacher guidance).

3. frustration level (level that thwarts or baffles).

4. capacity level (potential reading level).

The oral reading sequence in an informal reading inventory should begin on the level at which the child achieves 100 percent on a sight word recognition test. After the oral reading, the teacher asks questions about the selection; then the child reads the silent reading part and is asked questions about that selection.

Material is written at a child's *independent* reading level when he or she correctly pronounces 99 words in 100 (99 percent correct) and correctly responds to at least 90 percent of the questions. The material from which the child correctly pronounces 95 percent of the words and correctly answers at least 75 percent of the questions is roughly at the child's *instructional* level, the level at which teaching may effectively take place.

If a student needs help on more than one word out of ten (90 percent) or responds correctly to fewer than 50 percent of the questions, the material is too advanced and is at the child's *frustration* level. After the frustration level has been reached, the teacher should read aloud higher levels of material until the child reaches the highest reading level for which he or she can correctly answer 75 percent of the comprehension questions. The highest level achieved indicates the child's probable *capacity* (potential reading) level.

Teachers may make their own informal reading inventories, or they may use commercially prepared inventories. Example 11.9 shows a sample reading selection with comprehension questions and scoring aid from the *Burns/Roe Informal Reading Inventory*.

It is important to remember that the result of an informal reading inventory is an *estimate* of a reader's abilities. The percentages the child achieves are a significant indication of levels of performance, but the teacher's observations of the child taking the test are equally important.

SELF-CHECK: OBJECTIVE 6   What are some types of informal tests that a teacher might give? What information do these tests provide? (See Self-Improvement Opportunity 1.)

Miscue Analysis

Similar in form and procedures to the informal reading inventory, the *reading miscue inventory (RMI)* considers both the quantity and quality of *miscues*, or unexpected responses. Instead of simply considering the number of errors with equal weight for each, the teacher analyzes the RMI for the significance of each miscue. Knowing the type of miscue and what might have caused it provides more information about reading difficulties than knowing the number of miscues. (Some commercial IRIs, such as the one in Example 11.9, also include a qualitative analysis.)

Miscue analysis helps teachers gain insight into the reading process and helps them analyze students' oral reading (Goodman, Watson, and Burke, 1987). Analysis of the types of miscues each student makes helps the teacher interpret why students are having difficulties. To some extent, miscues are the result of the thought and language the student brings to the reading situation. Therefore, analyzing miscues in terms of the student's background or schemata enables the teacher to understand why some miscues were given and to provide appropriate instructional strategies that build on strengths.

Teachers should consider whether miscalled words indicate lack of knowledge about phonics or structural analysis, show inability to use context, reveal limited sight word knowledge, result from dialect differences, or suggest some other type

Example 11.9   *Reading Selection and Questions from an Informal Reading Inventory*

☆5 PASSAGE — FORM A — TEACHER 5☆

MOTIVATIONAL STATEMENT: Read this story to find out about a harbor seal pup that has a special problem.

In the sea, a harbor seal pup learns to catch and eat fish by watching its mother. By the time it is weaned, at the age of four or five weeks, it is able to feed on its own.

Without a mother, and living temporarily in captivity, Pearson had to be taught what a fish was and how to swallow it. Eventually, he would have to learn to catch one himself.

Holly started his training with a small herring—an oily fish which is a favorite with seals. Gently, she opened his mouth and slipped the fish in headfirst. Harbor seals have sharp teeth for catching fish but no teeth for grinding and chewing. They swallow their food whole.

But Pearson didn't seem to understand what he was supposed to do. He bit down on the fish and then spit it out. Holly tried again. This time, Pearson got the idea. He swallowed the herring in one gulp and looked eagerly for more.

Within a week, he was being hand-fed a pound of fish a day in addition to his formula. This new diet made him friskier than ever. He chased the other pups in the outside pen. He plunged into the small wading pool and rolled in the shallow water, splashing both seals and people.

Source: Pearson, *A Harbor Seal Pup*, by Susan Meyers. New York: E. P. Dutton, 1980, pp. 15–16.

[Note: Do not count as a miscue mispronunciation of the name Pearson. You may pronounce this name for the student if needed.]

SCORING AID

WORD RECOGNITION

%—MISCUES	
99—3	
95—11	
90—22	
85—33	

COMPREHENSION

%—ERRORS	
100—0	
90—1	
80—2	
70—3	
60—4	
50—5	
40—6	
30—7	
20—8	
10—9	
0—10	

214 WORDS (for Word Recognition)

217 WORDS (for Rate)

$\frac{13020}{}$ WPM

COMPREHENSION QUESTIONS

_____ main idea
1. What is this story about? (teaching a harbor seal pup to catch and eat fish; teaching Pearson to catch and eat fish)

_____ detail
2. How does a harbor seal pup learn to catch and eat fish in the sea? (by watching its mother)

_____ vocabulary
3. What does the word "temporarily" mean? (for a short time; not permanently)

_____ vocabulary
4. What does the word "captivity" mean? (the condition of being held as a prisoner or captive; confinement; a condition in which a person or animal is not free)

_____ cause and effect/inference
5. What caused Pearson to need to be taught what a fish was and how to swallow it? (He didn't have a mother to show him.)

_____ inference
6. What is an oily fish that seals like? (herring)

_____ cause and effect/inference
7. What causes harbor seals to swallow their food whole? (They have no teeth for grinding and chewing.)

_____ sequence
8. Name in order the two things that Pearson did the first time Holly put a fish in his mouth. (bit down on the fish and then spit it out)

_____ inference
9. How fast did Pearson learn how to eat a fish? (He learned on the second try.)

_____ detail
10. What made Pearson get friskier? (his new diet of fish and formula; his new diet)

Source: Betty D. Roe, *Burns/Roe Informal Reading Inventory*, Fourth Edition. Copyright © 1993 by Houghton Mifflin Company. Used with permission.

of difficulty. Therefore, while listening to a child read, a teacher must evaluate the significance of different miscues. For example, the child who reads "The boys are playing" as "The boys is playing" may be a speaker of a nonstandard dialect and may be using his or her decoding ability to translate the printed text to meaning. This miscue does not intefere with meaning, but many miscues do reflect problems.

In studying the miscues, the teacher should check for specific items such as the following:

1. Is the miscue a result of the reader's dialect? If he says *foe* for *four,* he may simply be using a familiar pronunciation that does not affect meaning.

2. Does the miscue change the meaning? If the reader says *dismal* for *dismiss,* the meaning is likely changed and the substitution would not make sense.

3. Does the reader self-correct? If he says a word that does not make sense but self-corrects, he is trying to make sense of reading.

4. Is he using syntactic cues? If he says *run* for *chase,* he still shows some use of syntactic cues, but if he says *boy* for *beautiful,* he is probably losing the syntactic pattern.

5. Is he using graphic cues? Comparing the sounds and spellings of miscues and expected words in substitutions will reveal how a reader is using graphic cues. Examples of graphic miscues include *house* for *horse, running* for *run, is* for *it,* and *dogs* for *dog.*

Goodman, Watson, and Burke (1987) offer four forms of the RMI. Procedure II questions each miscue in terms of its syntactic acceptability, semantic acceptability, meaning change, graphic similarity, and sound similarity. The following two cases show how these questions may be applied to miscues.

Case 1
Sentence: My *father* and I went fishing.
The child reads: My *dad* and I went fishing.

Analyzing the miscue in terms of the above criteria, the teacher finds the possible significance of the miscue to be as follows:

Syntactic acceptability: acceptable
Semantic acceptability: acceptable
Meaning change: no meaning change
Graphic similarity: no graphic similarity
Sound similarity: no sound similarity
Conclusion: Since the meaning of the sentence is not changed, the miscue is of little importance. Probably the child simply translated the word *father* into the more familiar form *dad.* The child is reading for meaning.

Case 2
Sentence: My *father* and I went fishing.
The child reads: My *feather* and I went fishing.

Syntactic acceptability: acceptable
Semantic acceptability: unacceptable
Meaning change: yes

Graphic similarity: high degree of graphic similarity
Sound similarity: high degree of sound similarity
Conclusion: This child is focusing on phonics to decode words rather than on meaning. Unless the miscue is self-corrected, the reader may be having difficulties with comprehension.

An extension of miscue analysis is the probe technique suggested by Barr, Sadow, and Blachowicz (1990). When teachers are uncertain about the meaning of their evaluation, they may wish to "probe," or further analyze, one or more areas. The probe technique generally involves working with children individually to find out why they made miscues. The teacher might question a child about a miscue, ask her to look at the word again, provide additional clues, and analyze her responses to determine why she was having difficulty. The teacher might continue working with her on other miscues to further evaluate her miscue patterns. A teacher can also use the probe technique for analyzing a child's ability to use comprehension strategies by having her reread a passage and asking her leading questions about what she reads until she is able to read it with understanding.

SELF-CHECK: OBJECTIVE 7   What are five observations a teacher can make to analyze a child's reading miscue in the following sentence?

Printed sentence: At the zoo, I *had* my first view of a zebra.
Child reads as: At the zoo, I *heard* my first view of a zebra.

What does this miscue indicate? (See Self-Improvement Opportunity 11.)

Running Records

Similar to miscue analysis is the *running record*, a strategy that tells how well a student is reading (Clay, 1979). In this procedure, the child reads a selection from each of three books: a book he or she has just completed with 90 to 100 percent accuracy, a harder text, and an easier text. These samples provide insights into the student's strengths (from easier material) and weaknesses (from more difficult material).

The procedure for completing the running record is similar to that used with the IRI or RMI. While a child is reading, the teacher places a check above every word read correctly. When a child makes a miscue, the teacher uses a coding system to mark the type of miscue. After completing the running record for the three samples, the teacher considers why the child made each miscue by asking, "What made him/her say that?" Miscalled words are analyzed according to whether the child used semantics (meaning—m), syntax (language structure—s), or grapho-phonic (visual—v) cues to arrive at the word. The teacher then tabulates the types of miscues by letter to see the total number of times each type of cue was used (*Reading in Junior Classes*, 1985).

Further Considerations about Informal Assessment

Although informal assessment gives a great deal of information about how well a child uses reading strategies, it has some limitations that teachers should consider. First, informal assessment is subjective; that is, the teacher's personal biases may influence judgments about student performance. Therefore, it is possible for two teachers to assess the same work differently. Also, some teachers may not be knowledgeable about the use of informal strategies or may not have realistic expectations for students at a certain level, so their assessments may not be fair appraisals of student performance. Informal assessment can also place a heavy burden on teacher time if teachers write frequent narrative reports on student progress instead of simply assigning numerical or letter grades based on objective test results. In addition, teachers must know how to interpret and apply information from informal records to help children improve their reading strategies.

Another limitation of informal assessment becomes apparent when some parents and administrators insist on grade point records, which are not available through many types of informal assessment. School systems often stress accountability, which means that sets of scores must be available for each student. Thus, for a variety of reasons, most school systems require the use of formal tests along with informal assessment.

Criterion-Referenced Tests

A *criterion-referenced* (or objective-referenced) *test* is designed to yield scores that are interpretable in terms of specific performance standards, for example, to indicate that a student can identify the main idea of a paragraph 90 percent of the time. Such tests are intended to be used as guides for developing instructional prescriptions. For example, if a child cannot perform the task of identifying cause-and-effect relationships, the teacher should provide instruction in that area. Such specific applications make these tests useful in day-to-day decisions about instruction.

However, educators have important questions concerning criterion-referenced tests. How many correct answers are needed to show that the student has achieved an objective or performed up to standard? Should every child be expected to meet every objective? Most importantly, does knowing the skill mean that the child can apply it in authentic situations?

Criterion-referenced testing has both advantages and disadvantages. It is an effective way to diagnose a child's knowledge of reading skills, and it helps in prescribing appropriate instruction. Furthermore, students do not compete with other students, but only try to achieve mastery of each criterion or objective. On the other hand, reading can appear to be nothing more than a series of skills to be taught and tested, and skills may be taught in isolation rather than in combination. Knowledge gained in this way may be difficult for children to apply to actual reading situations.

Formal Assessment (Norm-Referenced Tests)

Norm-referenced tests provide objective data about reading achievement, scholastic aptitude, areas of strengths and weaknesses, and so on. Authors of these tests sample large populations of children to determine the appropriateness of test items. They seek to verify the *validity* and *reliability* of test results so that schools can be confident that the tests measure what they are intended to measure and that results will not vary significantly if students take the same test more than once.

Results of norm-referenced tests are most commonly expressed as grade equivalents (or grade scores), percentile ranks, and stanines. A *grade equivalent* indicates the grade level, in years and months, for which a given score was the average score in the standardization sample. For example, if a score of 25 has the grade equivalent of 4.6, that means that in the norm group 25 was the average score of students in the sixth month of the fourth grade. After the test has been standardized, if another student in the sixth month of the fourth grade takes the same test and scores 25 correct, his or her performance is "at grade level," or average for this grade placement. A student who gets 30 right, or a grade equivalent of 5.3, has done as well as the typical fifth grader in the third month on *that* test. Similarly, a 3.3 grade equivalent for a fourth grader means that the performance is equal to that of the average student in the third month of the third grade on that test. Many educators object to using grade equivalents because they believe that misuse of grade equivalents is more likely to lead to a misunderstanding of a student's ability than is use of other data.

Percentile rank (PR) expresses a score in terms of its position within a set of 100 scores. The PR indicates the percentage of scores in a reference group that is equal to or lower than the given score; therefore, a score ranked at the fortieth percentile is equal to or better than the scores of 40 percent of the people in the reference group.

On a *stanine scale,* the scores are divided into nine equal parts, with a stanine of 5 as the mean. The following interpretation for stanine scores shows a student's relationship to the rest of the group.

stanine 9: higher performance
stanines 7 and 8: above average
stanines 4, 5, and 6: average
stanines 2 and 3: below average
stanine 1: lower performance

Teachers should be concerned not only with a student's total achievement score but also with subtest scores. Two children may have the same total score but have different reading strengths and weaknesses, as revealed in subtest scores.

	Child A	Child B
Word recognition	2.8	4.5
Word meaning	3.6	2.5
Comprehension	4.1	3.5
Reading achievement score	3.5	3.5

When students read considerably below grade level, teachers should administer out-of-level tests, or tests designed for one grade level but given to students at another level. Students who cannot read achievement tests can only guess at

Norm-referenced tests can provide teachers with objective data about reading achievement, scholastic aptitude, and areas of strengths and weaknesses. (© *Jean Claude-Lejeune*)

answers, so their scores are not reliable. Testing these students at levels that correspond to their reading abilities enables them to avoid frustration and do their best work. Many manuals that accompany standardized tests contain directions and tables for out-of-level testing (Gunning, 1982; Koenke and McClellan, 1987; Smith et al., 1983).

Traditional Achievement Tests

Most schools administer *achievement tests* in the spring or fall every year to assess the gains in achievement of groups of children. Most of these tests are actually batteries, or collections of tests on different subjects, and should be given under carefully controlled conditions and over the course of several days. They may be sent to the publisher for machine scoring.

Many achievement tests contain subtests in reading and language, which provide useful information for identifying students' general strengths and weaknesses in reading. Some norm-referenced achievement tests for which separate reading subtests are available are:

Iowa Tests of Basic Skills, Complete and Survey Batteries. Chicago: Riverside Publishing Company, 1991. (grades 2 to 8)

California Achievement Test, 5th ed. CTB/McGraw-Hill, 1992. (grades K to 12.9)

Metropolitan Achievement Test, 7th ed. The Psychological Corporation, 1992. (grades K to 12.9)

A sample page from the *Stanford Achievement Test* indicating the scope and sequence of the reading portion of the test appears in Example 11.10.

Limitations of Norm-Referenced Tests

If norm-referenced tests are properly understood and interpreted, they can assist teachers in planning reading instruction. "When used intelligently as part of an overall evaluation, they are significant indicators of educational progress" (Calfee, 1987, p. 743). Teachers need to understand the limitations of standardized tests as they exist today, however, and they should begin by asking a series of questions about them.

Do tests really measure what we know about the reading process today? Standardized tests often do not reflect current thinking about reading comprehension as a sustained, interactive, strategic process. Teachers should ask themselves the following questions when evaluating the usefulness of standardized tests in terms of new research about the reading process:

1. Does the test check knowledge of vocabulary by asking students to find one of several words that most closely matches an isolated key word, or does it ask students to identify vocabulary in context, in the manner in which readers nearly always encounter words?

2. Does the test assess reading comprehension based on answers to series of short, unrelated paragraphs, or does it ask students to read longer passages as they would in real reading situations?

3. Does the test present material without regard for students' prior knowledge, or does it consider the way students' existing schemata interact with the text as students construct meaning?

How accurate are the scores? It is doubtful that teachers should accept the results of norm-referenced tests with great confidence. They should not assume that a grade score exactly indicates an actual performance level, since a single test score on a norm-referenced reading test frequently reflects the child's frustration level rather than his or her instructional or independent level. In other words, a child who achieves a fourth-grade score on a test may be unable to perform satisfactorily with fourth-grade content materials. This situation is particularly true for readers at the upper and lower ends of the class distribution.

Is the test fair to minority groups and inner-city children? Test publishers have been giving increasing attention to the question of the fairness of their tests. They do not want to state questions in a way that will give certain children an unfair advantage or discourage some children so that they will not do their best. Many writers and editors from different backgrounds are involved in testmaking, and members of several ethnic groups review questions to correct unintentional, built-in biases.

Example 11.10   Stanford Achievement Test Scope and Sequence for Reading

SUBTESTS	SESAT 1	SESAT 2	Primary 1	Primary 2	Primary 3	Inter. 1	Inter. 2	Inter. 3	Adv. 1	Adv. 2	Task 1	Task 2	Task 3
Level / Grade (Content)	1st Half K	2nd Half K / 1st Half 1	1	2	3	4	5	6	7	8	9	10	11-12
Sounds and Letters													
Auditory Recognition	X	X											
Symbol Recognition	X	X											
Word Study Skills													
Structural Analysis			X	X	X								
Phonetic Analysis			X	X	X								
Word Reading	X	X	X										
Sentence Reading		X											
Reading Vocabulary													
Synonyms				X	X	X	X	X	X	X	X	X	X
Context				X	X	X	X	X	X	X	X	X	X
Multiple Meanings				X	X	X	X	X	X	X	X	X	X
Reading Comprehension													
Two-Sentence Stories			X										
Short Reading Passages			X										
Short Reading Passages with Questions			X										
Recreational Reading				X	X	X	X	X	X	X	X	X	X
Textual Reading				X	X	X	X	X	X	X	X	X	X
Functional Reading				X	X	X	X	X	X	X	X	X	X
Literal Comprehension				X	X	X	X	X	X	X	X	X	X
Inferential Comprehension				X	X	X	X	X	X	X	X	X	X
Critical Comprehension				X	X	X	X	X	X	X	X	X	X

Source: Stanford Achievement Test: 8th Edition. Copyright © 1988 by The Psychological Corporation. Reproduced by permission. All rights reserved.

Emergence of Performance-Based Achievement Tests

For seventy years, traditional achievement tests have remained essentially the same (VanLeirsburg, 1993). Comprehension sections consist of series of short passages followed by multiple-choice questions, and tests require students to identify a single correct answer for each test item. Estimates of a child's reading ability are based on the number of correct answers as found in an answer key. Many educators believe standardized tests fail to measure thinking and problem-solving skills, in-depth knowledge of subjects, and students' ability to direct their own learning (Sugarman, Allen, and Keller-Cogan, 1993).

Recently, however, researchers have been seeking to establish more authentic ways to assess reading ability by taking into consideration students' thought processes and reading strategies. Educators believe that because test scores often are used to direct instruction and predict performance, tests should measure the high-level thinking strategies students actually employ when reading (Powell, 1989). Therefore, developers of standardized tests have been seeking ways to measure a student's ability to apply reading strategies in a variety of authentic reading tasks. Rather than focusing on single correct answers, researchers are considering the entire process of reading and the strategies used. Farr and Carey (1986) have identified three ways that test developers are beginning to adapt new ideas about comprehension to their tests. In one instance, reading comprehension tests include setting purposes for reading (*Metropolitan Achievement Test*); in another, analysis of incorrect responses to multiple-choice questions aids in diagnosing sources of difficulties (*California Achievement Tests*). Yet another alternative is assessing vocabulary by asking readers to identify words embedded in text instead of words in isolation.

Both Illinois and Michigan are at the forefront of developing new types of reading assessment that focus on larger concepts, such as problem solving and higher-order thinking skills, and on curriculum strands, such as language arts (VanLeirsburg, 1993). For statewide assessment in Illinois, students are encouraged to answer test questions strategically, that is, by using a variety of strategies to make sense out of what they read (Valencia and Pearson, 1987). These tests ask students to choose the best of three or four summaries of a selection, assess the value of several retellings of a selection for different audiences, select the most useful questions to help a peer understand important ideas about a passage, identify more than one acceptable answer to a question, and predict the likelihood of the inclusion of certain items on a specified topic. These testing strategies take into consideration the need to connect assessment procedures with current beliefs about reading instruction, including the importance of prior knowledge to reading comprehension and the acceptability of more than one correct response to a reading selection.

Other applications of performance-based assessment come from the 1992 National Assessment of Education Progress (NAEP) and the Arizona Student Assessment Program. In the NAEP revision, reading passages are longer and come from real texts. The tests consist of more open-ended responses, oral readings, interviews based on classwork, and discussions of reading selections (Flood and Lapp, 1993). In the Arizona program, one task requires students to read nonfiction and high-quality literature to solve problems. Because students must produce original thoughts about issues rather than repeat given information, they must use higher-order thinking skills (Peters, 1994).

An example of a performance-based standardized test is the *Integrated Literature and Language Arts Portfolio Program* (ILALAPP) (Chicago: Riverside Publishing Company, 1991). This program is designed to assess the language arts in the same manner in which research indicates they should be taught. For example, listening, reading, and writing are integrated; reading passages consist of illustrated, intact selections from good literature; and an open-ended testing format enables students to write free responses.

One feature of the ILALAPP is a section that precedes the narrative or expository selection students are to read. This feature prepares students for the actual reading by causing them to draw on their own experiences and to think about what the story will be like. Example 11.11 illustrates this feature for the informational piece that follows.

Example 11.11   *Prior Knowledge Predicting Content Feature from the Integrated Literature and Language Arts Portfolio*

Day 3: Before Reading

Before you begin to read "How Sound Effects Are Made," stop for a moment to think about the meaning of the term *sound effects*. It means sounds or imitations of sounds that are recorded and used for movies, television, or radio.

You have heard many examples of sound effects. Try your hand at creating some sound effects. Think about how you would use sound effects in the radio ads below. Write in the sounds you think fit best in each blank. Choose from: clock ticking, car horns blaring, pouring rain, soothing music, faucet dripping, screams and laughter.

Ad 1	*Sound Effects*
ANNOUNCER:	1a. _____
Time on your hands?	
Come to Thrills and Chills	
Amusement Park for the	1b. _____
TIME of your life!	
Ad 2	
ANNOUNCER: Stuck in traffic again?	2a. _____
Just stay tuned to our Lazy	2b. _____
Listening Channel 000.	

Source: p. 17 from Student Activity Booklet, Level 4, Form X, Riverside Publishing Co., 1991. *Integrated Literature and Language Arts Portfolio Program.* Copyright © 1991 by Houghton Mifflin Company. Used with permission of The Riverside Publishing Company, Chicago, Ill.

After students read the selection, they are asked to write the most interesting thing they learned, examples of concepts or information that appeared in the story, creative responses, and other types of reactions (at least one answer in full paragraph form). Scoring guides are available, but scorers will need to make careful decisions about the reasonableness of student responses to questions that have more than one acceptable answer. Ideally, student responses are evaluated by the classroom teacher, who is most interested in determining how a student arrived at a specific answer.

SELF-CHECK: OBJECTIVES 8 AND 9   Differentiate between traditional achievement tests and recent performance-based achievement tests. What are some advantages and disadvantages of each? (See Self-Improvement Opportunity 12.)

Summary

Assessment procedures are changing as educators seek ways to measure student progress in reading that reflect current authentic, or holistic, views of the reading process. More than ever before, assessment is merging with instruction as teachers continuously observe students, interact with them, and analyze their strengths and weaknesses.

Informal assessment can take many forms, and teachers can learn much about their students by using observation strategies. Daily observation, or kid-watching, is a key to effective assessment, and teachers can record their observations in a variety of ways, including anecdotal records and checklists. Rubrics make students aware of expectations by giving specific criteria for scoring their work. Portfolios are useful for keeping samples of student work, and self-appraisal helps students evaluate their own accomplishments.

Informal tests over specific areas, including teacher-made tests over content or skills and basal reader tests, provide information about student mastery of specific material. Teachers can also use computers in various ways to assess students' knowledge. The informal reading inventory, reading miscue inventory, and running record are similar forms of informal tests that help the teacher identify students' strengths and weaknesses.

The teacher can use criterion-referenced tests to determine how well a student has mastered a specific skill. Skill mastery, however, does not always indicate whether or not the student can apply the skill to actual reading situations.

Formal assessment consists of norm-referenced (standardized) tests that compare students with other students across the nation on the basis of test scores. Most schools require that achievement tests be given annually to measure the progress students have made in overall academic achievement. Most traditional standardized tests measure skill mastery, whereas newer performance-based standardized tests ask students to demonstrate their competence in performing a task or creating a product.

The following chart summarizes the purposes of informal and formal assessment:

Informal Assessment	Formal Assessment
Gives teacher useful day-to-day information about student progress	Compares students with other students across the nation
Informs teacher about planning instruction to meet students' needs	Provides accountability for school systems
Identifies individual strengths and weaknesses	Gives scores that can be interpreted statistically

The teacher's most useful assessment tool is day-to-day observation. Informal tests may be used to reinforce or supplement such observation, whereas norm-referenced tests are usually given only as mandated by the school system.

Test Yourself   *True or False*

_____ 1. Current practices in assessment correspond closely with what is known about the reading process.

_____ 2. Traditional standardized tests are more appropriate than performance assessment for outcome-based education.

_____ 3. Instruction and assessment should be separate procedures.

_____ 4. Teachers must devise their own informal reading inventories, since none are commercially available.

_____ 5. Basal reader programs usually include tests specific to each unit or reader.

_____ 6. Material written on a child's independent reading level is less difficult than material written on his or her instructional level.

_____ 7. Miscue analysis can help a teacher understand the nature of a child's unexpected responses in reading.

_____ 8. Self-questioning is an effective tool for reading and studying.

_____ 9. Percentile rank (PR) refers to the percentage of correct responses an examinee makes on a test.

_____ 10. A criterion-referenced assessment relates an individual's test performances to absolute standards rather than to the performances of others.

_____ 11. At present there are no computer programs for assessing reading skills.

———— 12. Major changes have been occurring in standardized testing for much of the past seventy years.

———— 13. Authentic assessment focuses on small, separate skills.

———— 14. Three significant aspects of informal evaluation are observation, interaction, and analysis.

———— 15. The term *kidwatching* refers to professional baby-sitting.

———— 16. Recordkeeping is an essential part of observation.

———— 17. Anecdotal records are written accounts of specific classroom incidents.

———— 18. Story retelling enables teachers to learn about a child's comprehension of a story.

———— 19. A rubric is used for scoring cloze tests.

———— 20. It is considered desirable for students to assess their own progress.

———— 21. In evaluating the results of a reading miscue inventory, the teacher focuses on the types of miscues rather than on the total number of miscalled words.

———— 22. A running record is a narrative report of a child's overall progress.

———— 23. A miscalled word is said to have semantic acceptability if the meaning is basically the same as that of the printed word.

———— 24. The cloze procedure is an example of a norm-referenced test.

———— 25. When using portfolios, samples of a student's work should be collected and reviewed by both the student and the teacher.

———— 26. The best questions for a teacher to ask during a student conference or interview are those that can be answered with *yes* or *no*.

———— 27. A student whose placement is in the first stanine is at or near the top of the class.

———— 28. Some recent standardized tests enable students to write responses to open-ended questions.

Self-Improvement Opportunities

1. Secure a published IRI and administer it to an elementary school student. Report the results to the class.

2. Prepare a rubric that includes criteria for writing that you believe are relevant for a specific grade level.

3. Discuss with a teacher and a librarian some ways to assess development of children's literary interests.

4. Read a journal article that deals with the status of assessment in relation to measuring current educational objectives, and write a critique of it. Share your findings and opinions with your peers.

5. Brainstorm a list of types of assessment. Consider whether or not each type gives information about the child's progress in learning to read, strengths and weaknesses, and use of language. After evaluating each type of assessment by these three criteria, decide which types are the best measures.

6. If you have access to an elementary classroom, write an anecdotal record about one child's behavior. Observe how the child works independently, interacts socially, and responds to the teacher.

7. Listen to a child read and use the oral reading checklist (Example 11.3) to evaluate his or her oral reading skill. You may wish to tape-record the oral reading so that you can check your impressions as you replay the tape.

8. Interview a child about his or her attitudes, interests, and progress in reading. Use the questions for conferencing and interviewing suggested in this text as a guide. Write the child's response to each question; then write your conclusions about the child's reading status.

9. Read a story to a child, and then ask her or him to tell you the story. Be sure to choose a story of high interest that is easy for the child to understand. When the child cannot think of anything more to say, you might ask some open-ended questions to elicit further information. Evaluate the child's understanding of the story based on the retelling.

10. Select samples of your work during a college term and organize them in a portfolio. Consider what you would include that would give a valid indication of your interests and achievement. At the end of the term, evaluate your class performance.

11. Compare and contrast the informal reading inventory, reading miscue inventory, and running record. (You may wish to find information from additional sources.) What are some strengths and weaknesses of each method?

12. Talk with a teacher about the norm-referenced tests used in his or her school district. Ask how teachers and administrators use these tests.

Chapter 12

Key Vocabulary

Pay close attention to these terms when they appear in the chapter.

achievement grouping

community of learners

cooperative learning

departmentalization

friendship grouping

heterogeneous grouping

homogeneous grouping

integrated language arts curriculum

interclass grouping

interest grouping

learning center

paraprofessional

peer tutoring

project or research groups

pupil pairs or partners

special skills or needs groups

student contract

teacher-researcher

thematic unit

theme cycle

whole language classroom

Classroom Organization and Management

Setting Objectives

When you finish reading this chapter, you should be able to

1. Explain some benefits of an integrated curriculum and how to implement it.

2. Discuss some features of whole language classrooms and strategies for cooperative learning.

3. Identify various ways teachers might group students for reading-related purposes.

4. Name some ways to use computers and media in the classroom.

5. Explain how the teacher can function as facilitator and manager of instruction, decision maker, researcher, and learner.

6. Describe some ways teachers can communicate with parents.

7. Explain the roles paraprofessionals and tutors play within the reading program.

Figure 12.1 *Chapter 12 Organization*

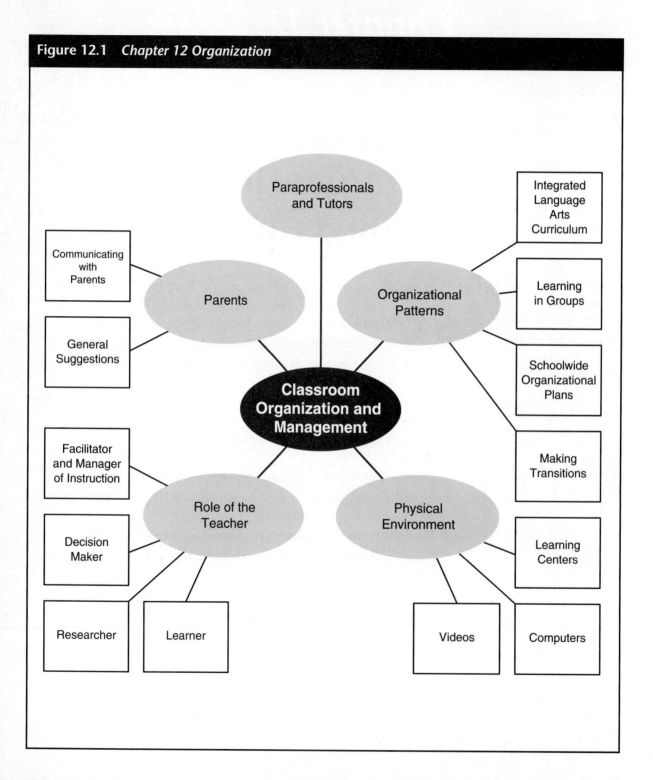

C lassroom organization does not directly involve the reading process or materials, methods, or approaches to teaching reading. Yet without good classroom organization and management, reading instruction may be totally ineffective. It is not enough for teachers to know what to teach; they must also know what organizational patterns and management techniques are conducive to learning.

This chapter presents various types of organizational plans and practical suggestions for forming and managing different kinds of groups. It considers an integrated language arts curriculum, a way to provide large blocks of time for students to learn and use language arts—reading, writing, listening, and speaking—meaningfully. It examines whole language classrooms and cooperative learning, as well as traditional classroom grouping arrangements. A variety of schoolwide organizational plans are presented, along with ideas for making transitions from one type of organization to another.

Next, the chapter recognizes the teacher as the most important variable in the classroom and introduces four major roles of the teacher: the teacher as facilitator and manager of instruction, as decision maker, as researcher, and as learner. The chapter also considers the influence of parents and the home environment on children's reading attitudes and achievement. Finally, the chapter explains the value of paraprofessionals and tutors in the school program.

Organizational Patterns

It is no secret that students within a single class vary a great deal in chronological age, maturity, cognitive abilities, interests, and personal experiences. In view of the obvious need to provide the most appropriate instruction for each learner, teachers must give careful consideration to plans that provide for both individual differences and a sense of community. Students should participate in small-group, individualized, partner, and whole-class activities.

As educational practices become more holistic, changes are occurring in classroom organization. Instead of scheduling reading groups in half-hour segments, teachers are reserving larger blocks of time for reading and writing activities. Rather than grouping children by ability or achievement, teachers are allowing children to work together in more flexible patterns. Instead of assigning seats for all-day use, teachers are encouraging children to work at centers and other locations where they are comfortable.

Following are some general guidelines for classroom organization:

1. Remember that no single classroom organization is better than all others.

2. Consider many criteria in deciding on a particular organizational plan, including children's needs and interests, your strengths and weaknesses, your educational philosophy, and specific goals of instruction.

3. Keep organizational plans and scheduling flexible; alter them as you discover improvements.

4. If you are using achievement groups, make low-ability groups smaller than high-ability groups so that you can give more attention to the special needs of low-achieving students.

5. Provide a consistent quality of instruction for all achievement groups.

6. Organize your classroom so that it is structured and orderly, but provide a supportive emotional climate.

7. Offer opportunities for individualized learning, making sure to manage independent activities for the benefit of all students.

8. Whenever possible, provide whole-class instruction so that all students experience a sense of community.

Integrated Language Arts Curriculum

reading-writing connection

An *integrated language arts curriculum* emphasizes relationships among reading, writing, listening, and speaking in authentic situations. Growth in one area is likely to result in growth in the others, and the language arts become the building blocks for content area learning. As language learning extends into the various subject areas, teachers can create a holistic and connected curricular approach to learning (Tchudi, 1994). Routman (1991) cautions, however, that teachers will find it difficult to achieve a fully integrated curriculum in which language, content, and concepts are interrelated across the entire curriculum all of the time.

A recent statement by the National Association for the Education of Young Children supports the concept of an integrated curriculum: "Children's learning does not occur in narrowly defined subject areas; their development and learning are integrated. Any activity that stimulates one dimension of development and learning affects other dimensions as well" (Ollila and Mayfield, 1992, p. 11). Integration of subjects is also supported by the associative theory of learning, which claims that students learn by associating material with other information, rather than by practicing isolated skills and memorizing facts (Cunningham and Allington, 1994). They learn by drawing on material from different but related sources to solve problems and reach goals.

thematic learning

Themes in an Integrated Curriculum

Teachers can help students make connections by using themes to integrate the curriculum. Unlike a unit, which is often relegated to an hour in the afternoon, a theme study is the core of the curriculum for an extended period of time (Gamberg et al., 1988). Most subjects can be integrated with the theme, although some subjects must receive additional attention because they do not fit into it naturally. "A thematic approach provides an organizational framework for students to learn language as well as to learn through language" (Pike, Compain, and Mumper, 1994, p. 272).

In *theme cycles,* teachers and students work together in negotiating the curriculum (Harste, Short, and Burke, 1988). Teachers bring their knowledge and experiences from encounters with experts and fields of study, and students bring their knowledge and experiences with life and learning. Together they plan what to study, make webs of "What We Know" and "What We Want to Know," and create lists of resources for obtaining information. As students explore a theme, they continue acquiring new information until they are ready to report their new knowledge to their classmates. The teacher's role is to help organize individual and group learning and to encourage students to consider new questions, search for resources, and discover different ways to present their ideas to their peers.

The teacher must choose themes, or topics, for an integrated curriculum by considering both curriculum guidelines and student interests. At the beginning of the school year, students might brainstorm topics they want to study. Using their ideas, the teacher tries to match them as closely as possible with the topics suggested in the curriculum framework. Themes should be broadly based to meet a variety of interests and individual differences so that students have choices within the theme structure (Pike, Compain, and Mumper, 1994). Topics should also be worthy of study; that is, they should have the potential for developing concepts that extend students' knowledge of their social and physical world. Examples are topics dealing with such issues as culture, energy, and social organization (Wilson et al., 1991).

reading-writing connection

One framework for integrating language arts across the curriculum is the use of a Topic Chart. The organizational structure in the following Classroom Scenario is adapted from the Data Charts used at Ivanhoe Boys' Grammar School in Melbourne, Australia, and from the I-Charts discussed in Chapter 6 (Hoffman, 1992). The theme, based on the students' choice and in keeping with the curriculum guide, is "Australia," which enables the students to understand a different land and culture.

**Classroom
Scenario**

Topic Charts

Jim Barlow reminds the students that they are beginning a theme study on Australia and reads them *My Place* by Nadia Wheatley, which traces the history of "my place" backwards from 1988 to the days of the aborigines. Mr. Barlow asks the students to brainstorm what they already know about Australia, and he begins recording their ideas in the form of a semantic map. When they finish, the major categories on the map are aborigines, animals and birds, cities, early settlers, famous people, and geography. These categories become topics for investigation.

Mr. Barlow has the students sign up for their first and second choices of topics. Then he forms groups of four students each, based on interest and without regard for achievement levels. He gives each group a Topic Chart on a large sheet of paper (see Example 12.1), and the students enter their topics and then select subtopics.

For instance, the geography group chooses the following subtopics: the Great Barrier Reef, the Outback, Oceans and Rivers, and Natural Resources. Together the children write what they already know about each subtopic in the appropriate square. They locate resource materials, and they each choose one of the sources to find the information needed. After selecting and reading the relevant material, each student records the bibliographic data from his or her source and summarizes information in the corresponding blocks.

When the members of a group complete their Topic Chart, they must decide how to present their information to the class. Some groups choose debates and panel discussions, one group uses maps and charts, another group presents a series of illustrated written reports, and the remaining group videotapes its presentation.

Analysis of Scenario

By using Topic Charts, the class became involved in a variety of language activities, including reading, writing, researching, note taking, and organizing material. Students also learned a great deal in social studies (the history and geography of Australia), as well as some math (measuring distances in kilometers), literature (books about Australia and by Australian authors), and science (animals and birds). They also had opportunities to work as a whole class, in groups, and independently. Topic Charts may be modified to include more or fewer subtopics and references, depending on students' abilities.

Scheduling

Scheduling for an integrated language arts curriculum calls for large blocks of time instead of small, fragmented, 15- or 20-minute chunks each for handwriting, spelling, grammar, and so forth. Ideally, this hour-and-a-half to two-hour block comes in the morning without interruption, providing time for a variety of language experiences. Many teachers are abandoning their segmented plan books in favor of larger, open-ended arrangements that allow more flexibility for language activities (Eisele, 1991). Scheduling is unique for each classroom; it is a reflection of how the teacher believes children learn and a response to their needs and interests.

One procedure for establishing a class schedule is to begin with a blank timetable and enter all of the special activities scheduled during the week, such as music, art, and library. Then enter any regularly scheduled events, such as lunch, recess, and Sustained Silent Reading. Block in a time for direct instruction in math, which is usually not covered adequately within a theme. Leave a few sessions open toward the end of the week for activities resulting from themes or unanticipated developments. Roughly outline plans for two or three weeks at a time, allowing learning to flow and providing flexibility from week to week. Display a large copy of the timetable for children to see so that they will be familiar with the routine and know how to plan their free activity time (Wilson et al., 1991).

Example 12.1 *Topic Chart*

Topic Chart

Students' Names:

Topic: Date:

Subtopics				
What I Already Know				
Reference 1 Title Author Call No. Pages				
Reference 2 Title Author Call No. Pages				
Reference 3 Title Author Call No. Pages				
Reference 4 Title Author Call No. Pages				

thematic learning

reading-writing connection

On the timetable shown in Example 12.2 is a large language arts block in the morning and a time for themes in the afternoon. Language arts time includes such activities as journal writing, process writing (including drafting, revising, and publishing), shared reading, author studies, reading and writing workshops, and literature response groups. Whenever possible, the language arts should be related to the theme or topic; that is, spelling words may be theme-related words, and reading, research, and writing activities may center on the topic as well. During the afternoon theme study, students will continue using language arts to investigate the topic, while also learning about social studies, science, and other areas of the curriculum.

Teachers may hold conferences with individual students any time during the day that children are working independently, to offer help and evaluate progress. Three ways to schedule conferences are daily; on a regular schedule, such as once or twice a week; or on an as-needed basis (Galda, Cullinan, and Strickland, 1993). Since students are not always aware that they need conferences and therefore do not request them, teachers should probably visit briefly with most or all students daily or schedule regular conferences with occasional unscheduled ones. Scheduled conferences enable both teacher and student to prepare in advance by gathering and reviewing pertinent materials. Although the length of time varies depending on the needs of the students, teachers usually average about five minutes per student. Thus, in a class of 30 students, a teacher could schedule conferences with six students each day within a half-hour's time. Teachers may go to students' desks or work areas, meet with students by calling them one by one to a

Example 12.2 *Schedule for an Integrated Language Arts Curriculum*

Time	Monday	Tuesday	Wednesday	Thursday	Friday
8:00– 8:30	Attendance, lunch money, announcements, sharing, story – – – – – – – – – – – –				
8:30–10:10	Language Arts	Language Arts	Language Arts	Language Arts	Language Arts
10:10–10:30	– – – – – – – – – – – – – – – – Recess –				
10:30–11:30	Math	Math / P.E.	Math	Library / Math	Math
11:30–12:05	– – – – – – – – – – – – – – – – Lunch –				
12:05–12:25	SSR	SSR	SSR	SSR	SSR
12:25– 2:25	Theme Study	Theme Study	Theme Study	Art / Theme Study	Theme Study / Music
2:25– 3:00	Free activity time (extension of theme, independent or group projects, free reading)				

designated area (not the teacher's desk), or assemble the group scheduled for that day at a conference table.

Whole Language Classrooms

reading-writing connection

An integrated language arts curriculum is a basic tenet of whole language classrooms. The language arts, along with the content areas, are taught in purposeful ways during flexible blocks of time. Children read and write throughout the day as they work independently, with partners, or in small groups.

A whole language classroom might seem disorganized to the casual observer, but in reality it is carefully structured. For whole language to work, teachers, along with their students, must develop and implement a basic management and organizational plan. Such a plan considers room arrangement, availability and location of resources, and time allocations (Baumann, 1992; Garan, 1994). Effective whole language teachers are well organized, aware of each child's needs, and able to provide situations that promote student-directed learning. Following are some guidelines for whole language teachers to use in organizing and managing a classroom (*Whole Language*, 1990):

1. Know the books in your class and school libraries.

2. Provide opportunities for children to take responsibility for their own reading and writing.

3. Encourage risk taking, predicting, confirming, and self-correcting strategies during reading.

4. Involve students in self-evaluation and evaluation of the class program.

5. Offer praise to children who are taking small steps in the right direction.

6. Recognize cultural diversity among students, and include books that deal with various cultures.

reading-writing connection

Resources in a whole language classroom consist of authentic reading and writing materials arranged so that students can access them easily. Reading materials may include newspapers and magazines (both children's and adults'), a large quantity of trade books, reference materials (atlases, dictionaries, almanacs, and so forth), student-published books, tape-recorded stories with accompanying books, scrapbooks, and textbooks. Writing materials include lined and unlined paper, simply constructed booklets, computer paper, mailboxes to hold individual correspondence, a variety of writing tools (felt-tipped markers, pencils, pens), and a message board for students' messages. Because students often participate in organizing, storing, and maintaining these materials, they feel responsible for them and thus tend to take good care of them.

Students should also be involved in organizing the classroom environment so that it satisfies their needs for independent and group learning. An area where the whole class can meet is essential, as are special interest areas or centers. Furniture should be arranged to provide many options for reading and writing activities.

reading-writing connection The following Classroom Scenario illustrates the organization of a whole language classroom.

**Classroom
Scenario**

Whole Language Classroom

The children in Melanie Childress's third grade are busily involved in a variety of reading and writing activities. Most children are working independently or with one another, while Ms. Childress acts as a consultant to children who need help. On the board, Ms. Childress has written "mystery questions" for which the children must find answers by searching through newspapers. She has also given them the option of writing letters to Miss Beth and Ms. Ann or of completing the following assignment: You are a pioneer. You can have three animals. What three animals would you choose, and why?

Other children are getting ready to publish books they have been working on for several weeks. Ms. Childress is helping them with their final drafts, while classmates also offer editorial advice.

One girl attaches herself to a visitor and eagerly reads the book she has written. She points out that her book is patterned after another story but uses different names for the characters and a slightly different sequence of events. Another child enthusiastically shows the classroom library to a visitor and picks up a milk crate full of books by Robert Munsch, the children's favorite author. Meanwhile, three boys excitedly approach a visitor and offer to act out a play that a fourth member of their group has written.

Analysis of Scenario
In Ms. Childress's classroom, children are enthusiastic about a multitude of reading and writing experiences. The classroom is neither quiet nor obviously organized, but each child has found some type of purposeful language project to pursue. Ms. Childress has provided an environment in which children are free to choose, take risks, and explore their own interests in reading and writing.

Program Evaluation

In moving toward an integrated language arts classroom, teachers might ask themselves some of the following questions to determine their progress (Vogt, 1991): Am I . . .

- modeling my own pleasure in reading and writing?
- providing a wide variety of literary genres, including short stories, novels, informational books, and magazines?
- using themes to integrate the language arts?

- providing reading and writing skills instruction for students who need it, not in isolation but in meaningful contexts?

- providing time for daily, self-selected reading and writing?

- using various types of organizational patterns, such as whole class, partners, small groups, individualized learning, and cooperative learning?

- offering opportunities for students to listen for different purposes, such as sharing time, reports, and readers' theater?

- modeling and teaching language for different purposes, such as persuading, informing, evaluating, and predicting?

- providing an environment where creative thought, opinions, and sharing ideas are valued?

- observing and recording students' responses?

- communicating to parents the reasons for integrating the language arts?

Affirmative answers to these questions may take time to achieve, but are worth working toward in order to provide a meaningful, authentic learning environment.

SELF-CHECK: OBJECTIVE 1   What are some ways to organize classes for reading instruction? How can teachers justify and implement an integrated curriculum? (See Self-Improvement Opportunities 1 and 2.)

Learning in Groups

Students learn from one another as well as from the teacher and on their own. In many classrooms, children have opportunities throughout the day to work in different kinds of groups that may vary in purpose, format, and materials (Flood et al., 1992). Purposes for groups may be skill development or shared interest; formats may be teacher or student led with varying numbers of participants; and materials may be the same for all groups or differ according to levels and themes. This section begins with a discussion of cooperative learning groups, then moves into more traditional types of reading groups, and concludes with the whole class functioning as a community of learners.

Cooperative Learning.

In *cooperative learning,* students approach tasks cooperatively by working in mixed-ability groups to achieve certain goals. The organization of cooperative learning groups is generally highly structured, with students working in teams and assuming responsibility for their own learning, as well as for that of their teammates. Students must use social skills that enable them to interact productively, and they are accountable both individually and as a group. Five elements have been identified as essential for cooperative learning:

1. *Positive interdependence* exists when each group member realizes that success is impossible without the support and interaction of all members, that is, each one has an awareness of "sink or swim together."

2. *Face-to-face promotive interaction* occurs as students discuss concepts and strategies, share knowledge, and solve problems through mutual encouragement and support.

3. *Individual accountability and personal responsibility* refers to the teacher's monitoring of each group member and provision of feedback to ensure that each student is learning.

4. *Collaborative skills* include such group interaction skills as leadership, trust building, decision making, and communication.

5. *Group processing* occurs when students discuss their progress in reaching goals and analyze their working relationships within the group (Johnson, Johnson, and Smith, 1990).

Before initiating cooperative learning groups, the teacher should help children acquire the necessary social skills: speaking softly, showing respect for others, avoiding negative comments, appreciating other points of view, establishing trust, communicating accurately, and so forth (Johnson and Johnson, 1989/1990; Madden, 1988). The teacher is then ready to form mixed groups of three to six students and present the guidelines, such as equal participation by group members and attention to the task. Then the teacher explains the phases of the model and demonstrates each strategy with a group of students. The model consists of three phases: Connection (relating prior knowledge to new information), Guided Independent Reading (directing students' attention to the text), and Follow-Up (extending ideas). As children begin working, the teacher carefully observes their progress and sometimes intervenes when problems arise (Uttero, 1988).

reading-writing connection   One language arts–related application of cooperative learning for upper elementary grades is Cooperative Integrated Reading and Composition (CIRC). This model features integrated language arts with basal or literature-based readers. It involves teacher presentation, partner and independent practice activities, and testing. While the teacher works with one group, pairs of students from two different reading groups may engage in activities such as the following:

1. Partner reading, in which students first read silently, then take turns reading aloud, with the listener correcting the reader when necessary

2. Story structure and story-related reading, with students answering questions about story elements and making predictions about how the problem will be resolved

3. Story retellings, in which students summarize stories for their partners

4. Peer conferencing during writers' workshops (Slavin, Madden, and Stevens, 1989/1990; Slavin, 1991)

As measured by standardized and informal tests, students engaged in CIRC showed significant growth in decoding and comprehension, as well as consistently positive growth in writing and language (Roehler and Duffy, 1991).

Another popular model for cooperative learning is Jigsaw, in which six-member heterogeneous teams investigate academic material that has been divided into sections. Each team member is assigned a different section to study. During preparation time, students work individually to find the information they need. Those who have the same assignment are then placed together into "expert groups" to discuss their sections. Then the students are regrouped into their original teams to teach their teammates about their sections. Learning is evaluated by testing or through a team project, and teams receive recognition for their achievement (Slavin, 1991).

There is evidence that both high- and low-achieving students benefit from opportunities to learn together in mixed-ability groups (Pearson and Fielding, 1994). Research supports the use of cooperative learning for improving thinking skills, retaining information, earning higher achievement test scores, making decisions, and accepting responsibility for learning. There are also claims that cooperative learning increases students' eagerness to learn and helps low-achieving and mainstreamed students develop positive attitudes toward learning (Augustine, Gruber, and Hanson, 1989/1990; Slavin, 1989/1990; Slavin, 1991; Smith, 1989; Uttero, 1988; Wood, 1990). It promotes self-esteem as children experience success and receive the support of their group (Ellis and Whalen, 1990). The following Classroom Scenario demonstrates one form of cooperative learning for reading instruction.

Classroom Scenario

Cooperative Learning

Barbara Eldridge was using the CIRC model of cooperative learning with her fifth graders for the basal reader lesson, in which each child would work with a partner. During the teacher-presentation segment of the lesson, she led into the story by asking the children to share their experiences with animals and then to read the introductory paragraph and look at the pictures to predict what the story might be about. Ms. Eldridge went over the word mastery list of eleven words by pronouncing each word clearly and distinctly, having the students say the word, asking them to define it if they could, clarifying the definition, and once again pronouncing the word with the class.

Before the children moved into the partner activities, Ms. Eldridge reminded them that they would do silent reading to a predetermined page and then do oral partner reading in their "one-inch voices." The children found comfortable places in the room to read, some sitting on the floor, others in chairs with their feet up. As they finished reading, each child sat beside a partner, with the partners facing opposite directions, and read softly into the partner's ear. Partners discussed the answers to a short list of comprehension questions and then wrote their answers separately. Before resuming the same procedure for the second part of the story, the children made further predictions.

Analysis of Scenario
Ms. Eldridge had formed partnerships randomly except for her three poorest readers, whom she had paired with patient, better readers. The children thoroughly enjoyed reading with partners, and their teacher felt that they were doing very well in reading.

SELF-CHECK: OBJECTIVE 2   What are some features of whole language classrooms? What are two types of cooperative learning? (See Self-Improvement Opportunity 5.)

Grouping for Reading

To accommodate a wide range of reading levels, many teachers group children within their classrooms as a compromise between providing whole-class or totally individualized instruction. Teachers may form many types of groups for reading-related purposes. Table 12.1 summarizes grouping patterns by showing the composition of each group and the materials that are generally used by group members. A more complete discussion of various types of groups follows.

Achievement Groups.   *Ability* or *achievement grouping,* a method of grouping children according to the level of material they can read for instructional purposes, is

Table 12.1   *Grouping Patterns*

Type of Group	Basis for Membership	Material
Achievement	Similar reading levels	Basal readers, workbooks
Skills or needs	Common areas of skill deficiencies	Practice exercises
Interest	Shared interests	Books, materials on topic
Project and research	Participation in special project	Materials related to project
Friendship	Social preferences	Favorite stories
Pupil pairs or partners	Assigned or self-chosen partners	Trade books, journals, basal readers
Cooperative learning	Placement in mixed-ability teams	Trade books, basal readers, other materials

a popular practice. The teacher may divide the class into two, three, or four groups, usually using basal readers as the main fare because the manuals and workbooks provide a careful and detailed skill-building program. The teacher should continuously monitor students' progress within achievement groups and consider making changes in placement when a child's progress is either substantially slower or more rapid than that of the rest of the group. It is important to keep groupings flexible.

Placing students in the appropriate achievement group is not an easy task, but it is an important one. Small ability differences, perhaps individual developmental differences, in first grade become the basis for decisions about group placement that determine different rates of learning throughout school (Hoffman, 1991). Teachers must consider several factors and may want to wait from several days to a few weeks before making group assignments. Records from the previous year usually show which basal reader each child last completed, and the teacher can place the child in the next book in the series. Teachers can also use achievement test scores or informal assessment to help them place students.

Reading achievement group sessions are generally held near the beginning of the day for about an hour and a half, and frequently this time period is used for instruction with the basal reader. No optimal number of groups exists; Table 12.2 shows a possible schedule for a class with three achievement groups.

The morning instructional period may be used for other approaches along with or instead of the basal reader. For instance, first graders might benefit from alternating basal reader instruction on Mondays, Wednesdays, and Fridays with language experience lessons on Tuesdays and Thursdays, whereas older students might alternate basal reader lessons with self-selected reading. Children should not read for instructional purposes only; they should read and write for various purposes all day so that they will realize that reading is more than skill building—it conveys meaning.

Table 12.2   *A General Plan for Grouping Within the Classroom*

	Group A	Group B	Group C
10 min.	Introduction of daily reading activities by teacher		
30 min.	Teacher-directed activity	Independent work	Library reading
30 min.	Independent work	Library reading	Teacher-directed activity
30 min.	Library reading	Teacher-directed activity	Independent work
10 min.	Summary of daily reading activities by teacher		

Note: The table suggests that all groups possess the same ability to work independently. In actual classroom situations, more teacher-directed activities for the slower-learning reading group(s) may be needed.

Although ability or achievement is the most common basis for grouping children for reading instruction (Jongsma, 1985), this type of grouping only reduces, and in no way eliminates, individual differences. Students still differ in their rates of progress, attitudes toward reading, backgrounds of experience, and degrees of motivation.

Teachers should provide a consistent quality of instruction for all achievement groups, but in practice they often use poorer-quality teaching strategies in low groups. They expect low-achieving students to do more oral and less silent reading, and to read words on lists or flashcards without meaningful context. Teachers correct more of these children's oral reading mistakes and are more likely to give pronunciation rather than meaning clues for words the children do not recognize. Teachers also ask more literal questions and fewer questions that call for higher-order thinking when working with children in the low-achieving groups (Anderson et al., 1985; Brown, Palincsar, and Armbruster, 1994; Flood et al., 1992; Paris, Wasik, and Turner, 1991; Wiggins, 1994). Although most teachers do not intentionally teach differently, they often do so to avoid embarrassing slow learners and to help them complete the work (Hoffman, 1991).

Even if a teacher tries to conceal the identities of the high and low groups, children are well aware of each group's level. Many students remain in the low group over the years and form poor self-concepts as a result. Teachers should try to minimize the stigma these students feel because of their placement in the low group.

To avoid the potential difficulties inherent in achievement grouping, teachers are seeking supplements or alternatives, such as the integrated curriculum and cooperative learning discussed earlier. Realizing that many teachers are still comfortable with the basal reader format, Wiggins (1994) suggests an alternative that would provide large-group instruction to introduce the whole class to the story, followed by flexible, small-group follow-up reinforcement based on student needs. Another possibility for alleviating the low self-esteem felt by members of the low group is to place them in a variety of groups unrelated to achievement levels, such as the following.

Interest Groups.   Based on shared interests, *interest grouping* is recommended for investigating topics through reading, writing, and literature. Children who are familiar with a topic and have a special interest in it can usually read material about it at higher levels than they normally read (Anderson et al., 1985).

thematic learning

Project or Research Groups.   Another type of grouping is based on *projects* or *research*, usually related to a theme such as in the Topic Chart presented in Example 12.1. Students of varying ability levels work together by investigating a topic, pooling their information, and planning a presentation. Appropriate topics are space travel, types of mammals, community helpers, pioneer life, energy, environmental control, or something similar.

Friendship Groups.   A popular form of grouping among students is *friendship grouping*, in which good friends work together for a specific purpose and within a

Students of varying achievement levels may work together in project or research groups.
(*David Young Wolf/Photo Edit*)

specified time frame. Because friends understand one another, enjoy being together, and usually cooperate well, this type of group can be particularly effective.

Special Skills or Needs Groups.   As children show deficiencies in their use of reading strategies, the teacher may form *special skills* or *needs groups* for direct instruction. Each group includes children who need help with the same strategy, regardless of their placement within a high, middle, or low group. A teacher can assemble such groups on a temporary basis and present minilessons, followed by student applications of the strategy.

Pupil Pairs or Partners.   Yet another type of grouping involves *pupil pairs* or *partners*, who may work cooperatively on such activities as

1. reading orally and listening to stories from trade books.
2. revising and editing stories.
3. corresponding through buddy journals.
4. providing assistance when one partner is a more proficient reader than the other.

Whole-Class Activities

Teachers should also use whole-class activities whenever possible to reduce any negative psychological effects from grouping and to develop a sense of community. Developing a sense of community begins with letting the students get to know one another well, perhaps exchanging points of view through class meetings or dialogue circles (Letts, 1994). Together teacher and students establish the rules they perceive as necessary for reaching the goals for learning in their class (Roberts, 1993). When students feel part of a *community of learners*, they are likely to take risks, support one another, and control their behavior.

Membership in a community of learners varies, but usually consists of the teacher and the students within the class and often extends to supplementary teachers and reading buddies from another class (Knight, 1994). The teacher is viewed as the "senior member" of the community of learners because he or she is more knowledgeable, experienced, and skilled in important learning processes. The teacher thus has an obligation to share and model ways to negotiate learning situations (Tierney and Pearson, 1994).

Many teachers begin and end each day with whole-class participation. Early morning is a good time for making announcements, letting students share, and reading aloud. Just before students go home, teachers may remind them of homework assignments and review what they have accomplished during the day. Among whole-class language activities are creative dramatics and choral reading, listening to stories read by the teacher or other students, taking part in Sustained Silent Reading, learning about reading study skills, going to the library, watching educational television, writing a class newspaper, creating a language experience story, watching and discussing a video of a story, sharing multiple copies of a student magazine or newspaper, and participating in a poetry hour.

SELF-CHECK: OBJECTIVE 3   What are several types of classroom grouping arrangements? What are some similarities and differences among the types of groups? (See Self-Improvement Opportunities 1, 3, and 5.)

Schoolwide Organizational Plans

Educators have made various attempts to create organizational plans for meeting the needs of all students in the most efficient ways possible. Some schools organize classrooms homogeneously so that children within each class are similar in achievement or ability. Other schools organize classrooms heterogeneously so that children within each class vary widely in achievement and ability. Research findings indicate that homogeneously grouped students show no significant gains or losses in overall achievement and that any gains made by high-achieving students are offset by losses for students in low reading groups (Otto, Wolf, and Eldridge, 1984). Within both classes that are intended to be homogeneous and heterogeneous, children exhibit a range of reading levels, although the spread is usually wider in heterogeneous classes, because it is not possible to construct perfectly homogeneous classes. This range of differences increases with each succeeding grade as some students fall further behind and others advance more rapidly.

Interclass Achievement Grouping

Interclass grouping involves parallel scheduling of reading lessons among several sections of a grade or grades. Groups go to different rooms and are divided according to general reading level. One teacher provides instruction for one achievement group, a second teacher works with another achievement level, and so on. This type of grouping can have negative effects on both low- and high-performing students. Lower achievers may be embarrassed to be grouped with younger students, whereas higher achievers may develop feelings of superiority.

Departmentalization

A *departmentalized* plan has a separate teacher for each subject, such as one teacher for reading (and possibly other language arts), one for social studies, one for science, and so forth. A teacher may teach the same subject for five to six classes a day, with one period free or devoted to giving individual help.

The advent of the middle school has created more departmentalized classrooms for students at earlier ages than before. Most research has not favored departmentalization for upper elementary students (Slavin, 1988).

Team Arrangement

A *team arrangement* involves combining two or three classes in one large area with a staff of several teachers. Team teaching developed from the belief that not all teachers are equally skilled or enthusiastic in all curricular areas. While one teacher instructs a large group in an area of his or her particular competence, the other teachers work with other groups or individuals on other subjects.

Multi-Age Classrooms

thematic learning

Some school systems are implementing *multi-age classrooms,* which often consist of primary classes with first-, second-, and third-grade students and intermediate classes for grades four and five. Although some new material is added at each grade level, many math, language arts, social studies, and science concepts are repeated within the combined grade levels. Theme studies allow students of varying levels to work together in all areas of the curriculum. The wide range of abilities in multi-age classes leads to a cooperative spirit, with younger students learning from older ones and older students reinforcing their own knowledge as they teach younger ones (Wall, 1994).

Cross-Grade Arrangements

Teachers find that by arranging partnerships between children at different grade levels, both younger and older students benefit from interacting in cooperative learning situations. *Cross-grade pairings* are often initiated and implemented by the teachers of the two classes involved, with meetings generally occurring during one or two class periods each week. This arrangement often results in personal growth and academic achievement for both older and younger learners. Partnerships across grades with low-achieving upper-grade students reading to kindergartners has proven to be worthwhile for both sets of partners (Labbo and Teale, 1990; Leland and Fitzpatrick, 1993/1994).

Making Transitions

For a variety of reasons, a teacher may wish to move from one organizational pattern to another. Some teachers become dissatisfied with their present organizational patterns and seek better plans, or beginning teachers wish to try some of the ideas they have learned in college, even though they vary from traditional organizational plans. Changing from one pattern to another requires careful consideration and study. Professional meetings, journal articles, books, and the experiences of other teachers can provide helpful information about both the theoretical basis for another type of classroom organization and ways to implement it. The Focus on Strategies that follows shows a teacher making the transition from traditional instruction to whole language instruction.

**Focus on
Strategies**

From Traditional to Whole Language Instruction

As Linda walked into the Fourth Street Elementary School library, she noticed she was among the first to arrive at the TAWL (Teachers Applying Whole Language) meeting. "Good," Linda thought to herself, "I like this informal get-together before the meeting starts because it gives me a chance to find out what other teachers are doing."

Linda had taken a graduate-level whole language course last summer and was committed to becoming a whole language teacher. Enthusiasm was contagious throughout the course, with nearly all of the students thinking of ways to implement this exciting, student-centered philosophy in their classrooms when school started. The professor had warned them, however, not to try too many new ideas at once— that it takes time to become a whole language teacher. He had also advised them to find a support group, another teacher, or someone else with whom they could share their triumphs and disappointments.

Spotting Carole, a former whole language classmate, looking at the display of professional books on whole language, Linda quickly walked over to her and asked, "How is it going? Are you trying some whole language strategies?"

Carole answered cautiously, "I am, but it's not easy. No one else is using whole language in my school, although some teachers seem interested. I've started journal writing, and I've given the class more time for free-choice reading."

Linda agreed that journal writing and SSR were good ways to begin. "I'm not using the basal much anymore either," said Linda, "although we sometimes use it because it has some really good stories."

Carole admitted that she was still using the basal two days a week. "We aren't using workbooks and skill charts now, though, and we never did do round-robin reading. That always seemed like such a poor way to teach, and so boring for all of us. What a waste of time to take turns reading aloud what the children had already read to themselves! I enjoy reading aloud to them more often, though. I had always felt somewhat guilty doing that, but we learned that reading aloud is really legitimate!" laughed Carole. "How about you?"

Linda replied, "I guess I'm lucky. Another fourth-grade teacher, Angelo, has been doing whole language for a few years, and he's sort of taken me under his wing. It's so helpful to be able to observe him and talk to him about what I'm trying to do. My students are writing in journals, too, and we've just started literature response groups. Angelo's class and mine share sets of books. He already had some sets, and I was able to get two more with PTO money."

"At least we have TAWL, even if I don't get much help at school," said Carole. "It's a great support group for me, and I get new ideas from each meeting."

"I couldn't help overhearing what you were saying, Carole, about not having much support in your school," said Beth. "Why don't you take a professional day and come to Brook Haven? We're a whole language pilot school, and all of us are trying it—with various degrees of success, of course! You're welcome to visit my classroom any time. You too, Linda."

Both Linda and Carole jumped at the opportunity. "We'd love to," they responded. "The best way for me to understand how whole language works is to see it in action," thought Linda.

As Linda and Carole wandered over to the refreshment table, they heard Rachel and Tom talking about theme studies. Rachel was saying, "We've started a theme on the solar system. The children came up with the topic after I showed them a film on outer space, and it fits into the curriculum framework. They are really excited about it, bringing in books and reference materials and volunteering to work on projects. I worry, though, that we're spending too much time on science and neglecting other areas of the curriculum."

Tom replied, "I'll bet you're covering more of the curriculum than you realize. There's a lot of math in calculating distances and speeds, and a lot of reading and writing with the reference materials they're investigating."

"There are even social studies applications if you consider possible cooperation among nations in exploring outer space," Linda added. "That's a great topic. I wonder if my fourth graders could do it."

Just then Sarah interrupted by placing a student-made big book in front of them. "You've just got to see what my fifth graders made for Dean's first graders! Look at these illustrations—and such a clever pattern for the story. They really did it all themselves after they looked at some big books in the library to get ideas." The book was indeed impressive; no wonder Sarah was proud of her students.

Linda noticed that Beverly, TAWL president, was trying to get everyone's attention to start the meeting, so she found a seat. The meeting usually began with some announcements about whole language events, and then someone read a new book—a shared pleasure for them all. Today's program was on portfolio assessment, something Linda knew a little about, and she was eager to learn more. She already had file folders and a few samples of student work, but she wasn't very clear about how to choose the samples and what to do with them. Now she had a chance to get some ideas for implementing portfolios in her classroom. That would be her next step in applying whole language philosophy.

Making changes is a difficult process for many reasons, and complete transitions are likely to take several years. The teacher must understand and be able to justify reasons for changing from one philosophical stance to another. Parents and administrators must be convinced that this move will benefit the students and that standardized test scores will not drop as a result (Pike, Compain, and Mumper, 1994).

Transitions allow teachers to move gradually from one theoretical position to another, implementing new ideas as they feel comfortable with them. Many basal reader teachers are moving toward literature-based instruction and then to whole language classrooms. In the process, they must make major changes in materials, planning, classroom organization, and assessment techniques (Sharer and Detwiler, 1992).

In his book *Reading in the Middle School*, Duffy (1990) includes several case studies in which schools have moved from traditional organizational patterns to other plans. In one middle school, teachers designed a reading curriculum that focused on developing reading strategies in cooperative learning groups (Monahan, 1990), and teachers in another school concentrated on integrating language with content across the curriculum (Roehler et al., 1990). Key points in effecting change were administrative support, careful planning, willingness to take risks, energy, time, and a background of information and knowledge about how to bring about change.

literature-centered reading   A single classroom incident caused Routman (1988) to rethink her traditional skills approach to reading and make a transition to a whole language classroom. During a remedial reading class for five second graders, Routman had read a favorite book aloud, and the children had begged her to let them read it. Because the readability level of the book was higher than the grade-level equivalents on their standardized test scores, Routman had told them they would not be able to read the book. Eventually, however, she had given in because the children had persisted. To her amazement, the children had been able to read it with practice and her guidance because of their intense motivation. Routman (1988) says, "I have continued to look closely at my own teaching, and to work with many teachers and children in moving away from basal textbooks and worksheets and into exciting children's books and children's own writing as a way of teaching young children to read and write" (p. 10).

Such changes occur gradually, often with doubts and apparent failures, and require understanding of both theory and practice before they are fully implemented. Here are some guidelines for changing organizational plans:

1. Learn all you can about the new plan, and make sure you are committed to it.

2. Find someone who supports you—your principal, another teacher, a university contact, or a member of a professional organization—with whom you can discuss your ideas.

3. Begin implementing the new plan gradually by using one or two appropriate activities. For instance, if you want to organize cooperative learning groups, begin with partner reading.

4. If you believe you have had an unsuccessful experience, analyze what you did and why it failed. Revise your plan or try a different approach. Be willing to take risks.

5. Get additional information from professional sources so that you can continue to expand your understanding and renew your enthusiasm.

Physical Environment

A classroom's furnishings and arrangement reflect a teacher's philosophy about how children learn (Wilson et al., 1991). Teachers who believe children learn from and with one another provide areas where the children can work in pairs and small groups. Teachers who understand that children have individual interests to pursue arrange quiet areas for independent work, and teachers who know that children need to work in groups of differing sizes and composition provide flexible room arrangements.

Teachers should consider many factors in creating a classroom's physical environment. Furniture should be arranged so that traffic flows easily, there are no safety hazards, and the teacher is able to see each child. Young children need well-defined areas, perhaps set off by a rug, marked with colored tape, or identified with bookcases and shelves set perpendicular to the walls (Mayfield, 1992). These classrooms may also need book racks for storing big books and easels for displaying them. The library area should be attractive, with comfortable chairs, large cushions, and displays of books and magazines. Many teachers are replacing individual student desks with tables, which permit more flexiblity but also necessitate setting up storage areas for students' books and supplies (Pike, Compain, and Mumper, 1994).

Learning Centers

Many classrooms have *learning centers,* which are areas of the classroom that contain sets of materials related to a theme. The materials may be attached to a piece of Masonite, hung on a pegboard, placed on shelves or in boxes, filed in kits, contained in folders or large envelopes, or displayed in some other way for children to use independently. Commercial kits are available for use at learning centers, but teachers often produce their own materials or collect those that are readily available from various sources. Learning centers should contain attractive, varied, and interesting materials that are inviting to children and are related to the theme. All centers should contain necessary supplies for carrying out activities and should include a comfortable place for children to work.

Learning centers require careful preparation and planning by the teacher. Students need to understand when they may go to the centers, how to use them, and where to place their completed work. They should be able to work independently or with classmates. Teachers need to provide protective coverings for frequently used materials, replenish supplies regularly, and replace center activities before children lose interest in them. Some types of learning centers that teachers may provide include library corners with a wide variety of reading materials and comfortable seating; computer centers; audiovisual stations with filmstrip projectors, tape recorders, and headphones; centers for puppet shows and creative drama; and well-equipped writing centers. More information on learning centers appears in Chapter 2.

Computers

Many schools face the dilemma of how to use a limited number of computers to best advantage. The number of computers in schools has increased rapidly in recent years, but even so, few students get sufficient exposure to computers. In some cases teachers allow more aggressive students to dominate the computers, thereby limiting their use by less assertive students. One solution to inequitable distribution of computer time is for the teacher to post a schedule chart with each student's name, class, and time for use so that students can take turns using the computer.

The location of computers in classrooms is important. Enough space for two or more children to work together should be provided so that children can work cooperatively. Ideally, a computer should either be housed on a rolling table for flexible placement or be placed in a carrel located at the side or back of the room where power outlets are available. Software should be kept either with the computer or at the teacher's desk, and a check-out system for using it should be in place. Posting a diagram of how to run a program, along with a short troubleshooting list, near the computer can help students solve simple operational problems (Caissy, 1987; Mayfield, 1992; Potter, 1989).

In setting up computer centers, whether in the classroom or the laboratory, teachers need to provide comfortable and safe conditions (Mayfield, 1992; Warren and Baritot, 1986). Here are some guidelines for working with computers:

1. Keep cords and plugs away from the children's reach.

2. Place the screen so that it is slightly below eye level.

3. Use chairs that provide proper back support.

4. Adjust screen brightness and contrast for viewing comfort.

5. Eliminate glare and screen reflection.

6. Locate the keyboard so that the user's wrist and lower arm are parallel to the floor.

7. Avoid having students face a window or other bright light source.

8. Allow students to take short breaks.

Computer-managed instruction (CMI) simplifies teachers' work by providing gradebook and test-development software (Yellin and Blake, 1994). Gradebook programs enable teachers to develop class lists, enter grades, and average grades quickly, and testmaking programs let teachers create a test bank from which they may select items to include on tests. More information about CMI appears in Chapter 7.

Videotapes

The videocassette recorder (VCR) provides many excellent opportunities for purposeful and motivational learning experiences. Relatively economical and easy to use, the VCR enables teachers to show videotapes, stop them at critical points so that students can discuss them, and then resume playing them or even rewind them to replay certain parts. Well-selected tapes can vastly enrich textbook information and create interest in learning social studies or science.

Teachers can use camcorders to record student performances, debates, interviews, and reports so that students can observe and evaluate themselves. Students may want to use the camcorders themselves to produce original television commercials, versions of newscasts or television shows, and plays. The steps in such productions resemble those of the writing process, since students must prewrite or plan, make initial revisions, tape with further revision and editing, and produce the video in its final form, which corresponds to publication (Yellin and Blake, 1994). Such videotapes can be shared with parents to inform them of class activities; they are also useful for keeping records of special events.

SELF-CHECK: OBJECTIVE 4   Identify several considerations in establishing the physical environment of the classroom. (See Self-Improvement Opportunities 1, 4, and 5.)

Role of the Teacher

Although organizational patterns do affect student learning, a competent teacher, not a particular structure, makes the major difference. Researchers have found that "about 15 percent of the variation among children in reading achievement at the end of the school year is attributable to factors that relate to the skill and effectiveness of the teacher," but only "about 3 percent of the variation in reading achievement at the end of the first grade was attributable to the overall approach of the program" (Anderson et al., 1985, p. 85). Thus, the most essential ingredient of a good reading program is the teacher.

The Teacher as Facilitator and Manager of Instruction

As a facilitator of instruction, the teacher must provide conditions that enable students to learn. The teacher should employ a variety of methods to meet the needs of a diverse student population, and she or he must consider both the requirements of the curriculum and students' needs and interests in planning instruction. Through such procedures as modeling and direct instruction, the teacher can help students acquire the strategies and knowledge they need to succeed. By providing a learner-centered environment, the teacher can support students in their efforts to become responsible, independent learners.

No matter how good a lesson is, students will learn little if the teacher is unable to manage their behavior. Classroom management is a crucial factor in learning, especially when instruction is individualized or conducted in groups. Clear, sensible, consistent procedures can contribute to an orderly classroom.

Near the beginning of the year, teacher and students should agree on rules of behavior, which should be stated positively whenever possible. Generally, students should have reasonable freedom of movement and be able to talk quietly about task-related topics, but low voices and quiet movements should be stressed. Children must know exactly what they are to do to be able work well independently and with their peers. After writing assignments on the chalkboard and/or discussing them with the students, the teacher should make sure the students understand what they are being asked to do. Students should also know what activities are available for them if they finish early.

One way that teachers manage their classrooms effectively is by modeling appropriate behavior and learning strategies. Their actions and words set expectations for students, and these expectations become powerful motivators. Teachers model by *inference* as they read along with students during SSR, and they model with *talk-alouds* by asking themselves questions out loud while performing academic tasks. When they use *think-alouds*, they model their reasoning by describing aloud their thought processes (Roehler and Duffy, 1991).

One way to manage or keep track of individual activities is through *student contracts*. Students may "contract" to complete certain projects designed to help them with their individual needs. The agreement, formalized through the use of a written contract and signed by teacher and child, simply states what the student is to do and when the task is to be completed. A teacher can prepare and have available contracts that call for a variety of assignments and tasks, from which children can select those that best suit their needs, or a student can propose a contract and negotiate it with the teacher. Once the terms have been agreed on, the student should complete the contract as specified. Example 12.3 illustrates one such contract.

Example 12.3   *Sample Student Contract Form*

1. After listening to the librarian read aloud *The Cay* by Theodore Taylor, read one of the following to learn more about the idea of survival.
   a. *Island of the Blue Dolphins* by Scott O'Dell
   b. *Stranded* by Matt Christopher
   c. *Hatchet* by Gary Paulsen
   d. *Call It Courage* by Armstrong Sperry
   e. *The Summer I Was Lost* by Philip Viereck

2. Share your research in one of these ways:
   a. Illustrate one incident in the story.
   b. Write a play dramatizing one incident.
   c. Make a model of an object that may be useful for survival.
   d. Interview an authority on the subject of some sort of survival technique, and write a report.
   e. Compare the character(s) of your story with Robinson Crusoe in terms of self-reliance.

Choose one book from Number 1 and one method from Number 2 for your contract.
I plan to do (1) _____ and (2) _____.
I will have this contract completed by _____.
Student's signature _____
Teacher's signature _____

Teachers also need a record of the activities students complete at learning centers. Since students do this work independently and check their own answers, teachers may not know exactly what the children are doing unless they keep account of their activities in some way. Example 12.4 presents one way for a child to record learning center work.

Teachers may post schedules or provide sign-up sheets for scheduling time for children to go to learning centers or work with computers. They may give students individual checklists for recording their activities or record sheets to complete and file in folders for checking later. Although organizing and managing independent work is not easy, it is worthwhile, because an important goal of education is to help students become good independent learners.

The Teacher as Decision Maker

Until recently, many commercial reading programs and models of teacher effectiveness prescribed what teachers should do and say and how they should do and say it. Many teachers believed that unless they used a manual with detailed

---

Example 12.4 *Sample Learning Center Record*

Name _____

I worked at the _____ center or station.

Time in _____ Time out _____

The work was _____. (good, fair, poor)

Activity:

I read _____

I worked on _____

I listened to _____

I read aloud with _____

I wrote _____

I also _____

---

instructions, their students would fail to learn (Tovey and Kerber, 1986). To a large extent, teachers were in danger of becoming managers of activities instead of professionals making their own decisions about goals, methods, and materials (Dreher and Singer, 1989). Although expert assistance may simplify teaching, it can also limit teachers' responsibilities as decision makers. The important point for teachers to consider is that they must use their own professional judgments in deciding how best to teach instead of implicitly following someone else's directions.

Classroom teachers make countless decisions daily as they manage their classrooms. Some decisions are made quickly and intuitively, but others require conscious reflection. Teachers may ask themselves:

How can I prevent potential behavior problems?

What is the best way to motivate these children?

What are the most appropriate materials to use?

What types of classroom organization will be most effective?

What teaching strategies are most appropriate to use?

What assessment techniques will tell me how well the children are learning?

What are the best ways to keep my students working productively?

How can I best meet individual needs?

How can I establish a supportive classroom environment?

What are the most effective ways to communicate with children, parents, and administrators?

Each of these concerns causes teachers to make decisions, and these decisions in turn affect students' learning and ultimate achievement (Otto, Wolf, and Eldridge, 1984; Smith, 1989; Harp and Brewer, 1991).

Although the teacher has the final authority in the classroom, students should also assume responsibility for their learning (Garan, 1994; Sumara and Walker, 1991). There should be a balance between teacher and student control. When students internalize the behavior and reading strategies modeled by the teacher, they are able to direct their own learning within certain limits. For example, classroom teachers may retain control of the kinds of tasks and when they are to be completed, but give students choices about how, with whom, and where to do them. These controlled choices can be successful within a predictable, safe structure (Sumara and Walker, 1991). Sharing control with students leads to the development of responsible, independent learners.

The Teacher as Researcher

Teachers may participate in two kinds of research: *action research* and *naturalistic research*. *Action research* is designed to improve instruction through controlled methods and statistical procedures; *naturalistic research* occurs within the teacher-researcher's setting through systematic observations and detailed recordkeeping. Essentially, research directly involving teachers may take three forms: individual teacher research conducted by a single teacher; collaborative action research carried out by a group of teachers working with a university professor or with staff development personnel; and schoolwide action research, in which an entire faculty works with a school consortium (Calhoun, 1993).

Many teachers have become more involved in research in order to improve their own educational practices by gaining a better understanding of how their students learn. Education today is focusing on the process of how students learn—how they approach a learning task, how they self-correct misunderstandings, and what strategies they use as they read and write. As teachers carefully observe and record what their students are doing, they gain insights into effective educational procedures (Strickland, 1988).

Based on her own experiences in a first-grade classroom, Avery (1990) suggests steps to follow in becoming a teacher-researcher:

1. *Begin with a question.* Often the question blends with other questions and evolves as the investigation unfolds.

2. *Listen and observe.* Children reveal much about how they learn through their words and behaviors.

3. *Talk.* Conversing with the children offers glimpses into their thinking processes.

4. *Write.* Recording observations while they are still fresh helps retain details.

5. *Read.* Reading about the question under investigation supports classroom observations and helps clarify connections between theory and practice.

From the teacher's viewpoint, the role of teacher-researcher is a constant reminder to analyze the environment, gather evidence about how children learn, and reconstruct beliefs about children's growth and development. From the researcher's point of view, this role enables the teacher to connect scholarly work with classroom investigations that are based on extensive, in-depth, long-term contact with students (Milz, 1989).

The Teacher as Learner

One of the most refreshing, yet challenging, truths about being a teacher is that the role is constantly evolving. Changing situations and different groups of children each year call for modifications of teaching strategies to meet student needs. Recently published research may point in fresh directions, and the administration may introduce new programs. Teachers who view themselves as learners ask questions and *want* to learn more about new ideas that may be useful to them in the classroom.

Jaggar (1989) has identified sources of knowledge and ways of learning that appear to be common among teachers as learners. The first is *theory and research*, a knowledge base that is useful for observing and interpreting student behavior. To be meaningful, however, research must be viewed in terms of the teacher's personal knowledge and experience. Teachers also learn through *practice* by reflecting on their teaching experiences. Careful *observation* of students in various settings informs teachers about students' prior knowledge, use of language, interests, and learning styles. From insights into students' capabilities and preferences, teachers can plan appropriate instruction. Finally, teachers learn through *social dialogue* as they share ideas about theory, research, and practice.

Students themselves help the teacher learn (Hansen, 1987; Newman, 1991). The teacher who learns from students creates an environment in which the students are free to express ideas and comment on how they learn. Then, by listening carefully, the teacher can learn about students' interests, learning strategies, and difficulties as the students question decisions, ask for information, comment on procedures, and make connections. By interacting with children at work, the observant teacher discovers what the students know and how to expand that knowledge. By engaging in reading and writing activities along with the students, the teacher helps establish a community of learners, of which the teacher is an active member.

Teachers also learn by interacting with other teachers. In addition to getting ideas from visiting other schools, teachers can arrange to meet at after-school meetings, during lunch periods set up to facilitate small-group meetings, while attending professional conferences, and at grade-level meetings during school hours while students are attending special classes such as music or art (Scharer and Detwiler, 1992).

Teachers can continue to learn and develop professionally in a variety of ways. They may take college courses for advanced degrees and recertification;

they may participate in in-service activities; and they may join professional organizations. Through these associations, they can subscribe to publications and participate in conferences to learn about and apply new ideas. Some professional organizations related to the interests of elementary reading teachers are listed here, along with their addresses and major publications.

American Library Association, 50 East Huron Street, Chicago, IL 60611. Various publications.

Association for Supervision and Curriculum Development, 1250 N. Pitt Street, Alexandria, VA 22314. *Educational Leadership.*

Children's Book Council, 568 Broadway, New York, NY 10012. *CBC Features.*

International Reading Association, 800 Barksdale Road, P.O. Box 8139, Newark, DE 19714. *The Reading Teacher, Journal of Reading, Reading Research Quarterly.*

National Association for the Education of Young Children, 1509 16th Street, N.W., Washington, DC 20036-1426. *Young Children.*

National Council of Teachers of English, 1111 W. Kenyon Road, Urbana, IL 61801-1096. *Language Arts, Primary Voices K–6,* and *Voices from the Middle.*

SELF-CHECK: OBJECTIVE 5 How do the roles of the teacher as decision maker, researcher, and learner reinforce one another? (See Self-Improvement Opportunity 6.)

Parents

Parents and teachers should work together to create a positive learning environment for children. A child's first learning experiences occur in the home, and the home continues to provide educational opportunities that supplement learning activities in the classroom. Therefore, it is important that teachers understand a child's home environment and communicate with those responsible for the child's well-being.

In a review of research, Wigfield and Asher (1984) concluded that parents exert a strong influence on children's acquisition of reading skills and orientation to achievement. These researchers also made several observations about the home reading environment and implications for helping children achieve success in reading. Children's reading ability correlates positively with the availability of appropriate reading materials at home and the ways parents and children interact with each other while using these materials. Parents who read to their children, take them to the library, model positive reading behaviors, and encourage their children to read increase their children's likelihood of becoming good readers. If parents provide these services for their children and have positive attitudes toward reading, their children should look on reading as a pleasurable activity and, as a result, read more. The amount of time spent reading with parents is one of the clearest predictions of early reading achievement (Paris, Wasik, and Turner, 1991).

Communicating with Parents

Schools that value parent participation have more effective programs, more positive attitudes, and higher achievement than schools that do not encourage parents to participate (Jones, 1991). Some information parents usually want to know includes goals of the school and the teacher, what the child is learning and how it is taught, attendance and homework policies, and the child's progress.

It is therefore important that teachers and parents establish and maintain communication. Among the traditional methods of communication are newsletters (carefully written letters and bulletins to keep the parents informed about happenings at school), school booklets (including rules and regulations and information parents need to know before and after sending their children to school), parent-teacher association meetings, written reports in the form of personal letters or checklists, telephone calls, parent-teacher conferences, home visits (which give parent and teacher a chance to discuss particular problems and acquaint the teacher with the child's home environment), and Open House days (when the parents visit in the child's classroom—with or without the child—to familiarize themselves with the materials, schedules, and routines of the school day). For years schools have utilized these methods, in various combinations, to foster communication between school and home.

The report card is the traditional way to inform parents and children about the child's performance in school, but report cards often give information that is incomplete and can be misunderstood. Simple A, B, or C grades for each subject tell very little about a student's interests, progress, attitudes, and effort. Example 12.5 shows a sample holistic report card for language arts with four grading periods.

Another option for communicating with parents is to use portfolios that contain samples of the children's work (Flood and Lapp, 1989). Parents often have difficulty understanding percentiles and standardized achievement test scores, but they can readily see the progress (or lack of progress) their children have made over time on informal measures such as writing samples. The portfolio should contain a broad array of children's work, including informal assessments, voluntary reading activities, self-evaluations, standardized test scores, and writing samples.

Many schools schedule parent-teacher conferences two or three times throughout the school year, but teachers can arrange conferences whenever they are necessary. During a conference, the teacher needs to listen to the parent's concerns, share samples of the child's schoolwork, show records of achievement (test scores, for example), and offer constructive suggestions for ways the parent and teacher can work together for the child's benefit. Parents may want to obtain ideas from the teacher for encouraging children to improve their reading skills by working with them in the home. Teachers should maintain informal records of major points discussed with parents, conclusions reached, and recommendations for the child by teacher and parents.

Parents are often interested in how homework is assigned. Most homework should be carefully planned and informal in nature, supplementing formal preparation in the classroom. It should be assigned only after children understand the

Example 12.5 *Holistic Report Card for Language Arts*

	1	2	3	4
Literature Appreciation				
Chooses appropriate literature				
Selects a variety of reading materials				
Reads willingly and with interest				
Responds creatively to literature				
Reading Strategies				
Reads for meaning				
Uses context clues				
Uses word structure clues				
Uses phonics clues				
Organizes ideas				
Recalls information				
Reads aloud fluently				
Draws conclusions				
Uses a variety of strategies				
Writing Strategies				
Expresses ideas clearly				
Organizes material				
Uses capitals and punctuation				
Revises and edits material				
Initiates and enjoys writing				
Listening and Speaking				
Communicates effectively				
Shows courtesy and respect				
Participates in class discussions				
Spelling				
Is learning dictionary skills				
Learns assigned words				
Uses correct spelling in revisions				
Handwriting				
Writes legibly and neatly				

Parents who read to their children, take them to the library, model positive reading behaviors, and encourage their children to read increase their children's likelihood of becoming good readers. (© *Elizabeth Crews*)

concepts and ideas and are motivated sufficiently to do the homework unaided. Ideally, most homework assignments should be personalized to the individual child, and there should be little or no regularly assigned drill homework for the entire class.

The fall conference or Open House is a good time to introduce parents to the reading materials used in the school and to describe the reading experiences and skills being emphasized that year. A teacher may want to explain how the reading program is organized and the general approaches he or she uses. The teacher may also point out what (if anything) will be required of the child in terms of homework, as well as what the parents can do when the child requests help.

Teachers also communicate with parents through letters, progress reports, and notices they send home with children. Some basal reader series provide letters for teachers to send home periodically as children complete units of work; the school may publish brochures informing parents of school policies and special events; libraries may provide lists of recommended recreational reading suitable for various age levels; professional societies may have helpful bulletins or pamphlets for teachers to send home; and children may write letters to their parents about a forthcoming event. The classroom teacher may write a personal note to a parent, especially to praise a child's performance; send home a summer calendar of reading-related activities for each day at the end of the school year; provide parents with activities to do with children that correspond to current reading objectives; or send a form letter, such as the following, that applies to a group or whole class of children:

Dear _____,

During the past six weeks, your child has been working on a folklore unit in reading class. He or she has studied the characteristics of tall tales and has attempted to write an original tall tale of his or her own after reading several examples and hearing other examples read by the teacher. Your child's story is attached to this report. You may wish to read it and discuss it with him or her. All the children produced tall tales that indicated an understanding of this form of literature.

Sincerely,

General Suggestions

Following are some general suggestions to offer parents for helping their children enjoy reading:

1. Keep in touch with the school about your child's reading so that you will know how to help.

2. Help your child study and do homework by providing space, time, materials, and assistance if necessary.

3. Listen to your child read a story aloud at home, and ask questions about it.

4. Encourage your child to look in books for answers to questions.

5. Read aloud to your child often, making comments and discussing interesting features with her or him.

6. Have a family reading time when everyone reads together.

7. Make library visits a family event. Check out books together, and encourage your child to participate in summer reading programs or story hours.

8. Read interesting passages from newspapers and magazines to your child.

9. Become involved with school activities by working as a parent volunteer or attending parent-teacher meetings.

10. If possible, help your child learn to use computers at home. Provide opportunities for using word processing to compose stories, activities to promote reading skill development, and games that encourage interest in reading.

11. Encourage your child to read and use a variety of materials, including brochures on special subjects, maps and tourist information about family trips, telephone directories, and catalogues.

12. Let your child subscribe to a children's magazine and/or become a member of a children's book club.

SELF-CHECK: OBJECTIVE 6   Describe several ways parents and teacher can work together for the benefit of the child. (See Self-Improvement Opportunities 7, 8, and 9.)

Paraprofessionals and Tutors

Many adults work as paid or volunteer assistants to the teacher by helping with individual or small-group instruction, grading workbooks or test papers, making displays, supervising computer-assisted instruction, and performing clerical tasks. Employment of *paraprofessionals* has increased steadily and duties have expanded in recent years so that paraprofessionals now work along with teachers to provide instruction and services (Pickett, Vasa, and Steckelberg, 1993). These paraprofessionals need some training in how to relate to children positively, how to teach simple skills, and how to judge student progress. Basically, the classroom teacher is responsible for the activities the assistant performs and for preparing the paraprofessional to carry out assigned activities.

The teacher and paraprofessional need to communicate regularly, perhaps through structured conferences and shared planning times. The teacher should consider the individual's experience and level of training when assigning duties and then supervise daily work and provide feedback (Pickett, Vasa, and Steckelberg, 1993).

Peer tutoring occurs when one child tutors another child of either the same or a different age, whereas *cross-age tutoring* refers only to students of different ages (Ehly and Larsen, 1984). Being a tutor and modeling teacherlike behavior boosts the confidence and self-esteem of a "problem student," and a good student benefits in a similar manner by teaching skills to other children. The tutee also profits from peer tutoring by learning in a more relaxed and informal way than is possible in the traditional classroom environment. Results of peer tutoring reveal improved academic achievement and better self-concepts for both tutor and tutee, improved social interactions between the partners, and more positive attitudes toward reading for both (Pearson and Fielding, 1991; Topping, 1989).

When matching peer tutors with students, teachers must consider both the academic strengths and the emotional behavior of each student pair so that the two will work well together. Each tutor should receive training in planning appropriate lessons, selecting materials, following acceptable teaching procedures, and assessing the progress of the tutee. During peer conferencing, students learn how to interact by observing the teacher's modeling so that they can ask one another helpful questions (Forman and Cazden, 1994).

SELF-CHECK: OBJECTIVE 7   Provide several examples of how paraprofessionals and tutors may be of assistance in the reading program. (See Self-Improvement Opportunity 12.)

Summary

Orderly, efficient classroom organization is an important component of effective reading instruction. Many teachers are moving toward an integrated language arts curriculum, which allows children to understand the relationships among reading, writing, listening, and speaking as they use them in meaningful situations. Teachers, with student input, select worthy themes as the focus of an integrated curriculum, and they use large blocks of time to schedule language arts and content area activities. Whole language classrooms usually follow the integrated curriculum model.

Several other possibilities exist for organizing a classroom, including different ways of grouping children. Cooperative learning is a structured program that allows children to work with partners and in small groups to meet academic goals. The most common type of reading group is the achievement group, which is based on children's reading levels. Although achievement groups generally meet all year to provide reading skills instruction, teachers should keep membership within these groups flexible. Other types of reading-related groups include interest groups, project or research groups, friendship groups, special skills or needs groups, and pupil pairs or partners. Teachers usually create these arrangements for a limited time and a specific purpose, and these groupings may help to alleviate negative self-concepts for low-achieving children. Students also benefit from whole-class instruction, which allows them to develop a sense of community.

Some schools form larger organizational patterns, including departmentalization, multi-age classrooms, and team arrangements. Just as there is no one best way to teach reading for all children, there is no one way to organize a class to suit the needs of every teacher or every group of children. Usually schools and teachers use a combination of plans because each plan has strengths and weaknesses. As teachers strive to find which organizational plans work best for them and their students, they may go through a transition period in which they gradually introduce new ideas.

The classroom's physical environment is an important factor in determining how well children learn. Some teachers use learning centers, computers, and videotapes as part of the instructional program.

Four roles of the teacher are featured in this chapter: as facilitator and manager of instruction, as decision maker, as researcher, and as learner. The teacher is the key figure in the classroom and makes countless decisions daily that affect student learning. In some cases, the teacher assumes the role of researcher by making systematic observations and records of student behaviors. The teacher is also a learner, always alert to information supplied by research and theory, professional interactions, and the children themselves.

Parents strongly influence children's acquisition of reading skills and their attitudes toward achievement. Teachers should communicate with parents frequently in a variety of ways, including parent-teacher conferences, report cards, meetings, and publications. Teachers can offer suggestions to parents to help them create supportive reading environments in the home.

Teachers can benefit from the assistance of both paraprofessionals and tutors in the classroom. Paraprofessionals can provide a variety of reading-related services, including listening to children read, grading papers, preparing instructional materials, and assisting children in locating and using reference materials. Peer tutoring, cross-age tutoring, and tutoring by adult volunteers are also effective for helping children learn to read.

Test Yourself   *True or False*

_____ 1. Once organizational patterns have been established, they should be consistently maintained.

_____ 2. Low reading achievement groups should have more students than high reading achievement groups.

_____ 3. A wider range of reading levels within a single classroom is more common at lower elementary grade levels than at higher ones.

_____ 4. Every classroom should contain three reading achievement groups.

_____ 5. Achievement grouping is a method of grouping children according to the level of reading material they can read comfortably.

_____ 6. Other than achievement groups, most groups are formed for limited times and specific purposes.

_____ 7. Members of the low reading achievement group should be separated from the rest of the class during other activities as well.

_____ 8. Organizational changes should be made slowly and gradually.

_____ 9. If reading skills are adequately covered during the reading instructional period, there is no need for any other type of reading during the day.

_____ 10. Classroom management is an important factor in how well students learn.

_____ 11. Even within groups based on reading achievement, diverse abilities exist.

_____ 12. Specific needs grouping puts together children who need to work on the same skill.

_____ 13. Learning centers allow children to carry out activities independently.

_____ 14. Computer-assisted instruction can be used only with one student for each computer.

_____ 15. According to current research and theory, children learn better when they can associate material with other information.

_____ 16. When implementing an integrated language arts curriculum, teachers allocate brief periods of time for teaching each of the language arts.

_____ 17. Student contracts are one method teachers can use to manage individual activities.

_____ 18. The best time to hold teacher-student conferences is before or after school.

_____ 19. The organizational pattern of a classroom is more important than the teacher.

_____ 20. In cooperative learning, students learn in partnerships or as teams.

_____ 21. Individual accountability is not a consideration in cooperative learning.

_____ 22. Jigsaw is a reading follow-up activity related to industrial arts.

_____ 23. CIRC is a form of cooperative learning for upper elementary students in the area of language arts.

_____ 24. Whole language classrooms have no organization or structure.

_____ 25. Active student participation in language learning is an important aspect of whole language classrooms.

_____ 26. Teachers who observe students and record information about them are acting as researchers.

_____ 27. Just as students learn from teachers, teachers learn from students.

_____ 28. In reality, parents are their children's first teachers of reading.

_____ 29. In reading to their children, parents provide a foundation for the school's reading program.

_____ 30. Sending bulletins or letters to parents is a valuable way for teachers to communicate about the school's reading program.

_____ 31. Teacher assistants should do only clerical work in the classroom.

Self-Improvement Opportunities

1. Talk to at least two teachers at different grade levels to determine how they organize their classes for reading instruction.

2. Write your own weekly schedule for an integrated language arts curriculum. Identify a theme and list ways the theme can correlate with various areas of the curriculum.

3. What are some things you would do to help a child in the low reading group overcome feelings of inferiority?

4. Survey the elementary schools near your home to find the following information about computer-assisted instruction:

   a. The number of computers for student use in relation to the number of children enrolled in the school

   b. The percentage of teachers who use computers

   c. The types of organization for computer use (classroom, computer labs, media centers, and other arrangements)

5. Visit classrooms in which you can observe traditional grouping, cooperative learning, and/or whole language instruction. Write a brief description of your observations, and state the type of organization you prefer. Give reasons for your preference.

6. Interview a teacher who is engaged in classroom research to find out what issues are being considered and what findings are emerging. Discuss what you learn in class, and identify a topic you might like to research when you teach.

7. Make a calendar of reading-related activities for children to take home at the end of the year and do during the month of June. Identify the grade level, and provide a wide variety of interesting tasks.

8. Interview the parents of a preschooler to find out if they are providing a positive environment for learning to read. Consider especially the reading materials in the home, story reading by the parents, and interactions between parents and child that promote interest in reading.

9. Prepare a letter or bulletin to parents about one of the topics suggested in this chapter.

10. Talk with a paraprofessional about his or her role in the reading program. Share your findings with members of your class.

Chapter 13

Readers with Special Needs

Key Vocabulary

Pay close attention to these terms when they appear in the chapter.

Americans with Disabilities Act (ADA)

attention-deficit hyperactivity disorder (ADHD)

bilingualism

dialect

English as a Second Language (ESL)

exceptional learner

gifted learner

hearing impairment

inclusion

Individuals with Disabilities Education Act (IDEA)

individualized education program (IEP)

learning disability

limited English proficiency (LEP)

mainstreaming

mental retardation

multidisciplinary team

multicultural students

PL 94-142

resource room

speech impairment

visual impairment

Setting Objectives

When you finish reading this chapter, you should be able to

1. Explain mainstreaming and inclusion and their effects in a regular classroom.

2. Identify learners who are classified as exceptional and suggest several guidelines for instructing them.

3. Name and briefly define several types of disabilities commonly encountered in classrooms.

4. Describe some strategies that are generally effective in working with readers who have difficulties.

5. Explain some ways to adjust teaching strategies for gifted students.

6. Describe the effects of a child's culture on his or her reading achievement.

7. Discuss several important features and promising approaches to consider in a reading program for children with cultural or dialectal differences.

8. Describe some special needs of bilingual children and ways to meet these needs.

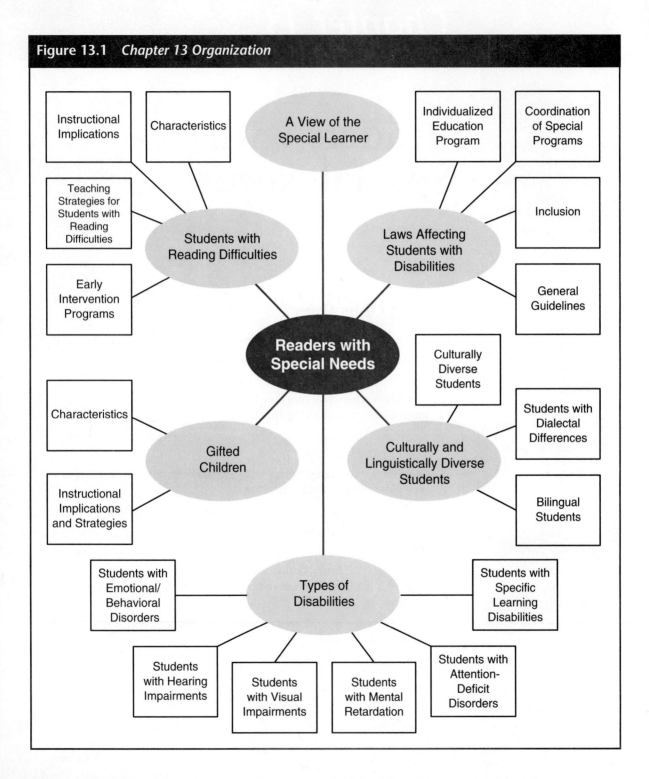

Figure 13.1 *Chapter 13 Organization*

Instructional Implications

Characteristics

A View of the Special Learner

Individualized Education Program

Coordination of Special Programs

Teaching Strategies for Students with Reading Difficulties

Students with Reading Difficulties

Laws Affecting Students with Disabilities

Inclusion

Early Intervention Programs

General Guidelines

Readers with Special Needs

Culturally Diverse Students

Characteristics

Students with Dialectal Differences

Gifted Children

Culturally and Linguistically Diverse Students

Instructional Implications and Strategies

Bilingual Students

Students with Emotional/ Behavioral Disorders

Types of Disabilities

Students with Specific Learning Disabilities

Students with Hearing Impairments

Students with Visual Impairments

Students with Mental Retardation

Students with Attention- Deficit Disorders

T his chapter considers exceptional learners, those who differ in some way from the majority of learners. These children also need well-balanced holistic reading instruction, but they may need some instructional modifications or supplements to help them reach their full potential. The chapter discusses special types of learners who may be mainstreamed or *included* in regular classrooms, but makes no attempt to cover children with severe disabilities. This chapter focuses on what the classroom teacher, rather than the specialist, can do.

Since many children who were formerly enrolled in special education classes are now being integrated into regular classes, teachers are responsible for working with more exceptional children than they were in the past. Educators today realize that association with children in a regular classroom may be beneficial for exceptional children, and schools are making special provisions for these children by placing them in the educational mainstream.

This chapter begins with a presentation of laws affecting students with disabilities, in particular, the Individuals with Disabilities Education Act (IDEA), based on Public Law 94-142, and its effects on the education of children with disabilities. Then it discusses inclusion and presents a list of guidelines for working with students who have special needs. Next, the chapter focuses on different types of exceptional learners: students with learning disabilities, attention-deficit disorders, or mental retardation; children with visual, hearing, or speech impairments; youngsters who are emotionally disturbed; children who are gifted, as well as those who are not proficient readers; and students with cultural and linguistic variations. The chapter concludes with a list of multicultural children's books to use with culturally different students.

A View of the Special Learner

Each child is an individual with a unique set of characteristics; there is no consensus on a definition of a typical child. Therefore, attempts to label learners and categorize them according to their special learning traits or difficulties are often futile. Instead of being concerned with how to classify special learners, teachers should provide the best possible learning experiences for each student.

Current views of reading and writing instruction support holistic approaches, which may be especially valuable for readers who are experiencing difficulties (Rhodes and Dudley-Marling, 1988; Scala, 1993; Truax and Kretschmer, 1993; Zucker, 1993). In traditional programs, readers with disabilities often spend years on meaningless drill-and-practice activities, which focus on their weaknesses. Holistic approaches, on the other hand, focus on strengths and place learning in meaningful contexts.

Although different types of disabilities and diversities are identified here, the reader should keep in mind that it is the individual learner, not the label, that is important. Students are more alike than they are different in their needs and interests, and caring teachers do their best to facilitate each child's ability to learn.

Laws Affecting Students with Disabilities

In recent years, Congress has passed laws to protect the rights of individuals with disabilities. *The Americans with Disabilities Act of 1990 (ADA)* is intended to eliminate discrimination against all individuals with disabilities. Its implications for schoolchildren include enabling them to participate more fully in all school programs and to learn more effectively by using telecommunication systems.

In 1975 Congress passed PL 94-142, the Education for All Handicapped Children Act, which altered the placement of students with disabilities in the public schools. Instead of being assigned to special rooms, many of these children are now being mainstreamed into regular classrooms. According to the U.S. Department of Education, more than 1.6 million of the 5 million children with disabilities who receive special services in the United States attend school in regular classrooms ("More Disabled Students . . . ," 1994). In 1990, Congress amended PL 94-142 by modifying some of the provisions and changing the terminology to reflect greater sensitivity to the individual, rather than focusing on the disability. The act was renamed the *Individuals with Disabilities Education Act (IDEA)* (Beirne-Smith, 1994; First and Curcio, 1993).

Individualized Education Program (IEP)

A major provision of the IDEA is the development of an *individualized education program (IEP)* for each child with disabilities who receives support through federal funding. The IEP states the child's present levels of educational performance, the projected starting date of the program, and the duration of the special services. It sets annual goals for the child's level of educational performance as well as short-term instructional objectives, which must be defined in measurable terms. The IEP also specifies educational services and special instructional media for the child.

The IEP is developed by a *multidisciplinary team*, sometimes called a *core evaluation team*, consisting of a representative (other than the child's teacher) of the local education agency (usually the school), the teacher, and one or both parents. The child and other professional personnel may be included when appropriate. The multidisciplinary team for children with specific learning disabilities must also include a person qualified to give individual diagnostic exams and, when available, an appropriate learning disabilities specialist.

One format for an IEP follows:

I. Summary of assessment

    A. Areas of strengths

    B. Areas of weaknesses

    C. Approaches that have failed

    D. Learning style(s)

    E. Recommended placement, general program outline, and assignment of personnel responsibility

  II. Classroom accommodations

    A. General teaching techniques

    B. Language arts modifications (and other subject matter modifications)

  III. Instructional plans

    A. Long-range (yearly) objectives, along with materials, strategies, and evidence of mastery

    B. Specific (one to three months) objectives

    C. Ancillary personnel and services

Coordination of Special Programs

When working with students who have disabilities, the classroom teacher should cooperate with other teachers, such as the resource or Chapter I teacher, who may provide special reading instruction for some children during part of the day. In fact, Chapter I, a federally funded compensatory education program, now requires its teachers to coordinate compensatory instruction with classroom instruction (Allington, 1993).

To coordinate a special learner's reading instructional program, the classroom teacher and the support teacher must communicate on a regular basis so that the support teacher's instruction supplements the instruction provided in the regular classroom. Sometimes children are in "pull-out" programs in which they go to resource rooms, and sometimes they are tutored in the regular classrooms by reading specialists or aides in an "in-class" program. Bean and Eichelberger (1985) studied both types of programs and found that reading specialists concentrated more on reinforcing classroom skills and less on diagnosing needs in in-class programs than they did in pull-out programs, but there were problems with having two teachers in one room and with implementing the program in terms of time and space. Neither program guarantees greater coordination among teachers; the important issue is that teachers communicate with one another about students' strengths and needs to provide an integrated reading program for each special learner (Allington and Shake, 1986).

Working together to plan instructional activities for exceptional children whenever possible, the support teacher and the classroom teacher may want to cooperate by drawing up a contract—a written agreement about specific measurable objectives, one or more activities for meeting each objective, and the date for completion (Wilhoyte, 1977). A contract helps the student focus on developing specific reading skills, keeping careful records, and accepting responsibility. It is based on his or her strengths and moves the child very gradually to a higher level of performance. Example 13.1 illustrates one possible reading contract.

Example 13.1 *Reading Contract*

READING CONTRACT

Larry H.
Student

Mrs. Morgan
Teacher

Objective	Activity	Date	Initials		Comments
			St.	Tch.	
To learn to read 3 new words.	Play word card game.	May 4	_LH_	_EM_	Good work!
To understand the events in a story.	Listen to a story at the listening station and tell someone about it.	May 6	_LH_	_EM_	You retold the story well.

Inclusion

Despite efforts to alleviate the difficulties that special learners often experience, results have been unimpressive (Allington, 1993; "Chapter I Gains Questioned," 1994; McGill-Franzen and Allington, 1991). The failure of many pull-out programs (the most common form of Chapter I assistance) may be due to fragmenting the school day, stigmatizing the student, wasting instructional time while students move through hallways, and inconsistent instruction offered by two teachers in two locations.

Because children with disabilities are not making the anticipated gains in pull-out programs, educators are considering *inclusion*, or in-class instructional support (Allington, 1993; "CEC Policy . . . ," 1993; Raynes, Snell, and Sailor, 1991; "Winners All," 1992). Inclusion means that students with disabilities are assigned to regular classrooms in a neighborhood school for the entire day and participate in all school activities. It differs from mainstreaming in that mainstreamed students move in and out of their regular classrooms during the day to receive special instruction. Inclusion requires adequate support services, such as physical accommodations, sufficient personnel, staff development and technical assistance, and collaboration among personnel involved. In some cases, a special education teacher joins the regular classroom teacher, not only to give support to students with disabilities, but to co-teach the entire class so that students are unaware that some of them need special assistance ("CEC Policy . . . ," 1993; Friend and Cook, 1992). Inclusion is still a new idea, however, and its effectiveness and full impact on the regular teacher cannot yet be measured (Smelter, Rasch, Yudewitz, 1994). The following Focus on Strategies and Classroom Scenario, both based on actual situations, show the effects of inclusion in two classrooms.

**Focus on
Strategies**

Inclusion

Long after the children had left, Faye sat at her desk reflecting on the year she had spent with this group of children. She remembered surveying her class of twenty-six second graders at the beginning of the year and thinking that this year would be quite a challenge. "It certainly has been," she thought, "and there was no way I could have predicted how it would turn out. I've had some very stressful experiences. It hasn't been easy."

Just before school started, Faye learned she would have two students in wheelchairs, Mickey with muscular dystrophy and Adam with spina bifida; Carlotta with attention-deficit hyperactivity disorder (ADHD); Yvonne, who was brain traumatized; and Leslie, who had been identified as seriously emotionally disturbed (SED). Ruby, a support teacher, would spend most of her time with Mickey but part of her time with Adam. Both children needed considerable help in completing their work.

One problem that demanded immediate attention was how to manage two wheelchairs and one or two additional adults in an already crowded classroom. Faye had tried several arrangements until she settled on one that seemed to work best. Maneuvering the wheelchairs to reading groups, learning centers, and special instructional areas had created some serious traffic jams! Faye had also found that she had to allow more time when preparing to leave the classroom for lunch and recess; it took time to position the wheelchairs and move them through the hallways.

It had been interesting to watch the children's relationships with Mickey and Adam develop. At first, they had eyed the two boys in wheelchairs somewhat suspiciously. Then they approached them cautiously, and finally warmed up to them. Mickey, with his bright, alert eyes, showed that he was eager to participate, and the children soon considered it a privilege to attend him. Adam was more reticent, being somewhat overprotected by his mother, who often sat with him in class, and the children found it more difficult to communicate with him.

Believing both boys were bright enough to do second-grade work, Faye held the same expectations for them that she did for the other children. Adam could speak well enough to answer her questions, but she found she had to modify his assignments because he was unable to track the work on the board to the paper on his tray. Mickey, on the other hand, could usually respond with only one or two words, so Ruby usually interpreted Mickey's answers for him. In small groups Mickey could speak more easily, perhaps as much as a sentence or two at a time.

Getting used to having another teacher in the room with her hadn't been easy either, Faye thought. Sometimes hearing another adult speaking at the same time she was talking had been quite disturbing; it was something she had had to get used to. Mickey needed Ruby's attention almost constantly in order to participate in the lessons. The only way he could take a spelling test was to spell the words to her so that she could write them down for him.

Recalling some of the better times, Faye thought of the way the class interacted with Mickey. "I really like the way the children took to Mickey," she thought. "They would bring him those toy trucks and stuffed animals to play with on his tray. Of course, he'd hit at them and knock them down when he'd try to pick them up because he couldn't control his arm movements, but the children didn't mind; they'd just pick them up for him. Mickey had a sparkle in his eye and was fun to be with."

One of the best ways the children worked with Mickey was as peer tutors during his therapy sessions. Pat, the physical therapist, would ask a couple of the children to accompany Mickey to therapy and teach them how to help Mickey with his body movements. On a few occasions, Mickey and his peer tutors went swimming at a nearby indoor pool during therapy sessions. That had been a real treat for the peer tutors as well as for Mickey.

Adam, however, hadn't benefited from the experience as much as Mickey had, Faye observed. Perhaps the children felt intimidated by his mother's presence, or maybe it was Adam's reluctance to participate in class activities. In any case, they seemed to prefer being with Mickey and spent little time with Adam voluntarily. Of course, they willingly pushed Adam's wheelchair when it was time for him to move to a different location.

Thinking back, Faye was well aware that Mickey and Adam certainly hadn't been the only children with special needs this year. Carlotta, Leslie, and Yvonne had been taking medication to help them control their behavior, but occasionally Carlotta's mother forgot to give her the medicine. On those days, Faye had to spend extra time helping Carlotta focus on her work.

Leslie's problems were more serious, sometimes causing her to be hospitalized for treatment for days or weeks at a time. After her first long-term hospitalization, Leslie had been reassigned to a special education self-contained room. Even though Leslie was being mainstreamed into Faye's room for periods of time each day, Faye recalled how much easier it had been to manage the class without Leslie's disruptive behaviors.

Getting the class to pay attention to her had been a constant struggle, too. The children were so easily distracted! Faye remembered the day she had used Mickey as an example of attentive behavior because of his eagerness and alertness. She recalled saying, "I really like the way Mickey is paying attention. Look at his eyes— they are always watching me when I'm talking." Looking over at Mickey, one of the children had said, "I know. Let's call him 'Eagle Eyes,'" and the nickname had stuck.

This year had been a learning experience for them all, Faye observed—probably more for herself than for the children. She had made it through somehow, but she hoped that accommodations would be made if she had so many children with special needs another year. A smaller class size would help, as would additional support teachers, even on a part-time basis. She would have also benefited from some training on how to work with these children. Although she had done her best, Faye believed that because of the special demands on her time and attention by a few children, the remaining children had been somewhat shortchanged.

**Classroom
Scenario**

Inclusion

Danny, who has cerebral palsy, has been admitted to Alan Stanton's third-grade class. Danny can move only his head and is unable to speak, but his IQ has been placed at 110. By moving his head and using his eyes, Danny indicates his wishes and answers questions. He also holds a pencil in his teeth to type written work, which is displayed along with the work of his peers, and he reads from an open book placed on a music stand.

Alan's positive attitude toward Danny and the children's eagerness to include him in *everything* they did created a positive learning environment. A larger child pushed his wheelchair so that Danny could go with them on field trips, take his turn as class leader, and participate in activities on the playground. When paired with a student of lower academic ability, Danny supplied the "brains" for a project while the other child carried out the plan. When the class learned folk dancing, Danny was the hub of the wheel and a child turned his chair. The children were protective, respectful, and accepting.

Analysis of Scenario
As a result of this experience, Danny benefited by being accepted as part of the class. Perhaps even more important, class members gained an appreciation of how much a student with disabilities can do.

As the two vignettes on inclusion indicate, children play an important role in terms of offering acceptance and support to the mainstreamed or included child. The teacher therefore should prepare students to accept these class members by frankly explaining the nature of the disabilities and each student's special needs. In addition, the teacher might read a story about a similar individual to help the class realize that even though a student has special needs, his or her feelings, interests, and goals are much like their own (Rubin, 1982). It is important that the child who is mainstreamed or included be fully accepted as an integral part of the class and not just occupy space in the classroom (Hoben, 1980). Students should become actively supportive by providing necessary services, tutoring when special help is needed, including the child in activities, and working with her or him in cooperative groups.

Cooperative learning strategies allow groups of students with varied abilities, including those who are mainstreamed or included, to work together on projects relating to the content areas (Maring, Furman, and Blum-Anderson, 1985). These strategies include such activities as preparing structured overviews, rewriting portions of the text in simpler language, making predictions about content based on headings and subheadings in the text, learning a task and teaching it to others, and developing relationships of concepts through a "list-group-label" activity.

Being included in these groups enables youngsters with disabilities to contribute to the activities, thereby improving their self-concepts, and to learn from their peers. The other children perceive them as part of their group and feel good about helping them learn.

SELF-CHECK: OBJECTIVE 1   Explain the impact of mainstreaming and inclusion on public schools. (See Self-Improvement Opportunity 2.)

General Guidelines

Most of the procedures and materials already recommended in this book can be effectively used with exceptional children when teachers make reasonable adjustments for particular difficulties. The exceptional child's basic needs and goals are not so different from those of the typical child, but the means of achieving those goals and fulfilling those needs may differ. The following general practices, which apply to all learners, are crucial in teaching exceptional children:

1. *Maintain a positive attitude toward exceptional learners.* Children with special needs require a great deal of encouragement and understanding. Show that you are interested in them: talk with them about their interests; have high but reasonable expectations; note things they have done; be friendly and encouraging. Give each child's personal worth and mental health primary consideration, and assist each child in every way possible to develop personally and socially as well as academically.

2. *Consider learning styles and modalities when planning instruction.* An exceptional child might be an auditory learner who readily associates sounds with symbols, a visual learner who remembers sight words easily, or a kinesthetic-tactile learner who needs to touch, manipulate, and move in order to learn to read. Such factors as lighting, space, time of day, and temperature may also affect children's ability to learn.

3. *Provide individualized instruction as needed.* Arrange individualized or small-group instruction, and use teaching strategies that match each child's strengths and needs. Some children will benefit from one-on-one tutoring.

4. *Offer meaningful, balanced instructional programs.* Help the children see a reason for learning to read, and emphasize skills through actual reading, not through artificial drills. Encourage them to use different strategies for getting meaning from text, to abandon a strategy that is not working, and to think aloud while reading. Avoid the temptation to focus exclusively on decoding skills, an obvious and immediate need for many exceptional children, at the expense of comprehension skills. Keep a balance between the two.

5. *Provide appropriate materials.* Use high-interest materials that the children are capable of using successfully. Do not use the types of reading materials with which the children have previously failed.

6. *Communicate with others who work with special children.* Be sure to coordinate each special learner's program with all others involved in his or her instruction, particularly Chapter I and resource teachers. Discuss the child's progress and needs, and work together to provide the best possible plan, with each teacher reinforcing and supplementing the work of the other. Where inclusion is used, make arrangements to co-teach so that children may benefit from the special skills and knowledge of each teacher.

7. *Provide a positive classroom environment.* Help the children in the regular classroom to accept and appreciate the unique qualities of children with disabilities by including the special learners in class activities and providing opportunities for them to make worthwhile contributions. Foster a climate of acceptance and appreciation for each child's uniqueness.

8. *Use varied instructional and assessment techniques.* Present concepts by means of concrete objects, manipulative devices, and multimedia presentations (films, television, videotapes, recordings) to make use of the child's five senses. Provide various opportunities for practicing skills in authentic situations (learning center activities, projects, school functions), various instructional techniques (science experiments, simulation activities, role playing), and various types of informal assessment.

9. *Provide opportunities for success in tasks.* Assign tasks at or below ability levels of exceptional children who have problems to ensure reasonable success. Provide short-term goals and give immediate feedback to encourage good work. Use progress charts to make growth apparent, and have children compete against their own records, not those of their classmates. Give praise for genuine efforts and successful completion of tasks. Make every effort to build self-confidence and avoid frustrating situations that may aggravate learning problems.

SELF-CHECK: OBJECTIVE 2 Describe several guidelines for working with learners who have special needs. (See Self-Improvement Opportunities 1 and 7.)

Types of Disabilities

In any classroom, a teacher is likely to find one or more students with some type of disability. This section discusses various disabilities and impairments, along with ways to adapt instruction for children with special needs.

Students with Specific Learning Disabilities

Over the past fifteen years, students with specific learning disabilities have comprised the largest group of students entitled to receive special education services (Wood, 1993). The most widely accepted definition of specific learning disabilities is from the *Federal Register*, 1977, p. 65083:

The term "children with specific learning disabilities" means those children who have a disorder in one or more of the basic psychological processes involved in understanding or in using language, spoken or written, which disorder may manifest itself in imperfect ability to listen, think, speak, read, write, spell, or do mathematical calculations. Such disorders include such conditions as perceptual handicaps, brain injury, minimal brain dysfunction, dyslexia, and developmental aphasia. Such term does not include children who have learning problems which are primarily the result of visual, hearing, or motor disabilities, of mental retardation, of emotional disturbance, or of environmental, cultural or economic disadvantage.

Although some students with learning disabilities have excellent verbal skills, many exhibit severe communication deficits in their oral language and reading performance. They may have difficulty with articulation, following oral and written directions, and accurately expressing their thoughts orally and in writing. Reading improvement is the most widely recognized academic need of the child with learning disabilities (Beattie, 1994; Gaskins, 1982). The general guidelines presented earlier apply to students with learning disabilities.

Students with Attention-Deficit Disorders (ADD)

Many students with learning disabilities have difficulty focusing on tasks and maintaining attention. Some of these children are said to have *attention-deficit hyperactivity disorder (ADHD)* if the behavior occurs much more frequently in them than in others of the same mental age and if the onset is before age seven. Sample criteria include impulsiveness, fidgeting and squirming, high distractibility, difficulty in waiting for turn or playing quietly, excessive talking and interrupting, and inability to pay attention (American Psychiatric Association, 1987; Gearheart and Gearheart, 1989; Richek, List, and Lerner, 1989). Another type of attention-deficit disorder, referred to as *undifferentiated attention-deficit disorder*, exists without hyperactivity and is characterized by marked inattention (Lerner, 1988).

Children who cannot concentrate are likely to have trouble learning to read and write. In some cases, doctors prescribe stimulant or antidepressant medication to help control behavior, but this has become a controversial practice. Children should realize that medication is used only for support and they are ultimately responsible for their own behavior (Fouse and Brians, 1993). Teachers who work with these children can help them manage their behavior by providing the following support (Fouse and Brians, 1993; Fowler, 1993; Wood, 1993):

1. Reward on-task behavior and ignore inappropriate behavior.

2. Give clear directions and ask students to paraphrase them back to you.

3. Use improvised study carrels to eliminate distractions.

4. Provide structure by adhering to schedules and routines.

5. Make reading sessions and assignments short.

6. Use contracts or progress charts.
7. Offer a multimodality approach.
8. Make instruction concrete whenever possible.
9. Monitor independent work carefully.
10. Provide alternate forms of assessment.

Students with Mental Retardation

A widely accepted definition of *mental retardation* states: "Mental retardation refers to significantly subaverage general intellectual functioning existing concurrently with deficits in adaptive behavior and manifested during the developmental period" (Grossman, 1983, p. 1). "Significantly subaverage general intellectual functioning" usually means a score of 70 or less on an intelligence test, and "adaptive behavior" refers to how the student functions in his or her social environment. Of the two criteria, the one dealing with adaptive behavior is more relevant to acceptable performance in the school environment (Kirk and Gallagher, 1989; Ysseldyke & Algozzine, 1990). Adaptive behavior includes such activities as doing chores, playing games, dressing, and using money. Students deficient in adaptive behavior lack acceptable and appropriate behavior for a particular age and culture and are unable to achieve standards of personal independence and social responsibility (Henley, 1985).

The primary characteristic of children with *mild mental retardation* is that they do not learn as readily as others of the same chronological age. They are usually unable to make complicated generalizations and learn material incidentally. According to Sedlak and Sedlak (1985), these children read less often than other children and choose material below their maturity levels. They are often deficient in oral and silent reading, locating details, recognizing main ideas, using context clues, and drawing conclusions, but can usually achieve word recognition skills, knowledge of word meanings, and reading rates on a par with others of the same mental age.

Students with Visual Impairments

A child who is *partially sighted* or *visually impaired* has visual acuity better than 20/200 but not better than 20/70 in the better eye with the best correction available. Educationally, the child who is partially sighted has difficulty but is able to learn to read print, as opposed to the blind child, who must learn to read braille.

Teachers can make provisions for children with visual impairments by adjusting lighting, providing tape-recorded stories and books with large print, and reading orally to the whole class frequently. They should refer children to visual specialists if they observe such symptoms as squinting, closing or covering one eye, rubbing eyes frequently, or making frequent errors when copying board work.

Students with Hearing Impairments

The term *hard of hearing* or *hearing impaired* applies to individuals whose sense of hearing is defective but adequate for ordinary purposes, with or without a hearing aid. Three factors related to hearing impairments affect a person's development (Schulz and Turnbull, 1984). The first factor is the *nature* or type of hearing difficulty, whether it involves frequency (pitch, or highness or lowness of sound) or intensity (loudness of a sound); the second factor is the *degree* of impairment, or the severity of the hearing loss; and the third factor is *age of onset.* The earlier the age of onset of hearing loss, the less opportunity a child has to learn language before beginning to read.

When providing reading instruction for children with hearing impairments, teachers should speak slowly, clearly, and with adequate volume; seat the child as far as possible from distracting sounds; use a whole-word approach to word recognition rather than a phonics approach because the child cannot hear sounds well; use the language experience approach to connect meaningful experiences to words; and supplement reading lessons with visual aids. Teachers should refer students to hearing specialists if they observe such symptoms as inattentiveness in class, requests for repetition of verbal information, frowning when trying to listen, or turning the head so that one or the other ear always faces the teacher.

Students with Speech Impairments

Speech is considered abnormal "when it deviates so far from the speech of other people that it calls attention to itself, interferes with communication, or causes the speaker or his listener to be distressed" (Van Riper, 1978, p. 43). Two of the most common *speech impairments* the classroom teacher encounters are articulation problems and stuttering. Articulation disorders are characterized by substituting one sound for another, omitting a sound, or distorting a sound. Children who stutter may have silent periods during which they are unable to produce any sound, or they may repeat a sound, a word, or a phrase or prolong the initial sound of a word.

Teachers of young children with articulation problems can make considerable use of rhymes, stories, and songs in groups, as well as planning more formal lessons organized around the speech sounds that are causing difficulties. In working with children who stutter, teachers should accept their speech and avoid prompting them.

Students with Emotional/Behavioral Disorders

Although all children sometimes misbehave, few children have emotional/behavioral disorders characterized by long-term, extremely unacceptable behaviors across many situations. These behaviors interfere with personal and social development, as well as with learning. Emotional/behavioral disorders are usually exhibited through aggressiveness and destructiveness or through withdrawal and anxiety (Deiner, 1993).

SELF-CHECK: OBJECTIVE 3   Name some types of disabilities that teachers may find in classrooms with students who are mainstreamed or included. (See Self-Improvement Opportunities 2, 3, 4, and 9.)

Instructional Implications and Strategies

The guidelines already given are useful for working with special learners, but each student has specific needs. When teachers identify students who appear to be having difficulties, they should refer them for special services (for example, auditory testing, psychological counseling) and use good judgment when helping them. The following section presents some instructional strategies for helping students who are experiencing difficulties with reading.

Students with Reading Difficulties

In any classroom some children are more likely to have problems learning to read than others. Educators have recommended a number of strategies to help these students.

Characteristics

A student who has difficulty learning to read may be labeled dyslexic, remedial, underachieving, at risk, disabled, retarded, impaired, or language learning disabled, but these labels are often difficult to apply accurately and serve no real purpose (Kamhi and Catts, 1989). The terms *learning disabled* and *remedial reader* are often confused, although the degree of underachievement for students with learning disabilities is more severe than that for remedial readers (Rhodes and Dudley-Marling, 1988). Some school systems consider any child who is achieving below grade level a nonproficient reader, whereas others consider whether or not the student is achieving below or up to potential before applying a label (Hargis, 1989).

In addition to problems with decoding and comprehension, these students often have behavioral and emotional problems (Beck, 1988). They may have difficulty initiating and completing tasks, working accurately, maintaining attention, remaining in their seats, and following oral and written directions. Emotional issues, such as low self-concept, poor frustration tolerance, and negative attitudes, may make these children unable to concentrate or unwilling to attempt learning tasks.

Instructional Implications

Strategies that are appropriate for teaching developmental readers, those who are making normal progress in reading, are generally the same as those for nonproficient readers. Instruction for readers with difficulties, however, may offer more individualized attention than they would normally receive in regular reading classes, highly specialized techniques for students with severe problems, and instruction that is based on a thorough diagnosis of the problem (Richek, List, and Lerner, 1989). Often these readers need opportunities to develop positive attitudes toward reading and to build positive self-concepts. In the following Classroom Scenario, an undergraduate student enrolled in a reading practicum course helped low-achieving readers find success and build self-esteem.

**Classroom
Scenario**

Providing Success for Nonproficient Readers

During her third-grade practicum, Molly Johnson had been assigned to work with three boys who hated to read and were reading at a first-grade level. After deciding to do a language experience chart with them, Molly began by reading Tomie de Paola's *The Quicksand Book* (Holiday House, 1977). After a discussion about quicksand, she involved the students in making quicksand in a large tub. The children made several charts related to the experience on such topics as what to do if trapped in quicksand, where quicksand is found, and the steps in conducting the experiment. When the three boys finished their work, Molly arranged for them to share their information with the rest of the class. They stood in the front of the classroom and read their charts to their peers, who were visibly impressed by what these boys had done.

Analysis of Scenario
By choosing an interesting topic and holding high expectations, Molly had found a way to motivate these students. They became excited about their special project and looked forward to the reading and writing activities related to their study of quicksand. By reading their charts in front of the room, they gained self-esteem and a measure of respect from their classmates.

Unfortunately, in many remedial reading programs instruction focuses on lower-level decoding skills instead of comprehension. Research indicates that readers in low groups spend most of their time in round-robin oral reading, are directed to focus their attention on recognizing words rather than constructing meaning, receive more drill on isolated words, respond to literal rather than higher-order questions, and are teacher directed rather than self-directed. Such instruction seems to be generally ineffective and only tends to make poor readers poorer (Weaver, 1990). Instead, these readers would benefit more from holistic instruction (Rhodes and Dudley-Marling, 1988; Weaver, 1990). In comparing holistic and traditional instruction for at-risk students, Stice and Bertrand (1990) found that students in whole language classrooms scored slightly higher on achievement tests than students from traditional classrooms and also outperformed them on less formal measures.

Instructional Strategies

For children who have difficulty grasping important concepts about the reading-writing process on their own, the teacher may occasionally need to provide direct instruction (Gaskins, 1988; Wong-Kam and Au, 1988). Such instruction is not a matter of asking children to complete skill sheets; instead it is a planned instructional sequence of explaining and modeling. By modeling mental processes, the teacher is helping readers understand the "invisible mental processes which are at the core of reading" (Duffy, Roehler, and Herrmann, 1988, p. 762). Direct instruction enables students to become independent readers by providing them with additional strategies for attacking unknown words and applying higher-level comprehension skills. Along with gaining control over written language, these students acquire self-confidence. (See Table 13.1 for examples of common reading difficulties and related direct instruction lessons.)

literature-centered reading Two uses of literature are particularly effective with students who have reading difficulties. Sustained Silent Reading (SSR), discussed in Chapter 8, enables them to choose familiar, predictable, or high-interest books that are easy to read. The basic plan for SSR can be modified for these students so that they may read their books orally to partners and discuss them in pairs (Ford and Ohlhausen, 1989; Rhodes and Dudley-Marling, 1988). Another useful strategy is repeated shared readings of predictable and repetitive stories and poetry, a procedure that enables students to sense language patterns (Ford and Ohlhausen, 1989; Wicklund, 1989). Students may then compose their own pieces based on the now familiar patterns.

Semantic mapping (explained in Chapters 4 and 5) is a particularly useful strategy for nonproficient readers because it helps them visualize relationships (Flood and Lapp, 1988; Pehrsson and Denner, 1989; Rhodes and Dudley-Marling, 1988). Semantic mapping may begin as a brainstorming session with ideas organized graphically according to major and minor points, interactions among elements or characters, or some other relationship. The teacher should model ways to make maps, but then children should struggle with creating their own designs to understand fully how to organize the material. This strategy has special value in content area reading.

reading-writing connection Journal writing and process writing are useful procedures for low-achieving students because they allow readers to choose their own topics, use invented spellings, and ignore writing conventions initially. By revising and editing selected pieces, even these students get to be published authors (Gaskins, 1988).

Table 13.1 *Common Reading Problems and Suggested Remedial Approaches*

If a student . . .	Let the student . . .
1. Reads word by word or uses incorrect phrasing.	a. Read easy, familiar, and interesting material.
	b. Tape-record a paragraph, listen to the tape, record it again with attention to units of meaning, and listen for improvement. Repeat this process until fluency is reached.
	c. Read orally with a good reader and imitate the good reader's phrasing and expression.
	d. Participate in choral reading or choral speaking.
	e. Read a part in a play; do readers' theater.
2. Lacks knowledge of sight words.	a. Associate pictures with words that have concrete referents.
	b. Identify names of familiar products that appear in advertisements.
	c. Read words from language experience charts and student-written stories as they appear both in context and on word cards.
	d. Build word banks of sight words and use them to create sentences or organize them by naming or action words. (See Chapter 7 for ideas about word banks.)
3. Has difficulty using context clues.	a. Watch the teacher modeling ways of using semantic and syntactic context clues.
	b. Fill in blanks with appropriate words in cloze selections. (See Chapter 10 for construction of cloze passages.)
	c. Brainstorm words that would make sense for the unknown word in a sentence and then consider phonics clues (especially beginning sound) in deciding on the word.
	d. Underline specific types of context clues, such as definition or comparison. (See Chapter 3 for more types of context clues.)
4. Cannot make inferences or draw conclusions.	a. Observe the teacher modeling ways to draw inferences by thinking aloud about clues for meaning.
	b. Look at pictures or collections of objects, find reasonable connections among them, and create stories from them.
	c. Listen to a story and predict what will happen next.
	d. Underline word and phrase clues that lead to making an inference. (What season is it? The <u>snow fell</u> and the streets <u>were icy</u>. It was <u>very cold outside</u>.)
	e. Solve short mysteries. (See Donald Sobol's Encyclopedia Brown books, for example.)

Table 13.1 *Common Reading Problems and Suggested Remedial Approaches (cont.)*

If a student . . .	Let the student . . .
5. Has a limited vocabulary.	a. Expand experiences by watching films and listening to stories that contain new concepts and words.
	b. Keep a file or notebook of new words with their meanings and use some of these words in writing.
	c. Play games that use word knowledge, such as *Password*.
	d. Brainstorm with other children lists of synonyms and antonyms.
	e. Compare figurative and literal meanings of figurative expressions.
	f. Experience a rich environment with many varied, concrete experiences.

Of special benefit during the writing process is peer conferencing, in which children help one another by offering suggestions and asking questions that lead to better composition (Wong-Kam and Au, 1988).

Involving children in authentic tasks promotes their understanding of reading and writing as meaning-making processes. The functional situations given in Example 13.2 and the list of activities that follows are appropriate for any reader who is having difficulties.

The following activities are most beneficial when students use them in purposeful and realistic situations:

Activities

1. Have the children set up a post office in which they write notes and address envelopes to their classmates.

2. Obtain multiple copies of last year's telephone directories, and let the students look up their own phone numbers; find emergency numbers; and look through the Yellow Pages to find restaurants, a skating rink, movie theaters, and other places that are familiar to them. Have each student make a telephone directory of these numbers.

3. Give children forms to fill out about themselves, including their names, addresses, telephone numbers, Social Security numbers, and so on.

4. Collect labels from different sizes and brands of the same product, and help children find which one is the most economical by comparing prices and amounts.

5. Make cards of words and phrases found in public places, such as *Wet Paint, No Trespassing, Danger, Ladies' Room,* and so on. Have the children see how many terms they can recognize.

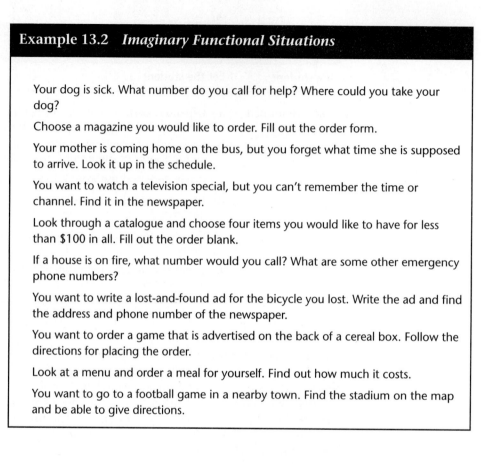

Example 13.2 *Imaginary Functional Situations*

Your dog is sick. What number do you call for help? Where could you take your dog?

Choose a magazine you would like to order. Fill out the order form.

Your mother is coming home on the bus, but you forget what time she is supposed to arrive. Look it up in the schedule.

You want to watch a television special, but you can't remember the time or channel. Find it in the newspaper.

Look through a catalogue and choose four items you would like to have for less than $100 in all. Fill out the order blank.

If a house is on fire, what number would you call? What are some other emergency phone numbers?

You want to write a lost-and-found ad for the bicycle you lost. Write the ad and find the address and phone number of the newspaper.

You want to order a game that is advertised on the back of a cereal box. Follow the directions for placing the order.

Look at a menu and order a meal for yourself. Find out how much it costs.

You want to go to a football game in a nearby town. Find the stadium on the map and be able to give directions.

6. Obtain city maps and let students locate landmarks. Simple map-reading skills involving their own school and neighborhood should precede work with a map of a larger area.

7. Ask the students to make a collection of grocery labels and product advertisements from magazines. Then let them pretend to go food shopping by selecting some of the labels and advertisements. They should tell you and other members of the group what they "bought." Have beginning readers match pictures and words from labels that have been cut apart.

8. Have students use newspapers to locate grocery store and other advertisements, find the classified section and look for items that are for sale and jobs that are available, use the index to find the comics page, read headlines, and look at the sports pages to find out about local athletic events.

9. Keep a collection of simple recipes, arranged alphabetically within categories, in a recipe box. Obtain basic ingredients and allow the children to make something.

10. Make a game of reading television schedules. Name a popular show and let children compete to see who can find the show first.

11. Collect coupons and distribute some to each child. Encourage children to figure out who will save the most money by using the coupons. Be sure they check expiration dates and any other specifications (such as two for the price of one).

Early Intervention Programs

As a result of a growing consensus that remedial reading instruction is often ineffective, particularly above second or third grade, a trend toward early intervention programs for students who are experiencing difficulty in learning to read is emerging (Hiebert and Taylor, 1994; Johnston and Allington, 1991; Pikulski, 1994; Pinnell, 1991). Reading educators contend that the emphasis should be on prevention rather than correction. Intensive early intervention followed by long-term, effective instruction appears to bring about lasting and substantial gains in reading achievement.

Intervention should begin as soon as a student shows signs of difficulty, usually in first grade. Typically, an intensive program is provided by a trained instructor and lasts for a short period of time, although some students may need additional intensive support beyond first grade. Two early intervention programs are briefly described here: Reading Recovery and Success for All.

Reading Recovery, developed in New Zealand by Marie Clay, is a temporary intervention program intended for first graders in the lowest 20 percent of the class (Clay, 1979; "Reading Recovery 1984–1988," 1988). A specially trained tutor works daily with each child for thirty minutes, usually for a period of twelve to sixteen weeks, until the child has developed effective strategies for independent learning and can function adequately in the regular classroom. From a selection of approximately 500 "little books," the tutor selects those that meet a student's particular interests and needs. Each lesson consists of having the child read many little books and compose a brief story or message. Research evidence indicates that Reading Recovery has enabled children to retain initial gains in reading and continue to make progress.

literature-centered reading

Success for All focuses on disadvantaged inner-city populations. This program involves school reorganization to provide excellent instruction from preschool through the primary grades (Slavin et al., 1994). Its three premises are innovative curriculum and instruction in reading, intensive one-on-one tutoring if reading problems emerge, and regrouping by reading level across the grades for ninety-minute reading instructional periods. The tutor reinforces the direct instruction provided by the regular classroom teacher, but also seeks to identify problems and find different strategies. In addition, a family support team attempts to involve parents, making them feel welcome in the school and providing special services. Research results are extremely positive and affirm the belief that reading failure in the primary grades is preventable.

SELF-CHECK: OBJECTIVE 4 What are some recommended strategies for helping poor readers? How are these strategies similar to or different from strategies used with any reader? (See Self-Improvement Opportunities 2 and 7.)

Gifted Children

Characteristics

Identifying the gifted and talented student can be a perplexing problem, with different school systems using various criteria to select those students entitled to special services. Commonly used criteria are high IQ scores; high overall grade point averages; outstanding performance in such areas as art, music, math, or science; or superior creative abilities (Davis and Rimm, 1989). In his theory of multiple intelligences, Howard Gardner claims there are seven or more forms of intelligence (Armstrong, 1994; Lazear, 1992). An individual may be gifted in any one or more of these areas:

1. *Linguistic intelligence*, the ability to use written and spoken words effectively

2. *Logical-mathematical intelligence*, the ability to reason, think deductively, and use numbers effectively

3. *Spatial intelligence*, the capacity to perceive visual-spatial aspects of the world accurately and to create mental images

4. *Body-kinesthetic intelligence*, knowledge of one's body and its physical movements

5. *Musical intelligence*, recognition of tonal patterns and sensitivity to rhythm

6. *Interpersonal intelligence*, the capacity to understand and relate to other people

7. *Intrapersonal intelligence*, knowledge of self, including metacognition, spirituality, and self-reflection

Teachers should encourage gifted students to use their intelligences by involving them in special projects.

Instructional Implications and Strategies

Gifted students need to be part of the community of learners within a classroom, participating in whole-class activities and working cooperatively with other students. Despite the widely recognized benefits of cooperative learning, however, gifted students also need opportunities to work alone and with their gifted peers on advanced projects related to their special abilities, as shown in the following Classroom Scenario. The current trend against grouping students by achievement or ability may actually have negative consequences for gifted students if they must always work in heterogeneous groups. In some school districts, special classes and programs for gifted children are being abolished (Davis and Rimm, 1994).

Classroom Scenario

Gifted Education Class

Sandy Smith, a countywide gifted education coordinator, schedules one-hour meetings with her classes each week. A creative person herself, she encourages her students to be creative and use higher-order thinking skills. As her group of fifth graders assembles, she poses a question: "If we value creativity in here, how can we share it with others? Let's brainstorm some ideas." Marcia says, "We could put on a play." Stephen suggests, "Let's teach some kids to make origami." "How about helping them make collages of their lives?" asks Karla. Thor excitedly calls out, "I know—let's tell stories creatively!" Ms. Smith asks, "What do you mean, creatively?" "You know," says Thor. "With sound effects and expression so that it's almost like drama." Several children begin talking about the stories they'd like to tell. "Whoa!" laughs Ms. Smith. "We didn't get very far with our brainstorming. Are there any other ideas?" After pausing a moment, Craig says he really likes the storytelling idea and thinks it would be good to share stories with other classes. Several of the others nod agreement.

"If that's what you want to do, let's see how we can work it out," says Ms. Smith. "First, does everyone agree?" The children eagerly affirm the choice. "Then what plans should we make?" asks Ms. Smith. "We'll need to decide which stories to tell," suggests Stephen. "How should we do that?" asks Ms. Smith. "We could have a sign-up sheet and write down our stories as soon as we've decided which ones to tell," offers Gretchen. "Is it okay if Amy and I do a tandem story together?" asks Marcia. "Of course," replies Ms. Smith. "I'd like to do our stories for a kindergarten," says Thor. "Why not?" Ms. Smith responds. "I'll ask Ms. Masters; she always likes us to come visit her kindergartners."

Analysis of Scenario
Although Ms. Smith meets each group of gifted education students only once a week, she presents them with challenging, thought-provoking ideas that they greet with brainstorming and other problem-solving techniques. Because they support one another and value everyone's ideas, the children are a community of enthusiastic learners. Ms. Smith encourages her students to take ideas back to their classes and share them, and she arranges to have them spend extra time in the library. She coordinates activities with the classroom teachers, librarians, and parents so that support for special activities comes from all directions. When doing a special storytelling project such as the one described here, the students prepare and practice during gifted education class, then later present their material to other students, especially to those in lower grades.

Whether or not a school system offers special programs for gifted students, the classroom teacher should challenge the gifted student to reach his or her potential. Even though gifted students are capable of completing their work more rapidly than other students, the teacher should not expect them to do more of the same kind of work if they finish their assignments early. Instead, the classroom teacher should provide a wide supply of resource materials, offer students opportunities to respond creatively to books, suggest long-term enrichment or research projects in their areas of special interest, develop a file of language puzzles and mindbenders for students to use, and plan many occasions for purposeful and extended reading and writing projects.

In a learner-centered classroom, the teacher may trust gifted students to be responsible for designing, researching, implementing, and reporting on their own projects. Because they are often highly motivated, gifted children are likely to respond enthusiastically to opportunities to develop their own learning experiences over an extended period of time.

Computers offer intellectually gifted students opportunities to think, create, and explore (Perry, 1989). Students should view computers as tools for helping them with writing assignments, keeping track of information, and comparing sets of data. Some types of software to use with gifted students are as follows:

1. Word-processing programs for enabling students to write drafts, revise, edit, and publish

2. Science simulations and experiments for engaging students in scientific inquiry and thinking skills

3. Graphics utilities for illustrating writing

4. Databases for organizing information such as

   a. Baseball cards or stamp collections

   b. Categories of historical information to analyze relationships among similar historical events for social studies

   c. Comparisons of political candidates' positions on election issues

   d. Scientific data for analysis to teach cause-and-effect explanations for experiments

   e. Classroom book lists for organizing books by categories and adding annotations as students read the books

5. Printing programs and desktop publishing programs for using graphics, multiple-column layouts, and various lettering fonts for such purposes as publishing newspapers, making posters and cards, creating letterheads, and putting written works into book form

6. Spreadsheets for organizing and calculating statistical information for such purposes as charting and analyzing class sales projects and forecasting population trends

SELF-CHECK: OBJECTIVE 5   List several characteristics of gifted learners. What are some appropriate instructional procedures to use with them? (See Self-Improvement Opportunity 8.)

Culturally and Linguistically Diverse Students

America has long been known as the "melting pot" because of its assimilation of people from all parts of the world. In recent years, this idea has been modified by people who believe in the "salad bowl" concept, or the rights of different minority groups to retain their cultural diversity within American society. The following discussions examine how children's backgrounds and specific language characteristics may affect the way they learn. They also consider the strategies teachers can use as they work with these children.

Culturally Diverse Students

Characteristics

Culturally diverse students differ from white Anglo-Saxon Americans in that they represent regional cultures, other ethnic groups, and religious minorities. Ethnic groups include

1. African Americans, whose origins are in Africa

2. Native Americans, whose origins are North American

3. Hispanic Americans, including those of Spanish descent or cultural heritage

4. Asian Americans, whose origins are in the Far East or Southeast Asia (Au, 1993; Norton, 1995; Wood, 1993)

In recent years the enrollment of minority students in public schools has increased dramatically (Wood, 1993), and the ethnic and racial composition of students has changed. The trend is toward an increase in Hispanic American, African American, and Asian American populations ("Why Multicultural Education?", 1994).

Children from some families may differ in their values, orientations toward school, and speech patterns from those in the American mainstream. Both their cultural and linguistic divergencies can influence how these children learn and consequently how they should be taught; thus, their presence and needs have affected educational policies in our schools.

Instructional Implications and Strategies

Multicultural education means developing an understanding and appreciation of various minority groups. This awareness should permeate the curriculum (Garcia, 1981). Children should be taught with consideration for their cultural heritages, their language preferences, and their lifestyles. On the other hand, too much attention to the cultural characteristics of special groups may lead to stereotyping and perhaps to a differentiated, segregated curriculum (Guild, 1994). It can also weaken the educational program. Thus, teachers need to concentrate on teaching the strategies and content necessary for all students to achieve success in American society (Thomas, 1981).

According to Banks (1994, p. 4), "[m]ulticultural education tries to create equal educational opportunities for all students by ensuring that the total school environment reflects the diversity of groups in classrooms, schools, and the society as a whole." Banks continues by saying that teachers implement multicultural education in different ways. The *contributions* approach deals with isolated facts about heroes from different cultures, and the *additive* approach adds units on special topics such as African Americans and the women's rights movement. Instead of these approaches, Banks recommends the *transformation approach*, which changes the curriculum so that students view content from the perspectives of a variety of groups. This approach involves fundamental changes in instructional materials and teaching techniques.

Following are some general guidelines for working with children of diverse cultural backgrounds (Au, 1993; Coelho, 1994, Ross, 1989; Wood, 1993).

1. *Learn about their cultures.* Find out about the children's language and learn cultural variations in word meanings. Learn about children's living conditions and what things are important to them. Try to discover cultural traits that affect how students learn. Show that you accept and value their cultures, even though they may differ from your own.

2. *Value their contributions.* Take an interest in what children bring to share, and listen to what they say. Create opportunities for their families to share their cultural heritages through learning experiences in the curriculum.

3. *Provide a supportive classroom environment.* Let the environment reflect the various cultures represented in the classroom by displaying multicultural materials and including instruction related to multicultural education.

4. *Provide opportunities for cooperative learning.* Let students work collaboratively to develop social and academic skills, understand and appreciate the diversity among themselves, and learn strategies to use in their interactions outside of school.

5. *Develop a learner-centered program.* Help students set personal goals for their own literacy learning. Placing students and their goals ahead of the skills mandated by scope and sequence charts should enable students to reach higher levels of achievement.

literature-centered reading

6. *Use multicultural literature.* When possible, choose stories related to students' cultural backgrounds. Exposure to such stories benefits both minority children, who gain self-esteem by reading about their own heritages, and mainstream American students, who broaden their concepts of the world and the people in it.

literature-centered reading

The use of multicultural literature merits special attention. Through literature, students can gain an understanding and appreciation of cultural diversity. Literature is a means of introducing global concepts and increasing the minority child's sense of dignity and self-worth (Stoddard, 1983). Children's literature represents a great variety of cultural views, thus enabling teachers to find books that are culturally meaningful to different groups represented in their classrooms (Holdaway, 1979).

The teacher is the key to any literature program that embraces cultural themes (Aiex, 1989). The approach to cultural diversity is usually either positive, reflecting a willingness to accept differences, or negative, projecting an attitude of rejection. The teacher should use literature that values cultural pluralism and avoid books that portray negative stereotypes. Books that perpetuate negative images of minorities or represent them inaccurately do more harm than good. Some questions for teachers to ask when evaluating books for stereotypes include the following:

1. Do the illustrations and text depict the character in the story as a distinct individual or as a stereotype of a particular ethnic group?

2. Do the settings always show conditions of poverty?

3. Are dialects used as a natural part of the story, or are they contrived to reinforce a stereotype?

4. Is the minority culture treated respectfully or portrayed as inferior?

5. Are minorities described authentically?

6. Is there diversity among characters within a particular cultural group?

Hadaway and Florez (1990) point out several ways to use multicultural literature. Teachers, with the help of librarians, should select books that represent minorities realistically and integrate these books into literature and social studies programs. As they tell or read the stories to the class, teachers can promote vocabulary, comprehension, writing, and values education. To orient students to the region of the world portrayed in a story, teachers should use maps so that students can visualize where stories are taking place. Some teachers may wish to keep a continuing record on a world map of the settings for various multicultural books and encourage minority students to identify the sites of their family origins.

To gain a better understanding of cultural variations, students may role-play situations or reactions. Particularly good choices of stories are folktales from various lands, stories of ethnic heroes, biographies of famous people who represent racial minorities, and stories of common individuals who realistically portray members of different cultural groups. The chapter appendix lists some multiethnic books that are classified by the four ethnic minority groups mentioned earlier in this section.

SELF-CHECK: OBJECTIVE 6   What are some problems that culturally diverse children encounter as they enter school? What are some ways teachers can help them? (See Self-Improvement Opportunities 5, 6, and 10.)

Students with Dialectal Differences

Children who exhibit cultural differences are also likely to show linguistic variations, often manifested as dialectal differences. A *dialect* is a variation of a language that is sufficiently different from the original to be considered a separate entity but not different enough to be classified as a separate language. Dialectal variations are usually associated with socioeconomic level, geographical region, or national origin. In truth, we all speak a dialect of some sort, and differences exist even within a regional pattern.

Characteristics

Differences in dialects occur in phonology (pronunciation), vocabulary, and grammatical construction. Examples of phonological dialect differences are *de* for *the, nofin'* for *nothing,* and *brovah* for *brother.* Regional usage determines whether the speaker says *sack, tote, poke,* or *bag.* Dialectal variations in grammatical construction often result from the influence of another language.

Each dialect is a complete and functional language system, and no dialect is superior or inferior to another for purposes of communication. However, for individuals to be accepted in some social classes and attain certain career goals, use of standard English is desirable. Standard language is the form of language recognized in dictionaries and grammar books, the "culturally dominant language in a country or region; language of well-educated people" (Harris and Hodges, 1981, p. 308). Teachers should therefore accept and respect children's dialects as part of their cultures and environments, but should make them aware of standard English as an important alternative. Currently, perhaps the most widely accepted view among linguists and educators is support of *bidialectalism,* which affirms both the value of home dialect and its use within the community and the value of teaching students standard English (Ovando and Collier, 1985). This means students should be able to speak their home dialects in school some of the time without being criticized.

Reading teachers should be familiar with the principal differences in pronunciation and syntactic rules of a child's dialect in order to evaluate oral reading. Without this knowledge, teachers cannot distinguish between a child's oral misreading that results from a lack of decoding skills and oral misreading that results from dialectal differences.

Instructional Implications and Strategies

The language experience approach (see Chapter 7) offers many advantages as a method for teaching reading to students whose dialect differs considerably from standard English. However, critics argue that it simply reinforces the dialect without providing contact with standard English. Gillet and Gentry (1983) propose a variation of this approach that values children's language but also provides exposure to standard English. The teacher transcribes the children's story exactly as dictated. The process continues in the traditional way, but later the teacher writes another version of the dictated chart in standard English with conventional sentence structure, using the same format and much of the same vocabulary. The teacher presents it as another story, not a better one, and children compare the two versions. The students then revise the original chart, making their sentences longer, more elaborate, and more consistent with standard English. They then practice echo reading and choral reading with this version until they can read it fluently and have acquired additional sight words.

For those readers who plan to teach in regions where children have divergent dialects, these classroom practices may be useful:

1. Provide purposeful literacy activities so that students can readily see applications for using language to communicate.

2. Relate reading to personal experiences and oral language forms that are familiar to the child.

3. Base instruction (particularly phonics) on a careful analysis of the child's language. Differentiate between oral reading miscues and specific speech patterns related to different linguistic backgrounds. (See the section "Miscue Analysis" in Chapter 11.)

4. Accept the student's nonstandard usage, but model standard English. For example, if a child says, "I ain't got no pencil," you might respond with "You don't have a pencil? I'll help you find one." Help the child to see purposes for learning standard English as an alternative.

5. Focus on the ideas the children are expressing rather than on their ways of expressing them.

6. Connect reading and writing whenever possible. Read stories to the children, let them write their own stories, and then have them read their stories to the class.

SELF-CHECK: OBJECTIVE 7   Explain what dialect is. Suggest some appropriate teaching strategies for children whose dialect differs significantly from standard English. (See Self-Improvement Opportunities 5, 6, and 10.)

Bilingual Students

The term *bilingualism* refers to the ability to speak or understand a language in addition to one's native tongue. Many people in the United States are bilingual or have non–English language backgrounds, and an estimated 6 to 8 million school-age children (about one out of every six) speak a non-English language at home (Hieshima, 1994; McKeon, 1994; "Why Multicultural Education?", 1994).

Characteristics

In the classroom, some bilingual students may speak very little English and others may speak English almost as well as they do their native language. A number of students give the impression of English competence in informal social settings but have not yet attained the standard English of the classroom, and many are unable to use their fragmented knowledge of home and school languages effectively in the classroom (Thonis, 1990). Ovando and Collier (1985) have identified four types of students commonly found in English as a Second Language (ESL) or bilingual classes:

1. *English-dominant students with a home language other than English.* These students may need to improve their academic achievement in English-speaking schools while continuing to develop the home language skills and cultural ties their parents wish them to maintain.

2. *Bilingual, bicultural students.* These students are generally fluent in both languages. Bilingual education merely enriches their academic experiences while reinforcing the cultural and linguistic identities of their families.

3. *Limited-English-proficient (LEP) students.* LEP students are perhaps most typical of those receiving bilingual and ESL instruction. They lack sufficient English language skills to achieve in a regular classroom and need special instruction to develop linguistic and academic skills.

4. *English-speaking monolingual students with no language minority background.* Since the law requires classes to be integrated, English-speaking students who do not speak a second language may also be in bilingual classes. They help to socialize minority students and also benefit personally from exposure to a second language.

Bilingual children may be from families of indigenous minorities, such as Native Americans; immigrants, who have left a country to settle permanently elsewhere; or refugees, who have fled a country to escape from an intolerable situation. Their home backgrounds and their families' attitudes toward language, school, and culture often affect how well they learn English as a second language.

Instructional Implications

The Bilingual Education Act (1968) brought about the widespread use of bilingual programs to provide equal educational opportunities for students with non–English-language backgrounds (Ovando and Collier, 1985). A bilingual education program attempts to do three things: (1) continue the development of the student's primary language, (2) help the student acquire a second language, and (3) provide instruction in content areas by using both English and the child's native language. This type of program includes historical and cultural components of both languages so that students can develop and maintain self-esteem and pride in both cultures.

English as a Second Language (ESL) instruction is a program for teaching English to students who live in an English-speaking environment but whose native language is not English. It is common for students in ESL programs to receive content instruction in English and to spend part of the day in pull-out programs

Example 13.3 *Sample Page from an ESL Book*

How Are You Today?

With Your Partner

Ask and answer with your partner.

1. Are you **happy** today?
   Yes, I am.
   No, I'm not.

2. Are you **sad** today?
   Yes, I am.
   No, I'm not.

3. Are you **angry** today?
   Yes, I am.
   No, I'm not.

4. Are you **nervous** today?
   Yes, I am.
   No, I'm not.

5. Are you **tired** today?
   Yes, I am.
   No, I'm not.

6. Are you **sick** today?
   Yes, _____
   No, _____

7. Are you **hot** today?
   Yes, _____
   No, _____

8. Are you **cold** today?
   Yes, _____
   No, _____

9. Are you **hungry** today?
   Yes, _____
   No, _____

10. Are you **thirsty** today?
    Yes, _____
    No, _____

Circle Dialogue

Sit in a circle. Ask the student on your right the first question. ("Are you happy today?") That student answers and then asks the student on his or her right the same question.

Teacher: "Are you happy today?"
Student 1: "Yes, I am." or "No, I'm not."
           "Are you happy today?"
Student 2: "Yes, I am. or "No, I'm not."
Continue around the circle. Repeat with all the questions on this page.

List on the Board: What Do You Do?

Ask the class these questions. Write a list on the board of all the different answers.

1. What do you do when you are happy?
2. What do you do when you are sad?
3. What do you do when you are hot?
4. What do you do when you are tired?
5. What do you do when you are cold?
6. What do you do when you are angry?

4

Source: Tina Kasloff Carver/Sandra Douglas Fotinos, *A Conversation Book: English in Everyday Life, Book I,* 2/E, © 1985, p. 4. Reprinted by permission of Prentice-Hall, Inc., Englewood Cliffs, New Jersey 07632.

with their LEP classmates to learn English (Willis, 1994). Example 13.3 is a page from an ESL workbook that uses familiar expressions for oral language, reading, and writing.

Many educators believe LEP children need to understand and speak English before they learn to read it (Lapp and Flood, 1986; Mace-Matluck, 1982; Thonis, 1976). There is no need, however, for bilingual students to *master* oral language before they are introduced to written language (Freeman and Freeman, 1988; Fitzgerald, 1993; Gonzales, 1994).

Research seems to indicate that minority students learn to read better if initial instruction is in their native language (Allen, 1994; Baca and Cervantes, 1989; Lapp and Flood, 1986; Mace-Matluck, 1982; Ovando and Collier, 1985; Schifini, 1994), and students who can already read and write in their native tongue generally learn to read much faster in English than those who are nonliterate in the language used at home. By beginning to read in the language they understand best, students are able to develop and use strategies that are effective for learning to read. Later they can transfer these same strategies or skills to reading material written in English. In addition, using a child's native language for instruction is likely to build a sense of identity and self-worth and reduce feelings of hostility or ambivalence toward English. According to Thonis (1976, p. 61), "The best predictor of success in a second language is success in the first language."

Gonzales (1994) found, however, that students can learn to read successfully in both their native language and English at the same time. Although it is easier for students to learn to read and write in their primary language, strategies for learning to read and write in English are similar to strategies used in other languages and can be mutually reinforcing.

Certain universal elements exist among languages that use the same alphabet, but the transfer of reading skills from one language to another does not occur automatically (Mace-Matluck, 1982; Lapp and Flood, 1986). Teachers need to identify those skills that are common to both the native language and English and then plan lessons to help students see how a particular reading skill can apply to both languages. Unless children realize they can use the same reading strategies, they may not transfer their knowledge. Once students perceive similarities in reading processes, they can transfer not only general reading strategies and attitudes, but also specific skills, such as awareness of text structure and knowledge of story grammar, from one language to the other.

Many teachers are monolingual and thus are unable to speak a bilingual child's primary language. In this case, there are several alternatives that still support language development (Freeman and Freeman, 1991). These include the following strategies:

1. Have bilingual aides or parent volunteers read and discuss literature in the child's primary language.

2. Ask older students who speak the child's first language to serve as peer tutors.

3. Encourage children to send pen-pal letters to students in another class who share the same primary language.

4. Pair students of the same primary language within a classroom so that the more proficient one can guide the other.

5. Place books in languages other than English in the classroom library.

6. Place signs or labels written in the children's native languages around the classroom, along with the English words.

7. Let children write in journals and ask a bilingual adult to respond to them.

In addition to the guidelines presented for teaching culturally and linguistically diverse students, the following suggestions are useful for working with bilingual students (Allen, 1994; Altwerger and Ivener, 1994; Au, 1993; Cummins, 1994; Fitzgerald, 1993):

1. *Provide a literate environment.* Set up a library corner with many predictable, repetitive books that are easy for children to read. Use words and sentences in meaningful ways, such as labeling objects and exhibits, writing directions for taking care of a pet, making class books of shared experiences, putting captions on bulletin board displays, and encouraging children to share books they write. On some occasions, present words in both English and the other language(s) the children speak.

2. *Involve parents.* Encourage parents to view themselves as partners in the education of their children in order to promote their academic and linguistic growth. If some parents are intimidated by the idea of coming to the school, ask them to listen to their children read books at home, help their children do research on their family backgrounds, and collaborate on writing projects.

3. *Encourage risk taking.* Let students experiment with using language without fear of embarrassment or ridicule. Emphasize the importance of communication, not the correctness of words and structure, during writing, conversation, and oral reading.

4. *Give feedback.* Reward students who are making efforts to communicate in English with praise and encouraging facial expressions and gestures. Be patient and realize that bilingual students may need more time to express themselves in English than many monolingual English students do.

5. *Use alternative forms of assessment.* Collect samples of students' writing, such as journal entries, reports, and published pieces, and keep records of their reading, including both reading of books and functional reading of recipes and directions. Tape-record oral reading and discussions, and keep observational records of students' progress in oral language development. Such informal assessment is more useful than standardized test scores.

6. *Encourage active participation.* Provide opportunities for students to become actively involved in class activities, take responsibility for their learning, work in cooperative groups, and make decisions about topics of study and classroom policies.

Instructional Strategies

Although research does not clearly indicate which approaches to bilingual instruction produce the best results, procedures based on whole language philosophy seem to be gaining support (Bird, 1991; Flores, 1990; Freeman and Freeman, 1988, 1992; Heald-Taylor, 1989; Thonis, 1990). Whole language philosophy values the diverse languages, cultures, and background experiences of bilingual students. Language tends to develop naturally as students work cooperatively with their peers on authentic tasks. Whole language teachers integrate learning across the curriculum so that students develop competency in oral language, reading, and writing as they learn content. Such teachers also provide a supportive classroom environment to encourage students to experiment and take risks in their use of English. The whole language classroom is a community of learners who actively participate in working on projects, sharing experiences, and learning language.

A major focus in both whole language theory and bilingual instruction is on language as a meaning-making process. Krashen (1991) uses the term *comprehensible input* to mean that it is important for the student to understand the meaning of the message instead of focusing on standard form and structure. Johns (1988) supports this view, asserting that language should be acquired naturally, not learned as a set of skills. According to Coelho (1994), the trend for second-language teaching is away from traditional instruction that focuses on information about language with many rules and examples.

The following specific strategies, along with those already presented for dialectal speakers, may benefit students with limited English proficiency as well.

Drama.   Through creative drama, bilingual students can interpret the stories they hear, thereby clarifying their understanding of story structure and vocabulary. Role playing enables them to experiment with vocabulary and sentence structure as they explore their feelings. These students can learn the meanings of prepositions by following directions on word cards that tell them to place objects *on, under,* or *beside* a table, and they can act out simple sentences such as "Carlos sits down." Songs, games, and choral readings with gestures also reinforce a child's understanding of word meanings.

Authentic Experiences.   Heidger (1991) suggests purposeful tasks for bilingual students: compiling bilingual dictionaries, reading children's books in primary languages, making books on the home or family supplemented with illustrations or photographs and captioned in both English and the home language, and listening to teacher-made or commercial audiotapes that accompany children's books written in English. Projects such as giving a party and inviting special people create many opportunities for using language (e.g., discussing plans, making lists, writing invitations, reading thank-you notes) and let children direct their own activities (Meyer, 1990). Direct experiences through field trips or classroom activities, along with such vicarious experiences as films and filmstrips, puppets, and pictures, enable children to learn language in meaningful ways.

Purposeful Writing.   Teachers should encourage bilingual students to write for authentic purposes even before they are proficient in English. The students may use a combination of symbols, drawings, and invented spellings to communicate their ideas. As they acquire new knowledge about English, they reveal their growth by moving toward conventional practices (Heald-Taylor, 1989).

The writing workshop (discussed in Chapter 8) provides many opportunities for language development (Au, 1993; Ruiz, 1991). Good literature provides models for writing, minilessons help students acquire the skills they need for writing, and conferences develop communication skills.

Dialogue journals (described in Chapter 8) are actually written conversations that enable teachers to move LEP children toward competency in English by providing them with a nonthreatening, nonstructured medium for exchanging ideas. Two important factors to consider in successfully implementing dialogue journals are (1) the child's freedom to choose the topic and (2) a positive relationship between teacher and student (De la Luz Reyes, 1990; Flores, 1990). In one classroom, each child chose a topic to write about every day. If the teacher could not read the entry, the child read it to the teacher, who then wrote a response and read it to the child. Studies have found that the use of dialogue journals results in substantial improvement in second-language students' writing (Farnan, Flood, and Lapp, 1994).

In addition to writing in journals, bilingual children can benefit from process writing instruction. Jonas Lindgren had completed one year of English in Sweden before coming to the United States, where he entered a sixth-grade ESL classroom. At the end of the year, Jonas wrote three drafts of a story about a subject that was very important to him. These drafts, which show his progress in making revisions, appear in Example 13.4.

Language Experience Approach.   The language experience approach (presented in Chapter 7) is particularly useful for helping LEP students learn to read (Heald-Taylor, 1989; Johns, 1988). Students who know very little English, however, need to acquire additional vocabulary and knowledge of oral language before they dictate sentences (Moustafa and Penrose, 1985). To increase students' vocabularies, teachers can ask them to touch, name, label, and talk about concrete objects. Teachers can also demonstrate the meanings of action words such as *look* by pointing to an object in the room and saying "Look!" while urging the children to look in that direction.

Literature.   When read aloud, literature offers bilingual students opportunities to hear the intonation and rhythm of the English language in meaningful contexts and to become familiar with the structure of the language. Of particular value to second-language learners are observing English print characteristics and directional patterns, making predictable stories into big books, and developing an awareness and appreciation of literature (Heald-Taylor, 1989). When selecting books for ESL students, teachers should choose

- concept books to introduce children to new vocabulary.

- well-illustrated books that provide clues to meaning.

- predictable books so that students can read along.

- high-interest books to motivate children to read.

- familiar stories to reinforce vocabulary and language patterns.

- informational books to supplement the curriculum.

- books linked to the children's cultures (Allen, 1994; Hough, Nurss, and Enright, 1986).

Example 13.4   *Process Writing Drafts by an ESL Student*

① The soccer final

It is year 2001 and Italy and Gurmeny is in the soccer final. Five minits in the game Gurmeny gets a very good clans, they kik the ball right outsid the gol. then Gurmeny gets a new clans 44 minits in the game. They cros it over to the mit spot of the penaty eria where ther mit for word is to hit it right in the kworner of the gol.

(then the first hafe finich) The sakend hafe was Itals hafe the started with a gol in the 23 mit and the finiched with a goll in the 43 menit. I italy won the world campion agen.

② The world campion soccer game

It is year 2001, and Italy and Gurmeny are in the world campion soccer final. Five minits in the game Gurmeny, gets a very good chance, they kik the ball it right outside the gol. Then Gurmany got a new chance 44 minits in the game They crost the ball over to the mit spot of the penelty eria where there mit forword was standig wating to hit the boll in the kworner of the gol. (Then the first half was finiched And he did it.

The sacend half was Italis half, they, started with a gol in the 23 mit and then finiched with a gol in the 43 minit.

Italy won the world cup agen

Example 13.4   *Process Writing Drafts by an ESL Student (cont.)*

Jonas Lindgren ③

The world champion soccer game

It is year 2009, and Italy and Germany are in the world champion soccer final.

Five minuts in the game Germany, gets a very good chance, they kick the ball right outside the goal.

Then Germany gets a new chance 44 minuts in the game, they crossed the ball over to the mit spot, in the middle of the penelty area, where there striker was standing waiting to hit it, in the corner of the goal, and he did it. (Then the first half was finiced.

The second half was Italys half, they started with a gool in the 23ᵈ minute and then they finiched with a gool in the 43ᵈ.

ITALY,
WON THE WORLD CUP AGAIN.

SELF-CHECK: OBJECTIVE 8 What are some factors to consider in working with bilingual children? (See Self-Improvement Opportunities 5, 6, 9, and 10.)

Summary

Every teacher should be aware of the needs of exceptional children, especially since the passage of the Education for All Handicapped Children Act (PL 94-142). This law was amended by the Individuals with Disabilities Education Act (IDEA), which provides for the mainstreaming or inclusion of many exceptional students into regular classrooms. Teachers work with other professionals in designing individualized education programs (IEPs) for children with disabilities. General guidelines for working with these children include providing opportunities for success, having positive attitudes toward them, providing appropriate instruction, using suitable materials, and communicating with others who work with them.

Several types of special learners are being integrated into regular classrooms. Children with learning disabilities usually show a significant discrepancy between achievement level and potential in one or more areas. Many have communication problems, and reading improvement is their greatest academic need. One form of learning disability is attention-deficit disorder (ADD), characterized by inattentive behaviors. Students with mental retardation do not learn as readily as other children do. Children with emotional/behavioral disorders exhibit a number of problems, often including aggressiveness or withdrawal. Teachers should also observe children carefully for possible visual or auditory impairments so that they can refer them for special services if needed. Two of the most common speech impairments are problems with articulation and stuttering.

Students who are having difficulty learning to read can benefit from well-balanced holistic instruction, including authentic reading and writing activities. Early intervention programs, such as Reading Recovery and Success for All, appear to be successful in helping young children overcome reading problems.

Gifted children can progress more rapidly than their peers and often show advanced development in one or more of the seven intelligences identified by Howard Gardner. Teachers should provide challenging tasks for these students and help them reach their full potential.

America's schools have children from a wide variety of ethnic, cultural, and racial origins who bring diverse backgrounds and experiences to the classroom. Many of them speak nonstandard dialects; others are English as a Second Language (ESL) students. The Bilingual Education Act has given rise to bilingual and ESL programs to provide equal educational opportunities for these students.

Carefully selected multicultural literature helps minority students develop an appreciation for their heritage. Many books are available for teachers to share in their classrooms.

Test Yourself   *True or False*

_____   1. The exceptional child's basic needs and goals are quite different from those of the average child.

_____   2. The language experience approach is generally a good approach to use with the exceptional learner.

_____   3. Many children who have been enrolled in special education classes are being integrated into regular classrooms.

_____   4. The IDEA is a modification of the Americans with Disabilities Act.

_____   5. Children who are being mainstreamed or included may have difficulty adjusting to a regular classroom.

_____   6. IEP stands for Instant Environmental Plan.

_____   7. A student with a learning disability has a low level of functioning in all areas.

_____   8. Two of the most common speech disorders the classroom teacher encounters are faulty articulation and stuttering.

_____   9. Children from different cultures are likely to exhibit linguistic differences.

_____   10. Understanding the backgrounds of multicultural students is a good way to begin relating to them.

_____   11. For purposes of general communication, some dialects are superior to others.

_____   12. ESL students appear to read better if they learn to read in their native language first.

_____   13. Many children with learning disabilities have severe communication deficits.

_____   14. Enrollment of minority students in public schools has decreased dramatically.

_____   15. If a child is identified as ADHD, it means visual and auditory problems are present.

_____   16. Reading Recovery is a program designed to help children with speech impairments pronounce words correctly during oral reading.

_____   17. The use of multicultural literature helps children of diverse cultural backgrounds gain self-respect.

_____   18. Teachers should choose multicultural literature that retains racial and ethnic stereotypes.

_____ 19. Cooperative learning strategies are generally effective for helping mainstreamed and included children adjust to the classroom.

_____ 20. When teaching students who are having difficulty with reading, teachers should focus on word attack skills without regard for meaning.

_____ 21. Nonproficient readers generally do better when their goals are long term rather than short term.

_____ 22. Predictable and repetitive stories are useful for helping low-achieving readers understand language patterns.

_____ 23. Computers offer many options for enabling gifted children to work up to their potential.

_____ 24. A student with mental retardation is generally considered to have poor adaptive behavior and an IQ score of 70 or below.

_____ 25. Teacher modeling is an effective strategy for helping students develop efficient mental processes for reading.

_____ 26. Because gifted children are capable of working more rapidly than their classmates, they should be assigned more of the same kind of work.

_____ 27. Chapter I teachers are required to coordinate instruction with classroom teachers.

_____ 28. Inclusion is an individualized educational plan designed especially for each child with a disability.

_____ 29. Standardized test scores are the most valid way to assess the achievement of bilingual students.

_____ 30. Whole language strategies seem to be effective for special learners.

_____ 31. The best way for ESL students to learn English is to memorize rules and practice skills.

Self-Improvement Opportunities

1. List the nine general guidelines given for instructing exceptional children in order of importance (in your opinion). Be prepared to justify your reasoning.

2. Visit a local school to find out how the needs of children with disabilities are met. Ask to visit a classroom where a student is being mainstreamed or included, and observe how this child participates in class activities and how he or she is accepted by classmates.

3. Talk with a speech correction teacher about the role of the regular classroom teacher in helping children with speech impairments.

4. Visit a classroom to see if any child appears to have ADHD. If there is such a child, observe how the teacher works with him or her.

5. Study the characteristics of the people who live in your area. How do their language patterns compare with standard English? What cultural and ethnic variations do you find? What implications do these findings have for teaching?

6. Get permission from a classroom teacher to work with a culturally or linguistically different child on a one-to-one basis for one week. Ask the teacher to help you plan an instructional program for this child.

7. Find a book you think would appeal to one type of exceptional child, and plan how you would present it.

8. Visit a local school to find out what provisions are made for different types of learners. Are resource rooms being used? Is there a program for gifted students? What special personnel are available to provide services?

9. If possible, interview a bilingual child about how he or she learned to read. Try to discover any problems or insights about learning to read from the child's point of view. Take notes on your findings and share them in class during group discussions.

10. If the region in which you live has a large number of families from a non-mainstream ethnic group, make an annotated bibliography of books that relate to this particular group's culture.

Chapter Appendix A

Multiethnic Literature

Books suitable for the primary level are marked *(P)*, those for the intermediate level are marked *(I)*, and those for all ages are marked *(A)*.

Asian American

Davis, Daniel S. *Behind Barbed Wire.* New York: Dutton, 1982. (I)
Friedman, Ina R. *How My Parents Learned to Eat.* Boston: Houghton Mifflin, 1984. (P)
Garland, Sherry. *The Lotus Seed.* San Diego: Harcourt Brace Jovanovich, 1993. (P)
Ishii, Momoko. *The Tongue-Cut Sparrow.* New York: Dutton, 1987. (I)
Mosel, Arlene. *The Funny Little Woman.* New York: Dutton, 1972. (P)
Say, Allen. *Grandfather's Journey.* Boston; Houghton Mifflin, 1993. (A)
Wallace, Ian. *Chin Chiang and the Dragon's Dance.* New York: Atheneum, 1984. (I)

Yee, Paul. *Tales from Gold Mountain: Stories of the Chinese in the New World.* New York: Macmillan, 1990. (I)
Yep, Lawrence. *Child of the Owl.* New York: Harper & Row, 1977. (I)
Yep, Lawrence. *The Rainbow People.* New York: Harper & Row, 1989. (I)
Yep, Lawrence. *Star Fisher.* New York: Morrow, 1991. (I)

African American

Aardema, Verna. *Bringing the Rain to Kapiti Plain: A Nandi Tale.* New York: Dial, 1981. (P)
Aardema, Verna. *Who's in Rabbit's House?* New York: Dial, 1977. (P)
Aardema, Verna. *Why Mosquitoes Buzz in People's Ears.* New York: Dial, 1975. (P)
Adoff, Arnold. *Black Is Brown Is Tan.* New York: Harper & Row, 1972. (P)
Adoff, Arnold. *In for Winter, Out for Summer.* San Diego: Harcourt Brace Jovanovich, 1991. (A)
Arkhurst, Joyce Cooper. *The Adventures of Spider: West African Folk Tales.* Boston: Little, Brown, 1964. (A)
Clifton, Lucille. *Everett Anderson's Goodbye.* New York: Holt, Rinehart and Winston, 1983. (P)
Courlander, Harold. *The Crest and the Hide: And Other African Stories of Heroes, Chiefs, Bards, Hunters, Sorcerers, and Common People.* New York: Coward-McCann, 1982. (A)
Davis, Ossie. *Langston.* New York: Delacorte, 1982. (I)
Feelings, Muriel. *Jambo Means Hello: Swahili Alphabet Book.* New York: Dial, 1974. (A)
Feelings, Muriel. *Moja Means One: Swahili Counting Book.* New York: Dial, 1971. (A)
Flournoy, Valerie. *The Patchwork Quilt.* New York: Dial, 1985. (P, I)
Greene, Bette. *Philip Hall Likes Me, I Reckon Maybe.* New York: Dial, 1974. (I)
Greenfield, Eloise. *Sister.* New York: Crowell, 1974. (I)
Guy, Rosa. *Mother Crocodile.* New York: Delacorte, 1981. (P, I)
Haley, Gail E. *A Story, a Story.* New York: Atheneum, 1970. (P)
Hamilton, Virginia. *The House of Dies Drear.* New York: Macmillan, 1968. (I)
Hamilton, Virginia. *M. C. Higgins, the Great.* New York: Macmillan, 1974. (I)
Hamilton, Virginia. *The People Could Fly: American Black Folktales.* New York: Knopf, 1985. (I)
Hamilton, Virginia. *The Planet of Junior Brown.* New York: Macmillan, 1971. (I)
Hamilton, Virginia. *Zeely.* New York: Macmillan, 1967. (I)
Harris, Joel Chandler. *The Adventures of Brer Rabbit.* Skokie, Ill.: Rand McNally, 1980. (P, I)
Hoffman, Mary. *Amazing Grace.* New York: Dial, 1991. (P)
Keats, Ezra Jack. *John Henry: An American Legend.* New York: Pantheon, 1965. (P, I)
Mathis, Sharon B. *The Hundred Penny Box.* New York: Viking, 1975. (P)
McDermott, Gerald. *Anansi the Spider: A Tale from the Ashanti.* New York: Holt, Rinehart and Winston, 1972. (P)
McKissack, Patricia. *The Dark-Thirty: Southern Tales of the Supernatural.* New York: Knopf, 1992. (I)
McKissack, Patricia. *Mirandy and Brother Wind.* New York: Knopf, 1988. (P)
Mendez, Phil. *The Black Snowman.* New York: Scholastic, 1989. (I)
Musgrove, Margaret. *Ashanti to Zulu, African Traditions.* New York: Dial, 1976. (P, I)

Myers, Walter Dean. *Scorpions*. New York: Harper & Row, 1988. (I)
Ringgold, Faith. *Aunt Harriet's Underground Railroad in the Sky*. New York: Crown, 1993. (P)
Ringgold, Faith. *Tar Beach*. New York: Crown, 1991. (P)
Stanley, Diane, and Peter Vennema. *Shaka: King of the Zulus*. New York: Morrow, 1988. (P, I)
Steptoe, John. *Stevie*. New York: Harper & Row, 1969. (P)
Taylor, Mildred. *Roll of Thunder, Hear My Cry*. New York: Dial, 1976. (I)
Williams, Sherley Anne. *Working Cotton*. San Diego: Harcourt Brace Jovanovich, 1992. (P)

Hispanic American

Belpre, Pura. *Once in Puerto Rico*. New York: Frederick Warne, 1973. (I)
Brown, Tricia. *Hello, Amigos!* New York: Henry Holt, 1986. (P)
de Paola, Tomie. *The Lady of Guadalupe*. New York: Holiday, 1980. (I)
Ehlert, Lois. *Moon Rope*. San Diego: Harcourt Brace Jovanovich, 1992. (A)
Garcia, Richard. *My Aunt Otila's Spirits*. Chicago: Children's Press, 1987. (P)
Griego, Margot. *Tortillas Para Mama and Other Nursery Rhymes: Spanish and English*. New York: Holt, 1981. (P)
Meltzer, Milton. *The Hispanic Americans*. New York: Crowell, 1982. (I)
Mohr, Nicholasa. *Felita*. New York: Dial, 1979. (I)
O'Dell, Scott. *Carlota*. Boston: Houghton Mifflin, 1981. (I)
Soto, Gary. *Baseball in April and Other Stories*. San Diego: Harcourt Brace Jovanovich, 1990. (I)
Soto, Gary. *Too Many Tamales*. New York: Putnam, 1993. (P)

Native American

Baker, Olaf. *Where the Buffaloes Begin*. New York: Murray, 1981. (P)
Baylor, Byrd. *When Clay Sings*. New York: Scribner's, 1972. (A)
Bierhorst, John. *The Ring in the Prairie, A Shawnee Legend*. New York: Dial, 1970. (A)
dePaola, Tomie. *The Legend of Bluebonnet*. New York: Putnam, 1983. (A)
Dixon, Ann. *How Raven Brought Light to People*. New York: Macmillan, 1993. (A)
Fritz, Gerald. *The Double Life of Pochahontas*. New York: Putnam, 1983. (I)
George, Jean Craighead. *The Talking Earth*. New York: Harper & Row, 1983. (I)
George, Jean Craighead. *Water Sky*. New York: Harper & Row, 1987. (I)
Goble, Paul. *Beyond the Ridge*. New York: Bradbury, 1989. (A)
Goble, Paul. *The Girl Who Loved Wild Horses*. New York: Bradbury, 1978. (A)
Highwater, Jamake. *Moonsong Lullaby*. New York: Lothrop, Lee and Shepard, 1981. (A)
Jeffers, Susan. *Brother Eagle, Sister Sky*. New York: Dial, 1991. (A)
Joosse, Barbara. *Mama, Do You Love Me?* New York: Chronicle, 1991. (P)
Martin, Bill, Jr., and John Archambault. *Knots on a Counting Rope*. New York: Henry Holt, 1987. (A)
McDermott, Gerald. *Raven: A Trickster Tale from the Pacific Northwest*. San Diego: Harcourt Brace Jovanovich, 1993. (A)

Miles, Miska. *Annie and the Old One.* Boston: Little, Brown, 1971. (P)

O'Dell, Scott. *Black Stars, Bright Dawn.* Boston: Houghton Mifflin, 1988. (I)

O'Dell, Scott. *Sing Down the Moon.* Boston: Houghton Mifflin, 1970. (I)

Paulsen, Gary. *Dogsong.* New York: Bradbury, 1988. (I)

Sneve, Virginia Driving Hawk. *Dancing Teepees: Poems of American Indian Youth.* New York: Holiday House, 1989. (A)

Speare, Elizabeth George. *The Sign of the Beaver.* Boston: Houghton Mifflin, 1983. (I)

Steptoe, John. *The Story of Jumping Mouse.* New York: Lothrop, Lee & Shepard, 1984. (A)

Bibliography

Aaron, Ira E., Jeanne S. Chall, Dolores Durkin, Kenneth Goodman, and Dorothy S. Strickland. "The Past, Present, and Future of Literacy Education: Comments from a Panel of Distinguished Educators, Part I." *The Reading Teacher,* 43 (January 1990), 302–311.

Aaron, Ira E., Jeanne S. Chall, Dolores Durkin, Kenneth Goodman, and Dorothy Strickland. "The Past, Present, and Future of Literacy Education: Comments from a Panel of Distinguished Educators, Part II." *The Reading Teacher,* 43 (February 1990), 370–380.

Adams, Marilyn Jager. *Beginning to Read: Thinking and Learning about Print.* Cambridge, Mass.: MIT Press, 1990.

Adams, Marilyn Jager. "Modeling the Connections Between Word Recognition and Reading." In *Theoretical Models and Processes of Reading,* 4th ed., edited by Robert B. Ruddell, Martha Rapp Ruddell, and Harry Singer. Newark, Del.: International Reading Association, 1994, pp. 838–863.

Adams, Marilyn Jager, et al. "*Beginning to Read*: A Critique by Literacy Professionals and a Response by Marilyn Jager Adams." *The Reading Teacher,* 44 (February 1991), 370–395.

Adelman, Howard S., and Linda Taylor. *An Introduction to Learning Disabilities.* Glenview, Ill.: Scott, Foresman, 1986.

Aiex, Nola Kortner. "Literature as Lessons on the Diversity of Culture." *ERIC Digest.* Bloomington, Ind.: ERIC Clearing House on Reading and Communication Skills, 1989.

Aiex, Nola Kortner. "Literature-Based Reading Instruction." *The Reading Teacher,* 41 (January 1988), 458–461.

Aiex, Nola Kortner. "Storytelling: Its Wide-Ranging Impact in the Classroom." In *ERIC DIGEST Number 9.* Bloomington, Ind.: ERIC Clearinghouse on Reading and Communication Skills, 1988.

Aliki. *A Weed Is a Flower: The Life of George Washington Carver.* Englewood Cliffs, N.J.: Prentice-Hall, 1965.

Allen, Elizabeth Godwin, Jone Perryman Wright, and Lester L. Laminack. "Using Language Experience to ALERT Pupils' Critical Thinking Skills." *The Reading Teacher,* 41 (May 1988), 904–910.

Allen, R. V. "The Language-Experience Approach." In *Perspectives on Elementary Reading: Principles and Strategies of Teaching,* edited by Robert Karlin. New York: Harcourt Brace Jovanovich, 1973.

Allen, Virginia. "Selecting Materials for the Reading Instruction of ESL Children." In *Kids Come in All Languages: Reading Instruction for ESL Students,* edited by Karen Spangenberg-Urbschat and Robert Pritchard. Newark, Del.: International Reading Association, 1994, pp. 108–131.

Allington, Richard. "Michael Doesn't Go Down the Hall Anymore." *The Reading Teacher,* 46 (April 1993), 602–604.

Allington, Richard L. "Oral Reading." In *Handbook of Reading Research,* edited by P. David Pearson. New York: Longman, 1984.

Allington, Richard L., and Mary C. Shake. "Remedial Reading: Achieving Curricular Congruence in Classroom and Clinic." *The Reading Teacher,* 39 (March 1986), 648–654.

Altwerger, Bess, Carole Edelsky, and Barbara Flores. "Whole Language: What's New?" *The Reading Teacher,* 41 (November 1987), 144–154.

Altwerger, Bess, and Bonnie Lee Ivener. "Self-Esteem: Access to Literacy in Multicultural and Multilingual Classrooms." In *Kids Come in All Languages: Reading Instruction for ESL Students,* edited by Karen Spangenberg-Urbschat and Robert Pritchard. Newark, Del.: International Reading Association, 1994, pp. 65–81.

Alvermann, Donna E. "The Discussion Web: A Graphic Aid for Learning Across the Curriculum." *The Reading Teacher,* 45 (October 1991), 92–99.

Alvermann, Donna E., and Paula R. Boothby. "Text Differences: Children's Perceptions at the Transition Stage in Reading." *The Reading Teacher,* 36 (December 1982), 298–302.

Anders, Patricia L., and Candace S. Bos. "Semantic Feature Analysis: An Interactive Strategy for Vocabulary Development and Text Comprehension." *Journal of Reading,* 29 (April 1986), 610–616.

Anderson, Gary, Diana Higgins, and Stanley R. Wurster. "Differences in the Free-Reading Books Selected by High, Average, and Low Achievers." *The Reading Teacher,* 39 (December 1985), 326–330.

Anderson, Nancy A. "Teaching Reading as a Life Skill." *The Reading Teacher,* 42 (October 1988), 92.

Anderson, Richard C., Elfrieda H. Hiebert, Judith A. Scott, and Ian A. G. Wilkinson. *Becoming a Nation of Readers: The Report of the Commission on Reading.* Washington, D.C.: National Institute of Education, 1985.

Anderson, Richard C., J. Mason, and L. Shirey. *The Reading Group: An Experimental Investigation of a Labyrinth.* Technical Report No. 271. Urbana–Champaign, IL: Center for the Study of Reading, University of Illinois, 1983.

Anderson, Richard C., and William E. Nagy. "Word Meanings." In *Handbook of Reading Research, Volume II,* edited by Rebecca Barr, Michael L. Kamil, Peter Mosenthal, and P. David Pearson. New York: Longman, 1991, pp. 690–724.

Anderson, Richard C., and P. David Pearson. "A Schema-Theoretic View of Basic Processes in Reading." In *Handbook of Reading Research,* edited by P. David Pearson. New York: Longman, 1984.

Anderson, Thomas H., and Bonnie B. Armbruster. "Studying." In *Handbook of Reading Research,* edited by P. David Pearson. New York: Longman, 1984.

Anderson-Inman, Lynne. "The Reading-Writing Connection: Classroom Applications for the Computer, Part I." *The Computing Teacher,* 14 (November 1986), 23–26.

Anderson-Inman, Lynne, Mark A. Horney, Der-Thang Chen, and Larry Lewin. "Hypertext Literacy: Observations from the Electro Text Project." *Language Arts,* 71 (April 1994), 279–287.

Angeletti, Sara Rappold. "Encouraging Students to Think about What They Read." *The Reading Teacher* 45 (December 1991), 288–296.

Ankney, Paul, and Pat McClurg. "Testing Manzo's Guided Reading Procedure." *The Reading Teacher,* 34 (March 1981), 681–685.

Antal, James. "To Simile or Not to Simile." *The Reading Teacher,* 41 (April 1988), 858–859.

Anthony, Robert J., Terry D. Johnson, Norma I. Mickelson, and Alison Preece. *Evaluating Literacy: A Perspective for Change.* Portsmouth, N.H.: Heinemann, 1991.

Armbruster, Bonnie B. "On Answering Questions." *The Reading Teacher,* 45 (May 1992), 724–725.

Armbruster, Bonnie B. "Readings about Reading to Learn." *The Reading Teacher,* 46 (April 1993), 598–600.

Armbruster, Bonnie B. "Science and Reading." *The Reading Teacher,* 46 (December 1992/January 1993), 346–347.

Armbruster, Bonnie B., T. H. Anderson, and J. Ostertag. "Does Text Structure/Summarization Instruction Facilitate Learning from Expository Text?" *Reading Research Quarterly,* 22 (1987), 331–346.

Armbruster, Bonnie B., Thomas H. Anderson, and Joyce Ostertag. "Teaching Text Structure to Improve Reading and Writing." *The Reading Teacher,* 43 (November 1989), 130–137.

Armbruster, Bonnie B., and William E. Nagy. "Vocabulary in Content Area Lessons." *The Reading Teacher,* 45 (March 1992), 550–551.

Armstrong, Thomas. *Multiple Intelligences in the Classroom.* Alexandria, Va.: Association for Supervision and Curriculum Development, 1994.

Arnold, Richard D. "Teaching Cohesive Ties to Children." *The Reading Teacher,* 42 (November 1988), 106–110.

Aron, Helen, and Ernest Balajthy. "Local Area Networks." *The Reading Teacher,* 42 (March 1989), 532–533.

Ashby-Davis, Claire. "Improving Students' Comprehension of Character Development in Plays." *Reading Horizons,* 26, no. 4 (1986), 256–261.

Ashton-Warner, Sylvia. *Teacher.* New York: Simon & Schuster, 1963.

Atwell, Nancie. *In the Middle: Writing, Reading, and Learning with Adolescents.* Upper Montclair, N.J.: Boynton/Cook, 1987.

Atwell, Nancie. "Writing and Reading from the Inside Out." In *Breaking Ground: Teachers Relate Reading and Writing in the Elementary School,* edited by Jane Hansen, Thomas Newkirk, and Donald Graves. Portsmouth, N.H.: Heinemann, 1985.

Au, Kathryn. *Literacy Instruction in Multicultural Settings.* Fort Worth: Harcourt Brace, 1993.

Au, Kathryn H. "An Overview of New Concepts of Assessment: Impact on Decision Making and Instruction." Paper presented at the International Reading Association Convention, Atlanta, May 6, 1990.

Au, Kathryn H., and Judith A. Scheu. "Guiding Students to Interpret a Novel." *The Reading Teacher,* 43 (November 1989), 104–110.

Augustine, Dianne, Kristin Gruber, and Lynda Hanson. "Cooperation Works!" *Educational Leadership,* 47 (December 1989/January 1990), 4–8.

Avery, Carol S. "First Grade Thinkers Becoming Literate." *Language Arts,* 64 (October 1987), 611–618.

Avery, Carol S. "Learning to Research/Researching to Learn." In *Opening the Door to Classroom Research,* edited by Mary W. Olson. Newark, Del.: International Reading Association, 1990.

Avery, Charles W., and Beth Faris Avery. "Merging Reading and Cooperative Strategies Through Graphic Organizers." *Journal of Reading,* 37 (May 1994), 689–690.

Babbs, Patricia J. "Monitoring Cards Help Improve Comprehension." *The Reading Teacher,* 38 (November 1984), 200–204.

Babbs, Patricia J., and Alden J. Moe. "Metacognition: A Key for Independent Learning from Text." *The Reading Teacher,* 36 (January 1983), 422–426.

Baca, Leonard, and Hermes T. Cervantes. *The Bilingual Special Education Interface,* 2d ed. Columbus, Ohio: Merrill, 1989.

Bader, Lois A. "Instructional Adjustments to Vision Problems." *The Reading Teacher,* 37 (March 1984), 566–569.

Bagford, Jack. "What Ever Happened to Individualized Reading?" *The Reading Teacher,* 39 (November 1985), 190–193.

Bailey, Mildred Hart. "The Utility of Phonic Generalizations in Grades One Through Six." *The Reading Teacher,* 20 (February 1967), 413–418.

Baker, Deborah Tresidder. "What Happened When? Activities for Teaching Sequence Skills." *The Reading Teacher,* 36 (November 1982), 216–218.

Baker, Linda, and Ann L. Brown. "Metacognitive Skills and Reading." In *Handbook of Reading Research,* edited by P. David Pearson. New York: Longman, 1984.

Balajthy, Ernest. *Computers and Reading.* Englewood Cliffs, N.J.: Prentice-Hall, 1989.

Balajthy, Ernest. "Keyboarding and the Language Arts." *The Reading Teacher,* 41 (October 1987), 86–87.

Balajthy, Ernest. *Microcomputers in Reading and Language Arts.* Englewood Cliffs, N.J.: Prentice–Hall, 1986.

Balajthy, Ernest. "Only One Computer in the Classroom?" *The Reading Teacher,* 41 (November 1987), 210–211.

Balajthy, Ernest. "Reinforcement and Drill by Microcomputer." *The Reading Teacher,* 37 (February 1984), 490–494.

Balajthy, Ernest. "What Are Basal Publishers Doing with Computer Based Instruction?" *The Reading Teacher,* 41 (December 1987), 344–345.

Balajthy, Ernest, and Gordon Link. "Desktop Publishing in the Classroom." *The Reading Teacher,* 41 (February 1988), 586–587.

Ball, E. W., and B. A. Blachman. "Does Phoneme Awareness Training in Kindergarten Make a Difference in Early Word Recognition and Developmental Spelling?" *Reading Research Quarterly,* 26, no. 1 (1991), 49–66.

Balsam, M., and C. Hammer. *Success with Reading.* New York: Scholastic, 1985.

Bank Street College of Education, F. E. Smith, and G. Brackett. *The Bank Street Writer for the Macintosh.* Jefferson City, Mo.: Scholastic Software, 1991.

Banks, James A. "Transforming the Mainstream Curriculum." *Educational Leadership,* 51 (May 1994), 4–8.

Barnard, Douglas P., and Robert W. Hetzel. *Selecting a Basal Reader Program: Making the Right Choice.* Lancaster, Pa.: Technomic Publishing, 1988.

Barnitz, John G. "Developing Sentence Comprehension in Reading." *Language Arts,* 56 (November/December 1979), 902–908, 958.

Baroni, Dick. "Have Primary Children Draw to Expand Vocabulary." *The Reading Teacher,* 40 (April 1987), 819–820.

Barr, Rebecca. "Beginning Reading Instruction." In *Handbook of Reading Research,* edited by P. David Pearson. New York: Longman, 1984.

Barr, Rebecca, and Robert Dreeben. "Grouping Students for Reading Instruction." In *Handbook of Reading Research,* *Vol. II,* edited by Rebecca Barr, Michael L. Kamil, Peter B. Mosenthal, and P. David Pearson. White Plains, N.Y.: Longman, 1991, pp. 885–910.

Barr, Rebecca, Marilyn Sadow, and Camille Blachowicz. *Reading Diagnosis for Teachers,* 2nd ed. New York: Longman, 1990.

Barrow, Lloyd H., Janice V. Kristo, and Barbara Andrew. "Building Bridges Between Science and Reading." *The Reading Teacher,* 38 (November 1984), 188–192.

Bash, Barbara. *Tree of Life: The World of the African Baobab.* Boston: Little, Brown, 1989.

Baskwill, Jane, and Paulette Whitman. *Evaluation: Whole Language, Whole Child.* Toronto: Scholastic, 1988.

Batzle, Janine. *Portfolio Assessment and Evaluation.* Cypress, Calif.: Creative Teaching Press, 1992.

Baumann, James. "Organizing and Managing a Whole Language Classroom." *Reading Research and Instruction,* 31 (Spring 1992), 3–14.

Baumann, James F., and P. Z. Ballard. "A Two Step Model for Promoting Independence in Comprehension." *Journal of Reading,* 30 (1987), 608–612.

Baumann, James F., Leah A. Jones, and Nancy Seifert-Kessell. "Using Think-Alouds to Enhance Children's Comprehension Monitoring Abilities." *The Reading Teacher,* 47 (November 1993), 184–193.

Baumann, James F., and Maribeth C. Schmitt. "The What, Why, How, and When of Comprehension Instruction." *The Reading Teacher,* 39 (March 1986), 640–646.

Baumann, James F., and Jennifer A. Stevenson. "Using Scores from Standardized Reading Achievement Tests." *The Reading Teacher,* 35 (February 1982), 528–533.

Beach, R., and S. Hynds. "Research on Response to Literature." In *Handbook of Reading Research, Vol. II,* edited by R. Barr, M.L. Kamil, P. Mosenthal, and P.D. Pearson. New York: Longman, 1991, pp. 453–489.

Bean, Rita, M., and R. Tony Eichelberger. "Changing the Role of Reading Specialists: From Pull-Out to In-Class Programs." *The Reading Teacher,* 38 (March 1985), 648–653.

Beattie, John. "Characteristics of Students with Disabilities and How Teachers Can Help." In *Teaching Reading to High-Risk Learners,* edited by Karen Wood and Bob Algozzine. Boston: Allyn & Bacon, 1994, pp. 99–121.

Beaty, Janice J. *Picture Book Storytelling.* Fort Worth: Harcourt Brace, 1994.

Beck, I. L., C. A. Perfetti, and M. G. McKeown. "Effects of Long-Term Vocabulary Instruction on Lexical Access and Reading Comprehension." *Journal of Educational Psychology,* 74 (1982), 506–521.

Beck, Isabel L. "Reading and Reasoning." *The Reading Teacher,* 42 (May 1989), 676–682.

Beck, Isabel L., and Margaret G. McKeown. "Learning Words Well—A Program to Enhance Vocabulary and Comprehension." *The Reading Teacher,* 36 (March 1983), 622–625.

Beck, Isabel L., and Margaret G. McKeown. "Research Directions: Social Studies Texts Are Hard to Understand: Mediating Some of the Difficulties." *Language Arts,* 68 (October 1991), 482–490.

Beck, Isabel, and Margaret McKeown. "Conditions of Vocabulary Acquisition." In *Handbook of Reading Research, Volume II,* edited by Rebecca Barr, Michael L. Kamil, Peter Mosenthal, and P. David Pearson. New York: Longman, 1991, pp. 789–814.

Beck, Judith S. "A Problem Solving Framework for Managing Poor Readers in Classrooms." *The Reading Teacher,* 41 (April 1988), 774–779.

Becker, Henry Jay. "Our National Report Card: Preliminary Results from the New Johns Hopkins Survey." *Classroom Computer Learning,* 6 (January 1986), 30–33.

Behrmann, Michael M., ed. *Handbook of Microcomputers in Special Education.* San Diego: College-Hill Press, 1984.

Bell, Barbara. "Literature Response Groups." Presentation at Richard C. Owen Workshop "Whole Language in the Classroom." Oak Ridge, Tennessee, June 12, 1990.

Bell, Kathy. "Books for Telling Time." *The Reading Teacher,* 42 (November 1988), 179.

Bell, Kathy. "Books to Supplement a Unit on Measurement." *The Reading Teacher,* 42 (December 1988), 256.

Bell, Kathy. "Using Literature to Teach Addition and Subtraction." *The Reading Teacher,* 42 (October 1988), 90.

Bellows, Barbara Plotkin. "Running Shoes Are to Jogging as Analogies Are to Creative/Critical Thinking." *Journal of Reading,* 23 (March 1980), 507–511.

Bennett, Rand Elliot. "Cautions for the Use of Informal Measures in the Educational Assessment of Exceptional Children." *Journal of Learning Disabilities,* 15 (June/July 1982), 337–339.

Berglund, Roberta L., and Jerry L. Johns. "A Primer on Uninterrupted Sustained Silent Reading." *The Reading Teacher,* 36 (February 1983), 534–539.

Bergquist, Leonard. "Rapid Silent Reading: Techniques for Improving Rate in Intermediate Grades." *The Reading Teacher,* 38 (October 1984), 50–53.

Berkowitz, S. J. "Effects of Instruction in Text Organization on Sixth-Grade Students' Memory for Expository Reading." *Reading Research Quarterly,* 18 (1986), 161–178.

Bernhardt, Bill. "Reading and Writing Between the Lines: An Interactive Approach Using Computers." *Journal of Reading,* 37 (March 1994), 458–463.

Beutler, Suzanne A. "Using Writing to Learn about Astronomy." *The Reading Teacher,* 41 (January 1988), 412–417.

Bidwell, Sandra M. "Ideas for Using Drama to Enhance Reading Instruction." *The Reading Teacher,* 45 (April 1992), 653–654.

Biehler, Robert F., and Jack Snowman. *Psychology Applied to Teaching,* 5th ed. Boston: Houghton Mifflin, 1986.

Bierne-Smith, Mary, James Patton, and Richard Ittenbach. *Mental Retardation,* 4th ed. New York: Merrill, 1994.

Bird, Lois. "Joyful Literacy at Fair Oaks School." In *The Whole Language Catalog,* edited by Kenneth Goodman, Lois Bird, and Yetta Goodman. Santa Rosa, Calif.: American School Publishers, 1991.

Bird, Lois. "Resource: Periodical." In *The Whole Language Catalog,* edited by Kenneth Goodman, Lois Bird, and Yetta Goodman. Santa Rosa, Calif.: American School Publishers, 1991.

Blachowicz, Camille L. Z. "C(2)QU: Modeling Context Use in the Classroom." *The Reading Teacher,* 47 (November 1993), 268–269.

Blachowicz, Camille L. Z. "Making Connections: Alternatives to the Vocabulary Notebook." *Journal of Reading,* 29 (April 1986), 643–649.

Blachowicz, Camille L. Z. "Showing Teachers How to Develop Students' Predictive Reading." *The Reading Teacher,* 36 (March 1983), 680–683.

Blachowicz, Camille L. Z. "Vocabulary Development and Reading: From Research to Instruction." *The Reading Teacher,* 38 (May 1985), 876–881.

Blachowicz, Camille L. Z., and John J. Lee. "Vocabulary Development in the Whole Literacy Classroom." *The Reading Teacher,* 45 (November 1991), 188–195.

Blachowicz, Camille L. Z., and Barbara Zabroske. "Context Instruction: A Metacognitive Approach for At-Risk Readers." *Journal of Reading,* 33 (April 1990), 504–508.

Blanchard, Jay S. "Computer-Assisted Instruction in Today's Reading Classrooms." *Journal of Reading,* 23 (February 1980), 430–434.

Blanchard, Jay S., and Claire J. Rottenberg. "Hypertext and Hypermedia: Discovering and Creating Meaningful Learning Environments." *The Reading Teacher,* 43 (May 1990), 656–661.

Blanton, William E., Gary B. Moorman, and Karen D. Wood. "A Model of Direct Instruction Applied to the Basal Skills Lesson." *The Reading Teacher,* 40 (December 1986), 299–304.

Blanton, William E., Karen D. Wood, and Gary B. Moorman. "The Role of Purpose in Reading Instruction." *The Reading Teacher,* 43 (March 1990), 486–493.

Blass, Rosanne J., Nancy Allan Jurenka, and Eleanor G. Zirzow. "Showing Children the Communicative Nature of Reading." *The Reading Teacher,* 34 (May 1981), 926–931.

Bloomfield, Leonard, and Clarence Barnhart. *Let's Read: A Linguistic Approach.* Detroit: Wayne State University Press, 1961.

Bode, Barbara A. "Dialogue Journal Writing." *The Reading Teacher,* 42 (April 1989), 568–571.

Bonds, Charles W., Lella Gant Bonds, and Walter Peach. "Metacognition: Developing Independence in Learning." *The Clearing House,* 66 (September/October 1992), 56–59.

Boodt, Gloria M. "Critical Listeners Become Critical Readers in Remedial Reading Class." *The Reading Teacher,* 37 (January 1984), 390–394.

Booth, David. *Classroom Voices*. Toronto: Harcourt Brace, 1994.

Bork, Alfred. "Computers in Education Today—and Some Possible Futures." *Phi Delta Kappan,* 66 (December 1984), 239–243.

Borkowski, J.G., and B.E. Kurtz. "Metacognition and Executive Control." *Cognition in Special Children: Comparative Approaches to Retardation, Learning Disabilities, and Giftedness,* edited by J.G. Borkowski and J.D. Day. Norwood, New Jersey: Ablex, 1987, 123–152.

Bormuth, J. R. "The Cloze Readability Procedure." In *Readability in 1968,* edited by J. R. Bormuth. Champaign, Ill.: National Council of Teachers of English, 1968.

Bouffler, Chrystine, and Bruce Knight. "Assessment and Evaluation in Reading." *PEN 81.* New South Wales, Australia: Primary English Teaching Association, 1991.

Boyd, Reta. "The Message Board." In *Whole Language: Theory in Use,* edited by Judith Newman. Portsmouth, N.H.: Heineman, 1985.

Boyle, Owen F., and Suzanne F. Peregoy. "Literacy Scaffolds: Strategies for First- and Second-Language Readers and Writers." *The Reading Teacher,* 44 (November 1990), 194–200.

Brackett, G. *Super Story Tree.* New York: Scholastic, 1989.

Bradley, L., and P. Bryant. "Categorizing Sounds and Learning to Read—A Causal Connection." *Nature,* 301 (1983), 419–421.

Bransford, John D., and Barry S. Stein. *The IDEAL Problem Solver.* New York: W. H. Freeman, 1984.

Braselton, Stephania, and Barbara C. Decker. "Using Graphic Organizers to Improve the Reading of Mathematics." *The Reading Teacher,* 48 (November 1994), 276–281.

Braun, C., B. J. Rennie, and G. D. Labercane. "A Conference Approach to the Development of Metacognitive Strategies." In *Solving Problems in Literacy: Learners, Teachers, and Researchers,* Thirty-Fifth Yearbook of the National Reading Conference, edited by J. A. Niles and R. V. Lalik. Rochester, N.Y.: National Reading Conference, 1986.

Breen, Leonard. "Connotations." *Journal of Reading,* 32 (February 1989), 461.

Brennan, A. D., and W. P. Dunlap. "What Are Prime Factors of Reading Mathematics?" *Reading Improvement,* 22 (1985), 152–159.

Bridge, Connie A. "Focusing on Meaning in Beginning Reading Instruction." In *Counterpoint and Beyond: A Response to Becoming a Nation of Readers,* edited by Jane L. Davidson. Urbana, Ill.: National Council of Teachers of English, 1988.

Bristow, Page Simpson. "Are Poor Readers Passive Readers? Some Evidence, Possible Explanations, and Potential Solutions." *The Reading Teacher,* 39 (December 1985), 318–325.

Bromley, Karen D. "Buddy Journals Make the Reading-Writing Connection." *The Reading Teacher,* 43 (November 1989), 122–129.

Bromley, Karen D'Angelo. "Teaching Idioms." *The Reading Teacher,* 38 (December 1984), 272–276.

Bromley, Karen D. *Webbing with Literature.* Boston: Allyn & Bacon, 1991.

Brown, A. L., and J. D. Day. "Macrorules for Summarizing Texts: The Development of Expertise." *Journal of Verbal Learning and Verbal Behavior,* 22, no. 1 (1983), 1–14.

Brown, A. L., J. D. Day, and R. Jones. "The Development of Plans for Summarizing Texts." *Child Development,* 54 (1983), 968–979.

Brown, Ann L., Annemarie Palincsar, and Bonnie Armbruster. "Instructing Comprehension." In *Theoretical Models and Processes,* 4th ed., edited by Robert Ruddell, Martha Rapp Ruddell, and Harry Singer. Newark, Del.: International Reading Association, 1994, pp. 757–787.

Brown, Carol S., and Susan L. Lytle. "Merging Assessment and Instruction: Protocols in the Classroom." In *Reexamining Reading Diagnosis: New Trends and Procedures,* edited by Susan Mandel Glazer, Lyndon W. Searfoss, and Lance M. Gentile. Newark, Del.: International Reading Association, 1988.

Brozo, William G., and Carl M. Tomlinson. "Literature: The Key to Lively Content Courses." *The Reading Teacher,* 40 (December 1986), 288–293.

Bruck, Maggie, and Rebecca Treiman. "Learning to Pronounce Words: The Limitations of Analogies." *Reading Research Quarterly,* 27, no. 4 (1992), 374–388.

Bufe, Bruce N. "Word Sort to Improve Comprehension." *The Reading Teacher,* 37 (November 1983), 209–210.

Bulletin Board Maker—Happy Habitats: The Pond. Fairfield, Conn.: Pelican, 1991.

Burchby, Marcia. "Literature and Whole Language." *The New Advocate,* 1 (Spring 1988), 114–123.

Burmeister, Lou E. *Foundations and Strategies for Teaching Children to Read.* Reading, Mass.: Addison-Wesley, 1983.

Burmeister, Lou E. "Usefulness of Phonic Generalizations." *The Reading Teacher,* 21 (January 1968): 349–356, 360.

Burns, Paul C., and Betty L. Broman. *The Language Arts in Childhood Education,* 5th ed. Boston: Houghton Mifflin, 1983, 1987.

Butler, Andrea, and Jan Turbill. *Towards a Reading-Writing Classroom.* Portsmouth, N.H.: Heinemann, 1987.

Butler, Dorothy, and Marie Clay. *Reading Begins at Home.* Auckland, New Zealand: Heinemann Educational Books, 1979.

Butler, Syd, and Barbara Cox. "DISKovery: Writing with a Computer in Grade One: A Study in Collaboration." *Language Arts,* 69 (December 1992), 633–640.

Cairney, T. *Teaching Reading Comprehension.* Milton Keynes, U.K.: Open University Press, 1990.

Cairney, Trevor. "Character Mug Sheets." *The Reading Teacher,* 41 (December 1987), 375–377.

Caissy, Gail. *Microcomputers and the Classroom Teacher.* Bloomington, Ind.: Phi Delta Kappa, 1987.

Caldwell, JoAnne. "A New Look at the Old Informal Reading Inventory." *The Reading Teacher,* 39 (November 1985), 168–173.

Calfee, Robert C. "The School as a Context for Assessment of Literacy." *The Reading Teacher,* 40 (April 1987), 738–743.

Calhoun, Emily. "Action Research: Three Approaches." *Educational Leadership,* 51 (October 1993), 62–65.

California State Department of Education. *English–Language Arts Framework.* Sacramento, Calif.: California State Department of Education, 1987.

Calkins, Lucy M. *Lessons from a Child.* Portsmouth, N.H.: Heinemann, 1983.

Cambourne, Brian. "Language, Learning and Literacy." In *Towards a Reading-Writing Classroom,* edited by Andrea Butler and Jan Turbill. Portsmouth, N.H.: Heinemann Educational Books, 1984.

Carlsen, Joanne M. "Between the Deaf Child and Reading: The Language Connection." *The Reading Teacher,* 38 (January 1985), 424–426.

Carney, J. J., D. Anderson, C. Blackburn, and D. Blessing. "Preteaching Vocabulary and the Comprehension of Social Studies Materials by Elementary School Children." *Social Education,* 48 (1984), 71–75.

Carnine, D., and D. Kinder. "Teaching Low-Performing Students to Apply Generative and Schema Strategies to Narrative and Expository Material." *Remedial and Special Education,* 6 (1985), 20–30.

Carnine, Douglas W. "Phonics Versus Look-Say: Transfer to New Words." *The Reading Teacher,* 30 (March 1977), 636–640.

Carr, Eileen. "The Vocabulary Overview Guide: A Metacognitive Strategy to Improve Vocabulary Comprehension and Retention." *Journal of Reading,* 21 (May 1985), 684–689.

Carr, Eileen, and Karen K. Wixson. "Guidelines for Evaluating Vocabulary Instruction." *Journal of Reading,* 29 (April 1986), 588–595.

Carr, Joan A. "Verbalizing Character Roles in Novels." *Journal of Reading,* 35 (October 1991), 145–146.

Carr, Kathryn S. "The Importance of Inference Skills in the Primary Grades." *The Reading Teacher,* 36 (February 1983), 518–522.

Carroll, John B., Peter Davies, and Barry Richman. *The American Heritage Word Frequency Book.* Boston: Houghton Mifflin, 1971.

Case, Elizabeth J., and Marty Christopher. *Pilot Study of the Writing to Read System.* Albuquerque: Albuquerque Public Schools, November 1989.

Cases in Literacy. Newark, Del.: International Reading Association, 1989.

Casteel, Carolyn P., and Bess A. Isom. "Reciprocal Processes in Science and Literacy Learning." *The Reading Teacher,* 47 (April 1994), 538–545.

Catterson, Jane. "Discourse Forms in Content Texts." *Journal of Reading,* 33 (April 1990), 556–558.

"CEC Policy on Inclusive Schools and Community Settings." Reston, Va.: The Council for Exceptional Children, 1993.

Ceprano, Maria A. "A Review of Selected Research on Methods of Teaching Sight Words." *The Reading Teacher,* 35 (December 1981), 314–322.

Chaney, Jeanne H. "Alphabet Books: Resources for Learning." *The Reading Teacher,* 47 (October 1993), 96–104.

"Chapter I Gains Questioned." *AAP Reading Initiative,* 4 (Winter 1994), 1–2.

Cheng, Pui-wan. "Metacognition and Giftedness: The State of the Relationship." *Gifted Child Quarterly,* 37 (Summer 1993), 105–112.

Chew, Charles. "Instruction Can Link Reading and Writing." In *Breaking Ground: Teachers Relate Reading and Writing in the Elementary School,* edited by Jane Hansen, Thomas Newkirk, and Donald Graves. Portsmouth, N.H.: Heinemann, 1985.

Ching, Doris C. *Reading and the Bilingual Child.* Newark, Del.: International Reading Association, 1983.

Chittenden, Edward, and Rosalea Courtney. "Assessment of Young Children's Reading: Documentation as an Alternative to Testing." In *Emerging Literacy: Young Children Learn to Read and Write,* edited by Dorothy Strickland and Lesley Morrow. Newark, Del.: International Reading Association, 1989.

Church, Susan M. "Is Whole Language Warm and Fuzzy?" *The Reading Teacher,* 47 (February 1994), 362–370.

Clark, L. K. "Invented Versus Traditional Spelling in First Graders' Writings: Effects on Learning to Spell and Read." *Research in the Teaching of English,* 22 (1988), 281–309.

Clay, Marie. "Concepts about Print in English and Other Languages." *The Reading Teacher,* 42 (January 1989), 268–276.

Clay, Marie. *The Early Detection of Reading Difficulties.* Auckland, New Zealand: Heinemann, 1979.

Clay, Marie. "Involving Teachers in Classroom Research." In *Teachers and Research,* edited by Gay Su Pinnell and Myna L. Matlin. Newark, Del.: International Reading Association, 1989.

Clay, Marie. *Reading: The Patterning of Complex Behavior,* 2d ed. Auckland, New Zealand: Heinemann, 1979.

Clymer, Theodore. "The Utility of Phonics Generalizations in the Primary Grades." *The Reading Teacher,* 16 (January 1963), 252–258.

Coate, Sheri, and Marrietta Castle. "Integrating LEA and Invented Spelling in Kindergarten." *The Reading Teacher,* 42 (March 1989), 516–519.

Coburn, Peter, et al. *Practical Guide to Computers in Education.* Reading, Mass.: Addison-Wesley, 1982.

Cochran-Smith, M., J. Kahn, and C. L. Paris. "When Word Processors Come into the Classroom." In *Writing* *with Computers in the Early Grades,* edited by J. L. Hoot and S. B. Silvern. New York: Teachers College Press, 1988.

Coelho, Elizabeth. *Learning Together in the Multicultural Classroom.* Markham, Ontario: Pippin, 1994.

Cohen, Ruth. "Self-Generated Questions as an Aid to Reading Comprehension." *The Reading Teacher,* 36 (April 1983), 770–775.

Collier, Calhoun C., and Lois A. Redmond. "Are You Teaching Kids to Read Mathematics?" *The Reading Teacher,* 27 (May 1974), 804–808.

Collins, Cathy. "Is the Cart Before the Horse? Effects of Preschool Reading Instruction on 4 Year Olds." *The Reading Teacher,* 40 (December 1986), 332–339.

Colt, Jacalyn M. "Support for New Teachers in Literature-Based Reading Programs." *Journal of Reading,* 34 (September 1990), 64–65.

Combs, Martha, and John D. Beach. "Stories and Storytelling: Personalizing the Social Studies." *The Reading Teacher,* 47 (March 1994), 464–471.

Commeyras, Michelle. "Promoting Critical Thinking through Dialogical-Thinking Reading Lessons." *The Reading Teacher,* 46 (March 1993), 486–493.

Commeyras, Michelle. "Using Literature to Teach Critical Thinking." *Journal of Reading,* 32 (May 1989), 703–707.

Committee on Geographic Education. *Guidelines for Geographic Education: Elementary and Secondary Schools.* Washington, D.C.: National Council for Geographic Education and the Association of American Geographers, 1983.

Conrad, Lori L. "Charting Effect and Cause in Informational Books." *The Reading Teacher,* 42 (February 1989), 451–452.

Cooper, Charles R., and Anthony R. Petrosky. "A Psycholinguistic View of the Fluent Reading Process." *Journal of Reading,* 20 (December 1976), 184–207.

Cooper, J. David. *Improving Reading Comprehension.* Boston: Houghton Mifflin, 1986.

Cooter, Robert B., Jr. *The Teacher's Guide to Reading Tests.* Scottsdale, Ariz.: Gorsuch Scarisbrick, 1990.

Cooter, Robert B., Jr., and Robert Griffith. "Thematic Units for Middle School: An Honorable Seduction." *Journal of Reading,* 32 (May 1989), 676–681.

Cordts, Anna D. *Phonics for the Reading Teacher.* New York: Holt, Rinehart and Winston, 1965.

Cowin, Gina. "Implementing the Writing Process with Sixth Graders, *Jumanji*: Literature Unit." *The Reading Teacher,* 40 (November 1986), 156–161.

Cox, Susan, and Lee Galda. "Multicultural Literature: Mirrors and Windows on a Global Community." *The Reading Teacher,* 43 (April 1990), 582–589.

Crafton, Linda K. "Comprehension Before, During, and After Reading." *The Reading Teacher,* 36 (December 1982), 293–297.

Criscuolo, Nicholas P. "Creative Vocabulary Building." *Journal of Reading,* 24 (December 1980), 260–261.

Crist, Barbara. "Tim's Time: Vocabulary Activities from Names." *The Reading Teacher,* 34 (December 1980), 309–312.

Crook, Patricia R., and Barbara A. Lehman. "Themes for Two Voices: Children's Fiction and Nonfiction as Whole Literature." *Language Arts,* 68 (January 1991), 34–41.

Cudd, Evelyn T., and Leslie L. Roberts. "A Scaffolding Technique to Develop Sentence Sense and Vocabulary." *The Reading Teacher,* 47 (December 1993/January 1994), 346–349.

Cudd, Evelyn T., and Leslie Roberts. "Using Writing to Enhance Content Area Learning in the Primary Grades." *The Reading Teacher,* 42 (February 1989), 392–404.

Cullinan, Bernice E. *Children's Literature in the Reading Program.* Newark, Del.: International Reading Association, 1987.

Cullinan, Bernice E. "Whole Language and Children's Literature." *Language Arts,* 69 (October 1992), 426–430.

Cullinan, Bernice E., and Lee Galda. *Literature and the Child,* 3d ed. Fort Worth: Harcourt Brace, 1994.

Cummins, Jim. "The Acquisition of English as a Second Language." In *Kids Come in All Languages: Reading Instruction for ESL Students.* Newark, Del.: International Reading Association, 1994, pp. 36–62.

Cunningham, James W., and Hunter Ballew. "Solving Word Problem Solving." *The Reading Teacher,* 36 (April 1983), 836–839.

Cunningham, James W., and Lisa K. Wall. "Teaching Good Readers to Comprehend Better." *Journal of Reading,* 37 (March 1994), 480–486.

Cunningham, Pat. "Improving Listening and Reading Comprehension." *The Reading Teacher,* 35 (January 1982a), 486–488.

Cunningham, Pat. "Knowledge for More Comprehension." *The Reading Teacher,* 36 (October 1982b), 98–101.

Cunningham, Patricia M. "A Compare/Contrast Theory of Mediated Word Identification." *The Reading Teacher,* 32 (April 1979), 774–778.

Cunningham, Patricia M. "Decoding Polysyllabic Words: An Alternative Strategy." *The Reading Teacher,* 21 (April 1978), 608–614.

Cunningham, Patricia M. *Phonics They Use: Words for Reading and Writing.* New York: HarperCollins, 1991.

Cunningham, Patricia M., and James W. Cunningham. "Content Area Reading-Writing Lessons." *The Reading Teacher,* 40 (February 1987), 506–512.

Cunningham, Patricia M., and James W. Cunningham. "Making Words: Enhancing the Invented Spelling-Decoding Connection." *The Reading Teacher,* 46 (October 1992), 106–115.

Cunningham, Patricia, and Richard Allington. *Classrooms that Work: They Can All Read and Write.* New York: HarperCollins, 1994.

Curtis, Mary E., and Linn McCart. "Fun Ways to Promote Poor Readers' Word Recognition." *Journal of Reading,* 35 (February 1992), 398–399.

Dailey, Kathleen, and Kimberly Owen. "Dramatic Play and Literacy Development." Presentation at International Reading Association Convention, Toronto, Canada, May, 1994.

Daisey, Peggy. "Three Ways to Promote the Values and Uses of Literacy at Any Age." *Journal of Reading,* 36 (March 1993), 436–440.

Dale, Edgar, and Jeanne S. Chall. "A Formula for Predicting Readability." *Educational Research Bulletin,* 27 (January 21, 1948), 11–20, 28; (February 18, 1948), 37–54.

Daneman, Meredyth. "Individual Differences in Reading Skills." In *Handbook of Reading Research, Vol. II,* edited by R. Barr, M. L. Kamil, P. Mosenthal, and P. D. Pearson. New York: Longman, 1991, pp. 512–538.

Daniel, Twyla. "Extending Literacy with School Libraries." *Language Arts,* 67 (November 1990), 746–749.

Danielson, Kathy E. *Dialogue Journals: Writing as Conversation.* Bloomington, Ind.: Phi Delta Kappa. 1988.

Danielson, Kathy Everts. "Picture Books to Use with Older Students." *Journal of Reading,* 35 (May 1992), 652–654.

Davidson & Associates. *Kid Works 2.* Torrance, Calif.: Davidson & Associates.

Davis, Gary, and Sylvia Rimm. *Education of the Gifted and Talented,* 2d ed. Englewood Cliffs, N.J.: Prentice-Hall, 1994.

Davis, Susan J. "Synonym Rally: A Vocabulary Concept Game." *Journal of Reading,* 33 (February 1990), 380.

Davis, Zephaniah T., and Michael D. McPherson. "Story Map Instruction: A Road Map for Reading Comprehension." *The Reading Teacher,* 43 (December 1989), 232–240.

Deaton, Cheryl D. "Idioms As a Means of Communication: Writing in the Middle Grades." *The Reading Teacher,* 45 (February 1992), 473.

DeFina, Allan A. *Portfolio Assessment.* New York: Scholastic, 1992.

DeGroff, Linda. "Computers in the Whole Language Classroom." Paper presented at the Florida Instructional Computing Conference, Orlando, Florida, January 1989.

DeGroff, Linda. "Informational Books: Topics and Structures." *The Reading Teacher,* 43 (March 1990), 496–501.

DeGroff, Linda. "Is There a Place for Computers in Whole Language Classrooms?" *The Reading Teacher,* 43 (April 1990), 568–572.

Deiner, Penny. *Resources for Teaching Children with Diverse Abilities.* Fort Worth: Harcourt Brace, 1993.

De la Luz Reyes, Maria. "'How Come Some Times You Don't Write Back?': Characteristics of Bilingual Students' Journal Writing." Paper presented at the annual conference of the International Reading Association, Atlanta, May 10, 1990.

DeSerres, Barbara. "Putting Vocabulary in Context." *The Reading Teacher,* 43 (April 1990), 612–613.

Dever, Christine T. "Press Conference: A Strategy for Integrating Reading with Writing." *The Reading Teacher,* 46 (September 1992), 72–73.

Dickerson, Dolores Pawley. "A Study of Use of Games to Reinforce Sight Vocabulary." *The Reading Teacher,* 36 (October 1982), 46–49.

Dickinson, David K. "Oral Language, Literacy Skills, and Response to Literature." In *The Dynamics of Language Learning,* edited by James R. Squire. Urbana, Ill.: ERIC Clearinghouse on Reading and Communication Skills, 1987.

D'Ignazio, Fred. "DISKovery: The Starship Enterprise: New Opportunities for Learning in the 1990's." *Language Arts,* 68 (March 1991), 248–252.

Dillner, Martha. "Using Hypermedia To Enhance Content Area Instruction." *Journal of Reading,* 37 (December 1993/January 1994), 260–270.

Dionisio, Marie. "Responding to Literary Elements through Mini-lessons and Dialogue Journals." *English Journal,* 80 (January 1991), 40–44.

Dionisio, Marie. "Write? Isn't This Reading Class?" *The Reading Teacher,* 36 (April 1983), 746–750.

Doiron, Ray. "Using Nonfiction in a Read-Aloud Program: Letting the Facts Speak for Themselves." *The Reading Teacher,* 47 (May 1994), 616–624.

Dougherty, Wilma Holden, and Rosalind E. Engel. "An 80s Look for Sex Equality in Caldecott Winners and Honor Books." *The Reading Teacher,* 40 (January 1987), 394–398.

Dowd, Cornelia A., and Richard Sinatra. "Computer Programs and the Learning of Text Structure." *Journal of Reading,* 34 (October 1990), 104–112.

Downing, John. "How Children Think about Reading." In *Psychological Factors in the Teaching of Reading,* compiled by Eldon E. Ekwall. Columbus, Ohio: Charles E. Merrill, 1973.

Downing, John. "Reading—Skill or Skills?" *The Reading Teacher,* 35 (February 1982), 534–537.

Doyle, Denis P. "The 'Unsacred' Texts: Market Forces that Work Too Well." *American Educator,* 8 (Summer 1984), 8–13.

Dreher, Joyce. "Character Contrast." *The Reading Teacher,* 42 (March 1989), 551–552.

Dreher, Mariam Jean, and Harry Singer. "Story Grammar Instruction Unnecessary for Intermediate Grade Students." *The Reading Teacher,* 34 (December 1980), 261–268.

Dreher, Miriam J., and Harry Singer. "The Teacher's Role in Students' Success." *The Reading Teacher,* 42 (April 1989), 612–617.

Dreyer, Lois G., Karen R. Futtersak, and Ann E. Boehm. "Sight Words for the Computer Age: An Essential Word List." *The Reading Teacher,* 39 (October 1985), 12–15.

Duchein, M. A., and D. L. Mealey. "Remembrance of Books Past . . . Long Past: Glimpses into Aliteracy." *Reading Research and Instruction,* 33, no. 1 (1993), 12–28.

Dudley-Marling, Curtis. "Microcomputers, Reading, and Writing: Alternatives to Drill and Practice." *The Reading Teacher,* 38 (January 1985), 388–391.

Duffelmeyer, Frederick A. "Effective Anticipation Guide Statements for Learning from Expository Prose." *Journal of Reading,* 37 (March 1994), 452–457.

Duffelmeyer, Frederick A. "The Influence of Experience-Based Vocabulary Instruction on Learning Word Meanings." *Journal of Reading,* 24 (October 1980), 35–40.

Duffelmeyer, Frederick A. "Introducing Words in Context." *The Reading Teacher,* 35 (March 1982), 724–725.

Duffelmeyer, Frederick A. "Teaching Word Meaning from an Experience Base." *The Reading Teacher,* 39 (October 1985), 6–9.

Duffelmeyer, Frederick A. "Word Maps and Student Involvement." *The Reading Teacher,* 41 (May 1988), 968–969.

Duffelmeyer, Frederick A., and Dale D. Baum. "The Extended Anticipation Guide Revisited." *Journal of Reading,* 35 (May 1992), 654–656.

Duffelmeyer, Frederick A., and Barbara Blakely Duffelmeyer. "Developing Vocabulary Through Dramatization." *Journal of Reading,* 23 (November 1979), 141–143.

Duffelmeyer, Frederick A., and Barbara Blakely Duffelmeyer. "Topic and Main Idea: Clearing Up the Confusion." *The Reading Teacher,* 45 (November 1991), 252–254.

Duffy, Gerald G. *Reading in the Middle School,* 2d ed. Newark, Del.: International Reading Association, 1990.

Duffy, Gerald G., and Laura R. Roehler. *Improving Classroom Reading Instruction.* New York: Random House, 1986.

Duffy, Gerald G., and Laura R. Roehler. "Improving Reading Instruction Through the Use of Responsive Elaboration." *The Reading Teacher,* 40 (February 1987), 514–520.

Duffy, Gerald G., Laura R. Roehler, and Beth Ann Herrmann. "Modeling Mental Processes Helps Poor Readers Become Strategic Readers." *The Reading Teacher,* 41 (April 1988), 762–767.

Duncan, Patricia H. "I Liked the Book Better: Comparing Film and Text to Build Critical Comprehension." *The Reading Teacher,* 46 (May 1993), 720–725.

Durkin, Dolores. "Reading Comprehension Instruction in Five Basal Reader Series." *Reading Research Quarterly,* 16 (1981a), 515–544.

Durkin, Dolores. "What Classroom Observations Reveal about Reading Comprehension Instruction." *Reading Research Quarterly,* 14 (1978/1979), 481–533.

Durkin, Dolores. "What Is the Value of the New Interest in Reading Comprehension?" *Language Arts,* 58 (January 1981b), 23–43.

Dwyer, Edward J. "Comprehending Figurative Language." *The Reading Teacher,* 45 (December 1991), 328–329.

Dwyer, Edward J. "Solving Verbal Analogies." *Journal of Reading,* 32 (October 1988), 73–75.

Dymock, Susan. "Reading But Not Understanding." *Journal of Reading,* 37 (October 1993), 86–91.

Eads, Maryann. "What to Do When They Don't Understand What They Read—Research-Based Strategies for Teaching Reading Comprehension." *The Reading Teacher,* 34 (February 1981), 565–571.

Ebel, Carolyn Williams. "An Update: Teaching Reading to Students of English as a Second Language." *The Reading Teacher,* 33 (January 1980), 403–407.

Edwards, Anthony T., and R. Allan Dermott. "A New Way with Vocabulary." *Journal of Reading,* 32 (March 1989), 559–561.

Egan, Margaret. "Capitalizing on the Reader's Strengths: An Activity Using Schema." *Journal of Reading,* 37 (May 1994), 636–640.

Egawa, Kathy. "Harnessing the Power of Language: First Graders' Literature Engagement with *Owl Moon.*" *Language Arts,* 67 (October 1990), 582–588.

Ehly, Stewart, and Stephen C. Larsen. "Peer Tutoring in the Regular Classroom." In *Readings on Reading Instruction,* 3d ed., edited by Albert J. Harris and Edward R. Sipay. New York: Longman, 1984.

Ehri, L. C. "Development of the Ability to Read Words." In *Handbook of Reading Research, Vol. II,* edited by R. Barr, M. L. Kamil, P. Mosenthal, and P. D. Pearson. New York: Longman, 1991, pp. 383–417.

Ehri, L. C., and C. Robbins. "Beginners Need Some Decoding Skill to Read Words by Analogy." *Reading Research Quarterly,* 27, no. 1 (1992), 13–26.

Ehri, L. C., and L. S. Wilce. "Does Learning to Spell Help Beginners Learn to Read Words?" *Reading Research Quarterly,* 22 (1987), 47–65.

Eisele, Beverly. *Lesson Plan Book for the Whole Language and Literature-Based Curriculum.* Cypress, Calif.: Creative Teaching Press, 1991.

Eisele, Beverly. *Managing the Whole Language Classroom.* Cypress, Calif.: Creative Teaching Press, 1991.

Ellis, DiAnn Waskul, and Fannie Wiley Preston. "Enhancing Beginning Reading Using Wordless Picture Books in a Cross-Age Tutoring Program." *The Reading Teacher,* 37 (April 1984), 692–698.

Ellis, Susan, and Susan Whalen. *Cooperative Learning.* New York: Scholastic, 1990.

Emans, Robert. "The Usefulness of Phonic Generalizations Above the Primary Grades." *The Reading Teacher,* 20 (February 1967), 419–425.

Englert, Carol Sue, and Chase C. Thomas. "Sensitivity to Text Structure in Reading and Writing: A Comparison Between Learning Disabled and Non–Learning Disabled Students." *Learning Disabilities Quarterly,* 10 (1987), 93–105.

Englot-Mash, Christine. "Tying Together Reading Strategies." *Journal of Reading,* 35 (October 1991), 150–151.

Esbensen, Thorwald. "Personal Computers: The Golden Mean in Education." *Personal Computing,* 5 (November 1981), 115–116, 120.

Evans, Carol. "*Monstruos, Pesadillas,* and Other Frights: A Thematic Unit." *The Reading Teacher,* 47 (February 1994), 428–430.

Faber, D. *Eleanor Roosevelt: First Lady of the World.* New York: Viking Kestrel, 1985.

Fagan, William T. "Empowered Students; Empowered Teachers." *The Reading Teacher,* 42 (April 1989), 572–578.

Faltis, Christian J. *Joinfostering: Adapting Teaching Strategies for the Multilingual Classroom.* New York: Merrill, 1993.

Farnan, Nancy, James Flood, and Diane Lapp. "Comprehending through Reading and Writing: Six Research-Based Instructional Strategies." In *Kids Come in All Languages: Reading Instruction for ESL Students,* edited by Karen Spangenberg-Urbschat and Robert Pritchard. Newark, Del.: International Reading Association, 1994, pp. 135–157.

Farr, Roger. "Portfolio Assessment." *The Reading Teacher,* 43 (December 1989), 264.

Farr, Roger. "Portfolios: Assessment in Language Arts." *ERIC Digest* (1991), 3 pp. [ED334603].

Farr, Roger. "Putting It All Together: Solving the Reading Assessment Puzzle." *The Reading Teacher,* 46 (September 1992), 26–37.

Farr, Roger, and Robert F. Carey. *Reading: What Can Be Measured?,* 2d ed. Newark, Del.: International Reading Association, 1986.

Farr, Roger, and Nancy Roser. *Teaching a Child to Read.* New York: Harcourt Brace Jovanovich, 1979.

Farr, Roger, and Bruce Tone. *Portfolio and Performance Assessment.* Fort Worth: Harcourt Brace, 1994.

Farrar, Mary Thomas. "Another Look at Oral Questions for Comprehension." *The Reading Teacher,* 36 (January 1983), 370–374.

Farrar, Mary Thomas. "Asking Better Questions." *The Reading Teacher,* 38 (October 1984a), 10–15.

Farrar, Mary Thomas. "Why Do We Ask Comprehension Questions? A New Conception of Comprehension Instruction." *The Reading Teacher,* 37 (February 1984b), 452–456.

Farris, Pamela J., and Carol J. Fuhler. "Developing Social Studies Concepts through Picture Books." *The Reading Teacher,* 47 (February 1994), 380–387.

Fay, Leo. "Reading Study Skills: Math and Science." In *Reading and Inquiry,* edited by J. Allen Figurel. Newark, Del.: International Reading Association, 1965.

Feitelson, D., B. Kita, and Z. Goldstein. "Effects of Listening to Series Stories on First Graders' Comprehension and Use of Language." *Research in the Teaching of English,* 20 (1986), 339–356.

Felber, Sheila. "Story Mapping for Primary Students." *The Reading Teacher,* 43 (October 1989), 90–91.

Ferguson, Anne M., and Jo Fairburn. "Language Experience for Problem Solving in Mathematics." *The Reading Teacher,* 38 (February 1985), 504–507.

Ferreiro, Emilia. "Literacy Development: Psychogenesis." In *How Children Construct Literacy: Piagetian Perspective,* edited by Yetta Goodman. Newark, Del.: International Reading Association, 1990.

Ferreiro, Emilia, and A. Teberosky. *Literacy Before Schooling.* Exeter, N.H.: Heinemann, 1982.

Field, James C., and David W. Jardine. "'Bad Examples' as Interpretive Opportunities: On the Need for Whole Language to Own Its Shadow." *Language Arts,* 71 (April 1994), 258–263.

Fielding, L. G., R. C. Anderson, and P. D. Pearson. *How Discussion Questions Influence Story Understanding* (Technical Report No. 490). Urbana–Champaign, Ill.: University of Illinois, Center for the Study of Reading, January 1990.

Fields, Marjorie, and Deborah Hillstead. "Whole Language in the Play Store." *Childhood Education,* 67 (Winter 1990), 73–76.

Finn, Patrick. *Helping Children Learn to Read.* New York: Random House, 1985.

First, Patricia, and Joan Curcio. *Implementing the Disabilities Acts: Implications for Educators.* Bloomington, Ind.: Phi Delta Kappa, 1993.

Fisette, Dolores. "Practical Authentic Assessment: Good Kid Watchers Know What to Teach Next." *The California Reader,* 26 (Summer 1993), 4–7.

Fish, John. *Special Education: The Way Ahead.* Philadelphia: Open University Press, 1985.

Fisher, Bobbi. "The Environment Reflects the Program." *Teaching K–8,* 20 (August/September 1989), 82, 84, 86.

Fisher, Bobbi. *Joyful Learning.* Portsmouth, N.H.: Heinemann, 1991.

Fitzgerald, Jill. "Enhancing Two Related Thought Processes: Revision in Writing and Critical Reading." *The Reading Teacher,* 43 (October 1989), 42–48.

Fitzgerald, Jill. "Helping Readers Gain Self-Control over Reading Comprehension." *The Reading Teacher,* 37 (December 1983), 249–253.

Fitzgerald, Jill. "Helping Young Writers to Revise: A Brief Review for Teachers." *The Reading Teacher,* 42 (November 1988), 124–129.

Fitzgerald, Jill. "Literacy and Students Who Are Learning English as a Second Language." *The Reading Teacher,* 46 (May 1993), 638–647.

Fitzgerald, Jill. "Research on Stories: Implications for Teachers." In *Children's Comprehension of Text: Research into Practice,* edited by K. Denise Muth. Newark, Del.: International Reading Association, 1989.

Flippo, Rona F., and Judy Anderson Smith. "Details, Details, Details." *The Reading Teacher,* 44 (November 1990), 276.

Flitterman-King, Sharon. "The Role of the Response Journal in Active Reading." *The Quarterly of the National Writing Project and the Center for the Study of Writing,* 10, no. 3 (1988), 4–11.

Flood, James. "The Text, the Student, and the Teacher: Learning from Exposition in the Middle Schools." *The Reading Teacher,* 39 (April 1986), 784–791.

Flood, James, and Diane Lapp. "Clearing the Confusion: A Closer Look at National Goals and Standards." *The Reading Teacher,* 47 (September 1993), 58–61.

Flood, James, and Diane Lapp. "Conceptual Mapping Strategies for Understanding Information Texts." *The Reading Teacher,* 41 (April 1988), 780–783.

Flood, James, and Diane Lapp. "Reading and Writing Relations: Assumptions and Directions." In *The Dynamics of Language Learning,* edited by James R. Squire. Urbana, Ill.: ERIC Clearinghouse on Reading and Communication Skills, 1987.

Flood, James, and Diane Lapp. "Reading Comprehension Instruction for At-Risk Students: Research-Based Practices That Can Make a Difference." *Journal of Reading,* 33 (April 1990), 490–496.

Flood, James, and Diane Lapp. "Reporting Reading Progress: A Comparison Portfolio for Parents." *The Reading Teacher,* 42 (March 1989), 508–514.

Flood, James, Diane Lapp, and Nancy Farnan. "A Reading-Writing Procedure that Teaches Expository Paragraph Structure." *The Reading Teacher,* 39 (February 1986), 556–562.

Flood, James, Diane Lapp, Sharon Flood, and Greta Nagel. "Am I Allowed to Group? Using Flexible Patterns for Effective Instruction." *The Reading Teacher,* 45 (April 1992), 608–616.

Flores, Barbara. "The Sociopsychogenesis of Literacy and Biliteracy." Paper presented at the annual conference of the International Reading Association, Atlanta, May 8, 1990.

Flynn, Linda L. "Developing Critical Reading Skills Through Cooperative Problem Solving." *The Reading Teacher,* 42 (May 1989), 664–668.

Flynn, Rosalind M., and Gail A. Carr. "Exploring Classroom Literature Through Drama: A Specialist and a Teacher Collaborate." *Language Arts,* 71 (January 1994), 38–43.

Ford, Michael, and Marilyn Ohlhausen. "Tips from Reading Clinicians for Coping with Disabled Readers in Regular Classrooms." *The Reading Teacher,* 42 (October 1988), 18–23.

Forell, Elizabeth. "The Case for Conservative Reader Placement." *The Reading Teacher,* 38 (May 1985), 857–862.

Forman, Ellice A., and Courtney B. Cazden. "Exploring Vygotskian Perspectives in Education: The Cognitive View of Peer Interaction." In *Theoretical Models and Processes of Reading,* 4th ed., edited by Robert Ruddell, Martha Rapp Ruddell, and Harry Singer. Newark, Del.: International Reading Association, 1994.

Fortescue, Chelsea M. "Using Oral and Written Language to Increase Understanding of Math Concepts." *Language Arts,* 71 (December 1994), 576–580.

Fouse, Beth, and Suzanne Brians. *A Primer on Attention Deficit Disorder.* Bloomington, Ind.: Phi Delta Kappa, 1993.

Fowler, Gerald. "Developing Comprehension Skills in Primary Students Through the Use of Story Frames." *The Reading Teacher,* 36 (November 1982), 176–179.

Fowler, Mary. *Maybe You Know My Kid.* New York: Carol Publishing Group, 1993.

Fox, Lynn H., and William G. Durden. *Educating Verbally Gifted Youth.* Bloomington, Ind.: Phi Delta Kappa, 1982.

Frager, Alan M. "Affective Dimensions of Content Area Reading." *Journal of Reading,* 36 (May 1993), 616–622.

Fredericks, Anthony D. "Mental Imagery Activities to Improve Comprehension." *The Reading Teacher,* 40 (October 1986), 78–81.

Freedman, Glenn, and Elizabeth G. Reynolds. "Enriching Basal Reader Lessons with Semantic Webbing." *The Reading Teacher,* 33 (March 1980), 667–684.

Freedman, R. *Lincoln: A Photobiography.* New York: Clarion, 1987.

Freeman, David E., and Yvonne S. Freeman. "Bilingual Learners: How Our Assumptions Limit Their World." Occasional paper. Tucson: Arizona Center for Research and Development, May 1988.

Freeman, Ruth H. "Poetry Writing in the Upper Elementary Grades." *The Reading Teacher,* 37 (December 1983), 238–243.

Freeman, Yvonne S. "The California Reading Initiative: Revolution or Merely Revision?" *The New Advocate,* 1 (Fall 1988), 241–249.

Freeman, Yvonne S., and David E. Freeman. "Ten Tips for Monolingual Teachers of Bilingual Students." In *The Whole Language Catalog,* edited by Kenneth Goodman, Lois Bird, and Yetta Goodman. Santa Rosa, Calif.: American School Publishers, 1991.

Freeman, Yvonne S., and David E. Freeman. *Whole Language for Second Language Learners.* Portsmouth, N.H.: Heinemann, 1992.

Frew, Andrew W. "Four Steps Toward Literature-Based Reading." *Journal of Reading,* 34 (October 1990), 98–102.

Fried, J., K. Grey, and S. Swanson. *Monsters & Make-Believe.* Fairfield, Conn.: Pelican, 1991.

Friend, Marilyn, and Lynne Cook. "The New Mainstreaming." *Instructor,* 101 (March 1992), 30–34.

Fritz, J. *What's the Big Idea, Ben Franklin?* New York: Coward, McCann & Geoghegan, 1976.

Fry, Edward. *Elementary Reading Instruction.* New York: McGraw-Hill, 1977.

Fry, Edward. "Fry's Readability Graph: Clarifications, Validity, and Extension to Level 17." *Journal of Reading,* 21 (December 1977), 249.

Fry, Edward. "Graphical Literacy." *Journal of Reading,* 24 (February 1981), 383–390.

Fry, Edward. "A Readability Formula for Short Passages." *Journal of Reading,* 33 (May 1990), 594–597.

Fuhler, Carol J. "Let's Move Toward Literature-Based Reading Instruction." *The Reading Teacher,* 43 (January 1990), 312–315.

Fuhler, Carol J. "Response Journals: Just One More Time with Feeling." *Journal of Reading,* 37 (February 1994), 400–405.

Furleigh, Mary A. "Teaching Comprehension with Editorials." *The Reading Teacher,* 44 (March 1991), 523.

Galda, Lee. "Children and Poetry." *The Reading Teacher,* 43 (October 1989), 66–71.

Galda, Lee. "History as Story: Books for the Social Studies." *The Reading Teacher,* 45 (November 1991), 224–233.

Galda, Lee. "Our Natural World." *The Reading Teacher,* 43 (January 1990), 322–326.

Galda, Lee. "Playing about a Story: Its Impact on Comprehension." *The Reading Teacher,* 36 (October 1982), 52–55.

Galda, Lee. "Readers, Texts and Contexts: A Response-Based View of Literature in the Classroom." *The New Advocate,* 1 (Spring 1988), 92–102.

Galda, Lee. "Saving Our Planet, Saving Ourselves." *The Reading Teacher,* 45 (December 1991), 310–317.

Galda, Lee. "What a Character!" *The Reading Teacher,* 43 (December 1989), 244–249.

Galda, Lee, Emily Carr, and Susan Cox. "The Plot Thickens." *The Reading Teacher,* 43 (November 1989), 160–166.

Galda, Lee, Bernice Cullinan, and Dorothy Strickland. *Language, Literacy and the Child.* Orlando: Harcourt Brace, 1993.

Galda, Lee, and Linda DeGroff. "Across Time and Place: Books for Social Studies." *The Reading Teacher,* 44 (November 1991), 240–246.

Galda, Lee, with Donna Diehl and Lane Ware. "One World, One Family." *The Reading Teacher,* 46 (February 1993), 410–419.

Galda, Lee, and Pat MacGregor. "Nature's Wonders: Books for a Science Curriculum." *The Reading Teacher,* 46 (November 1992), 236–245.

Galda, Lee, and Kathy G. Short. "Visual Literacy: Exploring Art and Illustration in Children's Books." *The Reading Teacher,* 46 (March 1993), 506–516.

Gale, David. "Why Word Play?" *The Reading Teacher,* 36 (November 1982), 220–222.

Gamberg, Ruth, Winnifred Kwak, Meredith Hutchings, Judy Altheim, and Gail Edwards. *Learning and Loving It: Theme Studies in the Classroom.* Portsmouth, N.H.: Heinemann, 1988.

Gambrell, Linda B. "How Much Time Do Children Spend Reading During Teacher-Directed Reading Instruction?" In *Changing Perspectives on Research in Reading/Language Processing and Instruction,* edited by Jerome A. Niles and Larry A. Harris. Rochester, N.Y.: National Reading Conference, 1984.

Gambrell, L., W. Pfeiffer, and R. Wilson. "The Effects of Retelling upon Reading Comprehension and Recall of Text Information." *Journal of Educational Research,* 78 (1985), 216–220.

Garan, Elaine. "Who's in Control? Is There Enough 'Empowerment' to Go Around?" *Language Arts,* 71 (March 1994), 192–199.

Garcia, Eugene. *Student Cultural Diversity.* Boston: Houghton Mifflin, 1994.

Garcia, Mary, and Kathy Verville. "Redesigning Teaching and Learning: The Arizona Student Assessment Program." In *Authentic Reading Assessment: Practices and Possibilities,* edited by Sheila Valencia, Elfrieda Hiebert, and Peter Afflerbach. Newark, Del.: International Reading Association, 1994.

Garcia, Ricardo L. *Education for Cultural Pluralism: Global Roots Stew.* Bloomington, Ind.: Phi Delta Kappa, 1981.

Gardner, Michael K., and Martha M. Smith. "Does Perspective Taking Ability Contribute to Reading Comprehension?" *Journal of Reading,* 30 (January 1987), 333–336.

Garrison, James W., and Kenneth Hoskisson. "Confirmation Bias in Predictive Reading." *The Reading Teacher,* 42 (March 1989), 482–486.

Gaskins, I. W., M. A. Downer, R. C. Anderson, P. M. Cunningham, R. W. Gaskins, M. Schommer, and The Teachers of Benchmark School. "A Metacognitive Approach to Phonics: Using What You Know to Decode What You Don't Know." *Remedial and Special Education* 9 (1988), 36–41.

Gaskins, Irene W. "Let's End the Reading Disabilities/Learning Disabilities Debate." *Journal of Learning Disabilities,* 15 (February 1982), 81–83.

Gaskins, Irene West. "Reading for Learning: Going Beyond the Basals in the Elementary Grades." *The Reading Teacher,* 35 (December 1981), 323–328.

Gaskins, Irene West, et al. "Classroom Talk about Text: Learning in Science Class." *Journal of Reading,* 37 (April 1994), 558–565.

Gaskins, Robert W. "The Missing Ingredients: Time on Task, Direct Instruction, and Writing." *The Reading Teacher,* 41 (April 1988), 750–755.

Gaskins, Robert W., Jennifer C. Gaskins, and Irene W. Gaskins. "A Decoding Program for Poor Readers—And the Rest of the Class, Too!" *Language Arts,* 68 (March 1991), 213–225.

Gauthier, Lane Roy. "A Strategy to Increase Punctuation Awareness." *Journal of Reading,* 36 (February 1993), 401–402.

Gauthier, Lane Roy. "Understanding Content Material." *The Reading Teacher,* 43 (December 1989), 266–267.

Gauthier, Lane Roy. "Using Capsulization Guides." *The Reading Teacher,* 42 (March 1989), 553–554.

Gauthier, Lane Roy. "Using Character Charts for Critical Thinking." *The Reading Teacher,* 45 (April 1992), 654–655.

Gauthier, Lane Roy. "Using Journals for Content Area Comprehension." *Journal of Reading,* 34 (March 1991), 491–492.

Gearheart, Bill R., and Carol J. Gearheart. *Learning Disabilities.* Columbus, Ohio: Merrill, 1989.

GEONews Handbook, November 11–17, 1990, 7.

Gill, J. Thomas, Jr. "Development of Word Knowledge as It Relates to Reading, Spelling, and Instruction." *Language Arts,* 69 (October 1992), 444–453.

Gilles, Carol. "Reading, Writing, and Talking: Using Literature Study Groups." *English Journal* (January 1989), 38–41.

Gillet, Jean Wallace, and J. Richard Gentry. "Bridges Between Nonstandard and Standard English with Extensions of Dictated Stories." *The Reading Teacher,* 36 (January 1983), 360–365.

Gipe, Joan P. "Use of a Relevant Context Helps Kids Learn New Word Meanings." *The Reading Teacher,* 33 (January 1980), 398–402.

Gitelman, Honore F., and Gayle Burgess Rasberry. "Bring on the Books: A Schoolwide Contest." *The Reading Teacher,* 39 (May 1986), 905–907.

Glass, Gerald G. "The Strange World of Syllabication." *The Elementary School Journal,* 67 (May 1967), 403–405.

Glynn, Shawn M. "The Teaching with Analogies Model." In *Children's Comprehension of Text: Research into Practice,* edited by K. Denise Muth. Newark, Del.: International Reading Association, 1989.

Gold, Lillian. *The Elementary School Publishing Center.* Bloomington, Ill.: Phi Delta Kappa. 1989.

Gold, Yvonne. "Helping Students Discover the Origins of Words." *The Reading Teacher,* 35 (December 1981), 350–351.

Golden, Joanne M. "Children's Concept of Story in Reading and Writing." *The Reading Teacher,* 37 (March 1984), 578–584.

Golden, Joanne M., Annyce Meiners, and Stanley Lewis. "The Growth of Story Meaning." *Language Arts,* 69 (January 1992), 22–27.

Goldenberg, Claude. "Instructional Conversations: Promoting Comprehension through Discussion." *The Reading Teacher,* 46 (December 1992/January 1993), 316–326.

Goldstein, Bobbye S. "Looking at Cartoons and Comics in a New Way." *Journal of Reading,* 29 (April 1986), 647–661.

Gonzales, Phillip. "Beginning English Reading for ESL Students." *The Reading Teacher,* 35 (November 1981), 154–162.

Gonzales, Phillip. "Second Language Literacy." *Illinois Reading Council Journal,* 22 (Winter 1994), 13–16.

Goodall, Marilyn. "Can Four Year Olds 'Read' Words in the Environment?" *The Reading Teacher,* 37 (February 1984), 478–482.

Goodman, Kenneth S. "As I See It: Evaluation in Whole Language." In *The Whole Language Catalog,* edited by Kenneth S. Goodman, Lois B. Bird, and Yetta M. Goodman. Santa Rosa, Calif.: American School Publishers, 1991.

Goodman, Kenneth S. "Reading: A Psycholinguistic Guessing Game." In *Perspectives on Elementary Reading,* edited by Robert Karlin. New York: Harcourt Brace Jovanovich, 1973.

Goodman, Kenneth S. "Reading, Writing, and Written Texts: a Transactional Sociopsycholinguistic View." In *Theoretical Models and Processes of Reading,* 4th ed., edited by Robert B. Ruddell, Martha Rapp Ruddell, and Harry Singer. Newark, Del.: International Reading Association, 1994, pp. 1093–1130.

Goodman, Kenneth S. "Unity in Reading." In *Theoretical Models and Processes of Reading,* 3d ed., edited by Harry Singer and Robert B. Ruddell. Newark, Del.: International Reading Association, 1985.

Goodman, Kenneth S. *What's Whole in Whole Language?* Portsmouth, N.H.: Heinemann Educational Books, 1986.

Goodman, Kenneth S. "Why Whole Language Is Today's Agenda in Education." *Language Arts,* 69 (September 1992), 354–363.

Goodman, Kenneth S., Yetta M. Goodman, and Wendy J. Hood, eds. *The Whole Language Evaluation Book.* Portsmouth, N.H.: Heinemann, 1989.

Goodman, Yetta. "Children Coming to Know Literacy." In *Emergent Literacy,* edited by William H. Teale and Elizabeth Sulzby. Norwood, N.J.: Ablex, 1986.

Goodman, Yetta M. "Evaluation of Students: Srehcaet fo Noitaulave." In *The Whole Language Evaluation Book,* edited by Kenneth S. Goodman, Yetta M. Goodman, and Wendy J. Hood. Portsmouth, N.H.: Heinemann, 1989.

Goodman, Yetta. "Kid Watching: An Alternative to Testing." *National Elementary Principal,* 57 (June 1978), 41–45.

Goodman, Yetta. "Kidwatching: Observing Children in the Classroom." In *Observing the Language Learner,* edited by Angela Jagger and M. T. Smith-Burke. Newark, Del.: International Reading Association, 1985.

Goodman, Yetta. "Test Review: Concepts about Print Test." *The Reading Teacher,* 34 (January 1981), 445–448.

Goodman, Yetta. "Using Children's Reading Miscues for New Teaching Strategies." *The Reading Teacher,* 23 (February 1970), 455–459.

Goodman, Yetta M., and Myna M. Haussler. "Literacy Environment in the Home and Community." In *Roles in Literacy Learning: A New Perspective,* edited by Duane R. Tovey and James E. Kerber. Newark, Del.: International Reading Association, 1986.

Goodman, Yetta M., Dorothy J. Watson, and Carolyn L. Burke. *Reading Miscue Inventory.* New York: Richard C. Owen, 1987.

Gordon, Christine J. "Teaching Narrative Text Structure: A Process Approach to Reading and Writing." In *Children's Comprehension of Text: Research into Practice,* edited by K. Denise Muth. Newark, Del.: International Reading Association, 1989.

Gordon, Christine, and P. David Pearson. *Effects of Instruction in Metacomprehension and Inferencing on Students' Comprehension Abilities* (Technical Report No. 269). Urbana–Champaign, Ill.: University of Illinois, Center for the Study of Reading, 1983.

Gordon, Naomi, ed. *Classroom Experiences: The Writing Process in Action.* Exeter, N.H.: Heinemann, 1984.

Gough, Philip B. "Word Recognition." In *Handbook of Reading Research,* edited by P. David Pearson. New York: Longman, 1984.

Gove, Mary. "Clarifying Teachers' Beliefs about Reading." *The Reading Teacher,* 37 (December 1983), 261–268.

Grabe, Mark, and Cindy Grabe. "The Microcomputer and the Language Experience Approach." *The Reading Teacher,* 38 (February 1985), 508–511.

Grabe, Nancy White. "Language Experience and Basals." *The Reading Teacher,* 34 (March 1981), 710–711.

Grace, Marsha. "Implementing a Portfolio System in Your Classroom." *Reading Today,* 10 (June/July 1993), 27.

Grady, Emily. *The Portfolio Approach to Assessment.* Bloomington, Ind.: Phi Delta Kappa, 1992.

Graves, D. H. *Investigate Nonfiction.* Portsmouth, N.H.: Heinemann, 1989.

Graves, Donald, and Jane Hansen. "The Author's Chair." *Language Arts,* 60 (February 1983), 176–183.

Graves, Michael F., and Maureen C. Prenn. "Costs and Benefits of Various Methods of Teaching Vocabulary." *Journal of Reading,* 29 (April 1986), 596–602.

Gray, Mary Ann. "Creatively Developing Research Writing Skills." *The Reading Teacher,* 42 (January 1989), 347.

Greaney, Vincent. "Parental Influences on Reading." *The Reading Teacher,* 39 (April 1986), 813–818.

Greenewald, M. Jane, and Rosalind L. Rossing. "Short-Term and Long-Term Effects of Story Grammar and Self-Monitoring Training on Children's Story Comprehension." In *Solving Problems in Literacy: Learners, Teachers, and Researchers,* edited by Jerome A. Niles and Rosary V. Lalik. Rochester, N.Y.: National Reading Conference, 1986.

Griffith, Priscilla, and Mary Olson. "Phonemic Awareness Helps Beginning Readers Break the Code." *The Reading Teacher,* 45 (March 1992), 516–523.

Groff, Patrick J. "Resolving the Letter Name Controversy." *The Reading Teacher,* 37 (January 1984), 384–388.

Groff, Patrick. "The Maturing of Phonics Instruction." *The Reading Teacher,* 39 (May 1986), 919–923.

Grossman, H., ed. *Manual on Terminology and Classification in Mental Retardation.* Washington, D.C.: American Association on Mental Deficiency, 1983.

Guild, Pat. "The Culture/Learning Style Connection." *Educational Leadership,* 51 (May 1994), 16–21.

Gunderson, Lee. "L2 Reading Instruction in ESL and Mainstream Classrooms." In *Issues in Literacy: A Research Perspective,* Thirty-Fourth Yearbook of the National Reading Conference, edited by Jerome A. Niles and Rosary V. Lalik. Rochester, N.Y.: National Reading Conference, 1985.

Gunning, Thomas G. "Wrong Level Test: Wrong Information." *The Reading Teacher,* 35 (May 1982), 902–905.

Guri-Rozenblit, Sarah. "Impact of Diagrams on Recalling Sequential Elements in Expository Text." *Reading Psychology,* 9, no. 2 (1988), 121–139.

Guthrie, John T. "Children's Reasons for Success and Failure." *The Reading Teacher,* 36 (January 1983), 478–480.

Guthrie, John T. "Models of Reading and Reading Disability." *Journal of Educational Psychology,* 65 (1973), 9–18.

Guthrie, John T. "Preschool Literacy Learning." *The Reading Teacher,* 37 (December 1983), 318–320.

Guzzetti, Barbara J., Barbara J. Kowalinski, and Tom McGowan. "Using a Literature-Based Approach to Teaching Social Studies." *Journal of Reading,* 36 (October 1992), 114–122.

Hacker, Charles J. "From Schema Theory to Classroom Practice." *Language Arts,* 57 (November/December 1980), 866–871.

Hadaway, Nancy L., and Terrell A. Young. "Content Literacy and Language Learning: Instructional Decisions." *The Reading Teacher,* 47 (April 1994), 522–527.

Hadaway, Nancy, and Viola Florez. "Teaching Multiethnic Literature, Promoting Cultural Pluralism." *The Dragon Lode,* 8 (Winter 1990), 7–13.

Hafner, Lawrence E., and Hayden B. Jolly. *Teaching Reading to Children.* 2nd ed. New York: Macmillan, 1982.

Haggard, Martha Rapp. "Developing Critical Thinking with the Directed Reading-Thinking Activity." *The Reading Teacher,* 41 (February 1988), 526–533.

Haggard, Martha Rapp. "The Vocabulary Self-Collection Strategy: Using Student Interest and World Knowledge to Enhance Vocabulary Growth." *Journal of Reading,* 29 (April 1986), 634–642.

Hahn, Amos L. "Teaching Remedial Students to Be Strategic Readers and Better Comprehenders." *The Reading Teacher,* 39 (October 1985), 72–77.

Hall, MaryAnne. "Teaching and Language Centered Programs." In *Roles in Literacy Learning,* edited by Duane Tovey and James Kerber. Newark, Del.: International Reading Association, 1986.

Hall, Nigel. *The Emergence of Literacy.* Portsmouth, N.H.: Heinemann Educational Books, 1987.

Haller, E. P., D. A. Child, and H. J. Walberg. "Can Comprehension Be Taught? A Quantitative Synthesis of 'Metacognitive' Studies." *Educational Researcher,* 17 (1988), 5–8.

Hamann, Lori S., Loree Schultz, Michael W. Smith, and Brian White. "Making Connections: The Power of Autobiographical Writing Before Reading." *Journal of Reading,* 35 (September 1991), 24–28.

Hancock, Marjorie R. "Character Journals: Initiating Involvement and Identification through Literature." *Journal of Reading,* 37 (September 1993), 42–50.

Hancock, Marjorie R. "Literature Response Journals: Insights Beyond the Printed Page." *Language Arts,* 69 (January 1992), 36–42.

Hansell, Stevenson F. "Stepping Up to Outlining." *Journal of Reading,* 22 (December 1978), 248–252.

Hansen, Jane. "The Effects of Inference Training and Practice on Young Children's Reading Comprehension." *Reading Research Quarterly,* 16, no. 3 (1981a), 391–417.

Hansen, Jane. "An Inferential Comprehension Strategy for Use with Primary Grade Children." *The Reading Teacher,* 34 (March 1981b), 665–669.

Hansen, Jane. "Literacy Portfolios Emerge." *The Reading Teacher,* 45 (April 1992), 604–607.

Hansen, Jane. "Organizing Student Learning: Teachers Teach What and How." In *The Dynamics of Language Learning,* edited by James R. Squire. Urbana, Ill.: National Council of Teachers of English, 1987.

Hansen, Jane. "Skills." In *Breaking Ground,* edited by Jane Hansen, Thomas Newkirk, and Donald Graves. Portsmouth, N.H.: Heinemann Educational Books, 1984.

Hansen, Jane. "Students' Evaluations Bring Reading and Writing Together." *The Reading Teacher,* 46 (October 1992), 100–105.

Hansen, Jane. *When Writers Read.* Portsmouth, N.H.: Heinemann, 1987.

Hansen, Jane, and Ruth Hubbard. "Poor Readers Can Draw Inferences." *The Reading Teacher,* 37 (March 1984), 586–589.

Hansen, Jane, Thomas Newkirk, and Donald Graves, eds. *Breaking Ground: Teachers Relate Reading and Writing in the Elementary School.* Portsmouth, N.H.: Heinemann, 1985.

Hansen, Jane, and P. David Pearson. "An Instructional Study: Improving the Inferential Comprehension of Fourth Grade Good and Poor Readers." *Journal of Educational Psychology,* 75, no. 6 (1983), 821–829.

Hare, Victoria Chou. "What's in a Word? A Review of Young Children's Difficulties with the Construct 'Word.'" *The Reading Teacher,* 37 (January 1984), 360–364.

Hargis, Charles. *Teaching Low Achieving and Disadvantaged Students.* Springfield, Ill.: Charles C. Thomas, 1989.

Hargis, Charles H., et al. "Repetition Requirements for Word Recognition." *Journal of Reading,* 31 (January 1988), 320–327.

Harlin, Rebecca, Sally Lipa, and Stephen Phelps. "Portfolio Assessment: Interpretations and Implications for Classroom Teachers and Reading Teachers." In *Literacy Research and Practice: Foundations for the Year 2000,* edited by Nancy Padak, Timothy Rasinsky, and John Logan. Pittsburg, Kan.: College Reading Association, 1992.

Harp, Bill. "When the Principal Asks, 'How Are We Using What We Know about Literacy Processes in the Content Areas?'" *The Reading Teacher,* 42 (May 1989), 726–727.

Harp, Bill. "When the Principal Asks, 'Why Are You Doing Guided Imagery During Reading Time?'" *The Reading Teacher,* 41 (February 1988), 588–590.

Harp, Bill. "When the Principal Asks: 'Why Are You Doing Piagetian Task Testing When You Have Given Basal Placement Tests?'" *The Reading Teacher,* 41 (November 1987), 212–214.

Harp, Bill. "When the Principal Asks: 'Why Aren't You Using the Phonics Workbooks?'" *The Reading Teacher,* 42 (January 1989), 326–327.

Harp, Bill. "When the Principal Asks, 'Why Don't You Ask Comprehension Questions?'" *The Reading Teacher,* 42 (April 1989), 638–639.

Harp, Bill, and Jo Ann Brewer. *Reading and Writing.* San Diego: Harcourt Brace Jovanovich, 1991.

Harris, Albert J., and Edward R. Sipay. *How to Increase Reading Ability,* 8th ed. New York: Longman, 1985.

Harris, Larry A., and Carl B. Smith. *Reading Instruction.* New York, Macmillan, 1986.

Harris, Theodore L., and Richard E. Hodges, eds. *A Dictionary of Reading and Related Terms.* Newark, Del.: International Reading Association, 1981.

Harris-Sharples, Susan D., Gail Kearns, and Margery Miller. "A Young Authors Program: One Model for Teacher and Student Empowerment." *The Reading Teacher,* 42 (April 1989), 580–583.

Harste, J. C., K. G. Short, and C. Burke. *Creating Classrooms for Authors: The Reading-Writing Connection.* Portsmouth, N.H.: Heinemann, 1988.

Harste, Jerome C. *New Policy Guidelines for Reading: Connecting Research and Practice.* Urbana, Ill.: National Council of Teachers of English and ERIC Clearinghouse on Reading and Communication Skills, 1989.

Hart, Leslie A. "Programs, Patterns and Downshifting in Learning to Read." *The Reading Teacher,* 37 (October 1983), 5–11.

Hayden, Carla, ed. *Venture into Cultures.* Chicago: American Library Association, 1992.

Hayes, David A. "Initiate Cartographic Literacy with the MAP Activity." *Journal of Reading,* 35 (May 1992), 659–661.

Heald-Taylor, Gail. *Whole Language Strategies for ESL Students.* San Diego: Dormac, 1989.

Hedges, William D. "Lightening the Load with Computer-Managed Instruction." *Classroom Computer News,* 1 (July/August 1981), 34.

Heffron, Kathleen. "Literacy with the Computer." *The Reading Teacher,* 40 (November 1986), 152–155.

Heide, F. "Rocks." In *By Myself,* compiled by L. B. Hopkins. New York: Crowell, 1980.

Heidger, Barbara. "No Need to Panic." In *The Whole Language Catalog,* edited by Kenneth Goodman, Lois Bridges, and Yetta Goodman. Santa Rosa, Calif.: American School Publishers, 1991.

Heimlich, Joan E., and Susan D. Pittelman. *Semantic Mapping: Classroom Applications.* Newark, Del.: International Reading Association, 1986.

Heine, Patricia. "The Power of Related Books." *The Reading Teacher,* 45 (September 1991), 75–77.

Helfeldt, John P., and William A. Henk. "Reciprocal Question-Answer Relationships: An Instructional Technique for At-Risk Readers." *Journal of Reading,* 33 (April 1990), 509–514.

Heller, Mary F. "Comprehending and Composing through Language Experience." *The Reading Teacher,* 42 (November 1988), 130–135.

Henk, William A. "Author Bias in the Balance." *The Reading Teacher,* 41 (February 1988), 620–621.

Henke, Linda. "Beyond Basal Reading: A District's Commitment to Change." *The New Advocate,* 1, no. 1 (1988), 42–51.

Henley, Martin. *Teaching Mildly Retarded Children in the Regular Classroom.* Bloomington, Ind.: Phi Delta Kappa, 1985.

Hennings, Dorothy Grant. "Reading Picture Storybooks in the Social Studies." *The Reading Teacher,* 36 (December 1982), 284–289.

Herman, Patricia A., Richard C. Anderson, P. David Pearson, and William E. Nagy. "Incidental Acquisition of Word Meaning from Expositions with Varied Text Features." *Reading Research Quarterly,* 22, no. 3 (1987), 263–284.

Herriott, John. "CAI: A Philosophy of Education and a System to Match." *Creative Computing,* 8 (April 1982), 80–86.

Herrmann, Beth Ann. "Two Approaches for Helping Poor Readers Become More Strategic." *The Reading Teacher,* 42 (October 1988), 24–28.

Hess, Mary Lou. "Understanding Nonfiction: Purpose, Classification, Response." *Language Arts,* 68 (March 1991), 228–232.

Hewett, Frank M., with Steven R. Forness. *Education of Exceptional Learners,* 3d ed. Boston: Allyn & Bacon, 1984.

Heymsfeld, Carla R. "Reciprocal Teaching Goes Co-op." *The Reading Teacher,* 45 (December 1991), 252–254.

Hickman, Janet. "Children's Response to Literature: What Happens in the Classroom." In *Readings on Reading Instruction,* edited by Albert J. Harris and Edward R. Sipay, 3d ed. New York: Longman, 1984.

Hiebert, Elfrieda H., and Barbara M. Taylor. "Interventions and the Restructuring of American Literacy Instruction." In *Getting Reading Right from the Start,* edited by Elfrieda H. Hiebert and Barbara M. Taylor. Boston: Allyn & Bacon, 1994.

Hiebert, Elfrieda H., and Jacalyn Colt. "Patterns of Literature-Based Reading Instruction." *The Reading Teacher,* 43 (October 1989), 14–20.

Hiebert, Elfrieda, and Terry Hutchison. "Research Directions: The Current State of Alternative Assessments for Policy and Instructional Uses." *Language Arts,* 68 (December 1991), 662–668.

Hiebert, Elfrieda, Sheila Valencia, and Peter P. Afflerbach. "Definitions and Perspectives." In *Authentic Reading Assessment: Practices and Possibilities,* edited by Sheila W. Valencia, Elfrieda H. Hiebert, and Peter P. Afflerbach. Newark, Del.: International Reading Association, 1994, pp. 6–21.

Hieshima, Joyce. "Literacy Instruction and ESL Learners: A Need for Re-examination." *Illinois Reading Council Journal,* 22 (Winter 1994), 17–20.

Hilbert, Sharon B. "Sustained Silent Reading Revisited." *The Reading Teacher,* 46 (December 1992/January 1993), 354–356.

Hills, Tynette. "Assessment in Context—Teachers and Children at Work." In *Early Childhood Education 94/95,* 15th ed., edited by Karen Paciorek and Joyce Munro. Guilford, Conn.: Dushkin, 1994, pp. 150–157.

Hoben, Mollie. "Toward Integration in the Mainstream." *Exceptional Children,* 47 (October 1980), 100–105.

Hoffman, James V. "Critical Reading/Thinking Across the Curriculum: Using I-Charts to Support Learning." *Language Arts,* 69 (February 1992), 121–127.

Hoffman, James V. "Leadership in the Language Arts: Am I Whole Yet? Are You?" *Language Arts,* 69 (September 1992), 366–371.

Hoffman, James V., and Sarah J. McCarthey. "Ongoing Research: Teachers' Practices and the New Basals." *NRRC News* (May 1995), 6–7.

Hoffman, James. "Teacher and School Effects on Learning to Read." In *Handbook of Reading Research, Vol. II,* edited by Rebecca Barr, Michael L. Kamil, Peter B. Mosenthal, and P. David Pearson. White Plains, N.Y.: Longman, 1991, pp. 911–950.

Holbrook, Hilary Taylor. "The Quality of Textbooks." *The Reading Teacher,* 38 (March 1985), 680–683.

Holdaway, Don. *The Foundations of Literacy.* Portsmouth, N.H.: Heinemann Educational Books, 1979.

Holdaway, Don. "Guiding a Natural Process." In *Roles in Literacy Learning,* edited by Duane R. Tovey and James E. Kerber. Newark, Del.: International Reading Association, 1986.

Holmes, Betty C. "A Confirmation Strategy for Improving Poor Readers' Ability to Answer Inferential Questions." *The Reading Teacher,* 37 (November 1983), 144–147.

Holzberg, Carol S. "Software Reviews: *Jack and the Beanstalk: An Animated Storybook.*" *The Apple IIGS Buyer's Guide,* Fall 1989, 57–58.

Hood, Joyce. "Why We Burned Our Basic Sight Vocabulary Cards." *The Reading Teacher,* 27 (March 1972), 579–582.

Hoppes, Ginny. "Spinning a Prereading Lesson." *The Reading Teacher,* 42 (February 1989), 450.

Hornsby, David, Deborah Sukarna, and Jo-Ann Parry. *Read On: A Conference Approach to Reading.* Portsmouth, N.H.: Heinemann, 1986.

Hough, Ruth A., Joanne R. Nurss, and D. Scott Enright. "Story Reading with Limited English Speaking Children in the Regular Classroom." *The Reading Teacher,* 39 (February 1986), 510–514.

Howell, Helen. "Language, Literature, and Vocabulary Development for Gifted Students." *The Reading Teacher,* 40 (February 1987), 500–504.

Hoyt, Linda. "Many Ways of Knowing: Using Drama, Oral Interactions, and the Visual Arts to Enhance Reading Comprehension." *The Reading Teacher,* 45 (April 1992), 580–584).

Huck, Charlotte S., Susan Hepler, and Janet Hickman. *Children's Literature in the Elementary School,* 5th ed. Fort Worth: Harcourt Brace, 1993.

Hughes, Sandra M. "Impact of Whole Language on Four Elementary School Libraries." *Language Arts,* 70 (September 1993), 393–399.

Humanities Software. *Great Scary Imaginings.* Hood River, Ore.: Humanities Software, 1991.

Humanities Software. *Terrible Days I.* Hood River, Ore.: Humanities Software, 1991.

Hunter-Grundin, Elizabeth. "Spoken Language in Emergent Literacy Learning." *Reading Today,* 7 (February/March 1990), 22.

Hutchins, Pat. *The Doorbell Rang.* New York: Mulberry Books, 1986.

"The Inclusive School." *Educational Leadership* (Special issue), 52 (December 1994/January 1995).

Ingham, Rosemary Oliphant. "Poetry Preferences with Great References." *Kentucky Reading Journal,* 5 (Spring 1984), 11–15.

International Business Machines. *Stories and More.* Atlanta: International Business Machines, 1991.

Irwin, Judith Westphal. "Implicit Connectives and Comprehension." *The Reading Teacher,* 33 (February 1980), 527–529.

Irwin, Judith Westphal. *Teaching Reading Comprehension Processes,* 2d ed. Englewood Cliffs, N.J.: Prentice-Hall, 1991.

Isaacson, Richard, et al., eds. *The Children's Catalog,* 16th ed. New York: H. W. Wilson, 1988.

Isaak, Troy, and John Joseph. "Authoring Software and Teaching." *The Reading Teacher,* 43 (December 1989), 254–255.

Iwicki, Ann L. "Vocabulary Connections." *The Reading Teacher,* 45 (May 1992), 736.

Jachym, Nora, Richard Allington, and Kathleen A. Broikou. "Estimating the Cost of Seatwork." *The Reading Teacher,* 43 (October 1989), 30–35.

Jaggar, Angela M. "Teacher as Learner: Implications for Staff Development." In *Teachers and Research,* edited by Gay Su Pinnell and Myna L. Matlin. Newark, Del.: International Reading Association, 1989.

Jasmine, Julia. *Portfolios and Other Assessments.* Huntington Beach, Calif.: Teacher Created Materials, 1993.

Jenkins, Barbara L., et al. "Children's Use of Hypothesis Testing When Decoding Words." *The Reading Teacher,* 33 (March 1980), 664–667.

Jenks, Carolyn, and Janice Roberts. "Reading, Writing, and Reviewing: Teacher, Librarian, and Young Readers Collaborate." *Language Arts,* 67 (November 1990), 742–745.

Jensen, Julie M., and Nancy L. Roser. "Are There Really 3 R's?" *Educational Leadership,* 47 (March 1990), 7–12.

Jett-Simpson, Mary. "Writing Stories Using Model Structures: The Circle Story." *Language Arts,* 58 (March 1981), 293–300.

Jiganti, Mary Ann, and Mary Anne Tindall. "An Interactive Approach to Teaching Vocabulary." *The Reading Teacher,* 39 (January 1986), 444–448.

Johns, Kenneth M. *How Children Learn a Second Language.* Bloomington, Ind.: Phi Delta Kappa, 1988.

Johns, Kenneth M., and Connie Espinoza. *Mainstreaming Language Minority Children in Reading and Writing.* Bloomington, Ind.: Phi Delta Kappa, 1992.

Johnson, Dale D., and James F. Baumann. "Word Identification." In *Handbook of Reading Research,* edited by P. David Pearson. New York: Longman, 1984.

Johnson, Dale D., and P. David Pearson. *Teaching Reading Vocabulary,* 2d ed. New York: Holt, Rinehart and Winston, 1984.

Johnson, Dale D., Susan D. Pittelman, and Joan E. Heimlich. "Semantic Mapping." *The Reading Teacher,* 39 (April 1986), 778–783.

Johnson, Dale D., and Bonnie von Hoff Johnson. "Highlighting Vocabulary in Inferential Comprehension Instruction." *Journal of Reading,* 29 (April 1986), 622–625.

Johnson, David, and Roger Johnson. "Social Skills for Successful Group Work." *Educational Leadership,* 47 (December 1989/January 1990), 29–33.

Johnson, David, Roger Johnson, and Karl Smith. "Cooperative Learning: An Active Learning Strategy." *Focus,* 5 (Spring 1990), 1, 8.

Johnson, Lori Beckmann. "Windows Computing: Finding the Right Words: Dictionaries, Thesauruses, and Quotations." *PC Novice,* 5 (September 1994), 21–23.

Johnson, Nancy M., and M. Jane Evert. "Time Travel Is Possible: Historical Fiction and Biography—Passport to the Past." *The Reading Teacher,* 45 (March 1992), 488–495.

Johnson, Terry D., and Daphne R. Louis. *Literacy Through Literature.* Portsmouth, N.H.: Heinemann, 1987.

Johnston, Francine R. "Improving Student Response in DR-TAs and DL-TAs." *The Reading Teacher,* 46 (February 1993), 448–449.

Johnston, Peter H. "Assessment in Reading." In *Handbook of Reading Research,* edited by P. David Pearson. New York: Longman, 1984.

Johnston, Peter, and Richard Allington. "Remediation." In *Handbook of Reading Research, Vol. II.,* edited by Rebecca Barr, Michael L. Kamil, Peter B. Mosenthal, and P. David Pearson. White Plains, N.Y.: Longman, 1991, pp. 984–1012.

Johnston, Peter H. *Constructive Evaluation of Literate Activity.* New York: Longman, 1992.

Johnston, Peter H. *Reading Comprehension Assessment: A Cognitive Basis.* Newark, Del.: International Reading Association, 1983.

Johnston, Peter H. "Teachers as Evaluation Experts." *The Reading Teacher,* 40 (April 1987), 744–748.

Jolly, Hayden B., Jr. "Teaching Basic Function Words." *The Reading Teacher,* 35 (November 1981), 136–140.

Jones, Linda L. "An Interactive View of Reading: Implications for the Classroom." *The Reading Teacher,* 35 (April 1982), 772–777.

Jones, Linda T. *Strategies for Involving Parents in Their Children's Education.* Bloomington, Ind.: Phi Delta Kappa, 1991.

Jones, Margaret B., and Denise D. Nessel. "Enhancing the Curriculum with Experience Stories." *The Reading Teacher,* 39 (October 1985), 18–22.

Jongsma, Eugene. "Grouping for Instruction." *The Reading Teacher,* 38 (May 1985), 918–920.

Jongsma, Kathleen S., and Eugene A. Jongsma. "Test Review: Commercial Informal Reading Inventories." *The Reading Teacher,* 34 (March 1981), 697–705.

Jongsma, Kathleen Stumpf. "Mathematics and Reading." *The Reading Teacher,* 44 (February 1991), 442–443.

Joranko, Joyce. "Reading and Writing Informational Texts." *The Reading Teacher,* 44 (November 1990), 276–277.

Josel, Carol Anne. "In a Different Context." *Journal of Reading,* 31 (January 1988), 375–377.

Jossart, Sarah A. "Character Journals Aid Comprehension." *The Reading Teacher,* 42 (November 1988), 180.

Judd, Dorothy H. "Avoid Readability Formula Drudgery: Use Your School's Microcomputer." *The Reading Teacher,* 35 (October 1981), 7–8.

Juel, Connie. "Beginning Reading." In *Handbook of Reading Research, Vol. II,* edited by R. Barr, M. L. Kamil, P. Mosenthal, and P. D. Pearson. New York: Longman, 1991, pp. 759–787.

Juel, Connie. "Learning to Read and Write: A Longitudinal Study of Fifty-four Children from First through Fourth Grade." *Journal of Educational Psychology,* 80 (1988), 437–447.

Kachuck, Beatrice. "Relative Clauses May Cause Confusion for Young Readers." *The Reading Teacher,* 34 (January 1981), 372–377.

Kaiden, Ellen, and Linda Rice. "Paragraph Patterns and Comprehension: A Tactical Approach." *Journal of Reading,* 30 (November 1986), 164–166.

Kaisen, Jim. "SSR/Booktime: Kindergarten and 1st Grade Sustained Silent Reading." *The Reading Teacher,* 40 (February 1987), 532–536.

Kamhi, Alan, and Hugh Catts. *Reading Disabilities: A Developmental Language Perspective.* Boston: Little, Brown, 1989.

Kaplan, Elaine M., and Anita Tuchman. "Vocabulary Strategies Belong in the Hands of Learners." *Journal of Reading,* 24 (October 1980), 32–34.

Karnowski, Lee. "Using LEA with Process Writing." *The Reading Teacher,* 42 (March 1989), 462–465.

Keegan, Suzi, and Karen Shrake. "Literature Study Groups: An Alternative to Ability Grouping." *The Reading Teacher,* 44 (April 1991), 542–547.

Keller, Paul F. G. "Maryland Micro: A Prototype Readability Formula for Small Computers." *The Reading Teacher,* 35 (April 1982), 778–782.

A Kid-Watching Guide: Evaluation for Whole Language Classrooms. Tucson, Ariz.: TAWL (Tucsonans Applying Whole Language), 1984.

Kimmel, Susan, and Walter H. MacGinitie. "Helping Students Revise Hypotheses While Reading." *The Reading Teacher,* 38 (April 1985), 768–771.

Kinman, Judith R., and Darwin L. Henderson. "An Analysis of Sexism in Newbery Medal Award Books from 1977 to 1984." *The Reading Teacher,* 38 (May 1985), 885–889.

Kinney, Martha A. "A Language Experience Approach to Teaching Expository Text Structure." *The Reading Teacher,* 38 (May 1985), 854–856.

Kirby, Dan, Dawn Latta, and Ruth Vinz. "Beyond Interior Decorating: Using Writing to Make Meaning in the Elementary School." *Phi Delta Kappan,* 69 (June 1988), 718–724.

Kitagawa, Mary M. "Improving Discussions or How to Get the Students to Ask the Questions." *The Reading Teacher,* 36 (October 1982), 42–45.

Klare, George R. "Readability." In *Handbook of Reading Research,* edited by P. David Pearson. New York: Longman, 1984.

Kleiman, Glenn, and Mary Humphrey. "Learning with Computers: Word Processing in the Classroom." *Compute,* 4 (March 1982), 96, 98–99.

Knight, Jenny. "Learning in a Community." *The Reading Teacher,* 47 (March 1994), 498–499.

Koeller, Shirley, and Samina Khan. "Going Beyond the Dictionary with the English Vocabulary Explosion." *Journal of Reading,* 24 (April 1981), 628–629.

Koenke, Karl, and Jane McClellan. "ERIC/RCS Report: Teaching and Testing the Reading Disabled Child." *Language Arts,* 64 (March 1987), 327–330.

Koeze, Scott. "The Dictionary Game." *The Reading Teacher,* 43 (April 1990), 613.

Koskinen, Patricia S., and Irene H. Blum. "Repeated Oral Reading and the Acquisition of Fluency." In *Changing Perspectives on Research in Reading/Language Processing and Instruction,* Thirty-Third Yearbook of the National Reading Conference, edited by Jerome A. Niles and Larry A. Harris. Rochester, N.Y.: National Reading Conference, 1984.

Koskinen, Patricia S., et al. "Retelling: A Strategy for Enhancing Students' Reading Comprehension." *The Reading Teacher,* 41 (May 1988), 892–896.

Koskinen, Patricia S., Robert M. Wilson, Linda B. Gambrell, and Susan B. Neuman. "Captioned Video and Vocabulary Learning: An Innovative Practice in Literacy Instruction." *The Reading Teacher,* 47 (September 1993), 36–43.

Kranz, Bella. *Identifying Talents among Multicultural Children.* Bloomington, Ind.: Phi Delta Kappa, 1994.

Krashen, Stephen D. "The Input Hypothesis and Language Education." In *The Whole Language Catalog,* edited by Kenneth Goodman, Lois Bridges, and Yetta Goodman. Santa Rosa, Calif.: American School Publishers, 1991.

Krieger, Evelyn. "Developing Comprehension Through Author Awareness." *Journal of Reading,* 33 (May 1990), 618–619.

Krushenisky, Cindy. "Lightening Your Load with Multimedia Encyclopedias." *PC Novice,* 4 (October 1993), 62–65.

Kubiszyn, Tom, and Gary Borich. *Educational Testing and Measurement,* 2d ed. Glenview, Ill.: Scott, Foresman, 1987.

Kuchinskas, G., and M. C. Radencich. *The Literary Mapper.* Gainesville, Fla.: Teacher Support Software, 1990.

Kuchinskas, G., and M. C. Radencich. *The Semantic Mapper.* Gainesville, Fla.: Teacher Support Software, 1986.

Kupiter, Karen, and Patricia Wilson. "Updating Poetry Preferences: A Look at the Poetry Children Really Like." *The Reading Teacher,* 47 (September 1993), 28–35.

Kuta, Katherine Wiesolek. "Teaching Text Patterns to Remedial Readers." *Journal of Reading,* 35 (May 1992), 657–658.

Kutzman, Sandra, and Rick Krutchinsky. "Improving Children's Math Vocabulary." *The Reading Teacher,* 35 (December 1981), 347–348.

Labbo, Linda, and William Teale. "Cross-age Reading: A Strategy for Helping Poor Readers." *The Reading Teacher,* 43 (February 1990), 362–369.

LaBerge, David, and S. Jay Samuels. "Toward a Theory of Automatic Information Processing in Reading." In *Theoretical Models and Processes of Reading,* 3d ed., edited by Harry Singer and Robert B. Ruddell. Newark, Del.: International Reading Association, 1985.

Lamme, Linda L. "Children's Literature: The Natural Way to Learn to Read." In *Children's Literature in the Reading Program,* edited by Bernice Cullinan. Newark, Del.: International Reading Association, 1987.

Lamme, Linda Leonard, and Linda Ledbetter. "Libraries: The Heart of Whole Language." *Language Arts,* 67 (November 1990), 735–741.

Lamme, Linda. "Authorship: A Key Facet of Whole Language." *The Reading Teacher,* 42 (May 1989), 704–710.

Landis, Ken. "Software Review: *Where in the World Is Carmen Sandiego?*" *The Apple IIGS Buyer's Guide,* Fall 1989, 59.

Lange, Bob. "Making Sense with Schemata." *Journal of Reading,* 24 (February 1981), 442–445.

Lapp, Diane, and James Flood. "Are There 'Real' Writers Living in Your Classroom? Implementing a Writer-Centered Classroom." *The Reading Teacher,* 48 (November 1993), 254–258.

Lapp, Diane, and James Flood. "Integrating the Curriculum: First Steps." *The Reading Teacher,* 47 (February 1994), 416–419.

Lapp, Diane, and James Flood. *Teaching Students to Read.* New York: Macmillan, 1986.

Larson, Jennifer. "Make New Friends: Introducing Children to Computers." *PC Novice,* September 1994, 34–36.

Larson, Jennifer. "Pick Up a Good Program: Reading Software for Children of All Ages." *PC Novice,* September 1994, 44–47.

Lathlaen, Peggy. "A Meeting of Minds: Teaching Using Biographies." *The Reading Teacher,* 46 (March 1991), 529–531.

Laughlin, Catherine E., and Mavis D. Martin. *Supporting Literacy.* New York: Teachers College Press, 1987.

Layton, Kent, and Martha E. Irwin. "Enriching Your Reading Program with Databases." *The Reading Teacher,* 42 (May 1989), 724.

Lazear, David. *Teaching for Multiple Intelligences.* Bloomington, Ind.: Phi Delta Kappa, 1992.

Leal, Dorothy L. "The Power of Literary Peer-Group Discussions: How Children Collaboratively Negotiate Meaning." *The Reading Teacher,* 47 (October 1993), 114–120.

The Learning Company. *The Children's Writing and Publishing Center.* Fremont, Calif.: The Learning Center, 1989.

Lee, Tosca Moon. "From Stories to Essays: Writing Software for School Children." *PC Novice,* September 1994, 44–47.

Leland, Christine, and Ruth Fitzpatrick. "Cross-Age Interaction Builds Enthusiasm for Reading and Writing." *The Reading Teacher,* 47 (December 1993/January 1994), 292–301.

Lerner, Janet. *Learning Disabilities,* 5th ed. Boston: Houghton Mifflin, 1988.

Letts, Nancy. "Building Classroom Unity." *Teaching K–8,* 25 (August/September 1994), 106–107.

Levine, Daniel U. "Successful Approaches to Improving Academic Achievement in Inner-City Elementary Schools." *Phi Delta Kappan,* 63 (April 1982), 523–526.

Levstick, Linda S. "Research Directions: Mediating Content Through Literary Texts." *Language Arts,* 67 (December 1990), 848–853.

Lewis, Maureen, David Wray, and Patricia Rospigliosi. " . . . And I Want It in Your Own Words." *The Reading Teacher,* 47 (April 1994), 528–536.

Lewkowicz, Nancy K. "The Bag Game: An Activity to Heighten Phonemic Awareness." *The Reading Teacher,* 47 (March 1994), 508–509.

Lipson, Marjorie Y., Sheila W. Valencia, Karen K. Wixon, and Charles W. Peters. "Integration and Thematic Teaching: Integration to Improve Teaching and Learning." *Language Arts,* 70 (April 1993), 252–263.

Lipson, Marjorie, and Karen Wixson. *Assessment and Instruction of Reading Disability.* New York: HarperCollins, 1991.

Long, Emily S. "Using Acrostic Poems for Research Reporting." *The Reading Teacher,* 46 (February 1993), 447–448.

Loughlin, Catherine E., and Mavis D. Martin. *Supporting Literacy.* New York: Teachers College Press, 1987.

Lundberg, I., J. Frost, and O. Peterson. "Effects of an Extensive Program for Stimulating Phonological Awareness in Preschool Children." *Reading Research Quarterly,* 23 (1988), 263–284.

Lynch-Brown, Carol. "Translated Children's Books: Voyaging to Other Countries." *The Reading Teacher,* 44 (March 1991), 486–492.

Mace-Matluck, Betty J. *Literacy Instruction in Bilingual Settings: A Synthesis of Current Research.* Los Alamitos, Calif.: National Center for Bilingual Research, 1982. [ED 222 079]

Macey, Joan Mary. "Word Lines: An Approach to Vocabulary Development." *The Reading Teacher,* 35 (November 1981), 216–217.

Maclean, Rod. "Two Paradoxes of Phonics." *The Reading Teacher,* 41 (February 1988), 514–517.

Macon, James M., Diane Bewell, and MaryEllen Vogt. *Responses to Literature: Grades K–8.* Newark, Del.: International Reading Association, 1991.

Madden, Lowell. "Improve Reading Attitudes of Poor Readers through Cooperative Reading Teams." *The Reading Teacher,* 42 (December 1988), 194–199.

Mallon, Barbara, and Roberta Berglund. "The Language Experience Approach: Recurring Questions and Their Answers." *The Reading Teacher,* 37 (May 1984), 867–871.

Mallow, Jeffry V. "Reading Science." *Journal of Reading,* 34 (February 1991), 324–338.

Mandler, J. M. *Stories, Scripts, and Scenes: Aspects of Schema Theory.* Hillsdale, N.J.: Erlbaum, 1984.

Mandler, Jean M., and Nancy S. Johnson. "Remembrance of Things Parsed: Story Structure and Recall." *Cognitive Psychology,* 9 (January 1977), 111–151.

Mangieri, John N., and Michael S. Kahn. "Is the Dolch List of 220 Basic Sight Words Irrelevant?" *The Reading Teacher,* 30 (March 1977), 649–651.

Manna, Anthony. "Making Language Come Alive Through Reading Plays." *The Reading Teacher,* 37 (April 1984), 712–717.

Manning, Gary L., and Maryann Manning. "What Models of Recreational Reading Make a Difference?" *Reading World,* 23 (May 1984), 375–380.

Manning, Maryann, Gary Manning, and Jackie Hughes. "Journals in 1st Grade: What Children Write." *The Reading Teacher,* 41 (December 1987), 311–315.

Manolakes, George. "Comprehension: A Personal Experience in Content Area Reading." *The Reading Teacher,* 42 (December 1988), 200–202.

Manzo, Anthony V. "The ReQuest Procedure." *Journal of Reading,* 13 (November 1969), 123–126.

Manzo, Anthony V. "Three 'Universal' Strategies in Content Area Reading and Language." *Journal of Reading,* 24 (November 1980), 147.

Maria, Katherine. "Developing Disadvantaged Children's Background Knowledge Interactively." *The Reading Teacher,* 42 (January 1989), 296–300.

Maric, K., and J. M. Johnson. "Correcting Misconceptions: Effect of Type on Text." In *Literacy Theory and Research: Analyses from Multiple Paradigms,* edited by S. McCormick and J. Zutell. Chicago: National Reading Conference, 1990.

Maring, Gerald H., Gail Chase Furman, and Judy Blum-Anderson. "Five Cooperative Learning Strategies for Mainstreamed Youngsters in Content Area Classrooms." *The Reading Teacher,* 39 (December 1985), 310–313.

Marshall, Nancy. "Using Story Grammar to Assess Reading Comprehension." *The Reading Teacher,* 36 (March 1983), 616–620.

Marston, Marilyn. "Bag the Magic E." *The Reading Teacher,* 42 (January 1989), 339.

Martinez, Miriam. "Motivating Dramatic Story Reenactments." *The Reading Teacher,* 46 (May 1993), 682–688.

Martinez, Miriam, and Marcia F. Nash. "Bookalogues: Talking about Children's Books." *Language Arts,* 68 (February 1991), 140–147.

Martinez, Miriam, and Marcia F. Nash. "Bookalogues: Talking about Children's Literature." *Language Arts,* 67 (October 1990), 599–606.

Martinez, Miriam, and Marcia F. Nash. "Bookalogues: Talking about Children's Literature." *Language Arts,* 67 (December 1990), 854–861.

Martinez, Miriam, and William H. Teale. "The Ins and Outs of a Kindergarten Writing Program." *The Reading Teacher,* 40 (January 1987), 444–451.

Marzano, Lorraine. "Connecting Literature with Cooperative Writing." *The Reading Teacher,* 43 (February 1990), 429–430.

Marzano, Robert J. "A Cluster Approach to Vocabulary Instruction: A New Direction from the Research Literature." *The Reading Teacher,* 38 (November 1984), 168–173.

Marzano, Robert J. "Lessons from the Field about Outcome-Based Performance Assessments." *Educational Leadership,* 51 (March 1994), 44–50.

Mason, George E. *Language Experience Recorder Plus.* Gainesville, Fla.: Teacher Support Software, 1987.

Mason, George. "The Word Processor and Teaching Reading." *The Reading Teacher,* 37 (February 1984), 552–553.

Mason, Jana M. "Early Reading from a Developmental Perspective." In *Reading Research Handbook,* edited by P. David Pearson et al. New York: Longman, 1984.

Mateja, John. "Musical Cloze: Background, Purpose, and Sample." *The Reading Teacher,* 35 (January 1982), 444–448.

Mathewson, Grover C. "Model of Attitude Influence upon Reading and Learning to Read." In *Theoretical Models and Processes of Reading,* 4th ed., edited by Robert B. Ruddell, Martha Rapp Ruddell, and Harry Singer. Newark, Del.: International Reading Association, 1994, pp. 1131–1161.

Mathewson, Grover C. "Teaching Forms of Negation in Reading and Reasoning." *The Reading Teacher,* 37 (January 1984), 354–358.

Mathison, Carla. "Activating Student Interest in Content Area Reading." *Journal of Reading,* 33 (December 1989), 170–176.

Maudeville, Thomas F. "KWLA: Linking the Affective and Cognitive Domains." *The Reading Teacher,* 47 (May 1994), 679–680.

Mavrogenes, Nancy A. "What Every Reading Teacher Should Know about Emergent Literacy." *The Reading Teacher,* 40 (November 1986), 174–178.

Mayfield, Margie. "The Classroom Environment: A Living-in and Learning-in Space." In *Emerging Literacy,* edited by Lloyd O. Ollila and Margie I. Mayfield. Boston: Allyn & Bacon, 1992, pp. 166–195.

Mayfield, Margie. "Organizing for Teaching and Learning." In *Emerging Literacy,* edited by Lloyd O. Ollila and Margie I. Mayfield. Boston: Allyn & Bacon, 1992, pp. 196–218.

McAloon, Noreen. "Prereading and Background Knowledge." *Journal of Reading,* 38 (October 1994), 142–144.

McAloon, Noreen. "Time for Nonfiction?" *Journal of Reading,* 36 (March 1993), 502–503.

McCallum, Richard D. "Don't Throw the Basals Out with the Bath Water." *The Reading Teacher,* 42 (December 1988), 204–208.

McCarthy, Robert. "Assessing the Whole Student." *Instructor Special Supplement* (May/June 1994), 18.

McClure, Amy A., and Connie S. Zitlow. "Not Just the Facts: Aesthetic Response in Elementary Content Area Studies." *Language Arts,* 68 (January 1991), 27–33.

McConaughy, Stephanie H. "Word Recognition and Word Meaning in the Total Reading Process." *Language Arts,* 55 (November/December 1978), 946–956, 1003.

McCord, D. "This Is My Rock." In *Anthology of Children's Literature,* 4th rev. ed., edited by E. Johnson, E. R. Sickels, and C. R. Sayers. Boston: Houghton Mifflin, 1970.

McCormick, S., and D. S. Hill. "An Analysis of the Effects of Two Procedures for Increasing Disabled Readers' Inferencing Skills." *Journal of Educational Research,* 77 (1984), 219–226.

McCracken, Robert, and Marlene McCracken. *Stories, Songs & Poetry to Teach Reading & Writing.* Winnipeg, Canada: Peguis, 1987.

McDonell, Gloria M., and E. Bess Osburn. "New Thoughts about Reading Readiness." In *Readings on Reading Instruction,* edited by Albert J. Harris and Edward R. Sipay. New York: Longman, 1984.

McGee, Lea M. "Exploring the Literature-Based Reading Revolution." *Language Arts,* 69 (November 1992), 529–537.

McGee, Lea M., and Donald J. Richgels. *Literacy's Beginnings.* Boston: Allyn & Bacon, 1990.

McGee, Lea M., and Donald J. Richgels. "Teaching Expository Text Structure to Elementary Students." *The Reading Teacher,* 38 (April 1985), 739–748.

McGee, Lea M., and Gail E. Tompkins. "The Videotape Answer to Independent Reading Comprehension Activities." *The Reading Teacher,* 34 (January 1981), 427–433.

McGill-Franzen, Anne. "'I Could Read the Words!': Selecting Good Books for Inexperienced Readers." *The Reading Teacher,* 46 (February 1993), 424–426.

McGill-Franzen, Anne, and Richard Allington. "Every Child's Right: Literacy." *The Reading Teacher,* 45 (October 1991), 86–89.

McGinley, William, and Daniel Madigan. "The Research 'Story': A Forum for Integrating Reading, Writing, and Learning." *Language Arts,* 67 (September 1990), 474–483.

McGuinness, Diane. *When Children Don't Learn.* New York: Basic Books, 1985.

McInnes, John. "Children's Quest for Literacy." In *Roles in Literacy Learning,* edited by Duane Tovey and James Kerber. Newark, Del.: International Reading Association, 1986.

McIntosh, Margaret E. "What Do Practitioners Need to Know about Current Inference Research?" *The Reading Teacher,* 38 (April 1985), 755–761.

McKenzie, Gary R. "Personalize Your Group Teaching." In *Readings on Reading Instruction,* 3d ed., edited by Albert J. Harris and Edward R. Sipay. New York: Longman, 1984.

McKeon, Denise. "When Meeting 'Common' Standards is Uncommonly Difficult." *Educational Leadership,* 51 (May 1994), 45–49.

McKeown, M. G., I. L. Beck, R. C. Omanson, and C. A. Perfetti. "The Effects of Long-Term Vocabulary Instruction on Reading Comprehension: A Replication." *Journal of Reading Behavior,* 15 (1983), 3–18.

McKeown, Margaret G., Isabel L. Beck, and M. Jo Worthy. "Grappling with Text Ideas: Questioning the Author." *The Reading Teacher,* 46 (April 1993), 560–566.

McKeown, Margaret G., Isabel L. Beck, Richard C. Omanson, and Martha T. Pople. "Some Effects of the Nature and Frequency of Vocabulary Instruction on the Knowledge and Use of Words." *Reading Research Quarterly,* 20, no. 5 (1985), 522–535.

McLane, Joan, and Gillian McNamee. *Early Literacy.* Cambridge, Mass.: Harvard University Press, 1990.

McMahon, Susan I., and Taffy E. Raphael. "Teacher Assessment Plan (TAP)." Paper presented at the International Reading Association Convention, Atlanta, May 6, 1990.

McMillan, Merna M., and Lance M. Gentile. "Children's Literature: Teaching Critical Thinking and Ethics." *The Reading Teacher,* 41 (May 1988), 876–878.

McNutt, Gaye, and Nancy Bukofzer. "Teaching Early Reading at McDonald's." *The Reading Teacher,* 35 (April 1982), 841–842.

McWhirter, Anna M. "Whole Language in the Middle School." *The Reading Teacher,* 43 (April 1990), 562–565.

MECC. *Story Book Weaver.* North Minneapolis, MN: MECC.

Meir, Margaret. "Comprehension Monitoring in the Elementary Classroom." *The Reading Teacher,* 37 (April 1984), 770–774.

Melnick, Steven A. "Electronic Encyclopedias on Compact Disk." *The Reading Teacher,* 44 (February 1991), 432–434.

Meltzer, Nancy S., and Robert Herse. "The Boundaries of Written Words as Seen by First Graders." *Journal of Reading Behavior,* 1 (Summer 1969), 3–14.

Memory, David M., and Carol Y. Yoder. "Improving Concentration in Content Classrooms." *Journal of Reading,* 31 (February 1988), 426–435.

Mendoza, Alicia. "Reading to Children: Their Preferences." *The Reading Teacher,* 38 (February 1985), 522–527.

Menke, Deborah J., and Michael Pressley. "Elaborative Interrogation: Using 'Why' Questions to Enhance the Learning from Text." *Journal of Reading,* 37 (May 1994), 642–645.

Meyer, Carol. "What's the Difference between *Authentic* and *Performance* Assessment?" *Educational Leadership,* 49 (May 1992), 39–40.

Meyer, Judy. "Integrating Second Language Students into the Classroom and Curriculum." Paper presented at the annual conference of the International Reading Association, Atlanta, May 9, 1990.

Miccinati, Jeannette L. "Using Prosodic Cues to Teach Oral Reading Fluency." *The Reading Teacher,* 39 (November 1985), 206–212.

Michener, Darlene M. "Test Your Reading Aloud IQ." *The Reading Teacher,* 42 (November 1988), 118–122.

Mickelson, Norma. "Adventures in Evaluation." Paper presented at the Whole Language Umbrella Conference, St. Louis, August 4, 1990.

Miholic, Vincent. "An Inventory to Pique Students' Metacognitive Awareness of Reading Strategies." *Journal of Reading,* 38 (October 1994), 84–86.

Mike, Dennis G. "Interactive Literacy." *Electronic Learning,* (May/June 1994), 50–52, 54.

Mikel, Vesta L. "Using Cooperative Learning in Teaching Content Reading." *Journal of Reading,* 36 (May 1993), 659–660.

Miller, Etta, Luther B. Clegg, and Bill Vanderhoff. "Creating Postcards from the Famous for Social Studies Class." *Journal of Reading,* 36 (October 1992), 134–135.

Miller, G. Michael, and George E. Mason. "Dramatic Improvisation: Risk-Free Role Playing for Improving Reading Performance." *The Reading Teacher,* 37 (November 1983), 128–131.

Miller, Kathleen K., and John E. George. "Expository Passage Organizers: Models for Reading and Writing." *Journal of Reading,* 35 (February 1992), 372–377.

Milz, Vera E. "Comments from a Teacher Researcher." In *Teachers and Research,* edited by Gay Su Pinnell and Myna L. Matlin. Newark, Del.: International Reading Association, 1989.

Mindplay. *Author! Author!* Danvers, Mass: Methods and Solutions, 1990.

Minnesota Educational Computing Consortium. *Story Book Weaver.* North Minneapolis, Minn.: MECC.

Moldofsky, Penny Baum. "Teaching Students to Determine the Central Story Problem: A Practical Application of Schema Theory." *The Reading Teacher,* 36 (April 1983), 740–745.

Monahan, Joy N. "Developing a Strategic Reading Program." In *Reading in the Middle Schools,* 2d ed., edited by Gerald G. Duffy. Newark, Del.: International Reading Association, 1990.

Moore, David W., and James W. Cunningham. "Task Clarity and Sixth-Grade Students' Main Idea Statements." In *Changing Perspectives on Research in Reading/Language Processing and Instruction,* edited by Jerome A. Niles and Larry A. Harris. Rochester, N.Y.: National Reading Conference, 1984.

Moore, David W., and John E. Readence. "Processing Main Ideas Through Parallel Lesson Transfer." *Journal of Reading,* 23 (April 1980), 589–593.

Moore, David W., and Greg P. Stefanich. "Middle School Reading: A Historical Perspective." In *Reading in the Middle School,* 2d ed., edited by Gerald G. Duffy. Newark, Del.: International Reading Association, 1990.

Moore, Margaret. "Computers Can Enhance Transactions Between Readers and Writers." *The Reading Teacher,* 42 (April 1989), 608–611.

Moore, Margaret. "Electronic Dialoguing: An Avenue to Literacy." *The Reading Teacher,* 45 (December 1991), 280–286.

Moore, Sharon Arthur, and David W. Moore. "Literacy through Content/Content through Literacy." *The Reading Teacher,* 43 (November 1989), 170–171.

Moore, Sharon Arthur, David W. Moore, and Jeanne Swafford. "Reading and Mathematics Comprehension." *The Reading Teacher,* 44 (May 1991), 684–686.

"More Disabled Students Now in Regular Classes." *Reading Today,* 11 (April/May 1994), 28.

Morrow, Lesley Mandel. "Manipulative Learning Materials: Merging Reading Skills with Content Area Objectives." *Journal of Reading,* 25 (February 1982), 448–453.

Morrow, Lesley Mandel. "Reading and Retelling Stories: Strategies for Emergent Readers." *The Reading Teacher,* 38 (May 1985), 870–875.

Morrow, Lesley Mandel. "Using Story Retelling to Develop Comprehension." In *Children's Comprehension of Text: Research into Practice,* edited by K. Denise Muth. Newark, Del.: International Reading Association, 1989.

Mosenthal P., and T. J. Na. "Quality of Text Recall as a Function of Children's Classroom Competence." *Journal of Experimental Child Psychology,* 30 (1980b), 1–21.

Mosenthal, P. "Children's Strategy Preference for Resolving Contradictory Story Information under Two Social Conditions." *Journal of Experimental Child Psychology,* 28 (1979), 323–443.

Mosenthal, P. "Reading Comprehension Research from a Classroom Perspective." In *Promoting Reading Comprehension,* edited by J. Flood. Newark, Del.: International Reading Association, 1984.

Mosenthal, P., and T. J. Na. "Quality of Children's Recall under Two Classroom Testing Tasks: Toward a Socio-Psycholinguistic Model of Reading Comprehension." *Reading Research Quarterly,* 15 (1980a), 501–528.

Mosenthal, Peter B. "Defining Reading: Freedom of Choice but Not Freedom from Choice." *The Reading Teacher,* 39 (October 1985), 110–112.

Mosenthal, Peter B. "Defining Reading: Operational Definitions and Other Oracles." *The Reading Teacher,* 39 (December 1985): 362–364.

Mosenthal, Peter B. "Defining Reading: Taxonomies and Stray Definitions." *The Reading Teacher,* 39 (November 1985), 238–240.

Mosenthal, Peter B. "Defining Reading: Translating Definitions of Reading in Research into Practice." *The Reading Teacher,* 39 (January 1986), 476–479.

Mosenthal, Peter B. "From Pyramid Taxonomy to Reading Theories: The Complexity of Simplification." *The Reading Teacher,* 39 (March 1986), 732–734.

Mosenthal, Peter B. "Improving Reading Practice with Reading Theory: The Procrustean Approach." *The Reading Teacher,* 40 (October 1986), 108–111.

Mosenthal, Peter B. "The Whole Language Approach: Teachers Between a Rock and a Hard Place." *The Reading Teacher,* 42 (April 1989), 628–629.

Mosenthal, Peter B., and Irwin S. Kirsch. "Understanding Documents: Understanding Graphs and Charts, Part I." *Journal of Reading,* 33 (February 1990), 371–373.

Mosenthal, Peter B., and Irwin S. Kirsch. "Understanding Documents: Understanding Graphs and Charts, Part II." *Journal of Reading,* 33 (March 1990), 454–457.

Mosenthal, Peter B., and Irwin S. Kirsch. "Understanding Documents: Understanding Thematic Maps." *Journal of Reading,* 34 (October 1990), 136–140.

Moss, Barbara. "Children's Nonfiction Trade Books: A Complement to Content Area Texts." *The Reading Teacher,* 45 (September 1991), 26–32.

Moss, Barbara, and Harry Noden. "Pointers for Putting Whole Language into Practice." *The Reading Teacher,* 47 (December 1993/January 1994), 342–344.

Moss, Joy F., and Sherri Oden. "Children's Story Comprehension and Story Learning." *The Reading Teacher,* 36 (April 1983), 784–789.

Mountain, Lee. "Math Synonyms." *The Reading Teacher,* 46 (February 1993), 451–452.

Moustafa, Margaret. "Comprehensible Input PLUS the Language Experience Approach: A Longterm Perspective." *The Reading Teacher,* 41 (December 1987), 276–286.

Moustafa, Margaret. "Recoding in Whole Language Reading Instruction." *Language Arts,* 70 (October 1993), 483–487.

Moustafa, Margaret, and Joyce Penrose. "Comprehensible Input PLUS the Language Experience Approach: Reading Instruction for Limited English Speaking Students." *The Reading Teacher,* 38 (March 1985), 640–647.

Muller, Dorothy H., and Liz Savage. "Mapping the Library." *The Reading Teacher,* 35 (April 1982), 840–841.

Mulligan, Patricia Alba, and Kay Gore. "DISKovery: Telecommunications: Education's Missing Link." *Language Arts,* 69 (September 1992), 379–384.

Munson, Jennie Livingston. "Story and Poetry Maps." *The Reading Teacher,* 42 (May 1989), 736–737.

Nagy, William E. *Teaching Vocabulary to Improve Reading Comprehension.* Urbana, Ill.: National Council of Teachers of English, 1988.

Nagy, William E., and Richard C. Anderson. "How Many Words Are There in Printed School English?" *Reading Research Quarterly,* 19, no. 3 (1984), 304–330.

Nagy, William E., Patricia A. Herman, and Richard C. Anderson. "Learning Words from Context." *Reading Research Quarterly,* 20, no. 2 (1985), 233–253.

Naughton, Victoria M. "Creative Mapping for Content Reading." *Journal of Reading,* 37 (December 1993/January 1994), 324–326.

Nelson, Olga. "Storytelling: Language Experience for Meaning Making." *The Reading Teacher,* 42 (February 1989), 386–390.

Nelson-Herber, Joan. "Expanding and Defining Vocabulary in Content Areas." *Journal of Reading,* 29 (April 1986), 626–633.

Nessel, Denise D. "Storytelling in the Reading Program." *The Reading Teacher,* 38 (January 1985), 378–381.

Neuman, Susan B., and Patricia S. Koskinen. "Captioned Television as Comprehensible Input: Effects of Incidental Word Learning in Context for Language Minority Students." *Reading Research Quarterly,* 27 (1992), 95–106.

Neuman, Susan, and Kathleen Roskos. *Language and Literacy Learning in the Early Years.* Orlando: Harcourt Brace Jovanovich, 1993.

Neville, Rita. "Critical Thinkers Become Critical Readers." *The Reading Teacher,* 35 (May 1982), 947–948.

Newman, Judith M. "Learning in Our Own Classrooms." In *The Whole Language Catalog,* edited by Kenneth S. Goodman, Lois Bridges Bird, and Yetta M. Goodman. Santa Rosa, Calif.: American School Publishers, 1991.

Newman, Judith M. "Online: From Far Away." *Language Arts,* 66 (1989), 791–797.

Newman, Judith M. "The Computer Is Only Incidental." *Language Arts,* 67 (April 1990), 439–444.

Newman, Judith M., and Susan M. Church. "Myths of Whole Language." *The Reading Teacher,* 44 (September 1990), 20–26.

Newman, Judith. "Insights from Recent Reading and Writing Research and Their Implications for Developing Whole Language Curriculum." In *Whole Language: Theory in Use,* edited by Judith M. Newman. Portsmouth, N.H.: Heinemann, 1985.

Nolan, Thomas E. "Self-Questioning and Prediction: Combining Metacognitive Strategies." *Journal of Reading,* 35 (October 1991), 132–138.

Nolte, Ruth Yopp, and Harry Singer. "Active Comprehension: Teaching a Process of Reading Comprehension and Its Effects on Reading Achievement." *The Reading Teacher,* 39 (October 1985), 24–31.

Noonan, Norma. "Parents as Partners in Reading Development." In *Readings on Reading Instruction,* 3d ed., edited by Albert J. Harris and Edward R. Sipay. New York: Longman, 1984.

Norton, Donna E. "Circa 1942 and the Integration of Literature, Reading, and Geography." *The Reading Teacher,* 46 (April 1993), 610–614.

Norton, Donna E. *The Impact of Literature-Based Reading.* New York: Merrill, 1992.

Norton, Donna E. "Modeling Inferencing of Characterization." *The Reading Teacher,* 46 (September 1992), 64–67.

Norton, Donna E. "Teaching Multicultural Literature in the Reading Curriculum." *The Reading Teacher,* 44 (September 1990), 28–40.

Norton, Donna E. *Through the Eyes of a Child,* 2d ed. Columbus, Ohio: Merrill, 1987, 1991, 1995.

Norton, Donna E. "Understanding Plot Structures." *The Reading Teacher,* 46 (November 1992), 254–258.

Norton, Donna E. "Webbing and Historical Fiction." *The Reading Teacher,* 46 (February 1993), 432–436.

Noyce, Ruth M. "Team Up and Teach with Trade Books." *The Reading Teacher,* 32 (January 1979), 442–448.

Nurss, Joanne. "Evaluation of Language and Literacy." In *Emerging Literacy,* edited by Lloyd Ollila and Margie Mayfield. Boston: Allyn & Bacon, 1992, pp. 229–252.

O'Brien, Kathy, and Darleen K. Stoner. "Increasing Environmental Awareness through Children's Literature." *The Reading Teacher,* 41 (October 1987), 14–19.

Ogle, Donna M. "K-W-L: A Teaching Model that Develops Active Reading of Expository Text." *The Reading Teacher,* 39 (February 1986), 564–570.

Ogle, Donna M. "The Know, Want to Know, Learn Strategy." In *Children's Comprehension of Text: Research into Practice,* edited by K. Denise Muth. Newark, Del.: International Reading Association, 1989.

Oldfather, Penny. "What Students Say about Motivating Experiences in a Whole Language Classroom." *The Reading Teacher,* 46 (May 1993), 672–681.

Oleneski, Sue. "Using Jump Rope Rhymes to Teach Reading Skills." *The Reading Teacher,* 46 (October 1992), 173–175.

Ollila, Lloyd O., and Margie I. Mayfield. *Emerging Literacy: Preschool, Kindergarten, and Primary Grades.* Boston: Allyn & Bacon, 1992, pp. 166–195.

Ollmann, Hilda E. "Cause and Effect in the Real World." *Journal of Reading,* 33 (December 1989), 224–225.

Ollmann, Hilda E. "Integrating Content Area Skills with Fiction Favorites." *Journal of Reading,* 34 (February 1991), 398–399.

Olson, Mary W., and Thomas C. Gee. "Content Reading Instruction in the Primary Grades: Perceptions and Strategies." *The Reading Teacher,* 45 (December 1991), 298–307.

Olson, Mary W., and Bonnie Longnion. "Pattern Guides: A Workable Alternative for Content Teachers." *Journal of Reading,* 25 (May 1982), 736–741.

O'Neil, John. "'Inclusive' Education Gains Adherents." *ASCD Update,* 35 (November 1993), 1, 3–4.

O'Neil, John. "Making Assessment Meaningful." *ASCD Update,* 36 (August 1994), 1, 4–5.

O'Neil, John. "Portfolio Assessment Bears the Burden of Popularity." *ASCD Update,* 35 (October 1993), 3, 8.

O'Neil, John. "The Promise of Portfolios." *ASCD Update,* 35. (September 1993), 1, 5.

"Open to Suggestion: Electronic Access to the Library of Congress in Washington, D.C." *Journal of Reading,* 37 (May 1994), 691.

Otto, Wayne, Anne Wolf, and Roger G. Eldridge. "Managing Instruction." In *Handbook of Reading Research,* edited by P. David Pearson. New York: Longman, 1984.

Ovando, Carlos J., and Virginia P. Collier. *Bilingual and ESL Classrooms.* New York: McGraw-Hill, 1985.

Owston, R. D., S. Murphy, and H. H. Wideman. "The Effects of Word Processing on Students' Writing Quality and Revision Strategies." *Research in the Teaching of English,* 26 (1992), 249–276.

Pace, Glennellen. "When Teachers Use Literature for Literacy Instruction: Ways That Constrain, Ways That Free." *Language Arts,* 68 (January 1991), 12–25.

Padek, Nancy D. "The Language and Educational Needs of Children Who Speak Black English." *The Reading Teacher,* 35 (November 1981), 144–151.

Pahl, Michele M., and Robert J. Monson. "In Search of Whole Language: Transforming Curriculum and Instruction." *Journal of Reading,* 35 (April 1992), 518–524.

Palincsar, Annemarie Sullivan, and Ann L. Brown. "Interactive Teaching to Promote Independent Learning from Text." *The Reading Teacher,* 39 (April 1986), 771–777.

Palmer, Barbara. "Dolch List Still Useful." *The Reading Teacher,* 38 (March 1985), 708–709.

Palmer, Gerry. "Process Writing Is Alive and Well." *Teaching K–8,* 20 (May 1990), 86–87.

Pardo, Laura S., and Taffy E. Raphael. "Classroom Organization for Instruction in Content Areas." *The Reading Teacher,* 44 (April 1991), 556–565.

Paris, Scott G., Barbara Wasik A., and Julianne C. Turner. "The Development of Strategic Readers." In *Handbook of Reading Research, Vol. II,* edited by Rebecca Barr,

Michael L. Kamil, Peter B. Mosenthal, and P. David Pearson. White Plains, N.Y.: Longman, 1991, pp. 609–640.

Pearson, P. David. "Changing the Face of Comprehension Instruction." *The Reading Teacher,* 38 (April 1985), 724–738.

Pearson, P. David. "Focus on Research: Teaching and Learning Reading: A Research Perspective." *Language Arts,* 70 (October 1993), 502–511.

Pearson, P. David, et al. *The Effect of Background Knowledge on Young Children's Comprehension of Explicit and Implicit Information.* Urbana–Champaign, Ill.: University of Illinois, Center for the Study of Reading, 1979.

Pearson, P. David, and Kaybeth Camperell. "Comprehension of Text Structures." In *Comprehension and Teaching: Research Reviews,* edited by John T. Guthrie. Newark, Del.: International Reading Association, 1981.

Pearson, P. David, and Kaybeth Camperell. "Comprehension of Text Structures." In *Theoretical Models and Processes of Reading,* 4th ed., edited by Robert Ruddell, Martha Rapp Ruddell, and Harry Singer. Newark, Del.: International Reading Association, 1994, pp. 448–468.

Pearson, P. David, and Linda Fielding. "Comprehension Instruction." In *Handbook of Reading Research, Volume II,* edited by Rebecca Barr, Michael L. Kamil, Peter Mosenthal, and P. David Pearson. New York: Longman, 1991.

Pearson, P. David, and Linda Fielding. "Comprehension Instruction." In *Theoretical Models and Processes of Reading,* 4th ed, edited by Robert Ruddell, Martha Rapp Ruddell, and Harry Singer. Newark, Del.: International Reading Association, 1994, 815–860.

Pearson, P. David, and Dale D. Johnson. *Teaching Reading Comprehension.* New York: Holt, Rinehart and Winston, 1978.

Peck, Jackie. "Using Storytelling to Promote Language and Literacy Development." *The Reading Teacher,* 43 (November 1989), 138–141.

Pehrsson, Robert, and Peter Denner. *Semantic Organizers: A Study Strategy for Special Needs Learners.* Rockville, Md.: Aspen, 1989.

Pelican Press. Fairfield, Conn.: Toucan, 1992.

Pellegrini, A. D., and Lee Galda. "The Effects of Thematic-Fantasy Play Training on the Development of Children's Story Comprehension." *American Educational Research Journal,* 19 (Fall 1982), 443–452.

Perry, Margaret. *Using Microcomputers with Gifted Students.* Bloomington, Ind.: Phi Delta Kappa, 1989.

Perry, Merry. *The New Talking Stickybear Alphabet. The Apple IIGS Buyer's Guide,* Fall 1989, 58–59.

Peters, Charles. "Commentary on Redesigning Teaching and Learning: The Arizona Student Assessment Program." In *Authentic Reading Assessment: Practices and Possibilities,* edited by Sheila Valencia, Elfrieda Hiebert, and Peter Afflerbach. Newark, Del.: International Reading Association, 1994, pp. 247–254.

Peters, L. *The Sun, the Wind, and the Rain.* New York: Holt, Rinehart and Winston, 1988.

Peterson, B. "Selecting Books for Beginning Readers." In *Bridges to Literacy: Learning from Reading Recovery,* edited by D. DeFord, C. Lyons, and G. S. Pinnell. Portsmouth, N.H.: Heinemann, 1991, pp. 119–147.

Peterson, Susan, and Patricia H. Phelps. "Visual-Auditory Links: A Structural Analysis Approach to Increase Word Power." *The Reading Teacher,* 44 (March 1991), 524–525.

Petrick, Pamela Bondi. "Creative Vocabulary Instruction in the Content Area." *Journal of Reading,* 35 (March 1992), 481–482.

Pettersen, Nancy-Laurel. "Grate/Great Homonym Hunt." *Journal of Reading,* 31 (January 1988), 374–375.

Pickert, Sarah M., and Martha L. Chase. "Story Retelling: An Informal Technique for Evaluating Children's Language." *The Reading Teacher,* 31 (February 1978), 528–531.

Pickett, Anna Lou, Stanley Vasa, and Allen Steckelberg. *Using Paraeducators Effectively in the Classroom.* Bloomington, Ind.: Phi Delta Kappa, 1993.

Piech, Pat. "Science Learning Centers: Seatwork Alternatives." *The Reading Teacher,* 44 (February 1991), 446–447.

Pierce, Kathryn Mitchell, and Kathy G. Short, eds. "Children's Books: Contemporary Social and Political Issues." *The Reading Teacher,* 47 (October 1993), 148–157.

Pierce, Kathryn Mitchell, and Kathy G. Short, eds. "Children's Books: Environmental Issues and Actions." *The Reading Teacher,* 47 (December 1993/January 1994), 328–335.

Pigg, John R. "The Effects of a Storytelling/Storyreading Program on the Language Skills of Rural Primary Students." Unpublished paper. Cookeville, Tenn.: Tennessee Technological University, 1986.

Pike, Kathy, Rita Compain, and Jean Mumper. *Connections: An Integrated Approach to Literacy.* New York: Harper-Collins, 1994.

Pikulski, John J. "Questions and Answers." *The Reading Teacher,* 42 (April 1989), 637.

Pikulski, John. "Preventing Reading Failure: A Review of Five Effective Programs." *The Reading Teacher,* 48 (September 1994), 30–39.

Pikulski, John. "The Assessment of Reading: A Time for Change?" *The Reading Teacher,* 43 (October 1989), 80–81.

Pikulski, John. "The Role of Tests in a Literacy Assessment Program." *The Reading Teacher,* 43 (May 1990), 686–688.

Pinnell, Gay Su. *Restructuring Beginning Reading with the Reading Recovery Approach.* Bloomington, Ind.: Phi Delta Kappa, 1991.

Pittelman, Susan D., Joan E. Heimlich, Roberta L. Bergund, and Michael T. French. *Semantic Feature Analysis: Classroom Applications.* Newark, Del.: International Reading Association, 1990.

Plisko, Valena White, and Joyce D. Stern, eds. "Educating Handicapped Students." *The Condition of Education.* Washington, D.C.: Statistical Report, National Center for Education Statistics, U.S. Department of Education, 1985.

Poe, Virginia L. "Mind Reading Made Easy: A Game for Practicing Word Recognition Skills." *The Reading Teacher,* 38 (April 1985), 822–824.

Poindexter, Candace. "Guessed Meanings." *Journal of Reading,* 37 (February 1994), 420–422.

Poindexter, Candace A., and Susan Prescott. "A Technique for Teaching Students to Draw Inferences from Text." *The Reading Teacher,* 39 (May 1986), 908–911.

Potter, Rosemary. *Using Microcomputers for Teaching Reading in the Elementary School.* Bloomington, Ind.: Phi Delta Kappa, 1989.

Powell, Janet L. "How Well Do Tests Measure Real Reading?" *ERIC Clearinghouse on Reading and Communication Skills* (June 1989), 1.

Powell, William R. "Teaching Vocabulary Through Opposition." *Journal of Reading,* 29 (April 1986), 617–621.

Powers, Anne. "Sharing a Language Experience Library with the Whole School." *The Reading Teacher,* 34 (May 1981), 892–895.

Preece, Alison. "Oral Language Competence and the Young Child." In *Emerging Literacy: Preschool, Kindergarten, and Primary Grades,* edited by Lloyd Ollila and Margie Mayfield. Needham Heights, Mass: Allyn and Bacon, 1992, pp. 42–70.

Prill, Pat. "Helping Students Use the Classroom Library." *The Reading Teacher,* 48 (December 1994/January 1995), 365.

Prince, A. T., and D. S. Mancus. "Enriching Comprehension: A Schema-Altered Basal Reading Lesson." *Reading Research and Instruction,* 27, no. 1 (1987), 45–54.

Probst, Robert E. "Transactional Theory in the Teaching of Literature." *Journal of Reading,* 31 (January 1988), 378–381.

Pugh, Sharon L., and Jesus Garcia. "Portraits in Black: Establishing African American Identity Through Nonfiction Books." *Journal of Reading,* 34 (September 1990), 20–25.

Rabin, Annette T. "Critical Reading." *Journal of Reading,* 24 (January 1981), 348.

Radebaugh, Muriel Rogie. "Using Children's Literature to Teach Mathematics." *The Reading Teacher,* 34 (May 1981), 902–906.

Radencich, Marguerite C. "Books That Promote Positive Attitudes Toward Second Language Learning." *The Reading Teacher,* 38 (February 1985), 528–530.

Ramsey, Patricia. *Teaching and Learning in a Diverse World.* New York: Teachers College Press, 1987.

Rand, Muriel K. "Story Schema: Theory, Research and Practice." *The Reading Teacher,* 37 (January 1984), 377–382.

Raphael, Taffy E. "Question-Answering Strategies for Children." *The Reading Teacher,* 36 (November 1982), 186–190.

Raphael, Taffy E. "Teaching Learners about Sources of Information for Answering Comprehension Questions." *Journal of Reading,* 27 (January 1984), 303–311.

Raphael, Taffy E. "Teaching Question-Answer Relationships, Revisited." *The Reading Teacher,* 39 (February 1986), 516–522.

Raphael, Taffy E., and P. David Pearson. *The Effect of Metacognitive Awareness Training on Children's Question Answering Behavior* (Technical Report No. 238). Urbana–Champaign, Ill.: University of Illinois, Center for the Study of Reading, 1982.

Raphael, Taffy, et al. "Research Directions: Literature and Discussion in the Reading Program." *Language Arts,* 69 (January 1992), 54–61.

Rasinski, Timothy V. "Mental Imagery Improves Comprehension." *The Reading Teacher,* 41 (April 1988), 867–868.

Rasinski, Timothy V. "The Role of Interest, Purpose, and Choice in Early Literacy." *The Reading Teacher,* 41 (January 1988), 396–400.

Rasinski, Timothy V., and Nancy D. Padak. "Multicultural Learning Through Children's Literature." *Language Arts,* 67 (October 1990), 576–580.

Raynes, Maria, Martha Snell, and Wayne Sailor. "A Fresh Look at Categorical Programs for Children with Special Needs." *Phi Delta Kappan,* 73 (December 1991), 326–331.

Readence, John E., R. Scott Baldwin, and Martha H. Head. "Direct Instruction in Processing Metaphors." *Journal of Reading Behavior,* 18, no. 4 (1986), 325–339.

Readence, John E., R. Scott Baldwin, and Martha H. Head. "Teaching Young Readers to Interpret Metaphors." *The Reading Teacher,* 40 (January 1987), 439–443.

Readence, John E., R. Scott Baldwin, Robert J. Rickelman, and G. Michael Miller. "The Effect of Vocabulary Instruction on Interpreting Metaphor." In *Solving Problems in Literacy: Learners, Teachers, and Researchers,* edited by Jerome A. Niles and Rosary V. Lalik. Rochester, N.Y.: National Reading Conference, 1986.

Reading in Junior Classes. Wellington, New Zealand: Department of Education, 1985.

"Reading Recovery 1984–1988." Columbus, Ohio: The Ohio State University, 1988.

Reading/Language in Secondary Schools Subcommittee of IRA. "A Reading-Writing Connection in the Content Areas." *Journal of Reading,* 33 (February 1990), 376–378.

Reardon, S. Jeanne. "The Development of Critical Readers: A Look Into the Classroom." *The New Advocate,* 1, no. 1 (1988), 52–61.

Recht, Donna. "Teaching Summarizing Skills." *The Reading Teacher,* 37 (March 1984), 675–677.

Reed, Arthea J. S. *Comics to Classics: A Parent's Guide to Books for Teens and Preteens.* Newark, Del.: International Reading Association, 1988.

Reimer, Beck L. "Recipes for Language Experience Stories." *The Reading Teacher,* 36 (January 1983), 396–401.

Reinking, D. *The Comprehension Connection.* St. Louis: Milliken, 1987.

Reissman, Rose. "Constitutional Comprehension Strategies: Using the Bill of Rights." *The Reading Teacher,* 45 (May 1992), 739–740.

Resnick, Lauren B. *Education and Learning to Think* (report). Washington, D.C.: National Academy Press, 1987.

Reutzel, D. Ray. "C^6: A Reading Model for Teaching Arithmetic Story Problem Solving." *The Reading Teacher,* 37 (October 1983), 28–34.

Reutzel, D. Ray. "Clozing in on Comprehension: The Cloze Story Map." *The Reading Teacher,* 39 (February 1986), 524–528.

Reutzel, D. Ray. "The Reading Basal: A Sentence Combining Composing Book." *The Reading Teacher,* 40 (November 1986), 194–199.

Reutzel, D. Ray. "Reconciling Schema Theory and the Basal Reading Lesson." *The Reading Teacher,* 39 (November 1985), 194–197.

Reutzel, D. Ray. "Story Maps Improve Comprehension." *The Reading Teacher,* 38 (January 1985), 400–404.

Reutzel, D. Ray, and Robert Cooter. "Organizing for Effective Instruction: The Reading Workshop." *The Reading Teacher,* 44 (April 1991), 548–554.

Reutzel, D. Ray, and Parker C. Fawson. "Using a Literature Webbing Strategy Lesson with Predictable Books." *The Reading Teacher,* 43 (December 1989), 208–215.

Rhodes, Lynn K. "I Can Read! Predictable Books as Resources for Reading and Writing Instruction." *The Reading Teacher,* 34 (February 1981), 511–518.

Rhodes, Lynn K., and Curt Dudley-Marling. *Readers and Writers with a Difference.* Portsmouth, N.H.: Heinemann, 1988.

Rhodes, Lynn, and Sally Nathenson-Mejia. "Anecdotal Records: A Powerful Tool for Ongoing Literacy Assessment." *The Reading Teacher,* 45 (March 1992), 502–509.

Richards, Janet Clarke, and Joan P. Gipe. "Activating Background Knowledge: Strategies for Beginning and Poor Readers." *The Reading Teacher,* 45 (February 1992), 474–478.

Richek, Margaret Ann. "Relating Vocabulary Learning to World Knowledge." *Journal of Reading,* 32 (December 1988), 262–267.

Richek, Margaret, Lynne List, and Janet Lerner. *Reading Problems.* Englewood Cliffs, N.J.: Prentice-Hall, 1989.

Richgels, Donald. "Experimental Reading with Invented Spelling (ERIS): A Preschool and Kindergarten Method." *The Reading Teacher,* 40 (February 1987), 522–529.

Richgels, Donald J., Lea M. McGee, and Edith A. Slaton. "Teaching Expository Text Structure in Reading and Writing." In *Children's Comprehension of Text: Research into Practice,* edited by K. Denise Muth. Newark, Del.: International Reading Association, 1989.

Rickelman, Robert J., William A. Henk, and Stephen A. Melnick. "Electronic Encyclopedias on Compact Disk." *The Reading Teacher,* 44 (February 1991), 432–434.

Ridout, Susan Ramp. "Sing Your Way to Better Reading." *The Reading Teacher,* 42 (October 1988), 95.

Riel, M. "The Impact of Computers in Classrooms." *Journal of Research on Computing in Education* (1989), 180–189.

Roberts, Patricia. *Counting Books Are More Than Numbers: An Annotated Action Bibliography.* Hamden, CT: Shoe String Press, 1990.

Roberts, Patricia. *A Green Dinosaur Day: A Guide for Developing Thematic Units in Literature-Based Instruction, K–6.* Boston: Allyn & Bacon, 1993.

Robinson, Francis P. *Effective Study,* rev. ed. New York: Harper & Row, 1961.

Robinson, H. Alan, Vincent Faraone, Daniel R. Hittleman, and Elizabeth Unruh. *Reading Comprehension Instruction: 1783–1987.* Newark, Del.: International Reading Association, 1990.

Roe, Betty D. *Use of Storytelling/Storyreading in Conjunction with Follow-up Language Activities to Improve Oral Communication of Rural First Grade Students: Phase I.* Cookeville, Tenn.: Rural Education Consortium, 1985.

Roe, Betty D. *Use of Storytelling/Storyreading in Conjunction with Follow-up Language Activities to Improve Oral Communication of Rural Primary Grade Students: Phase II.* Cookeville, Tenn.: Rural Education Consortium, 1986.

Roe, Mary F. "Reading Strategy Instruction: Complexities and Possibilities in Middle School." *Journal of Reading,* 36 (November 1992), 190–196.

Roehler, Laura, and Gerald Duffy. "Teachers' Instructional Actions." In *Handbook of Reading Research, Vol. II,* edited by Rebecca Barr, Michael L. Kamil, Peter B. Mosenthal, and P. David Pearson. White Plains, N.Y.: Longman, 1991, pp. 861–884.

Roehler, Laura R., Kathryn U. Foley, Mara T. Lud, and Carol A. Power. "Developing Integrated Programs." In *Reading in the Middle Schools,* 2d ed., edited by Gerald G. Duffy. Newark, Del.: International Reading Association, 1990.

Rogers, Wanda C. "Teaching for Poetic Thought." *The Reading Teacher,* 39 (December 1985), 296–300.

Romney, David M. *Dealing with Abnormal Behavior in the Classroom.* Bloomington, Ind.: Phi Delta Kappa, 1986.

Roney, R. Craig. "Background Experience Is the Foundation of Success in Learning to Read." *The Reading Teacher,* 38 (November 1984), 196–199.

Rose, David H., and Anne Meyer. "Focus on Research: The Role of Technology in Language Arts Instruction." *Language Arts,* 71 (April 1994), 290–294.

Rosenblatt, Louise M. *Literature as Exploration.* New York: Noble & Noble, 1938/1983.

Rosenblatt, Louise M. "Literature—S.O.S.!" *Language Arts,* 68 (1991), 444–448.

Rosenblatt, Louise M. *The Reader, the Text, and the Poem: The Transactional Theory of the Literary Work.* Carbondale, Ill.: Southern Illinois University Press, 1978.

Rosenblatt, Louise M. "The Transactional Theory of Reading and Writing." In *Theoretical Models and Processes of Reading,* 4th ed., edited by Robert B. Ruddell, Martha Rapp Ruddell, and Harry Singer. Newark, Del.: International Reading Association, 1994, pp. 1057–1092.

Rosenblatt, Louise M. "Viewpoints: Transaction Versus Interaction—A Terminological Rescue Operation." *Research in the Teaching of English,* 19 (February 1985), 96–107.

Rosenbloom, Cindy Shultz. "From *Ox-Cart Man* to *Little House in the Big Woods*: Response to Literature Shapes Curriculum." *Language Arts,* 68 (January 1991), 52–57.

Rosenholtz, Susan J., and Carl Simpson. "Classroom Organization and Student Stratification." *Elementary School Journal,* 85 (September 1984), 21–37.

Rosenshine, Barak, and Carla Meister. "Reciprocal Teaching: A Review of the Research." *Review of Educational Research,* 64 (Winter 1994), 479–530.

Rosenshine, Barak, and Robert Stevens. "Classroom Instruction in Reading." In *Handbook of Reading Research,* edited by P. David Pearson. New York: Longman, 1984.

Roser, N., and C. Juel. "Effects of Vocabulary Instruction on Reading Comprehension." In *New Inquiries in Reading Research and Instruction,* Thirty-First Yearbook of the National Reading Conference, edited by J. A. Niles and L. A. Harris. Rochester, N.Y.: National Reading Conference, 1982.

Roser, Nancy L., James Hoffman, Linda D. Labbo, and Cindy Forest. "Language Charts: A Record of Story Time Talk." *Language Arts,* 69 (January 1992), 44–52.

Roser, Nancy L., James V. Hoffman, and Cynthia Farest. "Language, Literature, and At-Risk Children." *The Reading Teacher,* 43 (April 1990), 554–559.

Roskos, Kathy, and Carol Vukelich. "Promoting Literacy in Play." *Day Care and Early Education,* 19 (Fall 1991), 30–34.

Ross, Elinor P. "Classroom Experiments with Oral Reading." *The Reading Teacher,* 40 (December 1986), 270–275.

Ross, Elinor P. "Culturally and Linguistically Different Learners." In *Classroom Reading Instruction,* edited by Richard A. Thompson. Dubuque, Iowa: Kendall/Hunt, 1989.

Ross, Elinor Parry. "Checking the Source: An Essential Component of Critical Reading." *Journal of Reading,* 24 (January 1981), 311–315.

Rosso, Barbara Rak, and Robert Emans. "Children's Use of Phonic Generalizations." *The Reading Teacher,* 34 (March 1981), 653–657.

Rouse, Michael W., and Julie B. Ryan. "Teacher's Guide to Vision Problems." *The Reading Teacher,* 38 (December 1984), 306–307.

Routman, Regie. *Invitations.* Portsmouth, N.H.: Heinemann, 1991.

Routman, Regie. *Transitions: From Literature to Literacy.* Portsmouth, N.H.: Heinemann, 1988.

Rowe, Deborah, and Jerome C. Harste. "Metalinguistic Awareness in Writing and Reading: The Young Child as Curricular Informant." In *Metalinguistic Awareness and Beginning Literacy,* edited by David B. Yaden, Jr., and Shane Templeton. Portsmouth, N.H.: Heinemann Educational Books, 1986.

Rubin, Dorothy. *A Practical Approach to Teaching Reading.* New York: Holt, Rinehart and Winston, 1982.

Rubino, Ann. "The Science/Language Connection: Why to Make It . . . How to Do It." *The Reading Teacher,* 45 (November 1991), 248–249.

Ruddell, Robert B. "A Whole Language and Literature Perspective: Creating a Meaning-Making Instructional Environment." *Language Arts,* 69 (December 1992), 612–620.

Ruddell, Robert B., and Norman J. Unrau. "Reading as a Meaning-Construction Process: The Reader, the Text, and the Teacher." In *Theoretical Models and Processes of Reading,* 4th ed., edited by Robert B. Ruddell, Martha Rapp Ruddell, and Harry Singer. Newark, Del.: International Reading Association, 1994, 996–1056.

Ruddiman, Joan. "The Vocab Game: Empowering Students Through Word Awareness." *Journal of Reading,* 36 (February 1993), 400–401.

Rude, Robert T. *Teaching Reading Using Microcomputers.* Englewood Cliffs, N.J.: Prentice–Hall, 1986.

Ruiz, Nadine. "Effective Instruction for Language Minority Children with Mild Disabilities." *ERIC Digest* #E499, 3 pp.

Rule, Audrey, and Joan Atkinson. "Choosing Picture Books about Ecology." *The Reading Teacher,* 47 (April 1994), 586–591.

Rumelhart, David E. "Schemata: The Building Blocks of Cognition." In *Comprehension and Teaching: Research Reviews,* edited by John T. Guthrie. Newark, Del.: International Reading Association, 1981.

Rumelhart, David. *Toward an Interactive Model of Reading* (Technical Report 56). San Diego, Calif.: Center for Human Information Processing, March 1976.

Rush, R. Timothy. "Assessing Readability: Formulas and Alternatives." *The Reading Teacher,* 39 (December 1985), 274–283.

Russell, David L. *Literature for Children,* 2d ed. New York: Longman, 1994.

Sabey, Brenda, and Linda Squier. "Environmental Print: Trash or Treasure." *Contemporary Issues in Reading,* 9 (Fall 1993), 45–51.

Sadow, Marilyn W. "The Use of Story Grammar in the Design of Questions." *The Reading Teacher,* 35 (February 1982), 518–522.

Sammons, Rebecca Bell, and Beth Davey. "Assessing Students' Skills in Using Textbooks: The Textbook Awareness and Performance Profile." *Journal of Reading,* 37 (December 1993/January 1994), 280–286.

Sampson, Mary Beth, Michael R. Sampson, and Wayne Linek. "Circle of Questions." *The Reading Teacher,* 48 (December 1994/January 1995), 364–365.

Samuels, S. Jay. "Decoding and Automaticity: Helping Poor Readers Become Automatic at Word Recognition." *The Reading Teacher,* 41 (April 1988), 756–760.

Samuels, S. Jay. "Toward a Theory of Automatic Information Processing in Reading, Revisited." In *Theoretical Models and Processes of Reading,* 4th ed., edited by Robert B. Ruddell, Martha Rapp Ruddell, and Harry Singer. Newark, Del.: International Reading Association, 1994, pp. 816–837.

Samuels, S. Jay, and Sumner W. Schachter. "Controversial Issues in Beginning Reading Instruction: Meaning Versus Subskill Emphasis." In *Readings on Reading Instruction,* edited by Albert J. Harris and Edward R. Sipay. New York: Longman, 1984.

Samway, Katherine Davies, et al. "Reading the Skeleton, the Heart, and the Brain of a Book: Students' Perspectives on Literature Study Circles." *The Reading Teacher,* 45 (November 1991), 196–205.

Sanacore, Joseph. "Creating the Lifetime Reading Habit in Social Studies." *Journal of Reading,* 33 (March 1990), 414–418.

Santino, Betsy H. "Improving Multicultural Awareness and Story Comprehension with Folktales." *The Reading Teacher,* 45 (September 1991), 77–79.

Savage, John F. *Teaching Reading Using Literature.* Madison, Wis.: WCB Brown & Benchmark, 1994.

Sawyer, John Michael. "Using Media Knowledge to Enhance the Literary Schema of Literarily Impoverished Students." *Journal of Reading,* 37 (May 1994), 683–684.

Scala, Marilyn. "What Whole Language in the Mainstream Means for Children with Learning Disabilities." *The Reading Teacher,* 47 (November 1993), 222–229.

Schachter, Summer W. "Using Workbook Pages More Effectively." *The Reading Teacher,* 35 (October 1981), 34–37.

Schaeffer, E. Marilyn. *Teaching Writing with the Microcomputer.* Bloomington, Ind.: Phi Delta Kappa, 1987.

Scharer, Patricia L., and Deana B. Detwiler. "Changing as Teachers: Perils and Possibilities of Literature-Based Language Arts Instruction." *Language Arts,* 69 (March 1992), 186–192.

Schatz, Elinore K., and R. Scott Baldwin. "Context Clues Are Unreliable Predictors of Word Meanings." *Reading Research Quarterly,* 21, no. 4 (1986), 439–453.

Schaudt, Barbara A. "Another Look at Sustained Silent Reading." *The Reading Teacher,* 36 (May 1983), 934–936.

Schell, Leo M. "Teaching Decoding to Remedial Readers." *Journal of Reading,* 31 (May 1978), 877–882.

Schell, Vicki J. "Learning Partners: Reading and Mathematics." *The Reading Teacher,* 35 (February 1982), 544–548.

Schifini, Alfredo. "Language, Literacy, and Content Instruction: Strategies for Teachers." In *Kids Come in All Languages: Reading Instruction for ESL Students,* edited by Karen Spangenberg-Urbschat and Robert Pritchard. Newark, Del.: International Reading Association, 1994, pp. 158–179.

Schipper, D., and K. Vincent. *Alexander and the Terrible, Horrible, No Good, Very Bad Day.* Pleasantville, N.Y.: Sunburst Communications, 1991.

Schmitt, M. C., and D. O'Brien. "Story Grammars: Some Cautions about the Translation of Research into Practice." *Reading Research Quarterly,* 26, no. 1 (1986), 1–8.

Schmitt, Maribeth Cassidy, and James F. Baumann. "How to Incorporate Comprehension Monitoring Strategies into Basal Reader Instruction." *The Reading Teacher,* 40 (October 1986), 28–31.

Schoenfeld, Florence G. "Instructional Uses of the Cloze Procedure." *The Reading Teacher,* 34 (November 1980), 147–151.

Schreiner, Robert. "The Computer, an Electronic Flash Card." *The Reading Teacher,* 39 (December 1985), 378–380.

Schuder, Ted, Suzanne F. Clewell, and Nan Jackson. "Getting the Gist of Expository Text." In *Children's Comprehension of Text: Research into Practice,* edited by K. Denise Muth. Newark, Del.: International Reading Association, 1989.

Schulz, Jane B., and Ann P. Turnbull. *Mainstreaming Handicapped Students.* 2d ed. Boston: Allyn & Bacon, 1984.

Schumm, Jeanne Shay. "Overcoming Students' Misconceptions about Science." *Journal of Reading,* 35 (October 1991), 161.

Schumm, Jeanne Shay. "Putting Ideas Together: Learning Disabled Students' Awareness of Text Structure." *Journal of Reading,* 35 (February 1992), 406.

Schumm, Jeanne Shay, and Linda Saumell. "Aliteracy: We Know It Is a Problem, But Where Does It Start?" *Journal of Reading,* 37 (May 1994), 701.

Schumm, Jeanne Shay, and Linda Saumell. "Word Processors: Their Impact on Process and Product." *Journal of Reading,* 37 (November 1993), 190.

Schwartz, David M. *How Much Is a Million?* New York: Scholastic, 1985.

Schwartz, Robert M. "Learning to Learn Vocabulary in Content Area Textbooks." *Journal of Reading,* 32 (November 1988), 108–118.

Schwartz, Robert M., and Taffy E. Raphael. "Concept of Definition: A Key to Improving Students' Vocabulary." *The Reading Teacher,* 39 (November 1985), 198–205.

Sebesta, Sam Leaton, James William Calder, and Lynne Nelson Cleland. "A Story Grammar for the Classroom." *The Reading Teacher,* 36 (November 1982), 180–184.

Seda, Ileana, and P. David Pearson. "Interviews to Assess Learners' Outcomes." *Reading Research and Instruction,* 31 (Fall 1991), 22–32.

Sedlak, Robert A., and Denise M. Sedlak. *Teaching the Educable Mentally Retarded.* Albany, N.Y.: State University of New York Press, 1985.

Seminoff, Nancy Wiseman. "Children's Periodicals Throughout the World: An Overlooked Educational Resource." *The Reading Teacher,* 39 (May 1986), 889–895.

Serebrin, Wayne. "A Writer and an Author Collaborate." *Language Arts,* 63 (March 1986), 281–283.

Shake, Mary C., and Richard L. Allington. "Where Do Teachers' Questions Come From?" *The Reading Teacher,* 38 (January 1985), 432–438.

Shanahan, Timothy. "Predictions and the Limiting Effects of Prequestions." In *Solving Problems in Literacy: Learners, Teachers, and Researchers,* edited by Jerome A. Niles and Rosary V. Lalik. Rochester, N.Y.: National Reading Conference, 1986.

Shanahan, Timothy. "The Reading-Writing Relationship: Seven Instructional Principles." *The Reading Teacher,* 41 (March 1988), 636–647.

Shanklin, Nancy L., and Lynn K. Rhodes. "Comprehension Instruction as Sharing and Extending." *The Reading Teacher,* 42 (March 1989), 496–500.

Shannon, Patrick. "Commentary: Teachers Are Researchers." In *Opening the Door to Classroom Research,* edited by Mary W. Olson. Newark, Del.: International Reading Association, 1990.

Sharp, Peggy Agostino. "Teaching with Picture Books Throughout the Curriculum." *The Reading Teacher,* 38 (November 1984), 132–137.

Shaw, Evelyn. "A Novel Journal." *The Reading Teacher,* 41 (January 1988), 489.

Shepard, Lorrie. "Why We Need Better Assessments." *Educational Leadership,* 46 (April 1989), 4–9.

Shoop, Mary. "InQuest: A Listening and Reading Comprehension Strategy." *The Reading Teacher,* 39 (March 1986), 670–674.

Silvers, Penny. "Process Writing and the Reading Connection." *The Reading Teacher,* 39 (March 1986), 684–688.

Silverstein, Alvin, and Virginia Silverstein. *Life in a Tidal Pool.* Boston: Little, Brown, 1990.

Sinatra, Richard, and Cornelia Dowd. "Using Syntactic and Semantic Clues to Learn Vocabulary." *Journal of Reading,* 35 (November 1991), 224–229.

Singer, Harry. "The Substrata-Factor Theory of Reading." In *Theoretical Models and Processes of Reading,* 4th ed., edited by Robert B. Ruddell, Martha Rapp Ruddell, and Harry Singer. Newark, Del.: International Reading Association, 1994, pp. 895–927.

Singer, Harry, John D. McNeil, and Lory L. Furse. "Relationship Between Curriculum Scope and Reading Achievement in Elementary Schools." *The Reading Teacher,* 37 (March 1984), 608–612.

Sippola, Arne E. "What to Teach for Reading Readiness—A Research Review and Materials Inventory." *The Reading Teacher,* 39 (November 1985), 162–167.

Slater, Wayne H., and Michael F. Graves. "Research on Expository Text: Implications for Teachers." In *Children's Comprehension of Text: Research into Practice,* edited by K. Denise Muth. Newark, Del.: International Reading Association, 1989.

Slaughter, Helen B. "Indirect and Direct Teaching in a Whole Language Program." *The Reading Teacher,* 42 (October 1988), 30–34.

Slavin, Robert E. "IBM's Writing to Read: Is It Right for Reading?" *Phi Delta Kappan,* 72 (November 1990), 214–216.

Slavin, Robert E., Nancy A. Madden, Nancy L. Karweit, Lawrence J. Dolan, and Barbara A. Wasik. "Success for All: Getting Reading Right the First Time." In *Getting Reading Right from the Start,* edited by Elfrieda H. Hiebert and Barbara M. Taylor. Boston: Allyn & Bacon, 1994, pp. 125–147.

Slavin, Robert E., Nancy L. Karweit, and Barbara A. Wasik. "Preventing Early School Failure: What Works?" *Educational Leadership,* 50 (December 1992/January 1993), 10–18.

Slavin, Robert, Nancy Madden, and Robert Stevens. "Cooperative Learning Models for the 3R's." *Educational Leadership,* 47 (December 1989/January 1990), 22–28.

Slavin, Robert. "Research on Cooperative Learning: Consensus and Controversy." *Educational Leadership,* 47 (December 1989/January 1990), 52–54.

Slavin, Robert. "Synthesis of Research on Cooperative Learning." *Educational Leadership,* 48 (February 1991), 71–82.

Slavin, Robert. "Synthesis of Research on Grouping in Elementary and Secondary Schools." *Educational Leadership,* 47 (September 1988), 67–77.

Smardo, Frances A. "Using Children's Literature to Clarify Science Concepts in Early Childhood Programs." *The Reading Teacher,* 36 (December 1982), 267–273.

Smelter, Richard, Bradley Rasch, and Gary Yudewitz. "Thinking of Inclusion for All Special Needs Students? Better Think Again." *Phi Delta Kappan,* 76 (September 1994), 35–38.

Smit, Edna K. "Teaching Theme to Elementary Students." *The Reading Teacher,* 43 (May 1990), 699–701.

Smith, Carl B. "Building a Better Vocabulary." *The Reading Teacher,* 42 (December 1988), 238.

Smith, Carl B. "Learning Through Writing." *The Reading Teacher,* 43 (November 1989), 172–173.

Smith, Carl B. "Prompting Critical Thinking." *The Reading Teacher,* 42 (February 1989), 424.

Smith, Carl B. "The Role of Different Literary Genres." *The Reading Teacher,* 44 (February 1991), 440–441.

Smith, Carl B. "Vocabulary Development in Content Area Reading." *The Reading Teacher,* 43 (March 1990), 508–509.

Smith, Carl, and Roger Sensenbaugh. "Helping Children Overcome Reading Difficulties." *ERIC Digest.* Bloomington, Ind.: ERIC Clearinghouse on Reading and Communication Skills, 1992. [ED344190]

Smith, Carl. "Shared Learning Promotes Critical Reading." *The Reading Teacher,* 43 (October 1989), 76–77.

Smith, Carl. "Teachers as Decision Makers." *The Reading Teacher,* 42 (April 1989), 632.

Smith, Frank. *Essays into Literacy.* Exeter, N.H.: Heinemann, 1983.

Smith, J. Lea, and Holly Johnson. "Models for Implementing Literature in Content Studies." *The Reading Teacher,* 48 (November 1994), 198–209.

Smith, Jamie. "DISKovery: Goin' Wild in HyperCard." *Language Arts,* 68 (December 1991), 674–680.

Smith, Lawrence L., Jerry L. Johns, Leonore Ganschow, and Nancy Browning Masztal. "Using Grade Level vs. Out-of-Level Reading Tests with Remedial Students." *The Reading Teacher,* 40 (February 1983), 550–553.

Smith, Marilyn, and Thomas W. Bean. "Four Strategies That Develop Children's Story Comprehension and Writing." *The Reading Teacher,* 37 (December 1983), 295–301.

Smith, Nancy. "The Word Processing Approach to Language Experience." *The Reading Teacher,* 38 (February 1985), 556–559.

Smith, Nancy J., M. Jean Greenlaw, and Carolyn J. Scott. "Making the Literate Environment Equitable." *The Reading Teacher,* 40 (January 1987), 400–407.

Smith, Richard J., et al. *The School Reading Program.* Boston: Houghton Mifflin, 1978.

Smith, William Earl, and Michael D. Beck. "Determining Instructional Reading Level with the 1978 Metropolitan Achievement Tests." *The Reading Teacher,* 34 (December 1980), 313–319.

Smolkin, Laura, and David Yaden, Jr. "*O* Is for Mouse: First Encounters with the Alphabet Book." *Language Arts,* 69 (October 1992), 432–441.

Smyers, Teresa. "Add SQ to the DRTA—Write." *The Reading Teacher,* 41 (December 1987), 372–374.

Solem, Maizie. "Junior First Grade: A Year to Get Ready." In *Prototypes,* edited by Stanley Elam. Bloomington, Ind.: Phi Delta Kappa, 1989.

Sorenson, Nancy L. "Basal Reading Vocabulary Instruction: A Critique and Suggestions." *The Reading Teacher,* 39 (October 1985), 80–85.

Spache, George D. *Good Reading for Poor Readers,* 6th ed. Champaign, Ill.: Garrard Press, 1966.

Spiegel, Dixie Lee, and Jill Fitzgerald. "Improving Reading Comprehension Through Instruction about Story Parts." *The Reading Teacher,* 39 (March 1986), 676–682.

Spiegel, Dixie Lee. "Adaptability and Flexibility of Literature Resource Materials." *The Reading Teacher,* 43 (April 1990), 590–592.

Spiegel, Dixie Lee. "Blending Whole Language and Systematic Direct Instruction." *The Reading Teacher,* 46 (September 1992), 38–44.

Spiegel, Dixie Lee. "Comprehension Materials: Quality of Directions and Instructional Language." *The Reading Teacher,* 43 (March 1990), 502–504.

Spiegel, Dixie Lee. "Content Bias in Reference and Study Skills." *The Reading Teacher,* 44 (September 1990), 64–66.

Spiegel, Dixie Lee. "Critical Reading Materials: A Review of Three Criteria." *The Reading Teacher,* 43 (February 1990), 410–412.

Spiegel, Dixie Lee. "Decoding and Comprehension Games." *The Reading Teacher,* 44 (November 1990), 258–261.

Spiegel, Dixie Lee. "Materials for Integrating Science and Social Studies with the Language Arts." *The Reading Teacher,* 44 (October 1990), 162–165.

Spiegel, Dixie Lee. "Materials to Introduce Children to Poetry." *The Reading Teacher,* 44 (February 1991), 428–430.

Spiegel, Dixie Lee. "Materials to Promote Vocabulary Development." *The Reading Teacher,* 44 (March 1991), 504–507.

Spiegel, Dixie Lee. "Reinforcement in Phonics Materials." *The Reading Teacher,* 43 (January 1990), 328–329.

Spiegel, Dixie Lee. "Six Alternatives to the Directed Reading Activity." *The Reading Teacher,* 34 (May 1981), 914–920.

Spiro, Rand J. *Etiology of Comprehension Style.* Urbana–Champaign, Ill.: University of Illinois, Center for the Study of Reading, 1979.

Squire, James. "Composing and Comprehending: Two Sides of the Same Basic Process." *Language Arts,* 60 (May 1983), 581–589.

Stahl, Steven A. "Saying the 'P' Word: Nine Guidelines for Exemplary Phonics Instruction." *The Reading Teacher,* 45 (April 1992), 618–625.

Stahl, Steven A. "Three Principles of Effective Vocabulary Instruction." *Journal of Reading,* 29 (April 1986), 662–668.

Stahl, Steven A., and Barbara A. Kapinus. "Possible Sentences: Predicting Word Meanings to Teach Content Area Vocabulary." *The Reading Teacher,* 45 (September 1991), 36–43.

Stahl, Steven A., Jean Osborn, and Fran Lehr. *Beginning to Read: Thinking and Learning about Print—A Summary.* Champaign, Ill.: University of Illinois, Center for the Study of Reading, 1990.

Stahl, Steven A., and Sandra J. Vancil. "Discussion Is What Makes Semantic Maps Work in Vocabulary Instruction." *The Reading Teacher,* 40 (October 1986), 62–67.

Stahl-Gemake, Josephine, and Francine Guastello. "Using Story Grammar with Students of English as a Foreign Language to Compose Original Fairy and Folktales." *The Reading Teacher,* 38 (November 1984), 213–216.

Stanger, D., P. Elseth, and S. Clough. *Magic Slate II.* Pleasantville, N.Y.: Sunburst Communications, 1988.

Stanovich, Keith. "Romance and Reality." *The Reading Teacher,* 47 (December 1993/January 1994), 280–291.

Starshine, Dorothy, and Laura R. Fortson. "First Graders Use the Computer: Great Word Processing." *The Reading Teacher,* 38 (November 1984), 241–243.

Staton, Jana. "ERIC/RCS Report: Dialogue Journals." *Language Arts,* 65 (February 1988), 198–201.

Stauffer, Russell G. "Reading as a Cognitive Process." *Elementary English,* 44 (April 1968), 348.

Stauffer, Russell G. *Teaching Reading as a Thinking Process.* New York: Harper & Row, 1969.

Stetson, Elton G., and Richard P. Williams. "Learning from Social Studies Textbooks: Why Some Students Succeed and Others Fail." *Journal of Reading,* 36 (September 1992), 22–30.

Stevens, Kathleen C. "Can We Improve Reading by Teaching Background Information?" *Journal of Reading,* 25 (January 1982), 326–329.

Stewart, Oran, and Dan S. Green. "Test-Taking Skills for Standardized Tests of Reading." *The Reading Teacher,* 36 (March 1983), 634–638.

Stewig, John Warren. *Children and Literature.* Chicago: Rand McNally, 1980.

Stice, Carole, and Nancy Bertrand. *Whole Language and the Emergent Literacy of At-Risk Children: A Two Year Comparative Study.* Nashville, Tenn.: Center of Excellence: Basic Skills, June, 1990.

Stoddard, Ann. "Teaching Worldmindedness through Children's Literature." Paper presented at the 21st Annual Meeting of the Florida Reading Association, 1983. [ED 243 152]

Stoll, Donald R., ed. *Magazines for Kids and Teens.* Glassboro, N.J.: Educational Press Association of America and Newark, Del.: International Reading Association, 1994.

Storey, Dee C. "Reading in the Content Areas: Fictionalized Biographies and Diaries for Social Studies." *The Reading Teacher,* 35 (April 1982), 796–798.

Stotsky, Sandra. "Research on Reading/Writing Relationships: A Synthesis and Suggested Directions." *Language Arts,* 60 (May 1983), 627–642.

Strange, Michael. "Instructional Implications of a Conceptual Theory of Reading Comprehension." *The Reading Teacher,* 33 (January 1980), 391–397. "A Talk with Marilyn Adams." *Language Arts,* 68 (March 1991), 206–212.

Strickland, Dorothy S. "The Teacher as Researcher: Toward the Extended Professional." *Language Arts,* 65 (December 1988), 754–764.

Strickland, Dorothy S., and Bernice E. Cullinan. "Literature and Language." *Language Arts,* 63 (March 1986), 221–225.

Strickland, Dorothy S., and Lesley Mandel Morrow. "Integrating the Emergent Literacy Curriculum with Themes." *The Reading Teacher,* 43 (April 1990), 604–605.

Strickland, Dorothy S., Rose M. Dillon, Leslie Funkhouser, Mary Glick, and Corrine Rogers. "Research Currents: Classroom Dialogue during Literature Response Groups." *Language Arts,* 66 (February 1989), 192–205.

Strickland, Dorothy, and Lesley Morrow. "Creating a Print Rich Environment." *The Reading Teacher,* 42 (November 1988), 156–157.

Strickland, Dorothy, and Lesley Morrow. "Family Literacy: Sharing Good Books." *The Reading Teacher,* 43 (March 1990), 518–519.

Strickland, Dorothy, and Lesley Morrow. "New Perspectives on Young Children Learning to Read and Write." *The Reading Teacher,* 43 (October 1988), 70–71.

Strickland, Dorothy, and Lesley Morrow. "The Daily Journal: Using Language Experience Strategies in an Emergent Literacy Curriculum." *The Reading Teacher,* 43 (February 1990), 422–423.

Strickland, Dorothy. "Emergent Literacy: How Young Children Learn to Read and Write." *Educational Leadership,* 47 (March 1990), 18–23.

Strickland, Dorothy. "Some Tips for Using Big Books." *The Reading Teacher,* 41 (May 1988), 966–968.

Sugarman, Jay, James Allen, and Meg Keller-Cogan. "Make Authentic Assessment Work for You." *Instructor,* 103 (July/August 1993), 66–68.

Sullivan, Joanne. "The Global Method: Language Experience in the Content Areas." *The Reading Teacher,* 39 (March 1986), 664–668.

Sulzby, Elizabeth. "I Can Write! Encouraging Emergent Writers." In *Early Childhood Education 94/95,* 15th ed., edited by Karen M. Paciorek and Joyce H. Munro. Guilford, Conn.: Dushkin, 1994, 204–207.

Sulzby, Elizabeth. "Using Children's Dictated Stories to Aid Comprehension." *The Reading Teacher,* 33 (April 1980), 772–778.

Sulzby, Elizabeth, and William Teale. "Emergent Literacy." In *Handbook of Reading Research, Vol. II,* edited by Rebecca Barr, Michael L. Kamil, Peter B. Mosenthal, and P. David Pearson. White Plains, N.Y.: Longman, 1991, pp. 727–758.

Sulzby, Elizabeth, William H. Teale, and George Kamberelis. "Emergent Writing in the Classroom: Home and School Connections." In *Emerging Literacy,* edited by Dorothy Strickland and Lesley Morrow. Newark, Del.: International Reading Association, 1989.

Sumara, Dennis, and Laurie Walker. "The Teacher's Role in Whole Language." *Language Arts,* 68 (April 1991), 276–285.

Sweet, Anne P. *State of the Art.* Washington, D.C.: Office of Educational Research and Improvement, 1993.

Sweet, M. *The Scholastic Process Writer.* New York: Scholastic, 1990.

"A Talk with Marilyn Adams." *Language Arts,* 68 (March 1991), 206–212.

Taylor, Barbara M. "A Summarizing Strategy to Improve Middle Grade Students' Reading and Writing Skills." *The Reading Teacher,* 36 (November 1982), 202–205.

Taylor, Barbara, and Elfrieda Hiebert. "Early Literacy Interventions: Aims and Issues." In *Getting Ready Right from the Start,* edited by Elfrieda Hiebert and Barbara Taylor. Boston: Allyn & Bacon, 1994, pp. 3–11.

Taylor, Barbara M., and Linda Nosbush. "Oral Reading for Meaning: A Technique for Word Identification." *The Reading Teacher,* 37 (December 1983), 234–237.

Taylor, Denny, and Dorothy S. Strickland. *Family Storybook Reading.* Portsmouth, N.H.: Heinemann, 1986.

Tchudi, Susan. *Integrated Language Arts in the Elementary School.* Belmont, Calif.: Wadsworth, 1994.

Teacher Support Software. *Great Beginnings* (rev. ed.). Gainesville, Fla.: Teacher Support Software, 1991.

Teale, William H., and Elizabeth Sulzby. *Emergent Literacy: Writing and Reading.* Norwood, N.J.: Ablex, 1986.

Teale, William H., Elfrieda H. Hiebert, and Edward A. Chittenden. "Assessing Young Children's Literacy Development." *The Reading Teacher,* 40 (April 1987), 772–777.

Teale, William, and Elizabeth Sulzby. "Emergent Literacy: New Perspectives." In *Emerging Literacy: Young Children Learn to Read and Write,* edited by Dorothy Strickland and Lesley Morrow. Newark, Del.: International Reading Association, 1989.

Temple, Charles, Ruth Nathan, Nancy Burris, and Frances Temple. *The Beginnings of Writing,* 2d ed. Boston: Allyn & Bacon, 1988.

Templeton, Shane. "Literacy, Readiness, and Basals." *The Reading Teacher,* 39 (January 1986), 403–409.

Thames, D. G., and J. E. Readence. "Effects of Differential Vocabulary Instruction and Lesson Frameworks on the Reading Comprehension of Primary Children." *Reading Research and Instruction,* 27, no. 2 (1988), 1–12.

Thelen, Judith N. "Vocabulary Instruction and Meaningful Learning." *Journal of Reading,* 29 (April 1986), 603–609.

Thomas, M. Donald. *Pluralism Gone Mad.* Bloomington, Ind.: Phi Delta Kappa, 1981.

Thompson, Deborah L. "The Alphabet Book as a Content Area Resource." *The Reading Teacher,* 46 (November 1992), 266–267.

Thompson, Stephen J. "Teaching Metaphoric Language: An Instructional Strategy." *Journal of Reading,* 30 (November 1986), 105–109.

Thonis, Eleanor Wall. *Literacy for America's Spanish Speaking Children.* Newark, Del.: International Reading Association, 1976.

Thonis, Eleanor Wall. "Teaching English as a Second Language." *Reading Today,* 7 (February/March, 1990), 8.

Tierney, R. J., and T. Shanahan. "Research on the Reading-Writing Relationship: Interactions, Transactions, and Outcomes." In *Handbook of Reading Research, Vol. II,* edited by R. Barr, J. L. Kamil, P. Mosenthal, and P. D. Pearson. New York: Longman, 1991, pp. 246–280.

Tierney, Robert J., and James W. Cunningham. "Research on Teaching Reading Comprehension." In *Handbook of Reading Research,* edited by P. David Pearson. New York: Longman, 1984.

Tierney, Robert J., and P. David Pearson. "A Revisionist Perspective on 'Learning to Learn from Text: A Framework for Improving Classroom Practice.'" In *Theoretical Models and Processes of Reading,* 4th ed., edited by Robert Ruddell, Martha Rapp Ruddell, and Harry Singer. Newark, Del.: International Reading Association, 1994, pp. 514–519.

Tipton, Juanita. "Extending Context Clues to Composition and Cooperative Learning." *Journal of Reading,* 35 (September 1991), 50.

Tompkins, Gail E., and Lea M. McGee. *Teaching Reading with Literature.* New York: Merrill, 1993.

Tompkins, Gail E., and Lea M. McGee. "Teaching Repetition as a Story Structure." In *Children's Comprehension of Text: Research into Practice,* edited by K. Denise Muth. Newark, Del.: International Reading Association, 1989.

Topping, Keith. "Peer Tutoring and Paired Reading: Combining Two Powerful Techniques." *The Reading Teacher,* 42 (March 1989), 488–494.

Tovey, Duane R. "Children's Grasp of Phonics Terms vs. Sound-Symbol Relationships." *The Reading Teacher,* 33 (January 1980), 431–437.

Tovey, Duane, and James Kerber, eds. *Roles in Literacy Learning.* Newark, Del.: International Reading Association, 1986.

Trachtenburg, Phyllis. "Using Children's Literature to Enhance Phonics Instruction." *The Reading Teacher,* 43 (May 1990), 648–654.

Trachtenburg, Phyllis, and Ann Ferruggia. "Big Books from Little Voices: Reaching High Risk Beginning Readers." *The Reading Teacher,* 42 (January 1989), 284–289.

Trelease, Jim. *The New Read-Aloud Handbook.* New York: Viking Penguin, 1989.

Truax, Roberta, and Richard Kretschmer, Jr. "Focus on Research: Finding New Voices in the Process of Meeting the Needs of All Children." *Language Arts,* 70 (November 1993), 592–601.

Tunnell, Michael O., and James S. Jacobs. "Using 'Real' Books: Research Findings on Literature-Based Reading Instruction." *The Reading Teacher,* 42 (March 1989), 470–477.

Tway, Eileen. *Writing Is Reading: 26 Ways to Connect.* Urbana, Ill.: National Council of Teachers of English, 1985.

Tyson, Eleanore S., and Lee Mountain. "A Riddle or Pun Makes Learning Words Fun." *The Reading Teacher,* 36 (November 1982), 170–173.

Unia, Sumitra. "From Sunny Days to Green Onions: On Journal Writing." In *Whole Language: Theory in Use,* edited by Judith M. Newman. Portsmouth, N.H.: Heinemann, 1985.

Unsworth, Len. "Meeting Individual Needs Through Flexible Within-Class Grouping of Pupils." *The Reading Teacher,* 38 (December 1984), 298–304.

Uttero, Debbra. "Activating Comprehension Through Cooperative Learning." *The Reading Teacher,* 41 (January 1988), 390–395.

Vacca, Jo Anne L., Richard T. Vacca, and Mary K. Gove. *Reading and Learning to Read.* Boston: Little, Brown, 1987.

Valencia, Sheila. "A Portfolio Approach to Classroom Reading Assessment: The Whys, Whats, and Hows." *The Reading Teacher,* 43 (January 1990), 338–340.

Valencia, Sheila, and P. David Pearson. "Reading Assessment: Time for a Change." *The Reading Teacher,* 40 (April 1987), 726–733.

Valentine, Sonia L. "Beginning Poets Dig for Poems." *Language Arts,* 63 (March 1986), 246–252.

Valeri-Gold, Maria. "Summarize It." *Journal of Reading,* 33 (October 1989), 53.

Valmont, William J. "Cloze Deletion Patterns: How Deletions Are Made Makes a Big Difference." *The Reading Teacher,* 37 (November 1983), 172–175.

VanLeirsburg, Peggy. "Standardized Reading Tests: Then and Now." In *Literacy: Celebration and Challenge,* edited by Jerry Johns. Bloomington, Ill.: Illinois Reading Council, 1993, pp. 31–54.

Van Riper, C. *Speech Correction: Principles and Methods,* 6th ed. Englewood Cliffs, N.J.: Prentice-Hall, 1978.

Varnhagen, Connie K., and Susan R. Goldman. "Improving Comprehension: Causal Relations Instruction for Learning Handicapped Learners." *The Reading Teacher,* 39 (May 1986), 896–904.

Vogt, MaryEllen. "An Observation Guide for Supervisors and Administrators: Moving toward Integrated Reading/Language Arts Instruction." *The Reading Teacher,* 45 (November 1991), 206–211.

Vukelich, Carol. "Parents' Role in the Reading Process: A Review of Practical Suggestions and Ways to Communicate with Parents." *The Reading Teacher,* 37 (February 1984), 472–477.

Wade, Suzanne E., and Ralph E. Reynolds. "Developing Metacognitive Awareness." *Journal of Reading,* 33 (October 1989), 6–14.

Walberg, Herbert J., Victoria Chou Hare, and Cynthia A. Pulliam. "Social-Psychological Perceptions and Reading Comprehension." In *Comprehension and Teaching: Research Reviews,* edited by John T. Guthrie. Newark, Del.: International Reading Association, 1981, pp. 140–159.

Walker-Dalhouse, Doris. "Using African-American Literature to Increase Ethnic Understanding." *The Reading Teacher,* 45 (February 1992), 416–422.

Wall, Bonnie. "Managing Your Multi-Age Classroom." *Teaching K–8,* 25 (August/September 1994), 68–73.

Waller, T. Gary. *Think First, Read Later! Piagetian Prerequisites for Reading.* Newark, Del.: International Reading Association, 1977.

Walmsley, Sean A. "Reflections on the State of Elementary Literature Instruction." *Language Arts,* 69 (November 1992), 508–514.

Walmsley, Sean A., and Ellen L. Adams. "Realities of 'Whole Language.'" *Language Arts,* 70 (April 1993), 272–280.

Walshe, R. D. "Donald Graves in Australia." In *Donald Graves in Australia—"Children Want to Write . . . ,"* edited by R. D. Walshe. Rozelle, NSW, Australia: Primary English Teaching Association, 1986.

Warren, Suzanne S., and Ellen E. Baritot. "Keeping Kids Working Comfortably." *Classroom Computer Learning,* 7 (September 1986), 52–54.

Watson, Dorothy J. "Whole Language: Why Bother?" *The Reading Teacher,* 47 (May 1994), 600–607.

Watson, Jerry J. "An Integral Setting Tells More Than When and Where." *The Reading Teacher,* 44 (May 1991) 638–646.

Waugh, Joyce Clark. "Using LEA in Diagnosis." *Journal of Reading,* 37 (September 1993), 56–57.

Waugh, R. P., and K. W. Howell. "Teaching Modern Syllabication." *The Reading Teacher,* 29 (October 1975), 20–25.

Weaver, Constance. *Psycholinguistics and Reading: From Process to Practice.* Cambridge, Mass.: Winthrop, 1980.

Weaver, Constance. *Understanding Whole Language.* Portsmouth, N.H.: Heinemann, 1990.

Weaver, Phyllis, and Fredi Shonhoff. "Subskill and Holistic Approaches to Reading Instruction." In *Readings on Reading Instruction,* edited by Albert J. Harris and Edward R. Sipay. New York: Longman, 1984.

Weber, Rose Marie. "Linguistic Diversity and Reading in American Society." In *Handbook of Reading Research, Vol. II,* edited by Rebecca Barr, Michael L. Kamil, Peter B. Mosenthal, and P. David Pearson. White Plains, N.Y.: Longman, 1991, pp. 97–119.

Webre, Elizabeth Cancienne. "Using Children's Choices Books to Enhance Math and Health Instruction." *The Reading Teacher,* 44 (February 1991), 445–446.

Weiss, Maria J. "Who Needs a Teacher's Guide?" *The Reading Teacher,* 41 (October 1987), 119–120.

Wepner, Shelley B. "Holistic Computer Applications in Literature-Based Classrooms." *The Reading Teacher,* 44 (September 1990), 12–19.

Wepner, Shelley B. "Linking Logos with Print for Beginning Reading Success." *The Reading Teacher,* 38 (March 1985), 633–639.

Wepner, Shelley B. "Technology and Author Studies." *The Reading Teacher,* 46 (April 1993), 616–619.

Wepner, Shelley B. "Technology and Textsets." *The Reading Teacher,* 46 (September 1992), 68–71.

Wepner, Shelley B. "Technology and Thematic Units: An Elementary Example on Japan." *The Reading Teacher,* 46 (February 1993), 442–445.

Wepner, Shelley B. "Technology and Thematic Units: A Primary Example." *The Reading Teacher,* 46 (November 1992), 260–263.

Wepner, Shelley B. "Technology Based Literature Plans for Elementary Students." *The Reading Teacher,* 45 (November 1991), 236–238.

Wepner, Shelley B. "Using Technology with Content Area Units." *The Reading Teacher,* 45 (April 1992), 644–646.

Wepner, Shelley B., Nancy E. Seminoff, and Jay Blanchard. "Navigating Learning with Electronic Encyclopedias." *Reading Today,* 12 (June/July 1995), 28.

Werner, Patrice Holden, and JoAnna Strother. "Early Readers: Important Emotional Considerations." *The Reading Teacher,* 40 (February 1987), 538–543.

Wertheim, Judy. "Teaching Guides for Novels." *The Reading Teacher,* 42 (December 1988), 262.

Whaley, Jill Fitzgerald. "Story Grammars and Reading Instruction." *The Reading Teacher,* 34 (April 1981), 762–771.

"What's in Store Software Guide." *Family Computing,* March 1986, 82–91.

Wheatley, Elizabeth A., Dorothy H. Muller, and Richard B. Miller. "Computer-Assisted Vocabulary Instruction." *Journal of Reading,* 37 (October 1993), 92–102.

White, Maureen C., and Susan Mary Lawrence. "Integrating Reading and Writing Through Literature Study." *The Reading Teacher,* 45 (May 1992), 740–743.

White, Thomas G., Joanne Sowell, and Alice Yanagihara. "Teaching Elementary Students to Use Word-Part Clues." *The Reading Teacher,* 42 (January 1989), 302–308.

Whitfield, Edie L., and Larry Hovey. "Integrating Reading and Science with Job Cards." *The Reading Teacher,* 34 (May 1981), 944–945.

Whitin, David J., and Sandra Wilde. *Read Any Good Math Lately? Children's Books for Mathematical Learning, K–6.* Portsmouth, N.H.: Heinemann, 1992.

Whitmer, Jean E. "Pickles Will Kill You: Use Humorous Literature to Teach Critical Reading." *The Reading Teacher,* 39 (February 1986), 530–534.

Whole Language in the Classroom. Katonah, N.Y.: Richard C. Owen, 1990.

"Why Multicultural Education?" *Program News.* Alexandria, Va.: Association for Supervision and Curriculum Development (May 1994), 4–5.

Wicklund, LaDonna. "Shared Poetry: A Whole Language Experience Adapted for Remedial Readers." *The Reading Teacher,* 42 (March 1989), 478–481.

Wiesendanger, Katherine D. "Comprehension: Using Anticipation Guides." *The Reading Teacher,* 39 (November 1985), 241–242.

Wiewandt, Thomas. *The Hidden Life of the Desert.* New York: Crown, 1990.

Wigfield, Allan, and Steven R. Asher. "Social and Motivational Influences on Reading." In *Handbook of Reading Research,* edited by P. David Pearson. New York: Longman, 1984.

Wiggins, Grant. *The Case for Authentic Assessment.* Washington, D.C.: ERIC Clearinghouse, 1990 [ED328611].

Wiggins, Robert A. "Large Group Lesson/Small Group Follow-Up: Flexible Grouping in a Basal Reading Program." *The Reading Teacher,* 47 (March 1994), 450–460.

Wilhoyte, Cheryl H. "Contracting: A Bridge Between the Classroom and Resource Room." *The Reading Teacher,* 30 (January 1977), 376–378.

Wilkinson, Phyllis A., and Del Patty. "The Effects of Sentence Combining on the Reading Comprehension of Fourth Grade Students." *Research in the Teaching of English,* 27 (February 1993), 104–125.

Williams, Mary Ann. "Teaching Vocabulary Through Rephrasing." *The Reading Teacher,* 41 (April 1988), 858–859.

Willis, Scott. "Teaching Language–Minority Students." *ASCD Update,* 36 (June 1994), 1, 4–5.

Wilson, Cathy Roller. "Teaching Reading Comprehension by Connecting the Known to the New." *The Reading Teacher,* 36 (January 1983), 382–390.

Wilson, Lorraine, David Malmgren, Shirl Ramage, and Leanne Schulz. *An Integrated Approach to Learning.* South Melbourne, Australia: Nelson, 1991.

Wilson, Patricia J., and Richard F. Abrahamson. "What Children's Literature Classics Do Children Really Enjoy?" *The Reading Teacher,* 41 (January 1988), 406–411.

Winkel, Lois, ed. *The Elementary School Library Collection: A Guide to Books and Other Media, Phases 1, 2, 3,* 15th ed. Williamsport, Pa.: Bro-Dart Foundation, 1986.

"Winners All." Alexandria, Va.: National Association of State Boards of Education, October, 1992.

Winograd, Peter N., Karen K. Wixson, and Marjorie Y. Lipson, eds. *Improving Basal Reading Instruction.* New York: Teachers College Press, 1989.

Winograd, Peter, and Karen W. Higgins. "Writing, Reading, and Talking Mathematics: One Interdisciplinary Possibility." *The Reading Teacher,* 48 (December 1994/January 1995), 310–318.

Winograd, Peter, Scott Paris, and Connie Bridge. "Improving the Assessment of Literacy." *The Reading Teacher,* 45 (October 1991), 108–116.

Winograd, Peter. "Developing Alternative Assessments: Six Problems Worth Solving." *The Reading Teacher,* 47 (February 1994), 420–423.

Wiseman, Donna L. "Helping Children Take Early Steps Toward Reading and Writing." *The Reading Teacher,* 37 (January 1984), 340–344.

Wittrock, Merlin C. "Process Oriented Measures of Comprehension." *The Reading Teacher,* 40 (April 1987), 734–737.

Wixson, Karen K. "Questions about a Text: What You Ask about Is What Children Learn." *The Reading Teacher,* 37 (December 1983), 287–293.

Wolchock, Carol. "Interpreting Idioms." *The Reading Teacher,* 43 (April 1990), 614–615.

Wolfe, Ronald, and Alice Lopez. "Structured Overviews for Teaching Science and Terms." *Journal of Reading,* 36 (December 1992/January 1993), 315–317.

Wollman-Bonilla, Julie E. "Reading Journals: Invitations to Participate in Literature." *The Reading Teacher,* 43 (November 1989), 112–120.

Wong Fillmore, Lily. "Research Currents: Equity or Excellence?" *Language Arts,* 63 (September 1986), 474–481.

Wong, B. Y. L. "Self-Questioning Instructional Research: A Review." *Review of Educational Research,* 55(1985), 227–268.

Wong, Jo Ann, and Kathryn Hu-pei Au. "The Concept-Text-Application Approach: Helping Elementary Students Comprehend Expository Text." *The Reading Teacher,* 38 (March 1985), 612–618.

Wong-Kam, Jo Ann, and Kathryn Au. "Improving a 4th Grader's Reading and Writing: Three Principles." *The Reading Teacher,* 41 (April 1988), 768–772.

Wood, Delores, and Joanne Nurss. "Print Rich Classrooms Support the Development of Print Awareness." *Georgia Journal of Reading,* 14 (Fall/Winter 1988), 21–23.

Wood, Judy. *Mainstreaming,* 2nd ed. Columbus, Ohio: Merrill, 1993.

Wood, Karen D. "Fostering Collaborative Reading and Writing Experiences in Mathematics." *Journal of Reading,* 36 (October 1992), 96–103.

Wood, Karen D. "Probable Passages: A Writing Strategy." *The Reading Teacher,* 37 (February 1984), 496–499.

Wood, Karen D., and John A. Mateja. "Adapting Secondary Level Strategies for Use in Elementary Classrooms." *The Reading Teacher,* 36 (February 1983), 492–496.

Wood, Karen, and Bob Algozzine, eds. *Teaching Reading to High-Risk Learners.* Boston: Allyn & Bacon, 1994.

Wood, Karen. "Collaborative Learning." *The Reading Teacher,* 43 (January 1990), 346–347.

Wood, Karen. "Using Cooperative Learning Strategies." *Middle School Journal,* 20 (May 1989), 23–26.

Wysocki, Katherine, and Joseph R. Jenkins. "Deriving Word Meanings Through Morphological Generalization." *Reading Research Quarterly,* 22, no. 1 (1987), 66–81.

Yatvin, J. *Developing a Whole Language Program.* Richmond, Va.: Virginia State Reading Association, 1991.

Yellin, David, and Mary Blake. *Integrating Language Arts: A Holistic Approach.* New York: HarperCollins, 1994.

Yonan, Barbara. "Encyclopedia Reports Don't Have to Be Dull." *The Reading Teacher,* 36 (November 1982), 212–214.

Yopp, Hallie Kay. "Developing Phonemic Awareness in Young Children." *The Reading Teacher,* 45 (May 1992), 696–703.

Yopp, R. E. "Questioning and Active Comprehension." *Questioning Exchange,* 2 (1988), 231–238.

Young, Terrell A., and Sylvia Vardell. "Weaving Readers Theatre and Nonfiction Into the Curriculum." *The Reading Teacher,* 46 (February 1993), 396–406.

Ysseldyke, James, and Bob Algozzine. *Introduction to Special Education,* 2d ed. Boston: Houghton Mifflin, 1990.

Zabrucky, Karen, and Hilary Horn Ratner. "Children's Comprehension Monitoring: Implications of Research Findings for the Classroom." *Reading Improvement,* 27 (Spring 1990), 46–53.

Zack, Vicki. "'It Was the Worst of Times': Learning about the Holocaust through Literature." *Language Arts,* 68 (January 1991), 42–48.

Zarillo, James. "Teachers' Interpretations of Literature-Based Reading." *The Reading Teacher,* 43 (October 1989), 22–28.

Zarnowski, Myra. "Learning about Fictionalized Biographies: A Reading and Writing Approach." *The Reading Teacher,* 42 (November 1988), 136–142.

Zastrow, Holly. "Word Play for 3rd to 7th Grade Readers." *The Reading Teacher,* 41 (January 1988), 495.

Zimet, Sara Goodman. "Teaching Children to Detect Social Bias in Books." *The Reading Teacher,* 36 (January 1983), 418–421.

Zirkelbach, Thelma. "A Personal View of Early Readig." *The Reading Teacher,* 37 (February 1984), 468–471.

Zogby, Grace. "Literature Groups: Empowering the Reader." Presentation at Whole Language Umbrella Conference, St. Louis, Missouri, August 4, 1990.

Zucker, Carol. "Using Whole Language with Students Who Have Language and Learning Disabilities." *The Reading Teacher,* 46 (May 1993), 660–670.

Glossary

achievement grouping Placing students into various groups on the basis of achievement.

achievement test A measure of the extent to which a person has assimilated a body of information.

affective Relating to attitudes, interests, values, appreciations, and opinions.

alphabetic principle Concept that letters represent speech sounds.

Americans with Disabilities Act (ADA) A law designed to eliminate discrimination against all individuals with disabilities.

analogies Comparisons of two similar relationships, stated in the form of the following example: *Author* is to *book* as *artist* is to *painting.*

analytic approach to phonics instruction Teaching the sounds of letters in already known words. Sight words are taught first; letter sounds second.

anaphora Use of a word as a substitute for another word or group of words.

anecdotal record Written account of specific incidents or behaviors in the classroom.

anticipation guides Sets of declarative statements related to materials about to be read that are designed to stimulate thinking and discussion.

antonyms A pair of words that have opposite meanings.

appositive A word or a phrase placed beside another word or phrase as an added explanation.

articulation Production of speech sounds.

assessment The collection of data, such as test scores and informal records, to measure student achievement.

attention-deficit hyperactivity disorder (ADHD) Syndrome characterized by inability to focus attention on tasks and maintain attention.

auditory acuity Sharpness of hearing.

auditory discrimination The ability to differentiate among sounds.

auditory memory The ability to recall information or stimuli that one has heard.

auditory perception The way the brain comprehends information it receives by sound.

auditory sense Sense of hearing.

authentic assessment Measurement of a student's performance on activities that reflect real-world learning experiences.

author's chair A chair in which children sit when they read their own books or trade books to an audience.

bandwagon technique An approach that utilizes the urge to do what others are doing. The impression is given that everyone else is participating in a particular activity.

bar graphs Graphs that use vertical or horizontal bars to compare quantities.

basal reader series Coordinated, graded set of textbooks, teacher's guides, and supplementary materials.

bidialectalism Ability to communicate in more than one dialect of a language.

big books Large books that the entire class can share together, often characterized by predictability, repetition, and rhyme.

bilingualism Ability to speak or understand another language in addition to one's native tongue.

bottom-up models Models that depict reading as being initiated by examination of the printed symbols, with little input being required from the reader.

Caldecott Award An annual award for excellence in illustration.

capacity level Potential reading level.

card stacking Telling only one side of a story by ignoring information favorable to the opposing point of view.

categorization Classification into related groups.

cause-and-effect pattern A writing pattern organized around causes and their effects.

characterization The way people come to life through words of the author.

checklist A convenient form on which the teacher can record observations about specific student behaviors or attitudes.

choral reading Dramatic reading of poetry in a group.

chronological order pattern A writing pattern based on time order.

cinquain A simple five line poem that follows a prescribed pattern.

circle or pie graphs Graphs that show relationships of individual parts to a whole circle.

classification pattern A writing pattern in which information is ordered under common headings and subheadings.

cloze procedure Method of estimating reading difficulty by omitting every nth (usually fifth) word in a reading passage and observing the number of correct words a reader can supply; an instructional technique in which words or other structures are deleted from a passage by the teacher, with blanks left in their places for students to fill in by using the surrounding context.

cognitive development The acquisition of knowledge.

community of authors A supportive and cooperative relationship among students and teacher during writing activities.

community of learners A cohesive group of class members who develop and pursue similar goals.

comparison/contrast pattern A writing pattern organized around likenesses and differences.

computer-assisted instruction Instruction that makes use of a computer to administer a programmed instructional sequence.

computer-managed instruction Use of the computer for such tasks as record-keeping, diagnosis, and prescription of individualized assignments.

concept-text-application approach A way to organize lessons to help elementary school students understand expository text.

concept/vocabulary development The acquisition of words and their meanings.

concrete experiences Direct experiences, involving all senses.

concrete-operational period Piaget's third stage of cognitive development (approximately ages seven to eleven).

connotations The feelings and shades of meaning that a word tends to evoke.

content area textbooks Textbooks in areas of information, such as literature, social studies, science, and mathematics.

context clues Clues to word meanings or pronunciations found in the surrounding words or sentences.

cooperative learning Learning through an instructional and grouping procedure utilizing mixed ability groups of students who work cooperatively to achieve certain goals.

creative dramatics Acting out stories spontaneously, without a script.

creative reading Reading beyond the lines.

criterion-referenced test Test designed to yield measurements interpretable in terms of specific performance standards.

critical reading Reading for evaluation.

cross-age tutoring Tutoring between those of different ages.

culturally diverse Pertaining to those who come from homes that differ economically, socially, and culturally.

database An organized body of information which can be sorted and searched electronically.

denotations Dictionary definitions.

departmentalization Instructional systems in which there is a different teacher for each major subject area.

derivatives Words formed by adding prefixes and suffixes to root words.

desktop publishing Application of computers combining text and graphics for classroom publishing.

dialect Regional or social modifications of a language; distinguishing features may include pronunciation, vocabulary, and syntax.

dialectal miscue Miscalling of a word due to dialect.

diorama A three-dimensional scene.

direct instruction Teacher control of learning environment through structured lessons, goal setting, choice of activities, and feedback.

directed inquiry activity A technique based upon the directed reading-thinking activity, in which predictions related to who, what, when, where, how, and why questions are made after previewing, but before reading, the content material, in order to set reading purposes.

directed reading activity A strategy in which detailed lesson plans are followed to teach the reading of stories.

directed reading-thinking activity A general plan for directing the reading of content area reading selections or basal reader stories and for encouraging children to think as they read, to predict, and to check their predictions.

directionality Reading from left to right and top to bottom.

drafting The second stage of the writing process, in which the author sets ideas on paper without regard for neatness or mechanics.

dramatic play Simulating real experiences, such as playing the mother or father in a housekeeping center.

eclectic approaches Approaches that combine desirable aspects of a number of different major approaches.

editing The fourth stage of the writing process, in which the author corrects spelling and mechanics.

ellipsis The omission of a word or group of words that are to be "understood" by the reader.

emergent literacy A developing awareness of the interrelatedness of oral and written language.

environmental print Words that children frequently see around them.

ESL (English as a second language) A program for teaching English language skills to those whose native language is not English.

etymology The origin and history of words.

euphemism The substitution of a less offensive word or phrase for an unpleasant term or expression.

exceptional child One who deviates from the majority of learners to such an extent that he or she cannot derive maximum benefit from regular classroom instruction; additional or different curriculum instruction or setting may be required.

expectation outline A categorized list of questions that children expect to be answered by a selection.

experience charts Written accounts about common experiences, dictated by the student(s) and recorded by the teacher.

experiential background Fund of total experiences that aid a reader in finding meaning in printed symbols.

explanation of a process pattern A writing pattern in which processes are described, frequently involving illustrations, such as pictures, charts, or diagrams, which are designed to clarify the textual material.

expository passage organizers (EPOs) Reading and writing process study guides designed to help students see the structure of expository text and use that knowledge in writing it.

expository style A precise, factual writing style.

expository text A text written in a precise, factual writing style.

fable A brief moral tale in which animals or inanimate objects speak.

figurative language Nonliteral language.

fixations Stops made by the eyes during reading in order to take in words and phrases and to react to them.

flexibility of reading habits Ability to adjust reading habits to fit the materials and purposes for reading.

formal (standardized) test Testing instrument based on extensive normative data and for which reliability and validity can be verified.

format The size, shape, design of pages, illustrations, typography, paper, and binding of a publication.

friendship grouping Allowing friends to work together for a specific purpose and within a specified time frame.

frustration level A level of reading difficulty with which a reader is unable to cope; when reading material is on this level, the reader usually recognizes 90 percent or less of the words he or she reads or comprehends 50 percent or less of what he or she reads.

genre A type of classification of literature, such as historical fiction, biography, or folktales.

gifted (intellectually) Possessing high intellectual development with a mental age that is above the norm.

glittering generalities Using vague phrases to influence a point of view without providing necessary specifics.

grade equivalent scores Test scores expressed in terms of grade level, comparing a student's score with average achievement of the population used to standardize the test (a score of 6.4 represents achievement equal to that of an average child in the fourth month of the sixth school year).

grapheme A written symbol that represents a phoneme.

graphic cue Clue provided by the written form of the word.

guide words Words used in dictionaries, encyclopedias, and other reference books to aid users in finding entries. The first guide word names the first entry on the page; the second guide word names the final entry on the page.

guided reading procedure A method designed to help readers improve organizational skills, comprehension, and recall.

hearing impaired One whose sense of hearing is defective but functional for ordinary purposes.

heterogeneous Different or unlike.

holistic assessment A process-oriented approach for evaluating a student's abilities to integrate separate skills in order to comprehend an entire selection.

homogeneous Similar or like.

homographs Words that have identical spellings but sound different and have different meanings.

homonyms Pairs or groups of words that are spelled differently but are pronounced alike; homophones.

hyperbole An extreme exaggeration.

idiom A group of words that, taken as a whole, has a meaning different from that of the sum of the meanings of the individual words.

IEP (Individual Education Program) A written account of objectives, strategies, curriculum modifications, and classroom accommodations for a student with learning problems.

improvisation Acting without a script.

inclusion The assignment of students with disabilities to regular classrooms in neighborhood schools for the entire school day. These children shall participate in all school activities.

independent level A level of reading difficulty low enough that the reader can progress without noticeable hindrance; the reader can ordinarily recognize at least 99 percent of the words and comprehend at least 90 percent of what he or she reads.

individualized reading approach An approach to reading instruction that is characterized by pupils' self-selection of reading materials and self-pacing and by pupil-teacher conferences.

Individuals with Disabilities Education Act (IDEA) An amended version of PL 94-142 that modifies some of the provisions and changes some terminology to show greater sensitivity for the individual.

inference Conclusion drawn from stated facts.

inflectional endings Endings that when added to nouns change the number, case, or gender; when added to verbs change the tense or person; and when added to adjectives change the degree.

informal assessment Nonstandardized measurement.

informal reading inventory An informal instrument designed to help the teacher determine a child's independent, instructional, frustration, and capacity levels.

Informal drama Spontaneous and unrehearsed acting.

InQuest Investigative Questioning, a comprehension strategy that combines student questioning with creative drama.

insertions Words that do not appear in the printed passage but are inserted by the reader.

instructional level A level of difficulty at which the reader can read with understanding with teacher assistance; the reader can ordinarily recognize at least 95 percent of the words in a selection and comprehend at least 75 percent of what he or she reads.

instructions for experiment pattern A writing pattern containing step-by-step procedures to be followed.

integrated curriculum A curriculum in which content and concepts are interrelated across subject areas.

integrated language arts curriculum The integration of purposeful reading, writing, listening, and speaking activities.

interactive processing Processing in which one uses both information supplied by the text and information from one's own prior world knowledge and background of experiences to interpret the text.

interactive theories Theories that depict reading as a combination of reader-based and text-based processing.

interclass grouping Forming groups from a number of classrooms.

interest grouping Placing pupils into various groups on the basis of common interests.

interest inventory Device used to assess a person's preferences in various areas.

interpretive reading Reading between the lines.

invented spellings Unconventional spellings resulting from children's attempts to associate sounds with letters.

irregularly spelled words Words not spelled the way they sound.

journals Written records of reflections, events, and ideas.

juncture Pauses in the flow of speech (marking the ends of phrases, clauses, or sentences)

kidwatching Observing children to gain insights into their learning.

knowledge-based processing Bringing one's prior world knowledge and background of experiences to the interpretation of the text.

K-W-L Teaching Model A teaching model for expository text; stands for What I *Know,* What I *Want* to Learn, What I *Learned.*

language arts Listening, speaking, reading, and writing skills.

language experience approach An approach in which reading and the other language arts are interrelated in the instructional program and the experiences of children are used as the basis for reading materials.

language experience story A story composed by a child or a group of children and recorded by them or the teacher.

language facility Listening comprehension, speaking ability, reading skill, and writing ability.

learning center An area containing several independent learning activities based on a theme.

learning disabled Having a developmental disorder that interferes with the ability to learn certain skills.

least restrictive environment A setting in which a child can master skills and content; it resembles the regular classroom as closely as possible.

legend (of a map) The map's key to symbols used.

limited English proficiency (LEP) Describing those who lack sufficient English language skills to achieve in a regular classroom and who thus require special instruction for developing linguistic and academic skills.

line graphs Graphs that show changes in amounts by connecting points representing the amounts with line segments.

linguistics The scientific study of human speech.

linguists Scientists who study human speech.

literal comprehension Understanding ideas that are directly stated.

literature-based approaches Approaches that use quality literature as a basis for reading instruction.

literature response groups Groups established to allow students to exchange ideas about books they are reading.

mainstreaming Integrating children who are disabled into the general reading program of the classroom.

mental retardation General intellectual ability that is significantly below average, coupled with deficits in adaptive behavior during the developmental period.

metacognition A person's knowledge of the functioning of his or her own mind and his or her conscious efforts to monitor or control this functioning.

metacognitive strategies Techniques for thinking about and monitoring one's own thought processes.

metalinguistic awareness The ability to think about language and manipulate it objectively.

metaphor A direct comparison not using the word *like* or *as*.

metaphoric language Nonliteral language.

minimally contrasting spelling patterns Words that vary in spellings by only a single letter.

miscue An unexpected oral reading response (error).

modality A sensory system for receiving and processing information (visual, auditory, kinesthetic, tactile).

morphemes The smallest units of meaning in a language.

motivation Incentive to act.

multicultural students Students who represent a variety of regional cultures, ethnic groups, and religious groups.

multidisciplinary team A group of people who construct an IEP for a student with disabilities.

multiethnic Pertaining to various racial and ethnic groups.

name calling Using derogatory labels to create a negative reaction without providing evidence to support such an impression.

Newbery Award An annual award for the most distinguished contribution to American literature for children.

nonrestrictive clauses Appositive clauses; clauses that do not restrict the information in the main clause but add information.

norm-referenced test Test designed to yield results interpretable in terms of a norm, the average or mean results of a sample population.

onsets and rimes Word parts, with onsets being the consonants or consonant clusters at the beginning of a syllable and rimes being the vowel(s) and any consonants that follow.

oral reading strategy A technique in which the teacher reads material to the students and has them restate it in their own words.

ownership A sense of complete responsibility for something, such as a piece of writing.

paired-associate learning Learning in which a stimulus is presented along with a desired response.

pantomime Dramatizing through movement without using words.

paraprofessional A teacher's assistant or other adult with some professional training who works in the classroom to assist the teacher.

peer tutoring One student helping another student learn.

percentile rank Test score expressed in terms of its position within a set of 100 scores.

perception The interpretation of sensory impressions.

performance-based assessment Measurement of a student's ability to create an assigned response or product to demonstrate her or his level of competence.

performance sampling Examples of children's work collected periodically for later analysis.

personification Giving the attributes of a person to an inanimate object or abstract idea.

phoneme The smallest unit of sound in a language.

phonemic awareness An understanding that speech consists of a series of small sound units.

phonemic segmentation The process of separating the sounds within words.

phonics The association of speech sounds with printed symbols.

picture graphs Graphs that express quantities with pictures.

pitch Highness or lowness of sound.

PL 94-142 The Education for All Handicapped Children Act, which provides federal assistance for the education of students who are disabled.

plain folks talk Relating a person or proposed program to the common people in order to gain their support.

plot The plan of a story.

poor reader One who has difficulty learning to read; also sometimes identified as dyslexic, remedial, underachieving, at-risk, disabled, retarded, impaired, or language learning disabled.

portfolio A collection of a child's work over a period of time.

potential reading level An estimate of a person's possible reading achievement level based upon intelligence or listening comprehension.

predictable books Books that use repetition, rhythmic language patterns, and familiar concepts.

preoperational period Piaget's second stage of cognitive development, extending from age two to age seven.

prewriting The first stage of the writing process in which the author prepares for writing by talking, reading, and thinking about the piece; organizing ideas; and developing a plan.

print conventions Generally accepted concepts about writing.

process-oriented assessment Measures a student's use of thought processes and reading strategies.

programmed instruction A method or presenting instructional material in which small, sequential steps; active involvement of the learner; immediate reinforcement; and self-pacing are emphasized.

project or research grouping Placing students of varying ability levels together so that they may investigate a topic.

propaganda techniques Techniques of writing used to influence people's thinking and actions, including bandwagon technique, card stacking, glittering generalities, name calling, plain folks talk, testimonials, and transfer techniques.

publishing The last stage of the writing process in which the writer puts the piece into finished form.

pupil pairs Partners who work cooperatively on activities.

question-only strategy A technique in which the students question the teacher about the topic of study and try to learn all they can in that way before reading the material on that topic.

readability An objective measure of the difficulty of written material.

readers' theater Reading aloud from scripts in a dramatic style.

reading and writing workshop Instructional procedure consisting of a minilesson, a status-of-the-class report, reading or writing, and sharing.

reading checklist Listing of significant reading behaviors and a convenient form for recording results of teacher observation.

reading miscue inventory An informal instrument that considers both the quality and quantity of miscues made by the reader.

reading rate Speed of reading, often reported in words per minute.

reading readiness The level of preparedness for formal reading instruction.

reading readiness test A test for predicting a child's readiness to begin formal reading instruction.

reading/study techniques Techniques designed to enhance comprehension and retention of written material.

realistic story A story that could have happened to real people.

reciprocal teaching A technique to develop comprehension and metacognition in which the teacher and students take turns being "teacher." They predict, generate questions, summarize, and clarify ideas.

ReFlex Action An approach for developing flexible readers.

regressions Eye movements back to a previously read word or phrase for the purpose of rereading.

reinforcement Something done to strengthen a response.

relative clauses Clauses that refer to an antecedent (may be restrictive or nonrestrictive).

reliability The degree to which a test gives consistent results.

remedial reader A reader whose reading achievement is two or more years behind reading expectancy.

ReQuest A technique in which the teacher and the students alternate asking questions about a passage.

resource room A classroom where children with disabilities spend a period of time on a regular basis, with instruction provided by the resource-room teacher.

restrictive clauses Clauses that restrict the information in the main clause by adding information.

reversals Changing the position or orientation of letters, parts of a word, or words.

reversibility The ability to reverse an operation to produce what was there initially.

revising The third stage of the writing process, in which the author makes changes in the initial draft.

rubric A set of criteria used to describe and evaluate a student's level of proficiency in a particular subject area.

running record A strategy for recording miscues during a student's oral reading.

SAVOR Procedure A procedure based upon the semantic feature analysis technique, but focusing on reinforcement of essential content area vocabulary.

scale (of a map) The part of a map showing the relationship of a given distance on a map to the same distance on the area represented.

schema A pre-existing knowledge structure developed about a thing, place, or idea.

selection aids References that identify and evaluate publications.

self-concept An individual's perception of himself or herself as a person, his or her abilities, appearance, performance, and so on.

semantic cues (or clues) Meaning clues.

semantic feature analysis A technique in which the presence or absence of particular features in the meaning of a word is indicated through symbols on a chart, allowing comparisons of word meanings.

semantic maps Graphic representations of relationships among words and phrases in written material.

semantic webbing Making a graphic representation of relationships in written material through the use of a core question, strands (answers), strand supports (facts and inferences from the story), and strand ties (relationships of the strands to each other).

sensory handicap Hearing and/or visual impairment.

sequence The order in which the events in a story occur.

setting The time and place of a story.

shared book experiences Reading and rereading books in a group activity for understanding and enjoyment.

sight words Words that are recognized immediately, without having to resort to analysis.

simile A comparison using *like* or *as*.

special skills (needs) grouping Placing pupils into various groups on the basis of skills deficiencies.

specific learning disability A developmental disorder exhibited by imperfect ability to learn certain skills.

speech impaired Those whose speech deviates sufficiently from normal speech to interfere with satisfactory oral communication.

SQRQCQ A study method consisting of six steps: Survey, Question, Read, Question, Compute, Question.

SQ3R A study method consisting of five steps: Survey, Question, Read, Recite, Review.

stanine scale A ranking of test scores on a scale of one through nine.

story grammar A set of rules that define story structures.

story mapping Making graphic representations of stories that make clear the specific relationships of story elements.

stress Degree of emphasis placed on a syllable or sound.

structural analysis Analysis of words by identifying prefixes, suffixes, root words, inflectional endings, contractions, word combinations forming compound words, and syllabication.

student contract Negotiated agreement about what the pupil is to do and when the task is to be completed.

study guides Duplicated sheets prepared by the teacher and distributed to the children to help guide reading in content fields and alleviate those difficulties that interfere with understanding.

stuttering A type of speech impairment characterized by hesitation, sound prolongations, and/or repetition.

style An author's mode of expressing thoughts in words.

subskill theories Theories that depict reading as a set of subskills that children must master and integrate.

survey test A test that measures general achievement in a given area.

Sustained Silent Reading (SSR) A program for setting aside a certain period of time daily for silent reading.

synonyms Groups of words that have the same, or very similar, meanings.

syntactic cues (or clues) Clues derived from the word order in sentences.

syntax The rules for combining words to form grammatical sentences.

synthetic approach to phonics instruction Teaching pupils to blend together individual known letter sounds in order to decode written words. Letter sounds are taught first; sight words second.

teacher research Teacher participation in classroom action or naturalistic research.

team arrangement Two or more classes combined with a staff of several teachers.

testimonial technique Using a highly popular or respected person to endorse a product or proposal.

text-based processing Trying to extract the information that resides in the text.

thematic unit An integrated learning experience with a topic or concept that is the core of the curriculum for an extended period of time.

theme The main idea that the writer wishes to convey to the reader.

theme cycle A theme study negotiated by the teacher and the students.

theory A set of assumptions or principles designed to explain phenomena.

top-down models Models that depict reading as beginning with the generation of hypotheses or predictions about the material by the reader.

topic sentence A sentence that sets forth the central thought of the paragraph in which it occurs.

topical order pattern A writing pattern organized around central themes or topics.

trade book A book for sale to the general public.

transactive theories Theories based on Rosenblatt's idea that every reading act is a transaction that involves a reader and a text and occurs at a particular time in a specific context, with meaning coming into being during the transaction between the reader and the text.

transfer technique Associating a respected organization or symbol with a particular person, project, or idea.

validity The extent to which a test represents a balanced and adequate sampling of the instructional outcomes it is intended to cover.

variants Words formed by adding inflectional endings to root words.

vicarious experiences Indirect experiences, not involving all five senses.

visual acuity Sharpness of vision.

visual discrimination Ability to differentiate between different shapes.

visual memory The ability to recall what one has seen.

visual perception The brain's processing and understanding of visual stimuli.

visualization Picturing events, places, and people described by the author.

visually impaired Those who are partially sighted but able to read print.

VLP An approach to prereading activities involving vocabulary, oral language, and prediction.

webbing A technique that graphically connects a central topic or theme to related ideas.

whole language A philosophy that supports an integrated curriculum, authentic learning tasks, social interactions, learner-centered classrooms, and the use of literature across the curriculum.

whole language classroom A child-centered environment where language is integrated with content through authentic experiences.

whole language philosophy A philosophy that advocates reading and writing of whole pieces of literature and student choice of reading and writing experiences that are personally meaningful.

word bank A collection of sight words that have been mastered by an individual pupil, usually recorded on index cards.

word configuration Word shape.

word webs Graphic representations of the relationships among words that are constructed by connecting the related terms with lines.

wordless picture books Picture books without words.

writing process A child-centered procedure for writing consisting of prewriting, drafting, revising, editing, and publishing.

Appendix

Answers to "Test Yourself"

Chapter 1   True-False

1. F	11. T	21. T
2. T	12. F	22. T
3. F	13. T	23. T
4. F	14. T	24. T
5. F	15. F	25. F
6. T	16. F	26. T
7. T	17. T	27. T
8. T	18. T	28. F
9. F	19. F	29. T
10. F	20. F	30. F

Chapter 2   True-False

1. T	11. F	21. F
2. F	12. T	22. F
3. T	13. T	23. T
4. T	14. F	24. F
5. F	15. F	25. T
6. F	16. F	26. T
7. F	17. F	27. T
8. T	18. F	28. F
9. F	19. T	
10. F	20. F	

Chapter 3   True-False

1. F	13. T	25. T
2. F	14. T	26. F
3. T	15. T	27. F
4. F	16. T	28. T
5. T	17. T	29. T
6. T	18. F	30. F
7. F	19. T	31. T
8. T	20. F	32. T
9. F	21. F	33. T
10. T	22. T	34. T
11. T	23. T	35. F
12. F	24. T	

Chapter 3   Multiple-Choice

1. a	5. c	9. b
2. c	6. a	10. b
3. a	7. c	11. a
4. b	8. b	

Chapter 4   True-False

1. F	11. T	21. T
2. T	12. F	22. F
3. F	13. T	23. T
4. F	14. T	24. T
5. T	15. T	25. T
6. T	16. T	26. F
7. T	17. T	27. T
8. T	18. T	28. F
9. T	19. T	
10. F	20. F	

Chapter 5   True-False

1. T	7. F	13. T
2. T	8. T	14. F
3. T	9. T	15. F
4. T	10. T	16. F
5. F	11. F	
6. T	12. T	

Chapter 6   True-False

1. T	8. F	15. F
2. T	9. T	16. F
3. T	10. F	17. F
4. F	11. T	18. T
5. T	12. T	19. T
6. F	13. F	20. F
7. T	14. T	

Chapter 7   *True-False*

1. F	9. T	17. T
2. T	10. F	18. F
3. F	11. T	19. F
4. F	12. T	20. F
5. T	13. T	21. T
6. T	14. F	22. T
7. F	15. T	23. F
8. T	16. T	24. F

Chapter 8   *True-False*

1. T	9. F	17. T
2. T	10. T	18. F
3. F	11. T	19. T
4. F	12. F	20. F
5. F	13. T	21. F
6. F	14. F	22. T
7. T	15. F	23. T
8. F	16. T	24. T

Chapter 9   *True-False*

1. F	11. T	21. T
2. T	12. T	22. T
3. T	13. F	23. F
4. T	14. T	24. F
5. F	15. F	25. T
6. T	16. F	26. T
7. F	17. T	27. F
8. F	18. T	28. T
9. T	19. F	
10. T	20. T	

Chapter 10   *True-False*

1. F	11. F	21. T
2. T	12. T	22. T
3. T	13. T	23. T
4. F	14. T	24. T
5. F	15. F	25. T
6. T	16. T	26. F
7. F	17. T	
8. F	18. T	
9. T	19. F	
10. T	20. T	

Chapter 11   *True-False*

1. F	11. F	21. T
2. F	12. F	22. F
3. F	13. F	23. T
4. F	14. T	24. F
5. T	15. F	25. T
6. T	16. T	26. F
7. T	17. T	27. F
8. T	18. T	28. T
9. F	19. F	
10. T	20. T	

Chapter 12   *True-False*

1. F	12. T	23. T
2. F	13. T	24. F
3. F	14. F	25. T
4. F	15. T	26. T
5. T	16. F	27. T
6. T	17. T	28. T
7. F	18. F	29. T
8. T	19. F	30. T
9. F	20. T	31. F
10. T	21. F	
11. T	22. F	

Chapter 13   *True-False*

1. F	12. T	23. T
2. T	13. T	24. T
3. T	14. F	25. T
4. F	15. F	26. F
5. T	16. F	27. T
6. F	17. T	28. F
7. F	18. F	29. F
8. T	19. T	30. T
9. T	20. F	31. F
10. T	21. F	
11. F	22. T	

Index

Aaron, Ira E., 22
Abrahamson, Richard F., 397
Accent marks, 148–149
Accentuation, 143–146, 148–149
Accountability, of tests, 23
Accuracy, of material, 286–287
Achievement groups, 590–592
Achievement tests, 539, 567–568, 569, 570–572
Acronyms, 189
Acting. See Creative dramatics; Dramatic play
Action research, by teacher, 605
Adams, Ellen L., 23
Adams, Marilyn Jager, 20, 65, 73, 93, 113, 114, 119, 122, 129, 207
Adequacy, of material, 286–287
Adverb referents, 267
Affective aspects, of reading, 8, 15–17
Affixes. See Prefixes; Suffixes
Afflerbach, Peter P., 539
Aiex, Nola Kortner, 334, 396, 645
ALERT, 291
Algozzine, Bob, 631
Allen, Elizabeth Godwin, 291
Allen, James Allen, 540, 570
Allen, R. V., 353
Allen, Virginia, 650, 651, 653
Allington, Richard L., 215, 580, 623, 624, 639
Alphabet books, 49
Alphabetical order, 440–442
Alphabetic principle, 65, 73
Altwerger, Bess, 651
Americans with Disabilities Act of 1990 (ADA), 622
Analogies: for content area reading, 485; for phonics instruction, 129, 130; for vocabulary instruction, 180–182, 183
Analysis, in informal assessment, 545
Analytic approach, to phonics instruction, 122–128, 129, 130, 134
Anaphora, 265–266, 267
Anders, Patricia L., 187
Anderson-Inman, Lynne, 210, 367
Anderson, Nancy A., 6

Anderson, Richard C., 8, 11, 14, 25, 31, 93, 111, 113, 142, 162, 175, 216, 395, 592, 602
Andrew, Barbara, 532
Anecdotes, 485, 543–544
Angeletti, Sara Rappold, 249
Ankney, Paul, 495
Anthony, Robert J., 551
Anticipation guides, 225–228, 494
Antonyms, 161, 199–200
Apostrophe, 142–143
Appendices, 439
Application, as postreading activity, 238
Appositive clues, 106
Appropriateness, of material, 287
Armbruster, Bonnie B., 162, 298, 528, 592
Armstrong, Thomas, 640
Art, responding to literature through, 405–406
Articulation disorders, 632
Ashby-Davis, Claire, 281
Asher, Steven R., 607
Ashton-Warner, Sylvia, 15, 64, 99
Assessment, 27, 539–541; criterion-referenced tests, 432, 565; of emergent literacy, 79–83; of reading, 17, 79–83; of writing, 79, 82. See also Informal assessment; Norm-referenced tests
Associational aspect, of reading, 8, 15, 17
Association method, for context clues, 174
Astigmatism, 10
Atkinson, Joan, 532
Atlases, 440
Attention-deficit disorders (ADD), 630–631
Attention-deficit hyperactivity disorder (ADHD), 630
Attitudes, toward reading, 8, 15–17
Atwell, Nancie, 335, 389
Au, Kathryn H., 486, 512, 555, 635, 637, 643, 644, 651, 652
Audience, comprehension and, 216
Audiovisual aids, 431. See also Graphic aids
Auditory acuity, 11, 12
Auditory discrimination, 12, 112, 114, 115–117

Auditory learners, 25
Auditory perception, 12
Auditory sense. See Hearing
Augustine, Dianne, 589
Authentic assessment, 80–83, 539, 540. See also Assessment
Authentic experiences, for bilingual students, 562
Author: evaluating factors on, 285–286; as thematic unit, 411, 413, 415–417
Authoring systems, for vocabulary instruction, 196
Author of the Week program, 77
Automaticity, 18–20
Avery, Beth Faris, 248
Avery, Carol S., 45, 605
Avery, Charles W., 248

Babbs, Patricia J., 229, 461, 555
Baca, Leonard, 650
Bagford, Jack, 347, 348
Bailey, Mildred Hart, 118
Baker, Deborah Tresidder, 261
Baker, Linda, 461, 555
Balajthy, Ernest, 363, 365, 391, 483
Baldwin, R. Scott, 174, 190, 191
Ball, E. W., 114
Ballew, Hunter, 523
Balsam, M., 366
Bandwagon technique, 290
Banks, James A., 644
Bar graphs, 466, 467, 468
Baritot, Ellen E., 600
Barnhart, Clarence, 319
Barnitz, John G., 266
Baroni, Dick, 170
Barr, Rebecca, 564
Barrow, Lloyd H., 532
Basal reader series, 313–320; for beginning readers, 69; books about the book written in, 369; changes in, 320; content texts vs., 477–478; language experience stories with, 370; phonics and, 113; readiness tests in, 80; shared reading of trade books

Basal reader series (*cont.*)
  with, 369; sight words and, 101; types of, 319; uses of, 316–318; writing and, 28
Baskwill, Jane, 543
Batzle, Janine, 546, 551
Baum, Dale D., 494
Baumann, James F., 122, 130, 231, 330, 461, 462, 585
Beach, John D., 485
Beach, R., 21–22
Bean, Rita M., 623
Bean, Thomas W., 246
Beattie, John, 630
Beaty, Janice J., 405
Beck, Isabel L., 161, 163, 165, 168, 262, 263, 281, 296, 478, 515
Beck, Judith S., 633
Becoming a Nation of Readers (Anderson), 395
Behavioral disorders, 632–633
Bell, Barbara, 399
Bell, Kathy, 525
Bellows, Barbara Plotkin, 181
Bennett, Taylor, 72–73
Berglund, Roberta, 356
Bergquist, Leonard, 434
Bernhardt, Bill, 247
Bertrand, Nancy, 635
Bibliographies, 439
Bidialectalism, 646
Bidwell, Sandra M., 244
Biehler, Robert F., 10
Big books, 66–67, 87–88
Bilingual Education Act, 648
Bilingual students, 646–656
Biographies, 516–517, 518
Bird, Lois, 651
Blachman, B. A., 114
Blachowicz, Camille L. Z., 163, 168–169, 172–173, 174, 333, 462, 566
Blake, Mary, 601
Blanchard, Jay S., 367, 446
Blanton, William E., 214, 215, 317
Blass, Rosanne J., 354
Blatt, 406
Bloomfield, Leonard, 319
Blum-Anderson, Judy, 627
Boehm, Ann E., 95, 98
Boodt, Gloria M., 279
Book reports, 404–405
Booth, David, 45, 67
Borich, Gary, 560
Borkowski, J. G., 230
Bormuth, J. R., 479
Bos, Candace S., 187
Bottom-up processing, 20–21
Bound morphemes, 176
Boyd, Reta, 384
Boyle, Owen F., 220
Bracket, G., 366
Bradley, L., 114

Brainstorming, 168, 248
Bransford, 210
Bransford, John D., 210, 296
Braselton, Stephania, 523
Bratcher, Suzanne, 552
Breen, Leonard, 199
Brewer, Jo Ann, 605
Brians, Suzanne, 630
Bridge, Connie, 540, 555
Bristow, Page Simpson, 30, 31, 211, 213, 230, 305
Bromley, Karen D'Angelo, 276, 277, 387, 408
Brown, Ann L., 234, 459, 461, 555, 592
Brown, Carol S., 540
Brozo, William G., 485
Bryant, P., 114
Buck, Maggie, 129–130
Buddy journals, 387, 388
Bufe, Bruce N., 180
Bukofzer, Nancy, 53
Burke, 406–407
Burke, Carolyn L., 384, 387, 399, 509, 549, 561, 563, 581
Burmeister, Lou E., 41, 118
Burns/Roe Informal Reading Inventory, 561, 562
Butler, Andrea, 62, 383
Butler, Syd, 364

Cairney, Trevor, 337, 499
Caissy, Gail, 600
Caldecott Award winners, 396–397
Calfee, Robert C., 568
Calhoun, Emily, 605
California Achievement Test, 567, 570
Cambourne, Brian, 42
Camperell, Kaybeth, 219
Capacity level, 560, 561
Card catalog, 449–451, 452
Card stacking, 290
Career education activities, 6
Carey, Robert F., 570
Carney, J. J., 161
Carnine, Douglas W., 111
Carr, Eileen, 163, 166, 172–175
Carr, Emily, 512
Carr, Gail A., 229
Carr, Kathryn S., 263
Carroll, John B., 142, 176
Cartoons, conclusions from, 275
Casteel, Carolyn P., 528
Castle, Marrietta, 71, 355
Catalogues, 448, 449
Categorization, 174, 179–180, 181
Catts, Hugh, 633
Cause-and-effect relationships, 271–272
Cazden, Courtney B., 612
C.D.'s Story Time, 79
Ceprano, Maria A., 103

Cervantes, Hernes T., 650
Chall, Jeanne S., 482
Chaney, Jeanne H., 508
Characterization: analysis of, 281–283; cooperative groups and, 248; responding to literature with, 403; for story comprehension, 246; teaching, 511–512
Character journal, 247
Checklists, for informal assessment, 544–546, 547
Cheng, Pui-wan, 230
Child-centered classroom, 41
Chittenden, Edward A., 81, 542
Choices, children having, 45
Choice time reading, 67–68
Church, Susan M., 23, 24
Circle graphs, 466, 467
Circle story, 246
Classics, 397
Classroom environment, 599–601; computers in, 600–601; learning centers in, 599–600, 603, 604; videotapes in, 601
Classroom organization, 579–599; cross-grade, 595–596; integrated language arts curriculum, 580–587; multi-age, 595; transitions in, 596–599; whole-class activities, 594; whole language classroom and, 585–584, 596–598. *See also* Classroom environment; Groups, learning in; School-wide organizational plans
Clay, Marie, 48, 62, 80–83, 564, 639
Clegg, Luther B., 516
Closed-caption television programs, 74
Closed syllables, 145
Cloze procedure: context clue use and, 108; as during-reading activity, 236; for informal assessment, 559–560
Cloze tests, for textbook readability, 479–482
Clymer, Theodore, 118
Coate, Sheri, 71, 355
Coburn, Peter, 368
Cochran-Smith, M., 367
Coelho, Elizabeth, 644, 652
Cognitive development, 41–42
Cohen, Ruth, 305, 555
Collier, Virginia P., 646, 648, 650
Colt, Jacalyn, 334
Combs, Martha, 485
Commas, 220–221
Commeyras, Michelle, 281, 282, 283
Common-expression clues, 106–107
Communication, 6, 7. *See also* Reading product
Community, school literature program and, 415, 417
Community of learners, 594
Compain, Rita, 580, 581, 598, 599
Compare/contrast approach, to phonics instruction, 129, 130

Comparison clues, 106

Compositions, 514

Compound words, 143, 144, 175–176, 177–179

Comprehension, 7–8, 20, 205–309; audience for reading and, 216; cooperative learning for, 247–249; discussion for, 238–239; importance of task and, 216–217; knowledge-based processing and, 211–213; listening-reading transfer lesson for, 249; literal, 255, 257–261; of paragraphs, 221–222; punctuation and, 220–221; purposes of reading and, 214–216; questions based on, 299–301; reading situation and, 214–217; reading-writing connection and, 247; schemata for, 12, 209–214; semantic webbing for, 239–240, 241; of sentences, 217–221; story grammar activities for, 241–246; story mapping for, 239–241; text-based processing and, 211–213; of text patterns, 222–223. See also During-reading activities; Higher-order comprehension; Prereading activities; Questions

Computer-assisted instruction (CAI), 363, 364–366, 368, 370

Computer-managed instruction (CMI), 363, 368, 601

Computers, 361–369; in classrooms, 600–601; comments about reading using, 247; computer-assisted instruction, 363, 364–366, 368, 70; computer-managed instruction, 363, 368, 601; for content area reading, 500–501; databases, 362, 364, 366–367, 453–454; dictionaries on, 444–445; for drill-and-practice, 363; emergent literacy and, 78–79; for gifted students, 642; hypertext and hypermedia and, 367; for informal assessment, 560; interactive telecommunications, 367; for language experience approach, 359; language experience lesson and, 356–357; literature-based approach and, 366; multimedia programs and, 362–363, 368; multisensory approach of, 367; pairs of students working at, 367; synthetic speech and, 362; textbook readability tested with, 483; tutorial programs and, 196, 363–364; for visually-impaired, 362; for vocabulary instruction, 196; whole language classroom and, 366; word-processing programs, 196, 361, 364, 391; for writing, 78, 390–391

Concept cards, 169

Concepts, 28. See also Schemata

Concept-text-application (CTA) approach, 486

Conclusions, 274–276

Conferences, 343, 350; for informal assessment, 548–549; in integrated language arts curriculum, 584–585

Conrad, Lori L., 492

Consonant blends (clusters), 113

Consonant digraphs, 113, 120

Consonants, 113, 119–120

Consonant substitution, 132

Constructive aspect, of reading, 8, 17–18, 25

Content area reading, 14, 29, 75–485; readability of, 478–483, 484; textbooks vs. basal readers and, 477–478; trade books for, 406–408, 483, 485; vocabulary development for, 161–163, 169–170, 187. See also Content area reading techniques; Language arts reading; Mathematics reading; Science and health reading; Social studies reading; Textbooks

Content area reading techniques, 485–509; computers, 500–501; concept-text-application (CTA), 486; creative mapping, 496; Directed Inquiry Activity, 486–487; Directed Reading- Thinking Activity, 486–487; every-pupil-response activities, 496; expository paragraph frames, 499; feature matrix, 501–502; Global Method, 501; graphic organizers, 497–499; guided reading procedure, 495; integrating approaches, 504–505; K-W-L teaching model, 488, 489; language experience approach, 359–360, 501; learning logs, 503; literature-based units, 505, 509, 510; motivation strategies, 485; prereading, 503–504; Press Conference, 495; question-only strategy, 495; readers' theater, 496–497; structured overviews, 496; study guides, 431, 488–494; sustained silent reading, 497; text structure, 497–499; thematic units, 505–509; webs, 431, 497, 502–503; writing techniques for, 501–503. See also Study methods

Content-process guides, 488, 490

Context clues: picture, 104–105; semantic, 103, 105, 106–107; syntactic, 103, 105, 107; teaching strategies for, 107–110; for vocabulary instruction, 172–175; as word recognition aids, 99–100, 103–110

Context method, for context clues, 174

Contractions, 142–143

Contrast clues, 106

Cook, Lynne, 624

Cooperative Integrated Reading Composition (CIRC), 588–589

Cooperative learning, 587–590; for comprehension, 247–249; for problem solving, 296; for special needs children, 627–628

Cooper, Charles R., 22

Coordinated language experience approach, 60

Cooter, Robert, 389

Cordts, Anna D., 131

Core book, whole-class reading of, 335–339, 370

Courtney, Rosalea, 81

Cox, Barbara, 364

Cox, Susan, 397, 512

C(2)QU, 172–173

Crafton, Linda K., 211, 237

Creative dramatics, 55–56; for bilingual students, 652; as prereading activity, 229; responding to literature with, 402–403; for story comprehension, 242, 244. See also Dramatic play

Creative mapping, 496

Creative reading, 293–297

Creative response questions, 301

Criscuolo, Nicholas P., 195

Criterion-referenced tests, 432, 565

Critical reading, 278–293; for accuracy and adequacy, 286–287; for appropriateness, 287; for author's competence, 286; for author's purpose, 285; definition, 278; fact vs. opinion in, 287–289, 290; for point of view, 285; for propaganda, 289–291; retention improved with, 430; for style and tone, 286; teaching strategies for, 279–285; for timeliness, 286; value judgments made in, 291

Crook, Patricia R., 506

Cross-age tutoring, 612

Cross-grade arrangements, 595–596

Cross-grade pairings, 596

Cross-grade process writing programs, 385–386

Cudd, Evelyn T., 169, 499

Cullinan, Bernice E., 23, 314, 403, 584

Culturally diverse students, 643–645; language experience approach and, 353, 357; linguistically diverse students and, 646–656; multicultural literature for, 397, 644–645, 659–662; norm-referenced tests and, 568; successful reading experiences and, 31

Cummins, Jim, 651

Cumulative reading record, 550

Cunningham, James W., 73, 132–134, 214–215, 225, 235, 237, 270, 294, 501, 502, 523

Cunningham, Patricia M., 73, 111, 132–134, 210, 213, 249, 501, 502, 580

Curtis, Mary E., 157

Dailey, Kathleen, 53

Daisey, Peggy, 15

Dale, Edgar, 482

Dale-Chall Readability Formula, 482, 483

Daneman, Meredyth, 103

Danielson, Kathy Everts, 506

Dashes, 220–221

Databases, 362, 364, 366–367, 453–454

Davies, Peter, 142, 176

Davis, Gary, 640, 641

Davis, Susan J., 169
Davis, Zephaniah T., 239, 240
Dawson, Martha, 64
Day, D., 459
Days of week, as sight words, 100
Deaf children, 11
Deaton, Cheryl D., 277
Decker, Barbara C., 523
Deductive lesson plans, 127, 128
DeFina, Allan A., 554
Definition, concept of, 183–184, 185
Definition clues, 106
DeGroff, Linda, 78, 366, 367
Deiner, Penny, 633
De la Luz Reyes, Maria, 653
Demonstrations, schemata and, 165
Denner, Peter, 635
Departmentalization, 595
Derivatives, 443–444
Dermott, R. Allan, 174
DeSerres, Barbara, 108
Desktop publishing, 391
Detail questions, 300
Detwiler, Deana B., 335, 598, 606
Dever, Christine T., 495
Dewey Decimal System, 449
Diacritical markings, 147
Dialectal differences, students with, 646–647; bilingual students, 647–656
Dialogical-Thinking Reading Lessons (D-TRLs), 283–284
Dialogue journals, 387, 653
Dickerson, Dolores Pawley, 101
Dickinson, David K., 62
Dictionary, 146–150, 440–445; accent marks in, 148–149; alphabetical order in, 440–442; guide words in, 442–443; introduction to, 150, 151; phonetic respellings in, 147–148; picture, 100, 442; for pronunciation, 147; variants and derivatives in, 443–444; for vocabulary instruction, 187–189
Dictionary method, for context clues, 174
D'Ignazio, Fred, 368
Dillard, Jill, 337
Dillner, Martha, 367
Dionisio, Marie, 514
Diphthongs, 114, 121, 144
Directed Inquiry Activity (DIA), 486–487
Directed reading activity (DRA): with basal reader series, 313; with published reading series, 313, 329–331; schema activation and, 213
Directed Reading-Thinking Activity (DRTA): for content area reading, 486–487; with published reading series, 331–333; purpose for reading set by, 215; schema activation and, 213
Direct experiences, 59–60
Directions, following, 258, 262
Disabled children. *See* Special needs children

Discis Books, 78–79
Doiron, Ray, 396, 506
Dolch list, 95
Dowd, Cornelia A., 203, 500
Downing, John, 8, 130
Doyle, Denis P., 515
Drafting, 386
Dramatic play, 13, 52–55, 77. *See also* Creative dramatics
Dramatization, for vocabulary instruction, 169
Dreher, Joyce, 512
Dreher, Miriam Jean, 246, 604
Dreyer, Lois G., 95, 98
Drill-and-practice programs, 363
Drop Everything and Read (DEAR), 393
Duchein, M. A., 15
Dudley-Marling, Curtis, 365, 619, 633, 635
Duffelmeyer, Barbara Blakeley, 169, 269
Duffelmeyer, Frederick A., 169, 170–171, 172, 269, 494
Duffy, Gerald G., 230, 598, 602, 637
Duncan, Patricia H., 283
During-reading activities, 229–236
Durkin, Dolores, 209, 217, 255, 298
Duty chart, 47
Dwyer, Edward J., 182
Dymock, Susan, 207

Eads, Maryann, 207
Early intervention programs, 639
Ebert, M. Jane, 517
Eclectic approaches, 369–371
Editing, 387
Education for All Handicapped Children Act, 622
Edwards, Anthony T., 174
Egan, Margaret, 251
Egawa, Kathy, 335, 340
Ehly, Stewart, 612
Ehri, L. C., 129
Eichelberger, R. Tony, 623
Eisele, Beverly, 582
Eldridge, Roger G., 594, 605
Ellipsis, 267–268
Ellis, Susan, 589
Emans, Robert, 118, 119
Emergent literacy, 38–88; assessment of, 79–83; cognitive development and, 41–42; computers and, 78–79; creative dramatics and, 55–56; definition, 39–40; dramatic play and, 52–54; language learning and, 42–44; listening centers and, 51; listening comprehension and, 50–51; oral expression and, 51–52; parents and, 48–49; print-rich environment for, 43, 45–48, 56; reading readiness vs., 39
Emotional/behavioral disorders, 632–633
Encyclopedias, 440, 445–446
Ending sounds, 109

Englert, Carol Sue, 223
English as a Second Language (ESL) classes, 646–656
English classes/textbooks, 514
Englot-Mash, Christine, 233, 234
Enright, D. Scott, 653
Environment, trade books for, 407
Environmental print, 45–46, 79
Esbensen, Thorwald, 363
Essay tests, 432
Etymology, 187–188, 189–190
Euphemism, 190–191
Evaluation, 352–353, 539. *See also* Assessment
Evaluation questions, 300–301
Evans, Carol, 341
Every-pupil-response activities, 496
Example clues, 107
Exceptional learners. *See* Special needs children
Exclamation points, 220
Experience chart, 60, 62
Experiences: reading and, 8, 11–12, 13–14, 40, 58–62; schemata development and, 165, 166; vicarious, 13, 59–61, 166, 169; vocabulary instruction and, 170–171; writing about before reading, 229
Experience stories. *See* Language experience stories
Expository (explanatory) selections, 222, 477
Expository paragraph frames, 499
Expository passage organizers (EPOs), 492–493
Expressive phases, 27
Extending learning, 237
Eye movement, during reading, 11

Fables, 513
Fact, opinion vs., 287–289, 290
Failure, threat of, 31
Fairburn, Jo, 525
Fall conference, 610
Farest, Cynthia, 341
Farnan, Nancy, 653
Farr, Roger, 65, 540, 552, 554, 572
Farrar, Mary Thomas, 298
Farris, Pamela J., 516
Farsightedness, 10
Fawson, Parker C., 239
Fay, Leo, 430
Feature matrix, 501–502
Felber, Shiela, 240
Ferguson, Anne M., 525
Ferreiro, Emilia, 41–42
Fielding, Linda G., 215, 223, 330, 497, 589, 612
Fields, Marjorie, 53
Field trips, 165
Figurative language, 187; critical reading for, 286; interpreting, 276–278; teaching, 511;

for vocabulary instruction, 187, 190–192, 193
Film versions of stories, 246, 283
Finger puppets, 56
Fisette, Dolores, 549
Fisher, Bobbi, 47, 53, 62–63, 67
Fitzgerald, Jill, 239, 242, 246, 279, 461, 462, 649, 651
Fitzpatrick, Ruth, 596
Fixations, 11
Fleischman, Paul, 402
Flippo, Rona F., 260
Flitterman-King, Sharon, 336
Flood, James, 383, 384, 499, 506, 570, 587, 592, 608, 635, 649, 650, 653
Flores, Barbara, 651, 653
Florez, Viola, 645
Flow charts: content area reading and, 499; metacognition and, 233, 234
Flynn, Linda L., 296
Flynn, Rosalind M., 229
Folklore, 283, 284, 512–513
Footnotes, 439
Ford, Michael, 635
Forell, Elizabeth, 316
Formal assessment. See Norm-referenced tests
Forman, Ellice A., 612
Fortescue, Chelsea M., 525
Fortson, Laura R., 357
Fouse, Beth, 630
Fowler, Gerald L., 242, 243
Fowler, Mary, 630
Frager, Alan M., 22
Frame, in programmed instruction, 361
Fredericks, Anthony D., 294
Freedman, Glenn, 239
Freeman, David E., 650, 651
Freeman, Ruth H., 513
Freeman, Yvonne S., 650, 651
Free morphemes, 176
Friend, Marilyn, 624
Friendship groups, 590, 592–593
Frustration level: informal reading inventory and, 560, 561; textbook suitability and, 478–479, 482
Fry, Edward, 95, 96–97, 463, 482
Fry Readability Graph, 482, 483
Fuhler, Carol J., 318, 334, 336, 337, 340, 352, 516
Function words, 100–101
Furleigh, Mary A., 289
Furman, Gail Chase, 627
Furse, Lory L., 213
Futtersak, Karen R., 95, 98

Galda, Lee, 244, 397, 403, 405, 407, 511, 512, 513, 584
Gale, David, 194–195
Gallagher, 631
Gamberg, Ruth, 508

Gambrell, Linda B., 318
Games: for phonics instruction, 129, 134–136; for sight word recognition, 101, 102–103
Garan, Elaine, 585, 605
Garcia, Jesus, 518
Garcia, Mary, 546
Garcia, Ricardo L., 643
Gardner, Howard, 640
Gardner, Michael K., 302
Garrison, James W., 263
Gaskins, Irene West, 129, 496, 504, 505, 630
Gaskins, Robert W., 635
Gauthier, Lane Roy, 283, 503
Gearheart, Bill R., 630
Gearheart, Carol J., 630
Gee, Thomas C., 477
Genre, 411, 414
Gentile, Lance M., 281
Gentry, J. Richard, 646
Geography, themes in, 515–516
George, John E., 492–493
Gifted children, 230, 640–643
Gill, J. Thomas, Jr., 114
Gilles, Carol, 399
Gillet, Jean Wallace, 646
Gipe, Joan P., 174, 197, 234
Glass, Gerald G., 144
Glittering generalities, 289
Global Method, 501
Glossaries, 439
Gold, Yvonne, 190
Golden, Joanne M., 241, 246
Goldenberg, Claude, 238
Goldman, Susan R., 242
Gonzales, Phillip, 649, 650
Goodman, Kenneth S., 22, 23, 44–45, 353, 539, 543
Goodman, Yetta M., 540, 543, 549, 563, 563
Gordon, Christine, 239, 264
Gore, Kay, 500
Gough, Philip B., 103
Gove, Mary, 20, 21
Grabe, Cindy, 356, 357
Grabe, Mark, 356, 357
Grabe, Nancy White, 369
Grade equivalent, tests as, 566
Grammar, 23, 514
Graphemes, 15, 110
Graphic aids, 431, 462–470, 515; graphs, 466–467, 468; illustrations, 170, 470; maps, 463–466; tables, 467–469. See also Textbooks
Graphic organizers, 497–499, 523, 524
Graphophonic clues, 22
Graphs, 466–467, 468
Graves, 71
Graves, Michael F., 163, 167, 188, 197
Greek word parts, 177
Green, Dan S., 432
Greenewald, M. Jane, 246

Griffith, Priscilla, 65, 114
Groff, Patrick, 111
Grossman, H., 631
Group experience story, 355–359
Group journals, 78
Groups, learning in, 587–594; achievement groups, 590–592; friendship groups, 590, 592–593; interest groups, 590, 592; project/research groups, 590, 592; pupil pairs or partners and, 590, 593; for reading, 590–594; special skills/needs groups, 590, 593. See also Cooperative learning
Group thinking conferences, 279
Gruber, Kristin, 589
Guided imagery, 294
Guided reading procedure (GRP), 495
Guide words, 442–443
Guiding questions, 235–236
Guild, Pat, 644
Gunning, Thomas G., 567
Guthrie, John T., 19, 461
Guzzetti, Barbara J., 515
Gwynne, Fred, 199

Hacker, Charles J., 348, 354
Hadaway, Nancy L., 466, 499, 525, 645
Hafner, Lawrence E., 65
Haggard, Martha Rapp, 192–194, 333
Hall, Nigel, 39, 42, 62, 69
Hamann, Lori S., 229
Hammer, C., 366
Hancock, Marjorie R., 247, 340
Hansell, Stevenson F., 459
Hansen, Jane, 264, 298, 555, 606
Hanson, Lynda, 589
Hare, Victoria Chou, 20, 43
Hargis, Charles H., 101, 633
Harp, Bill, 41, 122, 294, 298, 486, 605
Harris, Albert J., 21
Harris, Theodore L., 646
Harris-Sharples, Susan D., 384
Harste, J. C., 384, 387, 399, 509, 581
Hart, Leslie A., 27, 31
Hayes, David A., 464
Head, Martha H., 190, 191
Heald-Taylor, Gail, 651, 652, 653
Hearing, 9, 11, 12
Hearing-impaired children, 11, 632
Hedges, William D., 368
Heffron, Kathleen, 364, 367
Heidger, Barbara, 652
Heimlich, Joan E., 182, 183
Heine, Patricia, 341
Heller, Mary F., 360
Henk, William A., 285
Henke, Linda, 334, 369
Henley, Martin, 631
Hennings, Dorothy Grant, 518
Hepler, Susan, 408
Herman, Patricia A., 175

Herriott, John, 363
Herrmann, Beth Ann, 230, 234, 635
Herse, Robert, 130
Hess, Mary Lou, 509
Heterogeneous classes, 594–595
Heymsfeld, Carla R., 248
Hickman, Janet, 392, 408
Hiebert, Elfrieda H., 334, 539, 542, 639
Hierarchical model, of perceptual learning, 19
Hieshima, Joyce, 647
Higgins, Karen W., 527, 528
Higher-order comprehension, 261–263. *See also* Creative reading; Critical reading; Interpretive reading
Hilbert, Sharon B., 335
Hill, D. S., 264
Hillstead, Deborah, 53
Historical fiction, 517
Hoben, Mollie, 627
Hodges, Richard E., 646
Hoffman, James V., 287, 288, 316, 341, 581, 591, 592
Holbrook, Hilary Taylor, 478
Holdaway, Don, 42, 47, 65, 67, 645
Holistic assessment. *See* Authentic assessment
Holzberg, Carol S., 365
Home environment: attitudes toward reading and, 15, 16, 17; experiences provided by, 13; literacy development and, 40, 48–49. *See also* Parents
Homework, 608, 610
Homogeneous classes, 594–595
Homographs, 110, 161, 198–199
Homonyms, 161, 195, 197–198
Homophones. *See* Homonyms
Hood, Wendy J., 543
Hornsby, David, 383
Hoskisson, Kenneth, 263
Hough, Ruth A., 653
Howard, Winter, 239, 240
Howell, Helen, 198, 199, 200
Howell, K. W., 146
Hoyt, Linda, 405
Hubbard, Ruth, 264
Huck, Charlotte S., 408
Hughes, Sanrda M., 453
Humor, for critical thinking, 280–281
Hunsucker, Stephanie, 489
Hunter-Grundin, Elizabeth, 52
Hyder, Gail, 488
Hynds, S., 21–22
Hyperbole, 190–191
HyperCard, 454
Hypermedia, 367
Hypertext, 367
Hypotheses, 264

IDEAL approach, 296
Idioms, 276–277
Illustrations, 170, 470

Imagery. *See* Visualization
Improvisation, 403
Inclusion, 623, 624–628
Independent level, 479, 482
Independent reading, 560, 561
Indexes, 436–438
Individualized education program (IEP), 622–624
Individualized reading approach, 343, 347–352, 370
Individuals with Disabilities Education Act (IDEA), 622
Inductive lesson plans, 127–128
Inference questions, 300
Inferences, 602. *See also* Interpretive reading
Inflectional endings, 137–139, 176
Inflectional suffixes, 137
Informal assessment, 79, 80, 81, 542–565; anecdotal records for, 543, 544; checklists for, 544–546, 547; cloze procedure for, 559–560; computers for, 560; conferences/interviews for, 548–549; informal reading inventories for, 560–561, 562; informal tests for, 559–564; kidwatching for, 543; limitation of, 564–565; of literary interests, 550–551; observation for, 542–549; portfolio assessment for, 551–554; probe technique for, 564; reading miscue inventory for, 561, 563–564; rubrics for, 546, 548; running records for, 564; self-appraisal for, 555–558
Informal reading inventories (IRIs) 480, 560–561, 562
Informational storybooks, 239
Information, locating, 435–454; in catalogues, 448, 449; in databases, 453–454; in library, 448–453; in magazines, 447; in newspapers, 446–447, 448. *See also* Reference books; Textbooks
Inquiry Charts, 287, 288
"Instant Words," 95, 96–97
Instructional conversations, 238
Instructional level: informal reading inventory for, 560, 561; of textbook, 479, 482
Instructional units. *See* Literature-based approaches; Thematic units
Integrated language arts curriculum, 380–383, 580–587
Integrated Literature and Language Arts Portfolio Program (ILALAPP), 571–572
Interaction, in informal assessment, 543
Interactive theories, 20–21
Interclass grouping, 595
Interest groups, 590, 592
Interest inventories: for individualized reading program, 348, 349; of reading interests, 396
Interests, attitude towards reading and, 15, 17
Interpretive reading, 247, 263–278; adverb referents in, 267; author's purpose detected in, 274; cause-and-effect in,

271–272; conclusion drawn in, 274–276; definition, 263; ellipsis in, 267–268; figurative language in, 276–278; main ideas and, 268–271; mood detected in, 273–274; pronoun referents in, 266–267; teaching strategies for, 263–266, 277–278
Interviews, for informal assessment, 548–549
Introduction, in textbook, 436
Introductory paragraphs, 223
Intuitive stage, 41
Invented spellings, 65, 71–77, 79, 114, 132–134, 355
Investigative Questioning Procedure (*InQuest*), 235–236
Iowa Tests of Basic Skills, 567
Irwin, Judith Westphal, 214, 216, 265, 267
Irwin, Martha E., 364, 453, 454
Isaak, Troy, 368
Isom, Bess A., 528
Italics, 220–221
Ivener, Bonnie Lee, 651
Iwicki, Ann L., 170

Jacobs, James S., 335
Jaggar, Angela M., 606
James, L. B., 464
Jenkins, Barbara L., 93
Jenkins, Joseph R., 175
Jenks, Carolyn, 350, 449
Jensen, Julie M., 380
Jett-Simpson, Mary, 246
Jiganti, Mary Ann, 197
Jigsaw, 589
Johns, Kenneth M., 652, 653
Johnson, 210
Johnson, Bonnie von Huff, 264
Johnson, Dale D., 122, 130, 182, 183, 185, 186, 207, 229, 264, 301
Johnson, David, 588
Johnson, Holly, 505, 506
Johnson, J. M., 531
Johnson, Lori Beckmann, 445
Johnson, Nancy M., 517
Johnson, Nancy S., 210, 241–242
Johnson, Roger, 588
Johnson, Terry D., 108
Johnston, Francine R., 332
Johnston, Peter H., 542, 549, 560, 639
Jolly, Hayden B., Jr., 65, 101
Jones, Leah A., 461, 462
Jones, Linda A., 103
Jones, Linda L., 161, 211
Jones, Linda T., 608
Jones, Margaret B., 369, 501
Jones, R., 459
Jongsma, Eugene, 592
Jongsma, Kathleen Stumpf, 527
Joranko, Joyce, 497
Joseph, John, 368

Jossart, Sarah A., 512
Journal writing, 387–388; for bilingual stu-
    dents, 653; learning logs, 503; literary ele-
    ments taught with, 512; literature response
    groups and, 340; purposeful writing and,
    77–78; for science programs, 532; for stu-
    dents with reading difficulties, 635; for
    whole-class reading of a core book, 337
Judd, Dorothy H., 483
Juel, Connie, 114, 161
Jurenka, Nancy Allan, 354

Kachuck, Beatrice, 218, 219
Kahn, Michael S., 95
Kaisen, Jim, 394
Kamberelis, George, 69, 71
Kamhi, Alan, 633
Kapinus, Barbara A., 169–170
Kaplan, Elaine M., 171, 175
Karnowski, Lee, 354
Kearns, Gail, 384
Keegan, Suzi, 340
Keller-Cogan, Meg, 540, 570
Kerber, James, 604
Key words, 129, 131–132
Khan, Samina, 200
Kidwatching, 543
Kimmel, Susan, 264
Kinesthetic learners, 25, 101
Kinney, Martha A., 360, 501
Kirby, Dan, 385
Kirk, 631
Kirsch, Irwin S., 464
Kitagawa, Mary M., 306
Knight, Jenny, 594
Knowledge-based processing, 211–213
Knowledge rating, 168
Koeller, Shirley, 200
Koenke, Karl, 567
Koskinen, Patricia S., 174, 238
Kowalinski, Barbara J., 515
Krashen, Stephen D., 652
Kretschmer, Richard, Jr., 619
Krieger, Evelyn, 285
Kristo, Janice V., 532
Krushenisky, Cindy, 446
Krutchinsky, Rick, 521
Kubiszyn, Tom, 560
Kuchinskas, G., 366
Kupiter, Karen, 397
Kurtz, B. E., 230
Kuta, Katherine Wiesolek, 223
Kutzman, Sandra, 521
K-W-L procedure: for content area reading,
    488, 489; thematic unit based on,
    408–409, 412–413

Labbo, Linda, 596
Labels, sight vocabulary and, 100

LaBerge, David, 19
Lamme, Linda Leonard, 385, 453
Lange, Bob, 263
Language arts, 27–28. See also Listening;
    under Reading; Speaking; under Writing
Language arts integration, 380–383, 582–587.
    See also Literature, language integration
    with
Language arts reading, 509, 511–514
Language centers, 52
Language charts, 341
Language development, 41–44
Language experience approach (LEA), 28,
    353–360; for bilingual students, 653; for
    content area reading, 501; evaluation of,
    360; in higher grades, 359–360; in kinder-
    garten, 354–355; for positive self-concept,
    16; in primary grades, 355–359; sight
    vocabulary and, 100
Language experience stories, 355–359, 369;
    standard English learned with, 13; text-
    book suitability and, 482; whole-class
    reading of core book and, 369
Language learning, 42–44
Lapp, Diane, 383, 384, 506, 570, 608, 635,
    649, 650, 653
Larsen, Stephen C., 612
Larson, Jennifer, 366
Latin word parts, 177
Latta, Dawn, 385
Lawrence, Susan Mary, 341
Layton, Kent, 364, 453, 454
Lazear, David, 640
Learning centers, 599–600, 603, 604
Learning disabilities, children with,
    629–630; literature-based approaches and,
    335; story parts taught to, 242; test pat-
    terns and, 223. See also Special needs
    children
Learning logs, 503. See also Journal writing
Ledbetter, Linda, 453
Lee, John L., 163
Lee, Tosca Moon, 366
Legend, of map, 463
Lehman, Barbara A., 506
Lehr, Fran, 119
Leland, Christine, 596
Lerner, Janet, 630, 634
Letters (of alphabet), 64–65, 71–77
Letters, parent-teacher communication by,
    610–611
Letts, Nancy, 594
Levstick, Linda S., 517
Lewis, Maureen, 499
Lewkowicz, Nancy K., 157
Liberman, Isabelle, 19
Librarians, 415, 448–453
Library, 53, 54; card catalog in, 449–451, 452;
    for classroom, 396–398; library center, 53,
    54; locating information in, 415, 448–453;
    reading center as, 65–66

Like and different, understanding of, 114–115
Limited-English-proficient (LEP) students,
    648. See also Bilingual students
Lindgren, Jonas, 653, 654–655
Line graphs, 466, 467
Linek, Wayne, 532
Linguistically diverse students, 646–656
Linguistics, basal reader series focusing on,
    319
Link, Gordon, 365, 391
Lipson, Marjorie Y., 80, 314, 340, 341
Listening, 27, 50
Listening centers, 51
Listening comprehension, 50–51
Listening-reading transfer lesson, 249
List, Lynne, 630, 634
Literacy, 30–31, 39, 40, 48–49. See also Emer-
    gent literacy
Literacy observation checklist, 544, 545
Literal comprehension, 255, 257–261, 262
Literary forms, 512–514
Literary journals, 387
Literature; child's reaction to, 550–551; com-
    plete selections of, 28–29; for mathemat-
    ics, 525–527; for science and health, 530;
    selecting, 396–398, 420–421; skills mas-
    tery and, 509, 511–514. See also Multicul-
    tural literature
Literature analysis, 281
Literature-based and language-integrated
    series, 320–329
Literature-based approaches, 5, 241, 333–353;
    computers and, 366; concerns with, 335;
    for content area reading, 505, 509, 510;
    evaluation concerns with, 335, 352–353;
    individualized reading approach, 343,
    347–352; literature response groups, 340;
    recreational reading and, 30; selecting
    books for, 334; Sustained Silent Reading
    in, 335; thematic literature units,
    340–343, 344–347, 370; trade books for,
    334; whole-class reading of a core book,
    335–339; whole language philosophy and,
    24
Literature circles. See Literature response
    groups
Literature, language integration with,
    391–417; across curriculum, 406–408; cre-
    ating environment for reading for,
    392–394; literature selection for, 396–398,
    420–421; magazines for, 398, 422; reading
    aloud for, 394–396; storytelling for, 396;
    support personnel for, 415, 417; thematic
    units for, 408–417; trade books for,
    406–408. See also Literature, responding to
Literature logs, 336, 337, 399, 400
Literature program, for culturally diverse
    students, 644–645, 653, 659–662
Literature, responding to, 391–398,
    407–408; art and music for, 405–406;
    drama for, 402–403; literature response

Literature, responding to (*cont.*)
groups for, 399–401; oral reading for,
401–402; written expression for, 404–405
Literature response groups, 340; evaluation
during, 546, 547; for responding to litera-
ture, 399–401; self-appraisal and, 555,
556–558
Literature webs. *See* Story mapping; Webs
Long, Emily S., 504
Longnion, Bonnie, 491
Look-and-say approach. *See* Sight words
Lopez, Alice, 496
Loughlin, Catherine E., 42, 71
Louis, Daphne R., 108
Lundberg, I., 114
Lytle, Susan L., 540

McAlcon, Noreen, 516
McCallum, Richard D., 315
McCarthey, Sarah J., 316
McCarthy, Robert, 560
McCart, Linn, 157
McClellan, Jane, 567
McClure, Amy A., 504
McClurg, Pat, 495
McConaughy, Stephanie H., 161
McCormick, S., 264
McCracken, Marlene, 68, 394
McCracken, Robert, 68, 394
McDonald, Frederick, 8
Mace-Matluck, Betty J., 649, 650
Macey, Joan Mary, 182
McGee, Lea M., 21, 78, 242, 246, 411, 497
McGill-Franzen, Anne, 99, 624
MacGinitie, Walter H., 264
McGowan, Tom, 515
MacGregor, Pat, 407
McIntosh, Margaret E., 264
McKeon, Denise, 647
McKeown, Margaret G., 161, 163, 167, 168,
285, 478, 515
Mackie, Beverly, 544
McLane, Joan, 40, 48
Maclean, Rod, 111
McMillan, Merna M., 281
McNamee, Gillian, 40, 48
McNeil, John D., 213
McNutt, Gaye, 53
McPherson, Michael D., 239, 240
Macrocloze activities, 242, 247
McWhirter, Anna M., 336
Madden, Lowell, 588
Madden, Nancy, 588
Magazines, 398, 422, 447
Main idea questions, 300
Main ideas, 61, 268–271
Mainstreaming, inclusion vs., 624
Making Words, 132–134
Mallon, Barbara, 356

Mallow, Jeffry V., 529
Mancus, D. S., 330
Mandler, Jean M., 210, 241–242, 246
Mangieri, John N., 95
Manipulatives, 169, 504
Manna, Anthony, 513, 514
Manzo, Anthony V., 306, 487, 495
MAP (Make-A-Place) activity, 464
Maps, 463–466. *See also* Semantic mapping
Maria, Katherine, 262
Maric, K., 531
Maring, Gerald H., 627
Marshall, Nancy, 303
Martin, Mavis D., 42, 71
Martinez, Miriam, 56, 77, 518
Marzano, Lorraine, 342
Marzano, Robert J., 180, 539
Mason, George E., 244, 359
Mateja, John, 175
Mathematical skills, dramatic play practic-
ing, 53
Mathematics reading, 520–528; trade books
for, 406. *See also* Graphic aids
Mathewson, Grover C., 15–16
Mathison, Carla, 485
Maudeville, Thomas F., 16
Mavrogenes, Nancy A., 40
Mayfield, Margie I., 51, 69, 580, 599, 600
Maze procedure, 236
Mealey, D. L., 15
Meaning vocabulary, 161. *See also* Vocabu-
lary development; Vocabulary instruction
Media center. *See* Library
Meir, Margaret, 461
Meister, Carla, 234
Melnick, Steven A., 446
Meltzer, Nancy S., 130
Memory, David M., 431
Menke, Deborah J., 235, 431
Mental retardation, 631
Metacognition: as directed reading activity,
330; as during-reading activity, 229–235;
self-appraisal and, 555
Metacognitive strategies, 31; for meaning
and reading for retention, 460–462
Metaphor, 190–191
Metropolitan Achievement Test, 568, 570
Meyer, Anne, 79, 362, 363
Meyer, Carol, 539
Meyer, Judy, 652
Michener, Darlene M., 395
Mickelson, Norma, 543
Miholic, Vincent, 462
Mike, Dennis G., 362
Mikel, Vesta L., 488
Miller, Etta, 516
Miller, G. Michael, 191, 244
Miller, Kathleen K., 492–493
Miller, Margery, 384
Milz, Vera E., 606

Miscue analysis. *See* Reading miscue inven-
tory
Mixed-ability groups, 587–590
Mnemonic devices, 431
Modalities, of instruction, 25
Modeling: metacognition and, 230; by
teachers, 602
Moe, Alden J., 229, 461, 555
Moldofsky, Penny Baum, 269, 271
Monahan, Joy N., 598
Monson, Robert J., 23
Mood, detecting, 273–274
Moore, David W., 270
Moore, Margaret, 340, 367
Moorman, Gary B., 317
Morphemes, 176
Morrow, Lesley Mandel, 49, 56–57, 65, 78,
238, 504
Mosenthal, Peter B., 23, 216, 217, 464
Moss, Barbara, 23, 478, 483, 485
Moss, Joy F., 276
Motivation, for reading, 14, 16, 485
Mountain, Lee, 195, 521
Moustafa, Margaret, 353, 653
Movies, for story comprehension, 246, 283
Mug sheets on characters, 337
Mulligan, Patricia Alba, 500
Multi-age classrooms, 595
Multicultural literature: for culturally diverse
students, 644–645, 659–662; literature-
based approach and, 334; in social studies
programs, 518. *See also* Culturally diverse
students
Multimedia computer software, 368
Mumper, Jean, 580, 581, 598, 599
Mundell, Dee, 294
Munson, Jennie Livingston, 240
Murphy, S., 364
Music, responding to literature through,
405–406
Musical cloze, 175
Myths, 513

Na, T. J., 216, 217
Nagy, William E., 142, 162, 163, 175, 189
Name calling, 289
Names of children, 100
Narrative (storylike) selections, 222, 477
Nash, Marcia F., 518
Nathenson-Mejia, Sally, 543
Naturalistic research, 605
Naughton, Victoria M., 496
Nearsightedness, 10
Needs groups, 590, 593
Nelson, Olga, 356
Nelson-Herber, Joan, 162–163, 167
Nessel, Denise D., 210, 369, 396, 501
Neuman, Susan B., 45, 55, 174
Neville, Rita, 293

Newbery Award winners, 396–397
Newman, Judith M., 23, 24, 367, 606
Newspapers, 258, 446–447, 448, 518–520
News period, 59
New Words, 200
Nigohosian, Elsie, 500
Noden, Harry, 23
Nolan, Thomas E., 230
Nolte, Ruth Yopp, 305
Nonliteral language. *See* Figurative language
Nonphonetic strings of letters, 71
Nonstandardized assessment. *See* Informal assessment
Norm-referenced tests, 23, 79–83, 540, 565–572; achievement tests, 567–568, 569, 570; limitations of, 568; performance-based achievement tests, 539, 570–572; preparation for, 23; for reading achievement levels, 482; strategies for taking, 432
Norton, Donna E., 242, 245, 246, 281, 397, 408, 512, 515, 643
Nosbush, Linda, 152
Note taking, 247, 431, 454–456
Notices, to parents, 610
Numbers, in mathematics, 521
Nurss, Joanne R., 47, 653

Objective-referenced tests. *See* Criterion-referenced tests
O'Brien, D., 246
Observation, for informal assessment, 542–549
Oden, Sherri, 276
Ogle, Donna M., 409, 488
Ohlhausen, Marilyn, 635
Oldfather, Penny, 23
Oleneski, Sue, 134
Ollila, Lloyd O., 51, 69, 580
Ollmann, Hilda E., 271, 503
Olson, Mary W., 65, 114, 477, 491
O'Neil, John, 546
Onsets, 129
Open-ended questions, 294
Open House, 610
Open syllables, 145
Opinion, facts vs., 287–289, 290
Oral context, context clues and, 105, 107–108
Oral reading, 19, 401–402
Oral reading checklist, 544, 545
Organic words, 64
Organizational techniques, 454–460; note taking, 454–456; outlining, 456–459; summarizing, 459–460
Osborn, Jean, 119
Otto, Wayne, 594, 605
Outcome-based education (OBE), 539
Outlining, 456–459

Ovando, Carlos J., 646, 648, 650
Overlearning, 431
Owen, Kimberly, 53
Owston, R. D., 364

Padak, Nancy D., 334, 518
Pahl, Michele M., 23
Palincsar, Annemarie Sullivan, 234, 592
Palmer, Barbara, 95
Pantomiming, 403
Paperback books, 397–398
Paper-bag puppets, 56
Paragraphs: cause-and-effect, 222; chronological order, 221; introductory, 223; organizational patterns in, 221–222; summary, 223; topical, 223
Paraprofessionals, 612
Parents, 607–612; children reading with, 607, 611–612; literacy development and, 48–49; school literature program and, 415, 417; teachers communicating with, 608–611. *See also* Home environment
Parent-teacher conferences, 608
Paris, Scott G., 461, 540, 555, 592, 607
Parry, Jo-Ann, 383
Partners, groups based on, 590, 593
Passive games, 101
Pattern guides, 489, 491–492
Patty, Del, 219
Pearson, P. David, 12, 65, 114, 182, 185, 186, 207, 209, 210, 215, 219, 223, 239, 247, 263, 264, 298, 301, 304, 330, 497, 541, 549, 570, 589, 594, 612
Peck, Jackie, 396
Peer conferencing, 637
Peer tutoring, 612
Pehrsson, Robert, 635
Pellegrini, A. D., 244
Penrose, Joyce, 353, 653
Percentile rank (PR), 566
Perceptual aspects, of reading, 8, 11–12; experiential aspects of reading and, 13–14
Peregoy, Suzanne F., 220
Perfetti, C. A., 161
Performance-based achievement tests, 539, 570–572
Periods, 220
Perry, Margaret, 365
Perry, Merry, 642
Personal reading record, 550
Personification, 190–191, 277–278
Peters, Charles, 571
Peterson, Susan, 177
Petrick, Pamela Bondi, 169
Petrosky, Anthony R., 22
Pettersen, Nancy-Laurel, 198
Petty, Pam, 344–347
Phelps, Patricia H., 177
Phonemes, 11, 12, 15, 110, 114

Phonemic awareness, 65, 71–77, 114
Phonetic respellings, 147–148
Phonics, 110–136; basal reader series and, 319; definition, 110; generalizations, 117–121, 130–131
Phonics instruction, 110, 112–113; analogy approach to, 129, 130; analytic approach to, 122–128, 129, 130, 134; associations in, 15; auditory discrimination and, 112, 114, 115–117; for beginning reading program, 12; consonant substitution for, 132; context clues and, 108, 109; games for, 129, 134–136; invented spelling for, 132–134; key words for, 129, 131–132; onsets and rimes and, 129; phoneme-grapheme correspondences for, 129–130; phonics generalizations for, 117–121, 130–131; prerequisites for, 114–115; reinforcement for, 112; relevance of, 113; synthetic approach to, 121–122, 129; teaching strategies for, 121–136; terminology for, 113–114; visual discrimination for, 112, 114, 115, 116; whole language philosophy and, 23
Phonograms, 129
Physically active games, 101, 102–103
Piaget, Jean, 41
Pickett, Anna Lou, 612
Picture books, 60, 516
Picture clues, 104–105
Picture dictionary, 100, 442
Picture graphs, 466, 467
Pictures, vicarious experiences from, 60, 61
Piech, Pat, 533
Pie graphs, 466, 467
Pierce, Kathryn M., 407, 532
Pigg, John R., 166–167, 210
Pike, Kathy, 580, 581, 598, 599
Pikulski, John J., 65, 540, 639
Pinnell, Gay Su, 639
Pittelman, Susan D., 182, 183
Plain-folks talk, 290
Plays, 513–514. *See also* Creative dramatics; Dramatic play
Plot, 511, 512
Plot diagrams, 244–246
Pocket chart, 68–69
Poetry, 397, 512, 513
Poindexter, Candace A., 230
Point of view, determining, 285
Portfolio assessment, 551–554
Portfolios, communicating with parents by, 608
Portmanteau words, 189
Positive reinforcement, 14, 15, 431
Possessive case, 139
Possible Sentences, 169–170
Postal system/penpal program, 77
Potter, Rosemary, 600
Powell, Janet L., 570

Powers, Anne, 357
Practice, 26; for associations, 15; for learning to read, 14; for subskills, 19–20
Preconceptual stage, 41
Predictable stories, 66, 87–88
Predicting: in directed reading activity, 330; in directed reading-thinking activity, 331–333; higher-order comprehension and, 262–263; metacognition and, 230; as prereading activity, 213, 247
Preface, 436
Prefixes, 139–142, 176–177
Prenn, Maureen C., 163, 167, 188, 197
Preoperational period, 41
Prephonetic stage, 71
Prereading activities, 225–229; anticipation guides, 225–228; for content area reading, 503–504; creative drama, 229; predicting, 213; purpose questions, 215–216; semantic mapping, 229; story previews, 225; writing before reading, 229
Prescott, Susan, 230
Press Conference, 495
Pressley, Michael, 235, 431
Previews. *See* Story previews
Prewriting, 386
Prince, A. T., 330
Principles, of teaching reading, 25–31
Print conventions, 62–63
Print-rich classroom environment, 43, 45–48, 66
Probe technique, 564
Problem solving, 295–296
Probst, Robert E., 21
Process-oriented assessment, of literacy development, 80–83
Process writing, 385–387, 635
Professional organizations, 607
Programmed instruction, 361
Progress reports, 610
Project groups, 592
Pronoun referents, 266–271
Pronunciation, 7–8, 117; context clarifying, 110; dictionary for, 147–148; phonics and, 111; syllabication/accent and, 143–146. *See also under* Phonics
Propaganda techniques, 289–291
Psycholinguistics, 22
Published reading series, 313–333; directed reading activity with, 313, 329–331; directed reading-thinking activity with, 331–333; literature-based and language-integrated series, 320–329. *See also* Basal reader series
Publishing, 387
Pugh, Sharon L., 518
Pulliam, Cynthia A., 20
Pull-out programs, 623, 624
Punctuation, 220–221
Pupil pairs, groups and, 590, 593
Puppets, 55–56, 403

Purposeful writing, 77–78, 562–563
Purpose, of author, 274, 285
Purpose questions, 215–216, 431
Purposes of reading, comprehension and, 214–216

Question-Answer Relationships (QARs), 304–305
Questioning the Author, 285
Question marks, 220
Question-only strategy, 495
Questions, 297–306; answering, 304–305; asking, 305–306; comprehension factors as bases for, 299–301; for content area reading, 499; for critical conferences, 279–280; guiding, 235–236; oral, 298; as postreading activity, 237; preparing, 298–304; purpose, 215–216, 431; story grammar as basis for, 299, 302–303; thinking guided by, 8, 14; types of, 300–302; written, 298. *See also* Self-questioning

Rabin, Annette T., 292
Radencich, M. C., 366
Rand, Muriel K., 210
Raphael, Taffy E., 183–184, 185, 304–305, 340
Rasch, Bradley, 624
Rasinski, Timothy V., 45, 295, 334, 518
Raynes, Maria, 624
Readability, assessment of: cloze tests for, 479–482; formulas for, 482–483, 484
Readability formulas, 482–483, 484
Readence, John E., 190, 191, 270, 330
Reader's Guide to Periodical Literature, 449
Readers' theater, 237, 403, 496–497
Reading, 27; attitude toward, 8, 15–17; creating environment for, 392–394; for enjoyment, *see* Recreational reading; functional, 5–6; importance of, 5–6; learning, 58–69, 70; purposes for, 214–216. *See also* Literature, language integration with
Reading act, 6–7. *See also* Reading process; Reading product
Reading aloud: attitudes towards reading and, 15; experience built by, 58; metacognition and, 462; by parents, 49; schema development and, 210; sharing big books as, 67; sight words taught with, 98; "talking like a book" and, 62; by teacher, 394–396; vocabulary development and, 166–167
Reading between the lines. *See* Interpretive reading
Reading centers, 65–66
Reading difficulties, children with, 633–640; experiential background and, 14; metacognitive strategies and, 230; reciprocal teaching for, 234; subskills and, 19;

success experienced by, 30–31; word recognition and, 93
Reading groups, 17, 280
Reading habits, flexibility of, 432–435
Reading interests, assessing, 396
Reading in the Middle School (Duffy), 598
Reading inventories: for individualized reading program, 348; informal, 480, 560–561, 562; reading miscue inventory, 561, 563–564. *See also* Interest inventories
Reading journals, 387
Reading levels, tests for, 482
Reading materials, 66–69
Reading miscue inventory (RMI), 561, 563–564
Reading process, 6, 7, 8–18; affective aspect of, 8, 15–17; associational aspect of, 7, 8, 15; comprehension and, 7–8; constructive aspect of, 8, 17–18, 25; experiential aspect of, 8, 11–12, 13–14, 40, 58–62; learning aspect of, 8, 14; perceptual aspect of, 8, 11–12; sensory aspect of, 8, 9–11; sequential aspect of, 8, 12; thinking aspect of, 8, 14. *See also* Reading product; Theories
Reading product, 6, 7–8
Reading rates, 433–435
Reading readiness: emergent literacy vs., 39; instructional activities considering, 30–31; tests of, 79–80
Reading Recovery Program, 99–100, 639
Reading situation, comprehension and, 214–217
Reading/study techniques, 427–428; metacognition, 460–462. *See also* Graphic aids; Information, locating; Organizational techniques; Reading habits, flexibility of; Study methods
Reading Teacher, The (Duffelmeyer), 171
Reading workshops, 388, 389
Reading-writing connection, 5, 247, 383–391; for comprehension, 241, 247; computers for writing and, 390–391; journal writing and, 387–388; process writing and, 385–387; producing new creations and, 297; reading and writing workshops and, 388–389
Reagan, Tiffany Nicole, 241
Reardon, S. Jeanne, 280
Receptive phases, of language, 27
Recht, Donna, 459
Reciprocal Questioning (ReQuest) procedure, 306
Reciprocal teaching, 234, 248–249
Recordkeeping, for observation, 542–543, 544
Record-keeping portfolio, 551
Recreational reading, 6, 29–30
Reference books, 439–448; atlases, 440; effective use of, 439–440; encyclopedias, 440, 445–446. *See also* Dictionary
Regressions, 11, 12

Reid, 130
Reimer, Beck L., 356
Reinforcement, 14, 15, 431
Reinking, D., 366
Reissman, Rose, 287
Relative clauses, 218–219
Reliability, of tests, 566
Remedial reading. See Reading difficulties, children with
Repetitions, sight words and, 99
Report card, 608, 609
Report writing. See Organizational techniques
Researcher, teacher as, 605–606
Research groups, 592
Resnick, Lauren B., 281
Retelling, 237–238, 549
Retention, improving, 430–431
Reutzel, D. Ray, 239, 241, 318, 330, 389, 523
Revising, 386
Reynolds, Elizabeth G., 239
Rhodes, Lynn K., 207, 543, 619, 633, 635
Rhymes, 115. See also Poetry
Richards, Janet Clarke, 234
Richards, Leslie Ann, 388
Richek, Margaret Ann, 200, 630, 634
Richgels, Donald J., 71, 78, 497
Richman, Barry, 142, 176
Rickelman, Robert J., 191, 445
Riddles, 195, 275
Riel, M., 367
Rimes, 129
Rimm, Sylvia, 640, 641
Robbins, C., 129
Roberts, Janice, 350, 449
Roberts, Leslie L., 169, 499
Roberts, Patricia A., 594
Robinson, Francis P., 428
Robinson, H. Alan, 161
Roe, Betty D., 166–167, 210, 385, 386, 562
Roe, Mary F., 207
Roehler, Laura R., 598, 602, 635
Roney, R. Craig, 209, 210
Rose, David H., 79, 362, 363
Rosenblatt, Louise M., 21, 22
Rosenbloom, Cindy Shultz, 509
Rosenshine, Barak, 234
Roser, Nancy L., 65, 161, 341, 380
Roskos, Kathleen, 45, 55
Ross, Elinor P., 286, 292, 644
Rossing, Rosalind L., 246
Rosso, Barbara Rak, 119
Rottenberg, Claire J., 367
Routman, Regie, 546, 548, 580, 598
Rubin, Dorothy, 627
Rubino, Ann, 532
Rubrics, 546, 548
Ruddell, Robert B., 16, 21, 334
Ruddman, Joan, 195
Rude, Robert T., 483

Rule, Audrey, 532
Rumelhart, David E., 21, 209, 302
Running records, 564
Rush, R. Timothy, 483
Russell, David L., 405
Rystrom, 212–213

Sabey, Brenda, 45
Sadow, Marilyn W., 302, 303, 564
Sailor, Wayne, 624
Sampson, Mary Beth, 532
Sampson, Michael R., 532
Samuels, S. Jay, 18, 19, 20, 93
Samway, Katherine Davies, 340
Santino, Betsy H., 283
Saumell, Linda, 15, 364
Savage, John F., 403, 411
Sawyer, John Michael, 246
Scala, Marilyn, 619
Scale, of map, 463
Scanning, 433
Schachter, Summer W., 19, 318
Schaeffer, E. Marilyn, 78
Scharer, Patricia L., 335, 598, 606
Schatz, Elinore K., 174
Schell, Leo M., 132
Schell, Vicki J., 522
Schemata, 12, 161; activation of, 213; for comprehension, 209–214; individualized reading approach and, 348; language experience approach and, 354; research findings about, 210–213; story, 210, 241, 302; for vocabulary development, 161, 163–167
Scheu, Judith A., 512
Schifini, Alfredo, 650
Schmitt, Maribeth Cassidy, 231, 46, 330
Schoenfeld, Florence G., 236
Schoolwide organizational plans, 594–596; cross-grade arrangements, 595–596; departmentalization, 595; heterogeneous vs. homogeneous, 594–595; interclass grouping, 595; multi-age classrooms, 595; team arrangement, 595
Schreiner, Robert, 560
Schulz, Jane B., 632
Schumm, Jeanne Shay, 15, 223, 364, 31
Schwartz, Robert M., 174, 175, 183–184, 185
Science and health reading, 528–533
Science centers, 51, 533
Science log, 532
Scriptually implicit questions, 301, 302
Sebesta, Sam Leaton, 246
Seda, Ileana, 549
Sedlak, Denise M., 631
Sedlak, Robert A., 631
Seifert-Kessell, Nancy, 461, 462
Selection aids, for selecting literature, 396
Self-appraisal, for informal assessment, 555–558

Self-collection strategy, for vocabulary instruction, 192–194
Self-concept: attitude towards reading and, 16, 17; language experience approach and, 360
Self-direction, of reading, 31
Self-monitoring, of reading, 31
Self-questioning: in directed reading activity, 330; learning, 305–306; metacognition and, 230
Semantic clues, 22, 103, 105, 106–107
Semantic feature analysis, 165, 169, 185–187
Semantic mapping: for content area reading, 499; in cooperative groups, 248; higher-order thinking and, 262; as prereading activity, 229; for students with reading difficulties, 635; for vocabulary instruction, 165, 182–184, 185
Semantic webbing, 239–240, 241
Seminoff, Nancy Wiseman, 398, 446
Sensory aspects, of reading, 8, 9–11
Sentence outlines, 456
Sentences: combining, 219; comprehension of, 217–221; concept of, 43, 44; difficulty factors in, 218–220; expanding, 169; patterns, 220; punctuation of, 220–221; relative clauses in, 218–219; in telegram form, 217, 218; topic, 268
Sequence, recognizing, 258, 261
Sequence questions, 300
Sequential aspects, of reading, 8, 12
Setting, 246, 511
Shake, Mary C., 215, 623
Shanahan, Timothy, 383, 384
Shanklin, Nancy L., 207, 237
Shankweiler, Donald, 19
Shared-book experience, 67
Shared reading lesson, 69, 70
Sharing, 357, 387
Sharing time, 50
Sharp, Peggy Agostino, 511, 512
Shaw, Evelyn, 337
Shepard, Lorrie, 540
Shonhoff, Fredi, 18, 19
Shoop, Mary, 235
Short, Kathy G., 384, 387, 399, 405, 407, 509, 532, 581
Showcase portfolio, 551
Shrake, Karen, 340
Sight words, 19, 63–64, 94–103
Simile, 190–191
Sinatra, Richard, 203, 500
Singer, Harry, 213, 246, 305, 604
Sipay, Edward R., 21
Sippola, Arne E., 114, 115
Skimming, 433
Slaughter, Helen B., 22
Slavin, Robert E., 367, 588, 589, 595, 639
Smardo, Frances A., 530
Smelter, Richard, 624
Smiley, Sandra, 461

Smit, Edna K., 512
Smith, Carl B., 184, 589, 605
Smith, Frank, 383, 567
Smith, J. Lea, 505, 506
Smith, Jamie, 454
Smith, Judy Anderson, 260
Smith, Karl, 588
Smith, Marilyn, 246
Smith, Martha M., 302
Smith, Nancy, 356
Smith, Richard J., 19
Smolkin, Laura, 49
Smyers, Teresa, 333
Snell, Martha, 624
Snowman, Jack, 10
Social studies reading, 514–520; Directed Reading-Thinking Activity for, 487; trade books for, 406. *See also* Graphic aids; Newspapers
Sock puppets, 56
Sowell, Joanne, 142, 176
Spaced practice, 431
Spache, George D., 482
Spache Readability Formula, 482
Speaking, 28, 50–52. *See also* Speech
Special needs children, 618–662; with attention-deficit disorders, 630–631; Chapter I, 623, 624; coordination of special programs for, 623–624; culturally and linguistically diverse students, 643–656, 659–662; early intervention programs for, 639; with emotional/behavioral disorders, 632–633; gifted children, 230, 640–643; guidelines for, 628–629; with hearing impairments, 11, 632; inclusion and, 624–628; individualized education program for, 622–623; laws affecting, 622–628; with mental retardation, 631; with speech impairments, 632; with visual impairments, 631. *See also* Learning disabilities, children with; Reading difficulties, children with
Special skills groups, 590, 593
Speech: development of, 42; impairments, 632; speaking, 28, 50
Spelling: invented, 65, 71–77, 79, 114, 132–134, 355; irregularity of, 117; whole language philosophy and, 23
Spiegel, Dixie Lee, 112, 117, 129, 217, 242, 246, 371, 451, 513
Spiro, Rand J., 211
SQRQCQ study method, 430
SQ3R study method, 213, 428–429
Squier, Linda, 45
Squire, James, 383
Stahl, Steven A., 94, 119, 129, 167, 169–170, 183
Standard English, 13, 646
Standardized tests. *See* Norm-referenced tests
Stanford Achievement Test, 568, 569

Stanine scale, 566
Stanovich, Keith, 65
Starshine, Dorothy, 357
Stated information, recognizing, 255–256
Stauffer, Russell G., 331
Steckelberg, Allen, 612
Stein, Barry S., 296
Stetson, Elton G., 515
Stevens, Kathleen C., 210
Stevens, Robert, 588
Stewart, Oran, 432
Stewig, John Warren, 511
Stice, Carole, 635
Stick puppets, 56
Stoddard, Ann, 645
Storey, Dee C., 516
Story frames, 242, 243
Story grammar, 241–246, 299, 302–303
Story(ies): concept of, 242; for creative dramatics, 55; definition, 302; elements of, 511–512; predictable, 66, 87–88; writing, 60–62. *See also* Reading aloud; Storytelling
Story mapping, 239–241
Story parts, 242
Story predictions, 247
Story previews, 225
Story problems, 522–525
Story reading. *See* Reading aloud
Story reenactments, 56
Story retelling. *See* Retelling
Story schema, 210, 241, 302
Storytelling: for content area reading, 485; schema development and, 210; by students, 396; by teachers, 396; vocabulary development and, 166–167
Stotsky, Sandra, 383
Strange, Michael, 213
Strickland, Dorothy S., 42, 49, 56–57, 65, 67, 78, 391, 399, 584, 605
Strohauer, Donna, 528
Structural analysis, 137–146, 175–179; compound words, 143, 144, 175–176, 177–179; context clues and, 108, 109; contractions, 142–143; inflectional endings, 137–139, 176; Latin or Greek word parts, 177; prefixes and suffixes, 139–142, 175, 176–177; syllabication/accents, 143–146, 175; for vocabulary instruction, 175–179; word meanings, 141
Structured overviews, for content area reading, 496
Student contracts, 602–603
Student-teacher conferences, 343, 350
Study guides, for content area instruction, 431, 488–494
Study methods, 428–432; retention techniques, 430–431; SQ3R, 428–429; SQRQCQ, 430; test-taking strategies, 432
Stuttering, 632

Style, 286, 511, 512
Subskill theories, 18–20, 23
Success, teaching for, 30
Success for All, 639
Suffixes, 109, 137, 139–142, 175, 176
Sugarman, Jay, 540, 570
Sukarna, Deborah, 383
Sullivan, Joanne, 501
Sulzby, Elizabeth, 39, 40, 42, 69, 71, 358
Sumara, Dennis, 605
Summarizing, 330, 431, 459–460
Summary paragraphs, 223
Supplementary reading, 29
Sustained Silent Reading (SSR), 393–394; for children with reading difficulties, 635; for content area reading, 497; in literature-based approaches, 335; whole language philosophy and, 24
Sweet, Anne P., 398
Syllabication, 143–146
Syllable, 144
Symbols, in mathematics, 521, 523
Synonyms, 161, 199, 200
Syntactic clues, 22, 103, 105, 107
Synthetic approach, to phonics instruction, 121–122, 129

Table of contents, 436
Tables, 467–469
Talk-alouds, 602
Tape recordings, 51
Taylor, Barbara M., 152, 639
Taylor, Denny, 391
Tchudi, Susan, 580
Teacher: communicating with parents, 608–611; paraprofessionals and, 612
Teacher, role of, 601–607; as decision maker, 603–605; as facilitator and manager of instruction, 602–603, 604; as learner, 606–607; as researcher, 605–606
Teale, William H., 39, 40, 42, 69, 71, 77, 542, 596
Team arrangement, 595
Teberosky, A., 41–42
Technical vocabulary, 161–162
Telecommunications software programs, 367
Telegram sentences, 217, 218
Testimonial technique, 290
Test-taking strategies, 432. *See also* Assessment
Text-based processing, 211–213
Textbooks, 435–439; appendices in, 439; basal readers vs., 477–478; bibliographies in, 439; cloze tests of, 479–483; for content areas, 29; footnotes in, 439; glossaries in, 439; indexes in, 436–438; informal reading inventories of, 480; preface/introduction in, 436; readability of, 478–483, 484; table of contents in,

Textbooks, table of contents in, (*cont.*) 436; trade books used with, 483, 485. *See also under* Content area reading

Text patterns, comprehension of, 222–223

Textset, 341

Text structure, textbook material learned with, 497–499

Textually explicit questions, 301, 302

Textually implicit questions, 301

Thames, D. G., 330

Thelen, Judith N., 165

Thematic learning approaches, 5

Thematic literature units, 340–343, 344–347, 370

Thematic maps, 463–464

Thematic units: for content area reading, 505–509; for literature, 340–343, 344–347, 370; within literature-centered instruction, 408–417

Theme cycles, 581

Themes: in integrated curriculum, 580–582; teaching, 511, 512

Theories: interactive, 20–21; subskill, 18–20, 23; transactive, 21–22, *see also* Whole language classrooms

Think-alouds: for context clues, 172; for figurative language instruction, 277–278; for interpretive reading instruction, 277–278; for metacognition, 231–232, 462; purpose for reading set by, 215; schema activation and, 213; teachers modeling by, 602

Thinking, reading and, 8, 14

Thomas, Chase C., 223

Thomas, Keith, 486

Thomas, M. Donald, 644

Thompson, Deborah L., 508

Thompson, Stephen J., 187, 190–191

Thonis, Eleanor Wall, 648, 649, 650, 651

Tierney, Robert J., 225, 235, 237, 294, 383, 594

Timeliness, of material, 286

Tindall, Mary Anne, 197

Tomlinson, Carl M., 485

Tompkins, Gail E., 242, 246, 411

Tone, 286

Tone, Bruce, 554

Top-down processing, 20, 21

Topic, main idea vs., 269

Topical paragraphs, 223

Topic Chart, 591–592, 593

Topic outlines, 456

Topic sentence, 268

Topping, Keith, 612

Tovey, Duane R., 130–131, 604

Trachtenburg, Phyllis, 122–125

Trade books: for literature-based programs, 334; literature integrated across the curriculum with, 406–408; for science and health programs, 530; for social studies

programs, 515, 517–518; with textbooks, 482, 485

Transactive theories, 21–22. *See also* Whole language classrooms

Transfer, phonics and, 111

Transfer technique, 290

Treiman, Rebecca, 129–130

Trelease, Jim, 396

Truax, Roberta, 621

Tuchman, Anita, 171, 175

Tunnell, Michael O., 335

Turbill, Jan, 62, 383

Turnbull, Ann P., 632

Turner, Julianne C., 461, 592, 607

Tutorial programs, computers for, 196, 363–364

Tutors, 612

Typewriters, 78

Tyson, Eleanor S., 195

Underlining, 220–221

Undifferentiated attention-deficit disorder, 630

Unrau, Norman J., 21

Uttero, Debbra, 248, 588, 589

Valencia, Sheila, 539, 541, 551, 570

Valeri-Gold, Maria, 459–460

Validity, 566

Valmont, William J., 236

Value judgments, 291–293

Vancil, Sandra J., 183

Vanderhoff, Bill, 516

VanLeirsburg, Peggy, 570

Van Riper, C., 632

Vardell, Sylvia, 496–497

Variants, 443–444

Varnhagen, Connie K., 242

Vasa, Stanley, 612

Venn diagrams: for content area reading, 499; film and text versions of stories compared with, 283; folk tales compared with, 283, 284

Verville, Kathy, 546

Vicarious experiences, 13, 59–61, 66, 169

Videotapes, 246, 601

Vinz, Ruth, 385

Vision, reading process and, 9, 10–11

Visual acuity, 10, 12

Visual discrimination, 12, 112, 114, 115; sight words and, 98

Visual impairments, 631–632

Visualization, creative reading and, 294–295

Visual learners, 25

Visual perception, 12

Visual representation, 237

Vocabulary Connections, 170

Vocabulary development, 28, 59, 161–162; for content area instruction, 161–163, 162, 169–170, 187; trade books for, 406–407. *See also* Vocabulary instruction

Vocabulary instruction, 161, 162–203; active approaches for, 168–170; analogies for, 180–182, 183; antonyms, 161, 199–200; categorization for, 179–180, 181; commercial materials for, 167–168; comparison of approaches to, 197; computers for, 196; context clues for, 172–175; dictionary use for, 187–189; in English classes, 514; etymology for, 187–188, 189–190; figurative language, 187, 190–192, 193; homographs, 161, 198–199; homonyms, 161, 195, 197–198; for mathematics, 520–521, 522; new words, 200; past experiences for, 170–171; schemata development and, 161, 163–167; in science and health, 528; semantic feature analysis for, 165, 169, 185–187; semantic mapping for, 165, 182–184, 185; in social studies, 514–515; structural analysis for, 175–179; student-centered techniques for, 171–172, 192–194; synonyms, 161, 199, 200; techniques for, 163, 167–197; vocabulary notebooks for, 194; word banks for, 194; word lines for, 182; word play for, 194–195; word webs for, 169, 184–185, 186

Vocabulary notebooks, 194

Vocabulary questions, 300

Vogel, Sheila, 74

Vogt, Mary Ellen, 586

Vowel digraphs, 113, 121

Vowels, 113, 120–121. *See also* Phonics instruction

Vukelich, Carol, 55

Walberg, Herbert J., 20

Walker, Laurie, 605

Walker, Trudy, 73

Walker-Dalhouse, Doris, 518

Wall, Bonnie, 595

Wall, Lisa K., 214–215

Waller, T. Gary, 41

Walmsley, Sean A., 23, 449

Walshe, R. D., 71

Warren, Suzanne S., 600

Wasik, Barbara A., 461, 592, 607

Watson, Dorothy J., 23, 549, 561, 563

Watson, Jerry J., 246

Waugh, Joyce Clark, 354

Waugh, R. P., 146

Weaver, 217

Weaver, Constance, 551, 635

Weaver, Phyllis, 18, 19

Webs, 408–409, 410; for content area reading, 431, 497, 501; for literary elements, 512; for outlining, 457–459; semantic

Webs (*cont.*)
  webbing and, 239–240, 241; word, 169, 184–185, 186
Weekly Reader, 519
Weiss, Maria J., 318
Wepner, Shelley B., 341, 366, 368, 390, 409, 446, 500
Wertheim, Judy, 338
Whalen, Susan, 589
Whaley, Jill Fitzberald, 242
Wheatley, Elizabeth A., 196
White, Maureen C., 341
White, Thomas G., 142, 176
Whitman, Paulette, 543
Whitmer, Jean E., 280
Whole-class activities, 594
Whole-class reading of a core book, 335–339, 370
Whole language classrooms, 22, 23–24, 371, 379–380, 585–586; for bilingual students, 651–652; computers and, 366; kindergarten literacy activities and, 57–58; mathematics and, 527; phonics and, 114; preoperational period and, 41; transition from traditional instruction to, 596
Whole word approach. *See* Sight words
"Why" questions, 431
Wicklund, LaDonna, 635
Wideman, H. H., 364
Wiesendanger, Katherine D., 225
Wigfield, Allan, 607
Wiggins, Grant, 540
Wiggins, Robert A., 314, 316, 318, 592
Wiggleworks: Scholastic Beginning Literacy System, 79
Wilhoyte, Cheryl H., 623
Wilkinson, Phyllis A., 219
Williams, Richard P., 515
Willis, Scott, 649
Wilson, Cathy Roller, 213, 461

Wilson, Lorraine, 581, 582, 599
Wilson, Patricia J., 397
Winograd, Peter, 527, 528, 540, 546, 555
Wiseman, Donna L., 66
Wixson, Karen K., 80, 163, 172–175, 298, 302
Wolf, Anne, 594, 605
Wolfe, Ronald, 496
Wollman-Bonilla, Julie E., 336, 387
Wong, B. Y. L., 235
Wong, Jo Ann, 486
Wong-Kam, Jo Ann, 635, 637
Wood, Delores, 47
Wood, Judy, 629
Wood, Karen D., 317, 361, 525, 589, 630, 643, 644
Word, concept of, 43
Word attack strategies, 93. *See also* Context clues; Dictionary; Phonics; Structural analysis
Word banks, 100, 194, 358
Word bingo, 101
Word cards, 64
Word configuration, 98–99
Word families, 115
Word lines, 182
Word maps, 183–184, 185
Word meanings, 17–18, 25, 141. *See also* Meaning vocabulary
Word play, 194
Word problems, 522–525
Word-processing programs, 196, 361, 364, 391
Word recognition strategies, 7, 26, 93–94, 150–152. *See also* Context clues; Dictionary; Phonics; Sight words; Structural analysis
Word trees, 190
Word wall, 64
Word webs, 169, 184–185, 186

Working portfolio, 551
Worksheets, sight words and, 101
Workshops, reading and writing, 388–389, 652
Writing: compositions, 514; computers for, 390–391; learning, 69, 71–79; in prereading phase, 247; process, 386–387; before reading, 229; reading and, 28, *see also* Language experience approach. *See also* Reading-writing connection
Writing centers, 78
Writing process, 386–387
Writing workshop, 388–389, 652
Wysocki, Katherine, 175

Yaden, David, Jr., 49
Yanagihara, Alice, 142, 176
Yatvin, J., 371
Yellin, David, 601
Yoder, Carol Y., 431
Yonan, Barbara, 445
Yopp, Hallie Kay, 65, 114
Yopp, R. E., 235
Young, Erin, 388
Young, Terrell A., 466, 496–497, 499, 525
Ysseldyke, James, 631
Yudewitz, Gary, 624

Zabroske, Barbara, 174, 462
Zack, Vicki, 509
Zarillo, James, 334, 342
Zarnowski, Myra, 516
Zimet, Sara Goodman, 280
Zirzow, Eleanor G., 354
Zitlow, Connie S., 504
Zogby, Grace, 399
Zucker, Carol, 335, 621

Student Response Form

Many of the changes made in the sixth edition of *Teaching Reading in Today's Elementary Schools* were based on feedback and evaluations of the earlier editions. Please help us respond to the interests and needs of future readers by completing the questionnaire below and returning it to: College Marketing, Houghton Mifflin Company, 222 Berkeley Street, Boston, MA 02116.

1. Please tell us your overall impressions of the text.

	Excellent	Good	Adequate	Poor
a. Was it written in a clear and understandable style?	____	____	____	____
b. Were difficult concepts well explained?	____	____	____	____
c. How would you rate the frequent use of illustrative Examples?	____	____	____	____
d. How comprehensive was the coverage of major issues and topics?	____	____	____	____
e. How does this book compare to other texts you have used?	____	____	____	____
f. How would you rate the activities?	____	____	____	____
g. How would you rate the study aids at the beginning and end of each chapter?	____	____	____	____

2. Please comment on or cite examples that illustrate any of your above ratings.

_____

_____

_____

3. Were there any topics that should have been included or covered more fully?

_____

_____

_____

4. Which chapters or features did you particularly like?

_____

_____

_____

5. Which chapters or features did you dislike?

_____

_____

_____

6. Which chapters taught you the most?

_____

_____

_____

7. What changes would you like to see in the next edition of this book?

_____

_____

_____

8. Is this a book you would like to keep for your classroom teaching experience? _____ Why or why not?

_____

_____

_____

9. Please tell us something about your background. Are you studying to be an
   elementary school classroom teacher or a reading specialist? Are you inservice or preservice? Are you an undergraduate or a graduate student?

_____

_____

_____

Thank you very much for your feedback.